Spring 3 With
Hibernate 4 Project
for Professionals

Spring 3 With
Hibernate 4 Project
for Professionals

Sharanam Shah
Vaishali Shah

THE
X
TEAM

SHROFF PUBLISHERS & DISTRIBUTORS PVT. LTD.
Mumbai   Bangalore   Kolkata   New Delhi

Spring 3 With Hibernate 4 Project for Professionals
by Sharanam Shah and Vaishali Shah

Copyright © 2012, Sharanam Shah

Series Editor: Ivan Bayross

First Edition: August 2012

ISBN 13: 978-93-5023--775-5

Published by **Shroff Publishers & Distributors Pvt. Ltd.** C-103, T.T.C. Industrial Area, M.I.D.C., Pawane, Navi Mumbai - 400 705. Tel.: (91-22) 2763 4290 Fax: (91-22) 2768 3337 E-mail: spdorders@shroffpublishers.com Printed at Decora Book Prints Pvt. Ltd., Mumbai.

Preface

Welcome to **Spring 3 With Hibernate 4 Project For Professionals**! Thank you for picking up this book.

This book is dedicated to **Janya**, our little princess. Thank you for coming to this world as our daughter. You are the most precious daughter we could ever ask for. We love you more than our life.

About This Book

Day by day, developers are able to get more done in less time. With today's high level languages, development environments, tools and the **rapid application development** mindset, both developers and managers have become accustomed to extremely fast development cycles.

Programmers are now more inclined to jump directly into development, fearing that every hour they are not writing code will result in an hour of overtime the weekend before the deadline.

The process of designing before coding is becoming outdated. Documenting designs is becoming even **rarer**. Many developers have never written a design document and cringe at the idea of doing so. Many who are required to, typically generate a lot of interaction diagrams and class diagrams, which do not often express the developer's thought process during the design phase.

This book aims serving students, developers, technical leads and to some extent project managers by demonstrating a structured documented modestly sized project, which will help communicate the software requirements and the design decisions.

What You'll Learn?

Reading this book, Java application developers will get an insight into how professional Web based projects are structured, documented and executed using:

- **MySQL** Community Server 5.5.25 as the data store
- **Java Server Pages** as the view technology
- **Spring 3** as the application development framework

   The most popular application development framework for enterprise Java, to create high performing, easily testable, reusable code without any lock-in.

❑   **Hibernate 4** as the <u>Object Relational Mapping</u> tool

A popular, powerful and a free, open source Object Relational Mapping library for the Java programming language which makes the application portable to all the SQL databases supported by Hibernate.

<u>All run on Microsoft Windows.</u>

We've tried to use our extensive application development experience to produce this book that should cover most of the areas that seem to puzzle developers from time to time in their application development career.

Any developer that acquires strong documentation and development skills using this framework will always be in demand and is sure of always being able to make a good living selling these skills to the highest bidder.

This book:

❑   Is a ready reference, with several add-ons and technologies, covering modestly sized project containing a **Back-end** with **Master** and **Transaction** data entry forms and a **Front-end** with application homepage and the **shopping cart**

❑   Addresses the following needs of developers:

How to **document:**

o   Case Study

o   Business Requirements

o   Software Requirement Specifications

o   Data Dictionary, Table Definitions and Directory Structure

o   End User Manual

o   Software Design Document

How to **implement** the following technologies:

o   Shopping Cart

o   Payment Gateway for accepting payments using Credit Cards [Google Checkout]

o   Tag Clouds

o   Session Management

o   Directory

o   Search

o   Dispatch Emails using the Java Mail API

o   Using BLOB to store images and PDF files

- o   Develop forms, validate form content and handle user requests
- o   Data Access Object Design Pattern
- o   Access based User Management using Spring Security
- o   Annotation-based programming model for MVC controllers
- o   Declarative transaction management capabilities
- o   Restricted page access protection
- o   Custom Error Pages
- ❑   Is suitable for students, developers, technical leads, project managers, consultants
- ❑   Assumes the reader with a good understanding of Java fundamentals and database programming using the Java Database Connectivity [JDBC] API and some familiarity with Spring and Hibernate

To true newcomers to Spring and/or Hibernate, we recommend that you read our earlier book called "**Spring 3 For Beginners**" before diving into project development.

Like all our earlier books, this book builds concepts using simple language, in a step by step, easy to follow manner.

The section that follows, presents a rundown of what the book delivers, as you work through its content.

This book contains **56** chapters held within **9** sections.

In the first section of the book we give a brief introduction to **Spring 3** and **Hibernate 4**.

The second section begins by defining the project's **Case Study** which describes the Software Development Life Cycle of the project. This section then delves deeply into the project in form of the **Software Requirement Specifications**, **Project Files** and the **Database Table Structure**.

Section 3 is dedicated to project's **End User Manual**. This section documents the steps [how to use/operate] of using this application/project.

After the reader is familiar with the application and its usage, this book moves towards explaining the actual processes [behind the scenes] that happen when an action is performed from the user interfaces [that are defined in the end user manual]. Section 4 takes care of the **Process Flow** for each module in the project.

The next two sections [fifth and sixth] of the book hold the **Software Design Documents**. Each module is a separate chapter, just to ensure that the reader, whilst reading, is focused on a single module.

The 7th section of this book holds the details of the project configuration files. This section helps understand what each configuration file does in the application.

Finally, section 8, depicts how to run the project. This is done by assembling [i.e. bringing all the files together] the project using the NetBeans IDE, followed by deploying and running the application.

The last section of this book [Appendix] holds a single chapter. This chapter documents the implementation procedure for Google **Checkout**.

This book's accompanying CD-ROM holds downloaded executables of the following:

❑ Java Development Kit [JDK] 7 Update 4
❑ NetBeans IDE 7.1.2 with:
  o Tomcat 7.0.22
  o GlassFish Server Open Source Edition 3.1.2
❑ Spring 3.2.0.M1
❑ Hibernate 4.1.4.Final
❑ MySQL 5.5.25
❑ MySQL Connector/J 5.1.20
❑ Spring Security 3.1.0.RELEASE

Writing this book has been one of the most challenging endeavors we've taken on and it would not have been possible without the help and support from several people.

Acknowledgments

Our sincere thanks go to:

❑ Our publisher Mr. Aziz Shroff for bringing up the X-Team concept that has brought enormous changes in our lives
❑ Ms. Rumaa Dey for entering our lives and making it more interesting and enthusiastic
❑ Our family for their patience, support and love
❑ The many programmers who read this book. We welcome both your brickbats and bouquets

❏   All those who helped through their comments, feedback and suggestions

If you have any questions, comments or just feel like communicating, please contact us at **enquiries@sharanamshah.com**.

We are now also available on Facebook [http://facebook.sharanamshah.com]. You can Sign up to connect with both of us.

We hope that you will enjoy reading and working through the project in this book as much as we enjoyed documenting and developing it.

For additional information on this book visit:

❏   http://www.sharanamshah.com

❏   http://www.vaishalishahonline.com

Sharanam & Vaishali Shah

How To Read This Book

This book documents a modestly sized project: **BookShop** - A web based **Book Management and Sales System** with a shopping cart tightly integrated with a payment gateway. This application is built using **Spring 3** as the application development framework and **Hibernate 4** as the Object Relational Mapping library with **MySQL Server 5** as the <u>data store</u>.

While Spring 3 and Hibernate 4 are incredibly powerful, they present a steep learning curve when you first encounter them. Steep learning curves are good. They impart profound insight once you have scaled them. Yet gaining that insight takes some perseverance and assistance. To help you up that learning curve, we strongly recommend that you read at least the basics prior moving on with the project. The basics can be found in one of our earlier books called **Spring 3 For Beginners** [**ISBN**: 978-93-5023-690-1].

Now about this book's road map, to make the driving easy, we recommend reading this book as follows:

1. Read through the **Section 1** called *Understanding the Framework* to gain a quick recap to Spring 3 as the application framework and Hibernate 4 as the ORM library

2. Follow Section 2. Since this is a project's book, the next section [**Section 2**] describes the project that this book helps you built. It does this by presenting a Case Study [SDLC of the project being built], followed by the **Software Requirements Specification**, database table structures and the project files. This section, makes the requirements of the project being built, crystal clear

3. Quickly run through **Section 3**: *End User Manual*. This section helps you visualize the actual application, how it appears and functions

4. After you are done with the first three sections, we strongly recommended to:

    a. Setup the development environment by installing the NetBeans IDE and the MySQL database server [both are available on this book's CDROM]

    b. Run the Application using **Section 8** [use the code spec from the Book's CDROM - <CDROM Drive>:/Code/BookShop]

This book's accompanying CDROM holds the project code spec [**BookShop**] in a ready to run state. It also holds a MySQL SQL script [**bms.sql**] file that can be imported to quickly bring up and start using this application. **Section 8** [in detail] explains the steps involved in running the application.

This approach will be very useful. It will let the readers have a running copy of the application, whilst going through the sections to follow. The readers will be able to quickly correlate every activity of the application with the following sections:

a.   **Section 4:** Process Flow

b.   **Section 5:** Backend [Administration] Software Design Documentation

c.   **Section 6:** Frontend [Customer Facing] Software Design Documentation

d.   **Section 7:** Project Configuration Files

Whilst going through these sections, you can refer the appendix, to understand the Google Wallet implementation [used in this project as the Payment Gateway].

Alright, let's dive in.

Sharanam & Vaishali Shah

Table Of Contents

Chapter 1

SECTION I: UNDERSTANDING THE FRAMEWORK

Introduction To Spring Framework

When considering Spring for Java, it's probably worth running through the history of the **Java web applications**.

The History Of The Java Web Applications

History begins with:

The Servlet API

Sun introduced the Servlet API in **1997**. The Servlet API marked Java's entry into Web application development. It provided a standard on which vendors could build Web containers and developers could implement a simple programming model for constructing Web pages.

The best part with Servlets was the dynamic construction of HTML documents. However, since the documents were constructed inside the Java source code, the maintenance was challenging. For example, changing the font or moving content within a page required updating the HTML inside the Servlet code and recompiling and redeploying it to the container.

Sun resolved this issue in **1999** by introducing JavaServer Pages [JSP].

JavaServer Pages And The Model 1 Architecture

Rather than implementing presentation code inside Servlets, JSP allows building HTML like documents that mingle Java code snippets to support dynamic content.

At runtime, JSPs are translated to Servlet source code, compiled and then deployed to a Web container dynamically. If any part of the JSP is changed, the container detects the change, recompiles the page and redeploys it. This architecture was called **Page-Driven** or **Model 1**.

In the Model 1 architecture, each page contains the business logic that is required to generate the dynamic content as well as the control logic to determine application flow.

Although conceptually simple, **Model 1** was not conductive to large scale application development as, this model:

❏ Duplicated a great deal of functionality in each JSP

❏ Unnecessarily tied together the business logic and presentation logic of the application

Thus the Model 2 architecture came into existence.

Model 2 Architecture

The Model 2 architecture separates the programmatic responsibilities into the technologies best suited for them. It adheres to the **MVC** Smalltalk design pattern, where:

❏ **M:** The **Model** represents the data or the objects with which the application is interacting

❏ **V:** The **View** is a visualization of the model

❏ **C:** The **Controller** manages the application flow and makes calls into business objects

In Java,

❏ **M:** The **Model** is typically a loose JavaBean or **P**lain **O**ld **J**ava **O**bject [POJO] that has getters and setters to manipulate its contents

❑ **V:** The **View** is usually a JSP page or some other view technology such as FreeMarker, Velocity, XML/XSLT and so on

❑ **C:** After the business logic is complete and the model has been generated, the **Controller** passes the **Model** to the **View** to be presented to the user. The **Controller** is typically implemented by a Servlet that calls into business services to perform some action

Enterprise JavaBeans

Later, Sun brought in middle-tier capabilities in Java by defining Enterprise JavaBeans, due to which Business Logic could be effectively developed in Java.

Over the past few years, EJB specification evolved significantly.

EJB 2.x gained wide adoption. It had reached a level of maturity which made it capable to embrace the requirements of many enterprise applications. Despite its relative success, it was considered overcomplicated due to:

❑ Lack of a good persistence strategy

❑ Long and tedious deployment descriptors

❑ Limited capacity for testing

This caused a considerable number of developers to look for alternative technologies/frameworks.

Sun Microsystems came up with a revised version of the specification, EJB 3.0.

Enterprise JavaBeans 3.0

EJB 3.0 dealt with most of the existing drawbacks and thus became a viable solution again and many developers who had once put it aside are now using it.

Even though its success, EJB 3.0 did not go as far as it could. It was facing a lot of challenges.

These challenges were met and EJB 3.1 was born.

Enterprise JavaBeans 3.1

EJB 3.1 is even easier to use. It promotes a POJO-based programming model and employs Dependency Injection and Aspect Oriented Programming.

But the EJB 3.1 move was **too late**. By the time the EJB 3.1 specification arrived, other POJO-based development frameworks had already established themselves as de facto standards in the Java community.

The Spring Project

Spring was one among the many alternative technologies/frameworks and a de facto standard in the Java community.

During the early days of Enterprise JavaBeans [EJB], developers led by Rod Johnson brought the idea of Spring project which appeared first in 2002. Spring is being developed till now, the current version being 3.1.

What Is The Purpose Of Spring?

Applications built using the Java EE Container are usually too heavy. Developers do not need to use all of its services, instead they should be allowed to choose the ones they desire to use and implement.

And so, Spring.

Spring easily manages Business Objects. Developers do not have to use a specific class or interface. This way the coupling between the clients and the Spring framework is cut down.

What Is The Spring Framework?

Spring is one of the most popular open source frameworks for developing enterprise applications. It addresses most infrastructure concerns of typical applications and provides comprehensive infrastructure support for developing Java applications. It aims to:

❑ Make building business applications with Java EE much easier compared with the classic Java frameworks and API's such as JDBC and JSP by providing a POJO-based programming model

❑ Improve the way the business applications are designed and implemented by:

  o Promoting good programming practices

  o Simplifying development

  o Reducing dependencies on external frameworks or even classes within an application

❑ Handle the infrastructure leaving the developer to focus on the application

The Spring framework consists of a container, a framework for managing components and a set of snap-in services for web user interfaces, transactions and persistence.

Technically, it covers everything from Plain-Old-Java-Object [POJO] development, to web application development, to enterprise application development, to persistence layer management and Aspect Oriented Programming [AOP]. It provides:

❑ Lightweight IoC container for lifecycle and dependency management of objects

❑ **Aspect Oriented Programming [AOP]** for modularizing cross-cutting concerns and providing services to Plain Old Java Object [POJOs] in a declarative fashion such as transaction management, logging, messaging and exposing POJO using one of the remote technologies such as RMI, HTTP, web services and so on

❑ Consistent abstraction layer, which provides integration with various standards such as JPA [Java Persistence API], JDBC, JMS and third party APIs such as Hibernate, Top Link, JDO

❑ MVC framework, which provides a highly configurable Model View Controller implementation via strategy interfaces and accommodates numerous view technologies including JSP, Portlets, Velocity, Tiles, iText and POI implementation

Although the Spring framework does not impose any specific programming model, it has become popular in the Java community as an alternative to, replacement for the Enterprise JavaBean model.

Origin Of Spring Framework

The Spring as a framework was released on the first day of spring, 2003, under the Apache 2.0 license. This release was based on Rod Johnson's bestselling publication called "Expert One-on-One J2EE Design and Development".

Thereafter:

❑ The first fully working release 1.0 came in March 2004, with further releases in September 2004 and March 2005

❑ The Spring 1.2.6 framework won a Jolt productivity award and a JAX Innovation Award in 2006

❑ Spring 2.0 was released in October 2006

❑ Spring 2.5 was released in November 2007

❑ Spring 3.0 GA was released in December 2009

❑ Spring 3.1 GA was released in December 2011

❑   Spring 3.2 M1 was released in May 2012

The current version is 3.1.2.RELEASE [as the latest 3.1 release] and 3.2.0.M1 [as the latest 3.2 release]. This book uses 3.2.0.M1.

Features Of The Spring Framework

Spring is **modular**. It allows the developers to use just about any of its component in isolation. This means the developers can choose to use certain components of Spring with some other components of some other framework, for example:

❑   **IoC** container of **Spring**

❑   **MVC** framework such as **Struts**

❑   **Persistence layer management** such as **Hibernate** or **JPA**

This shows that the Spring Framework does not impose any restriction on the framework selection, instead it works as glue and helps quickly integrate different frameworks to build an application.

Spring Framework supports **declarative transaction management** where transaction boundaries can be defined using annotations as well as XML based configuration. It is flexible enough to work with JTA, JTS or simple JDBC transition API for the transaction management.

The Spring Framework is **non-intrusive**. This makes the business logic code generally have no dependency on the Spring classes.

The Spring Framework allows using **POJO** classes in enterprise application development to create Controllers, Web services and so on.

Spring nicely **integrates with Persistence Layer Management** tools such as Hibernate, JDO and iBATIS.

Spring comes with **MVC web application framework**, built on the core Spring functionality. This framework is highly configurable via strategy interfaces and accommodates multiple view technologies such as JSP, Velocity, Tiles, iText and POI. It even integrates well with other MVC web frameworks such as Struts.

All About The Spring framework

Simplifies Java Enterprise Application Development

The Spring framework's main aim is to make Java EE easier to use. It addresses the complexity of enterprise application development and makes it possible to use POJO-based programming model to achieve things that were previously only possible with EJBs.

The Spring framework brings a lot to the table, however, when broken down to its core parts, it primarily brings in:

- **POJO:** Development with **P**lain **O**ld **J**ava **O**bjects
- **Dependency Injection [DI]:** Loose coupling
- **Aspect-Oriented Programming [AOP]:** Declarative programming
- **Templates:** Boilerplate reduction

Core Parts Of The Spring Framework

POJOs

The Spring framework allows using POJOs to develop the applications. Spring aims to deliver the middleware services to loosely coupled **P**lain **O**ld **J**ava **O**bjects [POJOs].

The Spring framework **wires** [creating associations between application components] application services to the POJOs by intercepting the execution context or injecting service objects to the POJOs at runtime.

The POJOs themselves are not concerned about the wiring and have little dependency upon the framework.

As a result, developers can focus on the business logic and unit test their POJOs without the framework. In addition, since POJOs do not need to inherit from framework classes or implement framework interfaces, the developers have a high degree of flexibility to build inheritance structures and construct applications.

Dependency Injection [DI] aka Inversion of Control [IoC]

DI or the IoC container is one of best ways to implement loosely coupled applications.

Using DI, the framework acts as an object factory to build service objects and injects those service objects to application POJOs based on some runtime configuration. From the application developer's point of view, the client POJO automatically obtains the correct service object, when it is required.

DI makes the code significantly simpler, easier to understand and easier to test. The IoC container manages the POJOs and its dependencies in the application. The application defines the dependency and these dependencies are then satisfied at runtime by the IoC container as follows:

❑   A caller asks the container for an object with a specific name or of a specific type

❑   The container injects these objects by name to other objects, via either constructors, properties or factory methods

This way,

❑   Objects are not expected to create or obtain their dependencies. Dependencies are injected into the objects that need them

❑   Classes are no longer required to be coupled to any specific implementation, which is the key benefit of DI, **Loose Coupling**. Since an object only knows about its dependencies by their interface, the dependency can thus be swapped out with a different implementation without the depending object knowing the difference

In Spring, there are many ways to wire components together, but a common approach has always been via XML. Typically, the container is configured by loading XML files with some runtime configuration containing Bean definitions which provide the information required to create the beans.

A Tightly Coupled Application

Example

Consider the following application:

Solution [Contest.java]:

```
1  package com.springforbeginners;
2
3  public interface Contest {
4      public String promptQuestion();
5  }
```

Explanation:

Contest interface exposes **promptQuestion()**.

Solution [StrutsContest.java]:

```
1  package com.springforbeginners;
2
3  public class StrutsContest implements Contest {
4      @Override
5      public String promptQuestion() {
6          return "Who invented Struts?";
7      }
8  }
```

Solution [SpringContest.java]:

```
1  package com.springforbeginners;
2
3  public class SpringContest implements Contest {
4      @Override
5      public String promptQuestion() {
6          return "Who invented Spring?";
7      }
8  }
```

Explanation:

StrutsContest and **SpringContest** classes implement the **Contest** interface and these classes generate questions related to Struts and Spring respectively.

Solution [ContestService.java]:

```
1  package com.springforbeginners;
2
3  public class ContestService {
4      private Contest contest = new SpringContest();
5
6      public void askQuestion() {
7          System.out.println(contest.promptQuestion());
8      }
9  }
```

Explanation:

ContestService displays the question to the user and it holds a reference to the **Contest** interface.

Solution [ContestApplication.java]

```
1  package com.springforbeginners;
2
3  public class ContestApplication {
4     public static void main(String[] args) {
5         ContestService contestService = new ContestService();
6         contestService.askQuestion();
7     }
8  }
```

Explanation:

ContestApplication conducts the contest. It creates an instance of ContestService and calls askQuestion().

Output [on the console]:

The components of this application are tightly coupled. An instance of **Contest** in **ContestService** is created as:

For Spring

private Contest contest = new SpringContest();

For Struts

private Contest contest = new StrutsContest();

A Loosely Coupled Application

To avoid tight coupling, use Dependency Injection, where the component only needs to choose a way to accept the resources and the container will deliver the resource to the components.

Example

The following is the rewritten version of the previous example. It demonstrates a loosely coupled application.

Solution [ContestService.java]:

```
1   package com.springforbeginners;
2
3   public class ContestService {
4       Contest contest;
5
6       public void setContest(Contest contest) {
7           this.contest = contest;
8       }
9
10      public void askQuestion() {
11          System.out.println(contest.promptQuestion());
12      }
13  }
```

Explanation:

ContestService now does not directly create an object of the Contest bean.

Instead it will now make use of the container to do this. The container will inject the required dependencies.

Dependencies are injected using the **setter** or **constructor** injection. **ContestService** uses the setter injection. The value for the Contest is set using **setContest()**.

HINT

 The Contest object is never instantiated in **ContestService**, but is still accessed. Usually this should throw a **NullPointerException**, but here the container instantiates the object and hence it works fine.

The container comes into picture and it helps injecting the dependencies.

To wire all these components, the bean configuration is written in beans.xml. The act of creating associations between application components is commonly referred to as wiring. In Spring, there are many ways to wire components together, but a common approach has always been via XML.

Solution [beans.xml]:

```
1  <?xml version="1.0" encoding="UTF-8"?>
2  <beans xmlns="http://www.springframework.org/schema/beans"
3      xmlns:xsi="http://www.w3.org/2001/XMLSchema-instance"
4      xsi:schemaLocation="http://www.springframework.org/schema/beans
        http://www.springframework.org/schema/beans/spring-beans-3.0.xsd">
5    <bean id="springContest" class="com.springforbeginners.SpringContest" />
6    <bean id="strutsContest" class="com.springforbeginners.StrutsContest" />
7    <bean id="contestService" class="com.springforbeginners.ContestService">
8      <property name="contest">
9        <ref local="springContest" />
10     </property>
11   </bean>
12 </beans>
```

Explanation:

Each bean is defined using the **bean** tag. The **id** attribute of the bean tag gives a logical name to the bean and the **class** attribute represents the actual bean class.

The **property** tag is used to refer the property of the bean. To inject a bean using the setter injection the **ref** tag is used.

In this example, a reference of SpringContest is injected into the Contest bean. Hence when this application is executed, it shows, "Who invented Spring?" on the console.

To make this Contest ask questions related to Struts, the only change required is the **ref** tag.

```
<bean id="contestService" class="com.springforbeginners.ContestService">
  <property name="contest">
    <ref local="strutsContest" />
  </property>
</bean>
```

In this way, the Dependency Injection helps in reducing the coupling between the components.

Aspect-Oriented Programming [AOP]

While DI ties software components together loosely, AOP captures functionality that is used throughout the application in reusable components.

AOP is a technique that promotes separation of concerns within an application.

Applications are usually made up of several components, each responsible for a specific piece of functionality. Often these components also carry additional responsibility [such as logging, transaction management and security] beyond their core functionality which overlaps the existing business logic. These additional responsibility or services are commonly referred to as **cross-cutting concerns** because they tend to cut across multiple components in an application.

AOP isolates the cross-cutting concerns from the application code thereby modularizing them as a different entity. In short, AOP is another way of organizing the application's structure.

Consider the following application:

Example

Solution [OperateBankAccount.java]:

```
1   public class OperateBankAccount{
2      public long deposit(long depositAmount){
3         newAmount = existingAccount + depositAccount;
4         currentAmount = newAmount;
5         return currentAmount;
6      }
7
8      public long withdraw(long withdrawalAmount){
9         if (withdrawalAmount <= currentAmount){
10           currentAmount = currentAmount - withdrawalAmount;
11        }
12        return currentAmount;
13     }
14  }
```

Explanation:

This is a simple application which provides the **deposit** and **withdrawal** services.

To bring in some additional services: Ensure that only users with the **Administrator** privilege are allowed to use the **deposit** and **withdrawal** services.

Solution [OperateBankAccount.java] [with Security service]:

```
1   public class OperateBankAccount{
2      public long deposit(long depositAmount){
3         User user = getContext().getUser();
4         if (user.getRole().equals("BankAdmin"){
5            newAmount = existingAccount + depositAccount;
6            currentAmount = newAmount;
7         }
8         return currentAmount;
9      }
10
11     public long withdraw(long withdrawalAmount){
12        User user = getContext().getUser();
13        if (user.getRole().equals("BankAdmin"){
14           if (withdrawalAmount <= currentAmount){
15              currentAmount = currentAmount - withdrawalAmount;
16           }
17        }
18        return currentAmount;
19     }
20  }
```

Explanation:

This application now invokes **getContext().getUser()** which returns the object of the current user invoking the operation. Using the return value, the application now mandates the requirement of **Administrator** privilege before performing the requested operation.

To bring in some more additional services: Log and manage the transactions for all the operations that take place using this application.

Solution [OperateBankAccount.java] [with Logging and Transaction Manager services]:

```
1   public class OperateBankAccount{
2     public long deposit(long depositAmount){
3       logger.info("Start of deposit method");
4       Transaction trasaction = getContext().getTransaction();
5       transaction.begin();
6       try{
7         User user = getContext().getUser();
8         if (user.getRole().equals("BankAdmin"){
9           newAmount = existingAccount + depositAccount;
10          currentAmount = newAmount;
11        }
12        transaction.commit();
13      }catch(Exception exception){
14        transaction.rollback();
15      }
16      logger.info("End of deposit method");
17      return currentAmount;
18    }
19
20    public long withdraw(long withdrawalAmount){
21      logger.info("Start of withdraw method");
22      Transaction trasaction = getContext().getTransaction();
23      transaction.begin();
24      try{
25        User user = getContext().getUser();
26        if (user.getRole().equals("BankAdmin"){
27          if (withdrawalAmount <= currentAmount){
28            currentAmount = currentAmount - withdrawalAmount;
29          }
30        }
31        transaction.commit();
32      }catch(Exception exception){
33        transaction.rollback();
34      }
35      logger.info("End of withdraw method");
36      return currentAmount;
37    }
38  }
```

Explanation:

This kind of application structuring has a few disadvantages.

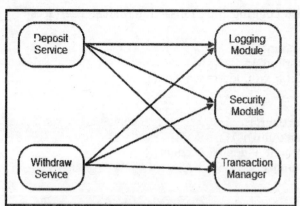

Business objects [Deposit and Withdraw] are intimately involved with the System services [**Logging, Security** and **Transaction Manager**]. Not only does each object know that it is being logged, secured and involved in a transactional context, but also each object is responsible for performing those services for itself.

On every new requirement, the methods and the logic changes which is against the Software Design principles. This is because every piece of newly added code has to undergo the Software Development Lifecycle of Development, Testing, Bug Fixing, Development, Testing and so on. This certainly cannot be encouraged in particularly big projects where a single line of code may have multiple dependencies between other components or other modules in the project.

Solution - AOP

The **OperateBankAccount** class provides the deposit and withdrawal services. But the implementation of these services does much more [such as User Checking, Logging and Transaction Management] than the normal business logic.

User Checking, Logging and Transaction Management services are never a part of the Deposit or the Withdrawal services.

AOP calls such additional system services that cross-cuts or overlaps the existing business logic as **Concerns** or **Cross-Cutting Concerns**.

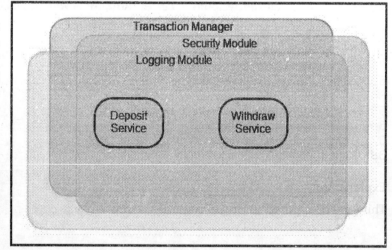

AOP's aim is to isolate the cross-cutting concerns from the application code thereby modularizing them as a different entity and then specifying some kind of relation between the original business code and the Concerns using some techniques.

With AOP, the core application can be covered with layers [**Logging, Security** and **Transaction Manager**] of functionality. These layers can be applied declaratively throughout the application in a flexible manner without the core application even knowing they exist.

Reduce Boilerplate Code Using Templates

Boilerplate is the term used to describe sections of code that have to be included in many places with little or no alteration.

An Application With Boilerplate Code

A lot of boilerplate code can be seen when using JDBC. For example, the following code uses JDBC to insert a customer record to the Customer database table. This shows the amount of code that is written to insert a simple record into the database using JDBC.

Solution [JDBCCustomersDAOImpl.java]:

```
 1   package com.springforbeginners;
 2
 3   import java.sql.Connection;
 4   import java.sql.PreparedStatement;
 5   import java.sql.ResultSet;
 6   import java.sql.SQLException;
 7   import javax.sql.DataSource;
 8   import com.springforbeginners.domain.Customer;
 9
10   public class JDBCCustomersDAOImpl implements CustomersDAO {
11       private DataSource dataSource;
12       public void setDataSource(DataSource dataSource) {
13           this.dataSource = dataSource;
14       }
15
16       public void insertData(Customer customer) {
17           String query = "INSERT INTO Customers (CustomerID, CustomerName,
             CustomerAddress) VALUES (?,?,?)";
18       \* Defining the connection and Prepared Statement parameters. *\
19           Connection connection = null;
20           PreparedStatement preparedStatement = null;
21           try {
22           \* Opening the connection. *\
23               connection = dataSource.getConnection();
24           \* Preparing the statement. *\
25               preparedStatement = connection.prepareStatement(query);
26           \* Binding the parameters to the Prepared Statement. *\
27               preparedStatement.setInt(1, customer.getCustomerId());
28               preparedStatement.setString(2, customer.getCustomerName());
```

```
29          preparedStatement.setString(3, customer.getCustomerAddress());
30      \* Executing the statement. *\
31          preparedStatement.execute();
32      } catch (SQLException e) {
33      \* Handling any exception. *\
34          e.printStackTrace();
35      } finally {
36          try {
37          \* Closing the Prepared Statement. *\
38              if (preparedStatement != null) {
39                  preparedStatement.close();
40              }
41          \* Closing the connection. *\
42              if (connection != null) {
43                  connection.close();
44              }
45          } catch (SQLException e) {
46          \* Handling any exception. *\
47              e.printStackTrace();
48          }
49      }
50  }
51 }
```

Explanation:
This JDBC code inserts a record in the Customer database table using an INSERT SQL query.

What's worth noting here is:
The small bit of code that's specific to inserting the record is concealed in a heap of other JDBC code.

To insert a single record into the database table, this program does the following:

1. Defines the connection and Prepared Statement parameters

2. Opens the connection

3. Prepares the statement

4. Binds the parameters to the Prepared Statement

5. Executes the statement

6. Handles any exception

7. Closes the Prepared Statement

8. Closes the connection

9. Handles any exception

Most of the code in this program is boilerplate code which is required to manage the resources and handle exceptions.

Boilerplate code makes the application hard to maintain, as the same code is written over and over again to accomplish common and otherwise simple tasks. This also makes the application potentially buggy.

JDBC is not alone in the boilerplate code business. Many activities such as JMS, JNDI and the consumption of REST services often involve a lot of commonly repeated code.

Spring comes to the rescue by offering templates. Templates help abstract the boilerplate code.

Spring helps eliminate such boilerplate code by encapsulating it in templates. Spring's **JdbcTemplate** makes it possible to perform database operations without all of the traditional JDBC code.

An Application Using Spring's JdbcTemplate

The same program is re-written using Spring's JdbcTemplate. This program now only focusses on the task of inserting customer data and not catering to the demands of the JDBC API.

Solution [CustomersDAOImpl.java]:

```
1   public class CustomersDAOImpl implements CustomersDAO {
2       private JdbcTemplate jdbcTemplate;
3       public void setDataSource(DataSource dataSource) {
4           this.jdbcTemplate = new JdbcTemplate(dataSource);
5       }
6
7       public void insertCustomers(Customer customer) {
8       \* Specifying the statement. *\
9           String query = "INSERT INTO Customers (CustomerID, CustomerName,
                CustomerAddress) VALUES (?,?,?)";
10      \* Specifying the values. *\
11          jdbcTemplate.update(query, new Object[] {
12              Integer.valueOf(customer.getCustomerId()),
13              customer.getCustomerName(), customer.getCustomerAddress() });
14      }
15  }
```

Explanation:

Since this program now uses JDBCTemplate, code is only written for inserting the data and all the other boilerplate code tasks are taken care by the template itself.

Several **update()** methods are available, implement the one that is simple and suites the requirement. The one that this program implements accepts an SQL query and an array of Object that contains values to be bound to indexed parameters of the query.

Spring Framework Modules

The Spring framework is created to address the complexity of enterprise application development. Spring as a framework consists of several well-defined modules which are constructed in a layered manner on the top of its **Core Container**, which define how beans are created, configured and managed.

One of the primary advantages of the Spring framework is its layered architecture. The layered architecture allows being selective about which of its modules are going to be used in the application being developed. This means the developer is free to choose the required modules or features and eliminate the modules which are of no use.

The Spring framework functionality can be used in any Java EE server and most of it is also adaptable to non-managed environments.

It aims to have reusable business and data-access objects that are not tied to specific Java EE services. Such objects can be thus reused across several Java EE environments such as Web, EJB, standalone applications and so on.

Each of the modules that comprise the Spring framework can stand on its own or be implemented jointly with one or more of the others. The functionality of each component is as follows:

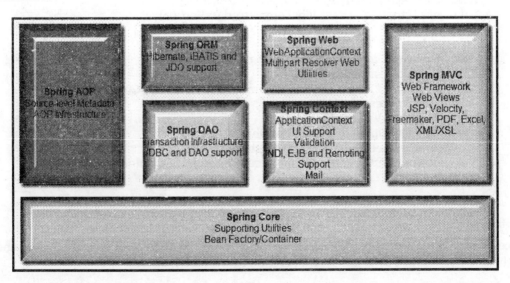

The Core Container

In an application built using the Spring framework, the application objects live within the Core container.

The container provides a consistent means of configuring and managing Java objects using callbacks. The container is responsible for managing object lifecycles such as:

❑   Creating objects

❑   Calling initialization methods

❑   Configuring objects by wiring them together

Objects created by the container are also called **Managed Objects** or **Beans**. Typically, the container is configured by loading XML files containing Bean definitions which provide the information required to create the bean. It uses Dependency Injection [DI] to manage the modules that make up an application.

Spring comes with several container implementations that can be categorized into:

Bean Factories [org.springframework.beans.factory.BeanFactory]

BeanFactory is an implementation of the Factory pattern which creates the bean as per the configurations provided by the developer in an XML file. BeanFactory applies the Inversion of Control [IoC] pattern to separate an application's configuration and dependency specification from the actual application code.

Application Contexts [org.springframework.context.ApplicationContext]

ApplicationContext is built on the notion of a bean factory by providing application framework services such as the ability to resolve textual messages from a properties file and the ability to publish application events to interested event listeners.

Application contexts are preferred over bean factories, as Bean factories are often too low-level for most applications.

Spring Context

The Spring context is a configuration file that provides context information to the Spring framework. The Spring context includes enterprise services such as JNDI, EJB, e-mail, internalization, validation and scheduling functionality.

Spring AOP

The AOP module brings in the aspect-oriented programming functionality into the Spring framework, through its configuration management feature. This module allows developers to define method-interceptors and point cuts to cleanly decouple code implementing functionality that should logically be separated.

With AOP, application-wide concerns such as transactions and security are decoupled from the objects to which they are applied.

Spring DAO

Working with JDBC often results in a lot of boilerplate code that obtains a database connection, creates a statement, processes a result set and then closes the database connection. All of this is abstracted by Spring's **Data Access Objects** [DAO] by providing a JDBC-abstraction layer to such low level tasks.

It also maintains a hierarchy of meaningful exceptions rather than throwing complicated error codes from specific database vendors. The exception hierarchy simplifies error handling and greatly reduces the amount of exception code that needs to be written such as opening and closing connections.

This module uses AOP to manage transactions. Since it integrates the transaction management framework, it is possible to set up a transactional system through configuration without having to rely on JTA or EJB.

The transactional framework also integrates with messaging and caching engines.

Spring ORM

For those who prefer using an **Object-Relational Mapping** [ORM] tool over straight JDBC, Spring provides the ORM module.

Spring does not provide its own ORM implementation, but its ORM module plugs in several popular object-relational mapping APIs including Hibernate, Java Persistence API, Java Data Objects and iBATIS SQL Maps. Spring's transaction management supports each of these ORM frameworks as well as JDBC.

Using the ORM module the developer can use all those O/R-mappers in combination with all the other features that the Spring framework offers.

Spring Web Module

The Spring Web module is part of Spring's web application development stack, which includes Spring MVC. The Web context module builds on top of the application context module, providing contexts for Web-based applications. As a result, the Spring framework supports integration with Jakarta Struts. The Web module also eases the tasks of handling multi-part requests and binding request parameters to domain objects.

Spring Web MVC

Spring comes with a capable MVC framework that eases the task of developing web applications and also promotes Spring's loosely coupled techniques in the web layer of an application. This framework comes in two forms:

❑ **Servlet**-based framework for conventional web applications

❑ **Portlet**-based application for developing against the Java Portlet API

Spring's MVC framework provides a clean separation between domain model code and web forms and allows the developer to use all the other features of the Spring framework.

Spring separates the roles of the controller, the model object, the dispatcher and the handler object which makes it easier to customize them. Spring's Web MVC does not push the user to use only JSPs for the view. The user has the flexibility to use JSPs, XSLT, Velocity templates and so on to render the view.

Spring also integrates very well with several popular MVC frameworks such as Struts, Tapestry, JSF, Wicket and so on.

Summary

This chapter gave a good idea of what Spring brings to the table. It gave a glimpse of Spring's framework architecture and scratched the surface of different Spring's modules. Now, let's understand what the Hibernate ORM does for us, in the very next chapter.

Chapter

2

SECTION I: UNDERSTANDING THE FRAMEWORK

Introduction To Hibernate 4

Persistence is one of the most vital piece of an application without which all the data is simply lost.

Often when choosing the persistence storage medium the following fundamental qualifiers are considered:

❑   The length of time data must be persisted

❑   The volume of data

For example,
An HTTP session can be considered when the life of a piece of data is limited to the user's session. However, persistence over several sessions or several users, requires a Database

Large amounts of data should not be stored in an HTTP session, instead a database should be considered.

The type of database that is chosen also plays an important influence on the architecture and design.

In today's object-oriented world, data is represented as OBJECTS. This is often called a DOMAIN model. However, the storage medium is based on a RELATIONAL paradigm. These objects have to be persisted to a relational database.

The inevitable mismatch between the object-oriented code spec [DOMAIN model] and the relational database requires writing a lot of code spec that maps one to the other. This code spec is often complex, tedious and costly to develop.

One of the most popular tools to address the mismatch problem is object-relational mappers.

An object-relational mapper is software used to transform an object view of the data into a relational one and provide persistence services such as **CREATE**, **READ**, **UPDATE** and **DELETE** [CRUD].

One of the most popular object-relational mappers is the open source Hibernate project. Hibernate acts as a layer between the application and the database by taking care of loading and saving of objects.

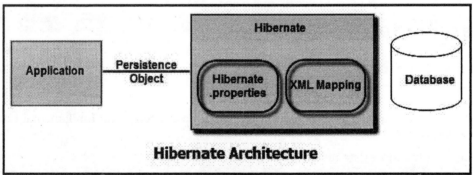

Hibernate Architecture

Diagram 2.1

About Hibernate

Hibernate applications are cheaper, more portable and more resilient to change.

Hibernate is a popular, powerful and a free, open source **Object Relational Mapping** library for the Java programming language. It can be used both in standalone Java applications and in Java EE applications using Servlets or EJB - Session Beans.

Hibernate was developed by a team of Java software developers around the world led by Gavin King, JBoss Inc. [now part of Red Hat] and later hired the lead Hibernate developers and worked with them in supporting Hibernate.

Hibernate allows the developer to focus on the objects and features of the application, without having to worry about how to store them or find them later.

Hibernate provides a framework for mapping an object oriented domain model to a traditional relational database.

Hibernate provides mapping between:

❑   The Java classes and the database tables

❑   The Java data types and SQL data types

Hibernate also provides data query and retrieval facilities. It generates the SQL calls and relieves the developer from manual result set handling and object conversion, keeping the application portable to all supported SQL databases, with database portability delivered at very little performance overhead.

When dealing with the database programming, it can significantly speed up the productivity and simplify the procedure of development.

To use Hibernate:

❑   Java bean classes [POJOs] that represents the table in the database are created

❑   The instance variables of the class are mapped to the columns in the database table

Hibernate allows performing operations SELECT, INSERT, UPDATE and DELETE on the database tables by automatically creating the required SQL query.

Architecture Of Hibernate

Hibernate is made up of the following three components:

Connection Management

Hibernate's Connection management service provides efficient management of the database connections. Database connection is the most expensive portion of an application that allows interacting with the database.

Transaction Management

Transaction management service provides the ability to execute more than one database statements at a time.

Object Relational Mapping

Object relational mapping is a technique of mapping the data representation from an object model to a relational data model. This part of Hibernate is used to SELECT, INSERT, UPDATE and DELETE records from the underlying database tables.

Usually a populated object of a POJO is passed to **Session.save()**. Hibernate reads the state of the variables of that object and executes the necessary SQL query.

A Quick Overview Of Hibernate

Hibernate makes use of persistent objects commonly called as **POJO** [Plain Old Java Object] along with XML mapping documents for persisting objects to the database layer.

HINT

POJO refers to a simple Java object that does not serve any other special role or implement any special interfaces of any of the Java frameworks such as EJB, JDBC, DAO and so on.

Hibernate uses runtime reflection to determine the persistent properties of a class. The objects to be persisted are defined in a mapping document, which serves to describe the persistent fields and associations, as well as any subclasses or proxies of the persistent object.

The mapping documents are compiled when the application starts. These documents provide the framework with the necessary information about a class. Additionally, they are used in support operations such as generating the database schema or creating stub Java source files.

Reviewing Typical Hibernate Code Spec

The Authors Table

This table stores the author details.

Column Name	Data Type	Size	Null	Default	Constraints
AuthorNo	Integer	10	No	- -	Primary Key
Description	An identity number of the author				
FirstName	Varchar	30	No	- -	- -
Description	The first name of the author				
LastName	Varchar	30	No	- -	- -
Description	The last name of the author				

Hibernate Configuration File [hibernate.cfg.xml]

Hibernate configuration file holds information needed to connect to the persistent layer and the linked mapping documents.

Here, either the data source name or JDBC details can be specified. These details are required for hibernate to make JDBC connection to the database.

<mapping-resource> refers to the mapping document that contains mapping for domain object and database table columns.

```
1   <?xml version="1.0" encoding="UTF-8"?>
2   <!DOCTYPE hibernate-configuration PUBLIC "-//Hibernate/Hibernate Configuration DTD 3.0//EN"
    "http://hibernate.sourceforge.net/hibernate-configuration-3.0.dtd">
3   <hibernate-configuration>
4    <session-factory>
5     <property name="hibernate.dialect">org.hibernate.dialect.MySQLDialect</property>
6     <property name="hibernate.connection.driver_class">com.mysql.jdbc.Driver</property>
7     <property name="hibernate.connection.url">jdbc:mysql://localhost:3306/bms</property>
8     <property name="hibernate.connection.username">root</property>
9     <property name="hibernate.connection.password">123456</property>
10    <property name="hibernate.default_catalog">bms</property>
11    <mapping resource="Authors.hbm.xml"/>
12   </session-factory>
13  </hibernate-configuration>
```

POJO [Authors.java]

To use Hibernate, it is required to create Java classes [POJO's] that represents the table in the database and then map the instance variables of the class with the columns in the database table. After which Hibernate can be used to perform operations on the database such as SELECT, INSERT, UPDATE and DELETE.

Hibernate automatically creates the SQL query to perform these operations.

```
1   package beans;
2
3   public class Authors {
4       private int AuthorNo;
5       private String FirstName, LastName;
6       public Authors() {
7       }
8       public int getAuthorNo() {
9           return AuthorNo;
10      }
11      public void setAuthorNo(int AuthorNo) {
12          this.AuthorNo = AuthorNo;
13      }
14      public String getFirstName() {
15          return FirstName;
16      }
17      public void setFirstName(String FirstName) {
18          this.FirstName = FirstName;
19      }
20      public String getLastName() {
21          return LastName;
22      }
23      public void setLastName(String LastName) {
24          this.LastName = LastName;
25      }
26  }
```

Hibernate is not restricted in its usage of property types. All Java JDK types and primitives such as String, char, Date and so on can be mapped, including classes from the Java collections framework.

These can be mapped as values, collections of values or associations to other entities.

Mapping Document [Authors.hbm.xml]

Each persistent class [POJO] needs to be mapped with its configuration file.

The following code spec represents Hibernate mapping file for the Authors class.

```
1   <?xml version="1.0" encoding="UTF-8"?>
2   <!DOCTYPE hibernate-mapping PUBLIC "-//Hibernate/Hibernate Mapping DTD 3.0//EN"
    "http://hibernate.sourceforge.net/hibernate-mapping-3.0.dtd">
3   <hibernate-mapping>
4     <class name="beans.Authors" table="authors">
5       <id name="AuthorNo" type="integer">
6         <column name="AuthorNo"/>
7         <generator class="increment"/>
8       </id>
9       <property name="FirstName" type="string">
10        <column length="30" name="FirstName" not-null="true"/>
11      </property>
12      <property name="LastName" type="string">
13        <column length="30" name="LastName" not-null="true"/>
14      </property>
15    </class>
16  </hibernate-mapping>
```

Hibernate mapping documents are straight forward.

<class> maps a table with corresponding class.

<id> represents the primary key column and its associated attribute in the domain object. It represents the database IDENTIFER [primary key] of that class, Hibernate can use identifiers only internally.

<property> represent all other attributes available in the domain object.

Performing Database Operations

Here is how Hibernate can be used in an application.

A typical Hibernate application begins with configuration that is required for Hibernate.

Hibernate can be configured in two ways, Programmatically or using a Configuration file.

In Configuration file based mode, Hibernate looks for configuration file **hibernate.cfg.xml** in the classpath.

Based on the resource mapping provided, Hibernate creates mapping of tables and domain objects.

In the programmatic configuration method, the details such as JDBC connection details and resource mapping details are supplied in the program using Configuration API.

Prior performing database operations, a Hibernate session needs to be created.

Creating The Session Factory

Here, the application retrieves the Hibernate Session.

Hibernate **Session** is the <u>main runtime interface</u> between a Java application and Hibernate.

SessionFactory allows applications to create hibernate session by reading hibernate configurations file **hibernate.cfg.xml**.

```
1  sessionFactory = new Configuration().configure().buildSessionFactory();
2
3  Session session = sessionFactory.openSession();
```

Performing A Database Operation [Insert]

```
1   Transaction tx = session.beginTransaction();
2
3   Authors newAuthor = new Authors();
4   newAuthor.setFirstName("Sharanam");
5   newAuthor.setLastName("Shah");
6
7   session.save(newAuthor);
8
9   tx.commit();
10
11  session.close();
```

After the Hibernate session is available, to insert data in the Authors table, a transaction is required.

After specifying the transaction boundaries, application can make use of persistent Java objects and use session for persisting to the database.

Hence, an object of the Authors class is created and the required data is assigned to that object using the SETTER methods.

Finally, the Authors object is passed to the Hibernate session object's **save()** to save this as a new record in the database table.

The transaction is committed and the session is closed.

REMINDER

AuthorNo is set to automatically increment in the Mapping document
<generator class="**increment**"/>

Hence, it's not set using the SETTER method.

Performing A Database Operation [Select]

```
 1   ArrayList arrayList = null;
 2
 3   String SQL_STRING = "FROM Authors";
 4
 5   Query query = session.createQuery(SQL_STRING);
 6
 7   ArrayList list = (ArrayList)query.list();
 8
 9   for(int i=0; i<list.size();i++)
10   {
11       System.out.println(list.get(i));
12   }
13
14   session.close();
```

Here, the domain object called Authors is queried.

Hibernate automatically generates the SELECT SQL query and returns the result.

This result is retrieved and placed in an ArrayList object. This object is typically used in a JSP to display the records available in that object.

Prerequisites

Hibernate is an amazing technology. With a little experience and the power of Java 5 annotations, it's possible to build a complex database-backed application with ease.

It's often noticed that once a developer builds an application using Hibernate, the developer will never ever want to go back to the traditional method.

To true newcomers to the Hibernate API, it's recommended to gain at-least some basic knowledge before diving into this book's project.

Chapter 20 of our earlier book called "**Spring 3 For Beginners**" will definitely help the newcomers gain the required knowledge on Hibernate 4 and its **integration** with Spring 3.

Chapter

3

SECTION II: ABOUT THE PROJECT
The Project Case Study

The Web has come a long way in the last few years. Today, visitors want more than a pretty website design. They need meaningful and efficient E-Commerce websites packed with interactive elements that let them indicate their requirements to the business houses.

Running an online business requires flexible tools that are at the cutting edge of technology.

One such popular E-Commerce Web application is an **Online Shopping Cart**.

Online Shopping has made the life of the customers easier. Now, the customers have more variety, easier way of searching and browsing and more consistent modes of payment.

Building an online shopping cart has become possible due to enhancement of Internet technologies used to develop Web applications. These Web applications are some business supporting websites which make a product accessible to the customer in an easier and efficient manner.

A standard online shopping Web application must:

❑   Support the customers efficiently

- ❑ Successfully market the products
- ❑ Support online credit card processing
- ❑ Provide easy payment and checkout options
- ❑ Provide detailed transaction/sales reports

These features make the e-business thrive in a relentlessly competitive Web environment.

This book demonstrates developing an Online Shopping web application, which can be used to search and buy products online. Both the customer and the owner can benefit by the use of this web application which helps them to commence their transactions in a better, consistent and reliable manner.

The application being built will provide a large range of categories and products for the customers. It will change the business domain of the client from local to international. Customers from all over the world can search and browse for the available products. A customer can select the desired products, place an order and make the payment for the selected products.

Software Requirements

This web application will be built using the following applications and frameworks:
- ❑ JDK 7 Update 4
- ❑ NetBeans 7.1.2
- ❑ Spring 3.2.0.M1
- ❑ Hibernate 4.1.4.Final
- ❑ MySQL 5.5.25
- ❑ MySQL Connector/J 5.1.20
- ❑ Spring Security 3.1.0.RELEASE

Software Development Life Cycle Of The Project

This project is a Web application, which will be developed using **Spring 3** as the Web Application Framework and **Hibernate 4** as the Object-Relational Mapping [ORM] library.

Requirement Analysis

This is the first part in the life cycle of any project. Here the requirements of the end user are gathered and analyzed. The project development is based on this analysis.

Usually the client is asked the following questions:

❑ What are their requirements?

❑ What requirements are expected to be fulfilled by the project?

These are the questions, which must be answered before moving on to the next stage of the project development.

Client Side Requirements

The client is a book shop owner who desires to make their products [books] accessible to the customers in an efficient manner.

This application should help them in:

❑ Maintaining a detailed record of the following:

    o Available categories and products [in this case books] associated with each category

    o Authors who have written these books

    o Publishers who have published these books

❑ Making each book available for all customers to see, browse and buy online

❑ Adding, deleting, modifying various categories of books

❑ Adding, deleting, modifying the book details

❑ Adding, deleting, modifying various authors of books

❑ Adding, deleting, modifying various publishers of books

❑ Accepting orders and payments from customers

❑ Viewing transactions [orders placed] performed by the customers

Customer Side Requirements

The customers must be able to access the application to browse the required books. They must be able to search the available books, add them into the shopping cart, place order and make online payment using a credit card.

The requirements once analyzed help in creating a platform to design the software.

Software Design

The software designing phase can be divided into two separate phase i.e. high level and low level. In the high level phase, all the interfaces and forms are designed and the way of input and output is decided.

The formats of input and output are finalized and a framework of all the interfaces or the Web pages is designed.

This high level designing is done according to the requirement specification. All the interfaces should be designed, keeping in mind the need and convenience of the user.

Based upon the output of the high level design phase, a detailed design of the application is developed. This is called the low level design phase, which gives proper details such as functions of various modules of the application, number of classes and so on.

The Design Pattern

This application will follow the Model View Controller [MVC] design paradigm separating the application in three layers:

❑   **Model:** Application State

❑   **View:** Presentation Layer [JSP]

❑   **Controller:** Routing of Application Flow

In this book, *Section 4: Process Flow*, *Section 5: Backend [Administration] Software Design Documentation* and *Section 6: Frontend [Customer Facing] Software Design Documentation* take care of the High Level and Low Level Software Design phase.

The best thing about this project is that it is developed using Spring and Hibernate, which is becoming standard for developing well-structured Java based Web applications.

This application [based on these requirements] can be bifurcated as:

❑   Backend [Administration - For the client]

❑   Frontend [Customer facing]

Backend [Administration - For The Client]

This includes various functionalities related to the administrator who will be the client and its employees.

A valid set of username and password from a person having appropriate privileges is required to log in to this module.

After gaining access to the system, the administrator can add, delete and update various items, categories, authors and publishers.

Customer Module

A customer is a user of the site who browses / searches the website for the books of choice. The customer can add the desired books into the shopping cart.

A customer can also place an order for the selected books and make an online payment using a credit card.

Data Flow Diagram

The Context level Data Flow Diagram [DFD], shown in diagram 3.1 can be helpful to understand the basic functioning of the project. The arrow shows the flow of data from one person to another through various processes.

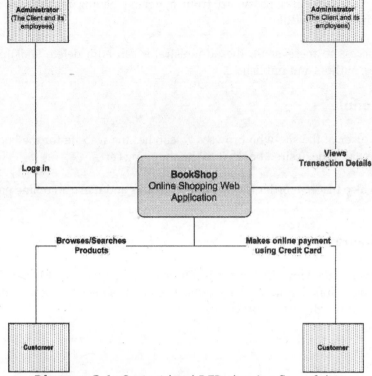

Diagram 3.1: Context level DFD showing flow of data

Development

In this phase, all the designed user interfaces and other supporting code files are written.

Various components like JSP pages, JavaBeans [POJO's] and some other classes are developed.

The code is written and compiled and all the developed components are put together in a standard manner to work together.

The project's complete source code can be found on this book's accompanying CDROM.

The project folder is named **BookShop**.

The reader can copy the project folder [BookShop], update the configuration files with the appropriate database username / password, build it using an IDE like NetBeans and deploy the .WAR on a Web server of choice.

Diagram 3.2 presents the home page of this Web application.

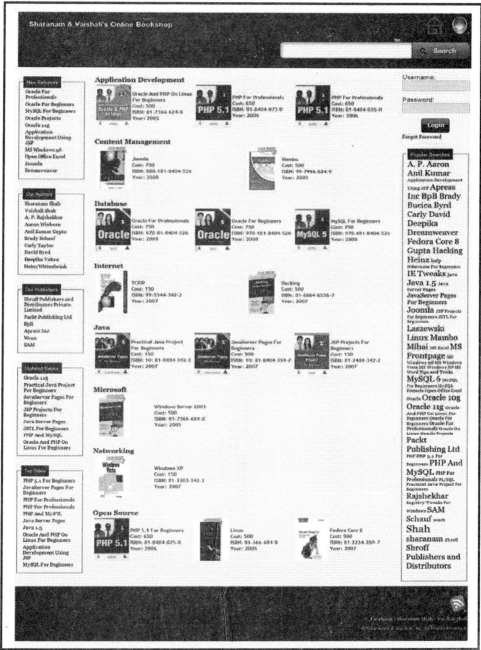

Diagram 3.2: Home page of the BookShop application

This chapter discussed the various phases of the software development life cycle of this project and also provided a brief description of the software requirements and what a reader should know prior to starting this project.

Every phase is critical. The development of the next phase totally depends upon the outcome of the previous one. Hence a proper requirement specification helps in a better design and a better design makes the life of developer easier.

Chapter

4

SECTION II: ABOUT THE PROJECT

Software Requirements Specification

Backend Modules

Login

Objective	To allow a system user to login to the system
Actors	Book shop employee, Book shop owner, System administrator
Pre-Condition	Person trying to log in should have the System User or the System Administrator privileges
Post-Condition	Actors successfully authenticate themselves and log in to the system

Steps

1. System User navigates to the homepage
2. System User clicks Administration

3. System displays the Administration Login Page with a data entry form to capture the following:

Form Field	Type	Unique	Required	Max Size
Username	Text box	Yes	Yes	- -
Password	Text box	Yes	Yes	- -

4. System User enters the username and the password
5. System User clicks Login [Refer A-1]
6. System authenticates the username and password. If found valid, the system displays Manage Transactions

Alternate Steps

A-1: Invalid User

System displays a message indicating that the username or password is not valid.

Data Validations

Basic form validation must be done before submitting the form:

a. Required fields
   i. Username
   ii. Password

Manage Countries

All the countries where authors, publishers or end users reside should be managed via the application.

This includes the ability to view all the countries, add a new country, edit and delete an existing country.

View Countries

Objective	To view a list of all Countries
Actors	Book shop employee, Book shop owner, System administrator
Pre-Condition	Users have sufficient privileges to view all countries
	At least one Country exists
Post-Condition	Actors view all the available countries

Steps

1. User navigates to the backend [site administration] login page

2. User logs in successfully

3. System displays the backend home page with Countries as one of the menu options

4. User selects the Countries option to view existing countries

5. System displays a list of all the countries currently in the system with the following information:

    ❑   Name of the Country

Add Countries

Objective	To add a new Country
Actors	Book shop employee, Book shop owner, System administrator
Pre-Condition	Users have sufficient privileges to add countries
Post-Condition	Actors successfully add a new country

Steps

1. User navigates to the backend [site administration] login page

2. User logs in successfully

3. System displays the backend home page with Countries as one of the menu options

4. User selects the Countries option to add a new country

5. System displays a data entry form to capture the following:

Form Field	Type	Unique	Required	Max Size
Country	Text box	Yes	Yes	25

6. User enters all the required information in the fields

7. User selects the option to save data [Refer A-1]

8. System saves the data and creates the new country [Refer A-2]

9. System refreshes the page to reflect the newly added countries

Alternate Steps

A-1: User selects Cancel

System does not save any user entered data.

System does not create a new country.

A-2: Duplicate Country

User enters a country name that already exists.
System displays a message that the country already exists.
System does not create a new country.

Edit Countries

Objective	To edit an existing Country
Actors	Book shop employee, Book shop owner, System administrator
Pre-Condition	Users have sufficient privileges to edit countries
Post-Condition	Actors successfully edit an existing country

Steps

1. User navigates to the backend [site administration] login page
2. User logs in successfully
3. System displays the backend home page with Countries as one of the menu options
4. User selects the Countries option to view and edit existing countries
5. Users clicks the Edit link of the desired country for editing
6. System displays a data entry form pre-populated with the existing form data
7. User edits the desired information in the fields
8. User selects option to save data [Refer A-1]
9. System saves the data and updates the existing country [Refer A-2]
10. System refreshes the page to reflect the updated list of countries

Alternate Steps

A-1: User selects Cancel

System does not save any user entered data.
System does not update the country.

A-2: Duplicate Country

User enters a country name that already exists.
System displays a message that the country already exists.

System does not update the country.

Delete Countries

Objective	To delete an existing Country
Actors	Book shop employee, Book shop owner, System administrator
Pre-Condition	Users have sufficient privileges to delete countries
Post-Condition	Actors successfully delete an existing country

Steps

1. User navigates to the backend [site administration] login page

2. User logs in successfully

3. System displays the backend home page with Countries as one of the menu options

4. User selects the Countries option to delete existing country

5. User selects the Delete link of the desired information to delete an existing country

6. System deletes the country only if that country is not referenced by a customer or an author or a publisher in the system [Refer A-1]

7. System refreshes the page to reflect the updated list of countries

Alternate Steps

A-1: Country is referenced by a customer, author and publisher

System displays a message indicating that the record(s) cannot be deleted as they are associated with exiting data.
System does not delete the country.

Data Validations

Basic form validation must be done before submitting the form:

a. Required fields

    i.   Country

b. Duplicate entries not allowed

    i.   Country

Manage States

All the states where authors, publishers or end users reside should be managed via the application.

This includes the ability to view all the states, add a new state, edit and delete an existing state.

View States

Objective	To view a list of all States
Actors	Book shop employee, Book shop owner, System administrator
Pre-Condition	Users have sufficient privileges to view all locations At least one State exists
Post-Condition	Actors view all the available states

Steps

1. User navigates to the backend [site administration] login page
2. User logs in successfully
3. System displays the backend home page with States as one of the menu options
4. User selects the States option to view existing states
5. System displays a list of all the states currently in the system

Add States

Objective	To add a new State
Actors	Book shop employee, Book shop owner, System administrator
Pre-Condition	Users have sufficient privileges to add states
Post-Condition	Actors successfully adds a new state

Steps

1. User navigates to the backend [site administration] login page
2. User logs in successfully
3. System displays the backend home page with States as one of the menu options
4. User selects the States option to add a new state

5. System displays a data entry form to capture the following:

Form Field	Type	Unique	Required	Max Size
State	Text box	No	Yes	25

6. User enters all required information in the fields

7. User selects the option to save data [Refer A-1]

8. System saves the data and creates the new state [Refer A-2]

9. System refreshes the page to reflect the newly added states

Alternate Steps

A-1: User selects Cancel

System does not save any user entered data.
System does not create a new state.

A-2: Duplicate State

User enters a state name that already exists.
System displays a message that the state already exists.
System does not create a new state.

Edit States

Objective	To edit an existing State
Actors	Book shop employee, Book shop owner, System administrator
Pre-Condition	Users have sufficient privileges to edit states
Post-Condition	Actors successfully edit an existing state

Steps

1. User navigates to the backend [site administration] login page

2. User logs in successfully

3. System displays the backend home page with States as one of the menu options

4. User selects the States option to view and edit existing states

5. Users clicks the Edit link of the desired state for editing

6. System displays a data entry form pre-populated with the existing form data

7. User edits the desired information in the fields

8. User selects the option to save data [Refer A-1]

9. System saves the data and updates the existing state [Refer A-2]

10. System refreshes the page to reflect the updated list of states

Alternate Steps

A-1: User selects Cancel

System does not save any user entered data.
System does not update the state.

A-2: Duplicate State

User enters a state name that already exists.
System displays a message that the state already exists.
System does not update the state.

Delete States

Objective	To delete an existing State
Actors	Book shop employee, Book shop owner, System administrator
Pre-Condition	Users have sufficient privileges to delete states
Post-Condition	Actors successfully delete an existing state

Steps

1. User navigates to the backend [site administration] login page

2. User logs in successfully

3. System displays the backend home page with States as one of the menu options

4. User selects the States option to delete existing state

5. User selects the Delete link of the desired information to delete an existing state

6. System deletes the state only if that state is not referenced by a customer or an author or a publisher in the system [Refer A-1]

7. System refreshes the page to reflect the updated list of states

Alternate Steps

A-1: State is referenced by a customer, author and publisher

System displays a message indicating that the record(s) cannot be deleted as they are associated with exiting data.
System does not delete the state.

Data Validations

Basic form validation must be done before submitting the form:

a. Required fields

i. State

b. Duplicate entries not allowed

i. State

Manage Authors

All the author's details should be managed via the application.

This includes the ability to view all the authors, add a new author, edit and delete an existing author.

View Authors

Objective	To view a list of all Authors
Actors	Book shop employee, Book shop owner, System administrator
Pre-Condition	Users have sufficient privileges to view all authors
	At least one Author exists
Post-Condition	Actors view all the available authors

Steps

1. User navigates to the backend [site administration] login page

2. User logs in successfully

3. System displays the backend home page with Authors as one of the menu options

4. User selects the Authors option to view existing authors

5. System displays a list of all the authors currently in the system with the following information:

    ❑   Name of the Author

    ❑   Specialty of the Author

    ❑   Photograph of the Author

Add Authors

Objective	To add a new Author
Actors	Book shop employee, Book shop owner, System administrator
Pre-Condition	Users have sufficient privileges to add authors
Post-Condition	Actors successfully add a new author

Steps

1. User navigates to the backend [site administration] login page

2. User logs in successfully

3. System displays the backend home page with Authors as one of the menu options

4. User selects the Authors option to add a new author

5. System displays a data entry form to capture the following:

Form Field	Type	Unique	Required	Max Size
First Name	Text box	No	Yes	25
Last Name	Text box	No	Yes	25
Address Line 1	Text box	No	No	50
Address Line 2	Text box	No	No	50
Country	Drop down list box	No	No	- -
State	Drop down list box	No	No	- -
City	Text box	No	No	50
Pincode	Text box	No	No	15
Birthdate	Text box	No	No	25
Degree	Text box	No	No	25
Email Address	Text box	Yes	Yes	50
Photograph	File upload	No	No	- -
Speciality	Text Area	No	No	55 cols 5 rows

6. User enters all the required information in the fields

7. User selects the option to save data [Refer A-1]

8. System saves the data and creates the new author [Refer A-2]

9.   System refreshes the page to reflect the newly added authors

Alternate Steps

A-1: User selects Cancel

System does not save any user entered data.
System does not create a new author.

A-2: Duplicate Email Address

User enters an email address that already exists.
System displays a message that the email address already exists.
System does not create a new author.

Edit Authors

Objective	To edit an existing Author
Actors	Book shop employee, Book shop owner, System administrator
Pre-Condition	Users have sufficient privileges to edit authors
Post-Condition	Actors successfully edit an existing author

Steps

1.   User navigates to the backend [site administration] login page

2.   User logs in successfully

3.   System displays the backend home page with Authors as one of the menu options

4.   User selects the Authors option to view and edit existing authors

5.   Users clicks the Edit link of the desired author for editing

6.   System displays a data entry form pre-populated with the existing form data

7.   User edits the desired information in the fields

8.   User selects the option to save data [Refer A-1]

9.   System saves the data and updates the existing author [Refer A-2]

10.   System refreshes the page to reflect the updated list of authors

Alternate Steps

A-1: User selects Cancel

System does not save any user entered data.
System does not update the author.

A-2: Duplicate Email Address

User enters an email address that already exists.
System displays a message that the email address already exists.
System does not update the author.

Delete Authors

Objective	To delete an existing Author
Actors	Book shop employee, Book shop owner, System administrator
Pre-Condition	Users have sufficient privileges to delete authors
Post-Condition	Actors successfully delete an existing author

Steps

1. User navigates to the backend [site administration] login page

2. User logs in successfully

3. System displays the backend home page with Authors as one of the menu options

4. User selects the Authors option to delete an existing author

5. User selects the Delete link of the desired information to delete existing authors

6. System deletes the author only if that author is not referenced by a book in the system [Refer A-1]

7. System refreshes the page to reflect the updated list of authors

Alternate Steps

A-2: Author is referenced by a book

System displays a message indicating that the record(s) cannot be deleted as they are associated with exiting data.
System does not delete the author.

Data Validations

Basic form validation must be done before submitting the form:

a.   Required fields

   i.   First Name

   ii.   Last Name

   iii.   Email Address

b.   Duplicate entries not allowed

   i.   Email Address

c.   Email Address should be well formed and valid

Manage Publishers

All the publisher's details should be managed via the application.

This includes the ability to view all the publishers, add a new publisher, edit and delete an existing publisher.

View Publishers

Objective	To view a list of all Publishers
Actors	Book shop employee, Book shop owner, System administrator
Pre-Condition	Users have sufficient privileges to view all publishers
	At least one Publisher exists
Post-Condition	Actors view all the available publishers

Steps

1.   User navigates to the backend [site administration] login page

2.   User logs in successfully

3.   System displays the backend home page with Publishers as one of the menu options

4.   User selects the Publishers option to view existing publishers

5.   System displays a list of all the publishers currently in the system with the following information:

   ❑   Name of the Publisher

   ❑   Email Address of the Publisher

Add Publishers

Objective	To add a new Publisher
Actors	Book shop employee, Book shop owner, System administrator
Pre-Condition	Users have sufficient privileges to add publishers
Post-Condition	Actors successfully add a new publisher

Steps

1. User navigates to the backend [site administration] login page
2. User logs in successfully
3. System displays the backend home page with Publishers as one of the menu options
4. User selects the Publishers option to add a new publisher
5. System displays a data entry form to capture the following:

Form Field	Type	Unique	Required	Max Size
Publisher Name	Text box	Yes	Yes	50
Email Address	Text box	Yes	Yes	50
Address Line 1	Text box	No	No	50
Address Line 2	Text box	No	No	50
Country	Drop down list box	No	No	- -
State	Drop down list box	No	No	- -
City	Text box	No	No	50
Pincode	Text box	No	No	15

6. User enters all the required information in the fields
7. User selects the option to save data [Refer A-1]
8. System saves the data and creates the new publisher [Refer A-2]
9. System refreshes the page to reflect the newly added publishers

Alternate Steps

A-1: User selects Cancel

System does not save any user entered data.
System does not create a new publisher.

A-2: Duplicate Email Address

User enters an email address that already exists.

System displays a message that the email address already exists.
System does not create a new publisher.

Edit Publishers

Objective	To edit an existing Publisher
Actors	Book shop employee, Book shop owner, System administrator
Pre-Condition	Users have sufficient privileges to edit publishers
Post-Condition	Actors successfully edit an existing publisher

Steps

1. User navigates to the backend [site administration] login page

2. User logs in successfully

3. System displays the backend home page with Publishers as one of the menu options

4. User selects the Publishers option to view and edit existing publishers

5. Users clicks the Edit link of the desired publisher for editing

6. System displays a data entry form pre-populated with the existing form data

7. User edits the desired information in the fields

8. User selects the option to save data [Refer A-1]

9. System saves the data and updates the existing publisher [Refer A-2]

10. System refreshes the page to reflect the updated list of publishers

Alternate Steps

A-1: User selects Cancel

System does not save any user entered data.
System does not update the publisher.

A-2: Duplicate Email Address

User enters an email address that already exists.
System displays a message that the email address already exists.
System does not update the publisher.

Delete Publishers

Objective	To delete an existing Publisher
Actors	Book shop employee, Book shop owner, System administrator
Pre-Condition	Users have sufficient privileges to delete publishers
Post-Condition	Actors successfully delete an existing publisher

Steps

1. User navigates to the backend [site administration] login page
2. User logs in successfully
3. System displays the backend home page with Publishers as one of the menu options
4. User selects the Publishers option to delete existing publisher
5. User selects the Delete link of the desired information to delete an existing publisher
6. System deletes the publisher only if that publisher is not referenced by a book in the system [Refer A-1]
7. System refreshes the page to reflect the updated list of publishers

Alternate Steps

A-1: Publisher is referenced by a book

System displays a message indicating that the record(s) cannot be deleted as they are associated with exiting data.
System does not delete the publisher.

Data Validations

Basic form validation must be done before submitting the form:

a. Required fields
   i. Publisher Name
   ii. Email Address
b. Duplicate entries not allowed
   i. Email Address
c. Email Address should be well formed and valid

Manage Categories

All the categories of the books should be managed via the application.

This includes the ability to view all the categories, add a new category, edit and delete an existing category.

View Categories

Objective	To view a list of all Categories
Actors	Book shop employee, Book shop owner, System administrator
Pre-Condition	Users have sufficient privileges to view all categories
	At least one Category exists
Post-Condition	Actors view all the available categories

Steps

1. User navigates to the backend [site administration] login page

2. User logs in successfully

3. System displays the backend home page with Categories as one of the menu options

4. User selects the Categories option to view existing categories

5. System displays a list of all the categories currently in the system with the following information:

   ❏ Name of the Category

   ❏ Description of the Category

Add Categories

Objective	To add a new Category
Actors	Book shop employee, Book shop owner, System administrator
Pre-Condition	Users have sufficient privileges to add categories
Post-Condition	Actors successfully add a new category

Steps

1. User navigates to the backend [site administration] login page

2. User logs in successfully

3. System displays the backend home page with Categories as one of the menu options

4. User selects the Categories option to add a new category

5. System displays a data entry form to capture the following:

Form Field	Type	Unique	Required	Max Size
Category	Text box	Yes	Yes	25
Description	Text area	No	Yes	80 cols 5 rows

6. User enters all the required information in the fields

7. User selects the option to save data [Refer A-1]

8. System saves the data and creates the new category [Refer A-2]

9. System refreshes the page to reflect the newly added categories

Alternate Steps

A-1: User selects Cancel

System does not save any user entered data.
System does not create a new category.

A-2: Duplicate Category

User enters a category name that already exists.
System displays a message that the category already exists.
System does not create a new category.

Edit Categories

Objective	To edit an existing Category
Actors	Book shop employee, Book shop owner, System administrator
Pre-Condition	Users have sufficient privileges to edit categories
Post-Condition	Actors successfully edit an existing category

Steps

1. User navigates to the backend [site administration] login page

2. User logs in successfully

3. System displays the backend home page with Categories as one of the menu options

4. User selects the Categories option to view and edit existing categories

5. Users clicks the Edit link of the desired category for editing

6. System displays a data entry form pre-populated with the existing form data

7. User edits the desired information in the fields

8. User selects the option to save data [Refer A-1]

9. System saves the data and updates the existing category [Refer A-2]

10. System refreshes the page to reflect the updated list of categories

Alternate Steps

A-1: User selects Cancel

System does not save any user entered data.
System does not update the category.

A-2: Duplicate Category

User enters a category name that already exists.
System displays a message that the category already exists.
System does not update the category.

Delete Categories

Objective	To delete an existing Category
Actors	Book shop employee, Book shop owner, System administrator
Pre-Condition	Users have sufficient privileges to delete categories
Post-Condition	Actors successfully delete an existing category

Steps

1. User navigates to the backend [site administration] login page

2. User logs in successfully

3. System displays the backend home page with Categories as one of the menu options

4. User selects the Categories option to delete existing category

5. User selects the Delete link of the desired information to delete an existing category

6. System deletes the category only if that category is not referenced by a book in the system [Refer A-1]

7. System refreshes the page to reflect the updated list of categories

Alternate Steps

A-1: Category is referenced by a book

System displays a message indicating that the record(s) cannot be deleted as they are associated with exiting data.
System does not delete the category.

Data Validations

Basic form validation must be done before submitting the form:

a. Required fields

    i. Category

    ii. Description

b. Duplicate entries not allowed

    i. Category

Manage Users

All the users of the administration department [Book shop employee, Book shop owner, System administrator] and all the customers who have registered with the site should be managed via the application.

This includes the ability to view all the users, add a new user, edit and delete an existing user.

View Users

Objective	To view a list of all Users
Actors	Book shop employee, Book shop owner, System administrator
Pre-Condition	Users have sufficient privileges to view all users
	At least one User exists
Post-Condition	Actors view all the available users

Steps

1. User navigates to the backend [site administration] login page
2. User logs in successfully

3. System displays the backend home page with Users as one of the menu options

4. User selects the Users option to view existing users

5. System displays a list of all the users [including the Customers who have registered using the Signup form in the frontend] currently in the system with the following information:

    ❏ Name of the User

    ❏ Username of the User

    ❏ Email Address of the User

    ❏ Authority of the User

Add Users

Objective	To add a new User
Actors	Book shop employee, Book shop owner, System administrator
Pre-Condition	Users have sufficient privileges to add users
Post-Condition	Actors successfully add a new user

Steps

1. User navigates to the backend [site administration] login page

2. User logs in successfully

3. System displays the backend home page with Users as one of the menu options

4. User selects the Users option to add a new user

5. System displays a data entry form to capture the following:

Form Field	Type	Unique	Required	Max Size
First Name	Text box	No	Yes	25
Last Name	Text box	No	Yes	25
Address Line 1	Text box	No	No	50
Address Line 2	Text box	No	No	50
Country	Drop down list box	No	No	- -
State	Drop down list box	No	No	- -
City	Text box	No	No	50
Pincode	Text box	No	No	15
Email Address	Text box	Yes	Yes	50
Birthday	Text box	No	No	25
Username	Text box	Yes	Yes	25

Form Field	Type	Unique	Required	Max Size
Password	Text box	No	Yes	8
New Releases	Check box	No	No	- -
Update Books	Check box	No	No	- -
Account Status (Active)	Check box	No	No	- -
Role	Drop down list box	No	Yes	- -

6. User enters all the required information in the fields

7. User selects the option to save data [Refer A-1]

8. System saves the data and creates the new user [Refer A-2]

9. System refreshes the page to reflect the newly added users

Alternate Steps

A-1: User selects Cancel

System does not save any user entered data.
System does not create a new user.

A-2: Duplicate Email Address and/or Username

User enters an email address and/or a username that already exists.
System displays a message that the email address or the username already exists.
System does not create a new user.

Edit Users

Objective	To edit an existing User
Actors	Book shop employee, Book shop owner, System administrator
Pre-Condition	Users have sufficient privileges to edit users
Post-Condition	Actors successfully edit an existing user

Steps

1. User navigates to the backend [site administration] login page

2. User logs in successfully

3. System displays the backend home page with Users as one of the menu options

4. User selects the Users option to view and edit existing users

5. Users clicks the Edit link of the desired user for editing

6. System displays a data entry form pre-populated with the existing form data

7. User edits the desired information in the fields

8. User selects the option to save data [Refer A-1]

9. System saves the data and updates the existing user [Refer A-2]

10. System refreshes the page to reflect the updated list of users

Alternate Steps

A-1: User selects Cancel

System does not save any user entered data.
System does not update the user.

A-2: Duplicate Email Address and/or Username

User enters an email address and/or a username that already exists.
System displays a message that the email address or the username already exists.
System does not update the user.

Delete Users

Objective	To delete an existing User
Actors	Book shop employee, Book shop owner, System administrator
Pre-Condition	Users have sufficient privileges to delete users
Post-Condition	Actors successfully deletes an existing user

Steps

1. User navigates to the backend [site administration] login page

2. User logs in successfully

3. System displays the backend home page with Users as one of the menu options

4. User selects the Users option to delete existing user

5. User selects the Delete link of the desired information to delete an existing user

6. System deletes the user only if the user being deleted is not Admin [Refer A-1]

7. System refreshes the page to reflect the updated list of users

Alternate Steps

A-1: Admin User being Deleted

System displays a message indicating that it cannot be deleted.
System does not delete the user.

Data Validations

Basic form validation must be done before submitting the form:

a.   Required fields

    i.   First Name

    ii.   Last Name

    iii.   Email Address

    iv.   Username

    v.   Password

    vi.   Authority

b.   Duplicate entries not allowed

    i.   Email Address

    ii.   Username

c.   Email Address should be well formed and valid

Manage Books

All the authored and published books should be managed via the application.

This includes the ability to view all the books, add a new book, edit and delete an existing book.

View Books

Objective	To view a list of all Books
Actors	Book shop employee, Book shop owner, System administrator
Pre-Condition	Users have sufficient privileges to view all books At least one Book exists
Post-Condition	Actors view all the available books

Steps

1. User navigates to the backend [site administration] login page
2. User logs in successfully
3. System displays the backend home page with Books as one of the menu options
4. User selects the Books option to view existing books
5. System displays a list of all the books currently in the system with the following information:
   - ❑ Name of the Book
   - ❑ ISBN of the Book
   - ❑ Synopsis of the Book
   - ❑ The image of the Cover Page of the Book
   - ❑ The Download links of TOC and Sample Chapter of the Book

Add Books

Objective	To add a new Book
Actors	Book shop employee, Book shop owner, System administrator
Pre-Condition	Users have sufficient privileges to add books
Post-Condition	Actors successfully add a new book

Steps

1. User navigates to the backend [site administration] login page
2. User logs in successfully
3. System displays the backend home page with Books as one of the menu options
4. User selects the Books option to add a new book
5. System displays a data entry form to capture the following:

Form Field	Type	Unique	Required	Max Size
Book	Text box	No	Yes	25
Publisher	Drop down list box	No	Yes	- -
Category	Drop down list box	No	Yes	- -
Cover Page Image	File upload	No	No	- -
ISBN	Text box	Yes	Yes	15
Edition	Text box	No	Yes	25
Year	Text box	No	Yes	4

Form Field	Type	Unique	Required	Max Size
Cost	Text box	No	Yes	8
First Author	Drop down list box	No	Yes	- -
Second Author	Drop down list box	No	No	- -
Third Author	Drop down list box	No	No	- -
Fourth Author	Drop down list box	No	No	- -
Synopsis	Text area	No	Yes	55 cols 5 rows
About Authors	Text area	No	Yes	55 cols 5 rows
Topics Covered	Text area	No	No	55 cols 5 rows
Contents of CDROM	Text area	No	No	55 cols 5 rows
TOC	File upload	No	No	- -
Sample Chapter	File upload	No	No	- -

6.   User enters all the required information in the fields

7.   User selects the option to save data [Refer A-1]

8.   System saves the data and creates the new book [Refer A-2 and A-3]

9.   System refreshes the page to reflect the newly added books

Alternate Steps

A-1: User selects Cancel

System does not save any user entered data.
System does not create a new book.

A-2: Duplicate ISBN

User enters ISBN that already exists.
System displays a message that the ISBN already exists.
System does not create a new book.

A-3: Notification by email

System sends email notifications to customers who have opted for being notified for new books.

Edit Books

Objective	To edit an existing Book
Actors	Book shop employee, Book shop owner, System administrator
Pre-Condition	Users have sufficient privileges to edit books
Post-Condition	Actors successfully edit an existing book

Steps

1. User navigates to the backend [site administration] login page
2. User logs in successfully
3. System displays the backend home page with Books as one of the menu options
4. User selects the Books option to view and edit existing books
5. Users clicks the Edit link of the desired book for editing
6. System displays a data entry form pre-populated with the existing form data
7. User edits the desired information in the fields
8. User selects the option to save data [Refer A-1]
9. System saves the data and updates the existing book [Refer A-2 and A-3]
10. System refreshes the page to reflect the updated list of books

Alternate Steps

A-2: User selects Cancel

System does not save any user entered data.
System does not update the book.

A-3: Duplicate ISBN

User enters ISBN that already exists.
System displays a message that the ISBN already exists.
System does not update the book.

A-3: Notification by email

System sends email notifications to customers who have opted for being notified for updated books.

Delete Books

Objective	To delete an existing Book
Actors	Book shop employee, Book shop owner, System administrator
Pre-Condition	Users have sufficient privileges to delete books
Post-Condition	Actors successfully delete an existing book

Steps

1. User navigates to the backend [site administration] login page
2. User logs in successfully
3. System displays the backend home page with Books as one of the menu options
4. User selects the Books option to delete existing book
5. User selects the Delete link of the desired information to delete an existing book
6. System deletes the book
7. System refreshes the page to reflect the updated list of books

Data Validations

Basic form validation must be done before submitting the form:

a. Required fields
   i. Book
   ii. Publisher
   iii. Category
   iv. ISBN
   v. Edition
   vi. Year
   vii. Cost
   viii. First Author
   ix. Synopsis
   x. About Authors
b. Duplicate entries not allowed
   i. ISBN

Manage Transactions

All the transactions that are performed by the customers should be managed via the application. This form should also be used to add the Google order number [received by email from Google Wallet] after the customer orders and makes a payment.

View Transactions

Objective	To view a list of transactions on a particular date or for a particular customer
Actors	Book shop employee, Book shop owner, System administrator
Pre-Condition	Users have sufficient privileges to view all transactions At least one Transaction exists
Post-Condition	Actors view the transactions for the chosen date

Steps

1. User navigates to the backend [site administration] login page

2. User logs in successfully

3. System displays the backend home page with Transactions as one of the menu options

4. User selects the Transactions option to view the transactions for a desired date or username

5. User enters a username or selects a date for which the transaction are to be viewed and clicks Search

6. System displays a list of transactions along with the transaction details with the following information:

   - Transaction Number
   - Transaction Date
   - Username
   - Google Order Number
   - Transaction Detail Number
   - Book Name
   - Amount
   - Quantity

Edit Transactions (Add Google Order Number)

Objective	To add the Google order number for a particular transaction
Actors	Book shop employee, Book shop owner, System administrator
Pre-Condition	Users have sufficient privileges to edit the transaction's google order number
	At least one Transaction exists
Post-Condition	Actors add the Google order number

Steps

1. User navigates to the backend [site administration] login page

2. User logs in successfully

3. System displays the backend home page with Transactions as one of the menu options

4. User selects the Transactions option to view and add the Google order number for a transaction

5. User enters a username or selects a particular date for which the transaction need to be viewed and then edited and clicks Search

6. System displays a list of transaction details along with the Google order number field for editing

7. Enter the Google order number and click Update

8. System updates the transaction

9. System switches back to the transactions page

Logout

Objective	To allow a system user to logout
Actors	Book shop employee, Book shop owner, System administrator
Pre-Condition	System User should have logged in to the system
Post-Condition	Actors successfully logout

Steps

1. System User clicks the Logout link to logout

2. System destroys the session

3. System displays the Administration Login Page after logout

Frontend Modules

Homepage

Homepage is the customer's entry point to the application. This page should serve the customers with their requirements.

The homepage is made up of the following:

Signup

Objective	To allow a visitor to signup and become a Customer
Actors	Visitors
Pre-Condition	None
Post-Condition	Actors successfully become a customer

Steps

1. Visitor navigates to the homepage and clicks Signup

2. System displays the Signup data entry form

3. Visitor enters the required information to sign-up and clicks Save [Refer A-1 and A-2]

4. System performs the necessary validations and if all fine, registers the customers details and dispatches an email to the customer

5. System displays a Thank you page

Alternate Steps

A-1: Already existing customer

System displays a message indicating that this customer [username or email address] is already available in the system.

A-2: User selects Cancel

System does not save any user entered data.
System does not register the customer.

Data Validations

Basic form validation must be done before submitting the form:

a. Required fields

    i. First Name

    ii. Last Name

    iii. Email Address

    iv. Username

    v. Password

b. Duplicate entries not allowed

    i. Email Address

    ii. Username

c. Email Address should be well formed and valid

Login

Objective	To allow a customer to login to the system
Actors	Customers
Pre-Condition	Person trying to log in should have signed up and thus is assumed to be a customer
Post-Condition	Actors successfully authenticate themselves and log in to the system

Steps

1. Customer navigates to the homepage

2. System displays a data entry form to capture the following:

Form Field	Type	Unique	Required	Max Size
Username	Text box	Yes	Yes	8
Password	Text box	Yes	Yes	8

3. Customer enters the username and the password

4. Customer clicks Login [Refer A-1]

5. System authenticates the username and password. If found valid, the system displays a welcome message and unlocks the shopping cart and download links for books

Alternate Steps

A-1: Invalid User

System displays a message indicating that the username or password is not valid.

Data Validations

Basic form validation must be done before submitting the form:

a.   Required fields

    i.   Username

    ii. Password

Forgot Password

Objective	To allow a customer to retrieve the forgotten password
Actors	Customers
Pre-Condition	Person trying to retrieve the forgotten password should be aware of the username Person trying to retrieve the forgotten password should be a customer
Post-Condition	Actors successfully retrieve the forgotten password

Steps

1.   Customer navigates to the homepage and clicks Forgot Password

2.   System displays a data entry form to capture the following:

Form Field	Type	Unique	Required	Max Size
Username	Text box	Yes	Yes	55

3.   Customer enters the required information and clicks Fetch

4.   System validates the information captured and if found valid, the system fetches and dispatches the password via email [Refer A-1]

Alternate Steps

A-1: Invalid Information

System displays a message indicating that the information entered is not valid.

Data Validations

Basic form validation must be done before submitting the form:

1. Required fields

    a. Username

Search

Objective	To allow a visitor to search for the required books
Actors	Visitors
Pre-Condition	None
Post-Condition	Actors successfully retrieve the required information if it is available in the system

Steps

1. Visitor navigates to the homepage
2. System displays a data entry form to capture the following:

Form Field	Type	Unique	Required	Max Size
Search For	Text box	Yes	Yes	- -

3. Visitor enters the required information and clicks Search
4. System fetches the required information from the database based on the search term entered by the visitor and displays the same on the Search page

Directory Of Books

Objective	To allow a visitor to browse through the available books by categories
Actors	Visitors
Pre-Condition	None
Post-Condition	Actors successfully view the book details of the chosen book

Steps

1. Visitor navigates to the homepage
2. System displays a list of books under category heads
3. Visitor glances through the list of book's cover page and clicks the desired book if one exists

OR

4. Visitor clicks the category name to view a list of all the available books under that category

5. System fetches the book details of the chosen book and displays it

Popular Searches

Objective	To allow a visitor to view search tags that were used the most
Actors	Visitors
Pre-Condition	None
Post-Condition	Actors successfully view the search results based on the search tags available in this section

Steps

1. Visitor navigates to the homepage

2. System displays a list of Popular search tags

3. Visitor glances through the list and clicks the desired tag [link to search results]

4. System fetches and displays the details [search results] of the chosen tag

New Releases

Objective	To allow a visitor to browse through the new books that are just released
Actors	Visitors
Pre-Condition	None
Post-Condition	Actors successfully view the book details of the chosen book

Steps

1. Visitor navigates to the homepage

2. System displays a list of new books

3. Visitor glances through the list of books and clicks the desired book name

4. System fetches the book details of the chosen book and displays it

Updated Books

Objective	To allow a visitor to browse through the books that are updated [New Edition]
Actors	Visitors
Pre-Condition	None
Post-Condition	Actors successfully view the book details of the chosen book

Steps

1. Visitor navigates to the homepage
2. System displays a list of updated books
3. Visitor glances through the list of books and clicks the desired book name
4. System fetches the book details of the chosen book and displays it

Top Titles

Objective	To allow a visitor to browse through the books that are most viewed
Actors	Visitors
Pre-Condition	None
Post-Condition	Actors successfully view the book details of the chosen book

Steps

1. Visitor navigates to the homepage
2. System displays a list of top titles books
3. Visitor glances through the list of books and clicks the desired book name
4. System fetches the book details of the chosen book and displays it

Our Authors

Objective	To allow a visitor to browse through the authors available in the system
Actors	Visitors
Pre-Condition	None
Post-Condition	Actors successfully view the author details of the chosen author

Steps

1. Visitor navigates to the homepage

2. System displays a list of available authors

3. Visitor glances through the list of authors and clicks the desired author name

4. System fetches the author and the details of the books written by that author and displays it

Our Publishers

Objective	To allow a visitor to browse through the publishers available in the system
Actors	Visitors
Pre-Condition	None
Post-Condition	Actors successfully view the publisher details of the chosen publishers

Steps

1. Visitor navigates to the homepage

2. System displays a list of available publishers

3. Visitor glances through the list of publishers and clicks the desired publisher name

4. System fetches the publisher and the details of the books published by that publisher and displays it

Add To Cart

Objective	To allow a customer to add books to the cart
Actors	Customers
Pre-Condition	Customer should have logged in to the system
Post-Condition	Actors successfully add the desired books to the cart

Steps

1. Customer navigates to the homepage

2. Customer opens the book details page by clicking a book name from one of the following sections on the home page:

    i. New Releases

    ii. Top Titles

    iii. Updated Books

    iv. Directory of Books

    v.   Popular Searches

    vi.   Our Authors → List of Books

    vii.   Our Publishers → List of Books

3.   Customer adds the desired book by clicking Add To Cart

4.   System adds the selected book to the Cart

Cart

Objective	To allow a customer to view the books available in the cart
Actors	Customers
Pre-Condition	Customer should have logged in to the system Customer must have added at least one book in the Cart
Post-Condition	Actors successfully view the books available in the cart

Steps

1.   Customer navigates to the homepage

2.   Customer clicks Show Cart

3.   System displays a list of books that are available in the cart [Refer A-1]

4.   Customer may choose to checkout by clicking Google Wallet

Alternate Steps

A-1: Empty Cart

System displays a message indicating that there are no books available in the cart.

Google Wallet

Objective	To allow a customer to checkout
Actors	Customers
Pre-Condition	Customer should have logged into the system Customer must have added at least one book in the Cart Customer must be desirous to buy the books available in the cart Customer must have a Google account Customer must have a valid Credit Card
Post-Condition	Actors successfully checkout and make the payment

Steps

1.   Customer navigates to the homepage

2. Customer clicks Show Cart

3. System displays a list of books that are available in the cart [Refer A-1]

4. Customer clicks Google Wallet

5. System sends the book details from the cart to the Google Payment gateway for processing

6. Customer is prompted to login to Google

7. Customer successfully logs in to Google

8. System prompts for the:
    i. Credit Card Number
    ii. Credit Card Expiry Date
    iii. Credit Card CVV Number

9. Customer enters the credit card information

10. Google authenticates and validates the card details and if all fine, processes the order and the payment [Refer A-2]

11. Google shows a Thank you page with a link to reach the site homepage if the customer desires

12. If the customer clicks the link, the site's home page is served

Alternate Steps

A-1: Empty Cart

System displays a message indicating that there are no books available in the cart.

A-2: Authentication Failure

System displays a message indicating that the card details are invalid.

Logout

Objective	To allow a customer to logout
Actors	Customers
Pre-Condition	Customer should have logged in to the system
Post-Condition	Actors successfully logout

Steps

1. Customer clicks the Logout link to logout
2. System destroys the session and the cart contents
3. System displays the site homepage after logout

Chapter 5

SECTION II: ABOUT THE PROJECT

Project Files

Based on the software requirements specification defined in *Chapter 04: Software Requirements Specification*, the application is held in the following directory structure.

Directory Structure - BookShop

Diagram 5.1

Dedicated Library Directory [lib]

This project holds all its libraries [.jar files] in a dedicated directory called **lib**, as shown in diagram 5.2.

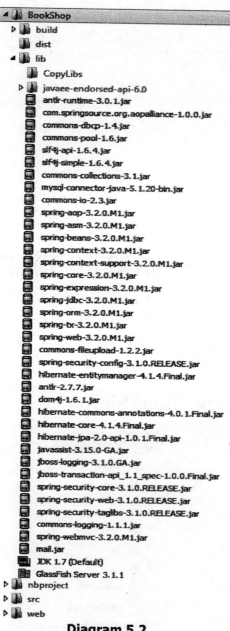

Diagram 5.2

Library File Name	Description
antlr-2.7.7.jar antlr-runtime-3.0.1.jar	ANTLR [Another Tool for Language Recognition] is a language tool that provides a framework for constructing recognizers, interpreters, compilers and translators from grammatical descriptions containing actions in a variety of target languages.
com.springsource.org.aopalliance-1.0.0.jar	AOP Alliance intends to facilitate and standardize the use of AOP to enhance existing middleware environments such as Java EE or development environments.
commons-dbcp-1.4.jar	A library for database connection pooling services.
commons-pool-1.6.jar	A generic object pooling component.
slf4j-api-1.6.4.jar slf4j-simple-1.6.4.jar	Simple Logging Facade for Java [SLF4J] serves as a simple facade or abstraction for various logging frameworks. For example: java.util.logging, log4j and logback, allowing the end user to plug in the desired logging framework at deployment time.
commons-collections-3.1.jar	Commons-Collections seek to build upon the JDK classes by providing new interfaces, implementations and utilities.
mysql-connector-java-5.1.20-bin.jar	MySQL Connector/J converts JDBC calls into the network protocol used by the MySQL database.
commons-io-2.3.jar	Commons IO is a library of utilities such as Utility classes, Filters, Comparators and Streams to assist with developing IO functionality.
commons-fileupload-1.2.2.jar	Commons FileUpload package makes it easy to add robust, high-performance, file upload capability to the Web applications.
commons-logging-1.1.1.jar	Commons Logging provides a Log interface that is intended to be both light-weight and an independent abstraction of other logging toolkits. It provides the middleware/tooling developer with a simple logging abstraction that allows the developer to plug in a specific logging implementation.
mail.jar	The JavaMail API provides a platform-independent and protocol-independent framework to build mail and messaging applications.
spring-aop-3.2.0.M1.jar	Core Spring AOP interfaces, built on AOP Alliance AOP interoperability interfaces.

Library File Name	Description
`spring-asm-3.2.0.M1.jar`	ASM is very small framework that is used to analyze and manipulate Java byte codes. It is used in Spring 3 framework to dynamically modify the Java bytecode and generate the new bye code in runtime.
`spring-beans-3.2.0.M1.jar`	Contains interfaces and classes for manipulating Java beans.
`spring-context-3.2.0.M1.jar`	This package builds on the beans package to add support for message sources and for the Observer design pattern and the ability for application objects to obtain resources using a consistent API.
`spring-context-support-3.2.0.M1.jar`	Classes supporting the org.springframework.context package such as abstract base classes for ApplicationContext implementations and a MessageSource implementation.
`spring-core-3.2.0.M1.jar`	Provides basic classes for exception handling and version detection and other core helpers that are not specific to any part of the framework.
`spring-expression-3.2.0.M1.jar`	The Spring's Expression API for writing and parsing SpEL [Spring Expression Language], which was created by Spring Framework community to work with all the Spring Framework products.
`spring-jdbc-3.2.0.M1.jar`	The classes in this package make JDBC easier to use and reduce the likelihood of common errors.
`spring-orm-3.2.0.M1.jar`	Root package for Spring's O/R Mapping integration classes.
`spring-tx-3.2.0.M1.jar`	Exception hierarchy for Spring's transaction infrastructure, independent of any specific transaction management system.
`spring-web-3.2.0.M1.jar`	Common, generic interfaces that define minimal boundary points between Spring's web infrastructure and other framework modules.
`spring-webmvc-3.2.0.M1.jar`	Standard controller implementations for the servlet MVC framework that comes with Spring.
`spring-security-config-3.1.0.RELEASE.jar`	Support classes for the Spring Security namespace.
`spring-security-core-3.1.0.RELEASE.jar`	Core classes and interfaces related to user authentication and authorization, as well as the maintenance of a security context.
`spring-security-web-3.1.0.RELEASE.jar`	Spring Security's web security module.

Library File Name	Description
spring-security-taglibs-3.1.0.RELEASE.jar	Security related tag libraries that can be used in JSPs and templates.
dom4j-1.6.1.jar	dom4j is an easy to use, open source library for working with XML, XPath and XSLT on the Java platform using the Java Collections Framework and with full support for DOM, SAX and JAXP.
hibernate-entitymanager-4.1.4.FINAL.jar	Hibernate EntityManager implements the standard Java Persistence: ❑ Management API ❑ Query Language ❑ Object lifecycle rules ❑ Configuration and packaging Hibernate EntityManager wraps the powerful and mature Hibernate Core.
hibernate-commons-annotations-4.0.1.FINAL.jar	This package ships the Hibernate Commons Annotations classes used by annotations based Hibernate sub-projects.
hibernate-core-4.1.4.FINAL.jar	Hibernate is a powerful, high performance object / relational persistence and query service. Hibernate allows developing persistent classes following object-oriented idiom including association, inheritance, polymorphism, composition and collections.
hibernate-jpa-2.0-api-1.0.1.FINAL.jar	This is the JAR containing the JPA 2.0 API. It provides all the interfaces and concrete classes that the specification defines as public API.
javassist-3.15.0.GA.jar	Javassist is a Java library providing means to manipulate the Java byte code of an application.
jboss-logging-3.1.0.GA.jar	JBoss Logging acts as a logging bridge. If there are no other logging libraries added to the project, it will delegate all logging calls it handles to the logging facility built into the Java platform [commonly referred to as JDK logging].
jboss-transaction-api_1.1_spec-1.0.0.FINAL.jar	The interfaces specified by the many transaction standards tend to be too low-level for most application programmers. Therefore, Sun Microsystems created Java Transaction API [JTA], which specifies higher-level interfaces to assist in the development of distributed transactional applications.

The Project Source Code Directory (src/java)

The project source code is placed under /src/java as shown in diagram 5.3.

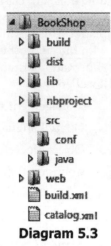

Diagram 5.3

Java Packages

The modules in this project are placed as shown in diagram 5.4.

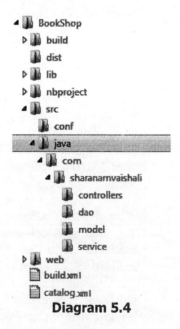

Diagram 5.4

Directory/Package Name	Description
com.sharanamvaishali.controllers	The Controller classes
com.sharanamvaishali.dao	The Data Access Object classes
com.sharanamvaishali.model	The Model/Entity classes
com.sharanamvaishali.service	The Service classes

Controllers (src\java\com\sharanamvaishali\controllers)

The **src\java\com\sharanamvaishali\controllers** directory of this project holds the following files as shown in diagram 5.5.

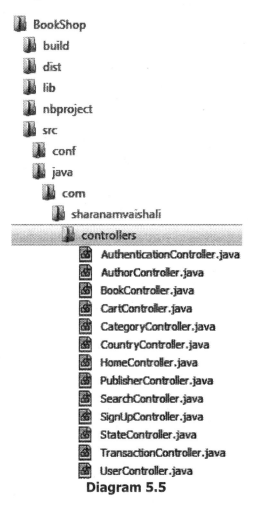

Diagram 5.5

File Name	Description
AuthenticationController.java	The controller that allows login and logout for the backend as well as the frontend users. It also allows retrieving the forgotten password.
AuthorController.java	The controller that allows performing insert, update, delete and view of the author details and download the photograph of an author.
BookController.java	The controller that allows performing insert, update, delete and view of the book details and download the cover page, toc and sample chapters of the book.
CartController.java	The controller that allows adding, removing and viewing cart items.
CategoryController.java	The controller that allows performing insert, update, delete and view categories.
CountryController.java	The controller that allows performing insert, update, delete and view countries.
HomeController.java	The controller that allows viewing homepage data.
PublisherController.java	The controller that allows performing insert, update, delete and view publishers.
SearchController.java	The controller that allows performing search and viewing the search results.
SignUpController.java	The controller that allows customer registration.
StateController.java	The controller that allows performing insert, update, delete and view states.
TransactionController.java	The controller that allows performing update and view transactions.
UserController.java	The controller that allows performing insert, update, delete and view users.

DAO Classes (src\java\com\sharanamvaishali\ dao)

The **src\java\com\sharanamvaishali\dao** directory of this project holds the following files as shown in diagram 5.6.

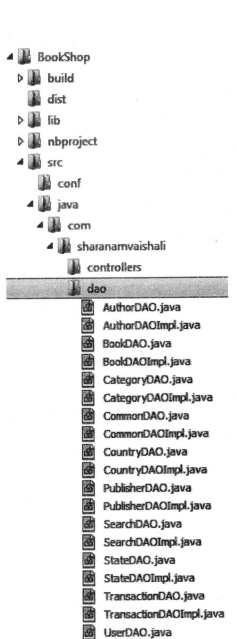

Diagram 5.6

Interface Name	Implementation Name
`AuthorDAO.java`	`AuthorDAOImpl.java`
Description	The DAO that performs actual insert, update, delete, view operation for authors using Hibernate. It also retrieves the list of authors and the books written by that author.
`BookDAO.java`	`BookDAOImpl.java`
Description	The DAO that performs actual insert, update, delete, view operation for books using Hibernate. It also retrieves the list of new releases, updated books and top titles.
`CategoryDAO.java`	`CategoryDAOImpl.java`
Description	The DAO that performs actual insert, update, delete, view operation for categories using Hibernate. It also retrieves the list of categories and the books available under that category.
`CommonDAO.java`	`CommonDAOImpl.java`
Description	The DAO that performs actual retrieving of the Blob images/PDFs using Hibernate.
`CountryDAO.java`	`CountryDAOImpl.java`
Description	The DAO that performs actual insert, update, delete, view operation for countries using Hibernate.
`PublisherDAO.java`	`PublisherDAOImpl.java`
Description	The DAO that performs actual insert, update, delete, view operation for publishers using Hibernate. It also retrieves the list of publishers and the books published by that publisher.
`SearchDAO.java`	`SearchDAOImpl.java`
Description	The DAO that fires the actual query using Hibernate to perform the search operation. It also retrieves the list of popular searches and deletes the records of popular searches.
`StateDAO.java`	`StateDAOImpl.java`
Description	The DAO that performs actual insert, update, delete, view operation for states using Hibernate.
`TransactionDAO.java`	`TransactionDAOImpl.java`
Description	The DAO that performs actual update and view operation for transactions using Hibernate.

UserDAO.java	UserDAOImpl.java
Description	The DAO that performs actual insert, update, delete, view operation for customers/system users using Hibernate.

Services Classes (src\java\com\sharanamvaishali\ service)

The **src\java\com\sharanamvaishali\service** directory of this project holds the following files as shown in diagram 5.7.

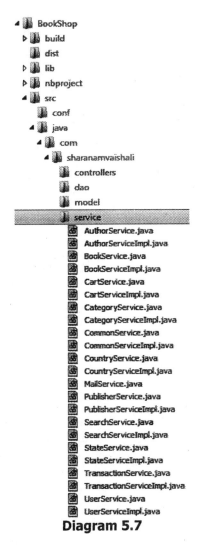

Diagram 5.7

Interface Name	Implementation Name
AuthorService.java	AuthorServiceImpl.java
Description	The Service that contains all the business logic related to authors.
BookService.java	BookServiceImpl.java
Description	The Service that contains all the business logic related to books.
CartService.java	CartServiceImpl.java
Description	The Service that contains all the business logic related to cart such as adding books to the cart, inserting the cart details and removing the books from the cart.
CategoryService.java	CategoryServiceImpl.java
Description	The Service that contains all the business logic related to categories.
CommonService.java	CommonServiceImpl.java
Description	The Service that contains all the business logic related to the Blob images/PDFs.
CountryService.java	CountryServiceImpl.java
Description	The Service that contains all the business logic related to countries.
- -	MailService.java
Description	The Service that contains all the business logic related to mails.
PublisherService.java	PublisherServiceImpl.java
Description	The Service that contains all the business logic related to publishers.
SearchService.java	SearchServiceImpl.java
Description	The Service that contains all the business logic related to perform the search operation.
StateService.java	StateServiceImpl.java
Description	The Service that contains all the business logic related to states.
TransactionService.java	TransactionServiceImpl.java
Description	The Service that contains all the business logic related to transactions.
UserService.java	UserServiceImpl.java
Description	The Service that contains all the business logic related to customers/system users.

Bean Classes (src\java\com\sharanamvaishali\model)

The **src\java\com\sharanamvaishali\model** directory of this project holds the following files as shown in diagram 5.8.

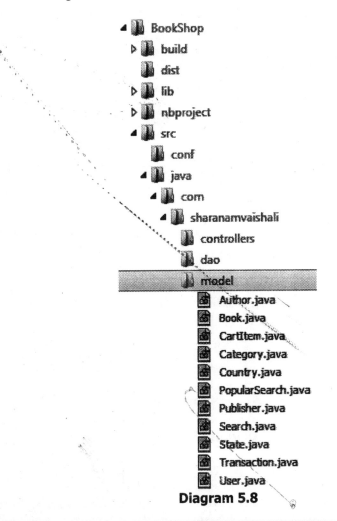

Diagram 5.8

File Name	Table Name
Author.java	Authors
Book.java	Books
CartItem.java	- -
Category.java	Categories
Country.java	Countries
PopularSearch.java	PopularSearches

File Name	Table Name
Publisher.java	Publishers
Search.java	- -
State.java	State
Transaction.java	Transactions
User.java	Users

Configuration and Properties Files (src\java*)

The configuration and properties files are available under **src\java** as shown in diagram 5.9.

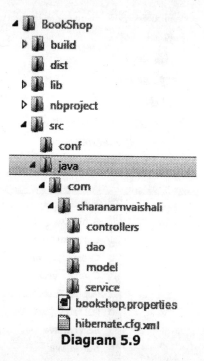

Diagram 5.9

File Name	Description
bookshop.properties	The properties [Resource Bundle] file that holds: **Email related variables:** googleMerchantID, emailFrom, emailUser, emailPasswd, emailHost, emailPort, sendMail **Database related variables:** dbUsername, dbPassword, dbURL, dbDriverClassName **Hibernate/SQL related variables:** showHQL
hibernate.cfg.xml	The Hibernate configuration file that holds references to the mappings between the model classes and the database tables.

The Web Directory (web\WEB-INF)

The web pages in this project are placed under **web\WEB-INF** as shown in diagram 5.10.

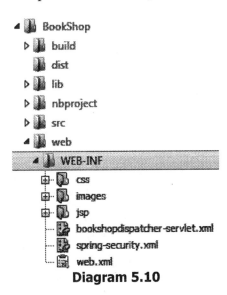

Diagram 5.10

The following table displays the details of the directory names under the **web\WEB-INF:**

Directory Name	Description
css	The cascading style sheet.
images	The images used by all the web pages.
jsp	The Backend [Administration] web based data entry forms. The Frontend [Customer facing] web pages. The common files for inclusion in the web pages that require them.

The following table displays the details of the file names under the **web\WEB-INF:**

File Name	Description
bookshopdispatcher-servlet.xml	The DispatcherServlet, which dispatches requests to handlers, with configurable handler mappings, view resolution, locale and theme resolution as well as support for upload files.
spring-security.xml	The Spring Security, which allows complete application security in just a few lines of XML.
web.xml	The Deployment Descriptor, which provides configuration and deployment information for the Web components that comprise a Web application.

Web Pages (web\WEB-INF\jsp)

The **web\WEB-INF\jsp** directory in this project holds the following files as shown in diagram 5.11.

Diagram 5.11

File Name	Description
adminAccessDenied.jsp	The Backend [Administration] access denied page.
adminFooter.jsp	The Backend [Administration] footer that appears on all the administrative web pages.
adminHeader.jsp	The Backend [Administration] header file that provides the menu bar.
adminLogin.jsp	The Backend [Administration] Login form.
allCategories.jsp	The directory of books according to the category wise page.
checkOut.jsp	The page that takes the customer to Google Checkout.
footer.jsp	The Frontend [Customer Facing] footer that appears on all the frontend web pages.
forgotPassword.jsp	The Forgot Password data entry form.
header.jsp	The Frontend [Customer Facing] header file that provides the menu and the search bar.
home.jsp	The home page.
leftMenu.jsp	The list of New Releases, Updated Books, Top Titles, Our Authors and Our Publishers shown in home page.
login.jsp	The Frontend [Customer Facing] Login form.
manageAuthors.jsp	The Backend [Administration] – Manage Authors data entry form that allows Add, View, Update and Delete.
manageBooks.jsp	The Backend [Administration] – Manage Books data entry form that allows Add, View, Update and Delete.
manageCategories.jsp	The Backend [Administration] – Manage Categories data entry form that allows Add, View, Update and Delete.
manageCountries.jsp	The Backend [Administration] – Manage Countries data entry form that allows Add, View, Update and Delete.
managePublishers.jsp	The Backend [Administration] – Manage Publishers data entry form that allows Add, View, Update and Delete.
manageStates.jsp	The Backend [Administration] – Manage States data entry form that allows Add, View, Update and Delete.
manageTransactions.jsp	The Backend [Administration] – Manage Transactions data entry form that allows Update and View.
manageUsers.jsp	The Backend [Administration] – Manage Users data entry form that allows Add, View, Update and Delete.
popularSearches.jsp	The list of popular searches shown in the home page.
searchResults.jsp	The page that allows searching and displays the search results.
showAuthorDetails.jsp	The page that displays author details for a particular author.
showBookDetails.jsp	The page that displays book details for a particular book.

File Name	Description
showCart.jsp	The page that shows the cart contents and allows deleting cart items and checking out via Google Wallet.
showCategoryDetails.jsp	The page that displays books and its details for a particular category.
showPublisherDetails.jsp	The page that displays publisher details for a particular publisher.
signUp.jsp	The Customer Registration data entry form.
signUpThankYou.jsp	The page that appears after a successful registration.

Cascading Style Sheet (web\WEB-INF\css)

The **web\css** directory in this project holds the following files as shown in diagram 5.12.

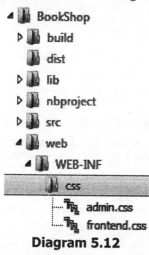

Diagram 5.12

File Name	Description
admin.css	The cascading style sheet that is applied to the administrative web pages.
frontend.css	The cascading style sheet that is applied to the frontend [customer facing] web pages.

Chapter

6

SECTION II: ABOUT THE PROJECT

Data Dictionary

This chapter documents:

❑ The **Entity Relationship Diagram** that helps understand the relationship between the database tables used in this project

❑ **Table Definitions** that provides the column attributes:

  o Constraints

  o Default Values

  o Data Type

  o Size

  o Null / Not Null

  o Description

HINT

 The Book's accompanying CDROM holds a .sql file that is a dump [export] of the entire database [all tables] with sample data that will be useful to begin using this project.

Entity Relationship Diagram

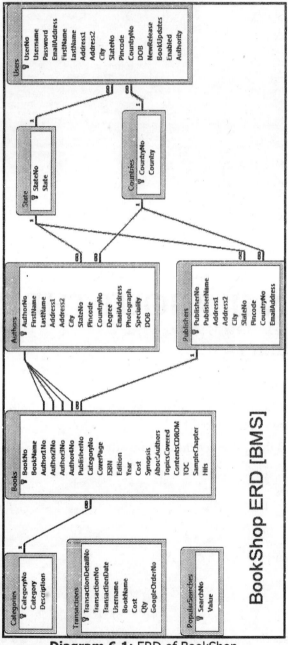

Diagram 6.1: ERD of BookShop

Table Definitions

Countries

This table stores the country name captured using the Manage Countries d/e form.

Column Name	Data Type	Size	Null	Default	Constraints
CountryNo	Integer	10	No	- -	Primary key
Description	An identity number of the country				
Country	Varchar	50	No	- -	Unique key
Description	The name of the country				

State

This table stores the state names captured using the Manage States d/e form.

Column Name	Data Type	Size	Null	Default	Constraints
StateNo	Integer	10	No	- -	Primary key
Description	An identity number of the state				
State	Varchar	50	No	- -	Unique Key
Description	The name of the state				

Categories

This table stores the category details captured using the Manage Categories d/e form.

Column Name	Data Type	Size	Null	Default	Constraints
CategoryNo	Integer	10	No	- -	Primary key
Description	An identity number of the category				
Category	Varchar	30	No	- -	Unique key
Description	The name of the category				
Description	Varchar	4000	No	- -	- - -
Description	The description of the category				

Authors

This table stores the author details captured using the Manage Authors d/e form.

Column Name	Data Type	Size	Null	Default	Constraints
AuthorNo	Integer	10	No	- -	Primary Key
Description	An identity number of the author				
FirstName	Varchar	30	No	- -	- -
Description	The first name of the author				
LastName	Varchar	30	No	- -	- -
Description	The last name of the author				
Address1	Varchar	50	Yes	NULL	- -
Description	The street address where the author resides				
Address2	Varchar	50	Yes	NULL	- -
Description	The street address where the author resides				
City	Varchar	50	Yes	NULL	- -
Description	The name of the city where the author resides				
StateNo	Integer	10	Yes	NULL	State(StateNo)
Description	An identity number of the State				
Pincode	Varchar	20	Yes	NULL	- -
Description	The pincode of the city where the author resides				
CountryNo	Integer	10	Yes	NULL	Countries(CountryNo)
Description	An identity number of the country				
Degree	Varchar	30	No	- -	- -
Description	The qualifications of the author				
EmailAddress	Varchar	50	No	- -	Unique key
Description	The email address of the author				
Photograph	MediumBlob	- -	Yes	NULL	- -
Description	The photograph of the author				
Speciality	Varchar	4000	Yes	NULL	- -
Description	The specialty of the author				
DOB	Varchar	15	Yes	NULL	- -
Description	The date of birth of the author				

Publishers

This table stores the publisher details captured using the Manage Publishers d/e form.

Column Name	Data Type	Size	Null	Default	Constraints
PublisherNo	Integer	10	No	- -	Primary Key
Description	An identity number of the publisher				
PublisherName	Varchar	50	No	- -	Unique key
Description	The name of the publisher				
Address1	Varchar	50	Yes	NULL	- -
Description	The street address where the publisher resides				
Address2	Varchar	50	Yes	NULL	- -
Description	The street address where the publisher resides				
City	Varchar	50	Yes	NULL	- -
Description	The name of the city where the publisher resides				
StateNo	Integer	10	Yes	NULL	State(StateNo)
Description	An identity number of the State				
Pincode	Varchar	20	Yes	NULL	- -
Description	The pincode of the city where the publisher resides				
CountryNo	Integer	10	Yes	NULL	Countries(CountryNo)
Description	An identity number of the country				
EmailAddress	Varchar	50	No	- -	Unique key
Description	The email address of the publisher				

PopularSearches

This table stores the search value of all the searches attempted by the user using the Search d/e form. These values are used to represent tag clouds under popular searches.

Column Name	Data Type	Size	Null	Default	Constraints
SearchNo	Integer	10	No	- -	Primary key
Description	An identity number of the search				
Value	Varchar	100	Yes	NULL	- -
Description	The value of the search				

Books

This table stores the book details captured using the Manage Books d/e form.

Column Name	Data Type	Size	Null	Default	Constraints
BookNo	Integer	10	No	- -	Primary Key
Description	An identity number of the book				
BookName	Varchar	255	No	- -	- -
Description	The name of the book				
Author1No	Integer	10	No	- -	Authors(AuthorNo)
Description	An identity number of the first author				
Author2No	Integer	10	Yes	NULL	Authors(AuthorNo)
Description	An identity number of the second author				
Author3No	Integer	10	Yes	NULL	Authors(AuthorNo)
Description	An identity number of the third author				
Author4No	Integer	10	Yes	NULL	Authors(AuthorNo)
Description	An identity number of the fourth author				
PublisherNo	Integer	10	No	- -	Publishers(PublisherNo)
Description	An identity number of the publisher				
CategoryNo	Integer	10	No	- -	Categories(CategoryNo)
Description	An identity number of the category				
CoverPage	MediumBlob	- -	Yes	NULL	- -
Description	The cover page image of the book				
ISBN	Varchar	20	No	- -	Unique key
Description	The ISBN of the book				
Edition	Varchar	20	No	- -	- -
Description	The edition of the book				
Year	Integer	4	No	- -	- -
Description	The year when the book was published				
Cost	Integer	12	No	- -	- -
Description	The cost of the book				
Synopsis	Varchar	4000	No	- -	- -
Description	The synopsis of the book				
AboutAuthors	Varchar	4000	No	- -	- -
Description	The information about the book authors				

TopicsCovered	Varchar	4000	Yes	NULL	- -
Description	The topics covered in the book				
ContentsCDROM	Varchar	4000	Yes	NULL	- -
Description	The contents of the CDROM of the book				
TOC	MediumBlob	- -	Yes	NULL	- -
Description	The Table of contents of the book in PDF format				
SampleChapter	MediumBlob	- -	Yes	NULL	- -
Description	The sample chapter of the book in PDF format				
Hits	Integer	11	Yes	0 [Zero]	- -
Description	The number of times the book was viewed				

Users

This table stores the user details captured using either the Signup d/e form or the Manage Users d/e form.

Column Name	Data Type	Size	Null	Default	Constraints
UserNo	Integer	10	No	- -	Primary key
Description	An identity number of the user				
Username	Varchar	30	No	- -	Unique key
Description	The username of the user				
Password	Varchar	30	No	- -	- -
Description	The password of the user				
EmailAddress	Varchar	50	No	- -	Unique key
Description	The email address of the user				
FirstName	Varchar	30	No	- -	- -
Description	The first name of the user				
LastName	Varchar	30	No	- -	- -
Description	The last name of the user				
Address1	Varchar	50	Yes	NULL	- -
Description	The street address where the user resides				
Address2	Varchar	50	Yes	NULL	- -
Description	The street address where the user resides				
City	Varchar	50	Yes	NULL	- -
Description	The name of the city where the user resides				
StateNo	Integer	10	Yes	NULL	State(StateNo)
Description	An identity number of the State				

Pincode	Varchar	20	Yes	NULL	- -
Description	The pincode of the city where the customer resides				

CountryNo	Integer	10	Yes	NULL	Countries(CountryNo)
Description	An identity number of the country				

DOB	Varchar	15	Yes	NULL	- -
Description	The date of birth of the user				

NewRelease	Tinyint	1	No	0 [Zero]	- -
Description	A flag to indicate if the customer has subscribed to New Releases				

BookUpdates	Tinyint	1	No	0 [Zero]	- -
Description	A flag to indicate if the customer has subscribed to Book Updates				

Enabled	Tinyint	1	No	1	- -
Description	A flag to indicate if the customer/user has permissions to login				

Authority	Varchar	45	Yes	CUSTOMER	- -
Description	The authority of the user, whether it is an administrator, a normal system user or a customer				

Transactions

This table stores the entries of the transactions [purchases] performed by the customers.

Column Name	Data Type	Size	Null	Default	Constraints
TransactionDetailNo	Integer	15	No	- -	Primary key
Description	An identity number of the transaction details				
TransactionNo	Integer	10	No	- -	- -
Description	An identity number of the transaction				
TransactionDate	TimeStamp	- -	No	- -	- -
Description	The date on which transaction is made				
Username	Varchar	25	No	- -	- -
Description	The username of the customer who made any purchases				
BookName	Varchar	255	No	- -	- -
Description	The name of the book				
Cost	Integer	12	No	- -	- -
Description	The cost of the book				

Qty	Integer	5	No	- -	- -
Description	The quantity of the book				
GoogleOrderNo	Varchar	50	Yes	NULL	- -
Description	The Google order number of the Google Wallet via which the customer checks out and makes payment				

Chapter

7

SECTION III: END USER MANUAL

Backend [Administration]

The backend consists of the following:

- Login
- Manage
  - Countries
  - States
  - Authors
  - Publishers
  - Categories
  - Users
  - Books
  - Transactions

To be able to use the backend [site administration], system users can be created using the Manage Users data entry form. By default a super user called **admin** is pre-created with the password set to **admin**. This user can always login to the system and <u>no other system users can delete this user</u>.

The Application's Homepage

To begin using this application, invoke it. The application's homepage appears, as shown in diagram 7.1, which holds a link to the **Administration** section.

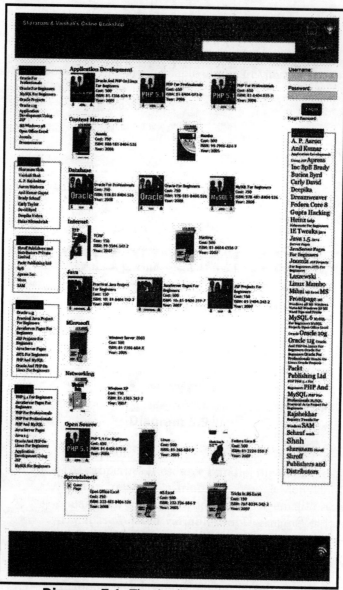

Diagram 7.1: The Application's Homepage

Backend [Administration] Login Page

Click  from the application's homepage. This delivers the login page, as shown in diagram 7.2.

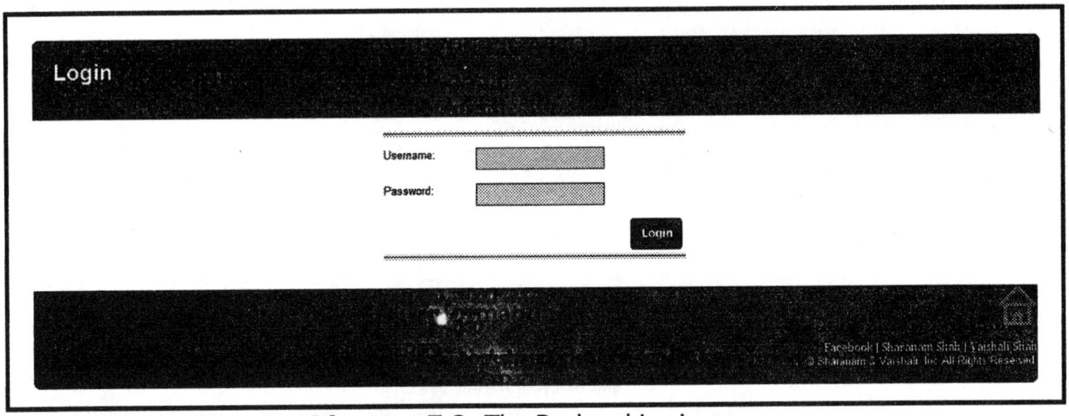

Login

Username: ▢

Password: ▢

Login

Facebook | Sharanam Shah | Vaishali Shah
© Sharanam & Vaishali. Inc All Rights Reserved

Diagram 7.2: The Backend Login page

Enter the username as **admin** and password as **admin**. Click  Login .
This is a super user account which is pre-created.

HINT

☺ Since this login was attempted using a super admin, all the menu options are available. However, this application allows restricting certain modules to certain system users using the Manage Users data entry form [explained later].

The system displays the Manage Transactions page after a successful login.

Manage Countries

Click  Countries . This delivers the Manage Countries data entry form, as shown in diagram 7.3.1.

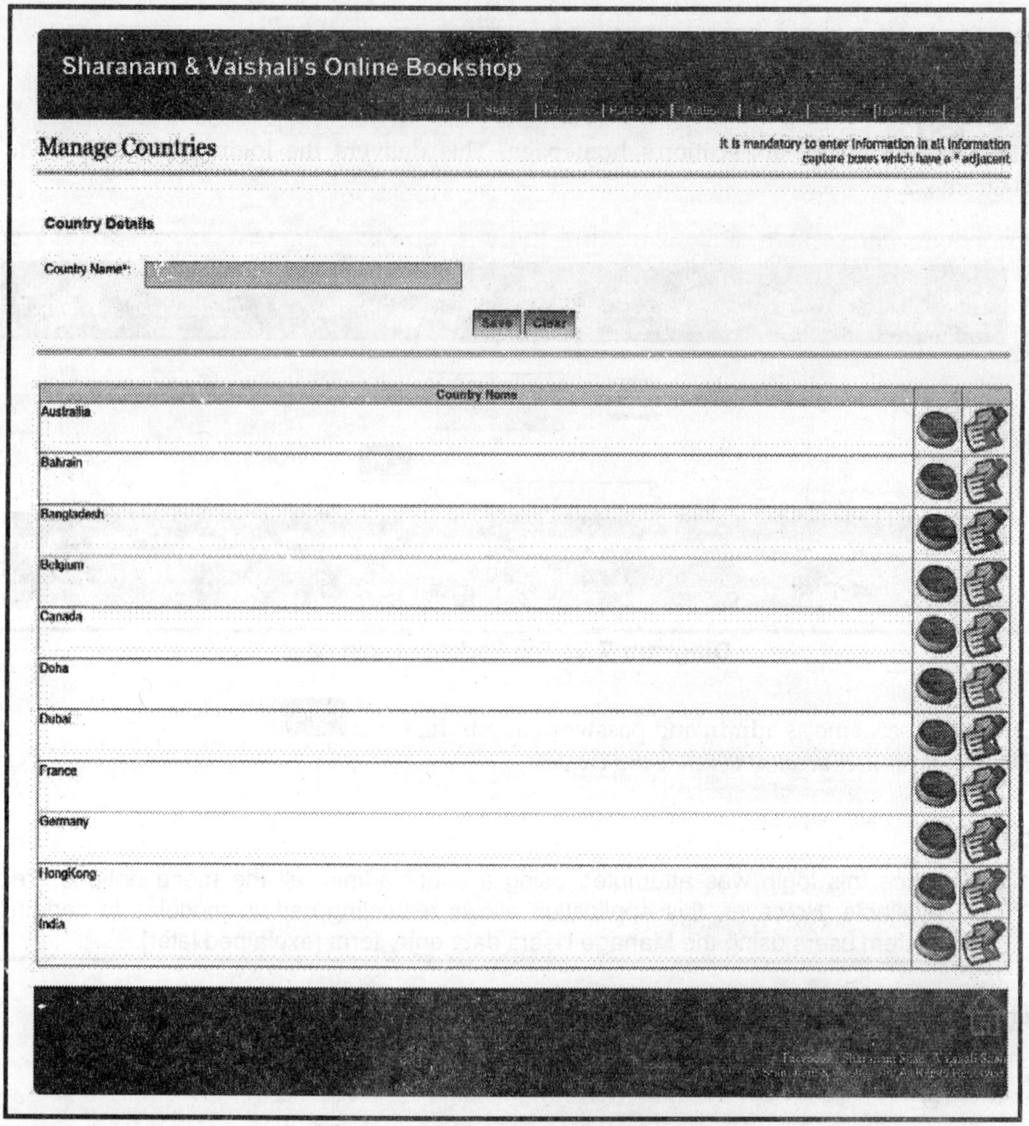

Diagram 7.3.1: Manage Countries

REMINDER

It is mandatory to enter information in all information capture boxes which have a * adjacent indicates entering values for all the form field labels that are marked * is mandatory.

Data entered in this form is used to populate the Country drop down list boxes in the following pages:

❑   Manage Authors

❑   Manage Publishers

❑   Manage Users

❑   Signup

Adding New Record

As soon as the data entry form loads in the web browser, it's ready to capture new records.

To add a new country, key in the required form field(s) and click **Save**.

Clicking **Save**, performs the following client side validations:

❑   Country name cannot be left blank

❑   Country name already exists

If any one of the above mentioned validations fails, an appropriate error message is displayed, as shown in diagram 7.3.2.

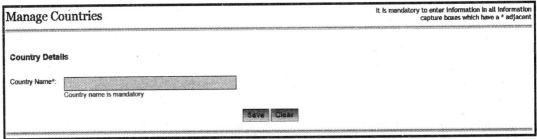

Diagram 7.3.2: Manage Countries [Error Message]

Correct the error. After doing so, click **Save** to save the entered data in the database.

If all the validations mentioned above go through without any errors, the data is saved in the database and the page is reloaded to reflect the newly added data.

Modifying Existing Record

To modify an already existing record, click ![hand icon] adjacent to the desired record from the GRID, as shown in diagram 7.3.3.

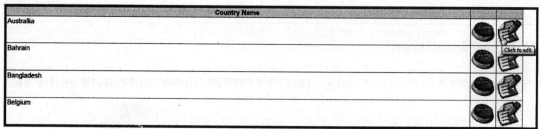

Diagram 7.3.3: Manage Countries [GRID for modification]

Doing so populates the record data in the data entry form, as shown in diagram 7.3.4.

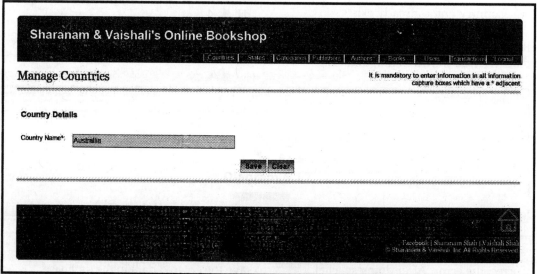

Diagram 7.3.4: Manage Countries [Data Populated]

Make the desired changes and click **Save**.

Clicking **Save**, performs the following client side validations:

❏ Country name cannot be left blank

❏ Country name already exists

If any one of the above mentioned validations fails, an appropriate error message is displayed, as shown in diagram 7.3.5.

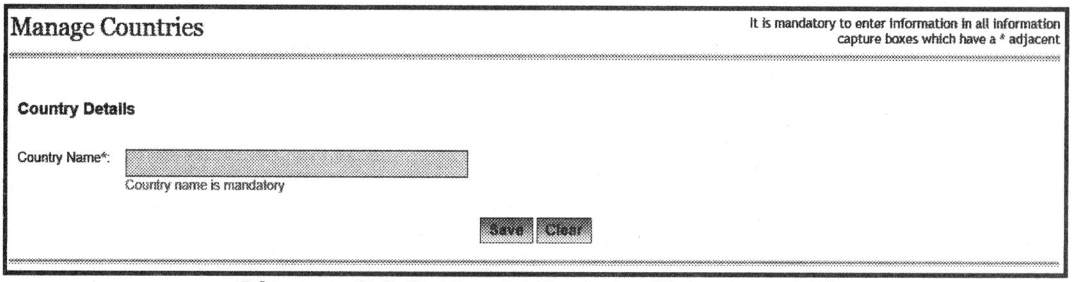

Manage Countries   It is mandatory to enter information in all information
                                                        capture boxes which have a * adjacent

Country Details

Country Name*:   [   ]
                  Country name is mandatory

                                              [Save] [Clear]

Diagram 7.3.5: Manage Countries [Error Message]

Correct the error. After doing so, click [Save] to save the entered data in the database.

If all the validations mentioned above go through without any errors, the data is updated in the database and the page is reloaded to reflect the modified data.

Deleting Existing Record

To delete an already existing record click [ ] adjacent to the desired record from the GRID, as shown in diagram 7.3.6.

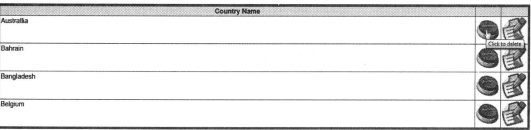

Diagram 7.3.6: Manage Countries [GRID for deletion]

Clicking [ ], performs the delete operation and reloads the page to reflect the deleted records.

If the user attempts to a delete record that is associated with the existing data, an error message appears indicating the same, as shown in diagram 7.3.7.

Deleting a master record that has been associated with detail records in this case Authors, Publishers and Users cannot be deleted.

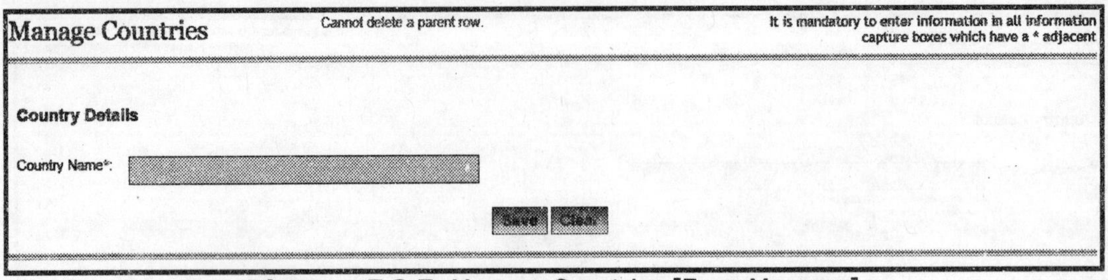

Manage Countries	Cannot delete a parent row.	It is mandatory to enter information in all information capture boxes which have a * adjacent

Country Details

Country Name*: [   ]

[Save] [Clean]

Diagram 7.3.7: Manage Countries [Error Message]

Manage States

Click [States]. This delivers the Manage States data entry form, as shown in diagram 7.4.1.

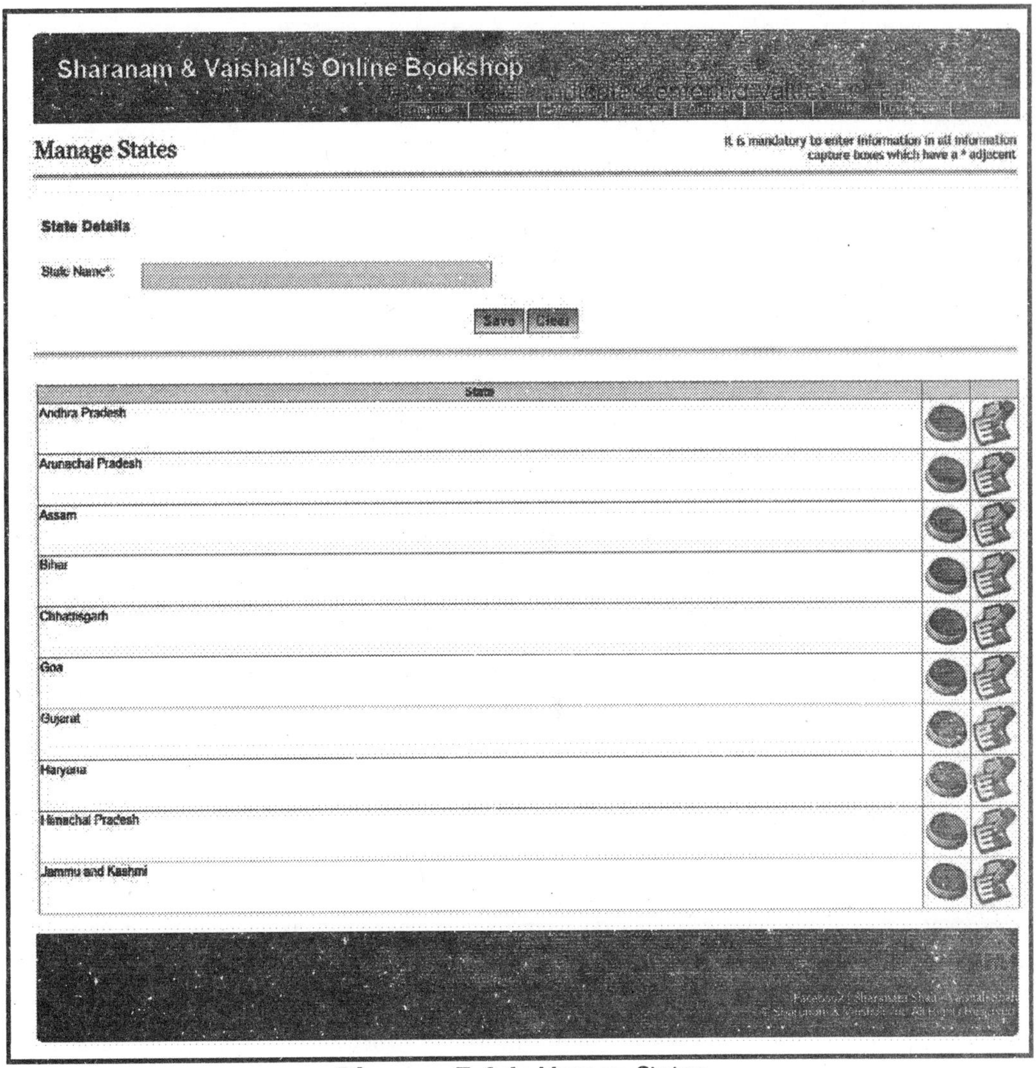

Sharanam & Vaishali's Online Bookshop

Manage States

It is mandatory to enter information in all information capture boxes which have a * adjacent

State Details

State Name*: [   ]

Save   Clear

State		
Andhra Pradesh		
Arunachal Pradesh		
Assam		
Bihar		
Chhattisgarh		
Goa		
Gujarat		
Haryana		
Himachal Pradesh		
Jammu and Kashmir		

Diagram 7.4.1: Manage States

REMINDER

 It is mandatory to enter information in all information capture boxes which have a * adjacent indicates entering values for all the form field labels that are marked * is mandatory.

Data entered in this form is used to populate the State drop down list boxes in the following pages:

❑ Manage Authors

- ❏ Manage Publishers
- ❏ Manage Users
- ❏ Signup

Adding New Record

As soon as the data entry form loads in the web browser, it's ready to capture new records.

To add a new state, key in the required form field(s) and click **Save**.

Clicking **Save**, performs the following client side validations:

- ❏ State name cannot be left blank
- ❏ State name already exists

If any one of the above mentioned validations fails, an appropriate error message is displayed, as shown in diagram 7.4.2.

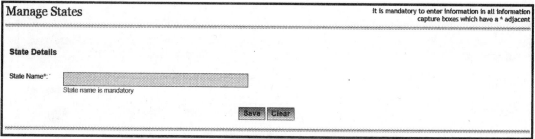

Diagram 7.4.2: Manage States [Error Message]

Correct the error. After doing so, click **Save** to save the entered data in the database.

If all the validations mentioned above go through without any errors, the data is saved in the database and the page is reloaded to reflect the newly added data.

Modifying Existing Record

To modify an already existing record, click 📝 adjacent to the desired record from the GRID, as shown in diagram 7.4.3.

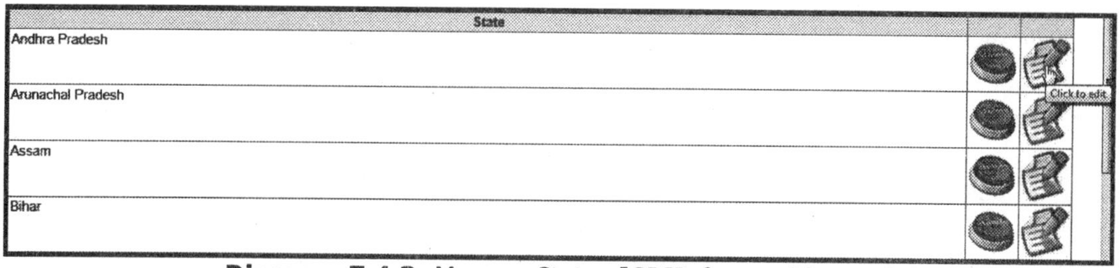

Diagram 7.4.3: Manage States [GRID for modification]

Doing so populates the record data in the data entry form, as shown in diagram 7.4.4.

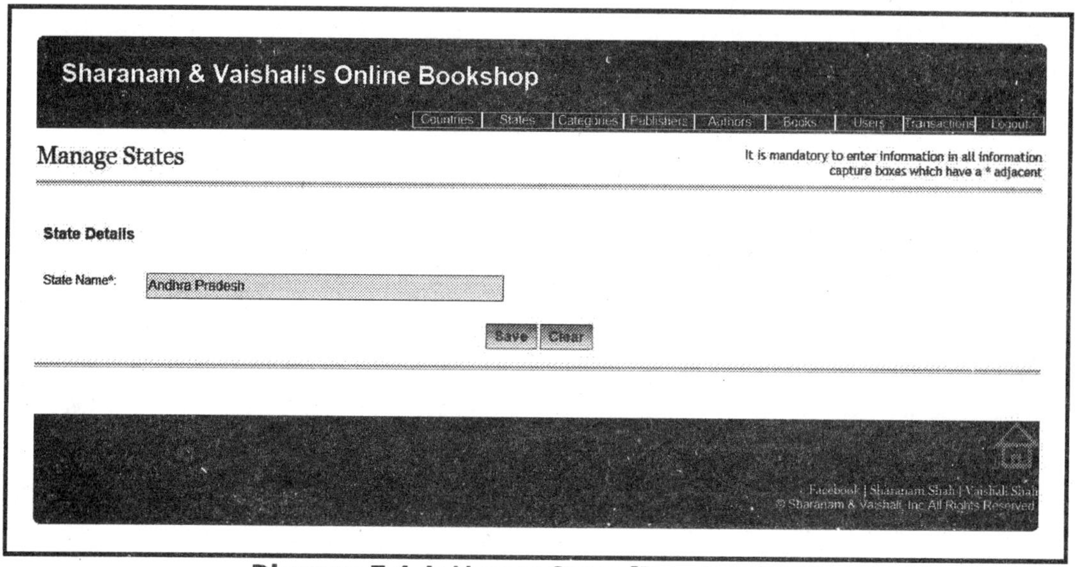

Diagram 7.4.4: Manage States [Data Populated]

Make the desired changes and click **Save**.

Clicking **Save**, performs the following client side validations:

❑ State name cannot be left blank
❑ State name already exists

If any one of the above mentioned validations fails, an appropriate error message is displayed, as shown in diagram 7.4.5.

Manage States

It is mandatory to enter information in all information capture boxes which have a * adjacent

State Details

State Name*:

State name is mandatory

Save   Clear

Diagram 7.4.5: Manage States [Error Message]

Correct the error. After doing so, click **Save** to save the entered data in the database.

If all the validations mentioned above go through without any errors, the data is updated in the database and the page is reloaded to reflect the modified data.

Deleting Existing Record

To delete an already existing record click  adjacent to the desired record from the GRID, as shown in diagram 7.4.6.

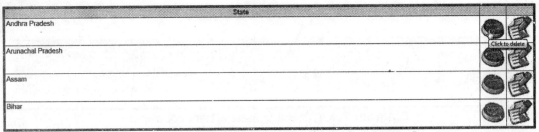

State		
Andhra Pradesh		
Arunachal Pradesh		Click to delete
Assam		
Bihar		

Diagram 7.4.6: Manage States [GRID for deletion]

Clicking  , performs the delete operation and reloads the page to reflect the deleted records.

If the user attempts to delete a record that is associated with the existing data, an error message appears indicating the same, as shown in diagram 7.4.7.

Deleting a master record that has been associated with detail records in this case Authors, Publishers and Users cannot be deleted.

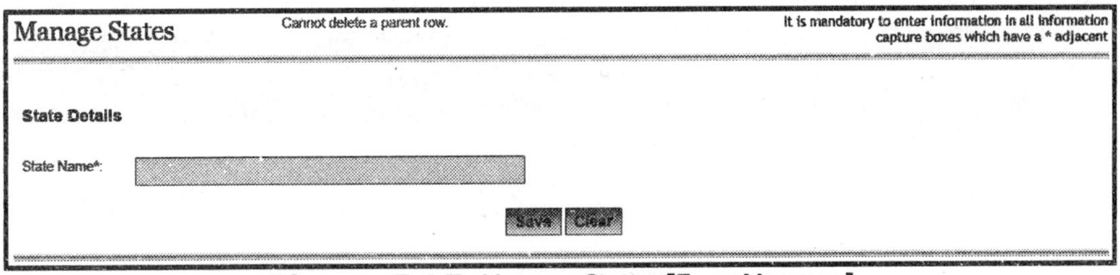

Manage States   Cannot delete a parent row.   It is mandatory to enter information in all information
                                                                capture boxes which have a * adjacent

State Details

State Name*: [   ]

Save Clear

Diagram 7.4.7: Manage States [Error Message]

Manage Categories

Click Categories. This delivers the Manage Categories data entry form, as shown in diagram 7.5.1.

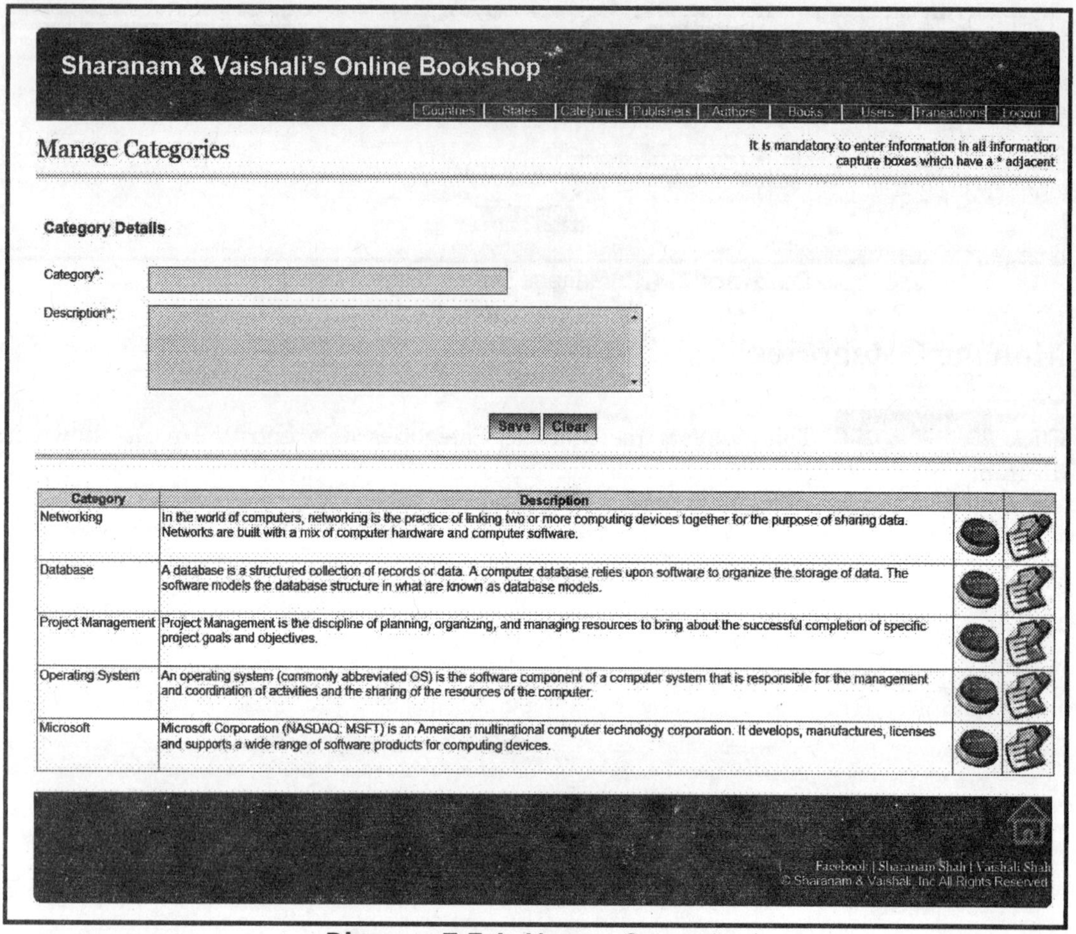

Diagram 7.5.1: Manage Categories

REMINDER

It is mandatory to enter information in all information capture boxes which have a * adjacent indicates entering values for all the form field labels that are marked * is mandatory.

Data entered in this form is used to populate the Category drop down list boxes in the Manage Books page.

Adding New Record

As soon as the data entry form loads in the web browser, it's ready to capture new records.

To add a new category, key in the required form field(s) and click **Save**.

Clicking **Save**, performs the following client side validations:

❑ Category name cannot be left blank

❑ Description cannot be left blank

❑ Category name already exists

If any one of the above mentioned validations fails, an appropriate error message is displayed, as shown in diagram 7.5.2.

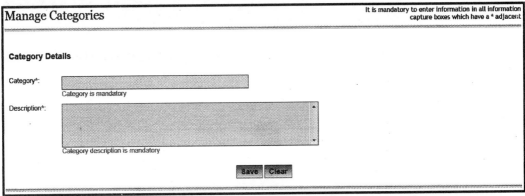

Diagram 7.5.2: Manage Categories [Error Message]

Correct the errors. After doing so, click **Save** to save the entered data in the database.

If all the validations mentioned above go through without any errors, the data is saved in the database and the page is reloaded to reflect the newly added data.

Modifying Existing Record

To modify an already existing record, click 🗒 adjacent to the desired record from the GRID, as shown in diagram 7.5.3.

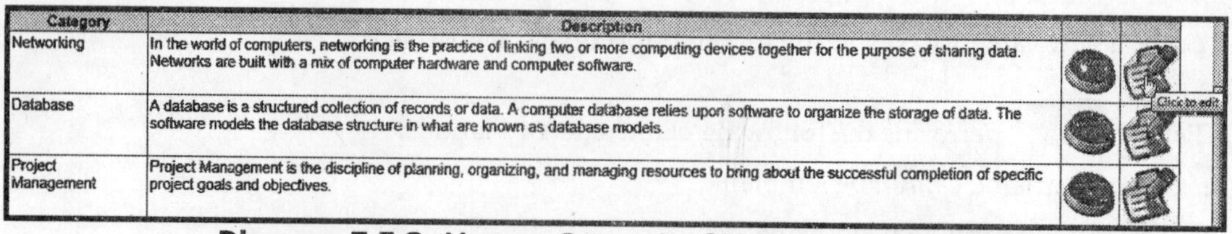
Category
Description
Networking
In the world of computers, networking is the practice of linking two or more computing devices together for the purpose of sharing data. Networks are built with a mix of computer hardware and computer software.
Click to edit
Database
A database is a structured collection of records or data. A computer database relies upon software to organize the storage of data. The software models the database structure in what are known as database models.
Project Management
Project Management is the discipline of planning, organizing, and managing resources to bring about the successful completion of specific project goals and objectives.

Diagram 7.5.3: Manage Categories [GRID for modification]

Doing so populates the record data in the data entry form, as shown in diagram 7.5.4.

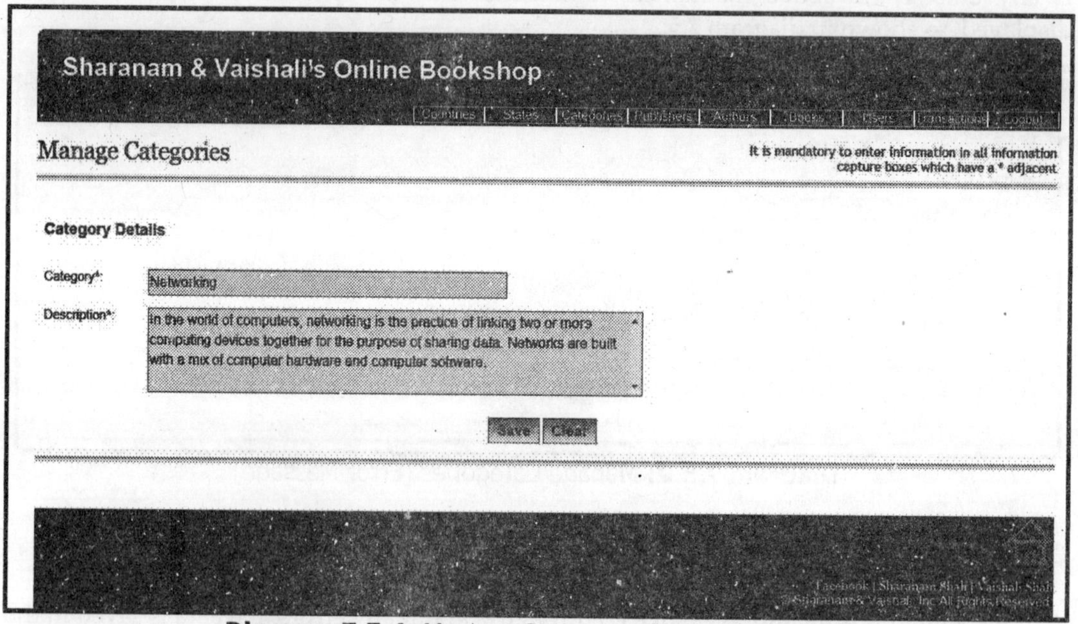
Sharanam & Vaishali's Online Bookshop
Countries | States | Categories | Publishers | Authors | Books | Users | Transactions | Logout
Manage Categories
It is mandatory to enter information in all information capture boxes which have a * adjacent
Category Details
Category*:
Networking
Description*:
In the world of computers, networking is the practice of linking two or more computing devices together for the purpose of sharing data. Networks are built with a mix of computer hardware and computer software.
Save
Clear

Diagram 7.5.4: Manage Categories [Data Populated]

Make the desired changes and click Save.

Clicking Save, performs the following client side validations:

- Category name cannot be left blank
- Description cannot be left blank
- Category name already exists

If any one of the above mentioned validations fails, an appropriate error message is displayed, as shown in diagram 7.5.5.

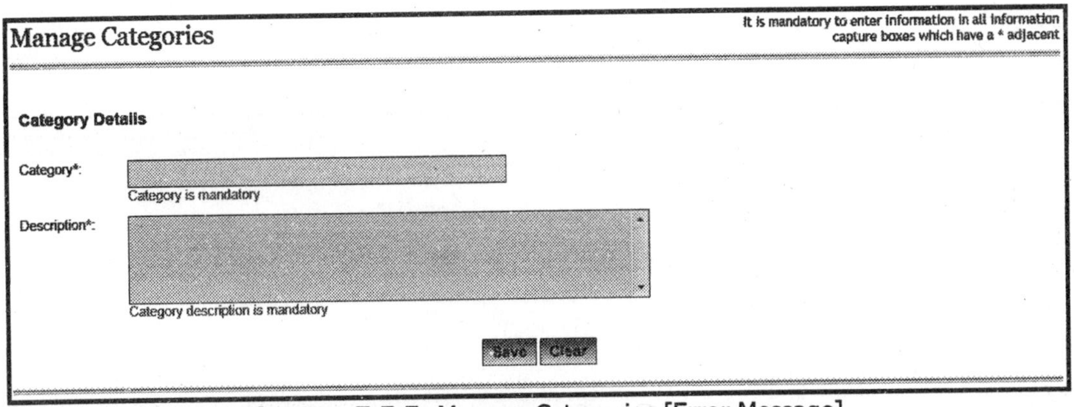

Diagram 7.5.5: Manage Categories [Error Message]

Correct the errors. After doing so, click **Save** to save the entered data in the database.

If all the validations mentioned above go through without any errors, the data is updated in the database and the page is reloaded to reflect the modified data.

Deleting Existing Record

To delete an already existing record click adjacent to the desired record from the GRID, as shown in diagram 7.5.6.

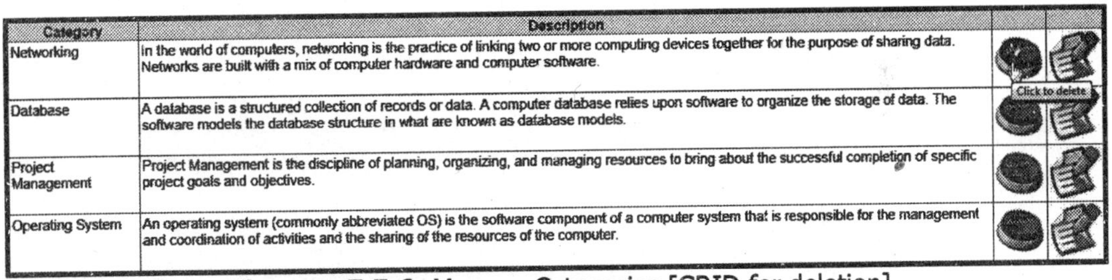

Diagram 7.5.6: Manage Categories [GRID for deletion]

Clicking , performs the delete operation and reloads the page to reflect the deleted records.

If the user attempts to a delete record that is associated with the existing data, an error message appears indicating the same, as shown in diagram 7.5.7.

Deleting a master record that has been associated with detail records in this case Books cannot be deleted.

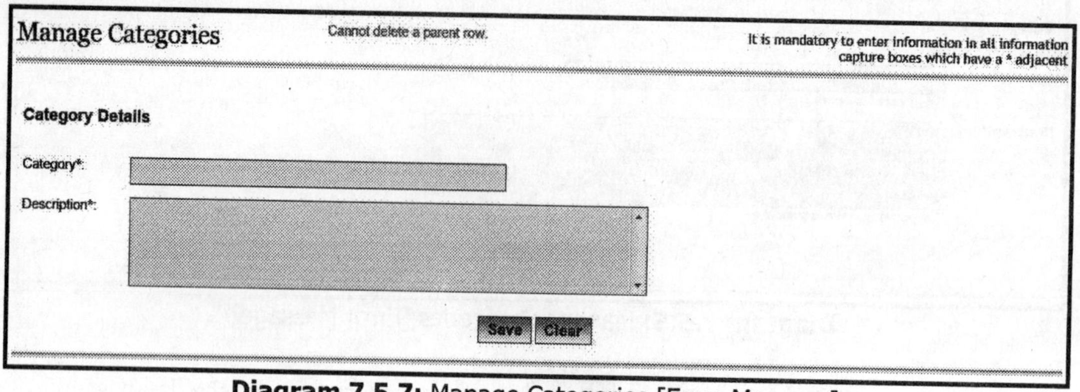

Manage Categories   Cannot delete a parent row.   It is mandatory to enter information in all information
                                                                                          capture boxes which have a * adjacent

Category Details

Category*: [   ]

Description*: [   ]

                                          [Save] [Clear]

Diagram 7.5.7: Manage Categories [Error Message]

Manage Publishers

Click [Publishers]. This delivers the Manage Publishers data entry form, as shown in diagram 7.6.1.

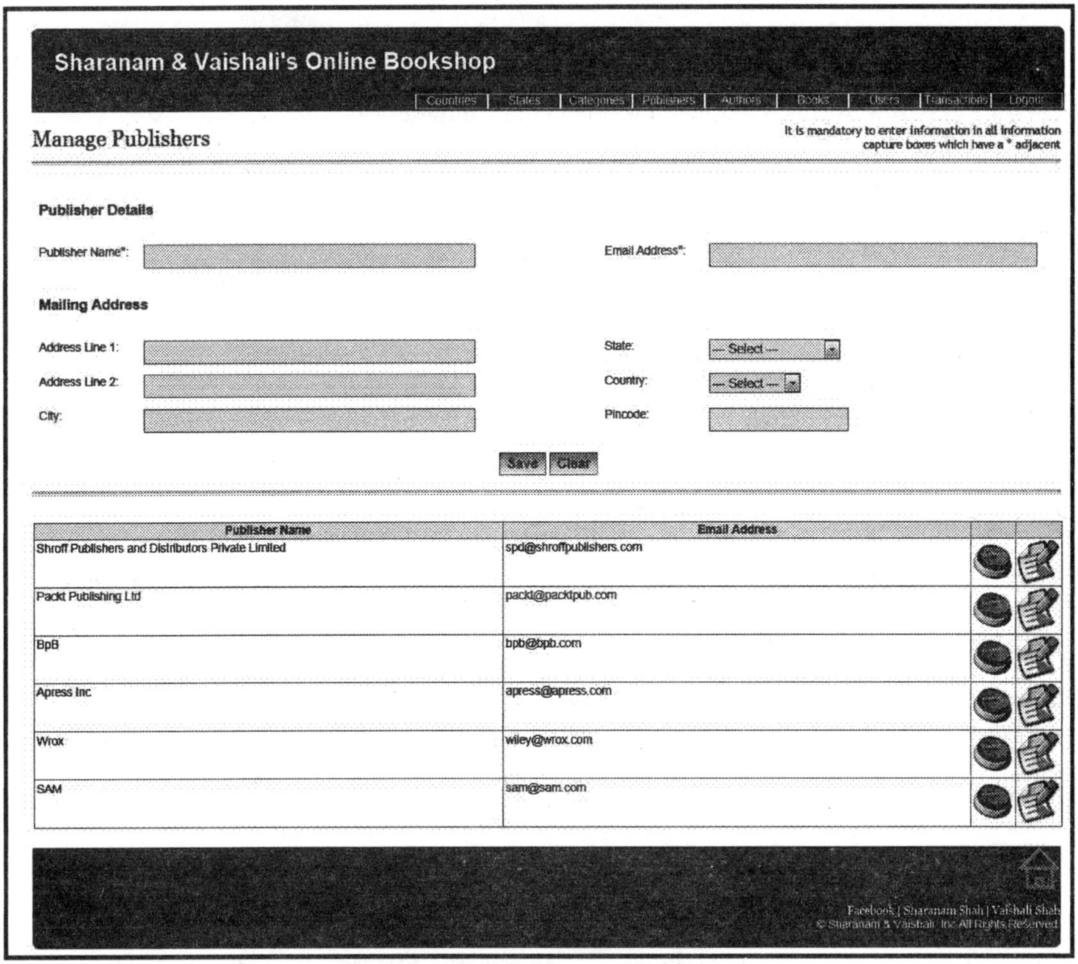

Diagram 7.6.1: Manage Publishers

Data entered in this form is used to populate the Publisher drop down list box in the Manage Books page.

Adding New Record

As soon as the data entry form loads in the web browser, it's ready to capture new records.

To add a new publisher, key in the required form field(s) and click [Save].

Clicking [Save], performs the following client side validations:

- ❑ Publisher name cannot be left blank
- ❑ Email address cannot be left blank
- ❑ Publisher name already exists
- ❑ Email address already exists

If any one of the above mentioned validations fails, an appropriate error message is displayed, as shown in diagram 7.6.2.

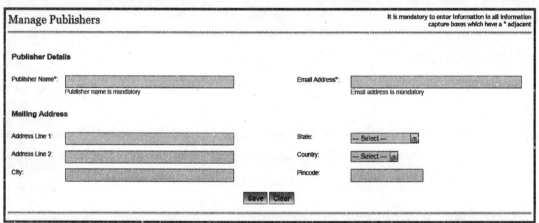

Diagram 7.6.2: Manage Publishers [Error Message]

Correct the errors. After doing so, click [Save] to save the entered data in the database.

If all the validations mentioned above go through without any errors, the data is saved in the database and the page is reloaded to reflect the newly added data.

Modifying Existing Record

To modify an already existing record, click [icon] adjacent to the desired record from the GRID, as shown in diagram 7.6.3.

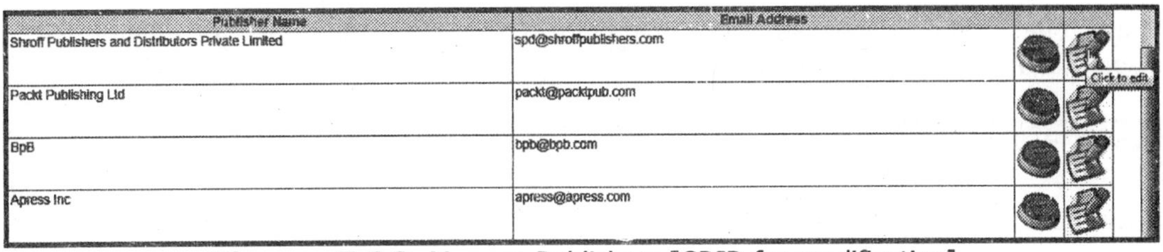

Publisher Name	Email Address	
Shroff Publishers and Distributors Private Limited	spd@shroffpublishers.com	
Packt Publishing Ltd	packt@packtpub.com	
BpB	bpb@bpb.com	
Apress Inc	apress@apress.com	

Diagram 7.6.3: Manage Publishers [GRID for modification]

Doing so populates the record data in the data entry form, as shown in diagram 7.6.4.

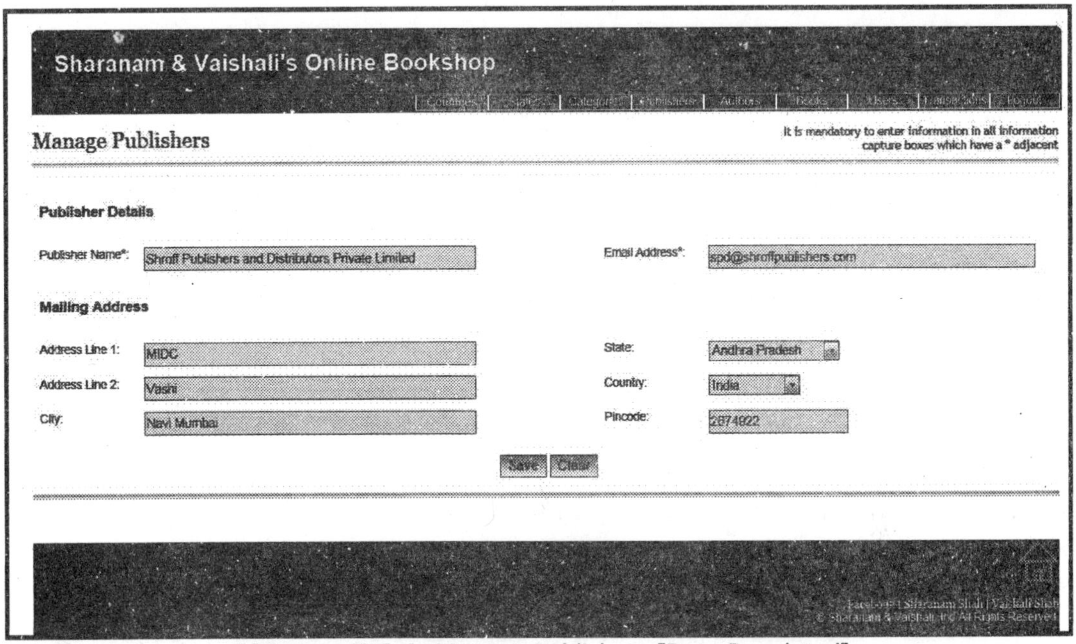

Diagram 7.6.4: Manage Publishers [Data Populated]

Make the desired changes and click **Save**.

Clicking **Save**, performs the following client side validations:

- Publisher name cannot be left blank
- Email address cannot be left blank
- Publisher name already exists
- Email address already exists

If any one of the above mentioned validations fails, an appropriate error message is displayed, as shown in diagram 7.6.5.

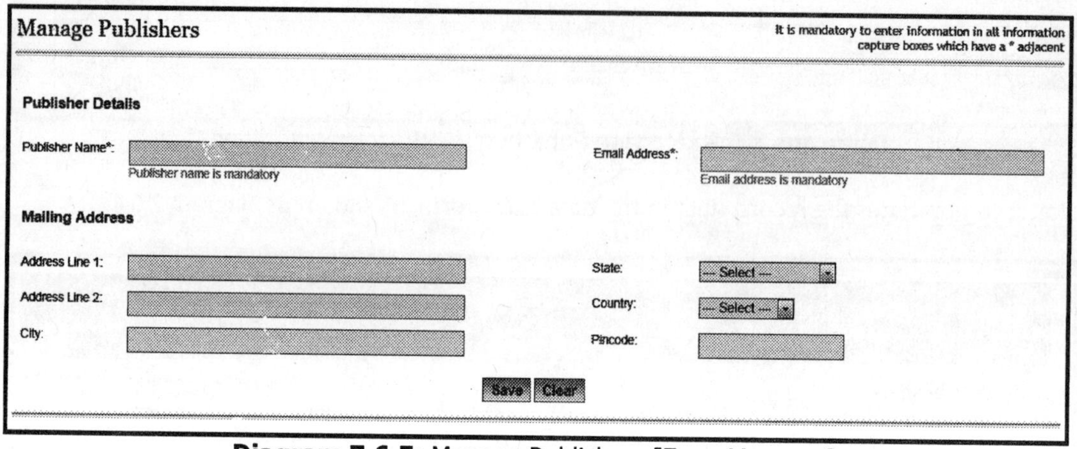

Diagram 7.6.5: Manage Publishers [Error Message]

Correct the error. After doing so, click **Save** to save the entered data in the database.

If all the validations mentioned above go through without any errors, the data is updated in the database and the page is reloaded to reflect the modified data.

Deleting Existing Record

To delete an already existing record click  adjacent to the desired record from the GRID, as shown in diagram 7.6.6.

Diagram 7.6.6: Manage Publishers [GRID for deletion]

Clicking  , performs the delete operation and reloads the page to reflect the deleted records.

If the user attempts to delete a record that is associated with the existing data, an error message appears indicating the same, as shown in diagram 7.6.7.

Deleting a master record that has been associated with detail records in this case Books cannot be deleted.

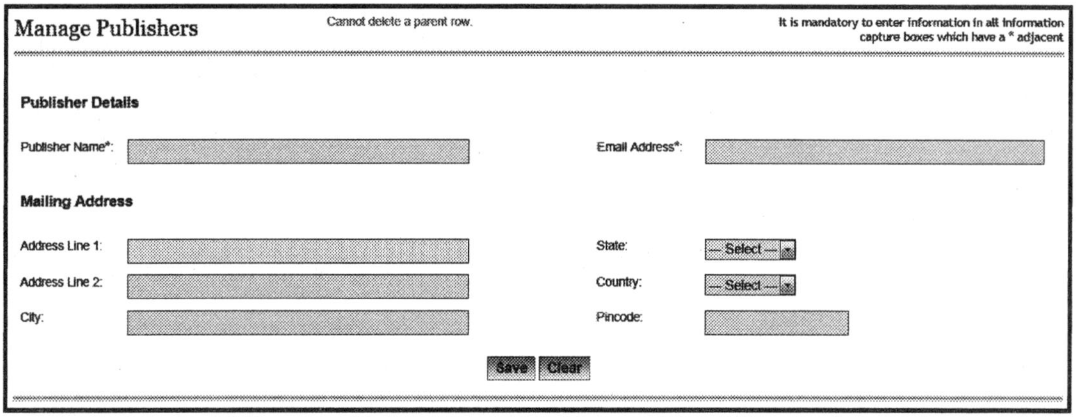

Manage Publishers	Cannot delete a parent row.	It is mandatory to enter information in all information capture boxes which have a * adjacent

Publisher Details

Publisher Name*: [   ]   Email Address*: [   ]

Mailing Address

Address Line 1: [   ]   State: [— Select — ▾]

Address Line 2: [   ]   Country: [— Select — ▾]

City: [   ]   Pincode: [   ]

[Save] [Clear]

Diagram 7.6.7: Manage Publishers [Error Message]

Manage Authors

Click [Authors]. This delivers the Manage Authors data entry form, as shown in diagram 7.7.1.

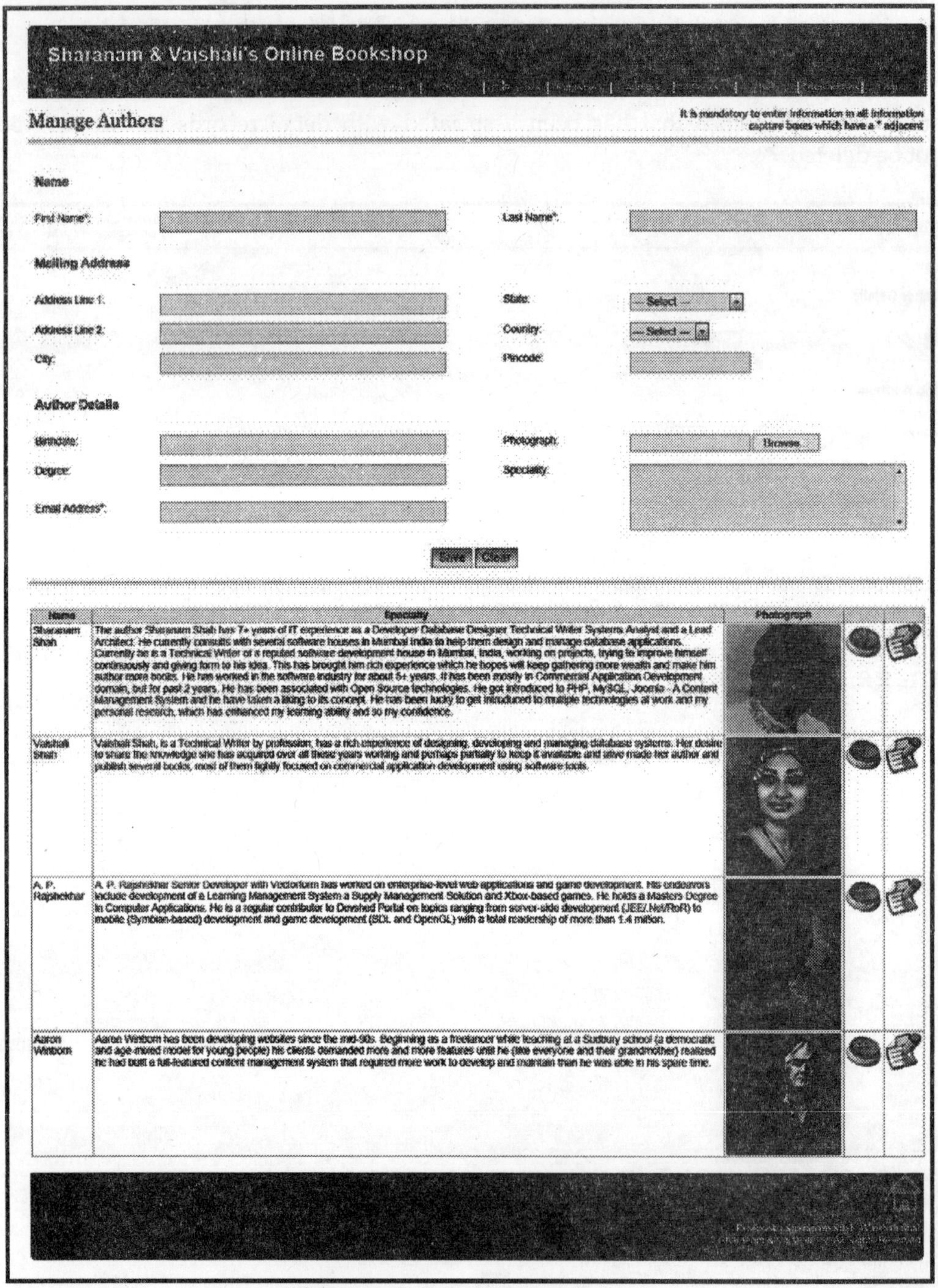

Diagram 7.7.1: Manage Authors

REMINDER

It is mandatory to enter information in all information
capture boxes which have a * adjacent indicates entering values for all the form field labels that are marked * is mandatory.

Data entered in this form is used to populate the Author drop down list box in the Manage Books page.

Adding New Record

As soon as the data entry form loads in the web browser, it's ready to capture new records.

To add a new author, key in the required form field(s) and click Save.

To upload the author photograph, click Browse... . Clicking Browse... opens the **File Upload** dialog box, as shown in diagram 7.7.1.1.

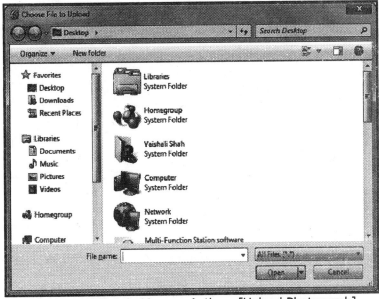

Diagram 7.7.1.1: Manage Authors [Upload Photograph]

Choose the desired image file and click Open.

Clicking **Save**, performs the following client side validations:

❑ First name cannot be left blank

❑ Last name cannot be left blank

❑ Email address cannot be left blank

❑ Email address already exists

If any one of the above mentioned validations fails, an appropriate error message is displayed, as shown in diagram 7.7.2.

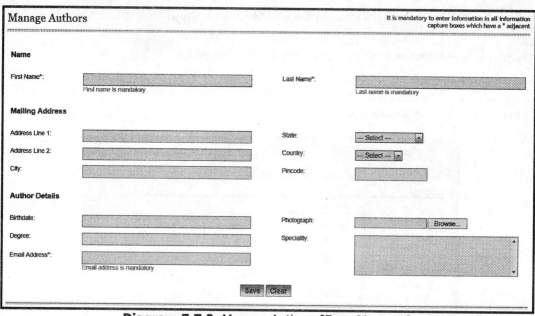

Diagram 7.7.2: Manage Authors [Error Message]

Correct the errors. After doing so, click **Save** to save the entered data in the database.

If all the validations mentioned above go through without any errors, the data is saved in the database and the page is reloaded to reflect the newly added data.

Modifying Existing Record

To modify an already existing record click ✎ adjacent to the desired record from the GRID, as shown in diagram 7.7.3.

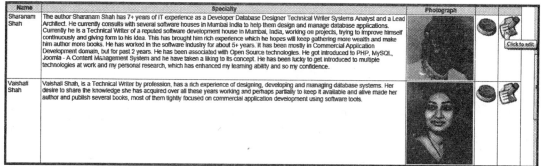

Name
Specialty
Photograph
Sharanam Shah
The author Sharanam Shah has 7+ years of IT experience as a Developer Database Designer Technical Writer Systems Analyst and a Lead Architect. He currently consults with several software houses in Mumbai India to help them design and manage database applications. Currently he is a Technical Writer of a reputed software development house in Mumbai, India, working on projects, trying to improve himself continuously and giving form to his idea. This has brought him rich experience which he hopes will keep gathering more wealth and make him author more books. He has worked in the software industry for about 5+ years. It has been mostly in Commercial Application Development domain, but for past 2 years. He has been associated with Open Source technologies. He got introduced to PHP, MySQL, Joomla - A Content Management System and he have taken a liking to its concept. He has been lucky to get introduced to multiple technologies at work and my personal research, which has enhanced my learning ability and so my confidence.
Click to edit
Vaishali Shah
Vaishali Shah, is a Technical Writer by profession, has a rich experience of designing, developing and managing database systems. Her desire to share the knowledge she has acquired over all these years working and perhaps partially to keep it available and alive made her author and publish several books, most of them tightly focused on commercial application development using software tools.

Diagram 7.7.3: Manage Authors [GRID for modification]

Doing so populates the record data in the data entry form, as shown in diagram 7.7.4.

Sharanam & Vaishali's Online Bookshop
Countries | States | Categories | Publishers | Authors | Books | Users | Transactions | Logout
Manage Authors
It is mandatory to enter information in all information capture boxes which have a * adjacent
Name
First Name*:
Sharanam
Last Name*:
Shah
Mailing Address
Address Line 1:
Some Building
State:
Andhra Pradesh
Address Line 2:
Some Road
Country:
India
City:
Mumbai
Pincode:
400016
Author Details
Birthdate:
2009-01-07
Photograph:
Browse...
Degree:
CDAC
Speciality:
The author Sharanam Shah has 7+ years of IT experience as a Developer Database Designer Technical Writer Systems Analyst and a Lead Architect. He currently consults with several software
Email Address*:
sharanams@gmail.com
Save
Clear
Facebook | Sharanam Shah | Vaishali Shah
© Sharanam & Vaishali, Inc. All Rights Reserved

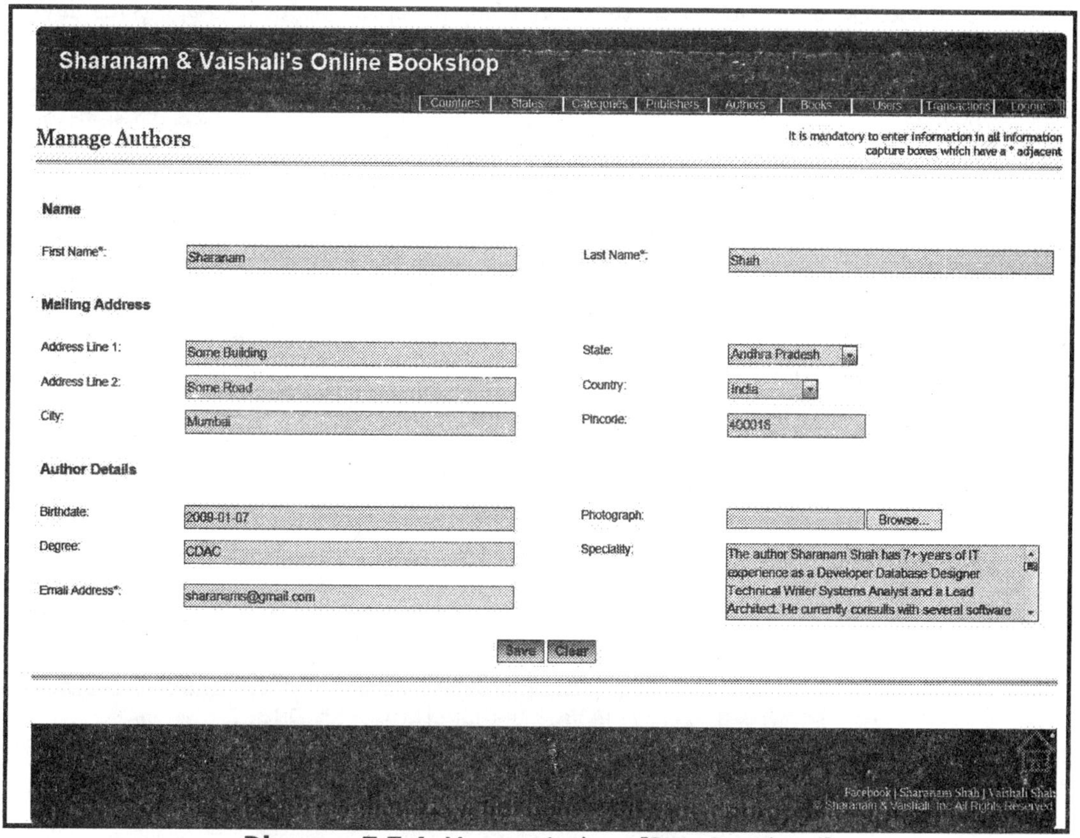

Diagram 7.7.4: Manage Authors [Data Populated]

If a new photograph is not uploaded [using **Browse...**] whilst updating the record, then the previous photograph is maintained in the database.

Make the desired changes and click **Save** .

Clicking **Save** , performs the following client side validations:

❑   First name cannot be left blank

❑   Last name cannot be left blank

❑   Email address cannot be left blank

❑   Email address already exists

If any one of the above mentioned validation fail, an appropriate error message is displayed, as shown in diagram 7.7.5.

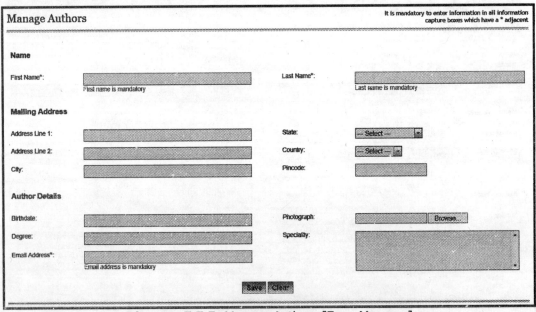

Diagram 7.7.5: Manage Authors [Error Message]

Correct the errors. After doing so, click **Save** to save the entered data in the database.

If all the validations mentioned above go through without any errors, the data is updated in the database and the page is reloaded to reflect the modified data.

Deleting Existing Record

To delete an already existing record click adjacent to the desired record from the GRID, as shown in diagram 7.7.6.

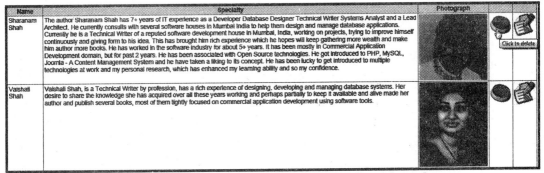

Diagram 7.7.6: Manage Authors [GRID for deletion]

Clicking , performs the delete operation and reloads the page to reflect the deleted records.

If the user attempts to delete a record that is associated with the existing data, an error message appears indicating the same, as shown in diagram 7.7.7.

Deleting a master record that has been associated with detail records in this case Books cannot be deleted.

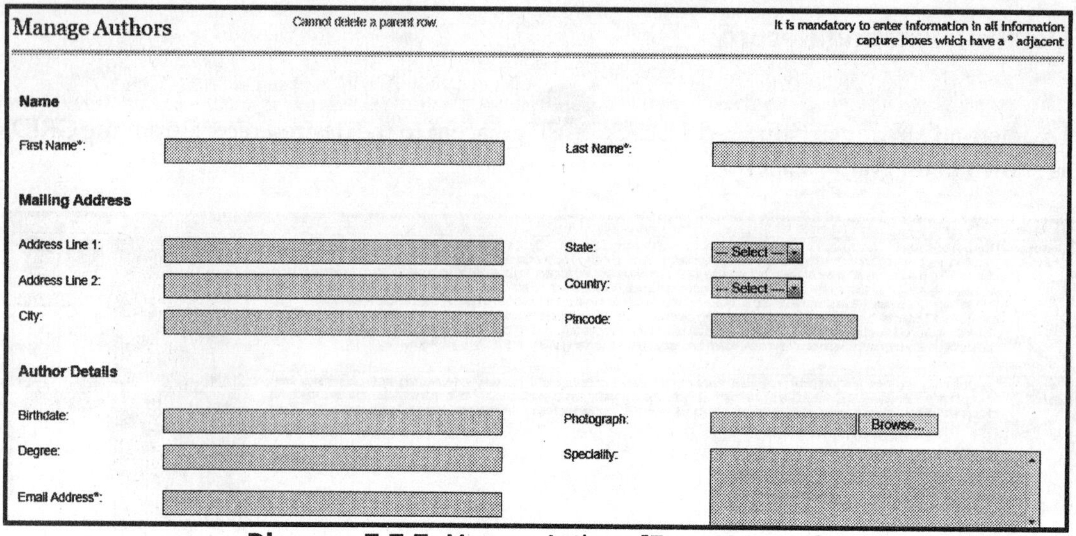

Diagram 7.7.7: Manage Authors [Error Message]

Manage Books

Click [Books] . This delivers the Manage Books data entry form, as shown in diagram 7.8.1.

Sharanam & Vaishali's Online Bookshop

| Courses | Stats | Categories | Publishers | Authors | Books | Users | Cancellations | Logout |

Manage Books

It is mandatory to enter information in all information capture boxes which have a * adjacent

Book Details

Book Name*:		Publisher*:	— Select —
Category*:	— Select —	Cover Page:	Browse...
ISBN*:		Edition*:	
Year*:		Cost*:	

Author Details

First Author*:	— Select —	Second Author:	— Select —
Third Author:	— Select —	Fourth Author:	— Select —

Description

Synopsis*:		About Authors*:	
Topics Covered:		CDROM:	

Downloads

TOC:	Browse...	Sample Chapter:	Browse...

Save   Clear

Book	ISBN	Synopsis	Cover Page	Downloads		
Oracle For Professionals	978-81-8404-026	Designed for new and experienced developers this book is an essential guide for putting Oracle SQL and PL/SQL to work. It provides all of the basics you would expect to find in an introductory text and at the same time serves those who want to harness the unexploited overlooked power of Oracle SQL and PL/SQL with an easy to follow format and numerous real examples based on most commonly used business database models.	Oracle	Sample TOC		
Practical Java Project For Beginners	10: 81-8404-342-2	This book can be useful for students pursuing B.E. M.C.A M.Sc. IGNOU BCA B.Sc. courses who have to make and submit a project as part of their curriculum.		Sample TOC		
JavaServer Pages For Beginners	10: 81-8404-359-7	The book has been written to provide genuine knowledge to programmers who wish to learn Java Server side Web based application development using Java Server Pages. Learning web development is done through a set of examples and hands on exercises		Sample TOC		

Diagram 7.8.1: Manage Books

REMINDER

it is mandatory to enter information in all information capture boxes which have a * adjacent indicates entering values for all the form field labels that are marked * is mandatory.

Adding New Record

As soon as the data entry form loads in the web browser, it's ready to capture new records.

To add a new book, key in the required form field(s) for the book being added and click `Save`.

To upload the book's cover page, click `Browse...`. Clicking `Browse...` opens the **File Upload** dialog box, as shown in diagram 7.8.1.1.

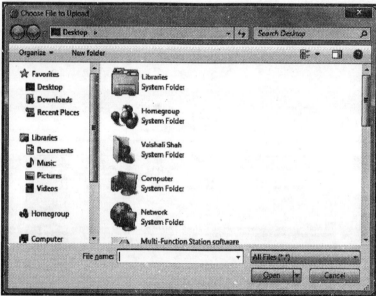

Diagram 7.8.1.1: Manage Books [Upload Cover Page]

Choose the desired image file and click `Open`. Similarly, TOC and Sample Chapter files can be uploaded.

Clicking `Save`, performs the following client side validations:

❑ Book name cannot be left blank

❑   Publisher name cannot be left blank

❑   Category name cannot be left blank

❑   ISBN cannot be left blank

❑   Edition cannot be left blank

❑   Year cannot be left blank

❑   Cost cannot be left blank

❑   First author cannot be left blank

❑   Synopsis cannot be left blank

❑   About authors cannot be left blank

❑   ISBN already exists

If any one of the above mentioned validations fails, an appropriate error message is displayed, as shown in diagram 7.8.2.

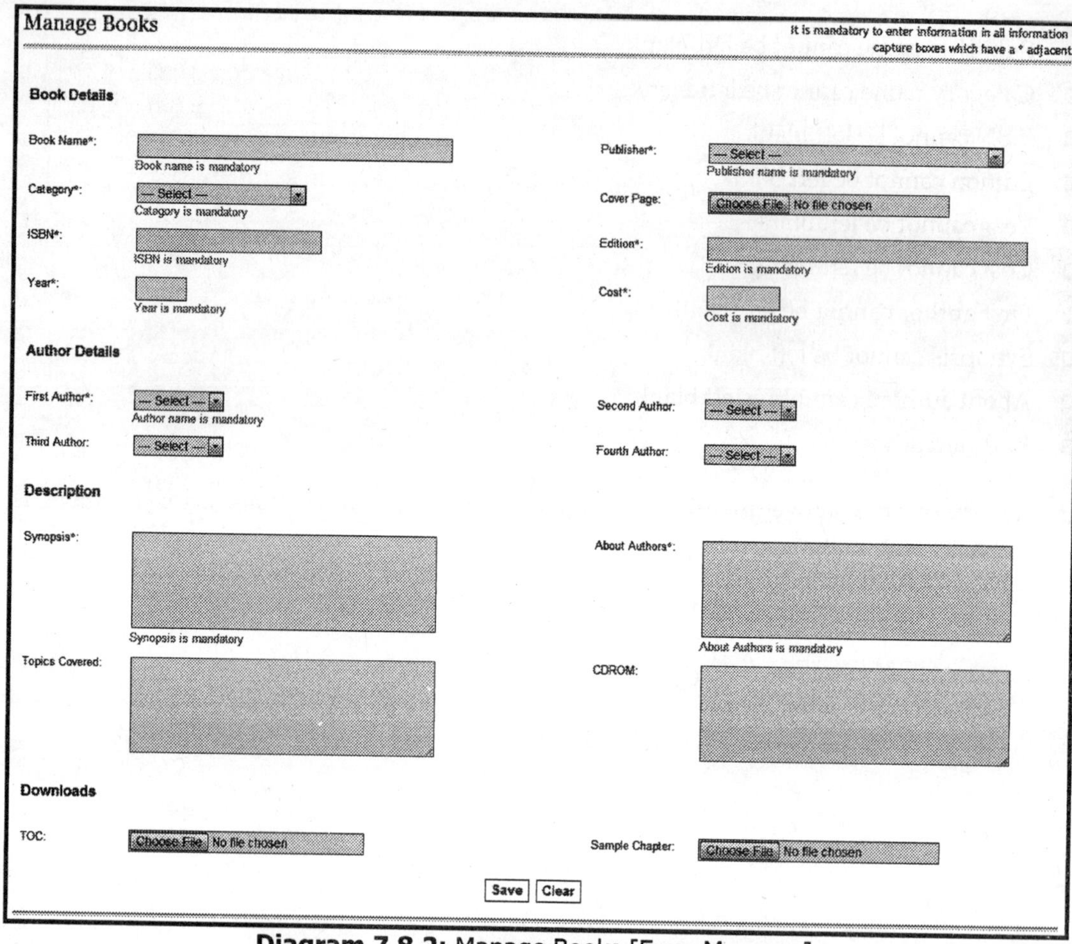

Manage Books

It is mandatory to enter information in all information capture boxes which have a * adjacent

Book Details

Book Name*:

Book name is mandatory

Publisher*:

— Select —

Publisher name is mandatory

Category*:

— Select —

Category is mandatory

Cover Page:

Choose File | No file chosen

ISBN*:

ISBN is mandatory

Edition*:

Edition is mandatory

Year*:

Year is mandatory

Cost*:

Cost is mandatory

Author Details

First Author*:

— Select —

Author name is mandatory

Second Author:

— Select —

Third Author:

— Select —

Fourth Author:

— Select —

Description

Synopsis*:

Synopsis is mandatory

About Authors*:

About Authors is mandatory

Topics Covered:

CDROM:

Downloads

TOC:

Choose File | No file chosen

Sample Chapter:

Choose File | No file chosen

Save   Clear

Diagram 7.8.2: Manage Books [Error Message]

Correct the errors. After doing so, click **Save** to save the entered data in the database.

If all the validations mentioned above go through without any errors, the data is saved in the database and the page is reloaded to reflect the newly added data.

After the book is added, an email as shown in diagram 7.8.3 is dispatched to all those customers who had subscribed for **New Releases** whilst signing up.

REMINDER

 The system dispatches emails only if, the **sendMail** attribute in the application's configuration file i.e. bookshop.properties is set to **true**, along with the other email attributes such as **emailFrom**, **emailUser** and **emailPasswd** that indicate the user credentials of the email ID.

Sharanam & Vaishali's Online Bookshop: Spring 3 For Beginners has been added.   Inbox x

s.v.onlinebookshop@gmail.com (12:40 PM (3 minutes ago)
to me

Dear Neil,

ISBN: 888-76587

Edition: First

Synopsis: Designed for beginners and intermediate developers, this book helps you come up to speed as quickly as possible with using the Spring 3 framework. It delves deeply into the core of the Spring 3 framework, providing a sound understanding of the components that make up the framework and the way they interact with each other.

Topics covered: Spring 3.1, Spring Security 3.1, Spring Web MVC, JDBC Templates, RESTful resources, MySQL 5.5, Hibernate 3

Thank you for using this site.

Regards,
Sharanam & Vaishali's Online Bookshop
THIS IS AN AUTOMATED MESSAGE; PLEASE DO NOT REPLY.

Sharanam & Vaishali Shah

Diagram 7.8.3: Email for New Releases

Modifying Existing Record

To modify an already existing record click ![icon] adjacent to the desired record from the GRID, as shown in diagram 7.8.4.

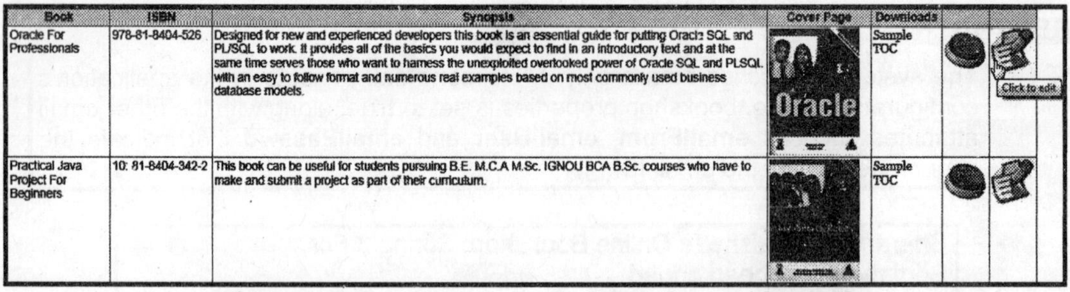

Book	ISBN	Synopsis	Cover Page	Downloads		
Oracle For Professionals	978-81-8404-526	Designed for new and experienced developers this book is an essential guide for putting Oracle SQL and PL/SQL to work. It provides all of the basics you would expect to find in an introductory text and at the same time serves those who want to harness the unexploited overlooked power of Oracle SQL and PLSQL with an easy to follow format and numerous real examples based on most commonly used business database models.		Sample TOC		Click to edit
Practical Java Project For Beginners	10: 81-8404-342-2	This book can be useful for students pursuing B.E. M.C.A M.Sc. IGNOU BCA B.Sc. courses who have to make and submit a project as part of their curriculum.		Sample TOC		

Diagram 7.8.4: Manage Books [GRID for modification]

Doing so populates the record data in the data entry form, as shown in diagram 7.8.5.

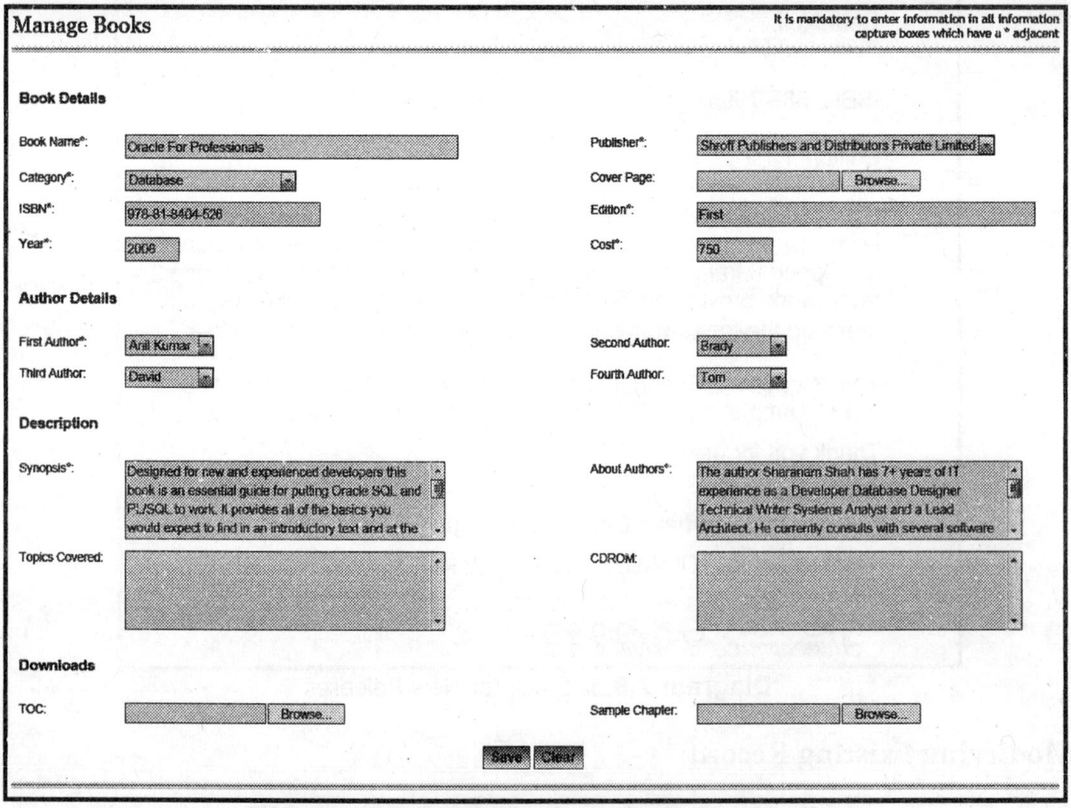

Manage Books

It is mandatory to enter information in all information capture boxes which have a * adjacent

Book Details

Book Name*:   Oracle For Professionals   Publisher*:   Shroff Publishers and Distributors Private Limited

Category*:   Database   Cover Page: Browse...

ISBN*:   978-81-8404-526   Edition*:   First

Year*:   2006   Cost*:   750

Author Details

First Author*:   Anil Kumar   Second Author: Brady

Third Author: David   Fourth Author: Tom

Description

Synopsis*:   Designed for new and experienced developers this book is an essential guide for putting Oracle SQL and PL/SQL to work. It provides all of the basics you would expect to find in an introductory text and at the

About Authors*:   The author Sharanam Shah has 7+ years of IT experience as a Developer Database Designer Technical Writer Systems Analyst and a Lead Architect. He currently consults with several software

Topics Covered:

CDROM:

Downloads

TOC: Browse...   Sample Chapter: Browse...

Save   Clear

Diagram 7.8.5: Manage Books [Data Populated]

Make the desired changes and click Save .

If the cover page, toc or sample chapter is not re-uploaded whilst editing the record, then the previous ones are deleted.

Clicking [Save], performs the following client side validations:

❑ Book name cannot be left blank

❑ Publisher name cannot be left blank

❑ Category name cannot be left blank

❑ ISBN cannot be left blank

❑ Edition cannot be left blank

❑ Year cannot be left blank

❑ Cost cannot be left blank

❑ First author cannot be left blank

❑ Synopsis cannot be left blank

❑ About authors cannot be left blank

❑ ISBN already exists

If any one of the above mentioned validations fails, an appropriate error message is displayed, as shown in diagram 7.8.6.

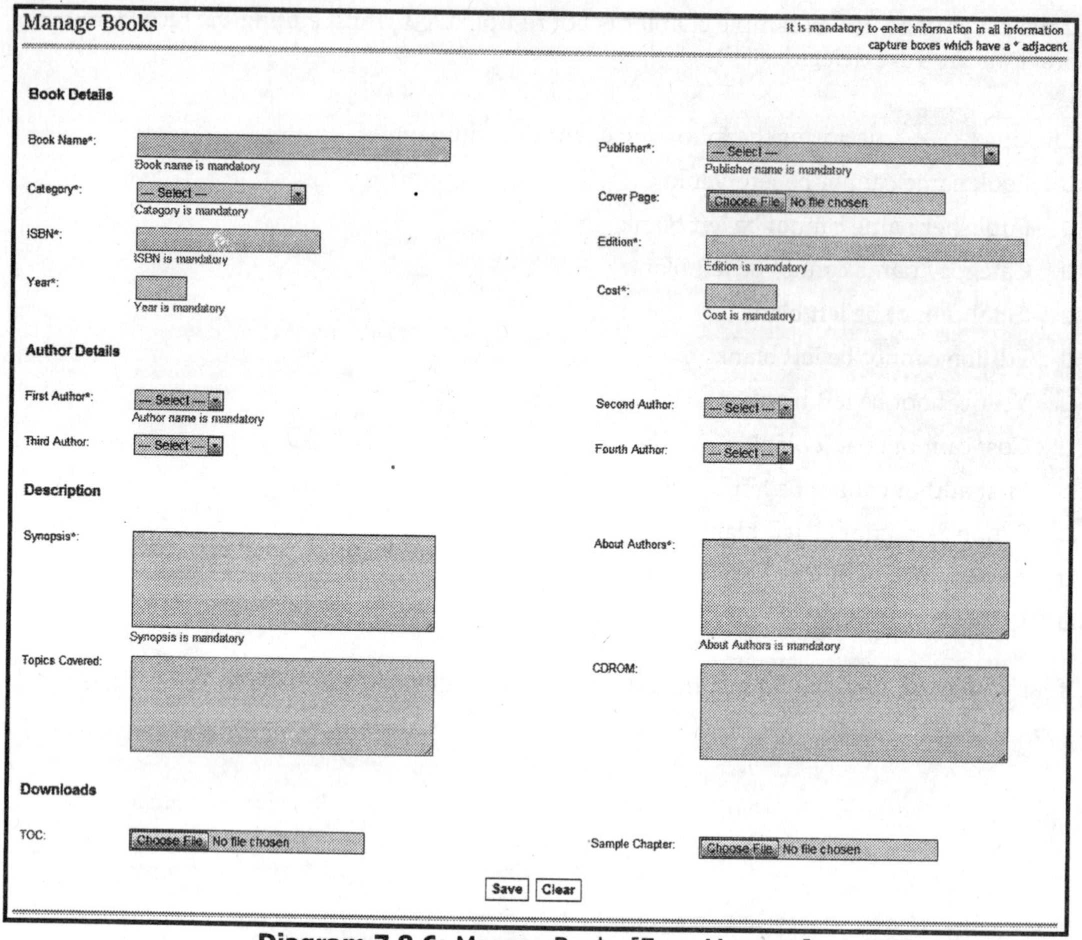

Manage Books   It is mandatory to enter information in all information
                                                                          capture boxes which have a * adjacent

Book Details

Book Name*:   Publisher*:   — Select —
Book name is mandatory   Publisher name is mandatory

Category*:   — Select —   Cover Page: Choose File   No file chosen
Category is mandatory

ISBN*:   Edition*:
ISBN is mandatory   Edition is mandatory

Year*:   Cost*:
Year is mandatory   Cost is mandatory

Author Details

First Author*:   — Select —   Second Author: — Select —
Author name is mandatory

Third Author: — Select —   Fourth Author: — Select —

Description

Synopsis*:   About Authors*:

Synopsis is mandatory   About Authors is mandatory

Topics Covered: CDROM:

Downloads

TOC: Choose File   No file chosen   Sample Chapter: Choose File   No file chosen

                              Save   Clear

Diagram 7.8.6: Manage Books [Error Message]

Correct the errors. After doing so, click **Save** to save the entered data in the database.

If all the validations mentioned above go through without any errors, the data is updated in the database and the page is reloaded to reflect the modified data.

After the book is updated, an email as shown in diagram 7.8.7 is dispatched to all those customers who had subscribed for **Book Updates** whilst signing up.

REMINDER

The system dispatches emails only if, the **sendMail** attribute in the application's configuration file i.**e**. bookshop.properties is set to **true**, along with the other email attributes such as **emailFrom**, **emailUser** and **emailPasswd** that indicate the user credentials of the email ID.

Sharanam & Vaishali's Online Bookshop: Spring 3 For Beginners has been updated. Inbox x

s.v.onlinebookshop@gmail.com   12:58 PM (0 minutes ago)

to me

Dear Neil,

ISBN: 888-76587

Edition: Second

Synopsis: Designed for beginners and intermediate developers, this book helps you come up to speed as quickly as possible with using the Spring 3 framework. It delves deeply into the core of the Spring 3 framework, providing a sound understanding of the components that make up the framework and the way they interact with each other.

Topics covered: Spring 3.1, Spring Security 3.1, Spring Web MVC, JDBC Templates, RESTful resources, MySQL 5.5, Hibernate 3, JPA, Transaction Management, Annotations, @AspectJ AOP, Classic AOP, Dependency Injection

Thank you for using this site.

Regards,
Sharanam & Vaishali's Online Bookshop

THIS IS AN AUTOMATED MESSAGE; PLEASE DO NOT REPLY.

Sharanam & Vaishali Shah

Diagram 7.8.7: Email for Book Updates

Deleting Existing Record

To delete an already existing record click  adjacent to the desired record from the GRID, as shown in diagram 7.8.8.

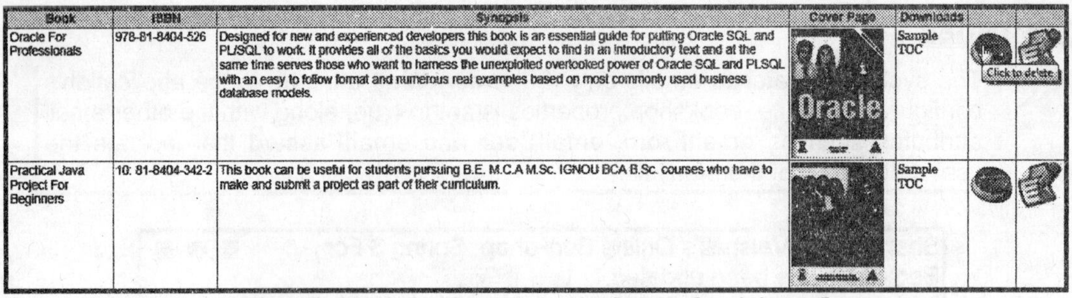

Book	ISBN	Synopsis	Cover Page	Downloads	
Oracle For Professionals	978-81-8404-526	Designed for new and experienced developers this book is an essential guide for putting Oracle SQL and PL/SQL to work. It provides all of the basics you would expect to find in an introductory text and at the same time serves those who want to harness the unexploited overlooked power of Oracle SQL and PLSQL with an easy to follow format and numerous real examples based on most commonly used business database models.	Oracle	Sample TOC	Click to delete
Practical Java Project For Beginners	10: 81-8404-342-2	This book can be useful for students pursuing B.E. M.C.A M.Sc. IGNOU BCA B.Sc. courses who have to make and submit a project as part of their curriculum.		Sample TOC	

Diagram 7.8.8: Manage Books [GRID for deletion]

Clicking ⬤, performs the delete operation and reloads the page to reflect the deleted records.

Manage Users

After the customer registers/signs up using the signup data entry form, the system user from the backend can modify, delete or view the customer details.

This form also allows adding, modifying or deleting system users.

Click **Users**. This delivers the Manage Users data entry form, as shown in diagram 7.9.1.

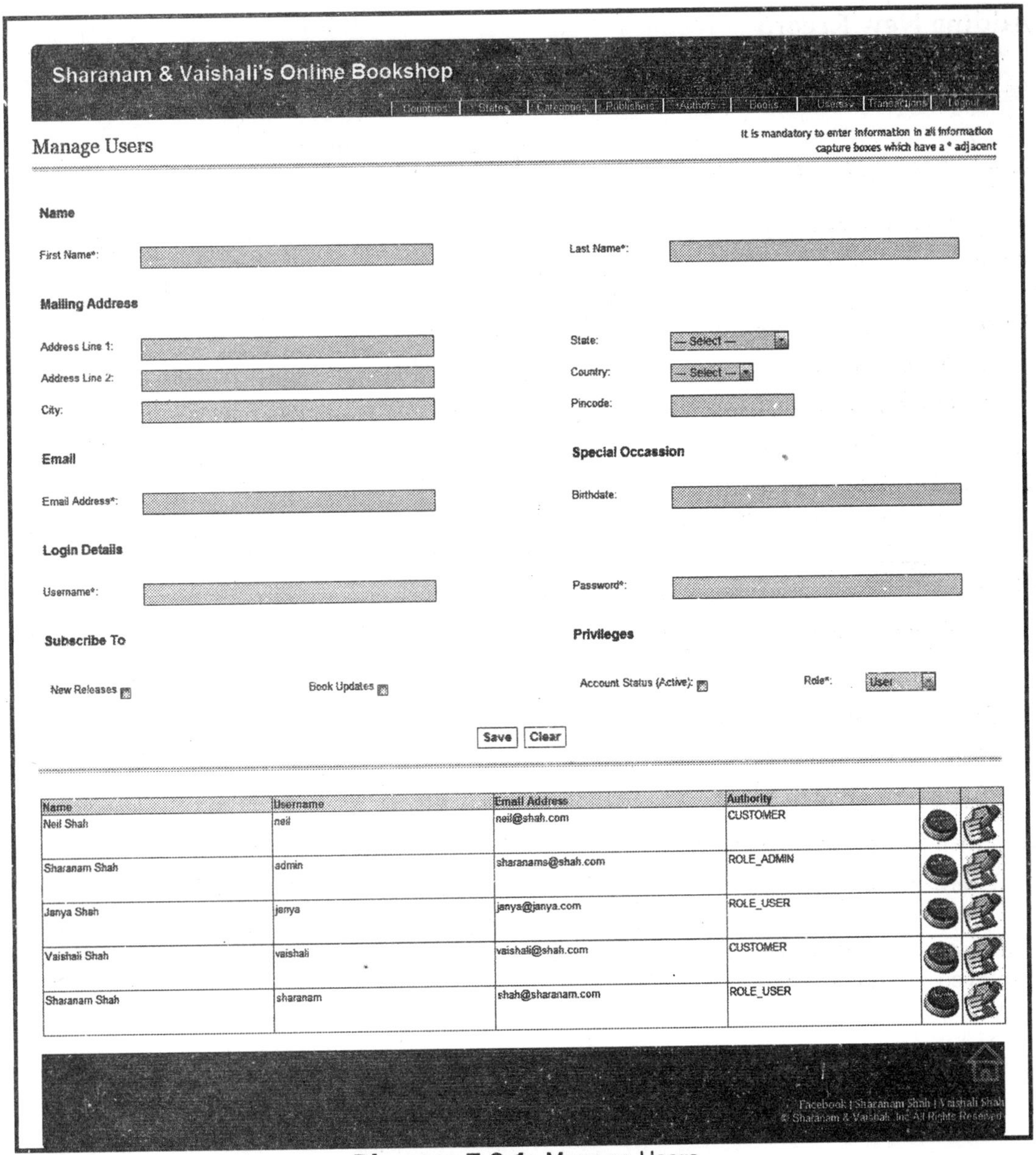

Sharanam & Vaishali's Online Bookshop

Countries | States | Categories | Publishers | Authors | Books | Users | Transactions | Logout

Manage Users

It is mandatory to enter information in all information capture boxes which have a * adjacent

Name

First Name*: [   ]

Last Name*: [   ]

Mailing Address

Address Line 1: [   ]

Address Line 2: [   ]

City: [   ]

State: [— Select — ▼]

Country: [— Select — ▼]

Pincode: [   ]

Email

Email Address*: [   ]

Special Occassion

Birthdate: [   ]

Login Details

Username*: [   ]

Password*: [   ]

Subscribe To

New Releases ☐   Book Updates ☐

Privileges

Account Status (Active): ☐   Role*: [User ▼]

[Save] [Clear]

Name	Username	Email Address	Authority		
Neil Shah	neil	neil@shah.com	CUSTOMER		
Sharanam Shah	admin	sharanams@shah.com	ROLE_ADMIN		
Janya Shah	janya	janya@janya.com	ROLE_USER		
Vaishali Shah	vaishali	vaishali@shah.com	CUSTOMER		
Sharanam Shah	sharanam	shah@sharanam.com	ROLE_USER		

Facebook | Sharanam Shah | Vaishali Shah
© Sharanam & Vaishali Inc All Rights Reserved

Diagram 7.9.1: Manage Users

REMINDER

It is mandatory to enter information in all information capture boxes which have a * adjacent indicates entering values for all the form field labels that are marked * is mandatory.

Adding New Record

As soon as the data entry form loads in the web browser, it's ready to capture new records.

To add a new user, key in the required form field(s) and click **Save**.

In this form, the **Privileges** section allows assigning rights to the user based on which access to appropriate data entry forms is granted to that user on login.

A user can have one of the following roles:

❏   **ADMIN:** All the management forms are accessible to the users with this role

❏   **USER:** All the management forms except the Manage Users form are accessible to the users with this role

❏   **CUSTOMER:** This is the default role for the users signing up as customers from the frontend. Users with this role cannot access the administration forms

Clicking **Save**, performs the following client side validations:

❏   First name cannot be left blank

❏   Last name cannot be left blank

❏   Email address cannot be left blank

❏   Username cannot be left blank

❏   Password cannot be left blank

❏   Email address already exists

❏   Username already exists

If any one of the above mentioned validations fails, an appropriate error message is displayed, as shown in diagram 7.9.2.

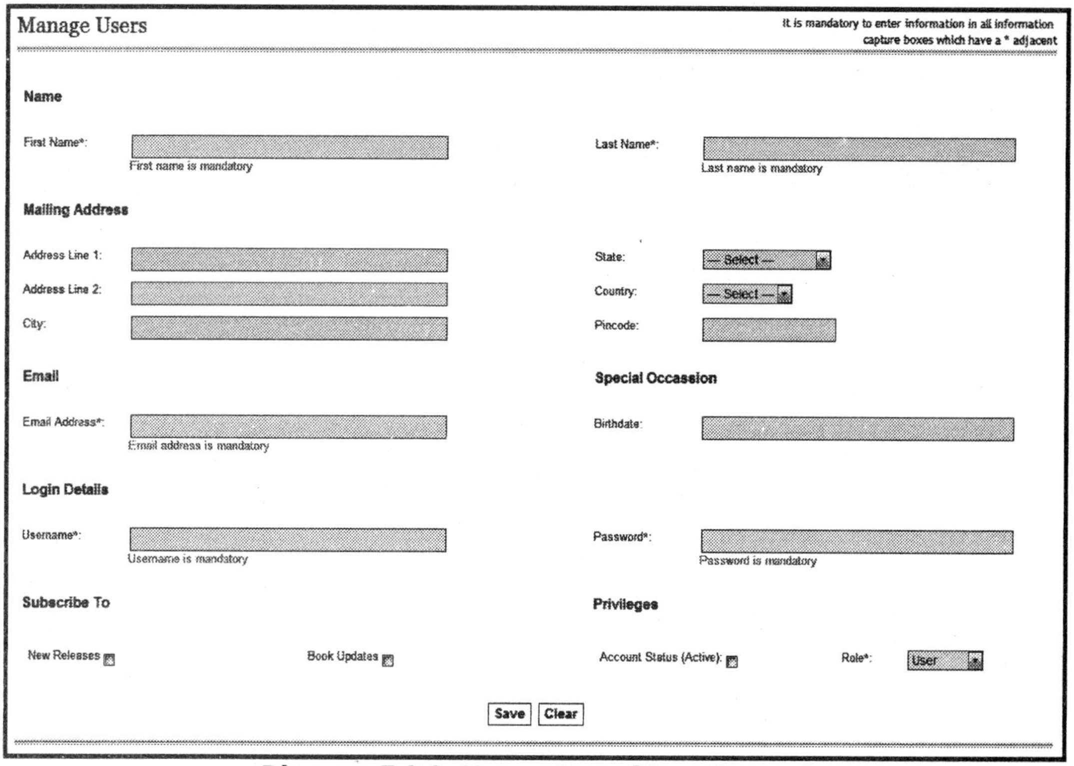

Diagram 7.9.2: Manage Users [Error Message]

Correct the errors. After doing so, click **Save** to save the entered data in the database.

If all the validations mentioned above go through without any errors, the data is saved in the database and the page is reloaded to reflect the newly added data.

Modifying Existing Record

To modify an already existing record click  adjacent to the desired record from the GRID, as shown in diagram 7.9.3.

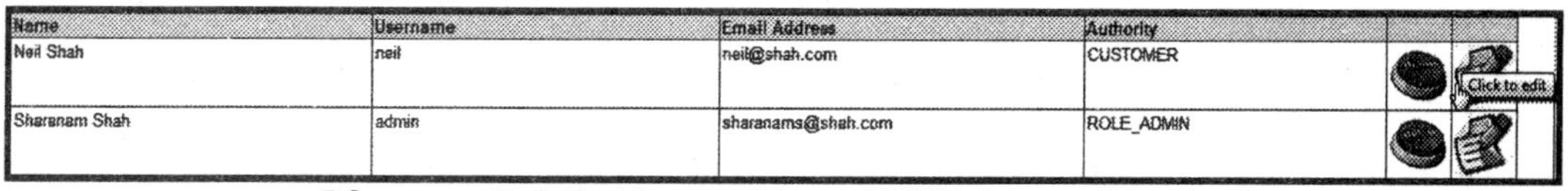

Name	Username	Email Address	Authority		
Neil Shah	neil	neil@shah.com	CUSTOMER		Click to edit
Sharanam Shah	admin	sharanams@shah.com	ROLE_ADMIN		

Diagram 7.9.3: Manage Users [GRID for modification]

Doing so populates the record data in the data entry form, as shown in diagram 7.9.4.

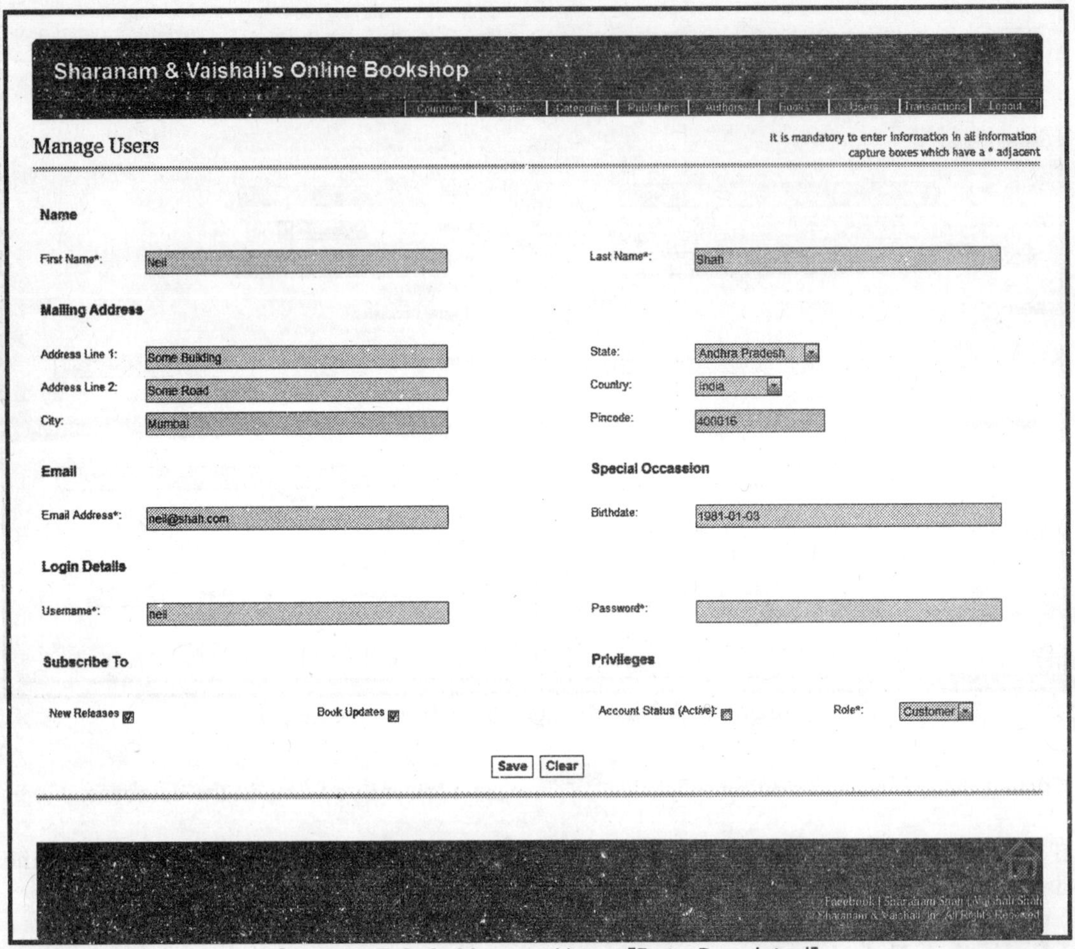

Diagram 7.9.4: Manage Users [Data Populated]

Make the desired changes and click **Save**.

Clicking **Save**, performs the following client side validations:

❑   First name cannot be left blank

❑   Last name cannot be left blank

❑   Email address cannot be left blank

❑   Username cannot be left blank

❑   Password cannot be left blank

❑ Email address already exists

❑ Username already exists

If any one of the above mentioned validations fails, an appropriate error message is displayed, as shown in diagram 7.9.5.

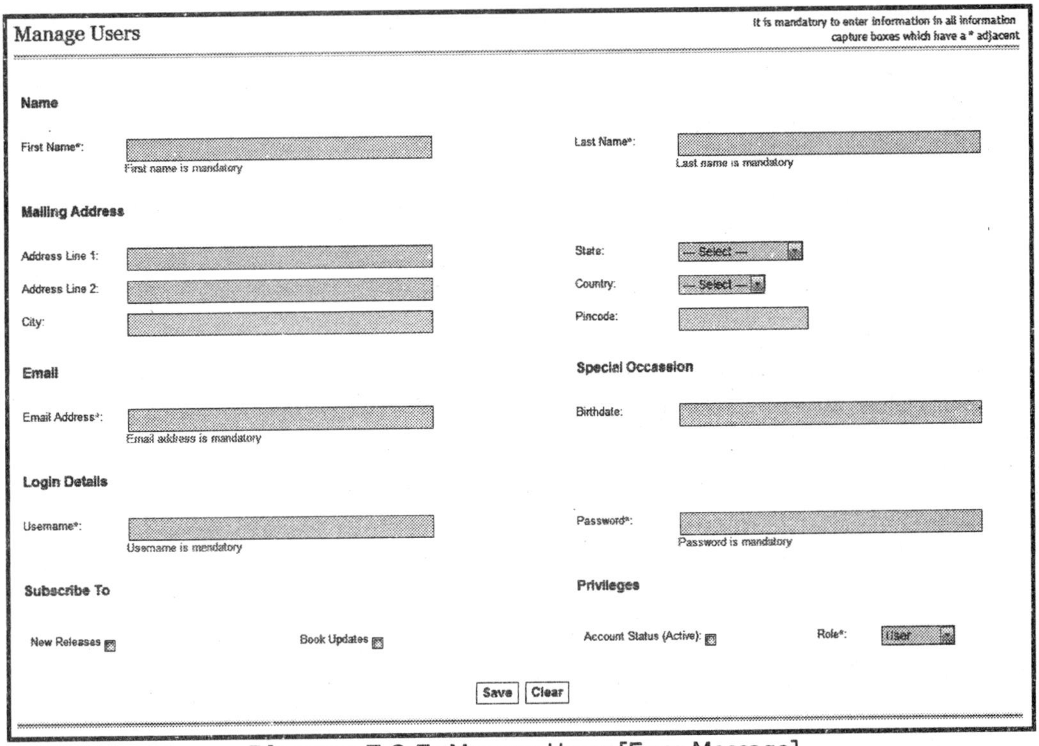

Diagram 7.9.5: Manage Users [Error Message]

Correct the error. After doing so, click [Save] to save the entered data in the database.

If all the validations mentioned above go through without any errors, the data is updated in the database and the page is reloaded to reflect the modified data.

Deleting Existing Record

To delete an already existing record click [image] adjacent to the desired record from the GRID, as shown in diagram 7.9.6.

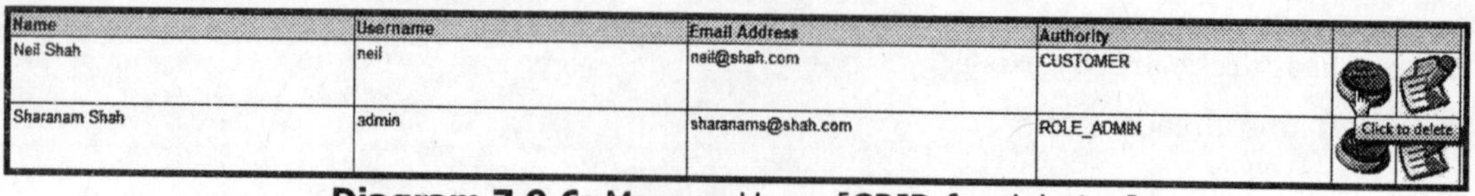

Name	Username	Email Address	Authority	
Neil Shah	neil	neil@shah.com	CUSTOMER	
Sharanam Shah	admin	sharanams@shah.com	ROLE_ADMIN	Click to delete

Diagram 7.9.6: Manage Users [GRID for deletion]

Clicking  , performs the delete operation and reloads the page to reflect the deleted records.

The ADMIN user [super user] record cannot be deleted. The system displays an error message, as shown in diagram 7.9.7

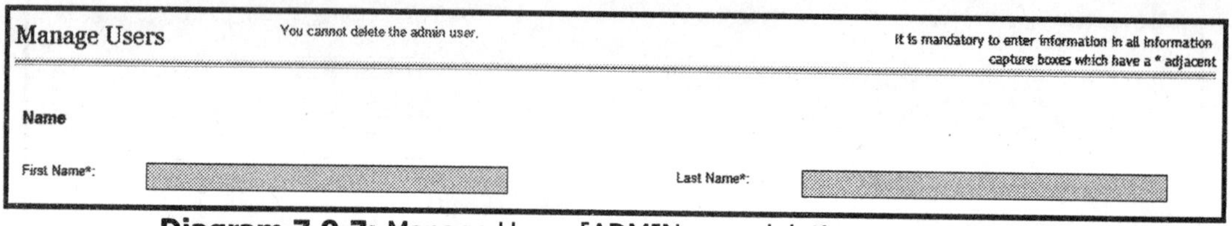

Manage Users   You cannot delete the admin user.   It is mandatory to enter information in all information capture boxes which have a * adjacent

Name

First Name*:   Last Name*:

Diagram 7.9.7: Manage Users [ADMIN user deletion error message]

Manage Transactions

Every transaction that takes place is logged by the application and is displayed under Site Administration [Backend] → Manage Transactions.

After the order is placed by the customer and an email is received, the seller [site owner] can ensure that the payment is received by receiving the Google order number. After the payment is received, Google Wallet sends the Google order number to the seller, which needs to be updated in the Manage Transactions form, to complete that transaction.

The site owner or the employee logs in to the backend and views such transactions that need to be updated in order to reflect the Google order number.

To manage transactions, click **Transactions**. This delivers the Manage Transactions data entry form, as shown in diagram 7.10.1.

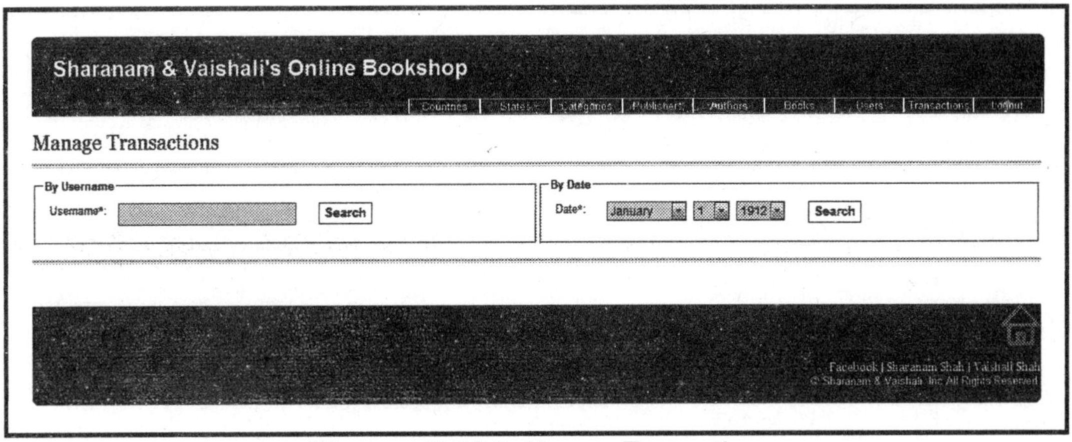

Diagram 7.10.1: Manage Transactions

Viewing The Transaction Reports

By Username

To view the transactions of a particular user [by username], enter the username in the text box and click Search .

This displays all the transactions details that were performed by that user, as shown in diagram 7.10.2.1.

Sharanam & Vaishali's Online Bookshop

Countries | States | Categories | Publishers | Authors | Books | Users | Transaction | Logout

Manage Transactions

By Username

Username*: [_____] [Search]

By Date

Date*: [January ▼] [1 ▼] [1912 ▼] [Search]

Transaction No.: 1
Transaction Date: 2008-07-15
Username: vaishali

Google Order No. [_____] [Update]

Detail No.	Book Name	Cost	Qty.
1	Fri Aug 15 18:58:03 IST 2008 - Oracle For Beginners	1	750
2	Fri Aug 15 18:58:02 IST 2008 - Oracle For Professionals	1	750
3	Fri Aug 15 18:52:22 IST 2008 - Oracle And PHP On Linux For Beginners	1	500
4	Fri Aug 15 18:52:27 IST 2008 - Struts For Beginners	1	500
5	Fri Aug 15 18:58:07 IST 2008 - MySQL Projects	1	650
6	Fri Aug 15 18:52:22 IST 2008 - PHP For Professionals	1	650
7	Fri Aug 15 18:52:26 IST 2008 - Struts For Beginners	1	500
8	Fri Aug 15 18:58:05 IST 2008 - Oracle 10g	1	150
9	Fri Aug 15 18:52:28 IST 2008 - PHP And MySQL	1	650
10	Fri Aug 15 18:52:24 IST 2008 - PHP And MySQL	1	650
		Total: 10	5750

Transaction No.: 15
Transaction Date: 2008-07-27
Username: vaishali

Google Order No. [_____] [Update]

Detail No.	Book Name	Cost	Qty.
41	Wed Aug 27 20:47:57 IST 2008 - MySQL For Beginners	1	750
42	Wed Aug 27 20:48:02 IST 2008 - Dreamweaver	1	750
43	Wed Aug 27 20:47:46 IST 2008 - PHP 5.1 For Beginners	1	650
		Total: 3	2150

Transaction No.: 16
Transaction Date: 2008-08-27
Username: vaishali

Google Order No. [_____] [Update]

Detail No.	Book Name	Cost	Qty.
44	Wed Aug 27 20:47:57 IST 2008 - MySQL For Beginners	1	750
45	Wed Aug 27 21:16:14 IST 2008 - Windows XP	1	150
46	Wed Aug 27 21:16:20 IST 2008 - JSP Projects For Beginners	1	150
47	Wed Aug 27 21:16:22 IST 2008 - JSTL For Beginners	1	500
48	Wed Aug 27 21:16:19 IST 2008 - Practical Java Project For Beginners	1	150
49	Wed Aug 27 20:47:46 IST 2008 - PHP 5.1 For Beginners	1	650
50	Wed Aug 27 20:48:02 IST 2008 - Dreamweaver	1	750
		Total: 7	3100

Diagram 7.10.2.1: Manage Transactions By Username

By Date

To view the transactions for a particular date, choose the date from the drop down list box and click [**Search**].

This displays all the transactions details that were performed on that date, as shown in diagram 7.10.2.2.

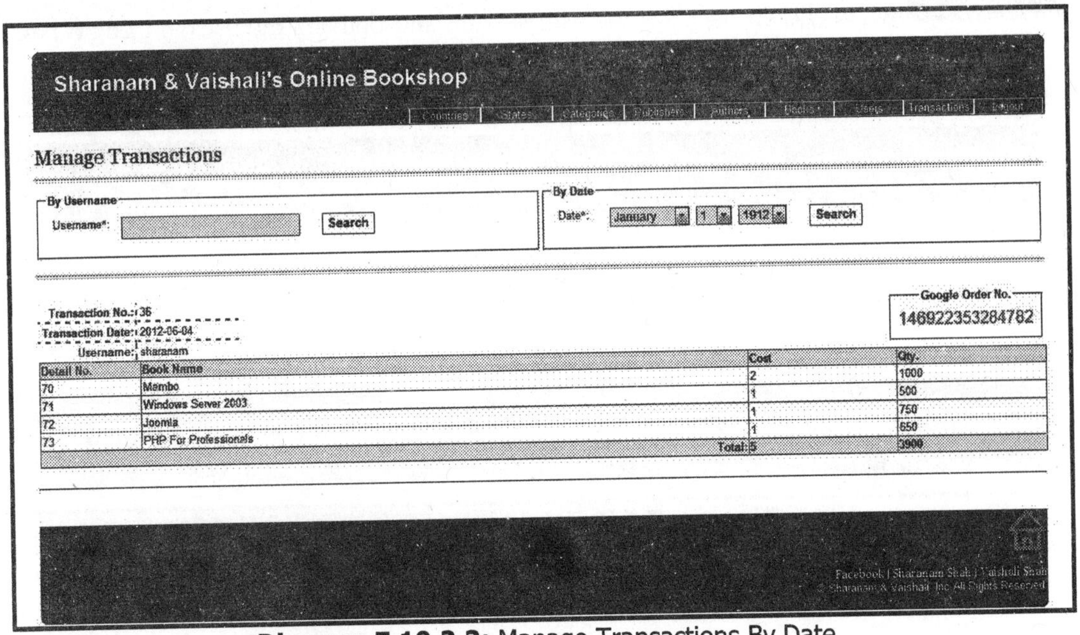

Diagram 7.10.2.2: Manage Transactions By Date

Updating The Transaction [Entering The Google Order Number]

To view the transactions:

☐ Enter the username in the text box and click **Search**

   Or

☐ Choose the date from the drop down list box and click **Search**

This displays the required transactions details. The Google Order No. field is empty for the ones which are yet to be confirmed. This field has to be filled up by the BookShop owner. Enter the Google Order No. from the email received from Google Wallet and click **Update**.

The Google Order Number is then displayed, as shown in diagram 7.10.2.2.

Logout

Logout when clicked destroys the user session and delivers the backend Login page, as shown in diagram 7.11.

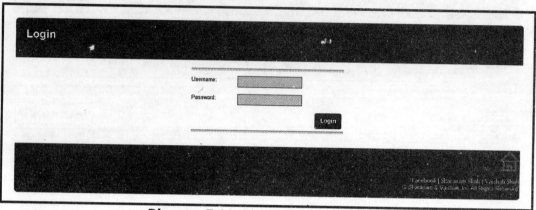

Diagram 7.11: The Backend Login page

Chapter

8

SECTION III: END USER MANUAL
Frontend [Customer Facing]

The frontend consists of the following:

- Login
  - o Forgot Password
- Signup
- New Releases

  Ability to view a list of book names that were recently released
- Updated Books

  Ability to view a list of book names that were recently updated
- Top Titles

  Ability to view a list of book names that were most viewed
- Our Authors

  Ability to view a list of available author names
- Our Publishers

  Ability to view a list of available publisher names

❑ Search

Using any keywords such as book name, author name, ISBN, cost of the book, synopsis, about authors

❑ Directory of available books [Category Wise]

Ability to view book names segregated under category heads

❑ Payment Gateway using Google Wallet

Ability to buy books using the shopping cart and transferring the information [book details: Book Name, Price, Qty] to Google Wallet for payment processing using Credit Card

To be able to use the frontend, master records need to be added to the database using the following data entry forms. The book's CDROM holds a .sql file which can be imported to have some sample data to work with:

❑ Manage

   o Countries

   o States

   o Authors

   o Publishers

   o Categories

   o Books

Frontend Home Page

The frontend homepage, as shown in diagram 8.1, can be reached by invoking the application.

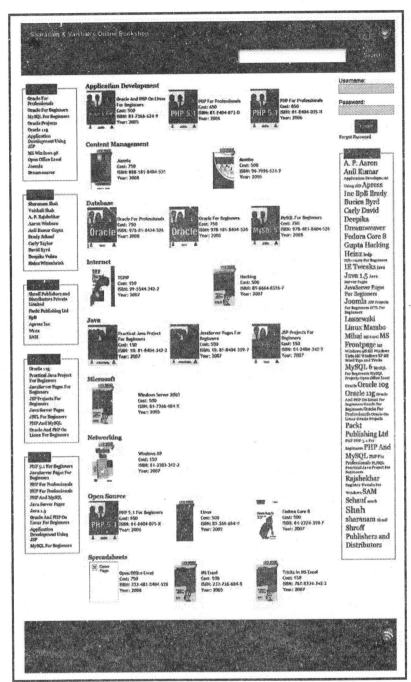

Diagram 8.1: The Frontend Homepage

This page allows visitors [who have not logged in] to:

❑ Login

❑ Retrieve Forgotten Password

❑ Signup

❑ Browse books using the Books directory

❑ Search

❑ View Book details

❑ View Author details

❑ View Publisher details

❑ View Popular Search Tags

This page allows customers [who have logged in] to:

❑ Search

❑ Browse books using Book directory

❑ View Book details

    ○ Download Sample Chapter

    ○ Download Table of Contents

    ○ Add to Cart

❑ View Author details

❑ View Publisher details

❑ View Popular Search Tags

❑ View Cart

❑ Checkout

❑ Logout

Forgot Password

To retrieve a forgotten password, click **Forgot Password**.

Forgot Password when clicked delivers the forgot password data entry form, as shown in diagram 8.2.1.

REMINDER

It is mandatory to enter information in all information
                  capture boxes which have a * adjacent indicates entering values for all the form
field labels that are marked * is mandatory.

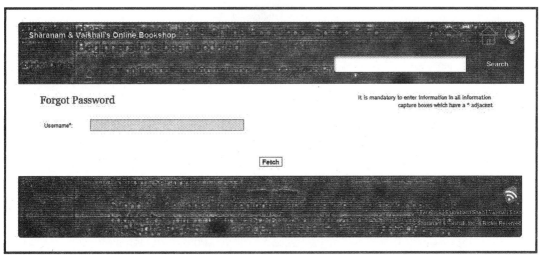

Diagram 8.2.1: The Forgot Password data entry form

Enter the username and click [**Fetch**]. Clicking [**Fetch**], validates the captured details and if all fine, an email is send with the registration details such as username and password, as shown in diagram 8.2.2.

REMINDER

The system dispatches emails only if, the **sendMail** attribute in the application's configuration file i.e. bookshop.properties is set to **true**, along with the other email attributes such as **emailFrom**, **emailUser** and **emailPasswd** that indicate the user credentials of the email ID.

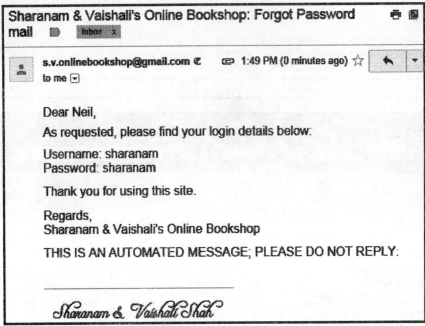

Diagram 8.2.2: The Forgot Password Email [Password retrieved]

Signup

Visitors can sign-up to the site using on the homepage.

when clicked delivers the Signup page, as shown in diagram 8.3.1.

Diagram 8.3.1: The Signup page

REMINDER

It is mandatory to enter information in all information capture boxes which have a * adjacent indicates entering values for all the form field labels that are marked * is mandatory.

Enter the required details as indicated in the data entry form and click Save .

Clicking Save , performs the following client side validations:

❏   First name cannot be left blank

❏   Last name cannot be left blank

❏   Email address cannot be left blank

❏   Email address should be unique

❏   Username cannot be left blank

❏   Username should be unique

❏   Password cannot be left blank

If any one of the above mentioned client side validations fail, an appropriate error message is displayed, as shown in diagram 8.3.2.

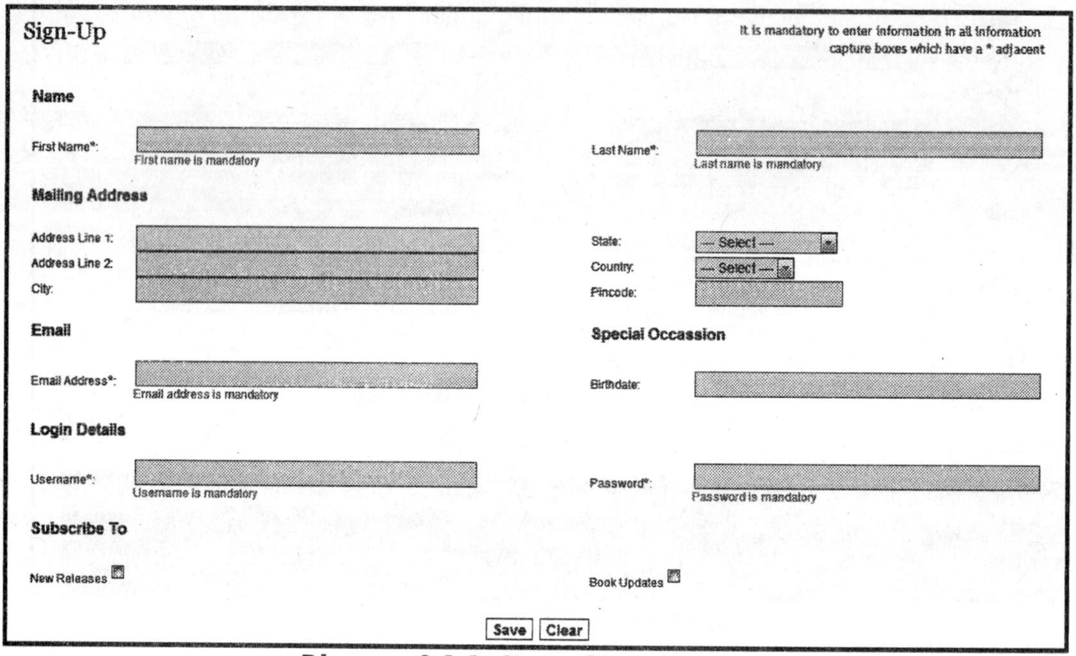

Diagram 8.3.2: Signup [Error Message]

Correct the errors. After doing so, click **Save** to save the entered data in the database.

If all the validations mentioned above go through without any errors, the data is saved in the database and the thank you page appears, as shown in diagram 8.3.3.

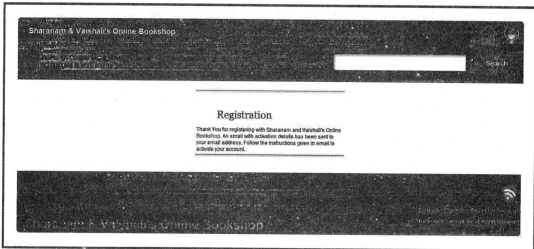

Diagram 8.3.3: Thank you page after registration

After successful registration, an email, as shown in diagram 8.3.4 is dispatched to the user.

REMINDER

The system dispatches emails only if, the **sendMail** attribute in the application's configuration file i.e. bookshop.properties is set to **true**, along with the other email attributes such as **emailFrom**, **emailUser** and **emailPasswd** that indicate the user credentials of the email ID.

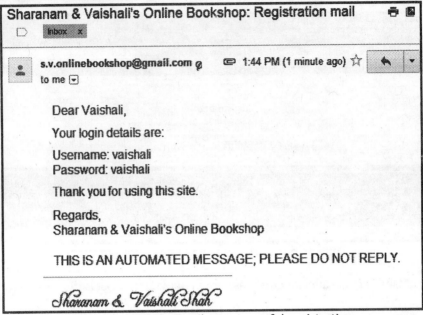

Diagram 8.3.4: Email on successful registration

Login

After a visitor registers and becomes a customer, the customer can login using the Login section in the homepage, as shown in diagram 8.4.1.

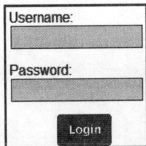

Diagram 8.4.1: The Frontend Homepage [Login]

Enter the appropriate username and password. Click .

Homepage After Logging In

Clicking [Login], authenticates the username and password and if found valid,

- Creates a user session
- Unlocks the download links to Sample Chapter and TOC under book details
- Unlocks the Add to Cart links under book details
- Unlocks the Cart link in the homepage to view the cart contents [if any]
- Unlocks the download links to Sample Chapter, TOC and Add to Cart link in the homepage
- Displays the Logout option
- Delivers the homepage with a welcome message, as shown in diagram 8.4.2

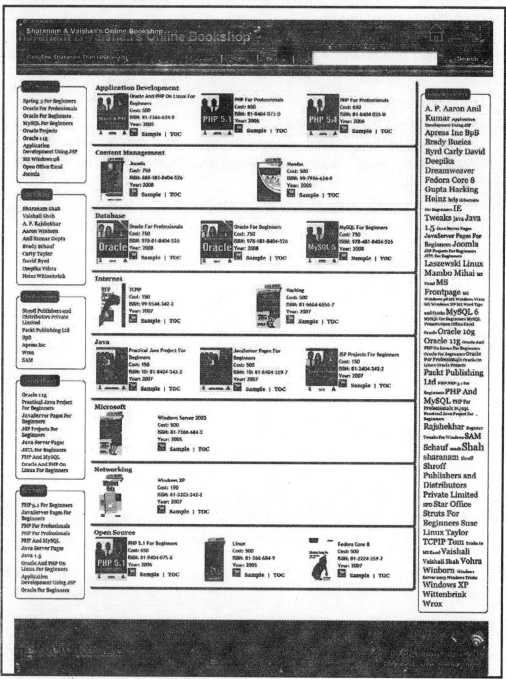

Diagram 8.4.2: The Homepage after logging in

Book Details

A visitor can view the book details of a book selected from one of the following sections:

Directory Listing

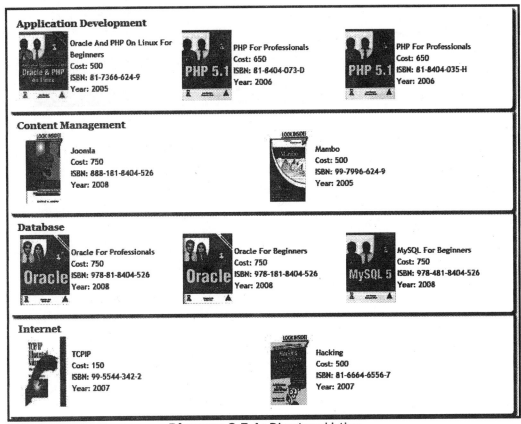

Diagram 8.5.1: Directory Listing

New Releases   *Updated Books*   *Top Titles*

New Releases	Updated Books	Top Titles
Spring 3 For Beginners	Oracle 11g	PHP 5.1 For Beginners
Oracle For Professionals	Practical Java Project For Beginners	JavaServer Pages For Beginners
Oracle For Beginners	JavaServer Pages For Beginners	PHP For Professionals
MySQL For Beginners	JSP Projects For Beginners	PHP And MySQL
Oracle Projects	Java Server Pages	Java Server Pages
Oracle 11g	JSTL For Beginners	Java 1.5
Application Development Using JSP	PHP And MySQL	Oracle And PHP On Linux For Beginners
MS Windows 98	Oracle And PHP On Linux For Beginners	Application Development Using JSP
Open Office Excel		Oracle For Beginners
Joomla		

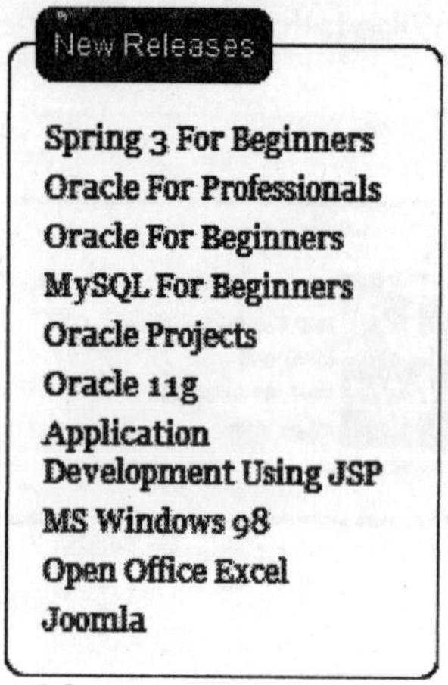

Diagram 8.5.2: New Releases   **Diagram 8.5.3:** Updated Books   **Diagram 8.5.4:** Top Titles

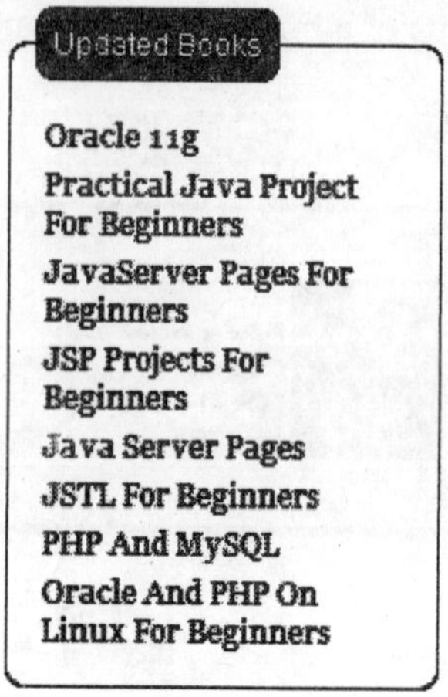

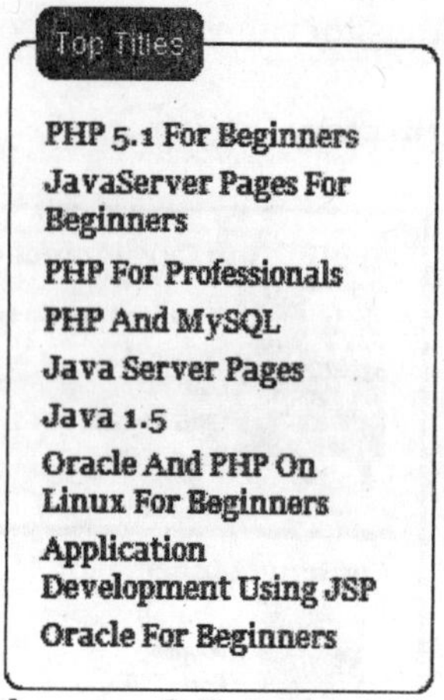

Book Details Without Logging In

A link identified by a book name in one of these sections when clicked, displays book details of the selected book, as shown in diagram 8.5.5.

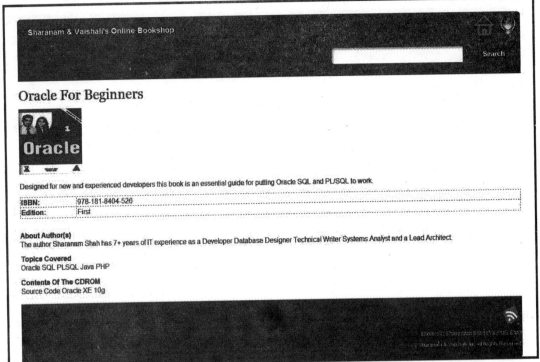

Diagram 8.5.5: Book Details page [without logged in]

Book Details After Logging In

If the customer has logged in and is viewing the book details page, then the page appears with additional options that allow adding the book to the cart, downloading sample chapters and TOC, as shown in diagram 8.5.6.

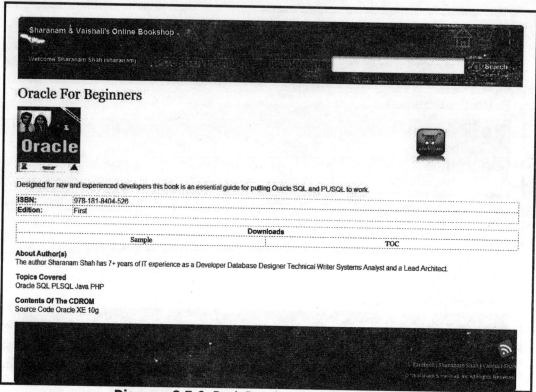

Diagram 8.5.6: Book Details page [after logging in]

Downloading Sample Chapter

Clicking the **Sample** link downloads the PDF file.

WARNING

 This requires a PDF file reader such as Adobe Acrobat.

Downloading TOC

Clicking the **TOC** link downloads the PDF file.

WARNING

 This requires a PDF file reader such as Adobe Acrobat.

Author Details

A visitor can view the author details from the following section on the homepage.

Diagram 8.6.1: Our Authors

A link identified by an author name in this section when clicked, displays author details of the selected author, as shown in diagram 8.6.2.

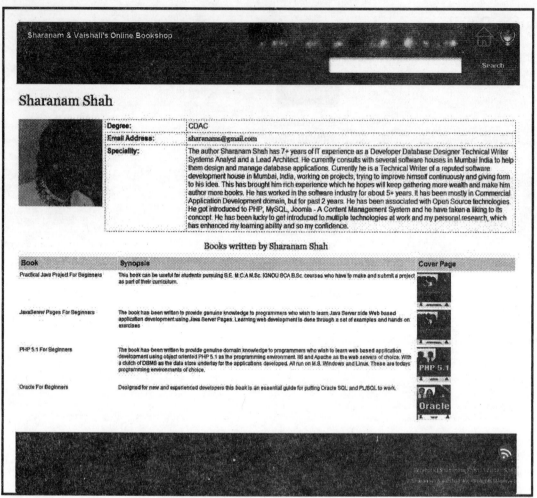

Diagram 8.6.2: Author Details page

This page shows Add To Cart link, as shown in diagram 8.6.3, for the logged in users.

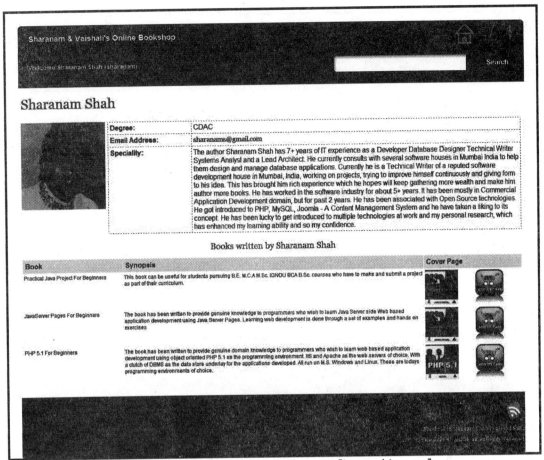

Diagram 8.6.3: Author Details page [Logged in user]

This page also displays a list of the books written by that author.

Clicking an entry from the list displays that book's details, as shown in diagram 8.6.4. Add To Cart appears for logged in users only.

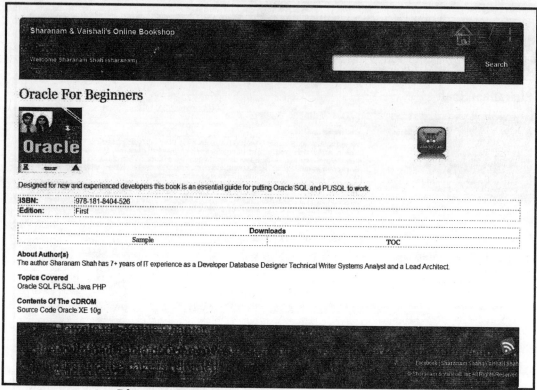

Diagram 8.6.4: Book Details page [after logging in]

Category Details

A visitor can view the books available under a category from the following section on the homepage.

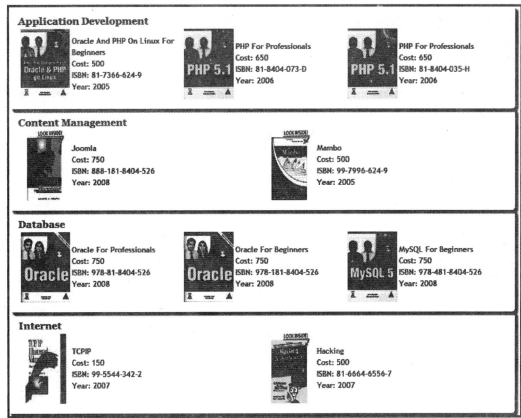

Diagram 8.7.1: Category wise books

A link identified by a category name in this section when clicked, displays books under that category, as shown in diagram 8.7.2.

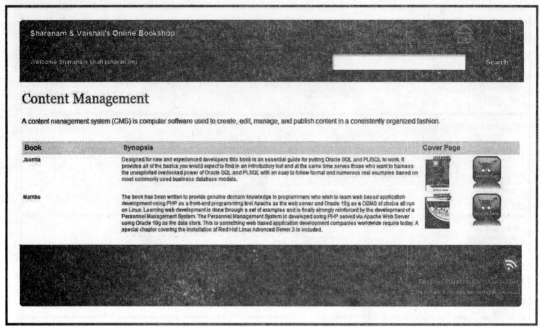

Diagram 8.7.2: Category Details page

Clicking an entry from the list displays that book's details, as shown in diagram 8.7.3. Add To Cart appears for logged in users only.

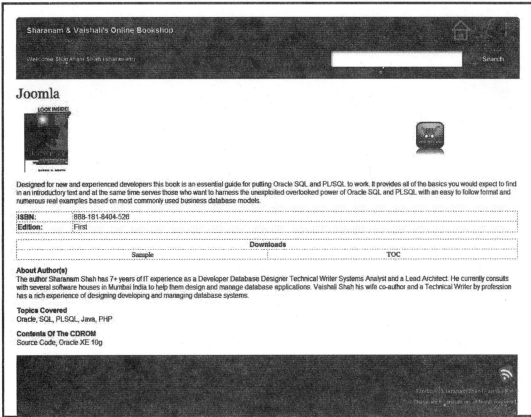

Diagram 8.7.3: Book Details page [after logging in]

Publisher Details

A visitor can view the publisher details from the following section on the homepage.

Diagram 8.8.1: Our Publishers

A link identified by a publisher name in this section when clicked, displays publisher details of the selected publisher, as shown in diagram 8.8.2.

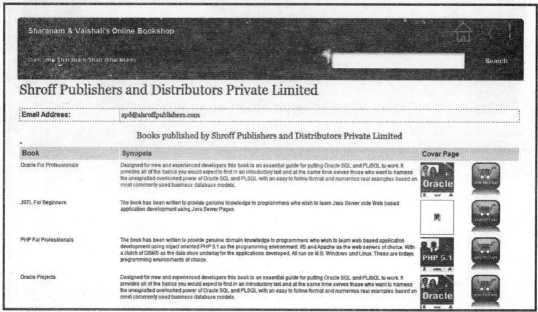

Diagram 8.8.2: Publisher Details page

This page also displays a list of the books published by that publisher.

Clicking an entry from the list displays that book's details, as shown in diagram 8.8.3. Add To Cart appears for logged in users only.

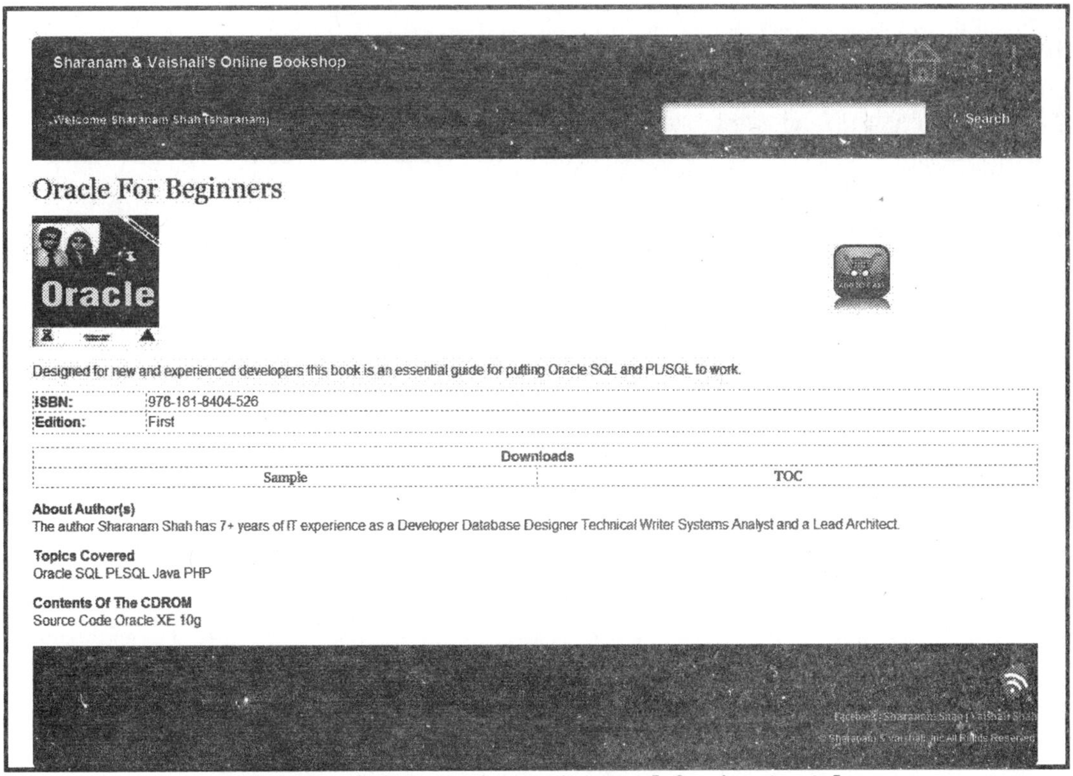

Diagram 8.8.3: Book Details page [after logging in]

Search

A visitor can search for the desired book, author or publisher by keyword using the search section available in the homepage, as shown in diagram 8.9.1.

Diagram 8.9.1: Search Section

Enter a keyword of choice and click [Search].

Clicking [Search], delivers the Search results, as shown in diagram 8.9.2.

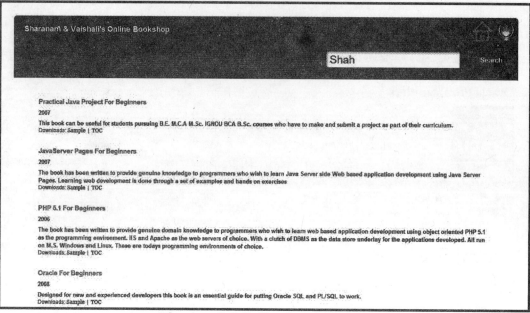

Diagram 8.9.2: The Search Results

Cart

A customer after logging in can click 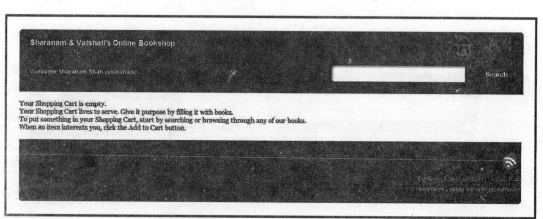 to view the content of the cart. If the customer has not added any books to the cart it will be empty, as shown in diagram 8.10.1.

Diagram 8.10.1: The Empty Cart

To add a book to the cart the customer needs to log in and click the book name link of the book of choice from the homepage. This delivers the book details page, as shown in diagram 8.10.2.

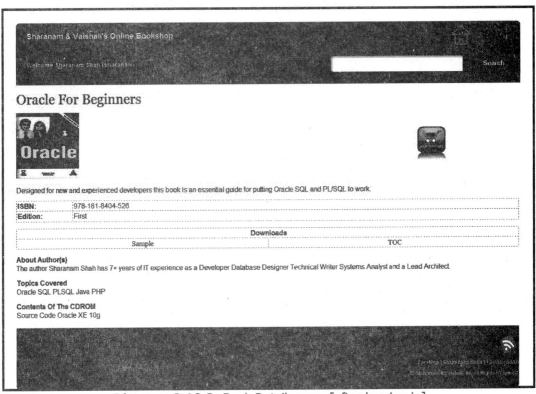

Diagram 8.10.2: Book Details page [after logging in]

Click ![add to cart] to add the chosen book to the cart. Repeat this for the desired books.

Now if the user clicks ![cart icon], it will be populated with the selected books, as shown in diagram 8.10.3.

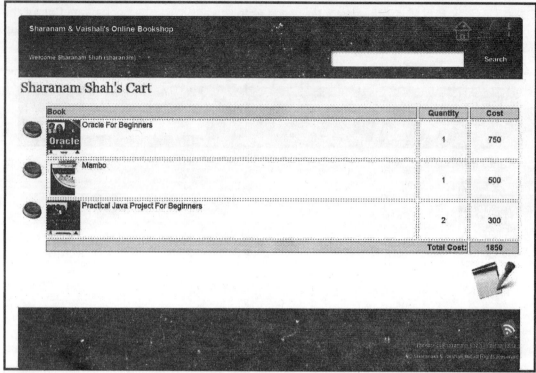

Diagram 8.10.3: The Cart with books added

 when clicked removes the book from the cart.

Checkout

WARNING

For demonstration purpose, this application uses Google Wallet in sandbox mode, hence actual orders and payments do not take place. In a production environment, the sandbox mode should be disabled and actual mode should be enabled via code spec.

After the cart holds the desired books, the user can choose to checkout. This application uses Google Wallet.

Click  . This sends the cart details to Google for further processing and payment, as shown in diagram 8.11.1.

WARNING

 If the Google Merchant ID is not set in the properties file, then the Google Wallet's Checkout option will not be available.

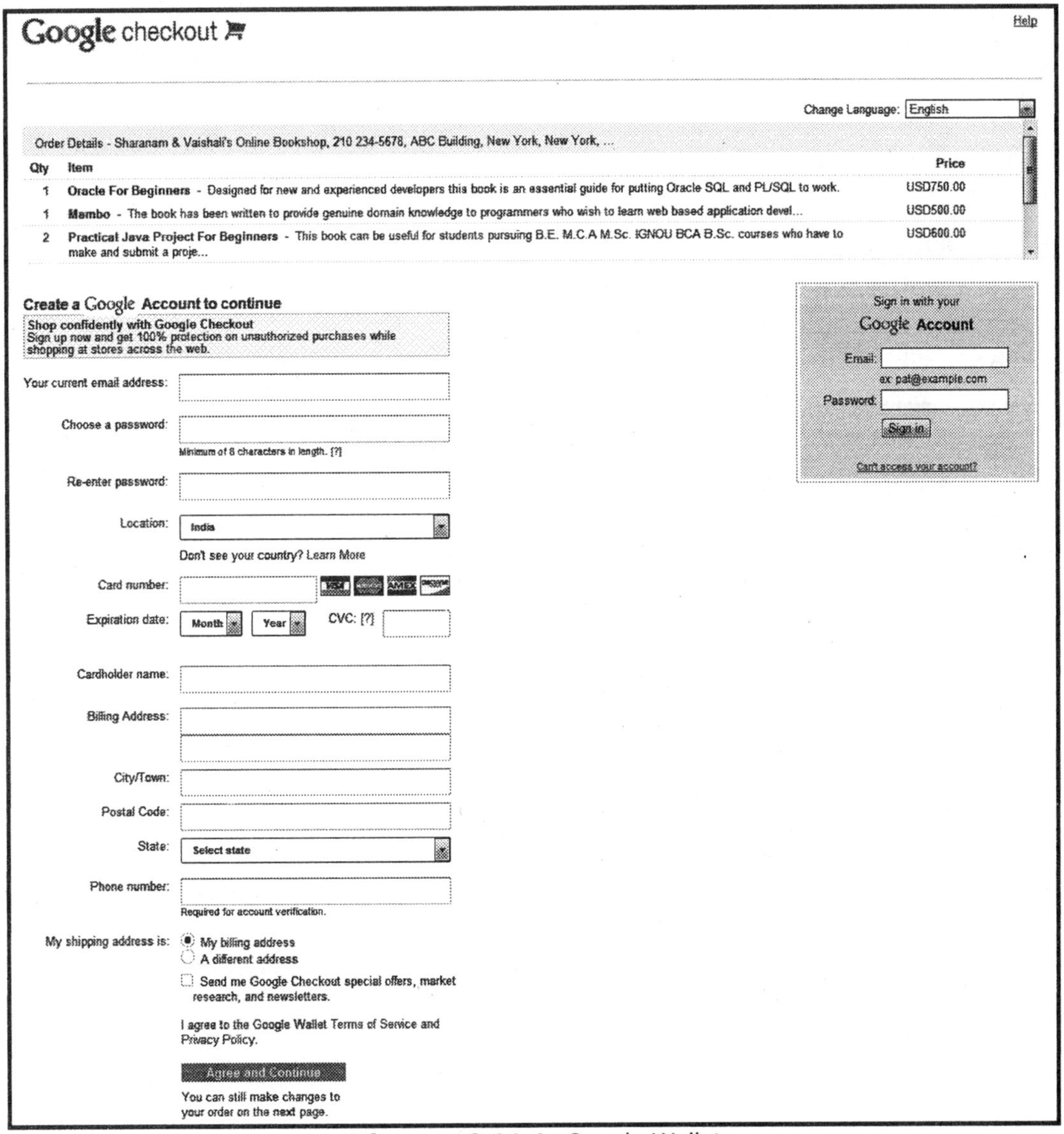

Google checkout ☰   Help

Change Language: English

Order Details - Sharanam & Vaishali's Online Bookshop, 210 234-5678, ABC Building, New York, New York, ...

Qty	Item	Price
1	**Oracle For Beginners** - Designed for new and experienced developers this book is an essential guide for putting Oracle SQL and PL/SQL to work.	USD750.00
1	**Mambo** - The book has been written to provide genuine domain knowledge to programmers who wish to learn web based application devel...	USD500.00
2	**Practical Java Project For Beginners** - This book can be useful for students pursuing B.E. M.C.A M.Sc. IGNOU BCA B.Sc. courses who have to make and submit a proje...	USD600.00

Create a Google Account to continue

Shop confidently with Google Checkout
Sign up now and get 100% protection on unauthorized purchases while shopping at stores across the web.

Your current email address:

Choose a password:
Minimum of 8 characters in length. [?]

Re-enter password:

Location: India
Don't see your country? Learn More

Card number:

Expiration date: Month Year   CVC: [?]

Cardholder name:

Billing Address:

City/Town:

Postal Code:

State: Select state

Phone number:
Required for account verification.

My shipping address is: ● My billing address
                          ○ A different address
□ Send me Google Checkout special offers, market research, and newsletters.

I agree to the Google Wallet Terms of Service and Privacy Policy.

Agree and Continue
You can still make changes to your order on the next page.

Sign in with your
Google Account

Email:
ex: pat@example.com
Password:

Sign in

Can't access your account?

Diagram 8.11.1: Google Wallet

HINT

 This requires having a Google Account. If it does not exist, then create one using the "Create a Google Account to complete this purchase" section. Refer to *Appendix A: Understanding Google Wallet* for more information on Google Wallet.

Login using the Google account or create a new account if one does not exist. Enter the credit card details.

Since this is a dummy [Sandbox] checkout, the following credit card details can be used:

❑ Credit card number: 4111-1111-1111-1111

❑ CVV number: Any three digits

❑ Card Expiry: Any month and year beyond the current date

Doing this delivers the page, as shown in diagram 8.11.2.

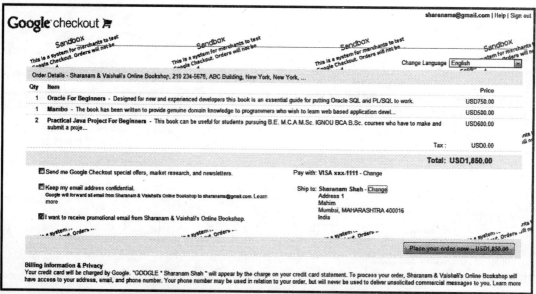

Diagram 8.11.2: Google Wallet - Place your order

Click **Place your order now – USD1,850.00** to place the order and make the payment.

This delivers the Thank you page, as shown in diagram 8.11.3.

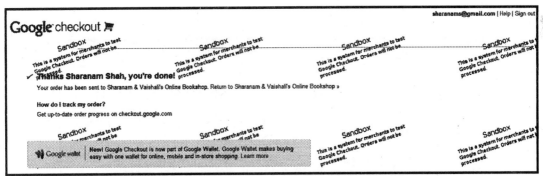

Diagram 8.11.3: Google Wallet - Thank you page

Click **Return to Sharanam & Vaishali's Online Bookshop »** to return to the site home page.

After the order is placed, Google Wallet delivers an email to the buyer as well as seller.

Buyer's Email

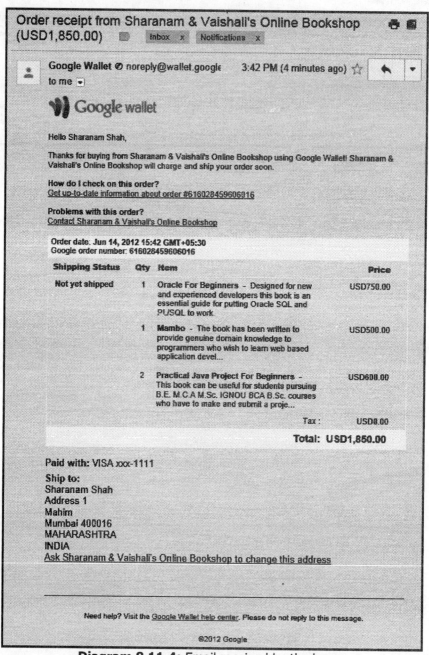

Diagram 8.11.4: Email received by the buyer

Seller's Email

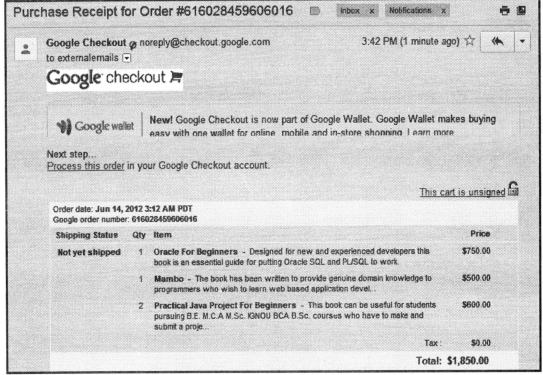

Diagram 8.11.5: Email received by the seller

After Placing The Order

After the order is placed and an email is received, the seller [site owner] ensures that the payment is received/credited to the bank account. If this is true, then the seller arranges to deliver the said books to the buyer [customer].

Every transaction that takes place is logged by the application and is displayed under Site Administration [Backend] → Manage Transactions.

The site owner or the employee logs in to the backend, views the transactions made by the customers and enters the Google Order No. to the appropriate transaction to mark the transaction complete.

Chapter

9

SECTION IV: PROCESS FLOW

The Application's Home Page [home.jsp]

HINT

 This section depicts the actual processes that take place while using the application.

To make the learning easy, it is recommended to run the project [available in Book's accompanying CDROM] prior moving on with this section. *Chapter 55: Assembling And Deploying The Project Using NetBeans IDE* of *Section VIII: Running The Project* documents the steps involved in bringing up the application.

After the application is up and running it will be very easy to correlate each and every activity of the application with the process flow documented in this section.

The application begins with the request **/home**. This means when a user keys in the application URL as http://localhost:8080/BookShop, the application serves up.

The application's homepage is served, as shown in diagram 9.1.

User Interface [/home → home.jsp]

Diagram 9.1

HomeController file holds a mapping to help the redirection.

```
33     @RequestMapping("/")
34     public String startHome() {
35         return "redirect:/home";
36     }
```

Using this mapping the control shifts to home.jsp via the **/home** request mapping and the homepage is served, as shown in diagram 9.1.

Process Flow

As soon as the application loading completes, home.jsp is served based on **/home** → **HomeController** → **showHome()**.

Here,

❑ **/home** is the request mapping, which invokes **showHome()** of **HomeController**

❑ **HomeController** is the controller, which holds a mapping to display the home page contents

❏ **showHome()** is the method available in the controller, which populates the List objects with the appropriate data. These List objects are made available to home.jsp

showHome() invokes the following methods of the Service layer:

Service	Method	Description
BookService	listNewReleases()	Holds the business logic to retrieve the newly released book details.
	listBook()	Holds the business logic to retrieve the book details.
	listUpdatedBooks()	Holds the business logic to retrieve the updated book details.
	listTopTitles()	Holds the business logic to retrieve the top titled book details.
AuthorService	listOurAuthors()	Holds the business logic to retrieve the author details.
PublisherService	listOurPublishers()	Holds the business logic to retrieve the publisher details.
CategoryService	listCategory()	Holds the business logic to retrieve the category details.
SearchService	listPopularSearches()	Holds the business logic to retrieve the popular searches details.

Service Layer in turn calls the DAO layer's methods.

The Service layer methods invoke the following methods of the DAO layer:

DAO	Method	Description
BookDAO	listNewReleases()	Does the actual retrieval of the available newly released books.
	listBook()	Does the actual retrieval of the available books.
	listUpdatedBooks()	Does the actual retrieval of the available updated books.
	listTopTitles()	Does the actual retrieval of the available top titled books.
AuthorDAO	listOurAuthors()	Does the actual retrieval of the available authors.
PublisherDAO	listOurPublishers()	Does the actual retrieval of the available publishers.
CategoryDAO	listCategory()	Does the actual retrieval of the available categories.
SearchDAO	listPopularSearches()	Does the actual retrieval of the available popular searches.

Diagram 9.2 depicts the use of these **List objects** to populate the various sections of home.jsp.

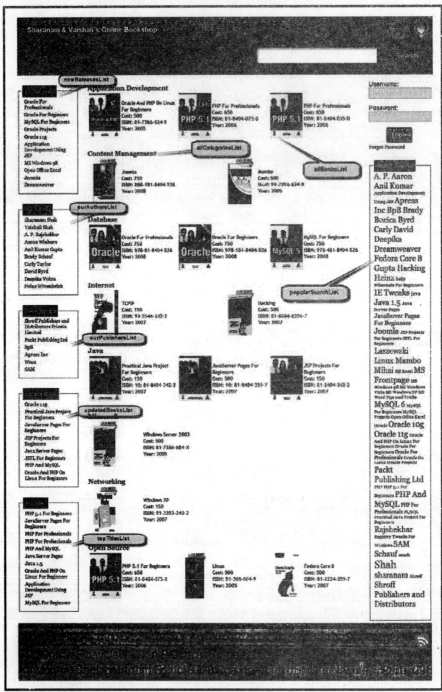

Diagram 9.2

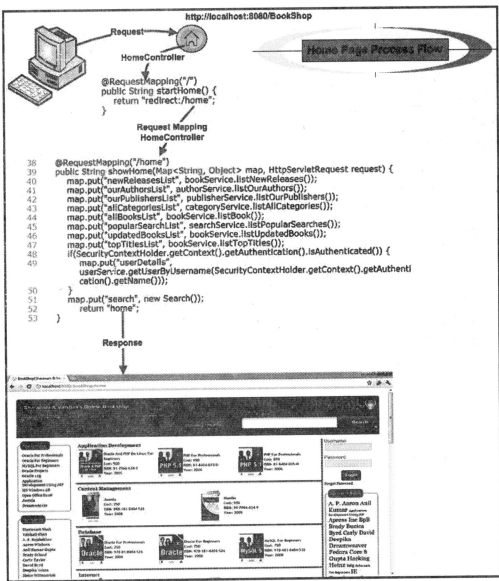

Diagram 9.3: Home Page Process Flow

Home Page Navigation [home.jsp]

After the home page loads completely, the user can navigate to other pages of the application using the hyperlinks.

The home page allows:

- ❏ Viewing Book Details
- ❏ Viewing Author Details
- ❏ Viewing Publisher Details
- ❏ Viewing Category Details
- ❏ Searching the required books
- ❏ View the Popular Searches
- ❏ Signing up as a customer
- ❏ Logging in & retrieving the forgotten password
- ❏ Viewing Cart & Google Wallet
- ❏ Logging out
- ❏ Access the Administration [BackOffice]
  - o Manage Countries
  - o Manage States
  - o Manage Authors
  - o Manage Publishers
  - o Manage Categories
  - o Manage Users
  - o Manage Books
  - o Manage Transactions

Chapter 10

SECTION IV: PROCESS FLOW
Book Details [showBookDetails.jsp]

To view the details of a book, the home page provides hyperlinks in the following sections:

New Releases	Updated Books	Top Titles
Oracle For Professionals	Oracle 11g	PHP 5.1 For Beginners
Oracle For Beginners	Practical Java Project For Beginners	JavaServer Pages For Beginners
MySQL For Beginners	JavaServer Pages For Beginners	PHP For Professionals
Oracle Projects	JSP Projects For Beginners	PHP And MySQL
Oracle 11g	Java Server Pages	Java Server Pages
Application Development Using JSP	JSTL For Beginners	Java 1.5
MS Windows 98	PHP And MySQL	Oracle And PHP On Linux For Beginners
Open Office Excel	Oracle And PHP On Linux For Beginners	Application Development Using JSP
Joomla		Oracle For Beginners
Dreamweaver		

Application Development

 Oracle And PHP On Linux For
Beginners
Cost: 500
ISBN: 81-7366-624-9
Year: 2005

 PHP For Professionals
Cost: 650
ISBN: 81-8404-073-0
Year: 2006

 PHP For Professionals
Cost: 650
ISBN: 81-8404-035-H
Year: 2006

Every hyperlink under the above mentioned sections invokes a controller using request mapping:

```
<a href="showBookDetails/${book.bookNo}">
    ${book.bookName}
</a>
```

To view the details of a particular book, **BookNo** is passed as a parameter [using the Spring's Expression tag] to the controller. This helps the controller determine the method to be invoked [based on the request mapping] which returns the appropriate book's details.

When the user clicks the hyperlink, showBookDetails.jsp is served, as shown in diagram 10.1.

User Interface [/showBookDetails/${bookNo} → showBookDetails.jsp]

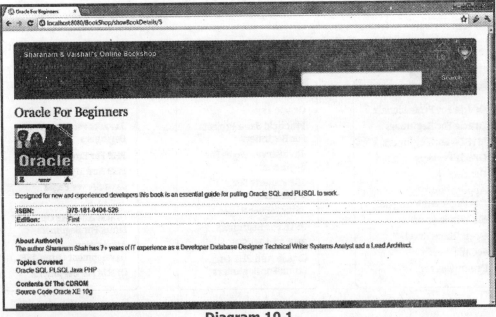

Diagram 10.1

Process Flow

Show Book Details displays the details of the book.

The book details in Show Book details is populated by **/showBookDetails/${bookNo}** → **HomeController** → **showBookDetails()**.

Here,

- **/showBookDetails/${bookNo}** is the request mapping, which invokes **showBookDetails()** of **HomeController**
- **HomeController** is the controller, which holds a mapping to help display the book details
- **showBookDetails()** is the method available in the controller, which retrieves the book details via BookService

showBookDetails() invokes the following methods of BookService:

Methods	Description
getBookById()	Holds the business logic to retrieve the book details.
updateHits()	Holds the business logic to update the Hits column of the Book object whenever a book is clicked for viewing its details.

The service layer i.e. BookService in turn invokes the DAO layer.

BookService's methods invoke the following methods of BookDAO:

Methods	Description
getBookById()	Returns the appropriate book's object from the Books database table using **BookNo** as the reference.
updateHits()	Updates the Hits column of the appropriate Book's object using BookNo as the reference.

Whilst populating these details in Show Book Details, the system checks if the user has logged in. Only if the user has logged in, additional links such as the following are displayed in Show Book Details:

- Add To Cart
- TOC and Sample Chapter download

This check is performed by accessing the username from the SESSION object.

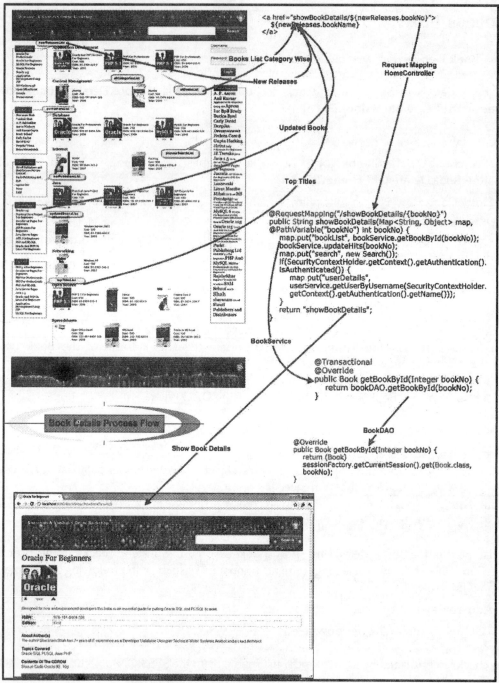

Diagram 10.2: Book Details Process Flow

SECTION IV: PROCESS FLOW

Author Details [showAuthorDetails.jsp]

To view details of an author, the home page provides hyperlinks in the following section:

Every hyperlink under the above mentioned section invokes a controller using request mapping:

```
<a href="showAuthorDetails/${ourAuthors.authorNo}">
   ${ourAuthors.firstName} ${ourAuthors.lastName}
</a>
```

To view the details of a particular author, **AuthorNo** is passed as a parameter [using the Spring's Expression tag] to the controller. This helps the controller determine the method to be invoked [based on the request mapping] which returns the appropriate author's details.

When the user clicks the hyperlink, showAuthorDetails.jsp is served, as shown in diagram 11.1.

User Interface [/showAuthorDetails/${authorNo} → showAuthorDetails.jsp]

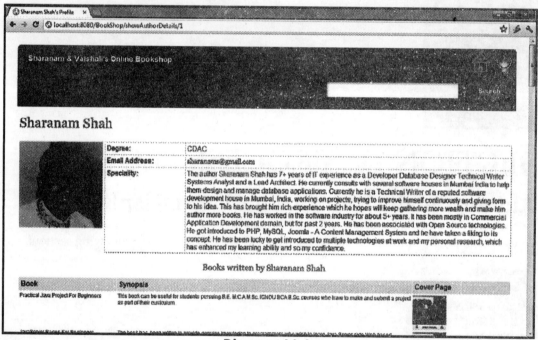

Diagram 11.1

Process Flow

Show Author Details displays the details of the author.

The author details in Show Author details is populated by **/showAuthorDetails/${authorNo} → HomeController → showAuthorDetails()**.

Here,

- **/showAuthorDetails/${authorNo}** is the request mapping, which invokes **showAuthorDetails()** of **HomeController**
- **HomeController** is the controller, which holds a mapping to help display the author details
- **showAuthorDetails()** is the method available in controller, which retrieves the author details via AuthorService

showAuthorDetails() invokes the following methods of AuthorService:

Methods	Description
getAuthorById()	Holds the business logic to retrieve the author details.
getAllBooksByAuthor()	Holds the business logic to retrieve the list of books written by that particular author.

The service layer i.e. AuthorService in turn invokes the DAO layer.

AuthorService's methods invoke the following methods of AuthorDAO:

Methods	Description
getAuthorById()	Returns the appropriate author's object from the Authors database table using **AuthorNo** as the reference.
getAllBooksByAuthor()	Returns the appropriate books List object from the Books database table using **AuthorNo** as the reference.

Whilst populating these details in Show Author Details, the system checks if the user has logged in. Only if the user has logged in, the additional link **Add To Cart** is displayed in Show Author Details.

This check is performed by accessing the username from the SESSION object.

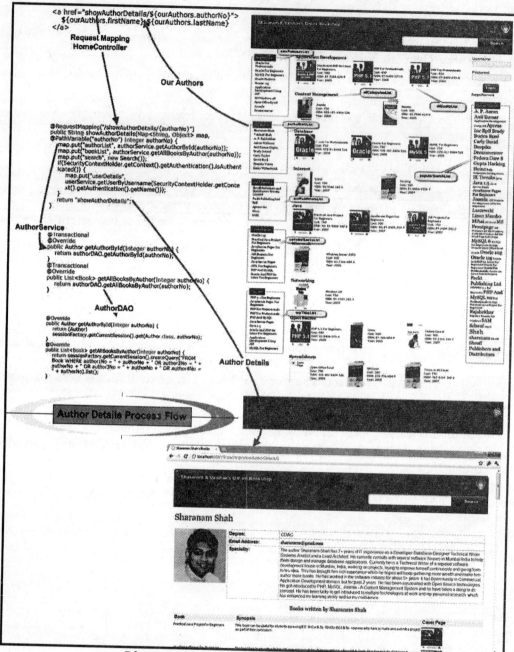

Diagram 11.2: Author Details Process Flow

SECTION IV: PROCESS FLOW

Publisher Details [showPublisherDetails.jsp]

To view the details of a publisher, the home page provides hyperlinks in the following section:

Every hyperlink under the above mentioned section invokes a controller using request mapping:

```
<a href="showPublisherDetails/${ourPublishers.publisherNo}">
   ${ourPublishers.publisherName}
</a>
```

To view the details of a particular publisher, **PublisherNo** is passed as a parameter [using the Spring's Expression tag] to the controller. This helps the controller determine the method to be invoked [based on the request mapping] which returns the appropriate publisher's details.

When the user clicks the hyperlink, showPublisherDetails.jsp is served, as shown in diagram 12.1.

User Interface [/showPublisherDetails/${publisherNo} → showPublisherDetails.jsp]

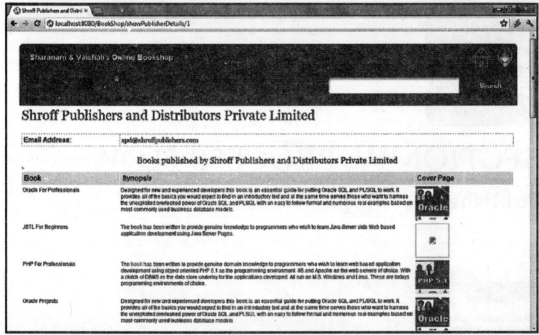

Diagram 12.1

Process Flow

Show Publisher Details displays the details of the publisher.

The publisher details in Show Publisher details is populated by **/showPublisherDetails/${publisherNo}** → **HomeController** → **showPublisherDetails()**.

Here,

- /showPublisherDetails/${publisherNo} is the request mapping, which invokes **showPublisherDetails()** of **HomeController**

- **HomeController** is the controller, which holds a mapping to help display the publisher details

- **showPublisherDetails()** is the method available in controller, which retrieves the publisher details via PublisherService

showPublisherDetails() invokes the following methods of PublisherService:

Methods	Description
getPublisherById()	Holds the business logic to retrieve the publisher details.
getAllBooksByPublisher()	Holds the business logic to retrieve the list of books published by that particular publisher.

The service layer i.e. PublisherService in turn invokes the DAO layer.

PublisherService's methods invoke the following methods of PublisherDAO:

Methods	Description
getPublisherById()	Returns the appropriate publisher's object from the Publishers database table using **PublisherNo** as the reference.
getAllBooksByPublisher()	Returns the appropriate books List object from the Books database table using **PublisherNo** as the reference.

Whilst populating these details in Show Publisher details, the system checks if the user has logged in. Only if the user has logged in, the additional link **Add To Cart** is displayed in Show Publisher Details.

This check is performed by accessing the username from the SESSION object.

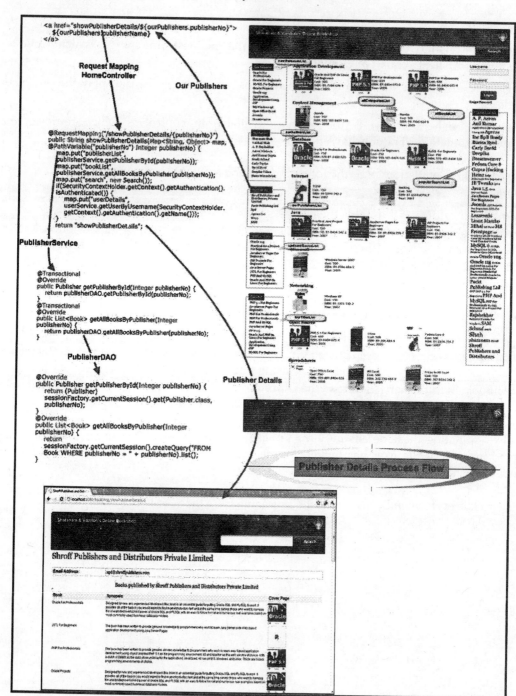

Diagram 12.2: Publisher Details Process Flow

Chapter 13

SECTION IV: PROCESS FLOW
Category Details [showCategoryDetails.jsp]

To view details of a category, the home page provides hyperlinks in the following section:

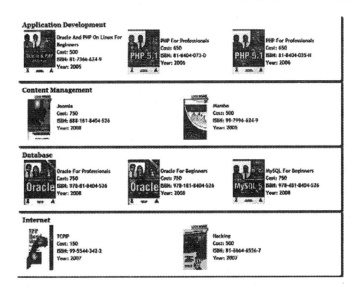

Every hyperlink [Category Name] under the above mentioned section invokes a controller using request mapping:

```
<a href="showCategoryDetails/${allCategories.categoryNo}"
title="${allCategories.description}" >
    ${allCategories.category}
</a>
```

To view the details of a particular category, **CategoryNo** is passed as a parameter [using the Spring's Expression tag] to the controller. This helps the controller determine the method to be invoked [based on the request mapping] which will return the appropriate category details.

When the user clicks the hyperlink, showCategoryDetails.jsp is served, as shown in diagram 13.1.

User Interface [/showCategoryDetails/${categoryNo} → showCategoryDetails.jsp]

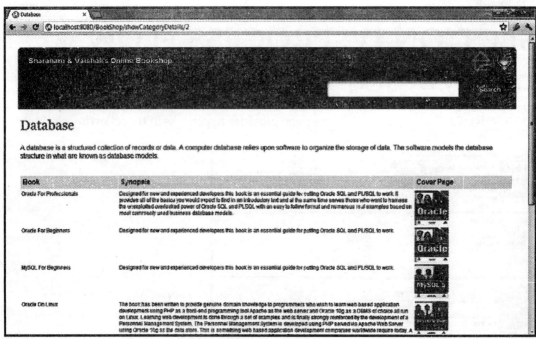

Diagram 13.1

Process Flow

Show Category Details displays the details of the category.

The category details in Show Category details is populated by /showCategoryDetails/${categoryNo} → **HomeController** → **showCategoryDetails()**.

Here,

- /showCategoryDetails/${categoryNo} is the request mapping, which invokes **showCategoryDetails()** of **HomeController**
- **HomeController** is the controller, which holds a mapping to help display the category details
- **showCategoryDetails()** is the method available in controller, which retrieves the category details via CategoryService

show·CategoryDetails() invokes the following methods of CatgeoryService:

Methods	Description
getCategoryById()	Holds the business logic to retrieve the category details.
getAllBooksByCategory()	Holds the business logic to retrieve the list of books categorized according to that particular category.

The service layer i.e. CategoryService in turn invokes the DAO layer.

CategoryService's methods invoke the following methods of CategoryDAO:

Methods	Description
getCategoryById()	Returns the appropriate category's object from the Categories database table using **CategoryNo** as the reference.
getAllBooksByCategory()	Returns the appropriate books List object from the Books database table using **CategoryNo** as the reference.

Whilst populating these details in Show Category Details, the system checks if the user has logged in. Only if the user has logged in, the additional link **Add To Cart** is displayed in Show Category Details.

This check is performed by accessing the username from the SESSION object.

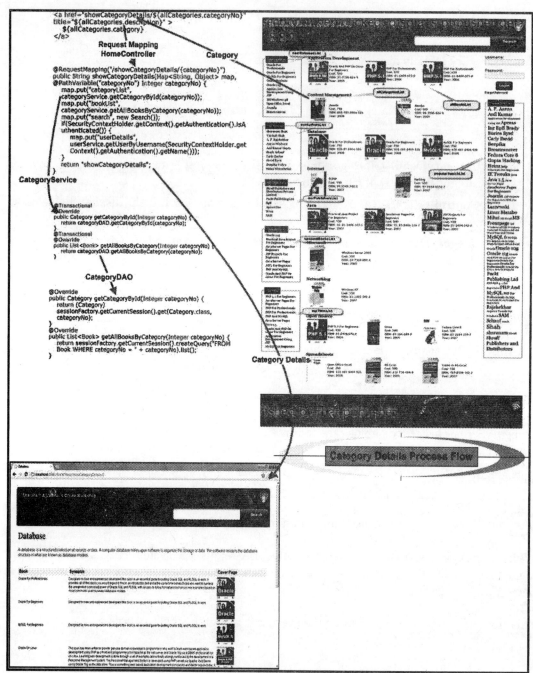

Diagram 13.2: Category Details Process Flow

Chapter

14

SECTION IV: PROCESS FLOW

Search [searchResults.jsp]

The header of the Frontend [customer facing] holds a Search data entry form.

The user can key in the desired search criteria and click **Search**.

Clicking **Search**, invokes a controller using request mapping:

```
<input id="button-search" class="search-button" type="button"
onclick="document.location.href='${pageContext.request.contextPath}/searchResults/'
+ document.forms[0].searchCriteria.value" title="Search" name="fulltext" value="" />
```

To view the search results, **SearchCriteria** is passed as a parameter to the controller. This helps the controller determine the method to be invoked [based on the request mapping] which returns the appropriate search results.

When the user clicks ![Search], searchResults.jsp is served, as shown in diagram 14.1.

Search By Criteria

User Interface [/searchResults/${searchCriteria} → searchResults.jsp]

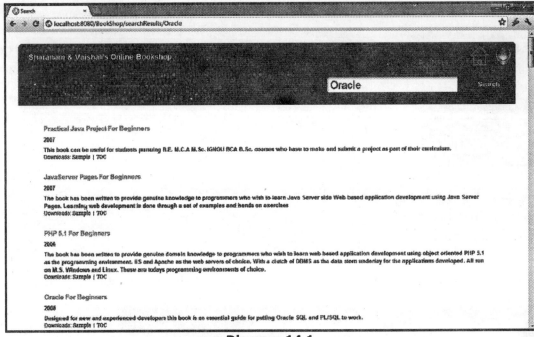

Diagram 14.1

Process Flow

When the customer keys in the search criteria and clicks ![Search], the search results are displayed in searchResults.jsp by **/searchResults/${searchCriteria}** → **SearchController** → **showSearchResultsByCriteria()**.

Here,

❑ **/searchResults/${searchCriteria}** is the request mapping, which invokes **showSearchResultsByCriteria()** of **SearchController**

❑ **SearchController** is the controller, which holds a mapping to help search the data according to the search criteria

❑   **showSearchResultsByCriteria()** is the method available in controller, which:

o   Displays the search results

o   Saves the search criteria in the PopularSearches database table

showSearchResultsByCriteria() in turn invokes the following methods of SearchService:

Methods	Description
searchResults()	Holds the business logic to retrieve the search results.
savePopularSearch()	Holds the business logic to save the SearchCriteria in the PopularSearches database table and deletes the old entries from the PopularSearches database table for housekeeping.

The service layer i.e. SearchService in turn invokes the DAO layer.

SearchService's methods invoke the following methods of SearchDAO:

Methods	Description
searchResults()	Returns the appropriate search results from the database tables using **SearchCriteria** as the reference.
savePopularSearch()	Does the actual saving of the SearchCriteria in the PopularSearches database table.
deletePopularSearches()	Deletes the old entries from the PopularSearches database table, if the total number of records crosses 600 entries.
getTotalPopularSearches()	Is called by deletePopularSearches() to retrieve the total number of records available in the PopularSearches database table.

Search Without Criteria

Process Flow

When the customer does not key in the search criteria and directly clicks , the search results are displayed in searchResults.jsp by **/searchResults → SearchController → showSearchResults() → SearchService [searchAllResults()] → SearchDAO [searchAllResults()]**.

Here,

❑   **/searchResults** is the request mapping, which invokes **showSearchResults()** of **SearchController**

❑   **SearchController** is the controller, which holds a mapping to help search the data

❑ **showSearchResults()** is the method available in controller, which displays the search results via SearchService

❑ **SearchService** is the service layer invoked by the controller

❑ **searchAllResults()** is the method available in service, which holds the business logic to retrieve all the search results

❑ **SearchDAO** is the Data Access Layer [DAO] invoked by the service

❑ **searchAllResults()** is the method available in DAO, which returns all the search results from the database table

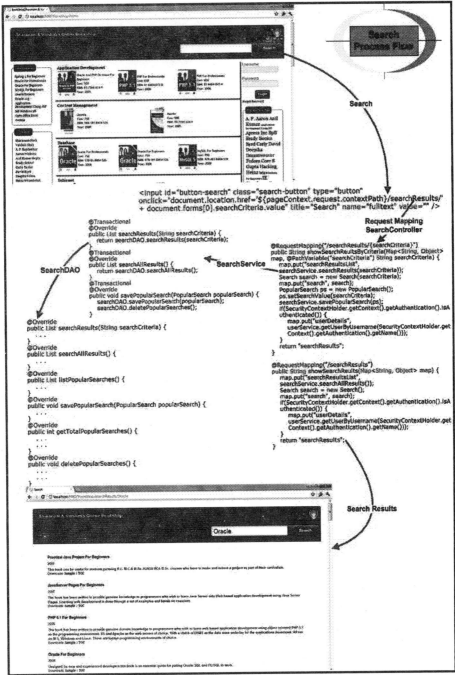

```
<input id="button-search" class="search-button" type="button"
onclick="document.location.href='${pageContext.request.contextPath}/searchResults/'
+ document.forms[0].searchCriteria.value" title="Search" name="fulltext" value="" />
```

```
@Transactional
@Override
public List searchResults(String searchCriteria) {
    return searchDAO.searchResults(searchCriteria);
}

@Transactional
@Override
public List searchAllResults() {
    return searchDAO.searchAllResults();
}

@Transactional
@Override
public void savePopularSearch(PopularSearch popularSearch) {
    searchDAO.savePopularSearch(popularSearch);
    searchDAO.deletePopularSearches();
}
```

SearchDAO

SearchService

```
@Override
public List searchResults(String searchCriteria) {
    ...
}

@Override
public List searchAllResults() {
    ...
}

@Override
public List listPopularSearches() {
    ...
}

@Override
public void savePopularSearch(PopularSearch popularSearch) {
    ...
}

@Override
public int getTotalPopularSearches() {
    ...
}

@Override
public void deletePopularSearches() {
    ...
}
```

Request Mapping SearchController

```
@RequestMapping("/searchResults/{searchCriteria}")
public String showSearchReultsByCriteria(Map<String, Object>
map, @PathVariable("searchCriteria") String searchCriteria) {
    map.put("searchResultsList",
    searchService.searchResults(searchCriteria));
    Search search = new Search(searchCriteria);
    map.put("search", search);
    PopularSearch ps = new PopularSearch();
    ps.setSearchValue(searchCriteria);
    searchService.savePopularSearch(ps);
    if(SecurityContextHolder.getContext().getAuthentication().isA
uthenticated()) {
        map.put("userDetails",
        userService.getUserByUsername(SecurityContextHolder.get
Context().getAuthentication().getName()));
    }
    return "searchResults";
}

@RequestMapping("/searchResults")
public String showSearchReults(Map<String, Object> map) {
    map.put("searchResultsList",
    searchService.searchAllResults());
    Search search = new Search();
    map.put("search", search);
    if(SecurityContextHolder.getContext().getAuthentication().isA
uthenticated()) {
        map.put("userDetails",
        userService.getUserByUsername(SecurityContextHolder.get
Context().getAuthentication().getName()));
    }
    return "searchResults";
}
```

Diagram 14.2: Search Process Flow

Chapter 15

SECTION IV: PROCESS FLOW

Popular Searches

The home page holds the Popular Searches section.

The user can click a desired search keyword to view the search results.

Every search keyword that is listed under the Popular Searches is hyperlinked to a controller using a request mapping.

```
<a href="searchResults/${popularSearch[0]}" class="popularSearch1" title="Click to
search for ${popularSearch[0]}">
    ${popularSearch[0]}
</a>
```

To view the search results for a particular popular search keyword, **SearchCriteria** is passed as a parameter to the controller. This helps the controller determine the method to be invoked [based on the request mapping] which returns the appropriate search results.

When the user clicks the desired hyperlink an appropriate searchResults.jsp is served, as shown in diagram 14.1 of *Chapter 14: Search [searchResults.jsp]*.

Process Flow

When the user clicks the desired hyperlink, the search results of that search criteria are displayed in searchResults.jsp by **/searchResults/${searchCriteria}** → **SearchController** → **showSearchResultsByCriteria()**.

Here,

❑ **/searchResults/${searchCriteria}** is the request mapping, which invokes **showSearchResultsByCriteria()** of **SearchController**

❑ **SearchController** is the controller, which holds a mapping to help search the data according to the search criteria

❑ **showSearchResultsByCriteria()** is the method available in controller, which:

   o Displays the search results

   o Saves the search criteria in the PopularSearches database table

showSearchResultsByCriteria() in turn invokes the following methods of SearchService:

Methods	Description
searchResults()	Holds the business logic to retrieve the search results.
savePopularSearch()	Holds the business logic to save the SearchCriteria in the PopularSearches database table and deletes the old entries from the PopularSearches database table for housekeeping.

The service layer i.e. SearchService in turn invokes the DAO layer.

SearchService's methods invoke the following methods of SearchDAO:

Methods	Description
searchResults()	Returns the appropriate search results from the database tables using **SearchCriteria** as the reference.
savePopularSearch()	Does the actual saving of the SearchCriteria in the PopularSearches database table.
deletePopularSearches()	Deletes the old entries from the PopularSearches database table, if the total number of records crosses 600 entries.
getTotalPopularSearches()	Is called by deletePopularSearches() to retrieve the total number of records available in the PopularSearches database table.

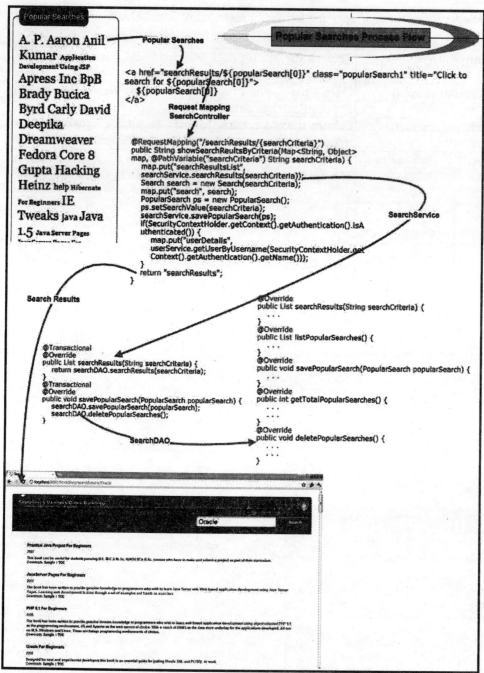

Diagram 15.1: Popular Searches Process Flow

Chapter

16

SECTION IV: PROCESS FLOW

Sign Up

Show Sign Up Page

The home page holds a hyperlink to the **Signup** page.

Sharanam & Vaishali's Online Bookshop

When the user clicks this link, the sign up page appears.

```
<a href="/BookShop/signUp">
    <img src="/BookShop/images/signup.png" title="Sign Up"/>
</a>
```

When the user clicks ![icon], signUp.jsp is served, as shown in diagram 16.1.

User Interface [/signUp → signUp.jsp]

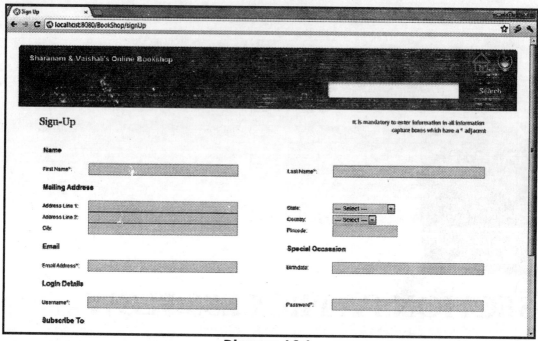

Diagram 16.1

Process Flow

After the user clicks 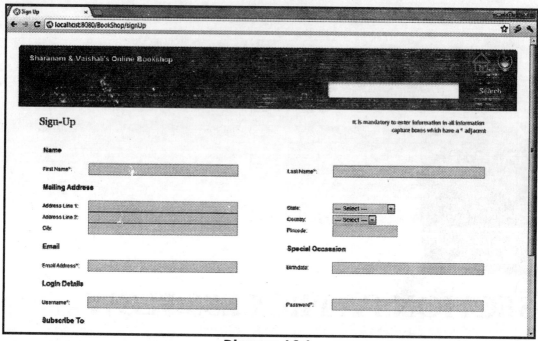, Sign Up is served by **/signUp** → **SignUpController** → **showSignUp()**.

Here,

- **/signUp** is the request mapping, which invokes **showSignUp()** of **SignUpController**
- **SignUpController** is the controller
- **showSignUp()** is the method available in controller, which retrieves the list of countries and states and then displays the sign up form for the user to sign up

showSignUp() invokes the following methods of the Service layer:

Service	Method	Description
CountryService	listCountry()	Holds the business logic to return the appropriate list of the available countries.
StateService	listState()	Holds the business logic to return the appropriate list of the available states.

Service Layer in turn calls the DAO layer's methods.

The Service layer methods invoke the following methods of the DAO layer:

DAO	Method	Description
CountryDAO	listCountry()	Does the actual retrieval of the available countries.
StateDAO	listState()	Does the actual retrieval of the available states.

Adding New Customer

After the user keys in the sign up data and clicks **Save**, signUpThankYou.jsp is served, as shown in diagram 16.2.

User Interface [/saveSignUp → /signUpThankYou → signUpThankYou.jsp]

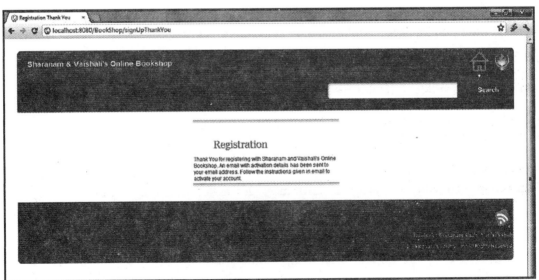

Diagram 16.2

Process Flow

This is a standard data entry form. By default, when the form loads, it's in the **INSERT** mode.

After SignUp loads, the user can simply key in the required data and click **Save**.

After the user keys in the required inputs and clicks **Save**, the FORM is submitted and the **save** operation is performed by **/saveSignUp** → SignUpController [registerCustomer()] → **/signUpThankYou** → SignUpController [showSignUpThankYou()].

Here,

☐ **/saveSignUp** is the request mapping, which invokes **registerCustomer()** of **SignUpController**

☐ **SignUpController** is the controller

☐ **registerCustomer()** is the method available in the controller, which does the saving of the captured data via UserService and then sends an email to the registered customer via MailService. **registerCustomer()** then upon successful registration redirects to **/signUpThankYou**

☐ **/signUpThankYou** is the request mapping, which invokes **showSignUpThankYou()** of **SignUpController**

☐ **showSignUpThankYou()** is the method available in the controller, which displays the Sign Up Thank You Page

registerCustomer() invokes the following methods of the Service layer:

Service	Method	Description
UserService	saveUser()	Holds the business logic to save the captured user details.
MailSerice	sendMail()	Holds the business logic to send an email.

UserService's **saveUser()** in turn calls **UserDAO**'s **saveUser()**, which does the actual saving of the user in the Users database table.

If the captured data is found to be invalid while saving the captured data, then the Sign Up Page is re-served with the appropriate error messages, as shown in diagram 16.3.

User Interface For Validation Errors [/saveSignUp → signUp.jsp]

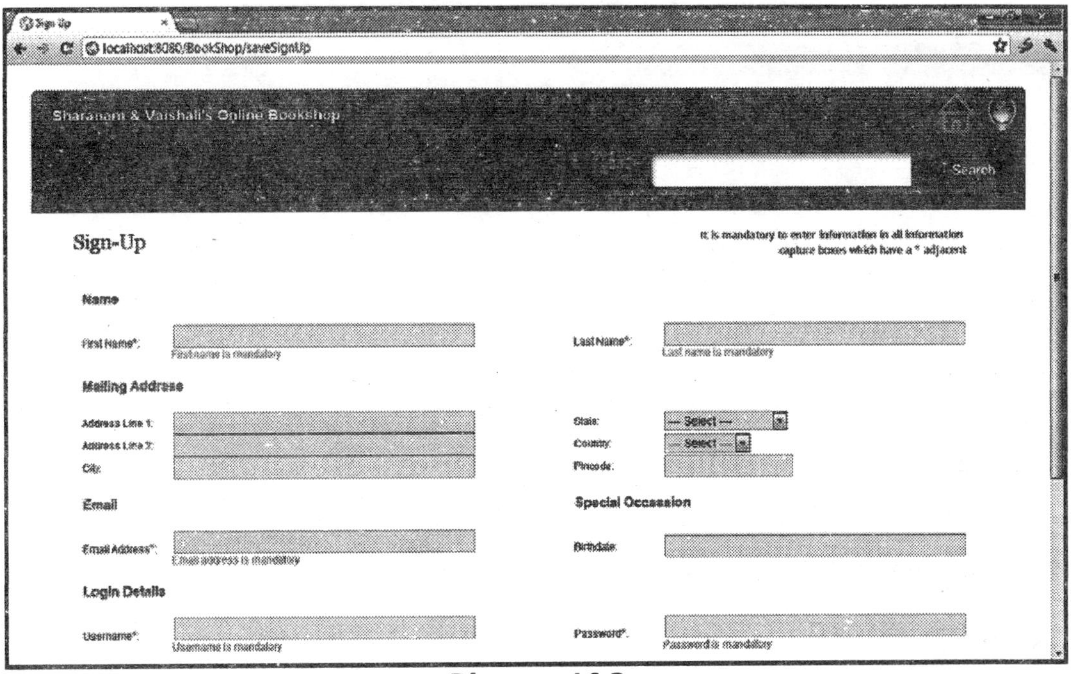

Diagram 16.3

Process Flow

If the captured data is found to be invalid, then Sign Up with appropriate error messages is served by **/saveSignUp → SignUpController [registerCustomer()]**.

Here,

☐ **/saveSignUp** is the request mapping, which invokes **registerCustomer()** of **SignUpController**

☐ **SignUpController** is the controller

☐ **registerCustomer()** is the method available in the controller, which traps the errors and forwards it to the Sign Up page

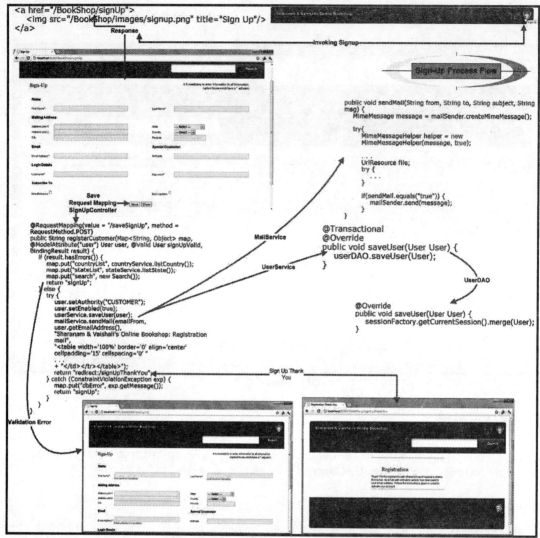

Diagram 16.4: Sign-Up Process Flow

Chapter

17

SECTION IV: PROCESS FLOW

Customer Login And Logout

Customer Login

The home page holds a Login data entry form.

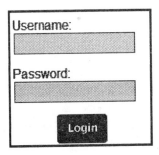

When the user keys in the login details and clicks **Login** the user is authenticated and if the user is found valid, home.jsp is served again with a welcome message.

When the user clicks , the Login form in home.jsp is submitted to the controller called **AuthenticationController** via a request mapping **/login**.

If the login attempted is successful, then home.jsp is served again with a welcome message and the login form disappears, as shown in diagram 17.1.

User Interface [/login → home.jsp]

Diagram 17.1

Process Flow

When the user clicks [icon], the login form is displayed by **spring-security.xml** → **/login** → **AuthenticationController** → **showLogin()**.

Here,

- □ spring-security.xml is the Spring Security configuration, which holds the mapping for displaying the login page
- □ **/login** is the request mapping, which invokes **showLogin()** of **AuthenticationController**
- □ **AuthenticationController** is the controller
- □ **showLogin()** is the method available in the controller, which returns the home page with the login form included in it

Successful Login

When the user keys in the username and password and clicks [Login], the user is authenticated and then on successful authentication, the application renders the home page, which is the startup page.

Process Flow

When the user keys in the username and password and clicks [Login], the login details are authenticated by **spring-security.xml** → **/j_spring_security_check**.

Here,

❑ spring-security.xml is the Spring Security configuration, which takes care of the login authentication

❑ **/j_spring_security_check** is the request mapping, which actually does the authentication process

After the login credentials are authenticated and are valid, the application renders the home page, which is the startup page.

/home returns the home page without the Login form.

Spring security has the default target URL in case of successful login, which in this case is **/home**:

```
<http auto-config="true" use-expressions="true">
    <form-login login-page="/login" login-processing-url="/j_spring_security_check"
    default-target-url="/home" authentication-failure-url="/loginFailed" />
    <logout logout-url="/j_spring_security_logout" logout-success-url="/home" />
</http>
```

Since the login details are available in the Session, some application features such as Add To Cart, Show Cart, Downloads of TOC and Sample Chapter are switched on based on the values available in the session which helps determine a valid authenticated user.

Login Failed

If the login attempted is un-successful then home.jsp is served again with an error message, as shown in diagram 17.2.

User Interface [/loginFailed → home.jsp]

Diagram 17.2

Process Flow

When the login credentials are found invalid, the login form is reserved along with the appropriate error messages by **spring-security.xml** → **/loginFailed** → **AuthenticationController** → **showLoginError()**.

Here,

❑ spring-security.xml is the Spring Security configuration, which takes care of the login authentication process

❑ **/loginFailed** is the request mapping, which invokes **showLoginError()** of **AuthenticationController**

❑ **AuthenticationController** is the controller

❑ **showLoginError()** is the method available in controller, which displays Home page along with the appropriate error messages

Logout

The user can choose to logout of the application by clicking .

Process Flow

when clicked destroys the session and redirects the user to the home page with the login form included using the request mapping **spring-security.xml** → **/j_spring_security_logout** → **/logout** → **AuthenticationController** → **showHomeAfterLogout()**.

Here,

❑ spring-security.xml is the Spring Security configuration, which takes care of the logout process

❑ **/j_spring_security_logout** is the request mapping, which actually does the logout process

❑ **/logout** is the request mapping, which invokes **showHomeAfterLogout()** of **AuthenticationController**

❑ **AuthenticationController** is the controller

❑ **showHomeAfterLogout** is the method available in the controller, which returns the user to Home page along with the login form included

Since logout destroys the session, some of the application features such as Add To Cart, Show Cart, Downloads of TOC and Sample Chapter are switched off.

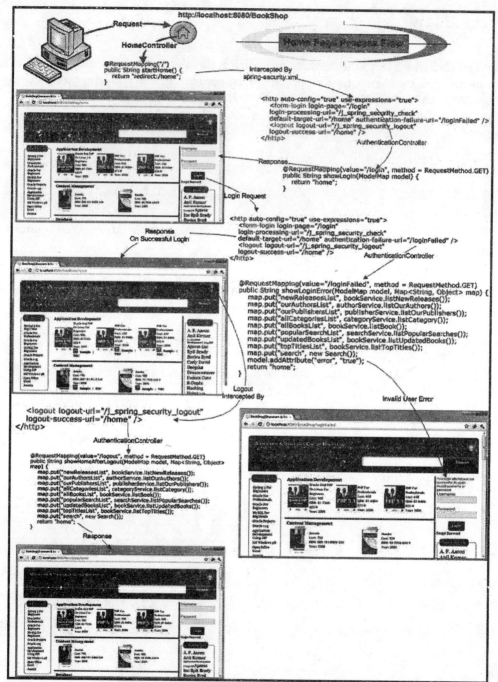

Diagram 17.3: Customer Login Process Flow

Chapter

18

SECTION IV: PROCESS FLOW

Forgot Password

Display Forgot Password Page

Forgot password data entry form retrieves the password for the customers who have forgotten it.

The home page holds a link to the Forgot Password data entry form.

Username:

Password:

Login

Forgot Password

This hyperlink invokes a controller using request mapping:

```
38  <a href="/BookShop/admin/forgotPassword">Forgot Password</a>
```

When the user clicks **Forgot Password**, forgotPassword.jsp is served, as shown in diagram 18.1.

User Interface [/forgotPassword → forgotPassword.jsp]

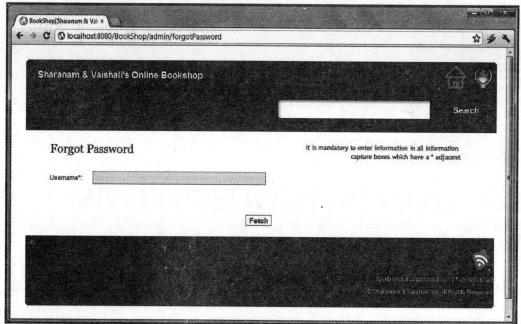

Diagram 18.1

Process Flow

When the user clicks **Forgot Password**, the application displays the Forgot Password data entry form by **/forgotPassword → UserController → showForgotPassword()**.

Here,

- **/forgotPassword** is the request mapping, which invokes **showForgotPassword()** of **UserController**
- **UserController** is the controller
- **showForgotPassword()** is the method available in controller, which displays the Forgot Password page

Retrieving Password

The user needs to key in the Username and click Fetch .

When the user clicks Fetch :

- ❑ The data entry form is submitted to **UserController** using a request mapping
- ❑ The data is validated. If data is found to be invalid, then forgotPassord.jsp is re-served along with an appropriate error message
- ❑ If data is valid, then the password of the customer is send via an email, if the username entered by the user is valid
- ❑ Finally, forgotPassword.jsp is re-served along with the message indicating success

Process Flow

When the user keys in the username and clicks Fetch , the captured username is authenticated by **/retrievePassword/${userName}** → **UserController** → **retrievePassword()**.

Here,

- ❑ **/retrievePassword/${userName}** is the request mapping, which invokes **retrievePassword()** of **UserController**
- ❑ **UserController** is the controller
- ❑ **retrievePassword()** is the method available in controller, which sends the password via an email on successful authentication of the captured data

retrievePassword() invokes the following methods of the Service layer:

Service	Method	Description
UserService	getUserByUsername()	Holds the business logic to return the appropriate details of the user according to the username entered by the customer.
MailService	sendMail()	Holds the business logic to send an email.

UserService's **getUserByUsername()** in turn calls **UserDAO**'s **getUserByUsername()**, which returns the appropriate user's details from the Users database table using **Username** as the reference.

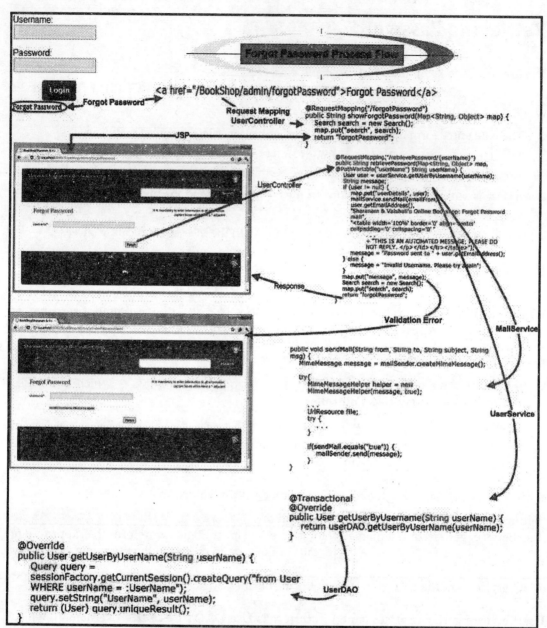

Diagram 18.2: Forgot Password Process Flow

SECTION IV: PROCESS FLOW

Cart [showCart.jsp]

Add To Cart

When the user logs in:

 appears in the home page, as shown in diagram 19.1

appears in the Show Book Details, ShowAuthor Details, Show Publisher Details and Show Category Details, as shown in diagram 19.2

User Interface [/addToCart/${userName}/${bookNo}]

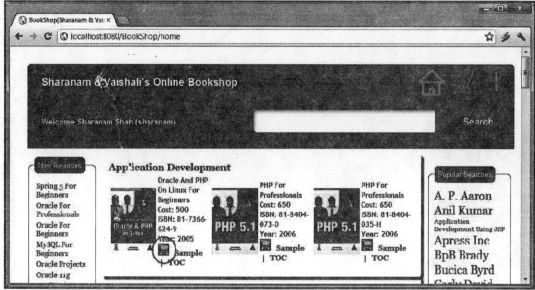

Diagram 19.1

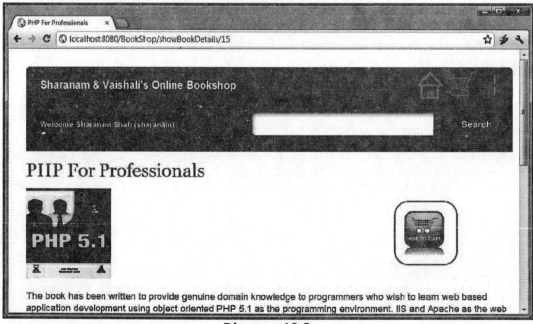

Diagram 19.2

Every hyperlink under the above mentioned section invokes a controller using request mapping:

```
<a href="addToCart/<sec:authorize access='isAuthenticated()'><sec:authentication
property='principal.username' /></sec:authorize>/${categoryWiseBooks.bookNo}">
    <img src="/BookShop/images/cart.jpg" class="imagePointer" border="0"/>
</a> 
```

Process Flow

When a user clicks [image] or [image], the book details are added to the cart by /addToCart/${userName}/{bookNo} → CartController [addToCart()] → CartService [addBookToCart()] → BookService [getBookById()] → BookDAO [getBookById()].

Here,

- /addToCart/${userName}/{bookNo} is the request mapping, which invokes **addToCart()** of **CartController**

- **CartController** is the controller

- **addToCart()** is the method available in the controller, which adds the book details such as the book name, cost, quantity to the CartList along with the session and username via **CartService**

- **CartService** is the service layer

- **addBookToCart()** is the method available in CartService, which adds all the book data i.e. username, book number, book name, synopsis, cost to the CartItem

- **BookService** is the service layer invoked by **CartService**

- **getBookById()** is the method available in BookService, which holds the business logic to retrieve the book details

- **BookDAO** is the DAO layer invoked by BookService

- **getBookById()** is the method available in BookDAO, which returns the appropriate book's object from the Books database table using **BookNo** as the reference

Show Cart

The home page holds a link to the Shopping Cart. The link appears only if the user has logged in.

After the books are added by **Add To Cart** link, the details about the books purchased are displayed in the **Show Cart** page.

When the user clicks 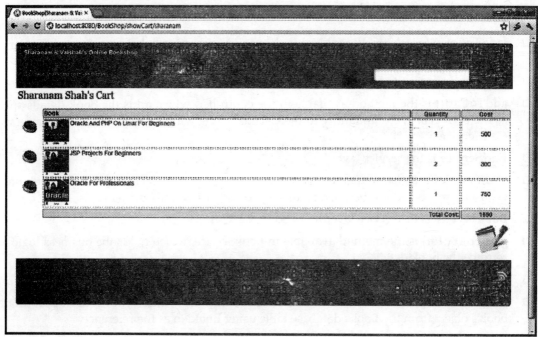, showCart.jsp is served, as shown in diagram 19.3.

User Interface [/showCart/${userName} → showCart.jsp]

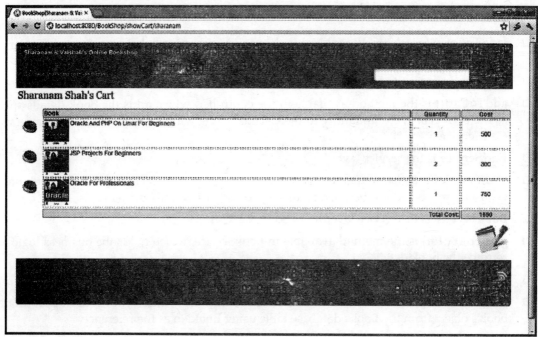

Diagram 19.3

Process Flow

Show Cart displays the details of the books added to the cart by the customer.

The book details in the JSP are populated by **/showCart/${userName}** → **CartController** → **showCart()**.

Here,

- **/showCart/${userName}** is the request mapping, which invokes **showCart()** of **CartController**
- **CartController** is the controller
- **showCart()** is the method available in the controller, which displays the list of books added to the cart by the customer

Removing The Cart Items [Books]

Every item [book] that is listed in showCart.jsp has  adjacent to it.

 is hyperlinked to a controller, named CartController, using a request mapping.

```
38  <a href="/BookShop/removeFromCart/<sec:authorize
    access='isAuthenticated()'><sec:authentication property='principal.username'
    /></sec:authorize>/${cart.bookNo}">
39      <img src="/BookShop/images/delete.jpg" alt="Click to remove the Book from the
        cart">
40  </a>
```

 when clicked removes the selected item and re-serves showCart.jsp.

Process Flow

Show Cart allows the user to delete/remove a book from the cart using . The deletion is done by **/removeFromCart/${userName}/{bookNo}** → **CartController** → **removeFromCart()** → **CartService** → **removeBookFromCart()**.

Here,

- **/removeFromCart/${userName}/{bookNo}** is the request mapping, which invokes **removeFromCart()** of **CartController**
- **CartController** is the controller
- **removeFromCart()** is the method available in the controller, which deletes/removes the book from the cart via **CartService**
- **CartService** is the service layer
- **removeBookFromCart()** is the method available in CartService, which holds the business logic to remove the book details from the CartItem

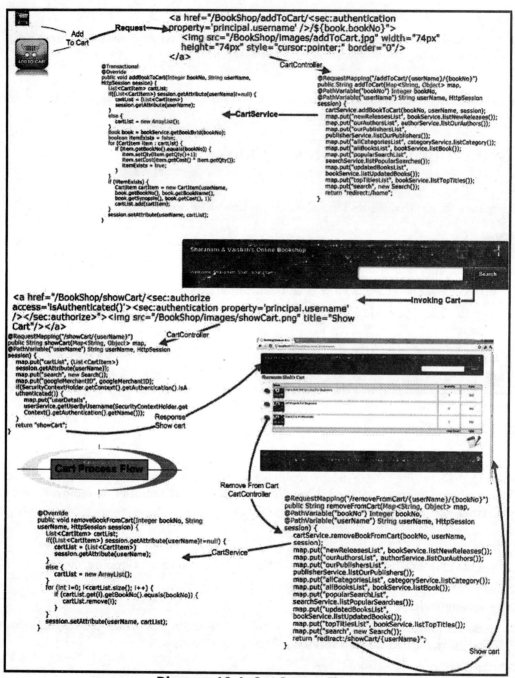

Diagram 19.4: Cart Process Flow

SECTION IV: PROCESS FLOW

Checkout

The Shopping Cart [showCart.jsp] holds a link to checkout.

When the user clicks this link, the Google Wallet is served, as shown in **diagram 20.1.**

User Interface [/saveCart/${userName} → /checkOut/${userName} → Google Wallet]

Diagram 20.1

Process Flow

When the user clicks the CheckOut link, the cart details are added to the database by **/saveCart/${userName}** → **CartController [saveCart()]** → **CartService [saveCart()]** → **TransactionService [saveTransaction()]** → **TransactionDAO [saveTransaction()]**.

Here,

☐ **/saveCart/${userName}** is the request mapping, which invokes **saveCart()** of **CartController**

☐ **CartController** is the controller

☐ **saveCart()** is the method available in the controller, which adds the book details such as the book name, cost, quantity to the Transactions database table via **CartService**

- ❏ **CartService** is the service layer
- ❏ **saveCart()** is the method available in the service layer, which holds the business logic to save the cart details as transactions via **TransactionService**
- ❏ **TransactionService** is the service layer
- ❏ **saveTransaction()** is the method available in the service layer, which holds the business logic to save the cart details via **TransactionDAO**
- ❏ **TransactionDAO** is the Data Access [DAO] Layer
- ❏ **saveTransaction()** is the method available in the DAO layer, which does the actual saving of the transaction [CartItem] in the Transactions database table

CartService's saveCart() also invokes **TransactionDAO's getNextTransactionNo()**, which retrieves the next TransactionNo from the underlying Transactions database table.

CartController's saveCart() after saving the cart items redirects to Google Wallet by /checkOut/${userName} → CartController → checkOut().

Here,

- ❏ **/checkOut/${userName}** is the request mapping, which invokes **checkOut()** of **CartController**
- ❏ **CartController** is the controller
- ❏ **checkOut()** is the method available in the controller, which displays the Google Wallet along with book details where the customer has to make the payment for the books purchased

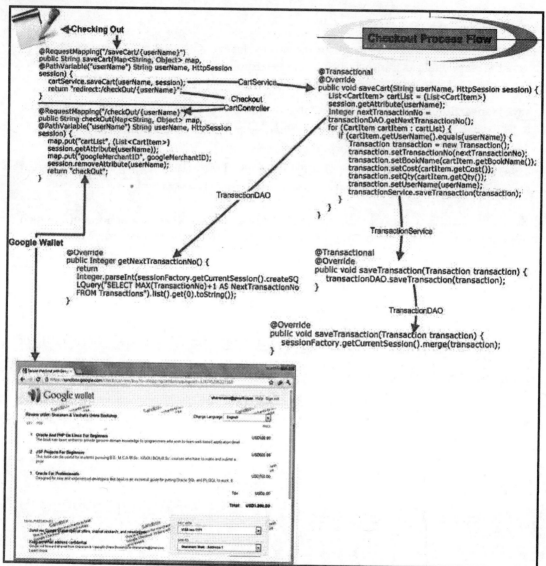

Diagram 20.2: Checkout Process Flow

SECTION IV: PROCESS FLOW

Administration Login And Logout

Administration Login

The home page holds a link to the application's back office [administration].

When the user clicks , adminLogin.jsp is served, as shown in diagram 21.1.

User Interface [/admin/adminLogin → adminLogin.jsp]

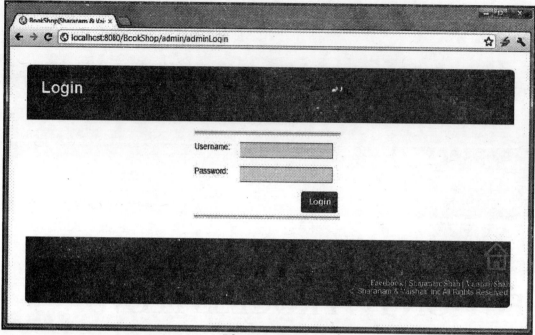

Diagram 21.1

Process Flow

When the user clicks ![icon], the login form is displayed by **spring-security.xml** → **/admin/adminLogin** → **AuthenticationController** → **showAdminLogin()**.

Here,

- spring-security.xml is the Spring Security configuration, which holds the mapping for displaying the administration login page
- **/admin/adminLogin** is the request mapping, which invokes **showAdminLogin()** of **AuthenticationController**
- **AuthenticationController** is the controller
- **showAdminLogin** is the method available in controller, which returns the Administration Login form

Successful Login

After the login credentials are authenticated and are valid, the application renders Manage Transactions, as shown in diagram 21.2.

User Interface [/admin/manageTransactions → manageTransactions.jsp]

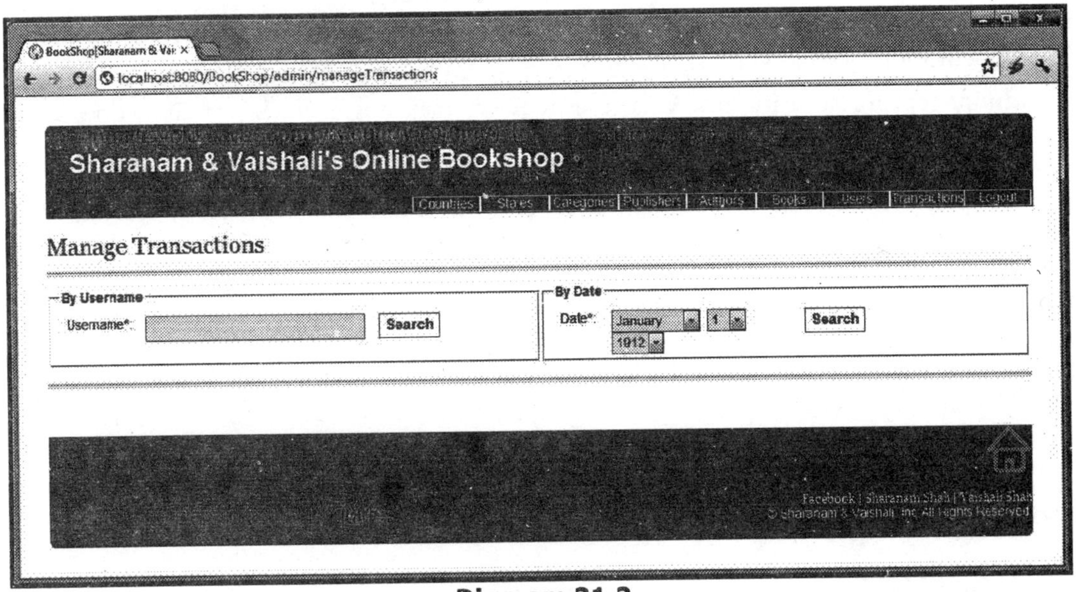

Diagram 21.2

The login data entry form allows the registered administration users to login to the backend application.

After an administration user logs in to the backend application, the user is allowed to manage:

- Countries
- States
- Authors
- Publishers
- Categories
- Users
- Books

❑   Transactions

Process Flow

When the user keys in the username and password and clicks [Login], the login details are authenticated by **spring-security.xml → /admin/j_spring_security_check**.

Here,

❑   spring-security.xml is the Spring Security configuration, which takes care of the login authentication

❑   **/admin/j_spring_security_check** is the request mapping, which actually does the authentication process

After the login credentials are authenticated and are valid, the application renders the Manage Transactions page, which is the startup page for the Administration section.

/admin/manageTransactions returns the Manage Transactions page.

Spring security has the default target URL in case of successful login, which in this case is the **/admin/manageTransactions**:

```
<form-login login-page="/admin/adminLogin"
login-processing-url="/admin/j_spring_security_check"
default-target-url="/admin/manageTransactions"
                                              ed" />
```

Login Failed

If the login attempted is un-successful then adminLogin.jsp is served again with an error message, as shown in diagram 21.3.

User Interface [/admin/adminLoginFailed → adminLogin.jsp]

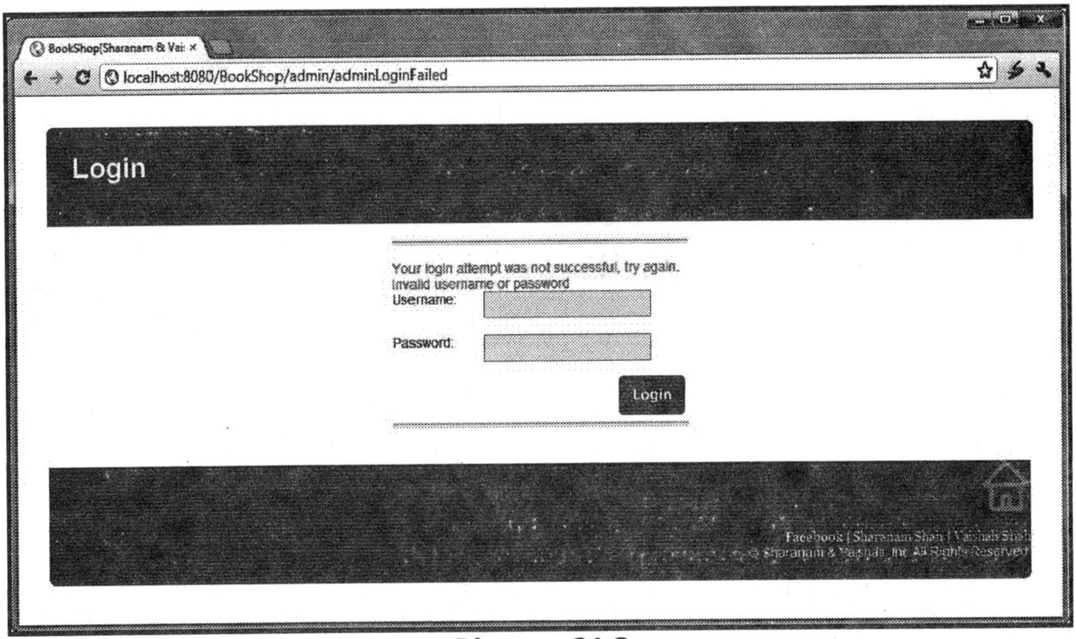

Diagram 21.3

Process Flow

When the login credentials are found invalid, the login form is returned along with the appropriate error messages by **spring-security.xml** → **/admin/adminLoginFailed** → **AuthenticationController** → **showAdminLoginError()**.

Here,

❑ spring-security.xml is the Spring Security configuration, which takes care of the login authentication process

❑ **/admin/adminLoginFailed** is the request mapping, which invokes **showAdminLoginError()** of **AuthenticationController**

❑ **AuthenticationController** is the controller

❑ **showAdminLoginError()** is the method available in the controller, which displays the administration login page along with the appropriate error messages

Access Denied

If the user other than the ROLE_ADMIN tries to click 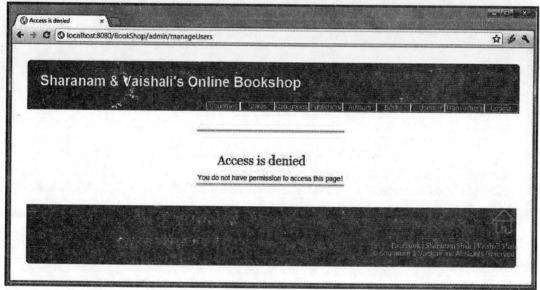 then adminAccessDenied.jsp is served, as shown in diagram 21.4.

User Interface [/adminAccessDenied → adminAccessDenied.jsp]

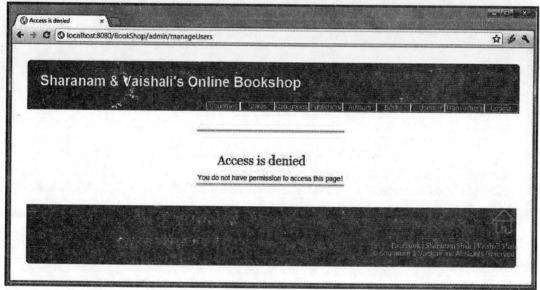

Diagram 21.4

Process Flow

After the login credentials are authenticated and are valid, the application renders the Manage Transactions page, which is the startup page for the Administration.

Spring Security checks the authority of the user i.e. whether the user is the ROLE_ADMIN or ROLE_USER. Based on that authority Spring Security intercepts the Manage forms.

Only ROLE_ADMIN has the authority to use Manage Users form.

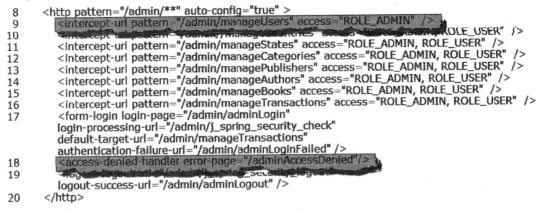

```
8     <http pattern="/admin/**" auto-config="true" >
9        <intercept-url pattern="/admin/manageUsers" access="ROLE_ADMIN" />
10       <intercept-url pattern="/admin/manageBranches" access="ROLE_USER" />
11       <intercept-url pattern="/admin/manageStates" access="ROLE_ADMIN, ROLE_USER" />
12       <intercept-url pattern="/admin/manageCategories" access="ROLE_ADMIN, ROLE_USER" />
13       <intercept-url pattern="/admin/managePublishers" access="ROLE_ADMIN, ROLE_USER" />
14       <intercept-url pattern="/admin/manageAuthors" access="ROLE_ADMIN, ROLE_USER" />
15       <intercept-url pattern="/admin/manageBooks" access="ROLE_ADMIN, ROLE_USER" />
16       <intercept-url pattern="/admin/manageTransactions" access="ROLE_ADMIN, ROLE_USER" />
17       <form-login login-page="/admin/adminLogin"
             login-processing-url="/admin/j_spring_security_check"
             default-target-url="/admin/manageTransactions"
             authentication-failure-url="/admin/adminLoginFailed" />
18       <access-denied-handler error-page="/adminAccessDenied" />
19       <logout logout-url="/admin/j_spring_security_logout"
             logout-success-url="/admin/adminLogout" />
20    </http>
```

When a user other than Administrator tries to enter Manage Users form, the application directs the user to the access denied page by **spring-security.xml** → **/adminAccessDenied** → **AuthenticationController** → **showAccessDeniedPage()**.

Here,

- spring-security.xml is the Spring Security configuration, which takes care of the access denied process

- /adminAccessDenied is the request mapping, which invokes **showAccessDeniedPage()** of **AuthenticationController**

- **AuthenticationController** is the controller

- **showAccessDeniedPage()** is the method available in the controller, which returns the Admin Access Denied page

Logout

The user can choose to logout of the administration section by clicking 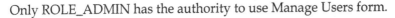.

Process Flow

 when clicked destroys the session and redirects the user to the administration login page using the request mapping **spring-security.xml** → **/admin/j_spring_security_logout** → **/admin/adminLogout** → **AuthenticationController** → **showAdminLoginAfterLogout()**.

Here,

- ❑ spring-security.xml is the Spring Security configuration, which takes care of the logout process
- ❑ **/admin/j_spring_security_logout** is the request mapping, which actually does the logout process
- ❑ **/admin/adminLogout** is the request mapping, which invokes **showAdminLoginAfterLogout()** of **AuthenticationController**
- ❑ **AuthenticationController** is the controller
- ❑ **showAdminLoginAfterLogout** is the method available in the controller, which returns the user to the administration login page

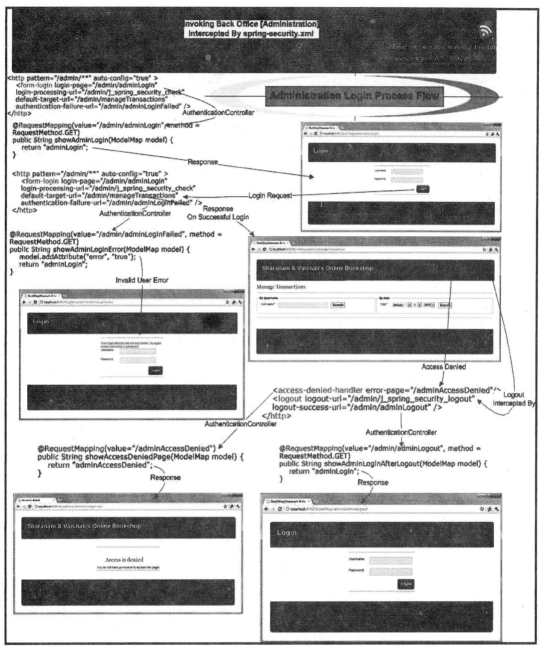

Diagram 21.5: Administration Login Process Flow

Chapter 22

SECTION IV: PROCESS FLOW

Manage Countries [manageCountries.jsp]

Manage Countries is the page that is served when **Countries** is clicked in the Administration section after successful administration login.

It displays:

- ❑ A data entry form to capture the country details
- ❑ List of countries available
- ❑ Delete link to delete a particular country record
- ❑ Edit link to edit a particular country record

Viewing Existing Country Details

When the user clicks **Countries**, manageCountries.jsp is served, as shown in diagram 22.1.

User Interface [/admin/manageCountries →
manageCountries.jsp]

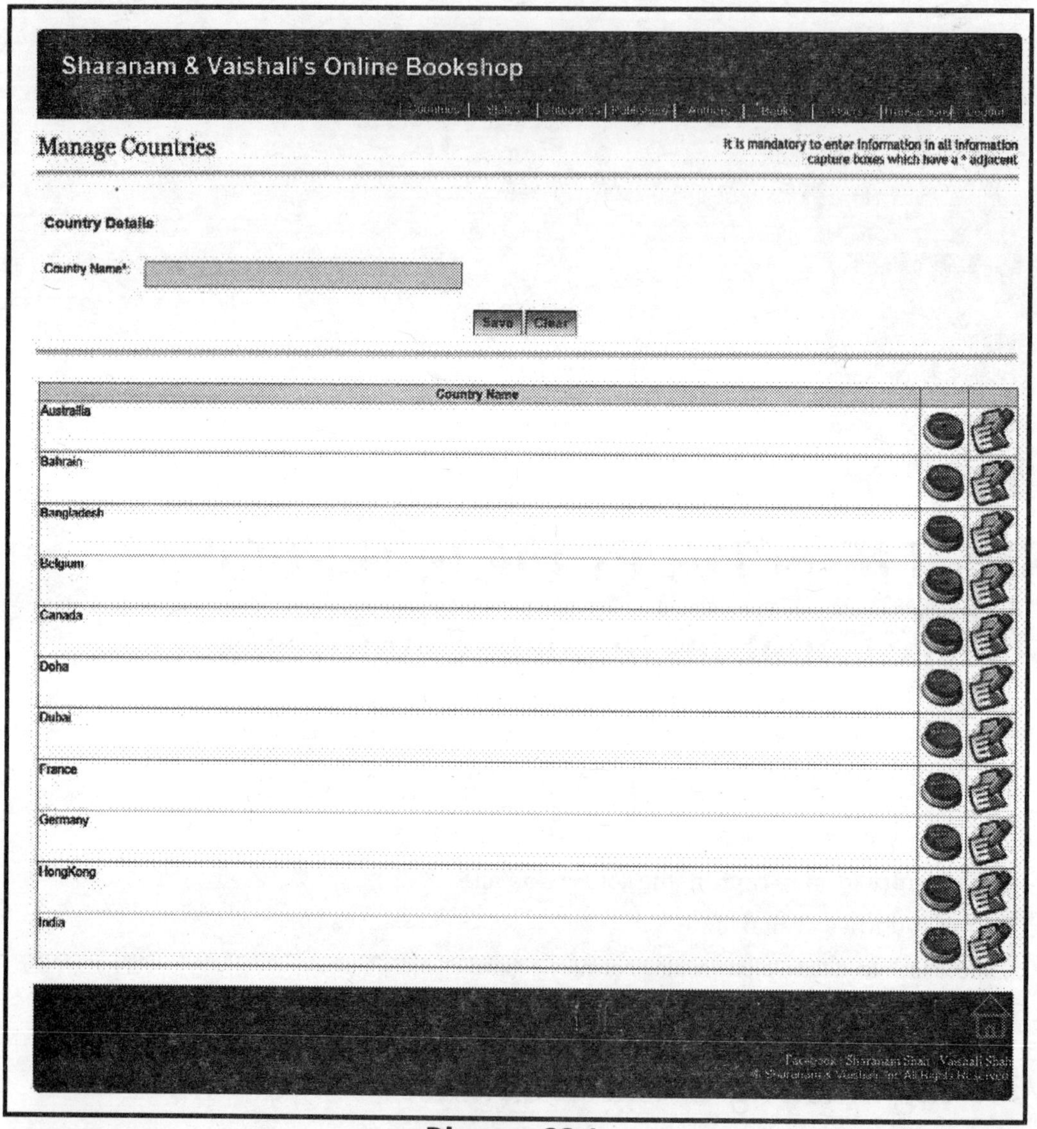

Diagram 22.1

This is a standard data entry form. By default when the form loads, it's in the **INSERT** and **VIEW** mode.

Process Flow

Manage Countries holds a data grid with a list of available records. This data grid serves the purpose of viewing.

The data grid is populated by **/admin/manageCountries** → **CountryController** **[showManageCountries()]** → **CountryService** **[listCountry()]** → **CountryDAO** **[listCountry()]**.

Here,

- **/admin/manageCountries** is the request mapping, which invokes **showManageCountries()** of **CountryController**
- **CountryController** is the controller
- **showManageCountries()** is the method available in the controller, which retrieves the list of countries via CountrySerive
- **CountryService** is the service layer
- **listCountry()** is the method available in **CountryService**, which holds the business logic to return the appropriate list of the available countries via CountryDAO
- **CountryDAO** is the Data Access Layer [DAO]
- **listCountry()** is the method available in **CountryDAO**, which does the actual retrieval of the available countries from the Countries database table

Adding New Country Details

After manageCountries.jsp loads, the user can key in the required data and click **Save**.

Process Flow

After the user keys in the required inputs and clicks **Save**, the FORM is submitted and the **save** operation is performed by **/admin/saveCountry** → **CountryController [saveCountry()]** → **CountryService [saveCountry()]** → **CountryDAO [saveCountry()]**.

Here,

- **/admin/saveCountry** is the request mapping, which invokes **saveCountry()** of **CountryController**
- **CountryController** is the controller

- ❑ **saveCountry()** is the method available in controller, which saves the captured data via CountrySerive
- ❑ **CountryService** is the service layer
- ❑ **saveCountry()** is the method available in **CountryService**, which holds the business logic to save the captured data via CountryDAO
- ❑ **CountryDAO** is the Data Access Layer [DAO]
- ❑ **saveCountry()** is the method available in **CountryDAO**, which does the actual saving of the captured data in the Countries database table

If there are any errors such as duplicate country name then manageCountries.jsp is re-served along with the error messages, as shown in diagram 22.2.

User Interface For Validation Errors [/admin/saveCountry → manageCountries.jsp]

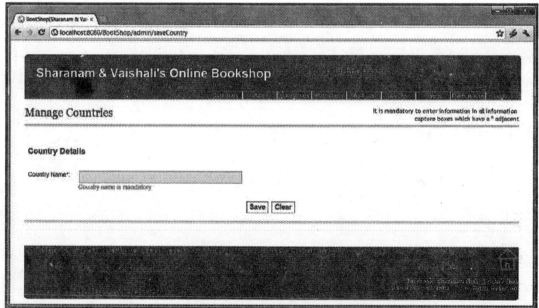

Diagram 22.2: Error messages [manageCountries.jsp]

Process Flow

If the captured data is found to be invalid, then Manage Countries with appropriate error messages is served by **/saveCountry → CountryController → saveCountry()**.

Here,

- **/saveCountry** is the request mapping, which invokes **saveCountry()** of **CountryController**
- **CountryController** is the controller
- **saveCountry()** is the method available in the controller, which traps the errors and forwards it to Manage Countries

Editing Existing Country Details

Every record that is listed in manageCountries.jsp holds 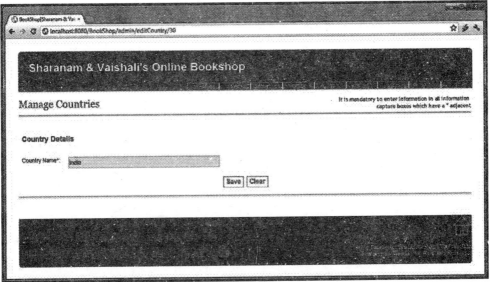 which is hyper linked to a mapping **/admin/editCountry/${countryNo}**.

```
79  <td><a href="/BookShop/admin/editCountry/${country.countryNo}"><img title="Click
    to edit" src="/BookShop/images/edit.jpg"/></a></td>
```

When the user clicks , manageCountries.jsp [pre-populated with the selected country's data] is served, as shown in diagram 22.3.

User Interface [/admin/editCountry/${countryNo} → manageCountries.jsp]

Diagram 22.3

Process Flow

The data population of the selected record for editing is done by the /admin/editCountry/${countryNo} → CountryController [editCountry()] → CountryService [getCountryById()] → CountryDAO [getCountryById()].

Here,

- /admin/editCountry/${countryNo} is the request mapping, which invokes **editCountry()** of **CountryController**
- **CountryController** is the controller
- **editCountry()** is the method available in the controller, which retrieves the country details based on CountryNo as reference via CountryService and re-serves Manage Countries with the required data
- **CountryService** is the service layer
- **getCountryById()** is the method available in **CountryService**, which holds the business logic to retrieve country details based on CountryNo via CountryDAO
- **CountryDAO** is the Data Access Layer [DAO]
- **getCountryById()** is the method available in **CountryDAO**, which returns the appropriate country's object from the Countries database table using **CountryNo** as the reference

After the data is populated and thus is available for editing in the data entry form, the user can make the desired changes and click **Save**.

After editing the country details, when the user clicks **Save**, saveCountry() of CountryController, followed by saveCountry() of CountryService, followed by saveCountry() of CountryDAO takes care of saving the updated country's details.

The data is **updated** in the underlying table and Manage Countries is re-served with the updated record.

Deleting Existing Country Details

Every record that is listed in manageCountries.jsp holds 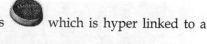 which is hyper linked to a mapping **/admin/deleteCountry/${countryNo}**.

```
78  <td><a href="/BookShop/admin/deleteCountry/${country.countryNo}"><img
    title="Click to delete" src="/BookShop/images/delete.jpg"/></a></td>
```

When the user clicks the selected record is deleted and manageCountries.jsp is re-served.

Process Flow

The record deletion is done by **/admin/deleteCountry/${countryNo}** → **CountryController [deleteCountry()]** → **CountryService [removeCountry()]** → **CountryDAO [removeCountry()]**.

Here,

❑ **/admin/deleteCountry/${countryNo}** is the request mapping, which invokes deleteCountry() of **CountryController**

❑ **CountryController** is the controller

❑ **deleteCountry()** is the method available in the controller, which deletes the country record based on CountryNo as reference via CountryService and re-serves Manage Countries with the available records

❑ **CountryService** is the service layer

❑ **removeCountry()** is the method available in **CountryService**, which holds the business logic to delete country details based on CountryNo via CountryDAO

❑ **CountryDAO** is the **Data Access Layer [DAO]**

❑ **removeCountry()** is the method available in **CountryDAO**, which deletes the appropriate country from the Countries database table based on **CountryNo** received as a reference

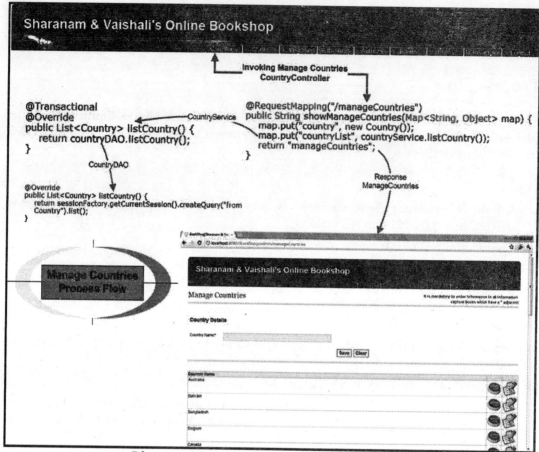

Diagram 22.4: Manage Countries Process Flow

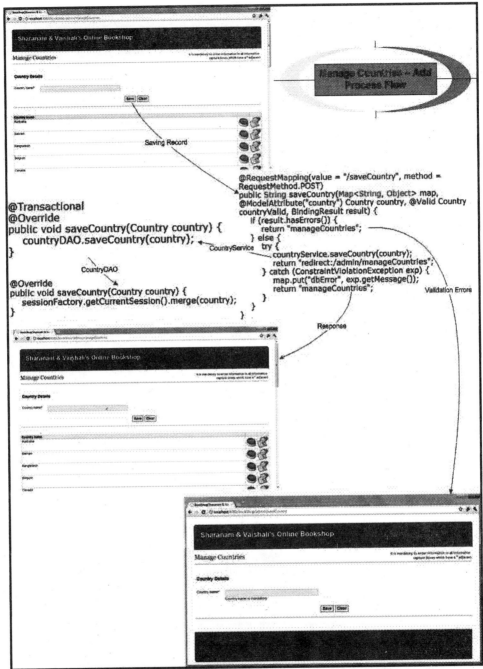

Diagram 22.5: Manage Countries - Add Process Flow

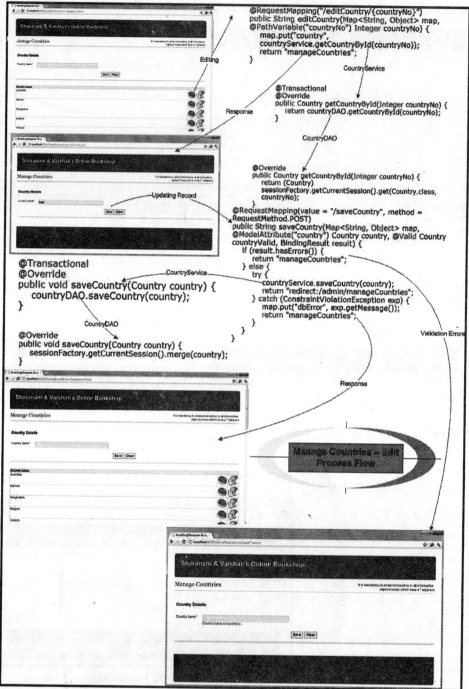

Diagram 22.6: Manage Countries - Edit Process Flow

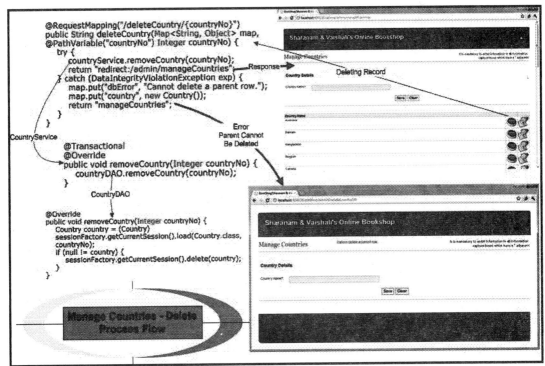

Diagram 22.7: Manage Countries - Delete Process Flow

Chapter

23

SECTION IV: PROCESS FLOW

Manage States [manageStates.jsp]

Manage States is the page that is served when States is clicked in the Administration section after successful administration login.

It displays:

- ❑ A data entry form to capture the state details
- ❑ List of states available
- ❑ Delete link to delete a particular state record
- ❑ Edit link to edit a particular state record

Viewing Existing State Details

When the user clicks States, manageStates.jsp is served, as shown in diagram 23.1.

User Interface [/admin/manageStates → manageStates.jsp]

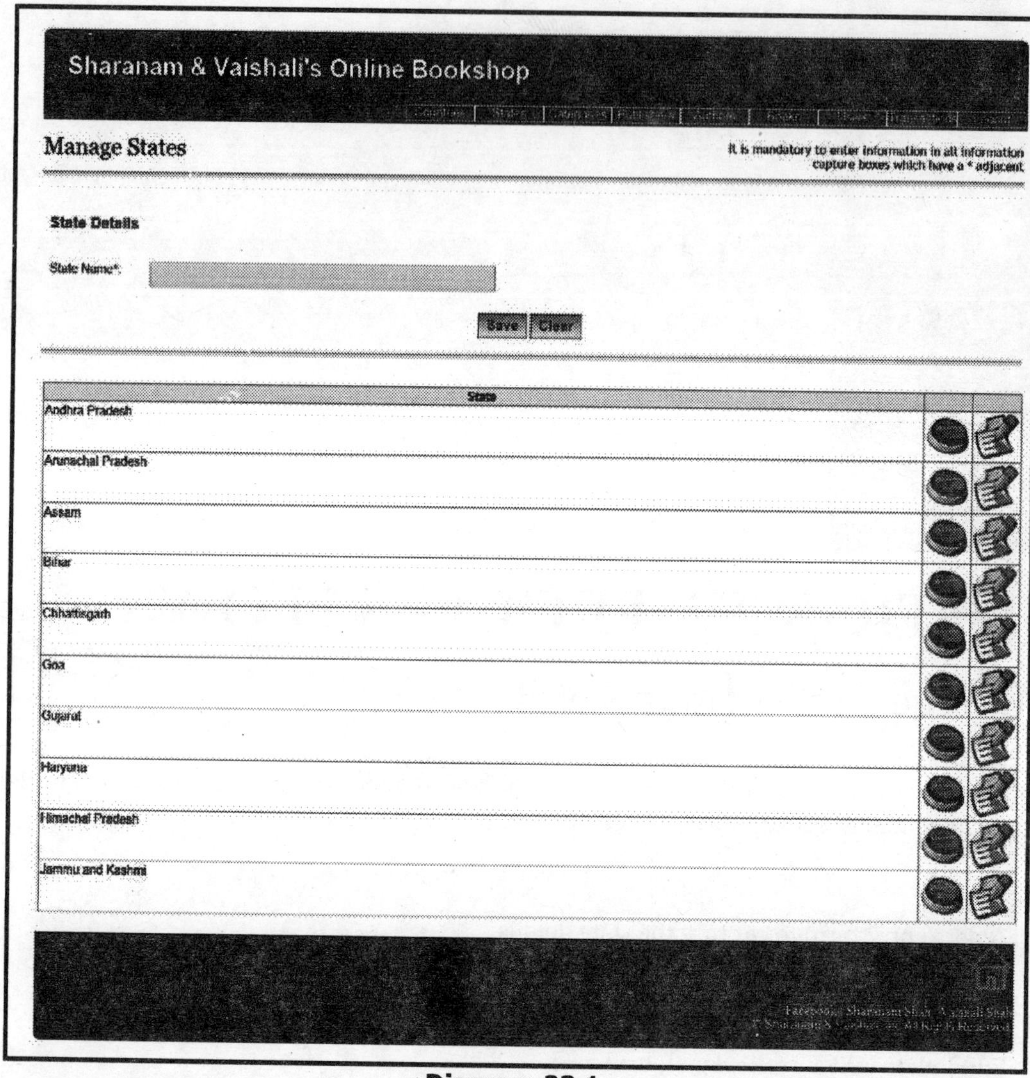

Diagram 23.1

This is a standard data entry form. By default when the form loads, it's in the **INSERT** and **VIEW** mode.

Process Flow

Manage States holds a data grid with a list of available records. This data grid serves the purpose of viewing.

The data grid is populated by **/admin/manageStates** → **StateController [showManageStates()]** → **StateService [listState()]** → **StateDAO [listState()]**.

Here,

- **/admin/manageStates** is the request mapping, which invokes **showManageStates()** of **StateController**
- **StateController** is the controller
- **showManageStates()** is the method available in the controller, which retrieves the list of states via StateService
- **StateService** is the service layer
- **listState()** is the method available in the service, which holds the business logic to return the appropriate list of the available states via StateDAO
- **StateDAO** is the Data Access Layer [DAO]
- **listState()** is the method available in DAO, which does the actual retrieval of the available states from the State database table

Adding New State Details

After **manageStates.jsp** loads, the user can key in the required data and click Save .

Process Flow

After the user keys in the required inputs and clicks Save , the FORM is submitted and the **save** operation is performed by **/admin/saveState** → **StateController [saveState()]** → **StateService [saveState()]** → **StateDAO [saveState()]**.

Here,

- **/admin/saveState** is the request mapping, which invokes **saveState()** of **StateController**
- **StateController** is the controller
- **saveState()** is the method available in the controller, which saves the captured data via StateService
- **StateService** is the service layer

❑ **saveState()** is the method available in the service, which holds the business logic to save the captured data via StateDAO

❑ **StateDAO** is the Data Access Layer [DAO]

❑ **saveState()** is the method available in DAO, which does the actual saving of the captured data in the State database table

If there are any errors such as duplicate state name then manageStates.jsp is re-served along with the error messages, as shown in diagram 23.2.

User Interface For Validation Errors [/admin/saveState → manageStates.jsp]

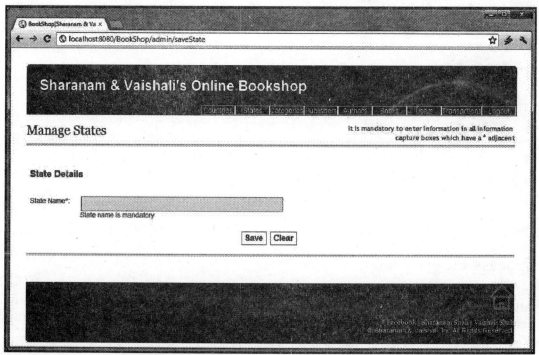

Diagram 23.2: Error messages [manageStates.jsp]

Process Flow

If the captured data is found to be invalid, then Manage States with appropriate error messages is served by **/saveState → StateController → saveState()**.

Here,

□ **/saveState** is the request mapping, which invokes **saveState()** of **StateController**

□ **StateController** is the controller

□ **saveState()** is the method available in the controller, which traps the errors and forwards it to Manage States

Editing Existing State Details

Every record that is listed in manageStates.jsp holds 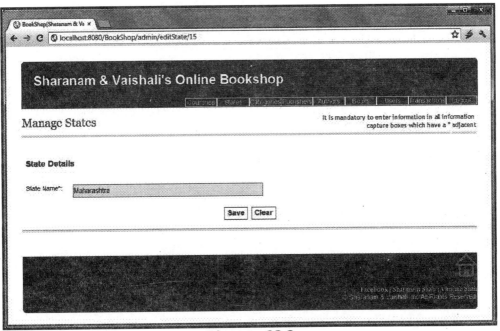, which is hyper linked to a mapping **/admin/editState/${stateNo}**.

79 `<td><a href="/BookShop/admin/editState/${state.stateNo}"><img title="Click to edit" src="/BookShop/images/edit.jpg"/></a></td>`

When the user clicks , manageStates.jsp [pre-populated with the selected state's data] is served, as shown in diagram 23.3.

User Interface [/admin/editState/${stateNo} → manageStates.jsp]

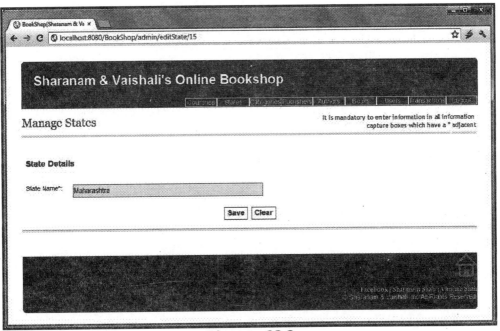

Diagram 23.3

Process Flow

The data population of the selected record for editing is done by the /admin/editState/${stateNo} → StateController [editState()] → StateService [getStateById()] → StateDAO [getStateById()].

Here,

- /admin/editState/${stateNo} is the request mapping, which invokes **editState()** of **StateController**, based on StateNo
- **StateController** is the controller
- **editState()** is the method available in the controller, which retrieves the state details based on StateNo as reference via StateService and re-serves Manage States with the required data
- **StateService** is the service layer
- **getStateById()** is the method available in the service, which holds the business logic to retrieve the state details based on StateNo via StateDAO
- **StateDAO** is the Data Access Layer [DAO]
- **getStateById()** is the method available in DAO, which returns the appropriate state's object from the State database table using **StateNo** as the reference

After the data is populated and thus is available for editing in the data entry form, the user can make the desired changes and click [Save].

After editing the state details, when the user clicks [Save], saveState() of StateController, followed by saveState() of StateService, followed by saveState() of StateDAO takes care of saving the updated states details.

The data is **updated** in the underlying table and Manage States is re-served with the updated record.

Deleting Existing State Details

Every record that is listed in manageStates.jsp holds [image] which is hyper linked to a mapping /admin/deleteState/${stateNo}.

```
78   <td><a href="/BookShop/admin/deleteState/${state.stateNo}"><img title="Click to
     delete" src="/BookShop/images/delete.jpg"/></a></td>
```

When the user clicks the selected record is deleted and manageStates.jsp is re-served.

Process Flow

The record deletion is done by **/admin/deleteState/${stateNo}** → **StateController [deleteState()]** → **StateService [removeState()]** → **StateDAO [removeState()]**.

Here,

- **/admin/deleteState/${stateNo}** is the request mapping, which invokes **deleteState()** of **StateController**
- **StateController** is the controller
- **deleteState()** is the method available in the controller, which deletes the state record based on StateNo as reference via StateService and re-serves Manage States with the available records
- **StateService** is the service layer
- **removeState()** is the method available in the service, which holds the business logic to delete state details based on StateNo via StateDAO
- **StateDAO** is the Data Access Layer [DAO]
- **removeState()** is the method available in DAO, which deletes the appropriate state from the State database table based on **StateNo** received as a reference

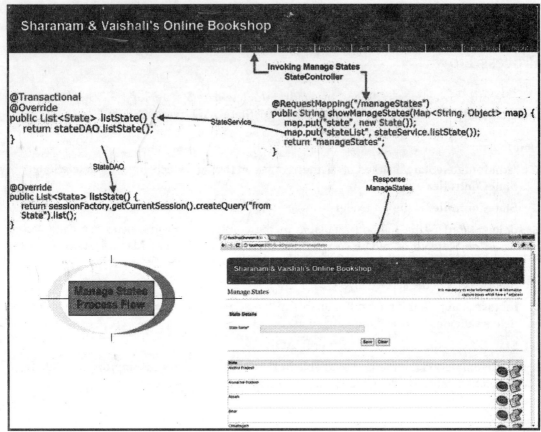

Diagram 23.4: Manage States Process Flow

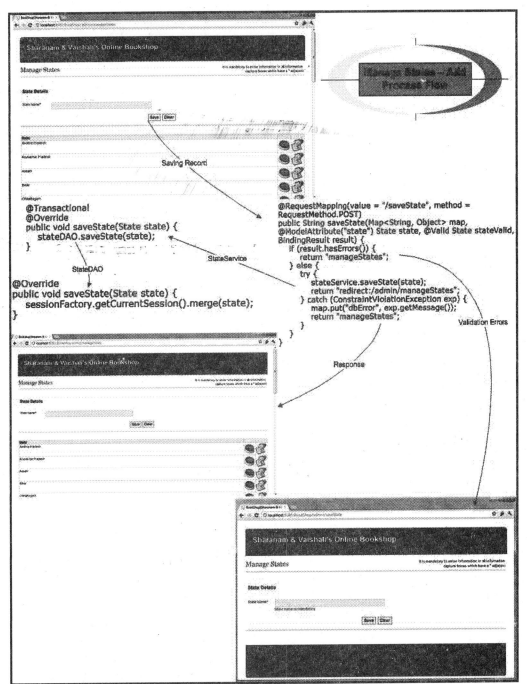

Diagram 23.5: Manage States - Add Process Flow

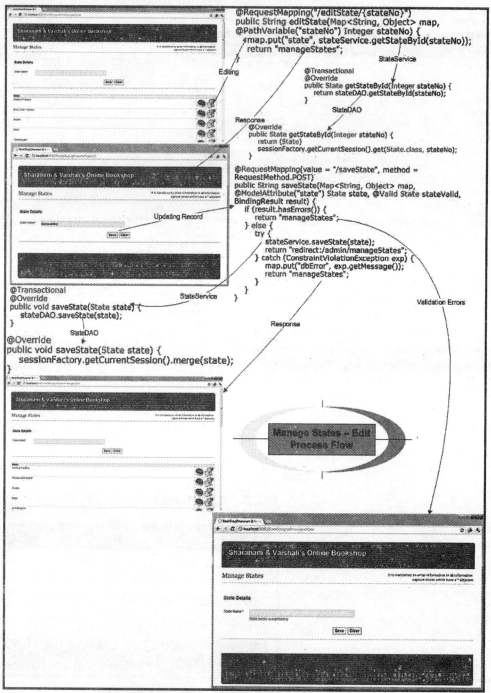

Diagram 23.6: Manage States - Edit Process Flow

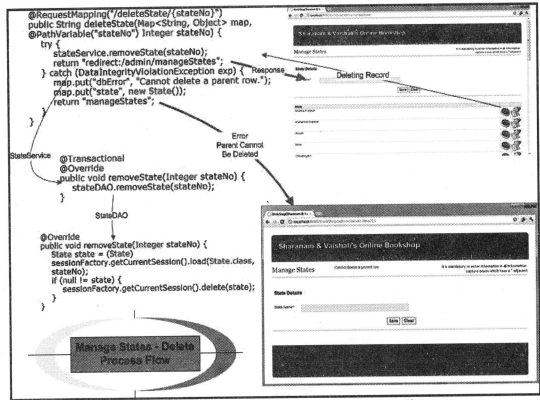

```
@RequestMapping("/deleteState/{stateNo}")
public String deleteState(Map<String, Object> map,
@PathVariable("stateNo") Integer stateNo) {
    try {
        stateService.removeState(stateNo);
        return "redirect:/admin/manageStates";
    } catch (DataIntegrityViolationException exp) {
        map.put("dbError", "Cannot delete a parent row.");
        map.put("state", new State());
        return "manageStates";
    }
}
```

StateService
```
@Transactional
@Override
public void removeState(Integer stateNo) {
    stateDAO.removeState(stateNo);
}
```

StateDAO
```
@Override
public void removeState(Integer stateNo) {
    State state = (State)
    sessionFactory.getCurrentSession().load(State.class,
    stateNo);
    if (null != state) {
        sessionFactory.getCurrentSession().delete(state);
    }
}
```

Manage States - Delete Process Flow

Diagram 23.7: Manage States - Delete Process Flow

Chapter 24

SECTION IV: PROCESS FLOW

Manage Categories [manageCategories.jsp]

Manage Categories is the page that is served when `Categories` is clicked in the Administration section after successful administration login.

It displays:

- ❑ A data entry form to capture the category details
- ❑ List of categories available
- ❑ Delete link to delete a particular category record
- ❑ Edit link to edit a particular category record

Viewing Existing Category Details

When the user clicks `Categories`, manageCategories.jsp is served, as shown in diagram 24.1.

User Interface [/admin/manageCategories →
manageCategories.jsp]

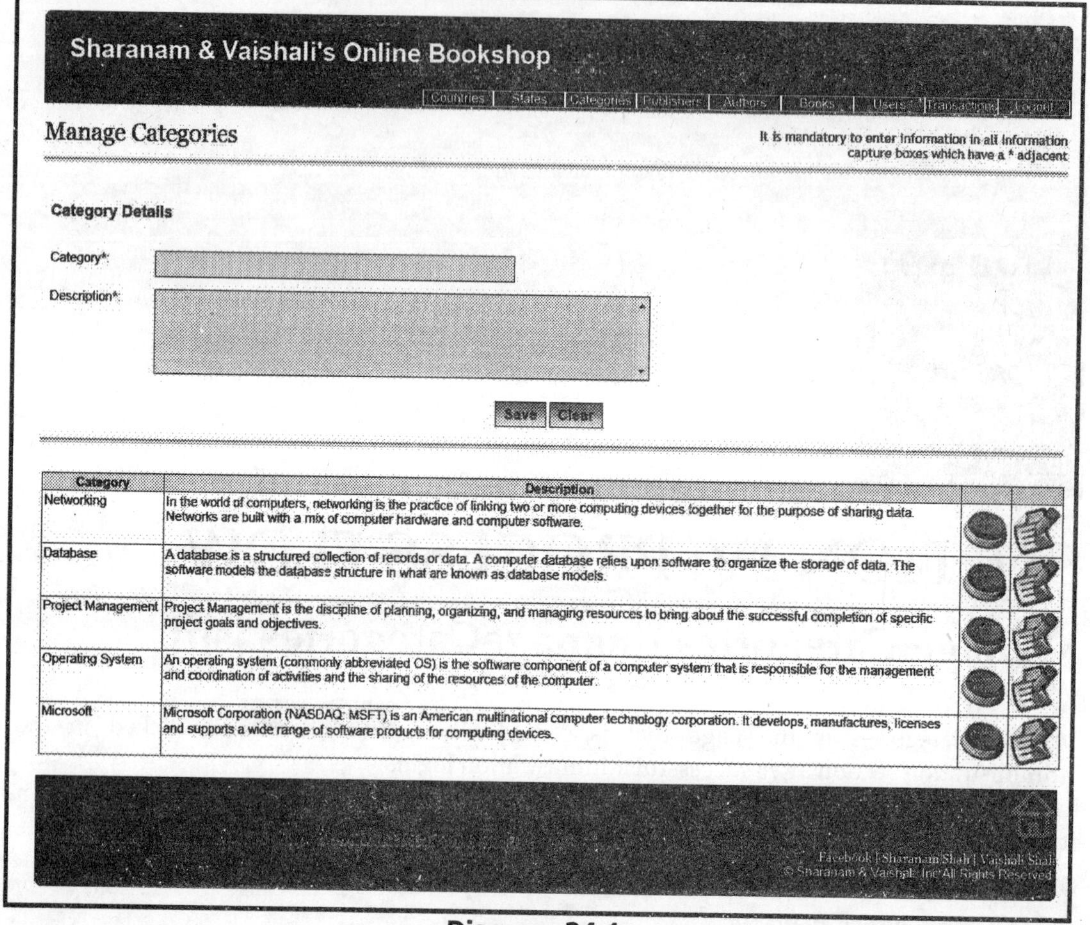

Diagram 24.1

This is a standard data entry form. By default when the form loads, it's in the **INSERT** and **VIEW** mode.

Process Flow

Manage Categories holds a data grid with a list of available records. This data grid serves the purpose of viewing.

The data grid is populated by **/admin/manageCategories** → **CategoryController** **[showManageCategories()]** → **CategoryService** **[listCategory()]** → **CategoryDAO** **[listCategory()]**.

Here,

- ❑ **/admin/ manageCategories** is the request mapping, which invokes showManageCategories() of **CategoryController**
- ❑ **CategoryController** is the controller
- ❑ **showManageCategories()** is the method available in the controller, which retrieves the list of categories via CategoryService
- ❑ **CategoryService** is the service layer
- ❑ **listCategory()** is the method available in the service, which holds the business logic to return the appropriate list of the available categories via **CategoryDAO**
- ❑ **CategoryDAO** is the Data Access Layer [DAO]
- ❑ **listCategory()** is the method available in DAO, which does the actual retrieval of the available categories from the Categories database table

Adding New Category Details

After manageCategories.jsp loads, the user can key in the required data and click 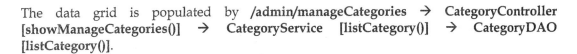.

Process Flow

After the user keys in the required inputs and clicks 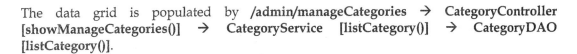, the FORM is submitted and the **save** operation is performed by **/admin/saveCategory** → **CategoryController** **[saveCategory()]** → **CategoryService** **[saveCategory()]** → **CategoryDAO** **[saveCategory()]**.

Here,

- ❑ **/admin/saveCategory** is the request mapping, which invokes **saveCategory()** of **CategoryController**
- ❑ **CategoryController** is the controller
- ❑ **saveCategory()** is the method available in the controller, which saves the captured data via CategorySerive
- ❑ **CategoryService** is the service layer
- ❑ **saveCategory()** is the method available in the service, which holds the business logic to save the captured data via CategoryDAO
- ❑ **CategoryDAO** is the Data Access Layer [DAO]

❑ **saveCategory()** is the method available in DAO, which does the actual saving of the captured data in the Categories database table

If there are any errors such as duplicate category name then manageCategories.jsp is re-served along with the error messages, as shown in diagram 24.2.

User Interface For Validation Errors [/admin/saveCategory → manageCategories.jsp]

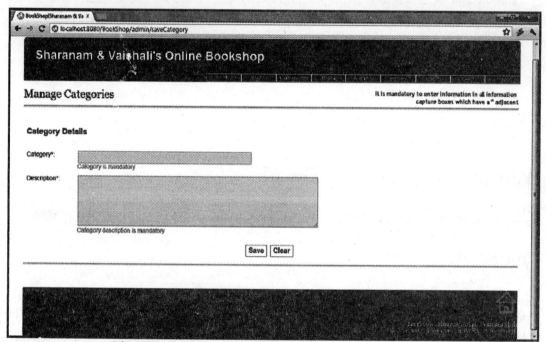

Diagram 24.2: Error messages [manageCategories.jsp]

Process Flow

If the captured data is found to be invalid, then Manage Categories with appropriate error messages is served by **/saveCategory → CategoryController → saveCategory()**.

Here,

❑ **/saveCategory** is the request mapping, which invokes **saveCategory()** of **CategoryController**

❑ **CategoryController** is the controller

□ **saveCategory()** is the method available in the controller, which traps the errors and forward it to Manage Categories

Editing Existing Category Details

Every record that is listed in manageCategories.jsp holds 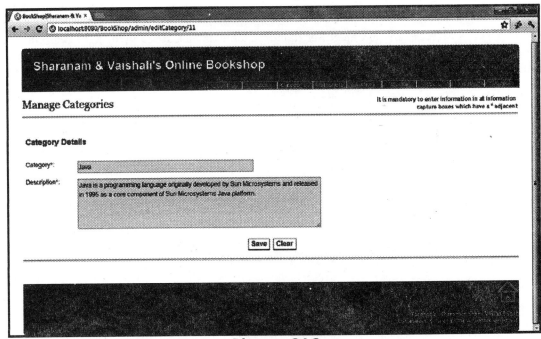, which is hyper linked to a mapping **/admin/editCategory/${categoryNo}**.

```
88  <td><a href="/BookShop/admin/editCategory/${category.categoryNo}"><img
    title="Click to edit" src="/BookShop/images/edit.jpg"/></a></td>
```

When the user clicks , manageCategories.jsp [pre-populated with the selected category's data] is served, as shown in diagram 24.3.

User Interface [/admin/editCategory/${categoryNo} → manageCategories.jsp]

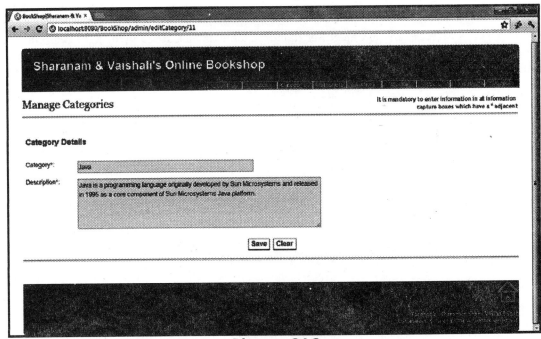

Diagram 24.3

Process Flow

The data population of the selected record for editing is done by the /admin/editCategory/${categoryNo} → CategoryController [editCategory()] → CategoryService [getCategoryById()] → CategoryDAO [getCategoryById()].

Here,

- **/admin/editCategory/${categoryNo}** is the request mapping, which invokes editCategory() of **CategoryController**
- **CategoryController** is the controller
- **editCategory()** is the method available in the controller, which retrieves the category details based on CategoryNo as reference via CategoryService and re-serves Manage Categories with the required data
- **CategoryService** is the service layer
- **getCategoryById()** is the method available in the service, which holds the business logic to retrieve category details based on CategoryNo via CategoryDAO
- **CategoryDAO** is the Data Access Layer [DAO]
- **getCategoryById()** is the method available in DAO, which returns the appropriate category's object from the Categories database table using **CategoryNo** as the reference

After the data is populated and thus is available for editing in the data entry form, the user can make the desired changes and click **Save**.

After editing the category details, when the user clicks **Save**, saveCategory() of CategoryController, followed by saveCategory() of CategoryService, followed by saveCategory() of CategoryDAO takes care of saving the updated categories details.

The data is **updated** in the underlying table and Manage Categories is re-served with the updated record.

Deleting Existing Category Details

Every record that is listed in manageCategories.jsp holds , which is hyper linked to a mapping **/admin/deleteCategory/${categoryNo}**.

```
87  <td><a href="/BookShop/admin/deleteCategory/${category.categoryNo}"><img
    title="Click to delete" src="/BookShop/images/delete.jpg"/></a></td>
```

When the user clicks , the selected record is deleted and manageCategories.jsp is re-served.

Process Flow

The record deletion is done by **/admin/deleteCategory/${categoryNo}** → **CategoryController [deleteCategory()]** → **CategoryService [removeCategory()]** → **CategoryDAO [removeCategory()]**.

Here,

- **/admin/deleteCategory/${categoryNo}** is the request mapping, which invokes **deleteCategory()** of **CategoryController**
- **CategoryController** is the controller
- **deleteCategory()** is the method available in the controller, which deletes the category record based on CategoryNo as reference via CategoryService and re-serves Manage Categories with the available records
- **CategoryService** is the service layer
- **removeCategory()** is the method available in the service, which holds the business logic to delete category details based on CategoryNo via CategoryDAO
- **CategoryDAO** is the Data Access Layer [DAO]
- **removeCategory()** is the method available in DAO, which deletes the appropriate category from the Categories database table based on **CategoryNo** received as a reference

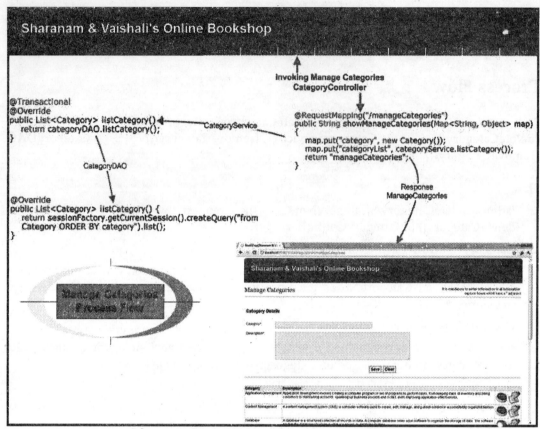

Diagram 24.4: Manage Categories Process Flow

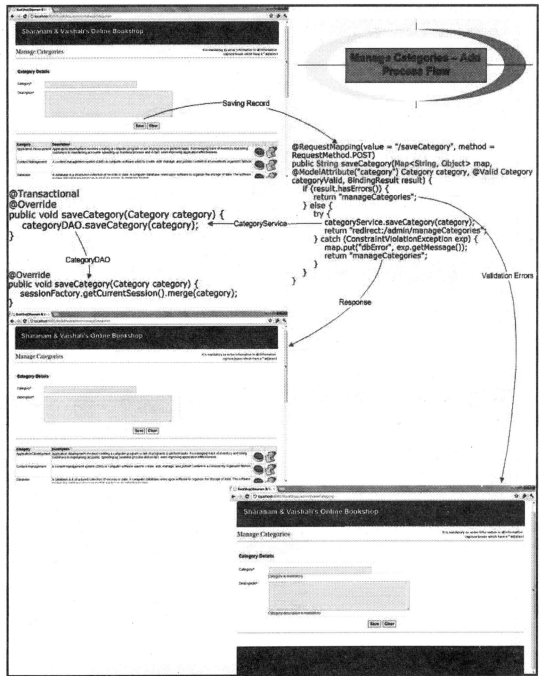

Diagram 24.5: Manage Categories - Add Process Flow

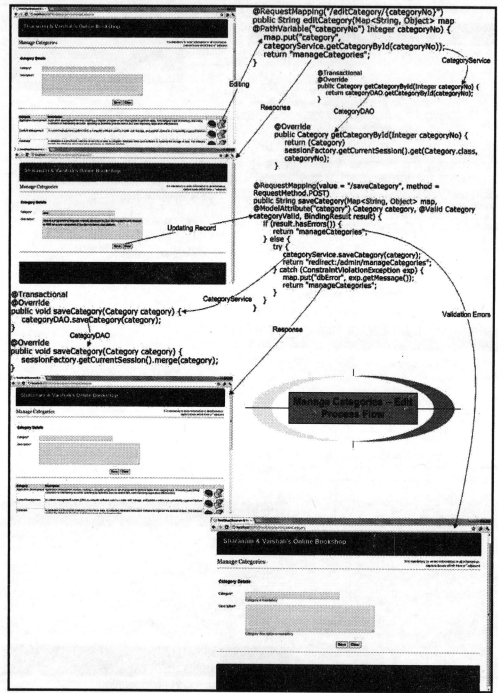

Diagram 24.6: Manage Categories - Edit Process Flow

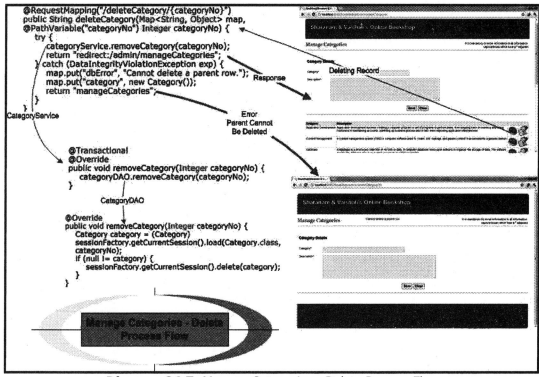

Diagram 24.7: Manage Categories - Delete Process Flow

SECTION IV: PROCESS FLOW

Manage Publishers [managePublishers.jsp]

Manage Publishers is the page that is served when **Publishers** is clicked in the Administration section after successful administration login.

It displays:

- ❑ A data entry form to capture the publisher details
- ❑ List of publishers available
- ❑ Delete link to delete a particular publisher record
- ❑ Edit link to edit a particular publisher record

Viewing Existing Publisher Details

When the user clicks **Publishers**, managePublishers.jsp is served, as shown in diagram 25.1.

User Interface [/admin/managePublishers →
managePublishers.jsp]

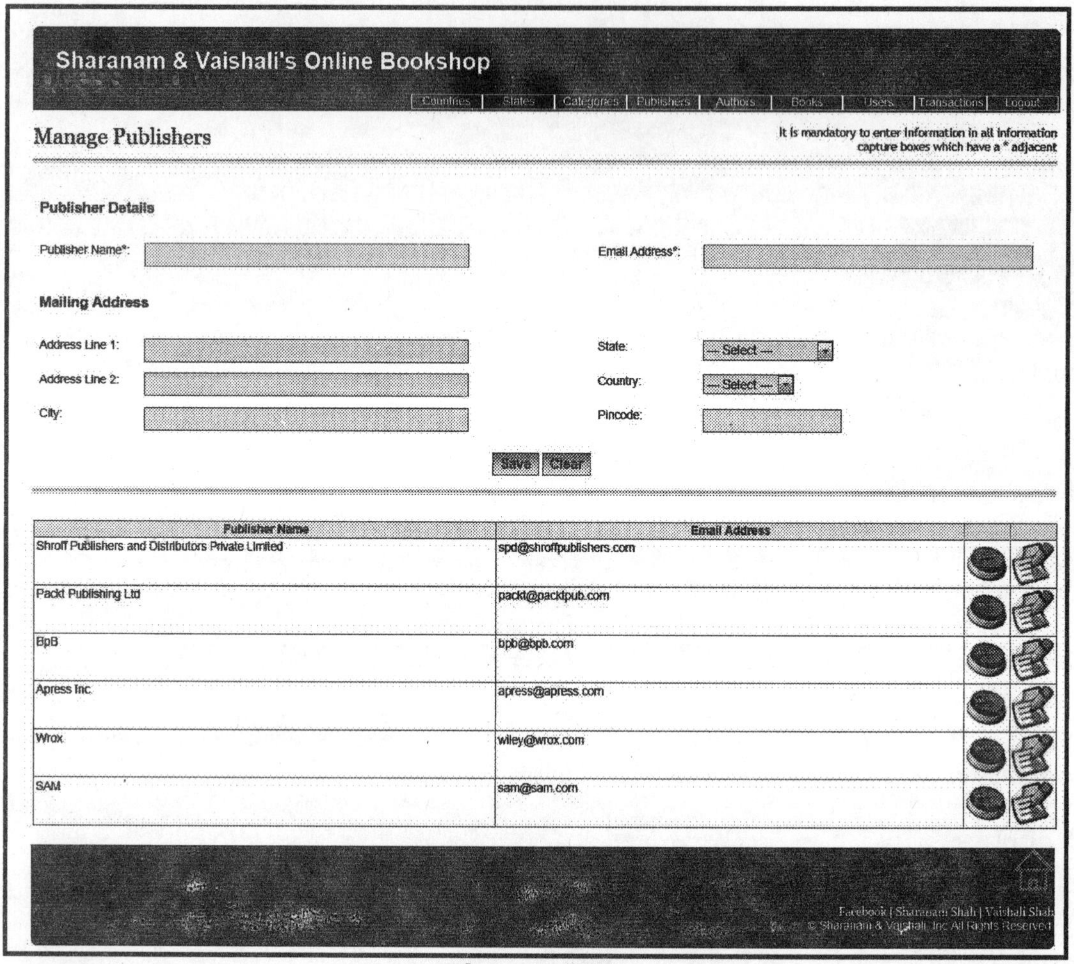

Diagram 25.1

This is a standard data entry form. By default when the form loads, it's in the **INSERT** and **VIEW** mode.

Process Flow

Manage Publishers holds a data grid with a list of available records. This data grid serves the purpose of viewing.

The data grid is populated by /admin/managePublishers → PublisherController [showManagePublishers()] → PublisherService [listPublisher()] → PublisherDAO [listPublisher()].

Here,

- /admin/ managePublishers is the request mapping, which invokes showManagePublishers() of **PublisherController**
- **PublisherController** is the controller
- **showManagePublishers()** is the method available in the controller, which retrieves the list of publishers via PublisherService
- **PublisherService** is the service layer
- **listPublisher()** is the method available in the service, which holds the business logic to return the appropriate list of the available publishers via **PublisherDAO**
- **PublisherDAO** is the Data Access Layer [DAO]
- **listPublisher()** is the method available in DAO, which does the actual retrieval of the available publishers from the Publishers database table

showManagePublishers() also invokes the following methods of the service layers:

Service	Method	Description
CountryService	listCountry()	Holds the business logic to retrieve the list of countries.
StateService	listState()	Holds the business logic to retrieve the list of states.

The Service Layer in turn calls the following methods of the DAO layer:

DAO	Method	Description
CountryDAO	listCountry()	Does the actual retrieval of the available countries from the Countries database table.
StateDAO	listState()	Does the actual retrieval of the available states from the State database table.

Adding New Publisher Details

After managePublishers.jsp loads, the user can key in the required data and click Save.

Process Flow

After the user keys in the required inputs and clicks **Save**, the FORM is submitted and the **save** operation is performed by **/admin/savePublisher** → **PublisherController** **[savePublisher()]** → **PublisherService** **[savePublisher()]** → **PublisherDAO** **[savePublisher()]**.

Here,

❑ **/admin/savePublisher** is the request mapping, which invokes **savePublisher()** of **PublisherController**

❑ **PublisherController** is the controller

❑ **savePublisher()** is the method available in the controller, which saves the captured data via PublisherSerive

❑ **PublisherService** is the service layer

❑ **savePublisher()** is the method available in the service, which holds the business logic to save the captured data via PublisherDAO

❑ **PublisherDAO** is the Data Access Layer [DAO]

❑ **savePublisher()** is the method available in DAO, which does the actual saving of the captured data in the Publishers database table

If there are any errors such as duplicate publisher name then managePublishers.jsp is reserved along with the error messages, as shown in diagram 25.2.

User Interface For Validation Errors [/admin/savePublisher → managePublishers.jsp]

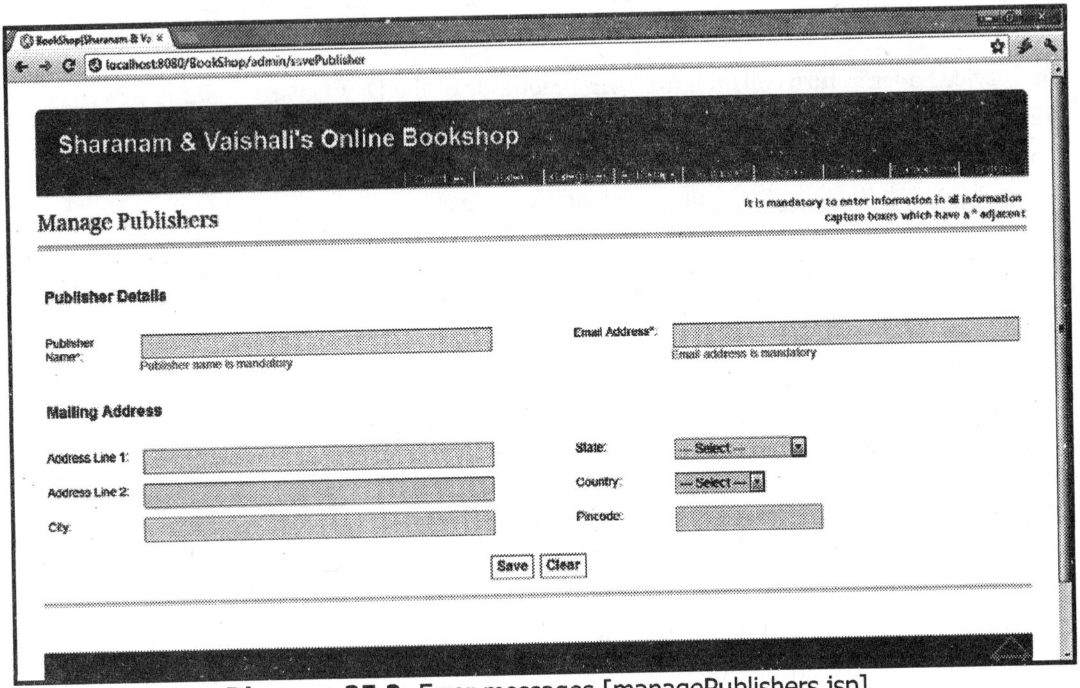

Diagram 25.2: Error messages [managePublishers.jsp]

Process Flow

If the captured data is found to be invalid, then Manage Publishers with appropriate error messages is served by **/savePublisher → PublisherController → savePublisher()**.

Here,

- **/savePublisher** is the request mapping, which invokes **savePublisher()** of **PublisherController**
- **PublisherController** is the controller
- **savePublisher()** is the method available in the controller, which traps the errors and forwards it to Manage Publishers

savePublisher() also invokes the following methods of the service layers:

Service	Method	Description
CountryService	listCountry()	Holds the business logic to retrieve the list of countries.
StateService	listState()	Holds the business logic to retrieve the list of states.

The Service Layer in turn calls the following methods of the DAO layer:

DAO	Method	Description
CountryDAO	listCountry()	Does the actual retrieval of available countries from the Countries database table.
StateDAO	listState()	Does the actual retrieval of available states from the State database table.

Editing Existing Publisher Details

Every record that is listed in managePublishers.jsp holds 🖱️, which is hyper linked to a mapping **/admin/editPublisher/${publisherNo}**.

```
127   <td><a href="/BookShop/admin/editPublisher/${publisher.publisherNo}"><img
      title="Click to edit" src="/BookShop/images/edit.jpg"/></a></td>
```

When the user clicks 🖱️, managePublishers.jsp [pre-populated with the selected publisher's data] is served, as shown in diagram 25.3.

User Interface [/admin/editPublisher/${publisherNo} →
managePublishers.jsp]

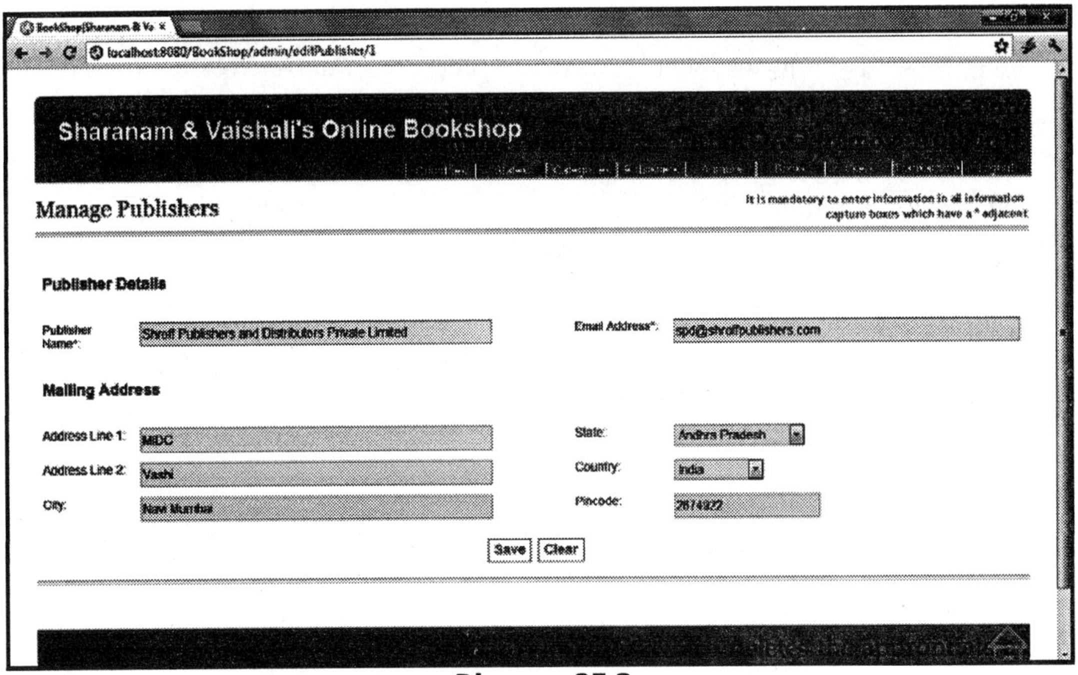

Diagram 25.3

Process Flow

The data population of the selected record for editing is done by the
/admin/editPublisher/${publisherNo} → **PublisherController [editPublisher()]** →
PublisherService [getPublisherById()] → **PublisherDAO [getPublisherById()]**.

Here,

- **/admin/editPublisher/${publisherNo}** is the request mapping, which invokes **editPublisher()** of **PublisherController**
- **PublisherController** is the controller
- **editPublisher()** is the method available in the controller, which retrieves the publisher details based on PublisherNo as the reference via PublisherService and re-serves Manage Publishers with the required data
- **PublisherService** is the service layer

❑ **getPublisherById()** is the method available in the service, which holds the business logic to retrieve publisher details based on PublisherNo via PublisherDAO

❑ **PublisherDAO** is the Data Access Layer [DAO]

❑ **getPublisherById()** is the method available in DAO, which returns the appropriate publisher's object from the Publishers database table using **PublisherNo** as the reference

editPublisher() invokes the following methods of the service layers:

Service	Method	Description
CountryService	listCountry()	Holds the business logic to retrieve the list of countries.
StateService	listState()	Holds the business logic to retrieve the list of states.

The Service Layer in turn calls the following methods of the DAO layer:

DAO	Method	Description
CountryDAO	listCountry()	Does the actual retrieval of available countries from the Countries database table.
StateDAO	listState()	Does the actual retrieval of available states from the State database table.

After the data is populated and thus is available for editing in the data entry form, the user can make the desired changes and click **Save**.

After editing the publisher details, when the user clicks **Save**, savePublisher() of PublisherController, followed by savePublisher() of PublisherService, followed by savePublisher() of PublisherDAO takes care of saving the updated publishers details.

The data is **updated** in the underlying table and Manage Publishers is re-served with the updated record.

Deleting Existing Publisher Details

Every record that is listed in managePublishers.jsp holds 🔘, which is hyper linked to a mapping **/admin/deletePublisher/${publisherNo}**.

```
126  <td><a href="/BookShop/admin/deletePublisher/${publisher.publisherNo}"><img
     title="Click to delete" src="/BookShop/images/delete.jpg"/></a></td>
```

When the user clicks 🔘, the selected record is deleted and managePublishers.jsp is re-served.

Process Flow

The record deletion is done by **/admin/deletePublisher/${publisherNo}** →
PublisherController [deletePublisher()] → **PublisherService [removePublisher()]** →
PublisherDAO [removePublisher()].

Here,

- **/admin/deletePublisher/${publisherNo}** is the request mapping, which invokes **deletePublisher()** of **PublisherController**
- **PublisherController** is the controller
- **deletePublisher()** is the method available in the controller, which deletes the publisher record based on PublisherNo as reference via PublisherService and re-serves Manage Publishers with the available records
- **PublisherService** is the service layer
- **removePublisher()** is the method available in the service, which holds the business logic to delete publisher details based on PublisherNo via PublisherDAO
- **PublisherDAO** is the **D**ata **A**ccess **L**ayer [DAO]
- **removePublisher()** is the method available in DAO, which deletes the appropriate publisher from the Publishers database table based on **PublisherNo** received as a reference

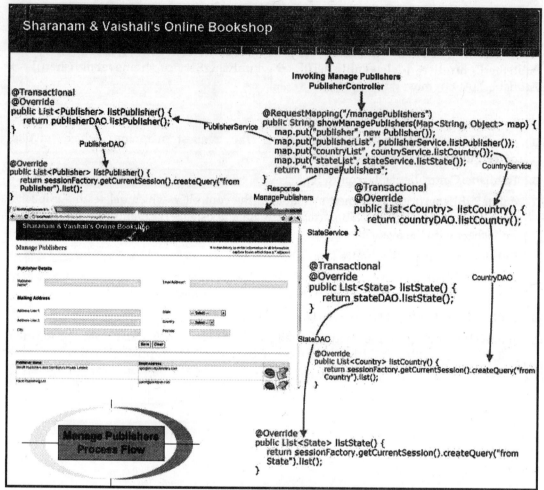

Diagram 25.4: Manage Publishers Process Flow

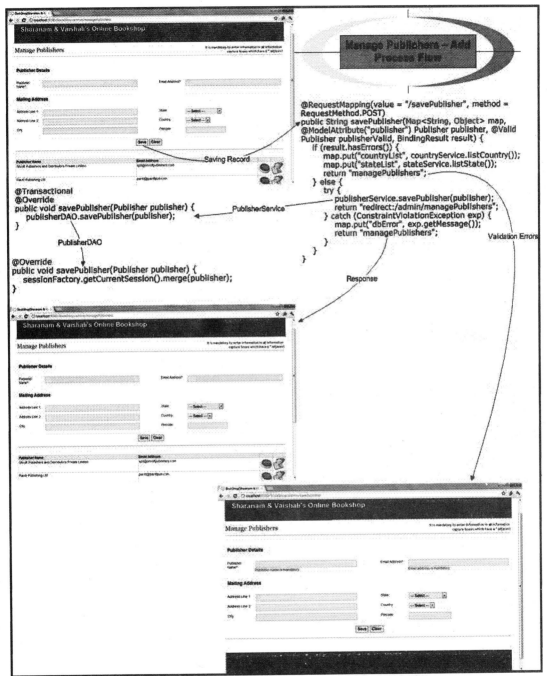

Diagram 25.5: Manage Publishers - Add Process Flow

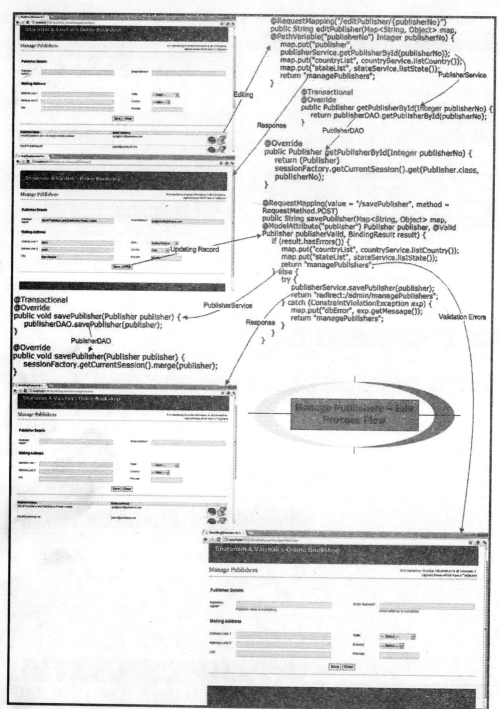

Diagram 25.6: Manage Publishers - Edit Process Flow

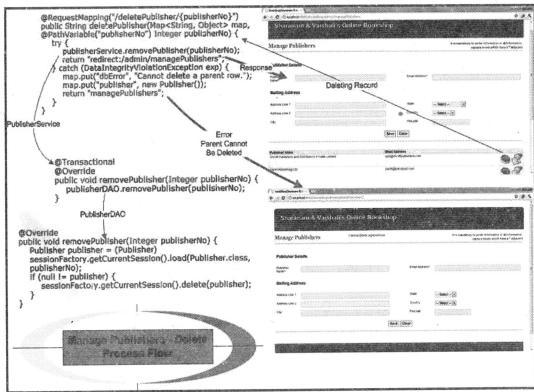

```
@RequestMapping("/deletePublisher/{publisherNo}")
public String deletePublisher(Map<String, Object> map,
@PathVariable("publisherNo") Integer publisherNo) {
    try {
        publisherService.removePublisher(publisherNo);
        return "redirect:/admin/managePublishers";
    } catch (DataIntegrityViolationException exp) {
        map.put("dbError", "Cannot delete a parent row.");
        map.put("publisher", new Publisher());
        return "managePublishers";
    }
}
```

PublisherService

```
@Transactional
@Override
public void removePublisher(Integer publisherNo) {
    publisherDAO.removePublisher(publisherNo);
}
```

PublisherDAO

```
@Override
public void removePublisher(Integer publisherNo) {
    Publisher publisher = (Publisher)
    sessionFactory.getCurrentSession().load(Publisher.class,
    publisherNo);
    if (null != publisher) {
        sessionFactory.getCurrentSession().delete(publisher);
    }
}
```

Manage Publishers - Delete Process Flow

Diagram 25.7: Manage Publishers - Delete Process Flow

Chapter

26

SECTION IV: PROCESS FLOW

Manage Authors [manageAuthors.jsp]

Manage Authors is the page that is served when  Authors is clicked in the Administration section after successful administration login.

It displays:

- ❑ A data entry form to capture the author details
- ❑ List of authors available
- ❑ Delete link to delete a particular author record
- ❑ Edit link to edit a particular author record

Viewing Existing Author Details

When the user clicks Authors, manageAuthors.jsp is served, as shown in diagram 26.1.

User Interface [/admin/manageAuthors → manageAuthors.jsp]

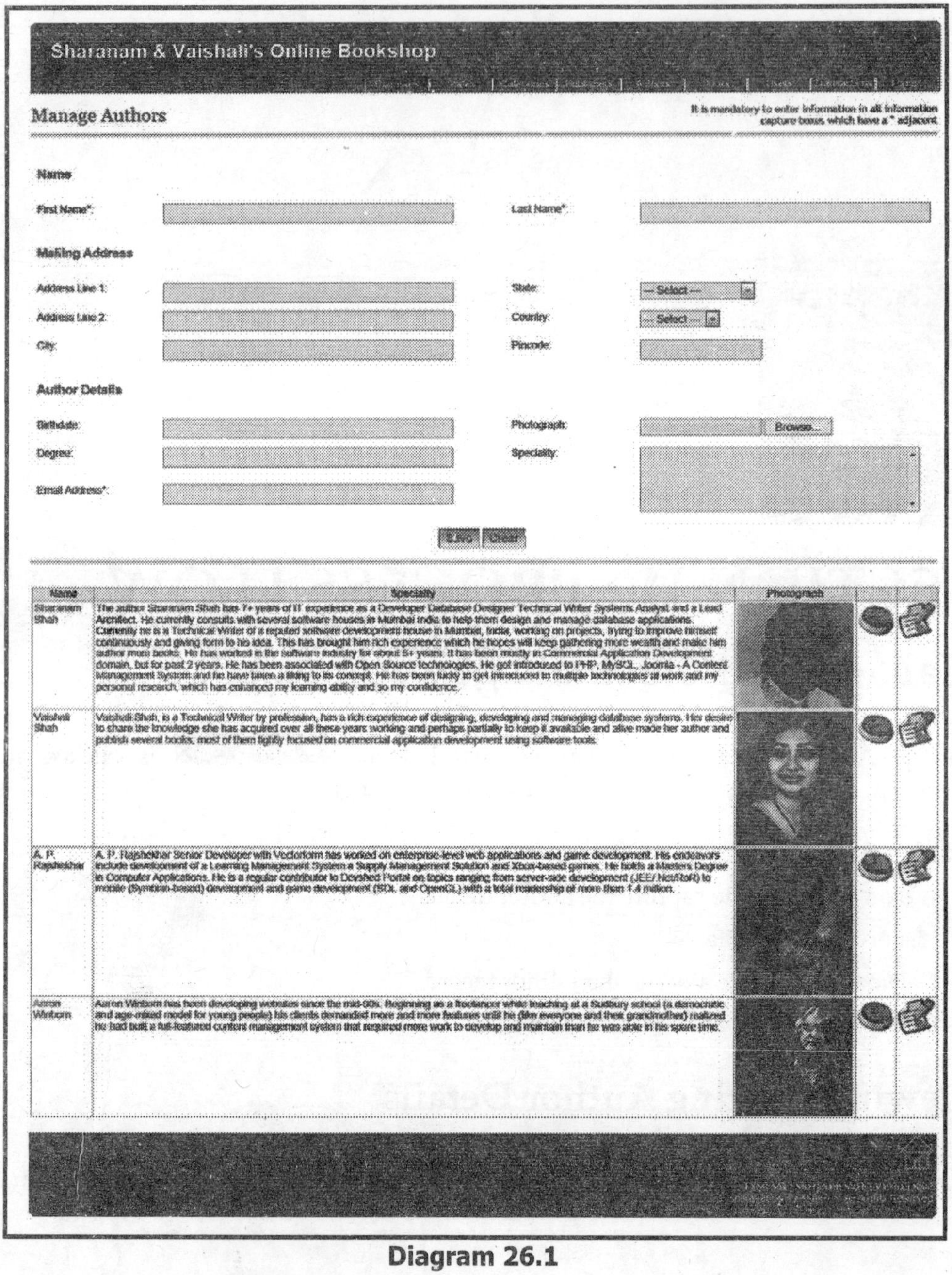

Diagram 26.1

This is a standard data entry form. By default when the form loads, it's in the **INSERT** and **VIEW** mode.

Process Flow

Manage Authors holds a data grid with a list of available records. This data grid serves the purpose of viewing.

The data grid is populated by **/admin/manageAuthors** → **AuthorController** **[showManageAuthors()]** → AuthorService **[listAuthor()]** → AuthorDAO **[listAuthor()]**.

Here,

❑ **/admin/ manageAuthors** is the request mapping, which invokes **showManageAuthors()** of **AuthorController**

❑ **AuthorController** is the controller

❑ **showManageAuthors()** is the method available in the controller, which retrieves the list of authors via AuthorService

❑ **AuthorService** is the service layer

❑ **listAuthor()** is the method available in the service, which holds the business logic to return the appropriate list of the available authors via **AuthorDAO**

❑ **AuthorDAO** is the Data Access Layer [DAO]

❑ **listAuthor()** is the method available in DAO, which does the actual retrieval of the available authors from the Authors database table

showManageAuthors() invokes the following methods of the service layers:

Service	Method	Description
CountryService	listCountry()	Holds the business logic to retrieve the list of countries.
StateService	listState()	Holds the business logic to retrieve the list of states.

The Service Layer in turn calls the following methods of the DAO layer:

DAO	Method	Description
CountryDAO	listCountry()	Does the actual retrieval of available countries from the Countries database table.
StateDAO	listState()	Does the actual retrieval of available states from the State database table.

Adding New Author Details

After manageAuthors.jsp loads, the user can key in the required data and click .

Process Flow

After the user keys in the required inputs and clicks , the FORM is submitted and the **save** operation is performed by **/admin/saveAuthor** → **AuthorController [saveAuthor()]** → **AuthorService [saveAuthor()]** → AuthorDAO [saveAuthor()].

Here,

- **/admin/saveAuthor** is the request mapping, which invokes **saveAuthor()** of **AuthorController**
- **AuthorController** is the controller
- **saveAuthor()** is the method available in the controller, which saves the captured data via AuthorSerive
- **AuthorService** is the service layer
- **saveAuthor()** is the method available in the service, which holds the business logic to save the captured data via AuthorDAO
- **AuthorDAO** is the Data Access Layer [DAO]
- **saveAuthor()** is the method available in DAO, which does the actual saving of the captured data in the Authors database table

If there are any errors such as duplicate email address of the author then manageAuthors.jsp is re-served along with the error messages, as shown in diagram 26.2.

User Interface For Validation Errors [/admin/saveAuthor → manageAuthors.jsp]

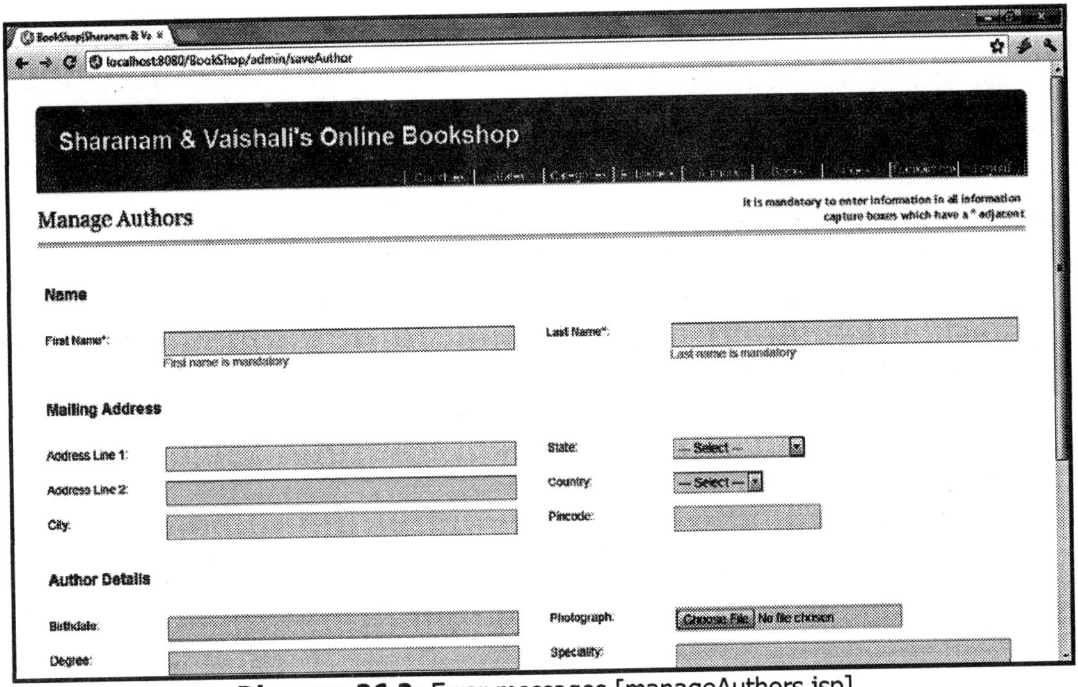

Diagram 26.2: Error messages [manageAuthors.jsp]

Process Flow

If the captured data is found to be invalid, then Manage Authors with appropriate error messages is served by **/saveAuthor** → **AuthorController** → **saveAuthor()**.

Here,

- **/saveAuthor** is the request mapping, which invokes **saveAuthor()** of **AuthorController**
- **AuthorController** is the controller
- **saveAuthor()** is the method available in the controller, which traps the errors and forwards it to Manage Authors

saveAuthor() invokes the following methods of the service layers:

Service	Method	Description
CountryService	listCountry()	Holds the business logic to retrieve the list of countries.
StateService	listState()	Holds the business logic to retrieve the list of states.

The Service Layer in turn calls the following methods of the DAO layer:

DAO	Method	Description
CountryDAO	listCountry()	Does the actual retrieval of available countries from the Countries database table.
StateDAO	listState()	Does the actual retrieval of available states from the State database table.

If the photographs are uploaded by the user, then the photographs are converted to Blob and saved in the Authors database table.

Process Flow

The photographs are converted by **AuthorController [saveAuthor()]** → **CommonService [getBlob()]** → **CommonDAO [getBlob()]**.

Here,

❑ **AuthorController** is the controller

❑ **saveAuthor()** checks whether the photographs are uploaded

❑ **CommonService** is the service layer

❑ **getBlob()** is the method available in the service, which reads the photograph files as byte[] and converts them to Blob via **CommonDAO**

❑ **CommonDAO** is the Data Access Layer [DAO]

❑ **getBlob()** is the method available in DAO, which does the actual conversion of photographs to Blob

Editing Existing Author Details

Every record that is listed in manageAuthors.jsp holds ![icon], which is hyper linked to a mapping /admin/editAuthor/${authorNo}.

```
161  <td><a href="/BookShop/admin/editAuthor/${author.authorNo}"><img title="Click
     to edit" src="/BookShop/images/edit.jpg"/></a></td>
```

When the user clicks ![icon], manageAuthors.jsp [pre-populated with the selected author's data] is served, as shown in diagram 26.3.

User Interface [/admin/editAuthor/${authorNo} → manageAuthors.jsp]

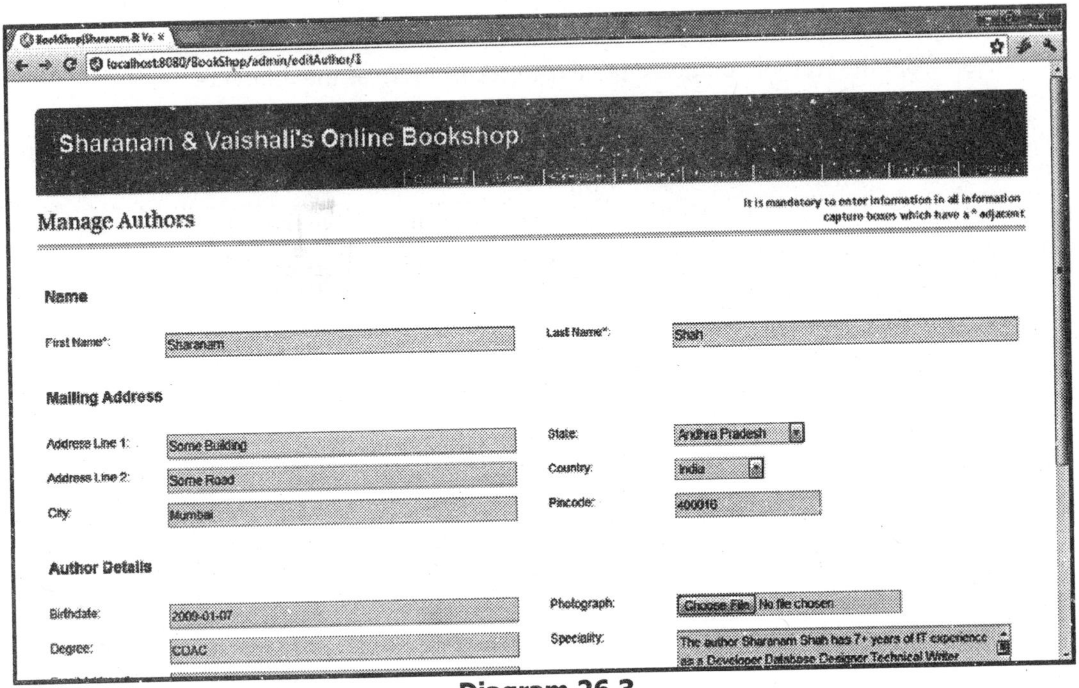

Diagram 26.3

Process Flow

The data population of the selected record for editing is done by the /admin/editAuthor/${authorNo} → **AuthorController** [editAuthor()] → **AuthorService** [getAuthorById()] → **AuthorDAO** [getAuthorById()].

Here,

☐ /admin/editAuthor/${authorNo} is the request mapping, which invokes **editAuthor()** of **AuthorController**

☐ **AuthorController** is the controller

☐ **editAuthor()** is the method available in the controller, which retrieves the author details based on AuthorNo as reference via AuthorService and re-serves Manage Authors with the required data

☐ **AuthorService** is the service layer

- **getAuthorById()** is the method available in the service, which holds the business logic to retrieve author details based on AuthorNo via AuthorDAO
- **AuthorDAO** is the Data Access Layer [DAO]
- **getAuthorById()** is the method available in DAO, which returns the appropriate author's object from the Authors database table using **AuthorNo** as the reference

editAuthor() invokes the following methods of the service layers:

Service	Method	Description
CountryService	listCountry()	Holds the business logic to retrieve the list of countries.
StateService	listState()	Holds the business logic to retrieve the list of states.

The Service Layer in turn calls the following methods of the DAO layer:

DAO	Method	Description
CountryDAO	listCountry()	Does the actual retrieval of available countries from the Countries database table.
StateDAO	listState()	Does the actual retrieval of available states from the State database table.

After the data is populated and thus is available for editing in the data entry form, the user can make the desired changes and click **Save**.

After editing the author details, when the user clicks **Save**, saveAuthor() of AuthorController, followed by saveAuthor() of AuthorService, followed by saveAuthor() of AuthorDAO takes care of saving the updated authors details.

If the user does not edit the photographs, then the original photographs are retained by retrieving them from the Authors database table by saveAuthor() of AuthorController.

The data is **updated** in the underlying table and Manage Authors is re-served with the updated record.

Deleting Existing Author Details

Every record that is listed in manageAuthors.jsp holds ⬤, which is hyper linked to a mapping **/admin/deleteAuthor/${authorNo}**.

```
160   <td><a href="/BookShop/admin/deleteAuthor/${author.authorNo}"><img
      title="Click to delete" src="/BookShop/images/delete.jpg"/></a></td>
```

When the user clicks , the selected record is deleted and manageAuthors.jsp is re-served.

Process Flow

The record deletion is done by **/admin/deleteAuthor/${authorNo}** → **AuthorController [deleteAuthor()]** → **AuthorService [removeAuthor()]** → **AuthorDAO [removeAuthor()]**.

Here,

- **/admin/deleteAuthor/${authorNo}** is the request mapping, which invokes **deleteAuthor()** of **AuthorController**
- **AuthorController** is the controller
- **deleteAuthor()** is the method available in the controller, which deletes the author record based on AuthorNo as reference via AuthorService and re-serves Manage Authors with the available records
- **AuthorService** is the service layer
- **removeAuthor()** is the method available in the service, which holds the business logic to delete author details based on AuthorNo via AuthorDAO
- **AuthorDAO** is the Data Access Layer [DAO]
- **removeAuthor()** is the method available in DAO, which deletes the appropriate author from the Authors database table based on **AuthorNo** received as a reference

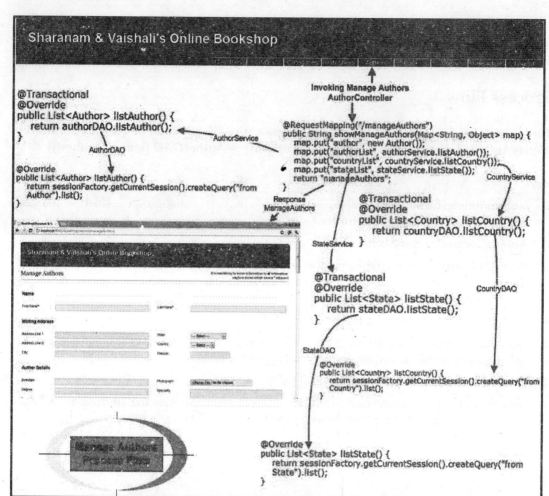

Diagram 26.4: Manage Authors Process Flow

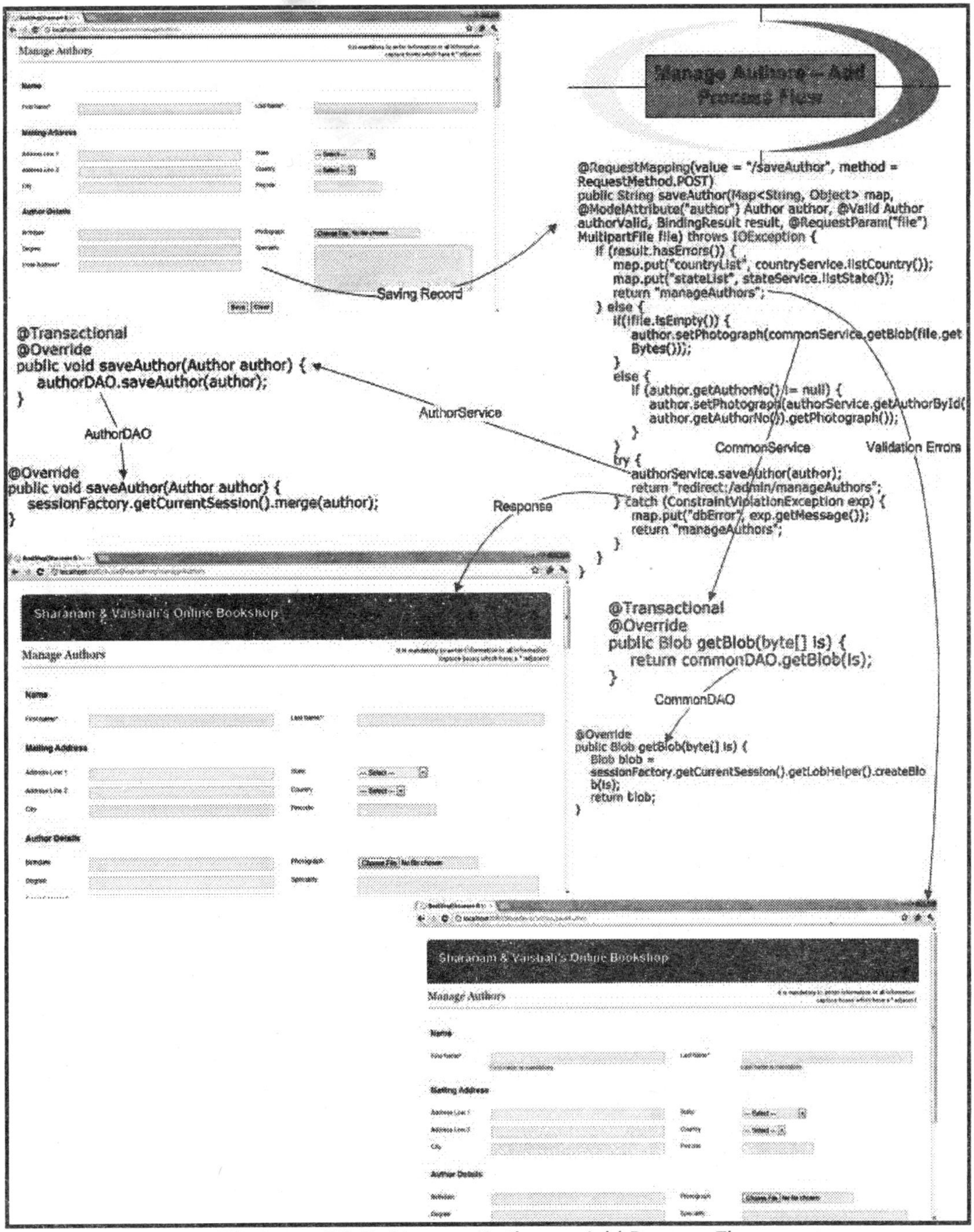

Diagram 26.5: Manage Authors - Add Process Flow

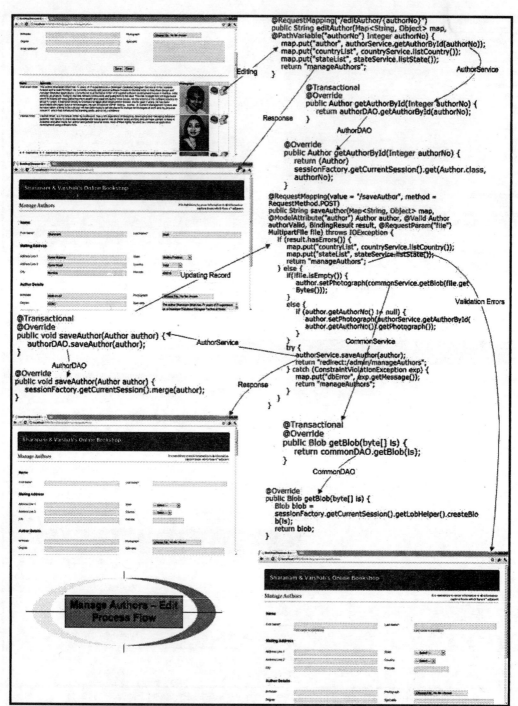

Diagram 26.6: Manage Authors - Edit Process Flow

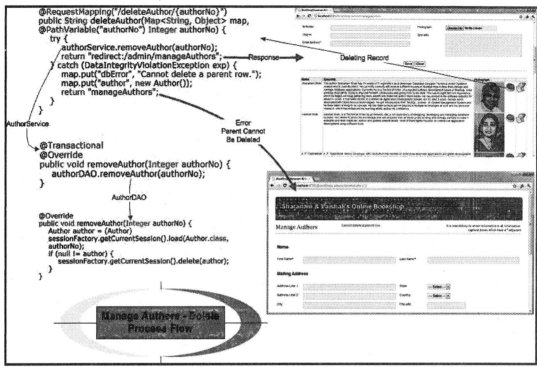

```
@RequestMapping("/deleteAuthor/{authorNo}")
public String deleteAuthor(Map<String, Object> map,
@PathVariable("authorNo") Integer authorNo) {
    try {
        authorService.removeAuthor(authorNo);
        return "redirect:/admin/manageAuthors";
    } catch (DataIntegrityViolationException exp) {
        map.put("dbError", "Cannot delete a parent row.");
        map.put("author", new Author());
        return "manageAuthors";
    }
}
```

AuthorService.

```
@Transactional
@Override
public void removeAuthor(Integer authorNo) {
    authorDAO.removeAuthor(authorNo);
}
```

AuthorDAO

```
@Override
public void removeAuthor(Integer authorNo) {
    Author author = (Author)
    sessionFactory.getCurrentSession().load(Author.class,
    authorNo);
    if (null != author) {
        sessionFactory.getCurrentSession().delete(author);
    }
}
```

Diagram 26.7: Manage Authors - Delete Process Flow

SECTION IV: PROCESS FLOW

Manage Books [manageBooks.jsp]

Manage Books is the page that is served when **Books** is clicked in the Administration section after successful administration login.

It displays:

- A data entry form to capture the book details
- List of books available
- Delete link to delete a particular book record
- Edit link to edit a particular book record

Viewing Existing Book Details

When the user clicks **Books**, manageBooks.jsp is served, as shown in diagram 27.1.

User Interface [/admin/manageBooks → manageBooks.jsp]

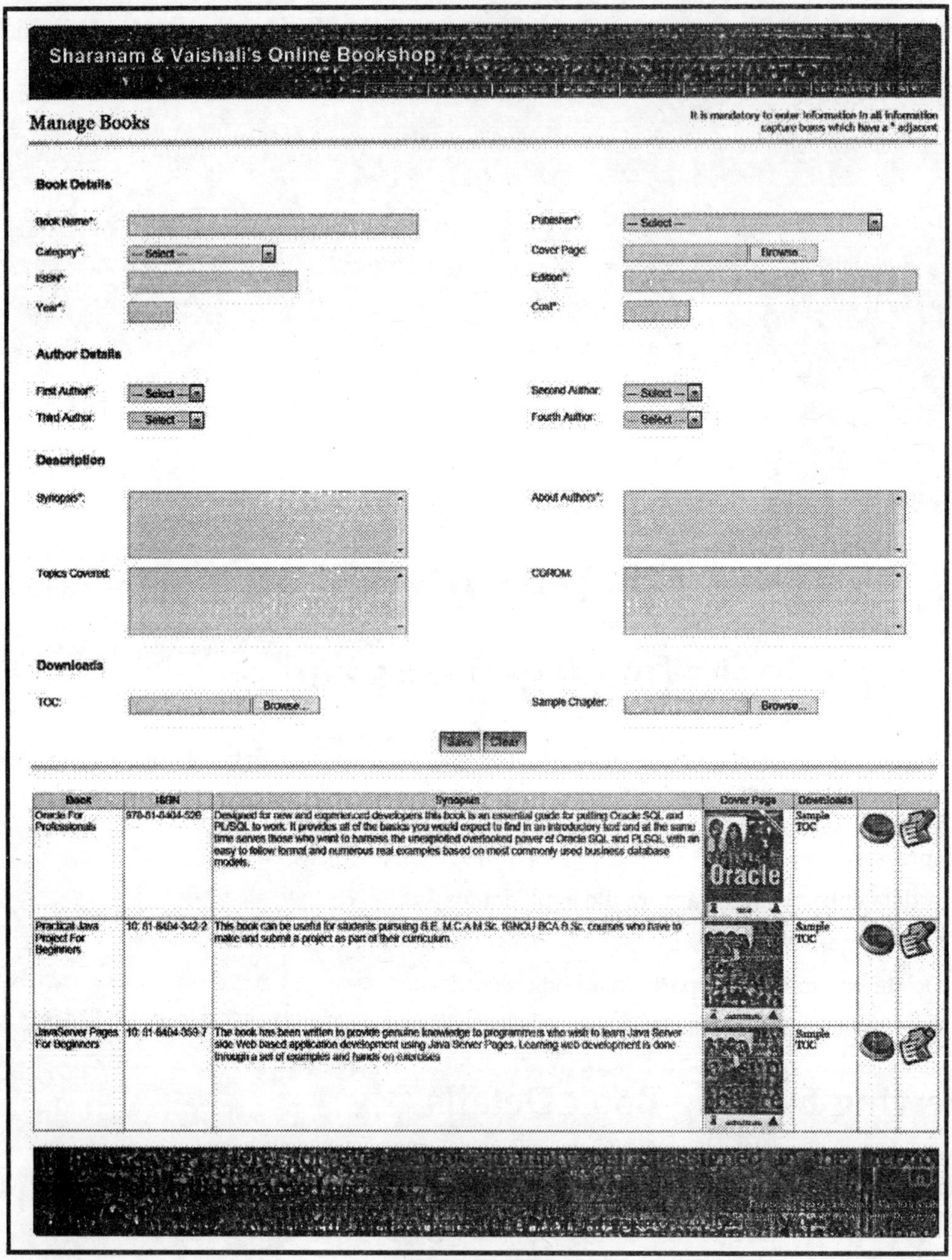

Diagram 27.1

This is a standard data entry form. By default when the form loads, it's in the **INSERT** and **VIEW** mode.

Process Flow

Manage Books holds a data grid with a list of available records. This data grid serves the purpose of viewing.

The data grid is populated by **/admin/manageBooks** → **BookController** **[showManageBooks()]** → **BookService [listBook()]** → **BookDAO [listBook()]**.

Here,

- **/admin/ manageBooks** is the request mapping, which invokes **showManageBooks()** of **BookController**
- **BookController** is the controller
- **showManageBooks()** is the method available in the controller, which retrieves the list of books via BookService
- **BookService** is the service layer
- **listBook()** is the method available in the service, which holds the business logic to return the appropriate list of the available books via **BookDAO**
- **BookDAO** is the Data Access Layer [DAO]
- **listBook()** is the method available in DAO, which does the actual retrieval of the available books from the Books database table

showManageBooks() invokes the following methods of the service layers:

Service	Method	Description
PublisherService	listPublisher()	Holds the business logic to retrieve the list of publishers.
CategoryService	listCategory()	Holds the business logic to retrieve the list of categories.
AuthorService	listAuthor()	Holds the business logic to retrieve the list of authors.

The Service Layer in turn calls the following methods of the DAO layer:

DAO	Method	Description
PublisherDAO	listPublisher()	Does the actual retrieval of available publishers from the Publishers database table.
CategoryDAO	listCategory()	Does the actual retrieval of available categories from the Categories database table.
AuthorDAO	listAuthor()	Does the actual retrieval of available authors from the Authors database table.

Adding New Book Details

After manageBooks.jsp loads, the user can key in the required data and click .

Process Flow

After the user keys in the required inputs and clicks , the FORM is submitted and the save operation is performed by **/admin/saveBook** → **BookController [saveBook()]** → **BookService [saveBook() and notifyCustomersByMail()]** → **BookDAO [saveBook()]**.

Here,

- **/admin/saveBook** is the request mapping, which invokes **saveBook()** of **BookController**
- **BookController** is the controller
- **saveBook()** is the method available in the controller, which saves the captured data via BookSerive
- **BookService** is the service layer
- **saveBook()** is the method available in the service, which holds the business logic to save the captured data via BookDAO
- **notifyCustomersByMail()** is the method available in the service, which notifies the customers about the new released books and updated books via MailService's **sendMail()**
- **BookDAO** is the Data Access Layer [DAO]
- **saveBook()** is the method available in DAO, which does the actual saving of the captured data in the Books database table
- **MailService** is the service layer
- **sendMail()** is the method available in MailService, which sends an email to the customer about the newly released books or the updated books

If there are any errors such as duplicate book name then manageBooks.jsp is re-served along with the error messages, as shown in diagram 27.2.

User Interface For Validation Errors [/admin/saveBook → manageBooks.jsp]

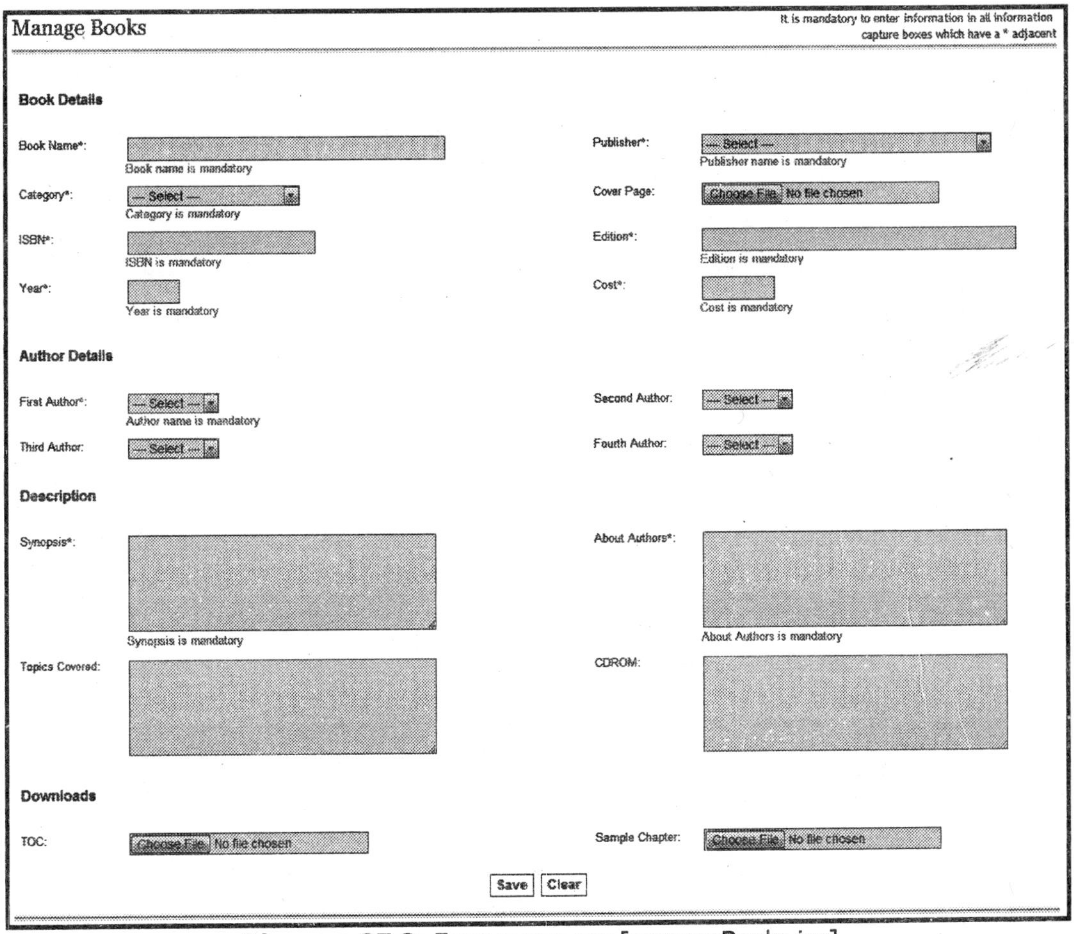

| Manage Books | It is mandatory to enter information in all information capture boxes which have a * adjacent |

Book Details

Book Name*:		Publisher*:	— Select —
Book name is mandatory		Publisher name is mandatory	
Category*:	— Select —	Cover Page:	Choose File No file chosen
Category is mandatory			
ISBN*:		Edition*:	
ISBN is mandatory		Edition is mandatory	
Year*:		Cost*:	
Year is mandatory		Cost is mandatory	

Author Details

First Author*:	— Select —	Second Author:	— Select —
Author name is mandatory			
Third Author:	— Select —	Fourth Author:	— Select —

Description

Synopsis*:		About Authors*:	
Synopsis is mandatory		About Authors is mandatory	
Topics Covered:		CDROM:	

Downloads

| TOC: | Choose File No file chosen | Sample Chapter: | Choose File No file chosen |

Save Clear

Diagram 27.2: Error messages [manageBooks.jsp]

Process Flow

If the captured data is found to be invalid, then Manage Books with appropriate error messages is served by **/saveBook → BookController → saveBook()**.

Here,

❏ **/saveBook** is the request mapping, which invokes **saveBook()** of **BookController**

❏ **BookController** is the controller

❑ **saveBook()** is the method available in the controller, which traps the errors and forwards it to Manage Books

saveBook() invokes the following methods of the service layers:

Service	Method	Description
PublisherService	listPublisher()	Holds the business logic to retrieve the list of publishers.
CategoryService	listCategory()	Holds the business logic to retrieve the list of categories.
AuthorService	listAuthor()	Holds the business logic to retrieve the list of authors.

The Service Layer in turn calls the following methods of the DAO layer:

DAO	Method	Description
PublisherDAO	listPublisher()	Does the actual retrieval of available publishers from the Publishers database table.
CategoryDAO	listCategory()	Does the actual retrieval of available categories from the Categories database table.
AuthorDAO	listAuthor()	Does the actual retrieval of available authors from the Authors database table.

If the files such as cover page, table of contents and sample chapter are uploaded by the user, then the cover page, table of contents and sample chapter are converted to Blob and saved in the Books database table.

Process Flow

The files are converted by **BookController [saveBook()]** → **CommonService [getBlob()]** → **CommonDAO [getBlob()]**.

Here,

❑ **BookController** is the controller

❑ **saveBook()** checks whether a file [such as cover page, table of contents and sample chapter] is uploaded

❑ **CommonService** is the service layer

❑ **getBlob()** is the method available in the service, which reads the files as byte[] and converts them to Blob via **CommonDAO**

❑ **CommonDAO** is the Data Access Layer [DAO]

❑ **getBlob()** is the method available in DAO, which does the actual conversion of photographs to Blob

Editing Existing Book Details

Every record that is listed in manageBooks.jsp holds 📑, which is hyper linked to a mapping **/admin/editBook/${bookNo}**.

212 <td><a href="/BookShop/admin/editBook/${book.bookNo}"><img title="Click to edit" src="/BookShop/images/edit.jpg"/></a></td>

When the user clicks 📑, manageBooks.jsp [pre-populated with the selected book's data] is served, as shown in diagram 27.3.

User Interface [/admin/editBook/${bookNo} → manageBooks.jsp]

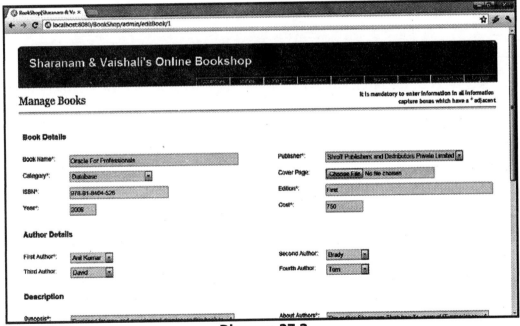

Diagram 27.3

Process Flow

The data population of the selected record for editing is done by the **/admin/editBook/${bookNo}** → **BookController** [editBook()] → **BookService** [getBookById()] → **BookDAO** [getBookById()].

Here,

- /admin/editBook/${bookNo} is the request mapping, which invokes **editBook()** of **BookController**

- **BookController** is the controller

- **editBook()** is the method available in the controller, which retrieves the book details based on BookNo as reference via BookService and re-serves Manage Books with the required data

- **BookService** is the service layer

- **getBookById()** is the method available in the service, which holds the business logic to retrieve book details based on BookNo via BookDAO

- **BookDAO** is the Data Access Layer [DAO]

- **getBookById()** is the method available in DAO, which returns the appropriate book's object from the Books database table using **BookNo** as the reference

editBook() invokes the following methods of the service layers:

Service	Method	Description
PublisherService	listPublisher()	Holds the business logic to retrieve the list of publishers.
CategoryService	listCategory()	Holds the business logic to retrieve the list of categories.
AuthorService	listAuthor()	Holds the business logic to retrieve the list of authors.

The Service Layer in turn calls the following methods of the DAO layer:

DAO	Method	Description
PublisherDAO	listPublisher()	Does the actual retrieval of available publishers from the Publishers database table.
CategoryDAO	listCategory()	Does the actual retrieval of available categories from the Categories database table.
AuthorDAO	listAuthor()	Does the actual retrieval of available authors from the Authors database table.

After the data is populated and thus is available for editing in the data entry form, the user can make the desired changes and click **Save**.

After editing the book details, when the user clicks **Save**, saveBook() of BookController, followed by saveBook() of BookService, followed by saveBook() of BookDAO takes care of saving the updated books details.

If the user does not edit the cover page, table of contents and sample chapter, then the original cover page, table of contents and sample chapter are retained by retrieving them from the Books database table by saveBook() of BookController.

The data is **updated** in the underlying table and Manage Books is re-served with the updated record.

Deleting Existing Book Details

Every record that is listed in manageBooks.jsp holds , which is hyper linked to a mapping **/admin/deleteBook/${bookNo}**.

```
211  <td><a href="/BookShop/admin/deleteBook/${book.bookNo}"><img title="Click to
     delete" src="/BookShop/images/delete.jpg"/></a></td>
```

When the user clicks , the selected record is deleted and manageBooks.jsp is re-served.

Process Flow

The record deletion is done by **/admin/deleteBook/${bookNo}** → **BookController [deleteBook()]** → **BookService [removeBook()]** → **BookDAO [removeBook()]**.

Here,

❑ **/admin/deleteBook/${bookNo}** is the request mapping, which invokes **deleteBook()** of **BookController**

❑ **BookController** is the controller

❑ **deleteBook()** is the method available in the controller, which deletes the book record based on BookNo as the reference via BookService and re-serves Manage Books with the available records

❑ **BookService** is the service layer

❑ **removeBook()** is the method available in the service, which holds the business logic to delete book details based on BookNo via BookDAO

❑ **BookDAO** is the Data Access Layer [DAO]

❑ **removeBook()** is the method available in DAO, which deletes the appropriate book from the Books database table based on **BookNo** received as a reference

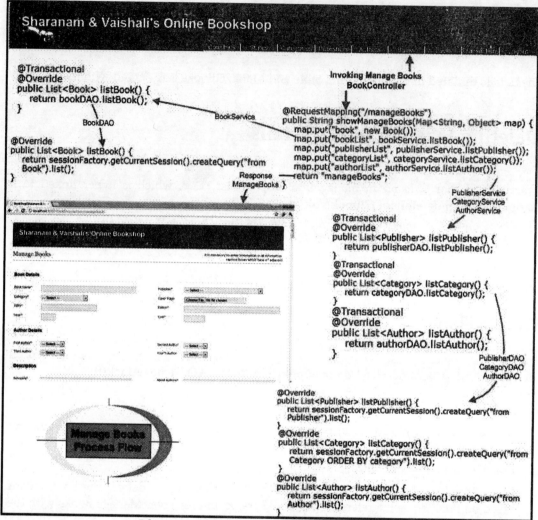

Diagram 27.4: Manage Books Process Flow

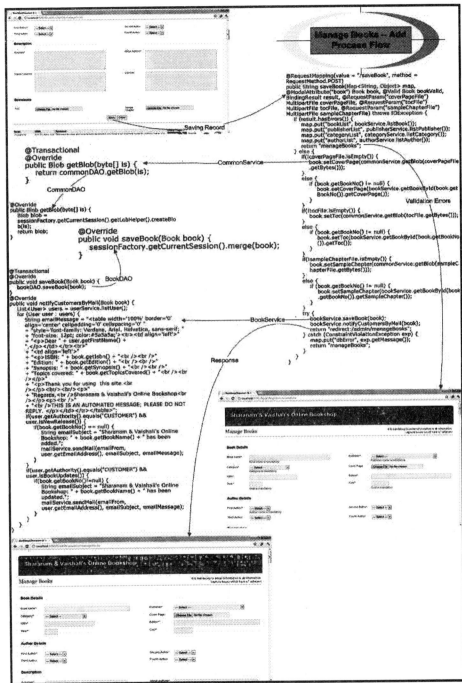

Diagram 27.5: Manage Books - Add Process Flow

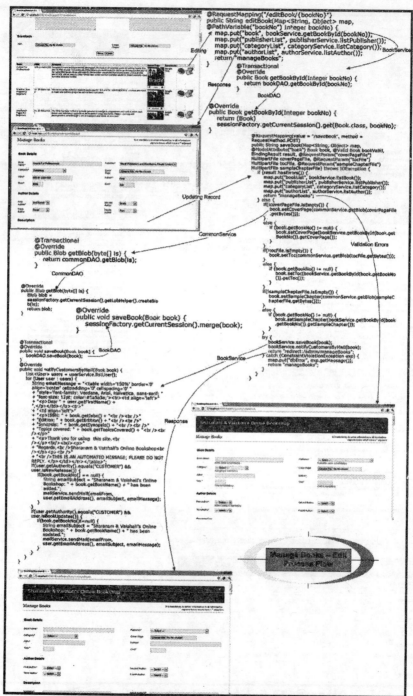

Diagram 27.6: Manage Books - Edit Process Flow

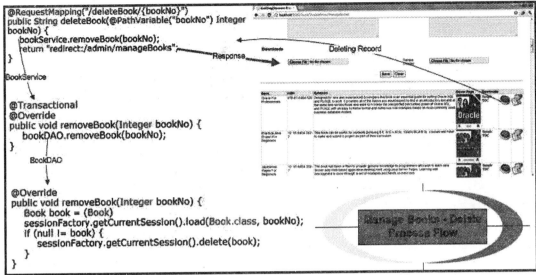

Diagram 27.7: Manage Books - Delete Process Flow

Chapter 28

SECTION IV: PROCESS FLOW
Manage Users [manageUsers.jsp]

Manage Users is the page that is served when  Users is clicked in the Administration section after successful administration login.

It displays:

- ❏ A data entry form to capture the user details
- ❏ List of users available
- ❏ Delete link to delete a particular user record
- ❏ Edit link to edit a particular user record

Viewing Existing User Details

When the user clicks Users , manageUsers.jsp is served, as shown in diagram 28.1.

User Interface [/admin/manageUsers → manageUsers.jsp]

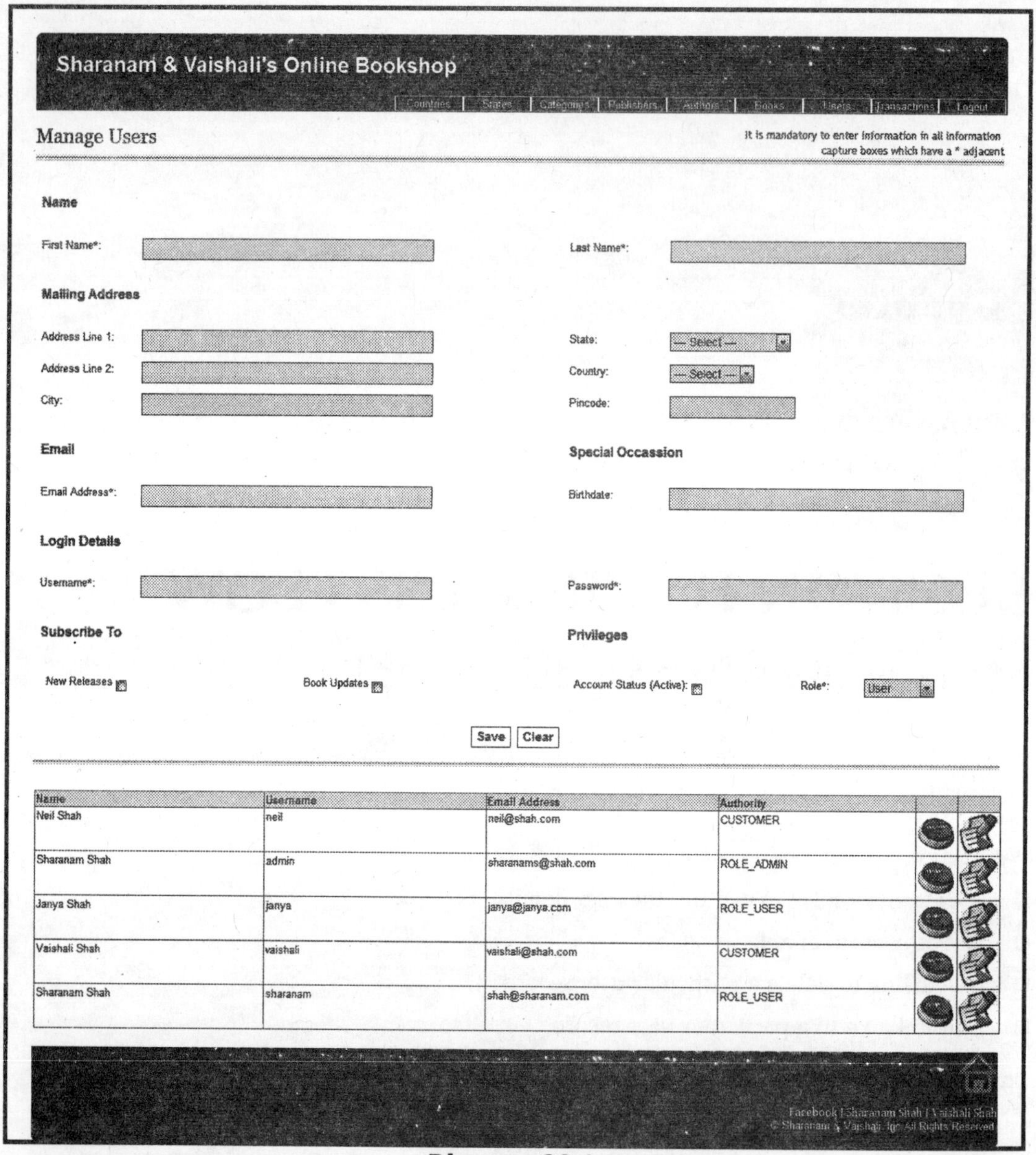

Diagram 28.1

This is a standard data entry form. By default when the form loads, it's in the **INSERT** and **VIEW** mode.

Process Flow

Manage Users holds a data grid with a list of available records. This data grid serves the purpose of viewing.

The data grid is populated by **/admin/manageUsers** → **UserController [showManageUsers()]** → **UserService [listUser()]** → **UserDAO [listUser()]**.

Here,

- **/admin/ manageUsers** is the request mapping, which invokes **showManageUsers()** of **UserController**
- **UserController** is the controller
- **showManageUsers()** is the method available in the controller, which retrieves the list of users via UserService
- **UserService** is the service layer
- **listUser()** is the method available in the service, which holds the business logic to return the appropriate list of the available users via **UserDAO**
- **UserDAO** is the Data Access Layer [DAO]
- **listUser()** is the method available in DAO, which does the actual retrieval of the available users from the Users database table

showManageUsers() invokes the following methods of the service layers:

Service	Method	Description
CountryService	listCountry()	Holds the business logic to retrieve the list of countries.
StateService	listState()	Holds the business logic to retrieve the list of states.

The Service Layer in turn calls the following methods of the DAO layer:

DAO	Method	Description
CountryDAO	listCountry()	Does the actual retrieval of the available countries from the Countries database table.
StateDAO	listState()	Does the actual retrieval of the available states from the State database table.

Adding New User Details

After manageUsers.jsp loads, the user can key in the required data and click **Save**.

On clicking **Save**, the **FORM** is submitted to **/admin/saveUser** and manageUsers.jsp is re-served.

Process Flow

After the user keys in the required inputs and clicks **Save**, the FORM is submitted and the **save** operation is performed by **/admin/saveUser** → **UserController [saveUser()]** → **UserService [saveUser()]** → **UserDAO [saveUser()]**.

Here,

□ **/admin/saveUser** is the request mapping, which invokes **saveUser()** of **UserController**

□ **UserController** is the controller

□ **saveUser()** is the method available in the controller, which saves the captured data via UserService

□ **UserService** is the service layer

□ **saveUser()** is the method available in the service, which holds the business logic to save the captured data via UserDAO

□ **UserDAO** is the Data Access Layer [DAO]

□ **saveUser()** is the method available in DAO, which does the actual saving of the captured in the Users database table

If there are any errors such as duplicate user name then manageUsers.jsp is re-served along with the error messages, as shown in diagram 28.2.

User Interface For Validation Errors [/admin/saveUser → manageUsers.jsp]

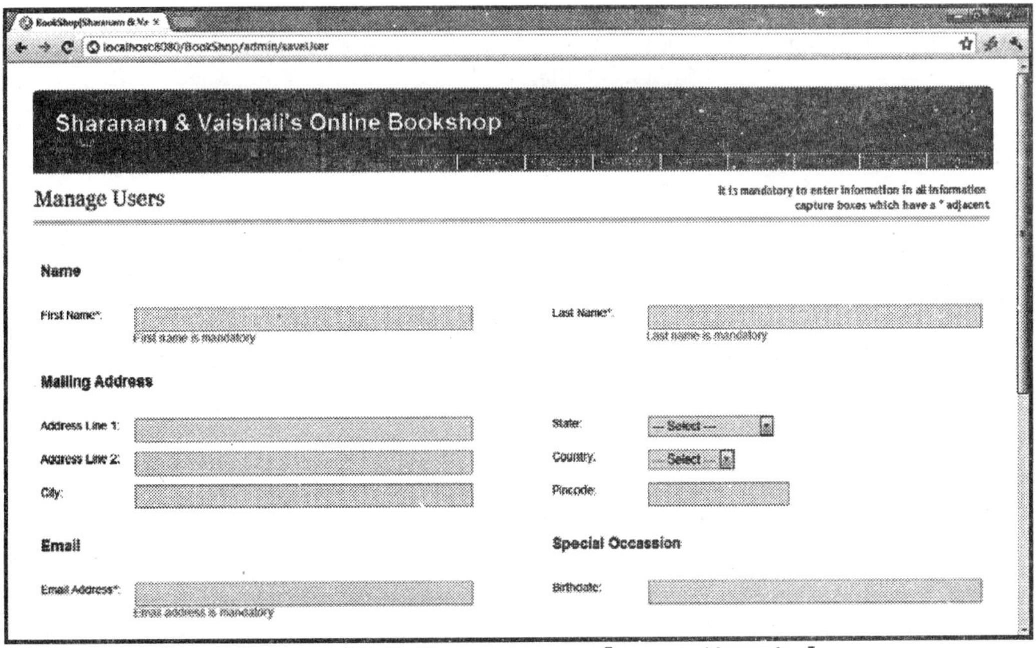

Diagram 28.2: Error messages [manageUsers.jsp]

Process Flow

If the captured data is found to be invalid, then Manage Users with appropriate error messages is served by **/saveUser → UserController → saveUser()**.

Here,

❑ **/saveUser** is the request mapping, which invokes **saveUser()** of UserController

❑ **UserController** is the controller

❑ **saveUser()** is the method available in the controller, which traps the errors and forwards it to Manage Users

saveUser() invokes the following methods of the service layers:

Service	Method	Description
CountryService	listCountry()	Holds the business logic to retrieve the list of countries.
StateService	listState()	Holds the business logic to retrieve the list of states.

The Service Layer in turn calls the following methods of the DAO layer:

DAO	Method	Description
CountryDAO	listCountry()	Does the actual retrieval of the available countries from the Countries database table.
StateDAO	listState()	Does the actual retrieval of the available states from the State database table.

Editing Existing User Details

Every record that is listed in manageUsers.jsp holds ![icon], which is hyper linked to a mapping **/admin/editUser/${userNo}**.

```
200  <td><a href="/BookShop/admin/editUser/${user.userNo}"><img title="Click to edit"
     src="/BookShop/images/edit.jpg"/></a></td>
```

When the user clicks ![icon], manageUsers.jsp [pre-populated with the selected user's data] is served, as shown in diagram 28.3.

User Interface [/admin/editUser/${userNo} → manageUsers.jsp]

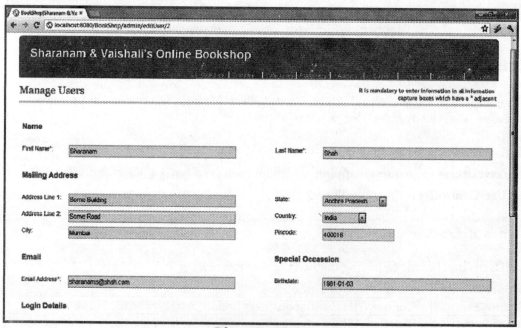

Diagram 28.3

Process Flow

The data population of the selected record for editing is done by the /admin/editUser/${userNo} → UserController [editUser()] → UserService [getUserById()] → UserDAO [getUserById()].

Here,

- /admin/editUser/${userNo} is the request mapping, which invokes **editUser()** of **UserController**
- **UserController** is the controller
- **editUser()** is the method available in the controller, which retrieves the user details based on UserNo as the reference via UserService
- **UserService** is the service layer
- **getUserById()** is the method available in the service, which holds the business logic to retrieve user details based on UserNo via UserDAO
- **UserDAO** is the Data Access Layer [DAO]
- **getUserById()** is the method available in DAO, which returns the appropriate user's object from the Users database table using **UserNo** as the reference

editUser() invokes the following methods of the service layers:

Service	Method	Description
CountryService	listCountry()	Holds the business logic to retrieve the list of countries.
StateService	listState()	Holds the business logic to retrieve the list of states.

The Service Layer in turn calls the following methods of the DAO layer:

DAO	Method	Description
CountryDAO	listCountry()	Does the actual retrieval of available countries from the Countries database table.
StateDAO	listState()	Does the actual retrieval of available states from the State database table.

After the data is populated and thus is available for editing in the data entry form, the user can make the desired changes and click **Save**.

After editing the user details, when the user clicks **Save**, saveUser() of UserController, followed by saveUser() of UserService, followed by saveUser() of UserDAO takes care of saving the updated users details.

The data is **updated** in the underlying table and Manage Users is re-served with the updated record.

Deleting Existing User Details

Every record that is listed in manageUsers.jsp holds ⬤ , which is hyper linked to a mapping **/admin/deleteUser/${userNo}**.

```
199  <td><a href="/BookShop/admin/deleteUser/${user.userNo}"><img title="Click to
     delete" src="/BookShop/images/delete.jpg"/></a></td>
```

When the user clicks ⬤ , the selected record is deleted and manageUsers.jsp is re-served.

Process Flow

The record deletion is done by **/admin/deleteUser/${userNo}** → **UserController [deleteUser()]** → **UserService [removeUser()]** → **UserDAO [removeUser()]**.

Here,

❑ **/admin/deleteUser/${userNo}** is the request mapping, which invokes **deleteUser()** of **UserController**

❑ **UserController** is the controller, which holds a mapping to help delete a user record from Manage Users

❑ **deleteUser()** is the method available in the controller, which deletes the user record based on UserNo as reference via UserService. deleteUser() first checks whether the user is admin. If the user is an admin, then the application displays an error and does not delete the user from the Users database table

❑ **UserService** is the service layer

❑ **removeUser()** is the method available in the service, which holds the business logic to delete user details based on UserNo via UserDAO

❑ **UserDAO** is the Data Access Layer [DAO]

❑ **removeUser()** is the method available in DAO, which deletes the appropriate user from the Users database table based on **UserNo** received as a reference

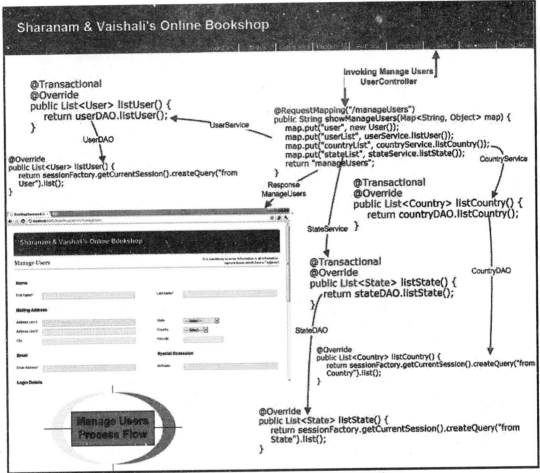

Diagram 28.4: Manage Users Process Flow

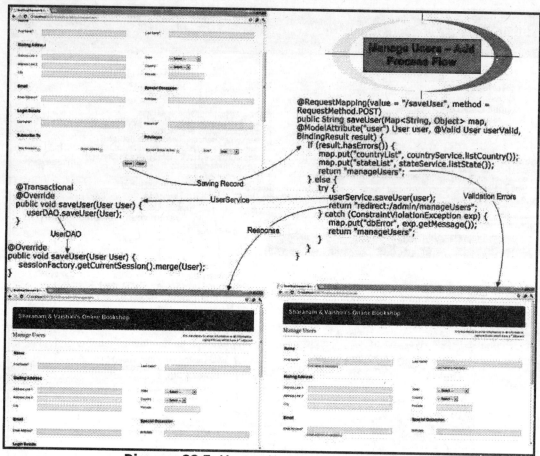

Diagram 28.5: Manage Users - Add Process Flow

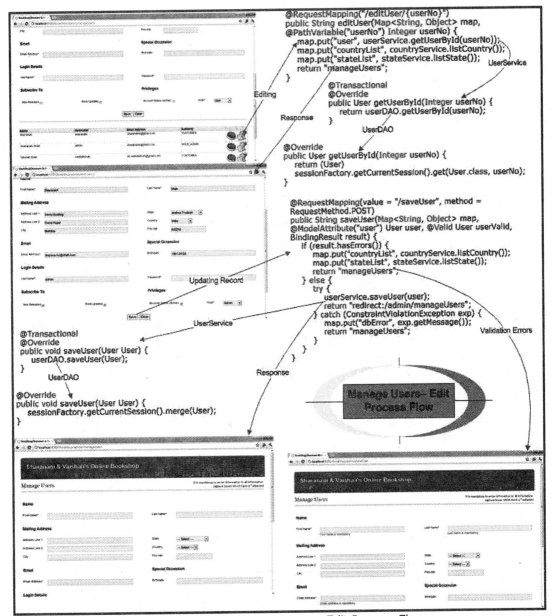

Diagram 28.6: Manage Users - Edit Process Flow

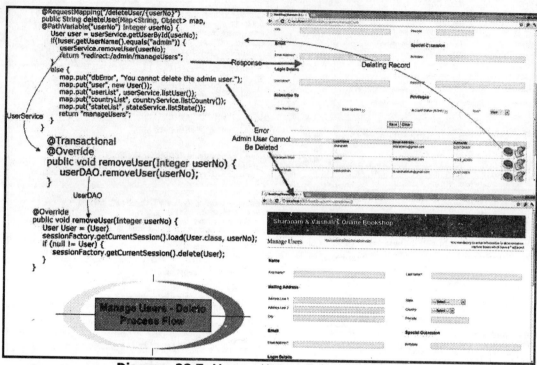

Diagram 28.7: Manage Users - Delete Process Flow

Chapter

29

SECTION IV: PROCESS FLOW

Manage Transactions [manageTransactions.jsp]

Manage Transactions is the page that is served when  Transactions is clicked in the Administration section after successful administration login.

Manage Transactions:

❑ Accepts the username and accordingly displays the transactions for that particular user

❑ Accepts the date and accordingly displays the transactions taken place on that particular day

❑ Allows updating the Google Order ID, once the seller receives the email from Google Wallet indicating the order and payment made by the customer

Displaying The Manage Transactions Page

When the user clicks Transactions, manageTransactions.jsp is served, as shown in diagram 29.1.

User Interface [/admin/manageTransactions → manageTransactions.jsp]

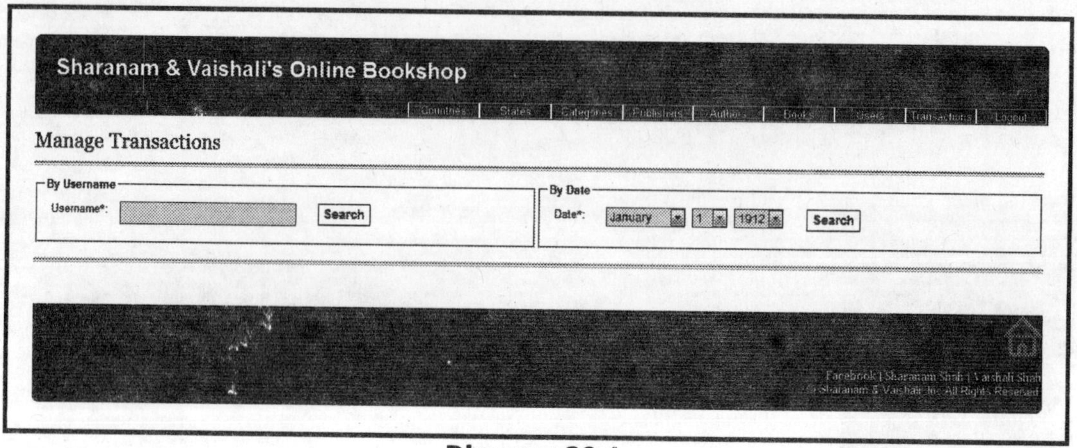

Diagram 29.1

Process Flow

Manage Transactions holds a data entry form which accepts the username/date.

The data entry form is displayed by **/admin/manageTransactions → TransactionController** **[showManageTransactions()]**.

Here,

- **/admin/ manageTransactions** is the request mapping, which invokes showManageTransactions() of **TransactionController**
- **TransactionController** is the controller
- **showManageTransactions()** is the method available in the controller, which displays the data entry form which accepts the username/date to display the list of transactions according to that particular username/date

Displaying Transactions According To Username

Displaying Only Particular User's Transactions

After manageTransactions.jsp loads, the user can key in the required username and click **Search**.

On clicking **Search**, the **FORM** is submitted to **/admin/searchTransactionsByUsername/${userName}** and manageTransactions.jsp is reserved.

User Interface [/admin/searchTransactionByUsername/${userName} → manageTransactions.jsp]

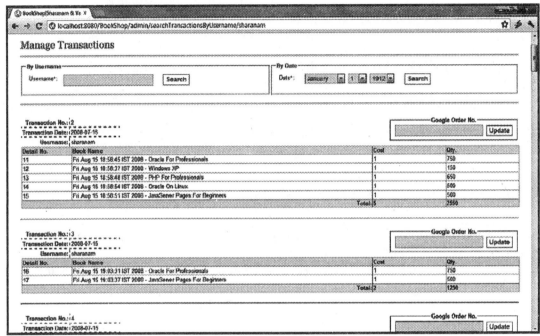

Diagram 29.2

Process Flow

After the user keys in the required inputs and clicks **Search**, the FORM is submitted and the **search** operation is performed by **/admin/searchTransactionByUsername/${userName}** → **TransactionController [showTransactionsByUsername()]**.

Here,

☐ **/admin/searchTransactionsByUsername/${userName}** is the request mapping, which invokes **showTransactionsByUsername()** of **TransactionController**

☐ **TransactionController** is the controller

❑ **showTransactionsByUsername()** is the method available in the controller, which displays the list of transactions based on the Username

showTransactionsByUsername() invokes the following methods of **TransactionService:**

Method	Description
listGroupedTransactionsByUsername()	Holds the business logic to retrieve the list of transactions made by the customer.
listTransactionsByUsername()	Holds the business logic to retrieve the details of the listed transactions.

TransactionService's methods in turn call the following methods of TransactionDAO:

Method	Description
listGroupedTransactionsByUsername()	Does the actual retrieval of the available transactions made by the customer.
listTransactionsByUsername()	Does the actual retrieval of the available transactions details.

Displaying All User's Transactions

After manageTransactions.jsp loads, the user can click Search without entering a username.

On doing so, the **FORM** is submitted to **/admin/searchTransactionsByUsername** and manageTransactions.jsp is re-served.

User Interface [/admin/searchTransactionByUsername → manageTransactions.jsp]

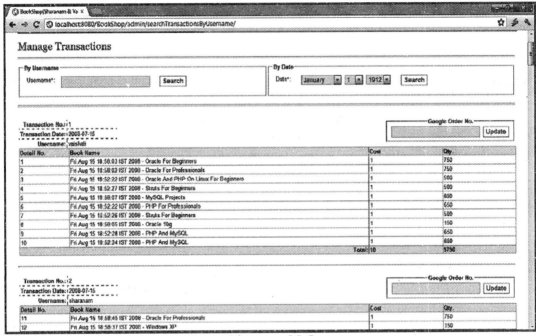

Diagram 29.3

Process Flow

After the user clicks **Save**, the FORM is submitted and the **search** operation is performed by **/admin/searchTransactionByUsername → TransactionController [showTransactions()]**.

Here,

- **/admin/searchTransactionsByUsername** is the request mapping, which invokes **showTransactions()** of **TransactionController**
- **TransactionController** is the controller
- **showTransactions()** is the method available in the controller, which displays a list of all transactions

showTransactions() invokes the following methods of **TransactionService**:

Method	Description
listGroupedTransactions()	Holds the business logic to retrieve the list of all transactions.
listTransactions()	Holds the business logic to retrieve the details of the listed transactions.

TransactionService's methods in turn call the following methods of TransactionDAO:

Method	Description
listGroupedTransactions()	Does the actual retrieval of the available transactions.
listTransactions()	Does the actual retrieval of the available transactions details.

Displaying Transactions According To Date

After manageTransactions.jsp loads, the user can key in the required date and click Search .

On clicking Search , the FORM is submitted to /admin/searchTransactionsByDate/${year}/${month}/${day} and manageTransactions.jsp is re-served.

User Interface
[/admin/searchTransactionByDate/${year}/${month}/${day} →
manageTransactions.jsp]

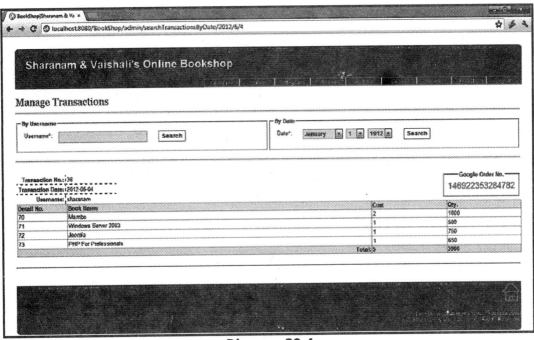

Diagram 29.4

Process Flow

After the user keys in the required inputs and clicks **Search**, the FORM is submitted and the **search** operation is performed by **/admin/searchTransactionByDate/${year}/${month}/${day} → TransactionController [showTransactionsByDate()]**.

Here,

- **/admin/searchTransactionsByDate/${year}/${month}/${day}** is the request mapping, which invokes **showTransactionsByDate()** of **TransactionController**

- **TransactionController** is the controller

- **showTransactionsByDate()** is the method available in the controller, which displays the list of transactions based on the date showTransactionsByDate() invokes the following methods of **TransactionService:**

Method	Description
listGroupedTransactionsByDate()	Holds the business logic to retrieve the list of transactions made on a particular date.
listTransactionsByDate()	Holds the business logic to retrieve the details of the listed transactions.

TransactionService's methods in turn call the following methods TransactionDAO:

Method	Description
listGroupedTransactionsByDate()	Does the actual retrieval of the available transactions made on a particular date.
listTransactionsByDate()	Does the actual retrieval of the available transactions details.

Updating Google Order Number

Every transaction that is listed in manageTransactions.jsp holds the Google Order No. section, which displays or accepts the Order number given by Google Wallet [via an email to the seller].

If this section does not show an existing Google Order Number, it shows the Google Order Number text field where the user can enter the order number [received from Google Wallet] and click **Update**.

After manageTransactions.jsp loads along with the list of transactions according to the username/date, the user can key in the required Google Order Number and click **Update**.

On clicking **Update**, the FORM is submitted to **/admin/updateGoogleOrderNo/${transactionNo}/${orderNo}** and manageTransactions.jsp is re-served.

Process Flow

The Google Order Number of the selected transaction is updated by the **/admin/updateGoogleOrderNo/${transactionNo}/${orderNo}** → TransactionController **[updateGoogleOrderNo()]** → TransactionService **[updateGoogleOrderNo()]** → TransactionDAO **[updateGoogleOrderNo()]**.

Here,

- **/admin/updateGoogleOrderNo/${transactionNo}/${orderNo}** is the request mapping, which invokes **updateGoogleOrderNo()** of **TransactionController**

- **TransactionController** is the controller

- **updateGoogleOrderNo()** is the method available in the controller, which updates the Google order number of a transaction based on TransactionNo as the reference via TransactionService and re-serves Manage Transactions form

- **TransactionService** is the service layer

- **updateGoogleOrderNo()** is the method available in the service, which holds the business logic to update the Google order number of a transaction based on TransactionNo via TransactionDAO

- **TransactionDAO** is the Data Access Layer [DAO]

- **updateGoogleOrderNo()** is the method available in DAO, which updates the appropriate transaction details in the Transactions database table using **TransactionNo** as the reference

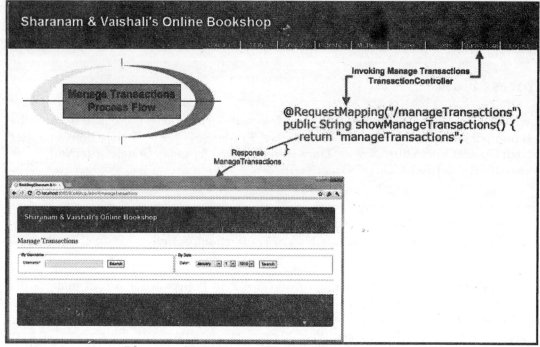

Diagram 29.5: Manage Transactions Process Flow

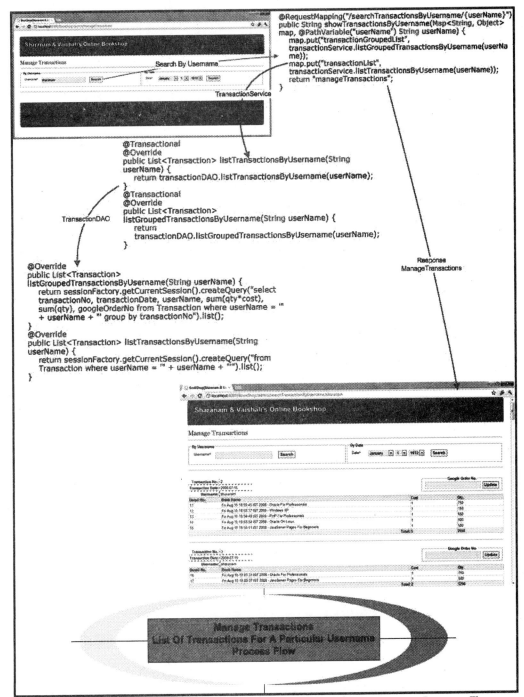

Diagram 29.6: Manage Transactions - For A Particular Username Process Flow

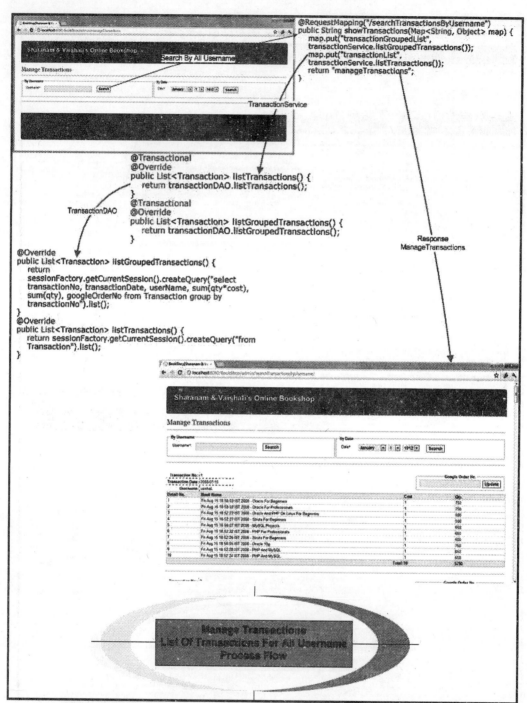

Diagram 29.7: Manage Transactions - For All Username Process Flow

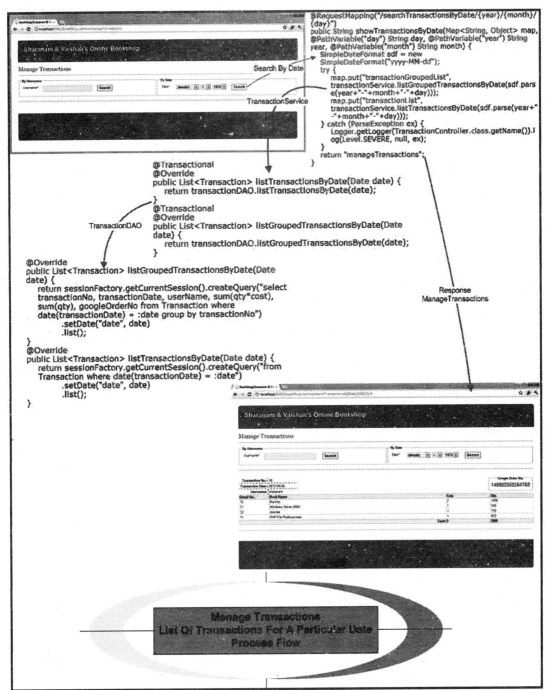

```
@RequestMapping("/searchTransactionsByDate/{year}/{month}/
{day}")
public String showTransactionsByDate(Map<String, Object> map,
@PathVariable("day") String day, @PathVariable("year") String
year, @PathVariable("month") String month) {
    SimpleDateFormat sdf = new
    SimpleDateFormat("yyyy-MM-dd");
    try {
        map.put("transactionGroupedList",
        transactionService.listGroupedTransactionsByDate(sdf.pars
        e(year+"-"+month+"-"+day)));
        map.put("transactionList",
        transactionService.listTransactionsByDate(sdf.parse(year+
        "-"+month+"-"+day)));
    } catch (ParseException ex) {
        Logger.getLogger(TransactionController.class.getName()).l
        og(Level.SEVERE, null, ex);
    }
    return "manageTransactions";
}
```

```
@Transactional
@Override
public List<Transaction> listTransactionsByDate(Date date) {
    return transactionDAO.listTransactionsByDate(date);
}

@Transactional
@Override
public List<Transaction> listGroupedTransactionsByDate(Date
date) {
    return transactionDAO.listGroupedTransactionsByDate(date);
}
```

```
@Override
public List<Transaction> listGroupedTransactionsByDate(Date
date) {
    return sessionFactory.getCurrentSession().createQuery("select
    transactionNo, transactionDate, userName, sum(qty*cost),
    sum(qty), googleOrderNo from Transaction where
    date(transactionDate) = :date group by transactionNo")
        .setDate("date", date)
        .list();
}
@Override
public List<Transaction> listTransactionsByDate(Date date) {
    return sessionFactory.getCurrentSession().createQuery("from
    Transaction where date(transactionDate) = :date")
        .setDate("date", date)
        .list();
}
```

Diagram 29.8: Manage Transactions - For A Particular Date Process Flow

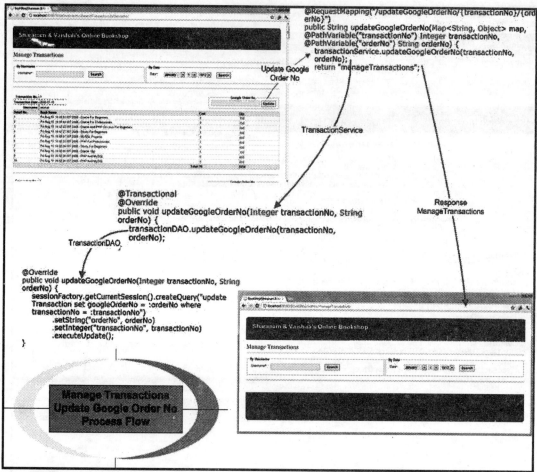

Diagram 29.9: Manage Transactions – Update Google Order Number Process Flow

Chapter

30

SECTION V: BACKEND [ADMINISTRATION] SOFTWARE DESIGN DOCUMENTATION

Administration Login And Logout

Administration Login is a Login data entry form which allows the administration users to login to the backend section to add, update or delete the master records.

This module uses the bms.Users table to perform the above operations.

This module is made up of the following:

Type	Name	Description
JSP	adminLogin.jsp	The data entry form
Spring		
Controller	AuthenticationController.java	Controller that facilitates data operations using request mapping
Spring Security Configuration	spring-security.xml	Spring Security configuration file

JSP [adminLogin.jsp]

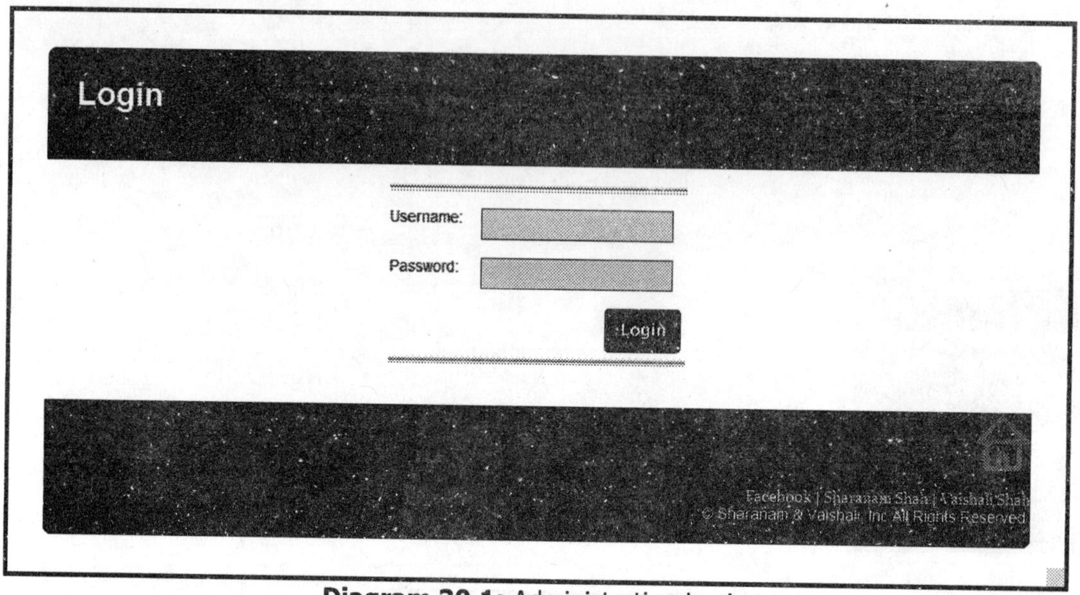

Diagram 30.1: Administration Login

This is a JSP which holds a data entry form, as shown in diagram 30.1. This form appears when the user clicks ▨ available on the footer of the frontend section of the application.

Form Specifications

File Name	adminLogin.jsp
Title	BookShop [Sharanam & Vaishali Shah] - Admin Login
Bound To Table	bms.Users
Form Name	adminLoginForm
Action	<c:url value='j_spring_security_check'/>
Method	POST

Data Fields

Login Details			
Label	**Name**	**Bound To**	**Validation Rules**
Username	j_username	Users.Username	Cannot be left blank
Password	j_password	Users.Password	Cannot be left blank

Data Controls

Object	Label	Name
submit	Login	submit

Code Spec

```
1   <%@page contentType="text/html" pageEncoding="UTF-8"%>
2   <%@taglib uri="http://java.sun.com/jsp/jstl/core" prefix="c"%>
3   <!DOCTYPE HTML PUBLIC "-//W3C//DTD HTML 4.01 Transitional//EN"
4     "http://www.w3.org/TR/html4/loose.dtd">
5   <html>
6     <head>
7       <meta http-equiv="Content-Type" content="text/html; charset=UTF-8">
8       <title>BookShop[Sharanam & Vaishali Shah] - Admin Login</title>
9       <link rel="stylesheet" href="/BookShop/css/admin.css" type="text/css">
10    </head>
11    <body onload='document.f.j_username.focus();'>
12      <div id="headerDiv">
13        <table class="headerTable" border="0" width="100%">
14          <tr><td><h1>Login</h1></td></tr>
15        </table>
16      </div>
17      <form name='adminLoginForm' action="<c:url value='j_spring_security_check'/>"
      method='POST'>
18        <table width="30%" align="center" border="0" cellpadding="0"
          cellspacing="0">
19          <tr><td width="100%" colspan="2"> </td></tr>
20          <tr><td class="hrLine" width="100%" colspan="2"> </td></tr>
21          <tr>
22            <td colspan="2">
23              <c:if test="${not empty error}">
24                <div class="error">
25                  Your login attempt was not successful, try again.<br />
26                  Invalid username or password
27                </div>
28              </c:if>
29            </td>
30          </tr>
31          <tr>
32            <td width="30%">Username:</td>
33            <td>
34              <input type='text' name='j_username' value=''>
35            </td>
36          </tr>
37          <tr><td width="100%" colspan="2"> </td></tr>
38          <tr>
39            <td width="30%">Password:</td>
40            <td>
41              <input type='password' name='j_password' />
42            </td>
```

```
43              </tr>
44              <tr><td width="100%" colspan="2"> </td></tr>
45              <tr>
46                 <td width="100%" colspan="2" class="loginButtonAlign">
47                    <input type="submit" name="submit" title="Login"
                          class="loginButton" value="" />
48                 </td>
49              </tr>
50              <tr><td class="hrLine" width="100%" colspan="2"> </td></tr>
51           </table>
52        </form>
53        <%@ include file="/WEB-INF/jsp/adminFooter.jsp" %>
54     </body>
55  </html>
```

Explanation:

Administration Login is served when the user clicks 📶, which is available in the footer of the application's home page.

This is a simple JSP page which holds a HTML form to capture the login credentials. These credentials are passed to the Spring Security check which takes care of authenticating the user credentials and if found valid takes the user in.

The login data entry form allows the registered administration users to login to the backend application.

After an administration user logs in to the backend application, the user is allowed to:

❑ Manage Countries

❑ Manage States

❑ Manage Authors

❑ Manage Publishers

❑ Manage Categories

❑ Manage Users

❑ Mange Books

❑ Manage Transactions

Controller [AuthenticationController.java]

This is a controller with the following specifications.

Controller Specifications

Class Name	Package
AuthenticationController	com.sharanamvaishali.controller

Methods		
Method Name	Request Mapping	Return Values
showAdminLogin()	/admin/adminLogin	adminLogin.jsp
showAdminLoginError()	/admin/adminLoginError	adminLogin.jsp
showAdminLoginAfterLogout()	/admin/adminLogout	adminLogin.jsp
showAccessDeniedPage()	/adminAccessDenied	adminAccessDenied.jsp

Code Spec

```
1   package com.sharanamvaishali.controllers;
2
3   import java.util.Map;
4   import org.springframework.stereotype.Controller;
5   import org.springframework.ui.ModelMap;
6   import org.springframework.web.bind.annotation.RequestMapping;
7   import org.springframework.web.bind.annotation.RequestMethod;
8
9   @Controller
10  public class AuthenticationController {
11      @RequestMapping(value="/admin/adminLogin", method = RequestMethod.GET)
12      public String showAdminLogin(ModelMap model) {
13          return "adminLogin";
14      }
15
16      @RequestMapping(value="/admin/adminLoginFailed", method =
        RequestMethod.GET)
17      public String showAdminLoginError(ModelMap model) {
18          model.addAttribute("error", "true");
19          return "adminLogin";
20      }
21
22      @RequestMapping(value="/admin/adminLogout", method = RequestMethod.GET)
23      public String showAdminLoginAfterLogout(ModelMap model) {
24          return "adminLogin";
25      }
26
27      @RequestMapping(value="/adminAccessDenied")
28      public String showAccessDeniedPage(ModelMap model) {
29          return "adminAccessDenied";
30      }
31  }
```

Explanation:

The following section describes the above code spec.

showAdminLogin()

When the user clicks 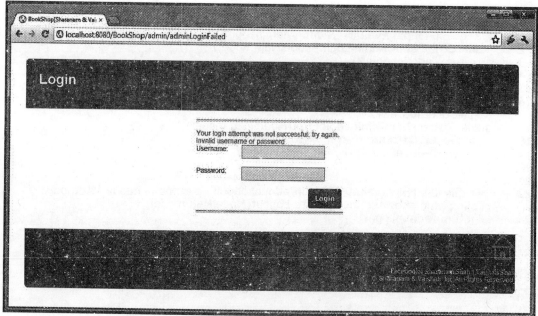, the request mapping **/admin/adminLogin** invokes **showAdminLogin()** via Spring Security.

showAdminLogin() displays the administration login form.

showAdminLoginError()

When the user clicks **Login**, the Login form is submitted to authenticate the user.

If the login attempted is un-successful, the request mapping **/admin/adminLoginFailed** invokes **showAdminLoginError()** via Spring Security.

showAdminloginError() sets the error flag to true [to inform the Spring's Security module that this login form has errors which need to be shown to the user] and returns the Administration Login form with an error message, as shown in diagram 30.2.

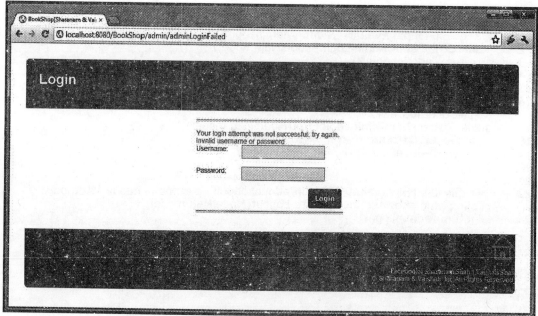

Diagram 30.2: Error message for unsuccessful login

showAdminLoginAfterLogout()

The user can choose to logout of the administration section by clicking **Logout**.

When user clicks **Logout**, the request mapping **/admin/adminLogout** invokes **showAdminLoginAfterLogout()**.

showAdminLoginAfterLogout() returns the Administration Login page after logging the user out of the administration section.

Logout in the View points to **/admin/j_spring_security_logout**.

```
51   <a href='<c:url value="/admin/j_spring_security_logout"/>' title="Logout">Logout</a>
```

Spring's Security module takes care of performing the logout process and then requesting **/admin/adminLogout** when it encounters **/admin/j_spring_security_logout**.

showAccessDeniedPage()

After the login credentials are authenticated and are valid, the application renders Manage Transactions, which is the startup page for the Administration.

Spring Security checks the authority of the user i.e. whether the user is the ROLE_ADMIN or ROLE_USER. Based on that authority Spring Security intercepts the Manage forms.

Only the user with the ROLE_ADMIN role can use the Manage Users form.

```
8       <http pattern="/admin/**" auto-config="true" >
9         <intercept-url pattern="/admin/manageUsers" access="ROLE_ADMIN" />
10                                                                    ROLE_USER" />
11        <intercept-url pattern="/admin/manageStates" access="ROLE_ADMIN, ROLE_USER" />
12        <intercept-url pattern="/admin/manageCategories" access="ROLE_ADMIN, ROLE_USER" />
13        <intercept-url pattern="/admin/managePublishers" access="ROLE_ADMIN, ROLE_USER" />
14        <intercept-url pattern="/admin/manageAuthors" access="ROLE_ADMIN, ROLE_USER" />
15        <intercept-url pattern="/admin/manageBooks" access="ROLE_ADMIN, ROLE_USER" />
16        <intercept-url pattern="/admin/manageTransactions" access="ROLE_ADMIN, ROLE_USER" />
17        <form-login login-page="/admin/adminLogin"
                login-processing-url="/admin/j_spring_security_check"
                default-target-url="/admin/manageTransactions"
                authentication-failure-url="/admin/adminLoginFailed" />
18        <access-denied-handler error-page="/adminAccessDenied" />
19        <logout                              security_logout
                logout-success-url="/admin/adminLogout" />
20      </http>
```

So, if the Admin user has logged in, then that user has access to the Manage Users form.

The other users are directed to the Access Denied page, if they attempt to access the Manage Users form.

The request mapping **/adminAccessDenied** invokes **showAccessDeniedPage()** via Spring Security.

showAccessDeniedPage() displays the Access Denied page for the users other than the Admin users, as shown in diagram 30.3.

Diagram 30.3

Spring Security [spring-security.xml]

Spring Security handles authentication and authorization at both the web request level and at the method invocation level.

Authentication helps establishing a user, device or some other system which can perform an action in the application. Authorization helps deciding whether that user, device or some other system is allowed to perform an action within the application.

Code Spec

```
1   <beans:beans xmlns="http://www.springframework.org/schema/security"
2      xmlns:beans="http://www.springframework.org/schema/beans"
3      xmlns:xsi="http://www.w3.org/2001/XMLSchema-instance"
4      xsi:schemaLocation="http://www.springframework.org/schema/beans
5      http://www.springframework.org/schema/beans/spring-beans-3.1.xsd
6      http://www.springframework.org/schema/security
7      http://www.springframework.org/schema/security/spring-security-3.1.xsd">
8      <http pattern="/admin/**" auto-config="true" >
9         <intercept-url pattern="/admin/manageUsers" access="ROLE_ADMIN" />
10        <intercept-url pattern="/admin//manageCountries" access="ROLE_ADMIN,
          ROLE_USER" />
11        <intercept-url pattern="/admin/manageStates" access="ROLE_ADMIN,
          ROLE_USER" />
12        <intercept-url pattern="/admin/manageCategories" access="ROLE_ADMIN,
          ROLE_USER" />
13        <intercept-url pattern="/admin/managePublishers" access="ROLE_ADMIN,
          ROLE_USER" />
14        <intercept-url pattern="/admin/manageAuthors" access="ROLE_ADMIN,
          ROLE_USER" />
15        <intercept-url pattern="/admin/manageBooks" access="ROLE_ADMIN,
          ROLE_USER" />
16        <intercept-url pattern="/admin/manageTransactions" access="ROLE_ADMIN,
          ROLE_USER" />
17        <form-login login-page="/admin/adminLogin"
          login-processing-url="/admin/j_spring_security_check"
          default-target-url="/admin/manageTransactions"
          authentication-failure-url="/admin/adminLoginFailed" />
18        <access-denied-handler error-page="/adminAccessDenied"/>
19        <logout logout-url="/admin/j_spring_security_logout"
          logout-success-url="/admin/adminLogout" />
20     </http>
21     <authentication-manager>
22        <authentication-provider>
23           <jdbc-user-service data-source-ref="dataSource"
24           users-by-username-query="select username, password, enabled from Users
             where username=?"
25           authorities-by-username-query="select username, authority from Users where
             username=?" />
26        </authentication-provider>
27     </authentication-manager>
28  </beans:beans>
```

Explanation:

The following section describes the above code spec.

Namespace Declaration In Spring Configuration File

It all begins with including the security namespace declaration in the XML file:

```
<beans:beans xmlns="http://www.springframework.org/schema/security"
    xmlns:beans="http://www.springframework.org/schema/beans"
    xmlns:xsi="http://www.w3.org/2001/XMLSchema-instance"
    xsi:schemaLocation="http://www.springframework.org/schema/beans
    http://www.springframework.org/schema/beans/spring-beans-3.1.xsd
    http://www.springframework.org/schema/security
    http://www.springframework.org/schema/security/spring-security-3.1.xsd">
```

With the security namespace as the primary namespace, **security:** prefixes can be avoided on all of the elements.

<http> Configuration

All that is required to enable web security to begin with is:

```
<http pattern="/admin/**" auto-config="true" >
    <intercept-url pattern="/admin/manageUsers" access="ROLE_ADMIN" />
    <intercept-url pattern="/admin//manageCountries" access="ROLE_ADMIN,
    ROLE_USER" />
    <intercept-url pattern="/admin/manageStates" access="ROLE_ADMIN,
    ROLE_USER" />
    <intercept-url pattern="/admin/manageCategories" access="ROLE_ADMIN,
    ROLE_USER" />
    <intercept-url pattern="/admin/managePublishers" access="ROLE_ADMIN,
    ROLE_USER" />
    <intercept-url pattern="/admin/manageAuthors" access="ROLE_ADMIN,
    ROLE_USER" />
    <intercept-url pattern="/admin/manageBooks" access="ROLE_ADMIN,
    ROLE_USER" />
    <intercept-url pattern="/admin/manageTransactions" access="ROLE_ADMIN,
    ROLE_USER" />
</http>
```

The above code spec configures the Spring security to intercept requests for all URLs as specified via <intercept-url> and restricts access to only authenticated users who have the ROLE_USER and ROLE_ADMIN roles.

<http> automatically sets up a FilterChainProxy [which is delegated to by the DelegatingFilterProxy, configured in web.xml, explained later in the chapter] and all of the filter beans in the chain.

pattern

The pattern which defines the URL path.

<http>'s pattern applied is:

```
<http pattern="/admin/**" auto-config="true" >
    <intercept-url pattern="/admin/manageUsers" access="ROLE_ADMIN" />
    <intercept-url pattern="/admin//manageCountries" access="ROLE_ADMIN,
    ROLE_USER" />
```

means that only the administration section is applied, where the controller class is mapped by:

```
23  @Controller
24  @RequestMapping("/admin")
25  public class AuthorController {
26      @Autowired
27      private CommonService commonService;
```

So, wherever the application encounters /admin/..., Spring security will refer to this <http> configuration.

auto-config

Setting the **auto-config** attribute to **true**, gives the application:

❑ A login page

❑ Support for HTTP Basic authentication

❑ Support for displaying access denied page

❑ Support for logging out

Setting **auto-config** to **true** is equivalent to:

```
<http pattern="/admin/**" auto-config="true" >
    <form-login />
    <http-basic />
    <access-denied-handler />
    <logout />
    <intercept-url pattern="/admin/manageUsers" access="ROLE_ADMIN" />
    <intercept-url pattern="/admin//manageCountries" access="ROLE_ADMIN,
    ROLE_USER" />
    <intercept-url pattern="/admin/manageStates" access="ROLE_ADMIN,
    ROLE_USER" />
    <intercept-url pattern="/admin/manageCategories" access="ROLE_ADMIN,
    ROLE_USER" />
    <intercept-url pattern="/admin/managePublishers" access="ROLE_ADMIN,
    ROLE_USER" />
```

```
<intercept-url pattern="/admin/manageAuthors" access="ROLE_ADMIN,
ROLE_USER" />
<intercept-url pattern="/admin/manageBooks" access="ROLE_ADMIN,
ROLE_USER" />
<intercept-url pattern="/admin/manageTransactions" access="ROLE_ADMIN,
ROLE_USER" />
</http>
```

<form-login> Configuration

Setting **auto-config** to true, automatically generates the administration login page.

This form can be accessed via the path **/spring_security_login** relative to the application's context URL. For example, http://localhost:8080/BookShop/**spring_security_login**

Alternatively, it is also possible to use a custom login form and just let Spring Security know about it, by configuring **<form-login>** to override the default behavior.

```
<http pattern="/admin/**" auto-config="true" >
   <form-login login-page="/admin/adminLogin"
   login-processing-url="/admin/j_spring_security_check"
   default-target-url="/admin/manageTransactions"
   authentication-failure-url="/admin/adminLoginFailed" />
</http>
```

login-page

login-page specifies a new context-relative URL for the login page.

login-page indicates that the login form resides at **/admin/adminLogin**. This is ultimately handled by a Spring MVC controller, which holds a method with an appropriate request mapping.

authentication-failure-url

Likewise, if authentication fails, **authentication-failure-url** is set to send the user back to the same administration login page.

login-processing-url

login-processing-url is set to **/admin/j_spring_security_check**, which indicates the URL to which the login form will submit back to authenticate the user.

REMINDER

 Even if the user chooses to use a custom login form, the username and password should be submitted in the request as fields named **j_username** and **j_password**.

default-target-url

default-target-url is set to **/admin/manageTransactions**, which indicates the URL to which the user will be send to if the authentication is valid.

Access Denied

<access-denied-handler> handles the access denied criteria.

```
<http pattern="/admin/**" auto-config="true" >
   <form-login login-page="/admin/adminLogin"
   login-processing-url="/admin/j_spring_security_check"
   default-target-url="/admin/manageTransactions"
   authentication-failure-url="/admin/adminLoginFailed" />
   <access-denied-handler error-page="/adminAccessDenied"/>
</http>
```

In this project, the ROLE_ADMIN has all the permissions to enter the manage forms. ROLE_USER have restrictions on using the manage users form and therefore, when it tries to use the restricted Manage Users form, the application will display the Access Denied page.

error-page

error-page is set to **/adminAccessDenied**, which indicates the URL to which the user is directed for accessing the restricted page.

Logging Out

<logout> sets up a Spring Security filter that invalidates a user session.

```
<http pattern="/admin/**" auto-config="true" >
   <form-login login-page="/admin/adminLogin"
   login-processing-url="/admin/j_spring_security_check"
   default-target-url="/admin/manageTransactions"
   authentication-failure-url="/admin/adminLoginFailed" />
   <access-denied-handler error-page="/adminAccessDenied"/>
   <logout logout-url="/admin/j_spring_security_logout"
   logout-success-url="/admin/adminLogout" />
</http>
```

logout-url

logout-url is internally mapped to **/admin/j_spring_security_logout**, which indicates the URL to invalidate a user session.

logout-success-url

logout-success-url is set to **/admin/adminLogout**, which indicates the URL to which the user is sent to, on a successful logout.

Intercepting Requests

<intercept-url> allows intercepting requests.

Its pattern attribute is given a URL pattern that is matched against incoming requests. If any requests match the pattern, then that <intercept-url>'s security rules are applied.

```
<intercept-url pattern="/admin/manageStates" access="ROLE_ADMIN, ROLE_USER" />
```

In this case, **pattern** is set to **/admin/manageStates**, to require ROLE_ADMIN as well as ROLE_USER access.

```
<intercept-url pattern="/admin/manageUsers" access="ROLE_ADMIN" />
```

In this case, Manage Users page is restricted to administrative users only.

REMINDER

 Multiple <intercept-url> entries can be used to secure various paths in the web application.

Authentication Services

Spring Security's **<jdbc-user-service>** helps having a JDBC based User Repository.

```
<jdbc-user-service id="userService" data-source-ref="dataSource" />
```

This configures a basic <jdbc-user-service> with an id so that it can be declared independently and wired into <authentication-provider>.

<jdbc-user-service> uses a JDBC data source wired in through its data-source-ref attribute, to query a database for user details.

The user service queries for user information using the following SQL:

```
select username, password, enabled from Users where username=?
```

Part of the authentication involves looking up the user's granted authorities. By default, the basic <jdbc-user-service> configuration uses the following SQL to look up authorities given a username:

```
select username, authority from Users where username=?
```

This is great, if the application's database happens to store user details and authorities in tables that match those queries. But this is usually never the case. Hence this default behavior does not work.

<jdbc-user-service> can easily be configured to use whatever queries best fit the application.

```
<jdbc-user-service data-source-ref="dataSource"
    users-by-username-query="select username, password, enabled from Users where
    username=?"
    authorities-by-username-query="select username, authority from Users where
    username=?" />
```

The following are the attributes that can be used to tweak <jdbc-user-service>'s behavior:

data-source-ref

The bean ID of the DataSource, mentioned in DispatcherServlet, which provides the required tables:

```
<bean id="dataSource" destroy-method="close"
class="org.apache.commons.dbcp.BasicDataSource">
    <property name="driverClassName" value="${dbDriverClassName}"/>
    <property name="url" value="${dbURL}"/>
    <property name="username" value="${dbUsername}"/>
    <property name="password" value="${dbPassword}"/>
</bean>
```

users-by-username-query

It holds the queries for a user's username, password and enabled status, given the username.

authorities-by-username-query

It holds the queries for a user's granted authorities, given the username.

Setting Up Spring Security Configuration In web.xml

Code Spec

```
1   <?xml version="1.0" encoding="UTF-8"?>
2   <web-app version="3.0" xmlns="http://java.sun.com/xml/ns/javaee"
    xmlns:xsi="http://www.w3.org/2001/XMLSchema-instance"
    xsi:schemaLocation="http://java.sun.com/xml/ns/javaee
    http://java.sun.com/xml/ns/javaee/web-app_3_0.xsd">
3       <listener>
4           <listener-class>org.springframework.web.context.ContextLoaderListener</listen
            er-class>
5       </listener>
6       <context-param>
7           <param-name>contextConfigLocation</param-name>
8           <param-value>
9               /WEB-INF/bookshopdispatcher-servlet.xml,
10              /WEB-INF/spring-security.xml
11          </param-value>
12      </context-param>
13      <filter>
14          <filter-name>springSecurityFilterChain</filter-name>
15          <filter-class>org.springframework.web.filter.DelegatingFilterProxy</filter-class>
16      </filter>
17      <filter-mapping>
18          <filter-name>springSecurityFilterChain</filter-name>
19          <url-pattern>/*</url-pattern>
20      </filter-mapping>
21  </web-app>
```

Explanation:

The following section describes the above code spec.

Spring Security's Configuration

Spring Security's configuration is done via an XML configuration file, which by default is named spring-security.xml and is expected to be in the web application's **/WEB-INF** directory of the application.

web.xml informs Spring where to find spring-security.xml:

```
<context-param>
   <param-name>contextConfigLocation</param-name>
   <param-value>
        /WEB-INF/bookshopdispatcher-servlet.xml,
        /WEB-INF/spring-security.xml
   </param-value>
</context-param>
```

<context-param>

<context-param> contains the declaration of a Web application's servlet context initialization parameters.

<param-name>

<param-name> defines parameter name.

<param-value>

<param-value> sets parameter value.

Spring Context Listener

Spring context listener provides more flexibility in terms of how an application is wired together. It uses the application's Spring configuration to determine what object to instantiate and loads the objects into the application context used by the servlet container.

When deploying application using the Spring context listener, the servlet container needs to load **org.springframework.web.context.ContextLoaderListener**. This is specified using <listener> and its <listener-class> child:

```
<listener>
    <listener-class>org.springframework.web.context.ContextLoaderListener</listener-class>
</listener>
```

org.springframework.web.context.ContextLoaderListener uses a context parameter called **contextConfigLocation** to determine the location of the Spring configuration file.

Servlet Filters

Before restricting access to users with certain privileges, there must be a way to know who is using the application. This thus requires the application to authenticate the user, prompting them to log in and identify themselves.

Spring Security supports these and many other forms of request-level security. To get started with web security in Spring, the servlet filters that provide the various security features need to be setup.

Spring Security employs several servlet filters to provide various aspects of security. To enable this, the following filter needs to be configured in the application's web.xml:

```
<filter>
    <filter-name>springSecurityFilterChain</filter-name>
    <filter-class>org.springframework.web.filter.DelegatingFilterProxy</filter-class>
</filter>
```

DelegatingFilterProxy

DelegatingFilterProxy is a special servlet filter which delegates to an implementation of javax.servlet.Filter. javax.servlet.Filter is registered as a <bean> in the Spring application context.

DelegatingFilterProxy allows configuring the actual filter in Spring and thus taking full advantage of Spring's support for dependency injection.

The value given as DelegatingFilterProxy's <filter-name> is the name used to look up the filter bean from the Spring application context. Spring Security automatically creates a filter bean whose ID is springSecurityFilterChain.

REMINDER

Spring Security relies on several servlet filters to provide different security features. But it is not required to explicitly declare the springSecurityFilterChain bean or any of the filters that it chains together. Spring Security automatically creates those beans when the <http> element is configured.

Web security services are configured using <http>.

Chapter

31

SECTION V: BACKEND [ADMINISTRATION] SOFTWARE DESIGN DOCUMENTATION

Manage Countries

This module allows performing the following operations:

❑ Adding new countries

❑ Editing existing countries

❑ Viewing existing countries

❑ Deleting existing countries

This module uses the bms.Countries table to perform the above operations.

This module is made up of the following:

Type	Name	Description
JSP	manageCountries.jsp	The data entry form
Spring		
Controller	CountryController.java	The controller class that facilitates data operations
Service Class	CountryService.java	The interface for the service layer.
	CountryServiceImpl.java	The implementation class for the service layer.
DAO Class	CountryDAO.java	The interface for the DAO layer.
	CountryDAOImpl.java	The implementation class that performs the actual data operations.
DispatcherServlet	bookshopdispatcher-servlet.xml	Central dispatcher for HTTP request handlers/controllers.
Hibernate		
Mapping	hibernate.cfg.xml	The mapping file that holds Model class mapping
Model Class	Country.java	The model class

JSP [manageCountries.jsp]

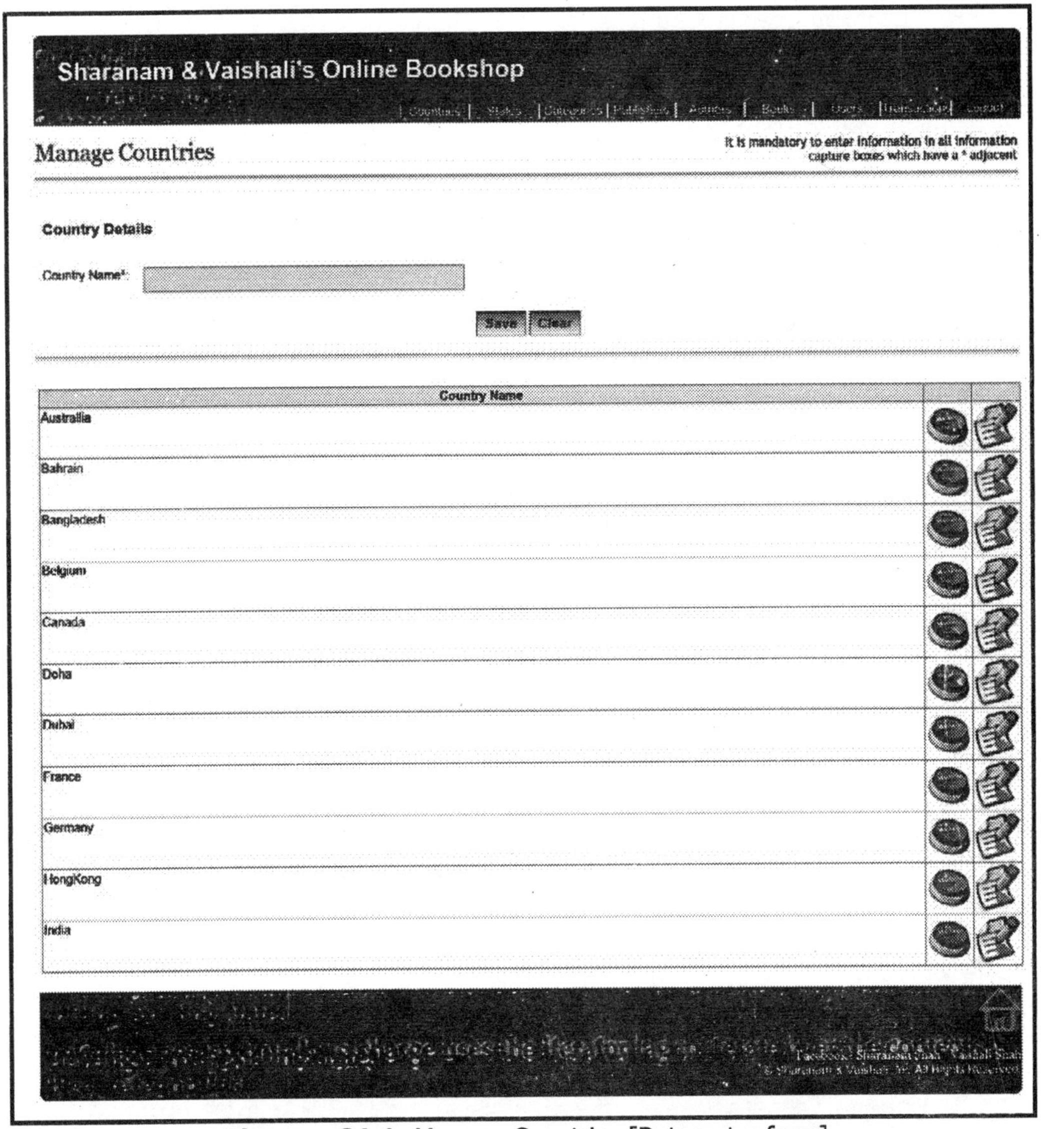

Diagram 31.1: Manage Countries [Data entry form]

This is a JSP which holds a data entry form, as shown in diagram 31.1. This form appears when the user clicks Countries .

Form Specifications

File Name	manageCountries.jsp
Title	BookShop[Sharanam & Vaishali Shah] - Manage Countries
Bound To Table	bms.Countries
Command Name	country
Action	${pageContext.request.contextPath}/admin/saveCountry
Method	POST

Data Fields

Label	Name	Bound To	Validation Rules
Country	Country.country	Countries.Country	Cannot be left blank

Micro-Help For Form Fields

Form Field	Micro Help Statement
Country.country	Enter the country name

Data Controls

Object	Label
Submit	Save
Reset	Clear

Code Spec

```
1   <%@page contentType="text/html" pageEncoding="UTF-8"%>
2   <%@taglib uri="http://www.springframework.org/tags/form" prefix="form"%>
3   <%@taglib uri="http://java.sun.com/jsp/jstl/core" prefix="c"%>
4   <!DOCTYPE HTML PUBLIC "-//W3C//DTD HTML 4.01 Transitional//EN"
5     "http://www.w3.org/TR/html4/loose.dtd">
6   <html>
7     <head>
8       <meta http-equiv="Content-Type" content="text/html; charset=UTF-8">
9       <title>BookShop[Sharanam & Vaishali Shah] - Manage Countries</title>
10      <link rel="stylesheet" href="/BookShop/css/admin.css" type="text/css">
11    </head>
12    <body>
13      <%@ include file="/WEB-INF/jsp/adminHeader.jsp" %>
14      <br/>
15      <form:form method="post"
          action="${pageContext.request.contextPath}/admin/saveCountry"
          commandName="country">
```

```
16      <form:hidden path="countryNo" />
17      <table width="100%" border="0" align="center" cellpadding="0"
        cellspacing="0">
18          <tr>
19            <td>
20              <table border="0" cellpadding="0" cellspacing="0" width="100%">
21                <tr>
22                  <td class="manageForms">Manage Countries</td>
23                  <td align="center" class="error">${dbError}</td>
24                  <td class="information">
25                      It is mandatory to enter information in all information
                        <br>capture boxes which have a <span
                        class="mandatory">*</span> adjacent
26                  </td>
27                </tr>
28              </table>
29            </td>
30          </tr>
31          <tr><td class="hrLine"> </td></tr>
32          <tr>
33            <td>
34              <table width="100%" border="0" align="center" cellpadding="0"
                cellspacing="0">
35                <tr>
36                  <td>
37                    <table width="100%" border="0" cellpadding="4"
                      cellspacing="4">
38                      <tr>
39                        <td class="sectionName" colspan="2">
40                          <br />Country Details<br /><br />
41                        </td>
42                      </tr>
43                      <tr>
44                        <td width="10%">Country Name<span
                          class="mandatory">*</span>:</td>
45                        <td>
46                          <form:input path="country" title="Enter the country
                            name" maxlength="25" size="50"/><br>
47                          <form:errors path="country" cssClass="error" />
48                        </td>
49                      </tr>
50                    </table>
51                  </td>
52                </tr>
53                <tr><td> </td></tr>
54                <tr>
55                  <td colspan="2" class="centerAlign">
56                    <input type="submit" class="groovybutton" value="Save" />
57                    <input type="reset" value="Clear" class="groovybutton"
                      onclick="javascript:document.location.href='/BookShop/admin
                      /manageCountries'" />
58                  </td>
59                </tr>
```

```
60                          </table>
61                      </td>
62                  </tr>
63              <tr><td> </td></tr>
64              <tr><td class="hrLine"> </td></tr>
65              <tr><td><br></td></tr>
66          </table>
67      </form:form>
68      <c:if test="${!empty countryList}">
69          <table class="data" width="100%">
70              <tr>
71                  <th width="94%">Country Name</th>
72                  <th width="3%"> </th>
73                  <th width="3%"> </th>
74              </tr>
75              <c:forEach items="${countryList}" var="country">
76                  <tr>
77                      <td>${country.country}</td>
78                      <td><a
                        href="/BookShop/admin/deleteCountry/${country.countryNo}"><img
                        title="Click to delete"
                        src="/BookShop/images/delete.jpg"/></a></td>
79                      <td><a
                        href="/BookShop/admin/editCountry/${country.countryNo}"><img
                        title="Click to edit" src="/BookShop/images/edit.jpg"/></a></td>
80                  </tr>
81              </c:forEach>
82          </table>
83      </c:if>
84      <%@ include file="/WEB-INF/jsp/adminFooter.jsp" %>
85  </body>
86  </html>
```

Explanation:

This is a standard data entry form, which captures the country details. By default, when the form loads, it is in the **INSERT** and **VIEW** mode. The form also has Delete and Edit options to delete and edit a particular country record.

To use the form tags, import the Spring's form tag library:

`<%@taglib uri="http://www.springframework.org/tags/form" prefix="form"%>`

\<form:form\>

\<form:form\> renders a HTML FORM tag and exposes a binding path to inner tags for binding. It puts the command object in the PageContext so that the command object can be accessed by inner tags. All the other tags in this library are nested tags of the form tag.

The HTTP POST method is used to submit the form:

```
<form:form method="post"
action="${pageContext.request.contextPath}/admin/saveCountry"
commandName="country">
```

The **action** of the form points to **/admin/saveCountry** request mapping.

The **commandName** of the form is the name of the form context object which is placed in the model by the controller.

<form:input>

<form:input> renders a HTML INPUT tag.

```
<form:input path="country" title="Enter the country
name" maxlength="25" size="50"/><br>
```

In this application, there is a domain object called Country. It is a JavaBean with property such as country. So, this is used as the form backing object of the form controller which returns manageCountries.jsp.

The country value is retrieved from the command object placed in the PageContext by the page controller.

manageCountries.jsp assumes that the variable name of the form backing object is **command**. If the form backing object is put into the model under another name, then the form can be bound to the named variable, which is the case in this application.

```
<form:form method="post"
action="${pageContext.request.contextPath}/admin/saveCountry"
commandName="country">
```

<form:input>'s **path** attribute is used to bind the form fields to the domain object.

<form:errors>

Spring's form binding JSP tag library is used to display the errors. <form:errors> is used to render field validation errors.

<form:errors>'s **path** attribute specifies the form field for which errors should be displayed.

For example: The following <form:errors> displays errors [if there are any] for the field country:

<form:errors path="country" cssClass="error" />

<form:errors>'s **cssClass** attribute refers to a class that is declared in CSS to display error messages in red so that it catches the user's attention.

Controller [CountryController.java]

This is a controller class with the following specifications.

Controller Specifications

Class Name	Package	
CountryController	com.sharanamvaishali.controllers	
Objects		
Object Name	Class Name	Object Type
countryService	CountryService	Service Layer
Methods		
Method Name	Request Mapping	
showManageCountries()	/admin/manageCountries	
saveCountry()	/admin/saveCountry	
deleteCountry()	/admin/deleteCountry/${countryNo}	
editCountry()	/admin/editCountry/${countryNo}	

Code Spec

```
1  package com.sharanamvaishali.controllers;
2
3  import com.sharanamvaishali.model.Country;
4  import com.sharanamvaishali.service.CountryService;
5  import java.util.Map;
6  import javax.validation.Valid;
7  import org.hibernate.exception.ConstraintViolationException;
8  import org.springframework.beans.factory.annotation.Autowired;
9  import org.springframework.dao.DataIntegrityViolationException;
10 import org.springframework.stereotype.Controller;
11 import org.springframework.validation.BindingResult;
12 import org.springframework.web.bind.annotation.ModelAttribute;
13 import org.springframework.web.bind.annotation.PathVariable;
14 import org.springframework.web.bind.annotation.RequestMapping;
15 import org.springframework.web.bind.annotation.RequestMethod;
16
17 @Controller
18 @RequestMapping("/admin")
```

```
19  public class CountryController {
20      @Autowired
21      private CountryService countryService;
22
23      @RequestMapping("/manageCountries")
24      public String showManageCountries(Map<String, Object> map) {
25          map.put("country", new Country());
26          map.put("countryList", countryService.listCountry());
27          return "manageCountries";
28      }
29
30      @RequestMapping(value = "/saveCountry", method = RequestMethod.POST)
31      public String saveCountry(Map<String, Object> map, @ModelAttribute("country")
        Country country, @Valid Country countryValid, BindingResult result) {
32          if (result.hasErrors()) {
33              return "manageCountries";
34          } else {
35              try {
36                  countryService.saveCountry(country);
37                  return "redirect:/admin/manageCountries";
38              } catch (ConstraintViolationException exp) {
39                  map.put("dbError", exp.getMessage());
40                  return "manageCountries";
41              }
42          }
43      }
44
45      @RequestMapping("/deleteCountry/{countryNo}")
46      public String deleteCountry(Map<String, Object> map, @PathVariable("countryNo")
        Integer countryNo) {
47          try {
48              countryService.removeCountry(countryNo);
49              return "redirect:/admin/manageCountries";
50          } catch (DataIntegrityViolationException exp) {
51              map.put("dbError", "Cannot delete a parent row.");
52              map.put("country", new Country());
53              return "manageCountries";
54          }
55      }
56
57      @RequestMapping("/editCountry/{countryNo}")
58      public String editCountry(Map<String, Object> map, @PathVariable("countryNo")
        Integer countryNo) {
59          map.put("country", countryService.getCountryById(countryNo));
60          return "manageCountries";
61      }
62  }
```

Explanation:

The following section describes the above code spec.

showManageCountries()

CountryController holds a mapping to help the viewing.

This means the list of country details is retrieved by the **CountryController** class's **showManageCountries()**.

showManageCountries() is invoked every time Manage Countries is served.

showManageCountries():

❑ Makes a provision for adding a new country [if the user chooses to] by instantiating an object of the Country entity class

❑ Retrieves the country details by invoking **listCountry()** of CountryService

❑ Returns the country details that **listCountry()** returns, to the View to render it, using **map.put()**

saveCountry()

CountryController holds a mapping to help the adding of countries.

```
@RequestMapping("/manageCountries")
public String showManageCountries(Map<String, Object> map) {
    map.put("country", new Country());
    map.put("countryList", countryService.listCountry());
    return "manageCountries";
}
```

As soon as Manage Countries is served, an object of the Country entity class is instantiated to make a provision for adding a new country. The user may view, edit, delete or choose to add a new country.

In case, the user chooses to add a new country, keys in the required country details and clicks **Save**, **CountryController** holds a mapping to help the saving of the newly captured country details.

saveCountry():

❑ Ensures that the captured data is valid

❑ Returns the control to the View along with the error messages [available in the BindingResult object], if the captured data is found to be invalid

❑ Saves the country details using CountryService's **saveCountry()**, if the captured data is valid and returns the control to the View to render Manage Countries

deleteCountry()

In case, the user chooses to delete a country and clicks , **CountryController** holds a mapping to help delete a country record from Manage Countries.

deleteCountry():

❑ Passes **CountryNo** of the country to be deleted [available as a @PathVariable] to CountryService's **removeCountry()**

❑ Checks if the record being deleted is referenced by a record in another database table and accordingly displays the error message indicating that this record cannot be deleted. This is done by catching the DataIntegrityViolation exception

❑ Returns the control to the View which renders Manage Countries with the updated data

editCountry()

CountryController holds a mapping to help the editing of existing countries. In case, the user chooses to edit a country and clicks , **CountryController** holds a mapping to help fill up the Manage Countries form with country details.

editCountry():

❑ Retrieves the appropriate Country's details using **CountryNo** as the reference. It calls CountryService's **getCountryById()** which returns the details of the country to be edited as a Country object. **CountryNo** is made available through **@PathVariable** [in the list of Country rendered by the View] when the user clicks to edit a particular country

❑ Returns the control to the View along with the data to be populated in the form. The data to be populated is made available using Map's **put()**, which is used to populate the countries object with the data that **getCountryById()** of CountryService returns

Service Class

Interface [CountryService.java]

This is a service interface with the following specifications.

Service Interface Specifications

Class Name	Package
CountryService	com.sharaṅamvaishali.service

Code Spec

```
1  package com.sharanamvaishali.service;
2
3  import com.sharanamvaishali.model.Country;
4  import java.util.List;
5
6  public interface CountryService {
7      public void saveCountry(Country country);
8      public List<Country> listCountry();
9      public void removeCountry(Integer countryNo);
10     public Country getCountryById(Integer countryNo);
11 }
```

Implementation Class [CountryService.java]

This is a service class with the following specifications.

Service Implementation Specifications

Class Name	Package	Implements
CountryServiceImpl	com.sharanamvaishali.service	CountryService
Objects		
Object Name	**Class Name**	**Object Type**
countryDAO	CountryDAO	Data Access Object Layer
Methods		
Method Name	**Arguments**	
saveCountry()	Country country	
listCountry()	- -	
removeCountry()	Integer countryNo	
getCountryById()	Integer countryNo	

Code Spec

```
1  package com.sharanamvaishali.service;
2
3  import com.sharanamvaishali.dao.CountryDAO;
4  import com.sharanamvaishali.model.Country;
5  import java.util.List;
6  import org.springframework.beans.factory.annotation.Autowired;
```

```
 7   import org.springframework.stereotype.Service;
 8   import org.springframework.transaction.annotation.Transactional;
 9
10   @Service
11   public class CountryServiceImpl implements CountryService {
12       @Autowired
13       private CountryDAO countryDAO;
14
15       @Transactional
16       @Override
17       public void saveCountry(Country country) {
18           countryDAO.saveCountry(country);
19       }
20
21       @Transactional
22       @Override
23       public List<Country> listCountry() {
24           return countryDAO.listCountry();
25       }
26
27       @Transactional
28       @Override
29       public void removeCountry(Integer countryNo) {
30           countryDAO.removeCountry(countryNo);
31       }
32
33       @Transactional
34       @Override
35       public Country getCountryById(Integer countryNo) {
36           return countryDAO.getCountryById(countryNo);
37       }
38   }
```

Explanation:

The following section describes the above code spec.

saveCountry()

saveCountry() holds the business logic to save the captured country details.

This method in turn invokes CountryDAO's **saveCountry()**.

listCountry()

listCountry() holds the business logic to return the appropriate list of the available countries.

This method in turn invokes CountryDAO's **listCountry()**.

removeCountry()

removeCountry() holds the business logic to delete country details based on CountryNo.

This method in turn invokes CountryDAO's **removeCountry()**.

getCountryById()

getCountryById() holds the business logic to retrieve country details based on CountryNo.

This method in turn invokes CountryDAO's **getCountryById()**.

DAO Class

Interface [CountryDAO.java]

This is a Data Access Object interface with the following specifications.

DAO Interface Specifications

Class Name	Package
CountryDAO	com.sharanamvaishali.dao

Code Spec

```
1   package com.sharanamvaishali.dao;
2
3   import com.sharanamvaishali.model.Country;
4   import java.util.List;
5
6   public interface CountryDAO {
7       public void saveCountry(Country country);
8       public List<Country> listCountry();
9       public void removeCountry(Integer countryNo);
10      public Country getCountryById(Integer countryNo);
11  }
```

Implementation Class [CountryDAOImpl.java]

This is a Data Access Object class with the following specifications.

DAO Implementation Specifications

Class Name	Package	Implements
CountryDAOImpl	com.sharanamvaishali.dao	CountryDAO

Objects	
Object Name	**Class Name**
sessionFactory	SessionFactory

Methods		
Method Name	**Arguments**	**Return Values**
saveCountry()	Country country	void
listCountry()	- -	List <Country>
removeCountry()	Integer countryNo	void
getCountryById()	Integer countryNo	Country

Code Spec

```
1  package com.sharanamvaishali.dao;
2
3  import com.sharanamvaishali.model.Country;
4  import java.util.List;
5  import org.hibernate.SessionFactory;
6  import org.springframework.beans.factory.annotation.Autowired;
7  import org.springframework.stereotype.Repository;
8
9  @Repository
10 public class CountryDAOImpl implements CountryDAO {
11     @Autowired
12     private SessionFactory sessionFactory;
13
14     @Override
15     public void saveCountry(Country country) {
16         sessionFactory.getCurrentSession().merge(country);
17     }
18
19     @Override
20     public List<Country> listCountry() {
21         return sessionFactory.getCurrentSession().createQuery("from Country").list();
22     }
23
24     @Override
25     public void removeCountry(Integer countryNo) {
26         Country country = (Country)
             sessionFactory.getCurrentSession().load(Country.class, countryNo);
27         if (null != country) {
28             sessionFactory.getCurrentSession().delete(country);
29         }
30     }
31
32     @Override
```

```
33    public Country getCountryById(Integer countryNo) {
34        return (Country) sessionFactory.getCurrentSession().get(Country.class,
          countryNo);
35    }
36 }
```

Explanation:

The following section describes the above code spec.

saveCountry()

saveCountry() does the actual saving of the country in the Countries database table.

This method uses **merge()** of SessionFactory, which takes care of adding as well as updating the country details, in case the user has edited an existing country and clicked Save .

listCountry()

listCountry() does the actual retrieval of the available countries.

This method fires a SELECT query that attempts to retrieve records from the Countries database table.

All the records that the query retrieves are extracted and returned as a **List** object.

This List object is returned to the calling method i.e. Service Layer's **listCountry():**

```
public List<Country> listCountry() {
    return countryDAO.listCountry();
}
```

This method in turn returns it to the CountryController's **showManageCountries():**

```
public String showManageCountries(Map<String, Object> map) {
    map.put("country", new Country());
    map.put("countryList", countryService.listCountry());
    return "manageCountries";
}
```

Finally, CountryController returns this List object to the View [using **map.put()**] which renders it.

manageCountries.jsp on taking charge uses the **iterator** tag to iterate over the contents of the List object **countryList**.

```
<c:forEach items="${countryList}" var="country">
   <tr>
      <td>${country.country}</td>
```

The countryList object holds all those records [meeting the search criteria] retrieved by the SQL query.

Each record's column values are extracted using $.

```
<td>${country.country}</td>
```

removeCountry()

removeCountry() deletes the appropriate country based on **CountryNo** received as a reference.

This method uses:

❑ **load()** of SessionFactory, which retrieves the appropriate Country to be deleted using CountryNo as a reference

❑ **delete()** of SessionFactory, which deletes the country from Countries database table

getCountryById()

getCountryById() returns the appropriate country's object from the Countries database table using **CountryNo** as the reference.

This method uses **get()** of SessionFactory, which returns the appropriate Country from Countries database table.

After editing the country details, when the user clicks **Save**, saveCountry() of CountryController, followed by saveCountry() of CountryService, followed by saveCountry() of CountryDAO takes care of saving the updated country's details.

Domain Class [Country.java]

This is a domain class with the following specifications.

Domain Specifications

Class Name	Package	Implements
Country	com.sharanamvaishali.model	java.io.Serializable

Properties		

Property Name	Property Type	Methods	
countryNo	Integer	getCountryNo()	setCountryNo()
country	String	getCountry()	setCountry()

Code Spec

```
1  package com.sharanamvaishali.model;
2
3  import javax.persistence.*;
4  import org.hibernate.validator.constraints.NotEmpty;
5
6  @Entity
7  @Table(name="COUNTRIES")
8  public class Country implements java.io.Serializable {
9      @Id
10     @GeneratedValue
11     @Column(name="COUNTRYNO")
12     private Integer countryNo;
13     @Column(name="COUNTRY")
14     @NotEmpty(message="Country name is mandatory")
15     private String country;
16
17     public String getCountry() {
18         return country;
19     }
20     public void setCountry(String country) {
21         this.country = country;
22     }
23
24     public Integer getCountryNo() {
25         return countryNo;
26     }
27     public void setCountryNo(Integer countryNo) {
28         this.countryNo = countryNo;
29     }
30 }
```

Chapter

32

SECTION V: BACKEND [ADMINISTRATION] SOFTWARE DESIGN DOCUMENTATION

Manage States

This module allows performing the following operations:

❑ Adding new states

❑ Editing existing states

❑ Viewing across existing states

❑ Deleting existing states

This module uses the bms.State table to perform the above operations.

This module is made up of the following:

Type	Name	Description
JSP	manageStates.jsp	The data entry form
Spring		
Controller	StateController.java	The controller class that facilitates data operations
Service Class	StateService.java	The interface for the service layer
	StateServiceImpl.java	The implementation class for the service layer.
DAO Class	StateDAO.java	The interface for the DAO layer
	StateDAOImpl.java	The implementation class that performs the actual data operations
DispatcherServlet	bookshopdispatcher-servlet.xml	Central dispatcher for HTTP request handlers/controllers
Hibernate		
Mapping	hibernate.cfg.xml	The mapping file that holds Model class mapping
Model Class	State.java	The model class

JSP [manageStates.jsp]

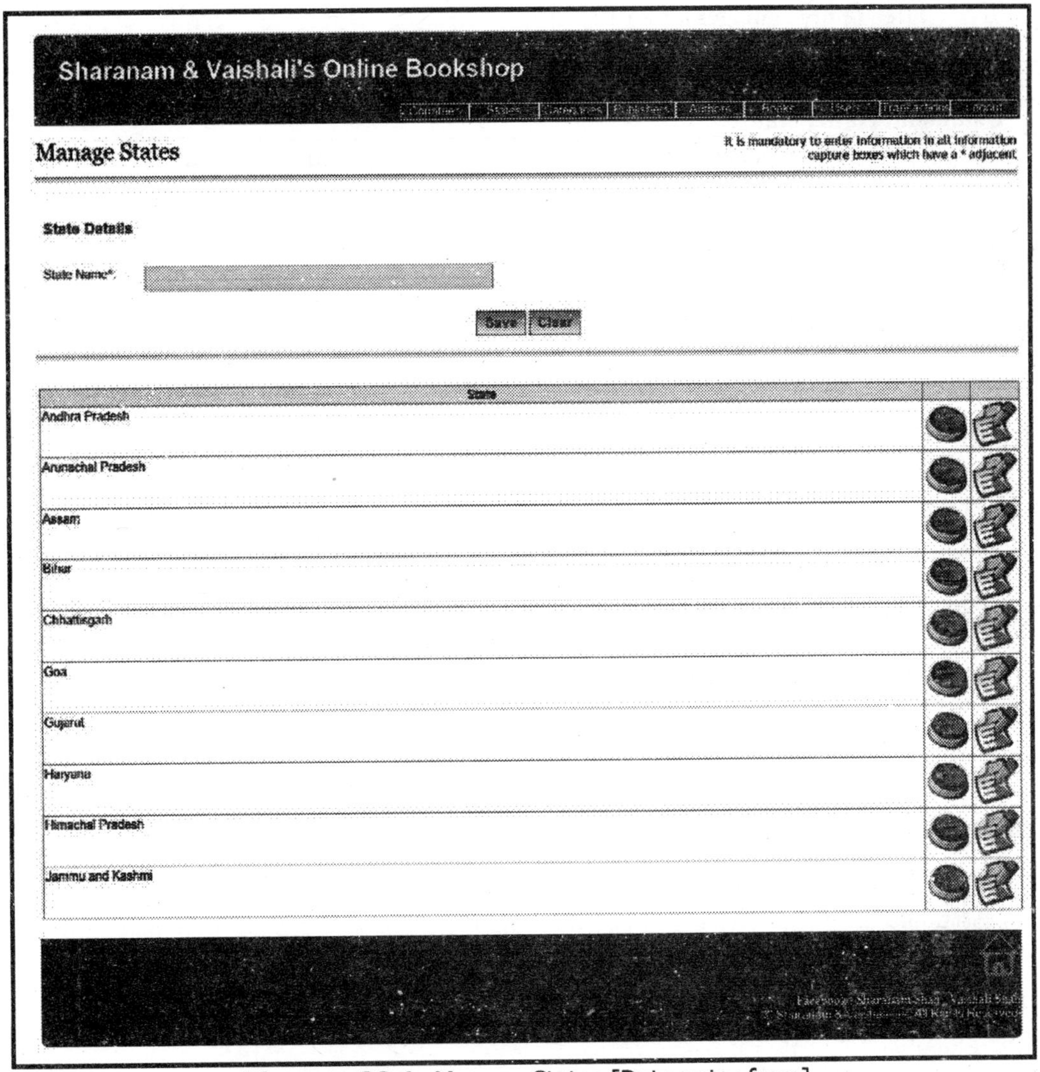

Diagram 32.1: Manage States [Data entry form]

This is a JSP which holds a data entry form, as shown in diagram 32.1. This form appears when the user clicks States .

Form Specifications

File Name	manageStates.jsp
Title	BookShop[Sharanam & Vaishali Shah] - Manage States
Bound To Table	bms.State
Command Name	state
Action	${pageContext.request.contextPath}/admin/saveState
Method	POST

Data Fields

Label	Name	Bound To	Validation Rules
State Name	State.state	State.State	Cannot be left blank

Micro-Help For Form Fields

Form Field	Micro Help Statement
State.state	Enter the state name

Data Controls

Object	Label
Submit	Save
Reset	Clear

Code Spec

```
1   <%@page contentType="text/html" pageEncoding="UTF-8"%>
2   <%@taglib uri="http://www.springframework.org/tags/form" prefix="form"%>
3   <%@taglib uri="http://java.sun.com/jsp/jstl/core" prefix="c"%>
4   <!DOCTYPE HTML PUBLIC "-//W3C//DTD HTML 4.01 Transitional//EN"
5     "http://www.w3.org/TR/html4/loose.dtd">
6   <html>
7     <head>
8       <meta http-equiv="Content-Type" content="text/html; charset=UTF-8">
9       <title>BookShop[Sharanam & Vaishali Shah] - Manage States</title>
10      <link rel="stylesheet" href="/BookShop/css/admin.css" type="text/css">
11    </head>
12    <body>
13      <%@ include file="/WEB-INF/jsp/adminHeader.jsp" %>
14      <br/>
15      <form:form method="post"
        action="${pageContext.request.contextPath}/admin/saveState"
        commandName="state">
```

```
16      <form:hidden path="stateNo" />
17      <table width="100%" border="0" align="center" cellpadding="0"
        cellspacing="0">
18          <tr>
19              <td>
20                  <table border="0" cellpadding="0" cellspacing="0" width="100%">
21                      <tr>
22                          <td class="manageForms">Manage States</td>
23                          <td align="center" class="error">${dbError}</td>
24                          <td class="information">
25                              It is mandatory to enter information in all information
                                <br>capture boxes which have a <span
                                class="mandatory">*</span> adjacent
26                          </td>
27                      </tr>
28                  </table>
29              </td>
30          </tr>
31          <tr><td class="hrLine"> </td></tr>
32          <tr>
33              <td>
34                  <table width="100%" border="0" align="center" cellpadding="0"
                    cellspacing="0">
35                      <tr>
36                          <td>
37                              <table width="100%" border="0" cellpadding="4"
                                cellspacing="4">
38                                  <tr>
39                                      <td class="sectionName" colspan="2">
40                                          <br />State Details<br /><br />
41                                      </td>
42                                  </tr>
43                                  <tr>
44                                      <td width="10%">State Name<span
                                        class="mandatory">*</span>:</td>
45                                      <td>
46                                          <form:input path="state" title="Enter the state
                                            name" maxlength="25" size="55"/><br>
47                                          <form:errors path="state" cssClass="error" />
48                                      </td>
49                                  </tr>
50                              </table>
51                          </td>
52                      </tr>
53                      <tr><td> </td></tr>
54                      <tr>
55                          <td colspan="2" class="centerAlign">
56                              <input type="submit" class="groovybutton" value="Save" />
57                              <input type="reset" value="Clear" class="groovybutton"
                                onclick="javascript:document.location.href='/BookShop/admin
                                /manageStates'" />
58                          </td>
59                      </tr>
```

```
60                    </table>
61                  </td>
62                </tr>
63                <tr><td> </td></tr>
64                <tr><td class="hrLine"> </td></tr>
65                <tr><td><br></td></tr>
66              </table>
67            </form:form>
68            <c:if test="${!empty stateList}">
69              <table class="data" width="100%">
70                <tr>
71                  <th width="94%">State</th>
72                  <th width="3%"> </th>
73                  <th width="3%"> </th>
74                </tr>
75                <c:forEach items="${stateList}" var="state">
76                  <tr>
77                    <td>${state.state}</td>
78                    <td><a
                        href="/BookShop/admin/deleteState/${state.stateNo}"><img
                        title="Click to delete"
                        src="/BookShop/images/delete.jpg"/></a></td>
79                    <td><a href="/BookShop/admin/editState/${state.stateNo}"><img
                        title="Click to edit" src="/BookShop/images/edit.jpg"/></a></td>
80                  </tr>
81                </c:forEach>
82              </table>
83            </c:if>
84            <%@ include file="/WEB-INF/jsp/adminFooter.jsp" %>
85        </body>
86    </html>
```

Explanation:

This is a standard data entry form, which captures the state details. By default when the form loads, it's in the **INSERT** and **VIEW** mode. The form also has Delete and Edit options to delete and edit a particular state record.

Controller [StateController.java]

This is a controller class with the following specifications.

Controller Specifications

Class Name	Package	
StateController	com.sharanamvaishali.controllers	
Objects		
Object Name	Class Name	Object Type
stateService	StateService	Service Layer

| Methods | |
Method Name	Request Mapping
showManageStates()	/admin/manageStates
saveState()	/admin/saveState
deleteState()	/admin/deleteState/${stateNo}
editState()	/admin/editState/${stateNo}

Code Spec

```
1  package com.sharanamvaishali.controllers;
2
3  import com.sharanamvaishali.model.State;
4  import com.sharanamvaishali.service.StateService;
5  import java.util.Map;
6  import javax.validation.Valid;
7  import org.hibernate.exception.ConstraintViolationException;
8  import org.springframework.beans.factory.annotation.Autowired;
9  import org.springframework.dao.DataIntegrityViolationException;
10 import org.springframework.stereotype.Controller;
11 import org.springframework.validation.BindingResult;
12 import org.springframework.web.bind.annotation.ModelAttribute;
13 import org.springframework.web.bind.annotation.PathVariable;
14 import org.springframework.web.bind.annotation.RequestMapping;
15 import org.springframework.web.bind.annotation.RequestMethod;
16
17 @Controller
18 @RequestMapping("/admin")
19 public class StateController {
20     @Autowired
21     private StateService stateService;
22
23     @RequestMapping("/manageStates")
24     public String showManageStates(Map<String, Object> map) {
25         map.put("state", new State());
26         map.put("stateList", stateService.listState());
27         return "manageStates";
28     }
29
30     @RequestMapping(value = "/saveState", method = RequestMethod.POST)
31     public String saveState(Map<String, Object> map, @ModelAttribute("state") State
       state, @Valid State stateValid, BindingResult result) {
32         if (result.hasErrors()) {
33             return "manageStates";
34         } else {
35             try {
36                 stateService.saveState(state);
37                 return "redirect:/admin/manageStates";
38             } catch (ConstraintViolationException exp) {
39                 map.put("dbError", exp.getMessage());
40                 return "manageStates";
```

```
41          }
42        }
43      }
44
45      @RequestMapping("/deleteState/{stateNo}")
46      public String deleteState(Map<String, Object> map, @PathVariable("stateNo")
        Integer stateNo) {
47          try {
48              stateService.removeState(stateNo);
49              return "redirect:/admin/manageStates";
50          } catch (DataIntegrityViolationException exp) {
51              map.put("dbError", "Cannot delete a parent row.");
52              map.put("state", new State());
53              return "manageStates";
54          }
55      }
56
57      @RequestMapping("/editState/{stateNo}")
58      public String editState(Map<String, Object> map, @PathVariable("stateNo") Integer
        stateNo) {
59          map.put("state", stateService.getStateById(stateNo));
60          return "manageStates";
61      }
62  }
```

Explanation:

The following section describes the above code spec.

showManageStates()

StateController holds a mapping to help the viewing.

This means the list of state details are retrieved by the **StateController** class's **showManageStates()**.

showManageStates() is invoked every time Manage States is served.

showManageStates():

❑ Makes a provision for adding a new state [if the user chooses to] by instantiating an object of the State entity class

❑ Retrieves the state details by invoking **listState()** of StateService

❑ Returns the state details that **listState()** returns, to the View to render it, using **map.put()**

saveState()

StateController holds a mapping to help the adding of states.

```
@RequestMapping("/manageStates")
public String showManageStates(Map<String, Object> map) {
    map.put("state", new State());
    map.put("stateList", stateService.listState());
    return "manageStates";
}
```

As soon as Manage States is served, an object of the State entity class is instantiated to make a provision for adding a new state. The user may view, edit, delete or choose to add a new state.

In case, the user chooses to add a new state, keys in the required state details and clicks **Save**, **StateController** holds a mapping to help the saving of the newly captured state details.

saveState():

❑ Ensures that the captured data is valid

❑ Returns the control to the View along with the error messages [available in the BindingResult object], if the captured data is found to be invalid

❑ Saves the state details using StateService's **saveState()**, if the captured data is valid and returns the control to the View to render Manage States

deleteState()

In case, the user chooses to delete a state and clicks ⬤, **StateController** holds a mapping to help delete a state record from Manage States.

deleteState():

❑ Passes **StateNo** of the state to be deleted [available as a @PathVariable] to StateService's **removeState()**

❑ Checks whether the record to be deleted is used by other database table and accordingly displays the error message indicating that this record cannot be deleted. This is done by catching the DataIntegrityViolation exception

❑ Returns the control to the View which renders Manage States with the updated data

editState()

StateController holds a mapping to help the editing of existing states. In case, the user chooses to edit a state and clicks 🖊, StateController holds a mapping to help fill up the Manage States form with state details.

editState():

☐ Retrieves the appropriate State's details using StateNo as the reference. It calls StateService's getStateById() which returns the details of the state to be edited as a State object. StateNo is made available through @PathVariable [in the list of State rendered by the View] when the user clicks 🖊 to edit a particular state

☐ Returns the control to the View along with the data to be populated in the form. The data to be populated is made available using Map's put(), which is used to populate the states object with the data that getStateById() of StateService returns

Service Class

Interface [StateService.java]

This is a service interface with the following specifications.

Service Interface Specifications

Class Name	Package
StateService	com.sharanamvaishali.service

Code Spec

```
1  package com.sharanamvaishali.service;
2
3  import com.sharanamvaishali.model.State;
4  import java.util.List;
5
6  public interface StateService {
7      public void saveState(State state);
8      public List<State> listState();
9      public void removeState(Integer stateNo);
10     public State getStateById(Integer stateNo);
11 }
```

Implementation Class [StateServiceImpl.java]

This is a service class with the following specifications.

Service Implementation Specifications

Class Name	Package	Implements
StateServiceImpl	com.sharanamvaishali.service	StateService

Objects		
Object Name	Class Name	Object Type
stateDAO	StateDAO	Data Access Object Layer

Methods	
Method Name	Arguments
saveState()	State state
listState()	- -
removeState()	Integer stateNo
getStateById()	Integer stateNo

Code Spec

```
1  package com.sharanamvaishali.service;
2
3  import com.sharanamvaishali.dao.StateDAO;
4  import com.sharanamvaishali.model.State;
5  import java.util.List;
6  import org.springframework.beans.factory.annotation.Autowired;
7  import org.springframework.stereotype.Service;
8  import org.springframework.transaction.annotation.Transactional;
9
10 @Service
11 public class StateServiceImpl implements StateService {
12     @Autowired
13     private StateDAO stateDAO;
14
15     @Transactional
16     @Override
17     public void saveState(State state) {
18         stateDAO.saveState(state);
19     }
20
21     @Transactional
22     @Override
23     public List<State> listState() {
24         return stateDAO.listState();
25     }
26
27     @Transactional
28     @Override
```

```
29    public void removeState(Integer stateNo) {
30        stateDAO.removeState(stateNo);
31    }
32
33    @Transactional
34    @Override
35    public State getStateById(Integer stateNo) {
36        return stateDAO.getStateById(stateNo);
37    }
38 }
```

Explanation:

The following section describes the above code spec.

saveState()

saveState() holds the business logic to save the captured state details.

This method in turn invokes StateDAO's **saveState()**.

listState()

listState() holds the business logic to return the appropriate list of the available states.

This method in turn invokes StateDAO's **listState()**.

removeState()

removeState() holds the business logic to delete state details based on StateNo.

This method in turn invokes StateDAO's **removeState()**.

getStateById()

getStateById() holds the business logic to retrieve state details based on StateNo.

This method in turn invokes StateDAO's **getStateById()**.

DAO Class

Interface [StateDAO.java]

This is a Data Access Object interface with the following specifications.

DAO Interface Specifications

Class Name	Package
StateDAO	com.sharanamvaishali.dao

Code Spec

```
1  package com.sharanamvaishali.dao;
2
3  import com.sharanamvaishali.model.State;
4  import java.util.List;
5
6  public interface StateDAO {
7      public void saveState(State state);
8      public List<State> listState();
9      public void removeState(Integer stateNo);
10     public State getStateById(Integer stateNo);
11 }
```

Implementation Class [StateDAOImpl.java]

This is a **Data Access Object** class with the following specifications.

DAO Implementation Specifications

Class Name	Package	Implements
StateDAOImpl	com.sharanamvaishali.dao	StateDAO

Objects	
Object Name	Class Name
sessionFactory	SessionFactory

Methods		
Method Name	Arguments	Return Values
saveState()	State state	void
listState()	- -	List <State>
removeState()	Integer stateNo	void
getStateById()	Integer stateNo	State

Code Spec

```
1  package com.sharanamvaishali.dao;
2
3  import com.sharanamvaishali.model.State;
4  import java.util.List;
5  import org.hibernate.SessionFactory;
6  import org.springframework.beans.factory.annotation.Autowired;
```

```
 7  import org.springframework.stereotype.Repository;
 8
 9  @Repository
10  public class StateDAOImpl implements StateDAO {
11      @Autowired
12      private SessionFactory sessionFactory;
13
14      @Override
15      public void saveState(State state) {
16          sessionFactory.getCurrentSession().merge(state);
17      }
18
19      @Override
20      public List<State> listState() {
21          return sessionFactory.getCurrentSession().createQuery("from State").list();
22      }
23
24      @Override
25      public void removeState(Integer stateNo) {
26          State state = (State) sessionFactory.getCurrentSession().load(State.class,
            stateNo);
27          if (null != state) {
28              sessionFactory.getCurrentSession().delete(state);
29          }
30      }
31
32      @Override
33      public State getStateById(Integer stateNo) {
34          return (State) sessionFactory.getCurrentSession().get(State.class, stateNo);
35      }
36  }
```

Explanation:

The following section describes the above code spec.

saveState()

saveState() does the actual saving of the state in the State database table.

This method uses **merge()** of SessionFactory, which takes care of adding as well as updating the state details, in case the user had edited an existing state and clicked Save.

listState()

listState() does the actual retrieval of the available states.

This method fires a SELECT query that attempts to retrieve records from the State database table.

All the records that the query retrieves are extracted and returned as a **List** object.

This List object is returned to the calling method i.e. Service Layer's **listState()**:

```
public List<State> listState() {
    return stateDAO.listState();
}
```

This method in turn returns it to the StateController's **showManageStates()**:

```
public String showManageStates(Map<String, Object> map) {
    map.put("state", new State());
    map.put("stateList", stateService.listState());
    return "manageStates";
}
```

Finally, StateController returns this List object to the View which renders it.

manageStates.jsp on taking charge uses the **iterator** tag to iterate over the contents of the List object **stateList**.

```
<c:forEach items="${stateList}" var="state">
    <tr>
        <td>${state.state}</td>
```

The stateList object holds all those records retrieved by the SQL query.

Each record's column values are extracted using $.

```
<td>${state.state}</td>
<td><a
```

removeState()

removeState() deletes the appropriate state based on **StateNo** received as a reference.

This method uses:

❑ **load()** of SessionFactory, which retrieves the appropriate State to be deleted using StateNo as a reference

❑ **delete()** of SessionFactory, which deletes the state from State database table *getStateById()*

getStateById() returns the appropriate state's object from the State database table using **StateNo** as the reference.

This method uses **get()** of SessionFactory, which returns the appropriate State from State database table.

After editing the state details, when the user clicks **Save** , saveState() of StateController, followed by saveState() of StateService, followed by saveState() of StateDAO takes care of saving the updated state's details.

Domain Class [State.java]

This is a domain class with the following specifications.

Domain Specifications

Class Name	Package	Implements
State	com.sharanamvaishali.model	java.io.Serializable

Properties			
Property Name	Property Type	Methods	
stateNo	Integer	getStateNo()	setStateNo()
state	String	getState()	setState()

Code Spec

```
1  package com.sharanamvaishali.model;
2
3  import javax.persistence.*;
4  import org.hibernate.validator.constraints.NotEmpty;
5
6  @Entity
7  @Table(name="STATE")
8  public class State implements java.io.Serializable {
9      @Id
10     @GeneratedValue
11     @Column(name="STATENO")
12     private Integer stateNo;
13     @Column(name="STATE")
14     @NotEmpty(message="State name is mandatory")
15     private String state;
16
17     public Integer getStateNo() {
18         return stateNo;
```

```
19      }
20      public void setStateNo(Integer stateNo) {
21          this.stateNo = stateNo;
22      }
23
24      public String getState() {
25          return state;
26      }
27      public void setState(String state) {
28          this.state = state;
29      }
30 }
```

Chapter

33

SECTION V: BACKEND [ADMINISTRATION] SOFTWARE DESIGN DOCUMENTATION

Manage Categories

This module allows performing the following operations:

- ❑ Adding new categories
- ❑ Editing existing categories
- ❑ Viewing across existing categories
- ❑ Deleting existing categories

This module uses the bms.Categories table to perform the above operations.

This module is made up of the following:

Type	Name	Description
JSP	manageCategories.jsp	The data entry form
Spring		
Controller	CategoryController.java	The controller class that facilitates data operations
Service Class	CategoryService.java	The interface for the service layer.
	CategoryServiceImpl.java	The implementation class for the service layer
DAO Class	CategoryDAO.java	The interface for the DAO layer
	CategoryDAOImpl.java	The implementation class that performs the actual data operations.
DispatcherServlet	bookshopdispatcher-servlet.xml	Central dispatcher for HTTP request handlers/controllers
Hibernate		
Mapping	hibernate.cfg.xml	The mapping file that holds Model class mapping
Model Class	Category.java	The model class

JSP [manageCategories.jsp]

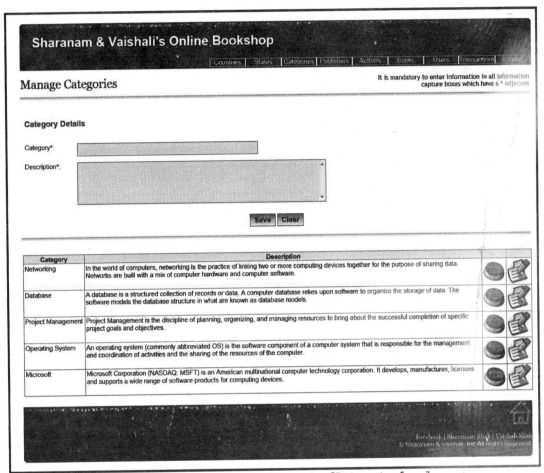

Diagram 33.1: Manage Categories [Data entry form]

This is a JSP which holds a data entry form, as shown in diagram 33.1. This form appears when the user clicks Categories.

Form Specifications

File Name	manageCategories.jsp
Title	BookShop[Sharanam & Vaishali Shah] - Manage Categories
Bound To Table	bms.Categories
Command Name	category
Action	${pageContext.request.contextPath}/admin/saveCategory
Method	POST

Data Fields

Label	Name	Bound To	Validation Rules
Category	Category.category	Categories.Category	Cannot be left blank
Description	Category.description	Categories.Description	Cannot by left blank

Micro-Help For Form Fields

Form Field	Micro Help Statement
Category.category	Enter the category name
Category.description	Enter the description of the category

Data Controls

Object	Label
Submit	Save
Reset	Clear

Code Spec

```
1  <%@page contentType="text/html" pageEncoding="UTF-8"%>
2  <%@taglib uri="http://www.springframework.org/tags/form" prefix="form"%>
3  <%@taglib uri="http://java.sun.com/jsp/jstl/core" prefix="c"%>
4  <!DOCTYPE HTML PUBLIC "-//W3C//DTD HTML 4.01 Transitional//EN"
5     "http://www.w3.org/TR/html4/loose.dtd">
6  <html>
7     <head>
8        <meta http-equiv="Content-Type" content="text/html; charset=UTF-8">
9        <title>BookShop[Sharanam & Vaishali Shah] - Manage Categories</title>
10       <link rel="stylesheet" href="/BookShop/css/admin.css" type="text/css">
11    </head>
12    <body>
13       <%@ include file="/WEB-INF/jsp/adminHeader.jsp" %>
14       <br/>
```

```
15      <form:form method="post"
        action="${pageContext.request.contextPath}/admin/saveCategory"
        commandName="category">
16        <form:hidden path="categoryNo" />
17        <table width="100%" border="0" align="center" cellpadding="0"
          cellspacing="0">
18          <tr>
19            <td>
20              <table border="0" cellpadding="0" cellspacing="0" width="100%">
21                <tr>
22                  <td class="manageForms">Manage Categories</td>
23                  <td align="center" class="error">${dbError}</td>
24                  <td class="information">
25                    It is mandatory to enter information in all information
                      <br>capture boxes which have a <span
                      class="mandatory">*</span> adjacent
26                  </td>
27                </tr>
28              </table>
29            </td>
30          </tr>
31          <tr><td class="hrLine"> </td></tr>
32          <tr>
33            <td>
34              <table width="100%" border="0" align="center" cellpadding="0"
                cellspacing="0">
35                <tr>
36                  <td>
37                    <table width="100%" border="0" cellpadding="4"
                      cellspacing="4">
38                      <tr>
39                        <td class="sectionName" colspan="2">
40                          <br />Category Details<br /><br />
41                        </td>
42                      </tr>
43                      <tr>
44                        <td width="10%">Category<span
                          class="mandatory">*</span>:</td>
45                        <td>
46                          <form:input path="category" title="Enter the
                            category name" maxlength="25" size="55"/><br>
47                          <form:errors path="category" cssClass="error" />
48                        </td>
49                      </tr>
50                      <tr>
51                        <td width="10%">Description<span
                          class="mandatory">*</span>:</td>
52                        <td>
53                          <form:textarea path="description" title="Enter the
                            description of the category" cols="80"
                            rows="5"/><br>
54                          <form:errors path="description" cssClass="error" />
55                        </td>
56                      </tr>
```

```
57                            </table>
58                          </td>
59                        </tr>
60                        <tr><td> </td></tr>
61                        <tr>
62                          <td colspan="2" class="centerAlign">
63                            <input type="submit" class="groovybutton" value="Save" />
64                            <input type="reset" value="Clear" class="groovybutton"
                             onclick="javascript:document.location.href='/BookShop/admin
                             /manageCategories'" />
65                          </td>
66                        </tr>
67                      </table>
68                    </td>
69                  </tr>
70                  <tr><td> </td></tr>
71                  <tr><td class="hrLine"> </td></tr>
72                  <tr><td><br></td></tr>
73                </table>
74              </form:form>
75              <c:if test="${!empty categoryList}">
76                <table class="data" width="100%">
77                  <tr>
78                    <th width="14%">Category</th>
79                    <th width="80%">Description</th>
80                    <th width="3%"> </th>
81                    <th width="3%"> </th>
82                  </tr>
83                  <c:forEach items="${categoryList}" var="category">
84                    <tr>
85                      <td>${category.category}</td>
86                      <td>${category.description}</td>
87                      <td><a
                        href="/BookShop/admin/deleteCategory/${category.categoryNo}"><i
                        mg title="Click to delete"
                        src="/BookShop/images/delete.jpg"/></a></td>
88                      <td><a
                        href="/BookShop/admin/editCategory/${category.categoryNo}"><img
                        title="Click to edit" src="/BookShop/images/edit.jpg"/></a></td>
89                    </tr>
90                  </c:forEach>
91                </table>
92              </c:if>
93              <%@ include file="/WEB-INF/jsp/adminFooter.jsp" %>
94          </body>
95  </html>
```

Explanation:

This is a standard data entry form, which captures the category details. By default when the form loads, it's in the **INSERT** and **VIEW** mode. The form also has Delete and Edit options to delete and edit a particular category record.

Controller [CategoryController.java]

This is a controller class with the following specifications.

Controller Specifications

Class Name	Package	
CategoryController	com.sharanamvaishali.controllers	

Objects		
Object Name	**Class Name**	**Object Type**
categoryService	CategoryService	Service Layer

Methods	
Method Name	**Request Mapping**
showManageCategories()	/admin/manageCategories
saveCategory()	/admin/saveCategory
deleteCategory()	/admin/deleteCategory/${categoryNo}
editCategory()	/admin/editCategory/${categoryNo}

Code Spec

```
1  package com.sharanamvaishali.controllers;
2
3  import com.sharanamvaishali.model.Category;
4  import com.sharanamvaishali.service.CategoryService;
5  import java.util.Map;
6  import javax.validation.Valid;
7  import org.hibernate.exception.ConstraintViolationException;
8  import org.springframework.beans.factory.annotation.Autowired;
9  import org.springframework.dao.DataIntegrityViolationException;
10 import org.springframework.stereotype.Controller;
11 import org.springframework.validation.BindingResult;
12 import org.springframework.web.bind.annotation.ModelAttribute;
13 import org.springframework.web.bind.annotation.PathVariable;
14 import org.springframework.web.bind.annotation.RequestMapping;
15 import org.springframework.web.bind.annotation.RequestMethod;
16
17 @Controller
18 @RequestMapping("/admin")
19 public class CategoryController {
20     @Autowired
21     private CategoryService categoryService;
22
23     @RequestMapping("/manageCategories")
24     public String showManageCategories(Map<String, Object> map) {
25         map.put("category", new Category());
26         map.put("categoryList", categoryService.listCategory());
27         return "manageCategories";
```

```
28     }
29
30     @RequestMapping(value = "/saveCategory", method = RequestMethod.POST)
31     public String saveCategory(Map<String, Object> map, @ModelAttribute("category")
       Category category, @Valid Category categoryValid, BindingResult result) {
32         if (result.hasErrors()) {
33             return "manageCategories";
34         } else {
35             try {
36                 categoryService.saveCategory(category);
37                 return "redirect:/admin/manageCategories";
38             } catch (ConstraintViolationException exp) {
39                 map.put("dbError", exp.getMessage());
40                 return "manageCategories";
41             }
42         }
43     }
44
45     @RequestMapping("/deleteCategory/{categoryNo}")
46     public String deleteCategory(Map<String, Object> map,
       @PathVariable("categoryNo") Integer categoryNo) {
47         try {
48             categoryService.removeCategory(categoryNo);
49             return "redirect:/admin/manageCategories";
50         } catch (DataIntegrityViolationException exp) {
51             map.put("dbError", "Cannot delete a parent row.");
52             map.put("category", new Category());
53             return "manageCategories";
54         }
55     }
56
57     @RequestMapping("/editCategory/{categoryNo}")
58     public String editCategory(Map<String, Object> map, @PathVariable("categoryNo")
       Integer categoryNo) {
59         map.put("category", categoryService.getCategoryById(categoryNo));
60         return "manageCategories";
61     }
62 }
```

Explanation:

The following section describes the above code spec.

showManageCategories()

CategoryController holds a mapping to help the viewing.

This means the list of category details are retrieved by the **CategoryController** class's **showManageCategories()**.

showManageCategories() is invoked every time Manage Categories is served.

showManageCategories():

☐ Makes a provision for adding a new category [if the user chooses to] by instantiating an object of the Category entity class

☐ Retrieves the category details by invoking **listCategory()** of CategoryService

☐ Returns the category details that **listCategory()** returns, to the View to render it, using **map.put()**

saveCategory()

CategoryController holds a mapping to help the adding of categories.

```
public String showManageCategories(Map<String, Object> map) {
    map.put("category", new Category());
    map.put("categoryList", categoryService.listCategory());
    return "manageCategories";
}
```

As soon as Manage Categories is served, an object of the Category entity class is instantiated to make a provision for adding a new category. The user may view, edit, delete or choose to add a new category.

In case, the user chooses to add a new category, keys in the required category details and clicks **Save**, **CategoryController** holds a mapping to help the saving of the newly captured category details.

saveCategory():

☐ Ensures that the captured data is valid

☐ Returns the control to the View along with the error messages [available in the BindingResult object], if the captured data is found to be invalid

☐ Saves the category details using CategoryService's **saveCategory()**, if the captured data is valid and returns the control to the View to render Manage Categories

deleteCategory()

In case, the user chooses to delete a category and clicks , **CategoryController** holds a mapping to help delete a category record from Manage Categories.

deleteCategory():

❏ Passes **CategoryNo** of the category to be deleted [available as a @PathVariable] to CategoryService's **removeCategory()**

❏ Checks whether the record to be deleted is used by other database table and accordingly displays the error message indicating that this record cannot be deleted. This is done by catching the DataIntegrityViolation exception

❏ Returns the control to the View which renders Manage Categories with the updated data

editCategory()

CategoryController holds a mapping to help the editing of existing categories. In case, the user chooses to edit a category and clicks , **CategoryController** holds a mapping to help fill up the Manage Categories form with category details.

editCategory():

❏ Retrieves the appropriate Category's details using **CategoryNo** as the reference. It calls CategoryService's **getCategoryById()** which returns the details of the category to be edited as a Category object. **CategoryNo** is made available through **@PathVariable** [in the list of Category rendered by the View] when the user clicks to edit a particular category

❏ Returns the control to the View along with the data to be populated in the form. The data to be populated is made available using Map's **put()**, which is used to populate the categories object with the data that **getCategoryById()** of CategoryService returns

Service Class

Interface [CategoryService.java]

This is a service interface with the following specifications.

Service Interface Specifications

Class Name	Package
CategoryService	com.sharanamvaishali.service

Code Spec

```
1  package com.sharanamvaishali.service;
2
3  import com.sharanamvaishali.model.Category;
4  import java.util.List;
5
6  public interface CategoryService {
7      public void saveCategory(Category category);
8      public List<Category> listCategory();
9      public void removeCategory(Integer categoryNo);
10     public Category getCategoryById(Integer categoryNo);
11 }
```

Implementation Class [CategoryServiceImpl.java]

This is a service class with the following specifications.

Service Implementation Specifications

Class Name	Package	Implements
CategoryServiceImpl	com.sharanamvaishali.service	CategoryService

Objects		
Object Name	Class Name	Object Type
categoryDAO	CategoryDAO	Data Access Object Layer

Methods	
Method Name	Arguments
saveCategory()	Category category
listCategory()	- -
removeCategory()	Integer categoryNo
getCategoryById()	Integer categoryNo

Code Spec

```
1  package com.sharanamvaishali.service;
2
3  import com.sharanamvaishali.dao.CategoryDAO;
4  import com.sharanamvaishali.model.Category;
5  import java.util.List;
6  import org.springframework.beans.factory.annotation.Autowired;
7  import org.springframework.stereotype.Service;
8  import org.springframework.transaction.annotation.Transactional;
9
10 @Service
11 public class CategoryServiceImpl implements CategoryService {
12     @Autowired
```

```
13      private CategoryDAO categoryDAO;
14
15      @Transactional
16      @Override
17      public void saveCategory(Category category) {
18          categoryDAO.saveCategory(category);
19      }
20
21      @Transactional
22      @Override
23      public List<Category> listCategory() {
24          return categoryDAO.listCategory();
25      }
26
27      @Transactional
28      @Override
29      public void removeCategory(Integer categoryNo) {
30          categoryDAO.removeCategory(categoryNo);
31      }
32
33      @Transactional
34      @Override
35      public Category getCategoryById(Integer categoryNo) {
36          return categoryDAO.getCategoryById(categoryNo);
37      }
38  }
```

Explanation:

The following section describes the above code spec.

saveCategory()

saveCategory() holds the business logic to save the captured category details.

This method in turn invokes CategoryDAO's **saveCategory()**.

listCategory()

listCategory() holds the business logic to return the appropriate list of the available categories.

This method in turn invokes CategoryDAO's **listCategory()**.

removeCategory()

removeCategory() holds the business logic to delete category details based on CategoryNo.

This method in turn invokes CategoryDAO's **removeCategory()**.

getCategoryById()

getCategoryById() holds the business logic to retrieve category details based on CategoryNo.

This method in turn invokes CategoryDAO's **getCategoryById()**.

DAO Class

Interface [CategoryDAO.java]

This is a Data Access Object interface with the following specifications.

DAO Interface Specifications

Class Name	Package
CategoryDAO	com.sharanamvaishali.dao

Code Spec

```
1  package com.sharanamvaishali.dao;
2
3  import com.sharanamvaishali.model.Category;
4  import java.util.List;
5
6  public interface CategoryDAO {
7      public void saveCategory(Category category);
8      public List<Category> listCategory();
9      public void removeCategory(Integer categoryNo);
10     public Category getCategoryById(Integer categoryNo);
11 }
```

Implementation Class [CategoryDAOImpl.java]

This is a Data Access Object class with the following specifications.

DAO Implementation Specifications

Class Name	Package	Implements
CategoryDAOImpl	com.sharanamvaishali.dao	CategoryDAO

Objects	
Object Name	**Class Name**
sessionFactory	SessionFactory

Methods		
Method Name	**Arguments**	**Return Values**
saveCategory()	Category category	void
listCategory()	- -	List <Category>
removeCategory()	Integer categoryNo	void
getCategoryById()	Integer categoryNo	Category

Code Spec

```
1  package com.sharanamvaishali.dao;
2
3  import com.sharanamvaishali.model.Category;
4  import java.util.List;
5  import org.hibernate.SessionFactory;
6  import org.springframework.beans.factory.annotation.Autowired;
7  import org.springframework.stereotype.Repository;
8
9  @Repository
10 public class CategoryDAOImpl implements CategoryDAO {
11     @Autowired
12     private SessionFactory sessionFactory;
13
14     @Override
15     public void saveCategory(Category category) {
16         sessionFactory.getCurrentSession().merge(category);
17     }
18
19     @Override
20     public List<Category> listCategory() {
21         return sessionFactory.getCurrentSession().createQuery("from Category ORDER BY
           category").list();
22     }
23
24     @Override
25     public void removeCategory(Integer categoryNo) {
26         Category category = (Category)
           sessionFactory.getCurrentSession().load(Category.class, categoryNo);
27         if (null != category) {
28             sessionFactory.getCurrentSession().delete(category);
29         }
30     }
31
32     @Override
33     public Category getCategoryById(Integer categoryNo) {
34         return (Category) sessionFactory.getCurrentSession().get(Category.class,
           categoryNo);
35     }
36 }
```

Explanation:

The following section describes the above code spec.

saveCategory()

saveCategory() does the actual saving of the category in the Categories database table.

This method uses **merge()** of SessionFactory, which takes care of adding as well as updating the category details, in case the user had edited an existing category and clicked ▮ Save ▮.

listCategory()

listCategory() does the actual retrieval of the available categories.

This method fires a SELECT query that attempts to retrieve records from the Categories database table.

All the records that the query retrieves are extracted and returned as a **List** object.

This List object is returned to the calling method i.e. Service Layer's **listCategory()**:

```
public List<Category> listCategory() {
    return categoryDAO.listCategory();
}
```

This method in turn returns it to the CategoryController's **showManageCategories()**:

```
public String showManageCategories(Map<String, Object> map) {
    map.put("category", new Category());
    map.put("categoryList", categoryService.listCategory());
    return "manageCategories";
}
```

Finally, CategoryController returns this List object to the View which renders it.

manageCategories.jsp on taking charge uses the **iterator** tag to iterate over the contents of the List object **categoryList**.

```
<c:forEach items="${categoryList}" var="category">
    <tr>
        <td>${category.category}</td>
        <td>${category.description}</td>
```

The categoryList object holds all those records retrieved by the SQL query.

Each record's column values are extracted using $.

```
<td>${category.category}</td>
<td>${category.description}</td>
```

removeCategory()

removeCategory() deletes the appropriate category based on **CategoryNo** received as a reference.

This method uses:

❑ **load()** of SessionFactory, which retrieves the appropriate Category to be deleted using CategoryNo as a reference

❑ **delete()** of SessionFactory, which deletes the category from Categories database table

getCategoryById()

getCategoryById() returns the appropriate category's object from the Categories database table using **CategoryNo** as the reference.

This method uses **get()** of SessionFactory, which returns the appropriate Category from Categories database table.

After editing the category details, when the user clicks **Save**, saveCategory() of CategoryController, followed by saveCategory() of CategoryService, followed by saveCategory() of CategoryDAO takes care of saving the updated category's details.

Domain Class [Category.java]

This is a domain class with the following specifications.

Domain Specifications

Class Name	Package	Implements
Category	com.sharanamvaishali.model	java.io.Serializable
Properties		
Property Name	Property Type	Methods
categoryNo	Integer	getCategoryNo() setCategoryNo()
category	String	getCategory() setCategory()
description	String	getDescription() setDescription()

Code Spec

```
 1  package com.sharanamvaishali.model;
 2
 3  import javax.persistence.*;
 4  import org.hibernate.validator.constraints.NotEmpty;
 5
 6  @Entity
 7  @Table(name="CATEGORIES")
 8  public class Category implements java.io.Serializable {
 9      @Id
10      @GeneratedValue
11      @Column(name="CATEGORYNO")
12      private Integer categoryNo;
13      @Column(name="CATEGORY")
14      @NotEmpty(message="Category is mandatory")
15      private String category;
16      @Column(name="DESCRIPTION")
17      @NotEmpty(message="Category description is mandatory")
18      private String description;
19
20      public String getCategory() {
21          return category;
22      }
23      public void setCategory(String category) {
24          this.category = category;
25      }
26
27      public Integer getCategoryNo() {
28          return categoryNo;
29      }
30      public void setCategoryNo(Integer categoryNo) {
31          this.categoryNo = categoryNo;
32      }
33
34      public String getDescription() {
35          return description;
36      }
37      public void setDescription(String description) {
38          this.description = description;
39      }
40  }
```

Chapter 34

SECTION V: BACKEND [ADMINISTRATION] SOFTWARE DESIGN DOCUMENTATION

Manage Publishers

This module allows performing the following operations:

- ❑ Adding new publishers
- ❑ Editing existing publishers
- ❑ Viewing across existing publishers
- ❑ Deleting existing publishers

This module uses the bms.Publishers table to perform the above operations.

This module is made up of the following:

Type	Name	Description
JSP	managePublishers.jsp	The data entry form.
Spring		
Controller	PublisherController.java	The controller class that facilitates data operations.
Service Class	PublisherService.java	The interface for the service layer.
	CountryService.java	
	StateService.java	
	PublisherServiceImpl.java	The implementation class for the service layer.
	CountryServiceImpl.java	
	StateServiceImpl.java	
DAO Class	PublisherDAO.java	The interface for the DAO layer.
	CountryDAO.java	
	StateDAO.java	
	PublisherDAOImpl.java	The implementation class that performs the actual data operations.
	CountryDAOImpl.java	
	StateDAOImpl.java	
DispatcherServlet	bookshopdispatcher-servlet.xml	Central dispatcher for HTTP request handlers/controllers.
Hibernate		
Mapping	hibernate.cfg.xml	The mapping file that holds Model class mapping.
Model Class	Publisher.java	The model class.
	Country.java	
	State.java	

JSP [managePublishers.jsp]

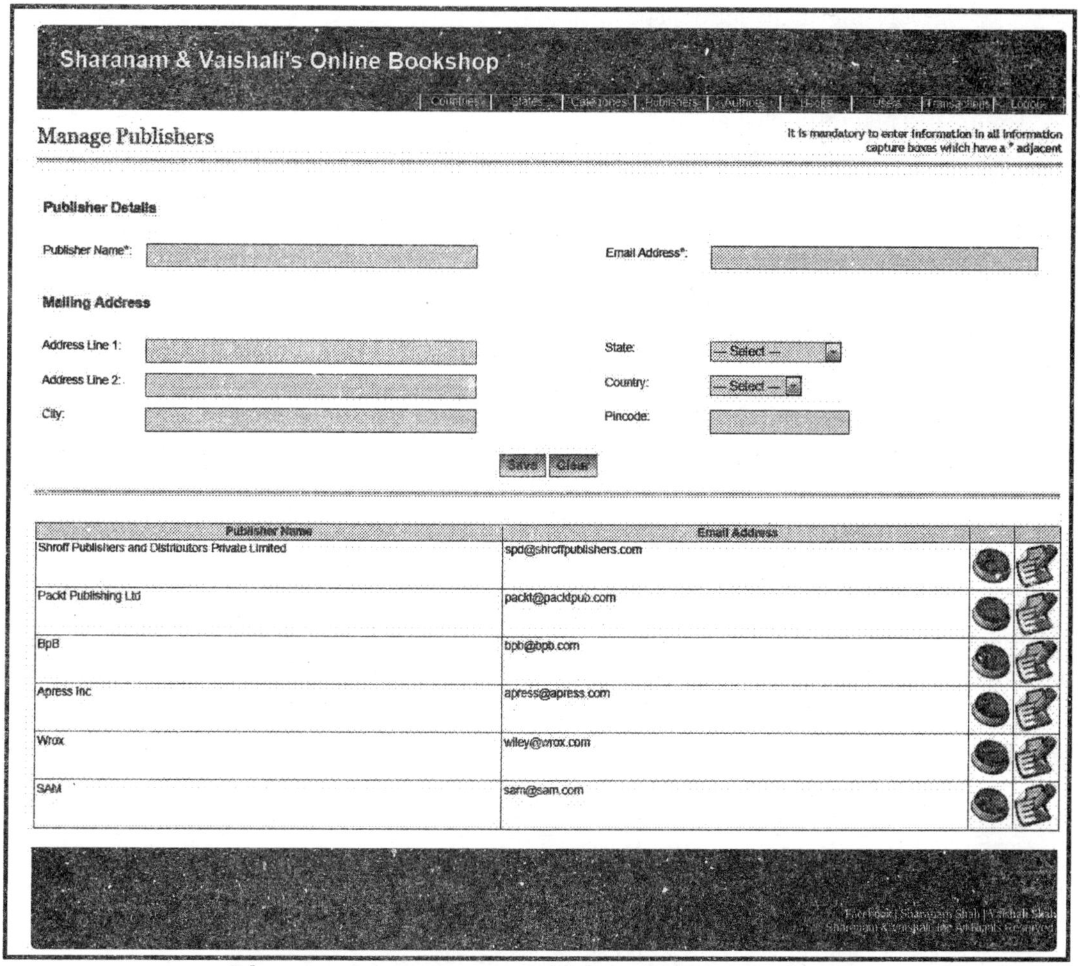

Diagram 34.1: Manage Publishers [Data entry form]

This is a JSP which holds a data entry form, as shown in diagram 34.1. This form appears when the user clicks ▮Publishers▮.

Form Specifications

File Name	managePublishers.jsp
Title	BookShop[Sharanam & Vaishali Shah] - Manage Publishers
Bound To Table	bms.Publishers
Command Name	publisher
Action	${pageContext.request.contextPath}/admin/savePublisher
Method	POST

Data Fields

Label	Name	Bound To	Validation Rules
Publisher Details			
Publisher Name	Publisher.publisherName	Publishers.PublisherName	Cannot be left blank
Email Address	Publisher.emailAddress	Publishers.EmailAddress	Cannot be left blank
Mailing Address			
Address Line 1	Publisher.address1	Publishers.Address1	- -
Address Line 2	Publisher.address2	Publishers.Address2	- -
City	Publisher.city	Publishers.City	- -
State	Publisher.stateNo	Publishers.StateNo	- -
Country	Publisher.countryNo	Publishers.CountryNo	- -
Pincode	Publisher.pincode	Publishers.Pincode	- -

Micro-Help For Form Fields

Form Field	Micro Help Statement
Publisher Details	
Publisher.publisherName	Enter the publisher name
Publisher.emailAddress	Enter the email address
Mailing Address	
Publisher.address1	Enter the street address
Publisher.address2	Enter the street address
Publisher.city	Enter the city
Publisher.stateNo	- -
Publisher.countryNo	- -
Publisher.pincode	Enter the pincode

Data Controls

Object	Label
Submit	Save
Reset	Clear

Code Spec

```
1   <%@page contentType="text/html" pageEncoding="UTF-8"%>
2   <%@taglib uri="http://www.springframework.org/tags/form" prefix="form"%>
3   <%@taglib uri="http://java.sun.com/jsp/jstl/core" prefix="c"%>
4   <!DOCTYPE HTML PUBLIC "-//W3C//DTD HTML 4.01 Transitional//EN"
5     "http://www.w3.org/TR/html4/loose.dtd">
6   <html>
7     <head>
8       <meta http-equiv="Content-Type" content="text/html; charset=UTF-8">
9       <title>BookShop[Sharanam & Vaishali Shah] - Manage Publishers</title>
10      <link rel="stylesheet" href="/BookShop/css/admin.css" type="text/css">
11    </head>
12    <body>
13      <%@ include file="/WEB-INF/jsp/adminHeader.jsp" %>
14      <br/>
15      <form:form method="post"
        action="${pageContext.request.contextPath}/admin/savePublisher"
        commandName="publisher">
16        <form:hidden path="publisherNo" />
17        <table width="100%" border="0" align="center" cellpadding="0"
          cellspacing="0">
18          <tr>
19            <td>
20              <table border="0" cellpadding="0" cellspacing="0" width="100%">
21                <tr>
22                  <td class="manageForms">Manage Publishers</td>
23                  <td align="center" class="error">${dbError}</td>
24                  <td class="information">
25                    It is mandatory to enter information in all information
                      <br>capture boxes which have a <span
                      class="mandatory">*</span> adjacent
26                  </td>
27                </tr>
28              </table>
29            </td>
30          </tr>
31          <tr><td class="hrLine"> </td></tr>
32          <tr>
33            <td>
34              <table width="100%" border="0" align="center" cellpadding="0"
                cellspacing="0">
35                <tr>
36                  <td>
```

```
37      <table width="100%" border="0" cellpadding="4"
        cellspacing="4">
38        <tr>
39          <td class="sectionName" colspan="4">
40            <br />Publisher Details<br /><br />
41          </td>
42        </tr>
43        <tr>
44          <td width="10%">Publisher Name<span
            class="mandatory">*</span>:</td>
45          <td width="45%">
46            <form:input path="publisherName" title="Enter the
              publisher name" maxlength="50" size="55"/><br>
47            <form:errors path="publisherName"
              cssClass="error" />
48          </td width="10%">
49          <td width="10%">Email Address<span
            class="mandatory">*</span>:</td>
50          <td width="45%">
51            <form:input path="emailAddress" title="Enter the
              email address" maxlength="50" size="55"/><br>
52            <form:errors path="emailAddress" cssClass="error"
              />
53          </td>
54        </tr>
55        <tr>
56          <td class="sectionName" colspan="4">
57            <br />Mailing Address<br /><br />
58          </td>
59        </tr>
60        <tr>
61          <td width="10%">Address Line 1:</td>
62          <td width="45%">
63            <form:input path="address1" title="Enter the
              street address" maxlength="50" size="55"/>
64          </td>
65          <td width="10%">State:</td>
66          <td width="45%">
67            <form:select path="stateNo">
68              <form:option value="" label="--- Select ---"/>
69              <form:options title="Select the state"
                items="${stateList}" itemValue="stateNo"
                itemLabel="state" />
70            </form:select>
71          </td>
72        </tr>
73        <tr>
74          <td width="10%">Address Line 2:</td>
75          <td width="45%">
76            <form:input path="address2" title="Enter the
              street address" maxlength="50" size="55"/>
77          </td>
78          <td width="10%">Country:</td>
79          <td width="45%">
```

```
80                              <form:select path="countryNo">
81                                  <form:option value="" label="--- Select ---"/>
82                                  <form:options title="Select the country"
                                    items="${countryList}" itemValue="countryNo"
                                    itemLabel="country" />
83                              </form:select>
84                          </td>
85                      </tr>
86                      <tr>
87                          <td width="10%">City:</td>
88                          <td width="45%">
89                              <form:input path="city" title="Enter the city"
                                    maxlength="50" size="55"/>
90                          </td>
91                          <td width="10%">Pincode:</td>
92                          <td width="45%">
93                              <form:input path="pincode" title="Enter the
                                    pincode" maxlength="15" size="20"/>
94                          </td>
95                      </tr>
96                  </table>
97              </td>
98          </tr>
99          <tr><td> </td></tr>
100         <tr>
101             <td colspan="2" class="centerAlign">
102                 <input type="submit" class="groovybutton" value="Save"
                        />
103                 <input type="reset" value="Clear" class="groovybutton"
                        onclick="javascript:document.location.href='/BookShop/admi
                        n/managePublishers'" />
104             </td>
105         </tr>
106     </table>
107 </td>
108 </tr>
109 <tr><td> </td></tr>
110 <tr><td class="hrLine"> </td></tr>
111 <tr><td><br></td></tr>
112 </table>
113 </form:form>
114 <c:if test="${!empty publisherList}">
115     <table class="data" width="100%">
116         <tr>
117             <th width="47%">Publisher Name</th>
118             <th width="47%">Email Address</th>
119             <th width="3%"> </th>
120             <th width="3%"> </th>
121         </tr>
122         <c:forEach items="${publisherList}" var="publisher">
123             <tr>
124                 <td>${publisher.publisherName}</td>
125                 <td>${publisher.emailAddress}</td>
```

```
126                    <td><a
                       href="/BookShop/admin/deletePublisher/${publisher.publisherNo}">
                       <img title="Click to delete"
                       src="/BookShop/images/delete.jpg"/></a></td>
127                    <td><a
                       href="/BookShop/admin/editPublisher/${publisher.publisherNo}"><i
                       mg title="Click to edit"
                       src="/BookShop/images/edit.jpg"/></a></td>
128                </tr>
129            </c:forEach>
130        </table>
131    </c:if>
132    <%@ include file="/WEB-INF/jsp/adminFooter.jsp" %>
133 </body>
134 </html>
```

Explanation:

This is a standard data entry form, which captures the publisher details. By default when the form loads, it's in the **INSERT** and **VIEW** mode. The form also has Delete and Edit options to delete and edit a particular publisher record.

Controller [PublisherController.java]

This is a controller class with the following specifications.

Controller Specifications

Class Name	Package	
PublisherController	com.sharanamvaishali.controllers	
Objects		
Object Name	Class Name	Object Type
publisherService	PublisherService	Service Layer
countryService	CountryService	Service Layer
stateService	StateService	Service Layer
Methods		
Method Name	Request Mapping	
showManagePublishers()	/admin/managePublishers	
savePublisher()	/admin/savePublisher	
deletePublisher()	/admin/deletePublisher/${publisherNo}	
editPublisher()	/admin/editPublisher/${publisherNo}	

Code Spec

```
1 package com.sharanamvaishali.controllers;
2
```

```
2
3   import com.sharanamvaishali.model.Publisher;
4   import com.sharanamvaishali.service.CountryService;
5   import com.sharanamvaishali.service.PublisherService;
6   import com.sharanamvaishali.service.StateService;
7   import java.util.Map;
8   import javax.validation.Valid;
9   import org.hibernate.exception.ConstraintViolationException;
10  import org.springframework.beans.factory.annotation.Autowired;
11  import org.springframework.dao.DataIntegrityViolationException;
12  import org.springframework.stereotype.Controller;
13  import org.springframework.validation.BindingResult;
14  import org.springframework.web.bind.annotation.ModelAttribute;
15  import org.springframework.web.bind.annotation.PathVariable;
16  import org.springframework.web.bind.annotation.RequestMapping;
17  import org.springframework.web.bind.annotation.RequestMethod;
18
19  @Controller
20  @RequestMapping("/admin")
21  public class PublisherController {
22      @Autowired
23      private PublisherService publisherService;
24
25      @Autowired
26      private CountryService countryService;
27
28      @Autowired
29      private StateService stateService;
30
31      @RequestMapping("/managePublishers")
32      public String showManagePublishers(Map<String, Object> map) {
33          map.put("publisher", new Publisher());
34          map.put("publisherList", publisherService.listPublisher());
35          map.put("countryList", countryService.listCountry());
36          map.put("stateList", stateService.listState());
37          return "managePublishers";
38      }
39
40      @RequestMapping(value = "/savePublisher", method = RequestMethod.POST)
41      public String savePublisher(Map<String, Object> map, @ModelAttribute("publisher")
        Publisher publisher, @Valid Publisher publisherValid, BindingResult result) {
42          if (result.hasErrors()) {
43              map.put("countryList", countryService.listCountry());
44              map.put("stateList", stateService.listState());
45              return "managePublishers";
46          } else {
47              try {
48                  publisherService.savePublisher(publisher);
49                  return "redirect:/admin/managePublishers";
50              } catch (ConstraintViolationException exp) {
51                  map.put("dbError", exp.getMessage());
52                  return "managePublishers";
53              }
54          }
```

```
55    }
56
57    @RequestMapping("/deletePublisher/{publisherNo}")
58    public String deletePublisher(Map<String, Object> map,
      @PathVariable("publisherNo") Integer publisherNo) {
59        try {
60            publisherService.removePublisher(publisherNo);
61            return "redirect:/admin/managePublishers";
62        } catch (DataIntegrityViolationException exp) {
63            map.put("dbError", "Cannot delete a parent row.");
64            map.put("publisher", new Publisher());
65            return "managePublishers";
66        }
67    }
68
69    @RequestMapping("/editPublisher/{publisherNo}")
70    public String editPublisher(Map<String, Object> map, @PathVariable("publisherNo")
      Integer publisherNo) {
71        map.put("publisher", publisherService.getPublisherById(publisherNo));
72        map.put("countryList", countryService.listCountry());
73        map.put("stateList", stateService.listState());
74        return "managePublishers";
75    }
76 }
```

Explanation:

The following section describes the above code spec.

showManagePublishers()

PublisherController holds a mapping to help the viewing.

This means the list of publisher details are retrieved by the **PublisherController** class's **showManagePublishers()**.

showManagePublishers() is invoked every time Manage Publishers is served.

showManagePublishers():

❑ Makes a provision for adding a new publisher [if the user chooses to] by instantiating an object of the Publisher entity class

❑ Retrieves the publisher details by invoking **listPublisher()** of PublisherService

❑ Retrieves the state names by invoking **listState()** of StateService, which is displayed in the drop down list box of State field

❑ Retrieves the country names by invoking **listCountry()** of CountryService, which is displayed in the drop down list box of Country field

❑ Returns the publisher, state and country details that **listPublisher()**, **listState()** and **listCountry()** return respectively, to the View to render it, using **map.put()**

savePublisher()

PublisherController holds a mapping to help the adding of publishers.

```
public String showManagePublishers(Map<String, Object> map) {
    map.put("publisher", new Publisher());
    map.put("publisherList", publisherService.listPublisher());
    map.put("countryList", countryService.listCountry());
    map.put("stateList", stateService.listState());
    return "managePublishers";
}
```

As soon as Manage Publishers is served, an object of the Publisher entity class is instantiated to make a provision for adding a new publisher. The user may view, edit, delete or choose to add a new publisher.

In case, the user chooses to add a new publisher, keys in the required publisher details and clicks ![Save], **PublisherController** holds a mapping to help the saving of the newly captured publisher details.

savePublisher():

❑ Ensures that the captured data is valid

❑ Returns the control to the View along with the error messages [available in the BindingResult object], if the captured data is found to be invalid.

 If the View is rendered along with the error messages, then the state and country names in the drop down list boxes are filled up by invoking listState() of StateService and listCountry() of CountryService respectively

❑ Saves the publisher details using PublisherService's **savePublisher()**, if the captured data is valid and returns the control to the View to render Manage Publishers

deletePublisher()

In case, the user chooses to delete a publisher and clicks ![icon], **PublisherController** holds a mapping to help delete a publisher record from Manage Publishers.

deletePublisher():

❑ Passes **PublisherNo** of the publisher to be deleted [available as a @PathVariable] to PublisherService's **removePublisher()**

❑ Checks whether the record to be deleted is used by other database table and accordingly displays the error message indicating that this record cannot be deleted. This is done by catching the DataIntegrityViolation exception

❑ Returns the control to the View which renders Manage Publishers with the updated data

editPublisher()

PublisherController holds a mapping to help the editing of existing publishers. In case, the user chooses to edit a publisher and clicks 📋, **PublisherController** holds a mapping to help fill up the Manage Publishers form with publisher details.

editPublisher():

❑ Retrieves the appropriate Publisher's details using **PublisherNo** as the reference. It calls PublisherService's **getPublisherById()** which returns the details of the publisher to be edited as a Publisher object. **PublisherNo** is made available through **@PathVariable** [in the list of Publisher rendered by the View] when the user clicks 📋 to edit a particular publisher

❑ Retrieves the state names by invoking **listState()** of StateService, which is displayed in the drop down list box of the State field

❑ Retrieves the country names by invoking **listCountry()** of CountryService, which is displayed in the drop down list box of the Country field

❑ Returns the control to the View along with the data to be populated in the form. The data to be populated is made available using Map's **put()**, which is used to populate the publishers object with the data that **getPublisherById()** of PublisherService returns. The same happens with the countryList and StateList objects

Service Class

Interface [PublisherService.java]

This is a service interface with the following specifications.

Service Interface Specifications

Class Name	Package
PublisherService	com.sharanamvaishali.service

Code Spec

```
1  package com.sharanamvaishali.service;
2
3  import com.sharanamvaishali.model.Publisher;
4  import java.util.List;
5
6  public interface PublisherService {
7      public void savePublisher(Publisher publisher);
8      public List<Publisher> listPublisher();
9      public void removePublisher(Integer publisherNo);
10     public Publisher getPublisherById(Integer publisherNo);
11 }
```

Implementation Class [PublisherServiceImpl.java]

This is a service class with the following specifications.

Service Implementation Specifications

Class Name	Package	Implements
PublisherServiceImpl	com.sharanamvaishali.service	PublisherService

Objects		
Object Name	Class Name	Object Type
publisherDAO	PublisherDAO	Data Access Object Layer

Methods	
Method Name	Arguments
savePublisher()	Publisher publisher
listPublisher()	- -
removePublisher()	Integer publisherNo
getPublisherById()	Integer publisherNo

Code Spec

```
1  package com.sharanamvaishali.service;
2
3  import com.sharanamvaishali.dao.PublisherDAO;
4  import com.sharanamvaishali.model.Publisher;
5  import java.util.List;
6  import org.springframework.beans.factory.annotation.Autowired;
```

```
 7  import org.springframework.stereotype.Service;
 8  import org.springframework.transaction.annotation.Transactional;
 9
10  @Service
11  public class PublisherServiceImpl implements PublisherService {
12      @Autowired
13      private PublisherDAO publisherDAO;
14
15      @Transactional
16      @Override
17      public void savePublisher(Publisher publisher) {
18          publisherDAO.savePublisher(publisher);
19      }
20
21      @Transactional
22      @Override
23      public List<Publisher> listPublisher() {
24          return publisherDAO.listPublisher();
25      }
26
27      @Transactional
28      @Override
29      public void removePublisher(Integer publisherNo) {
30          publisherDAO.removePublisher(publisherNo);
31      }
32
33      @Transactional
34      @Override
35      public Publisher getPublisherById(Integer publisherNo) {
36          return publisherDAO.getPublisherById(publisherNo);
37      }
38  }
```

Explanation:

The following section describes the above code spec.

savePublisher()

savePublisher() holds the business logic to save the captured publisher details.

This method in turn invokes PublisherDAO's **savePublisher()**.

listPublisher()

listPublisher() holds the business logic to return the appropriate list of the available publishers.

This method in turn invokes PublisherDAO's **listPublisher()**.

removePublisher()

removePublisher() holds the business logic to delete publisher details based on PublisherNo.

This method in turn invokes PublisherDAO's **removePublisher()**.

getPublisherById()

getPublisherById() holds the business logic to retrieve publisher details based on PublisherNo.

This method in turn invokes PublisherDAO's **getPublisherById()**.

REMINDER

CountryService's **listCountry()** is explained in the *Chapter 31: Manage Countries*, which retrieves the list of country names to be filled in the Country drop down list box.

StateService's **listState()** is explained in the *Chapter 32: Manage States*, which retrieves the list of state names to be filled in the State drop down list box.

DAO Class

Interface [PublisherDAO.java]

This is a Data Access Object interface with the following specifications.

DAO Interface Specifications

Class Name	Package
PublisherDAO	com.sharanamvaishali.dao

Code Spec

```
1  package com.sharanamvaishali.dao;
2
3  import com.sharanamvaishali.model.Publisher;
4  import java.util.List;
5
6  public interface PublisherDAO {
7      public void savePublisher(Publisher publisher);
8      public List<Publisher> listPublisher();
```

```
9     public void removePublisher(Integer publisherNo);
10    public Publisher getPublisherById(Integer publisherNo);
11 }
```

Implementation Class [PublisherDAOImpl.java]

This is a **Data Access Object** class with the following specifications.

DAO Implementation Specifications

Class Name	Package	Implements
PublisherDAOImpl	com.sharanamvaishali.dao	PublisherDAO

Objects	
Object Name	**Class Name**
sessionFactory	SessionFactory

Methods		
Method Name	**Arguments**	**Return Values**
savePublisher()	Publisher publisher	void
listPublisher()	- -	List <Publisher>
removePublisher()	Integer publisherNo	void
getPublisherById()	Integer publisherNo	Publisher

Code Spec

```
1     package com.sharanamvaishali.dao;
2
3     import com.sharanamvaishali.model.Publisher;
4     import java.util.List;
5     import org.hibernate.SessionFactory;
6     import org.springframework.beans.factory.annotation.Autowired;
7     import org.springframework.stereotype.Repository;
8
9     @Repository
10    public class PublisherDAOImpl implements PublisherDAO {
11        @Autowired
12        private SessionFactory sessionFactory;
13
14        @Override
15        public void savePublisher(Publisher publisher) {
16            sessionFactory.getCurrentSession().merge(publisher);
17        }
18
19        @Override
20        public List<Publisher> listPublisher() {
21            return sessionFactory.getCurrentSession().createQuery("from Publisher").list();
22        }
23
24        @Override
```

```
25    public void removePublisher(Integer publisherNo) {
26        Publisher publisher = (Publisher)
          sessionFactory.getCurrentSession().load(Publisher.class, publisherNo);
27        if (null != publisher) {
28            sessionFactory.getCurrentSession().delete(publisher);
29        }
30    }
31
32    @Override
33    public Publisher getPublisherById(Integer publisherNo) {
34        return (Publisher) sessionFactory.getCurrentSession().get(Publisher.class,
          publisherNo);
35    }
36 }
```

Explanation:

The following section describes the above code spec.

savePublisher()

savePublisher() does the actual saving of the publisher in the Publishers database table.

This method uses **merge()** of SessionFactory, which takes care of adding as well as updating the publisher details, in case the user had edited an existing publisher and clicked Save.

listPublisher()

listPublisher() does the actual retrieval of the available publishers.

This method fires a SELECT query that attempts to retrieve records from the Publishers database table.

All the records that the query retrieves are extracted and returned as a **List** object.

This List object is returned to the calling method i.e. Service Layer's **listPublisher()**:

```
public List<Publisher> listPublisher() {
    return publisherDAO.listPublisher();
}
```

This method in turn returns it to the PublisherController's **showManagePublishers()**:

```
public String showManagePublishers(Map<String, Object> map) {
    map.put("publisher", new Publisher());
    map.put("publisherList", publisherService.listPublisher());
    map.put("countryList", countryService.listCountry());
```

Finally, PublisherController returns this List object to the View which renders it.

managePublishers.jsp on taking charge uses the **iterator** tag to iterate over the contents of the List object **publisherList**.

```
<c:forEach items="${publisherList}" var="publisher">
   <tr>
      <td>${publisher.publisherName}</td>
      <td>${publisher.emailAddress}</td>
```

The publisherList object holds all those records retrieved by the SQL query.

Each record's column values are extracted using $.

```
<td>${publisher.publisherName}</td>
<td>${publisher.emailAddress}</td>
<td><a
```

removePublisher()

removePublisher() deletes the appropriate publisher based on **PublisherNo** received as a reference.

This method uses:

❏   **load()** of SessionFactory, which retrieves the appropriate Publisher to be deleted using PublisherNo as a reference

❏   **delete()** of SessionFactory, which deletes the publisher from Publishers database table

getPublisherById()

getPublisherById() returns the appropriate publisher's object from the Publishers database table using **PublisherNo** as the reference.

This method uses **get()** of SessionFactory, which returns the appropriate Publisher from Publishers database table.

After editing the publisher details, when the user clicks **Save**, savePublisher() of PublisherController, followed by savePublisher() of PublisherService, followed by savePublisher() of PublisherDAO takes care of saving the updated publisher's details.

<u>**REMINDER**</u>

 CountryDAO's **listCountry()** is explained in the *Chapter 31: Manage Countries*, which retrieves the list of country names to be filled in the Country drop down list box.

StateDAO's **listState()** is explained in the *Chapter 32: Manage States*, which retrieves the list of state names to be filled in the State drop down list box.

Domain Class [Publisher.java]

This is a domain class with the following specifications.

Domain Specifications

Class Name	Package	Implements
Publisher	com.sharanamvaishali.model	java.io.Serializable

Properties			
Property Name	**Property Type**	**Methods**	
publisherNo	Integer	getPublisherNo()	setPublisherNo()
publisherName	String	getPublisherName()	setPublisherName()
address1	String	getAddress1()	setAddress1()
address2	String	getAddress2()	setAddress2()
city	String	getCity()	setCity()
stateNo	Integer	getStateNo()	setStateNo()
pincode	String	getPincode(0	setPincode()
countryNo	Integer	getCountryNo()	setCountryNo()
emailAddress	String	getEmailAddress()	setEmailAddress()

Code Spec

```
1   package com.sharanamvaishali.model;
2
3   import javax.persistence.*;
4   import org.hibernate.validator.constraints.Email;
5   import org.hibernate.validator.constraints.NotEmpty;
6
7   @Entity
8   @Table(name="PUBLISHERS")
9   public class Publisher implements java.io.Serializable {
10      @Id
11      @GeneratedValue
12      @Column(name="PUBLISHERNO")
13      private Integer publisherNo;
14      @Column(name="PUBLISHERNAME")
```

```
15    @NotEmpty(message="Publisher name is mandatory")
16    private String publisherName;
17    @Column(name="ADDRESS1")
18    private String address1;
19    @Column(name="ADDRESS2")
20    private String address2;
21    @Column(name="CITY")
22    private String city;
23    @Column(name="STATENO")
24    private Integer stateNo;
25    @Column(name="PINCODE")
26    private String pincode;
27    @Column(name="COUNTRYNO")
28    private Integer countryNo;
29    @Column(name="EMAILADDRESS")
30    @NotEmpty(message="Email address is mandatory")
31    @Email(message="Invalid email address")
32    private String emailAddress;
33
34    public String getAddress1() {
35        return address1;
36    }
37    public void setAddress1(String address1) {
38        this.address1 = address1;
39    }
40
41    public String getAddress2() {
42        return address2;
43    }
44    public void setAddress2(String address2) {
45        this.address2 = address2;
46    }
47
48    public String getCity() {
49        return city;
50    }
51    public void setCity(String city) {
52        this.city = city;
53    }
54
55    public Integer getStateNo() {
56        return stateNo;
57    }
58    public void setStateNo(Integer stateNo) {
59        this.stateNo = stateNo;
60    }
61
62    public Integer getCountryNo() {
63        return countryNo;
64    }
65    public void setCountryNo(Integer countryNo) {
66        this.countryNo = countryNo;
67    }
68
```

```
69    public String getEmailAddress() {
70        return emailAddress;
71    }
72    public void setEmailAddress(String emailAddress) {
73        this.emailAddress = emailAddress;
74    }
75
76    public String getPincode() {
77        return pincode;
78    }
79    public void setPincode(String pincode) {
80        this.pincode = pincode;
81    }
82
83    public String getPublisherName() {
84        return publisherName;
85    }
86    public void setPublisherName(String publisherName) {
87        this.publisherName = publisherName;
88    }
89
90    public Integer getPublisherNo() {
91        return publisherNo;
92    }
93    public void setPublisherNo(Integer publisherNo) {
94        this.publisherNo = publisherNo;
95    }
96 }
```

REMINDER

Country.java [the model class] is explained in the *Chapter 31: Manage Countries*.
State.java [the model class] is explained in the *Chapter 32: Manage States*.

Chapter

35

SECTION V: BACKEND [ADMINISTRATION] SOFTWARE DESIGN DOCUMENTATION

Manage Authors

This module allows performing the following operations:

- ❏ Adding new authors
- ❏ Editing existing authors
- ❏ Viewing across existing authors
- ❏ Deleting existing authors

This module uses the bms.Authors table to perform the above operations.

This module is made up of the following:

Type	Name	Description
JSP	manageAuthors.jsp	The data entry form.
Spring		
Controller	AuthorController.java	The controller class that facilitates data operations.
Service Class	AuthorService.java	The interface for the service layer.
	CountryService.java	
	StateService.java	
	CommonService.java	
	AuthorServiceImpl.java	The implementation class for the service layer.
	CountryServiceImpl.java	
	StateServiceImpl.java	
	CommonServiceImpl.java	
DAO Class	AuthorDAO.java	The interface for the DAO layer.
	CountryDAO.java	
	StateDAO.java	
	CommonDAO.java	
	AuthorDAOImpl.java	The implementation class that performs the actual data operations.
	CountryDAOImpl.java	
	StateDAOImpl.java	
	CommonDAOImpl.java	
DispatcherServlet	bookshopdispatcher-servlet.xml	Central dispatcher for HTTP request handlers/controllers.
Hibernate		
Mapping	hibernate.cfg.xml	The mapping file that holds Model class mapping.
Model Class	Author.java	The model class.
	Country.java	
	State.java	

JSP [manageAuthors.jsp]

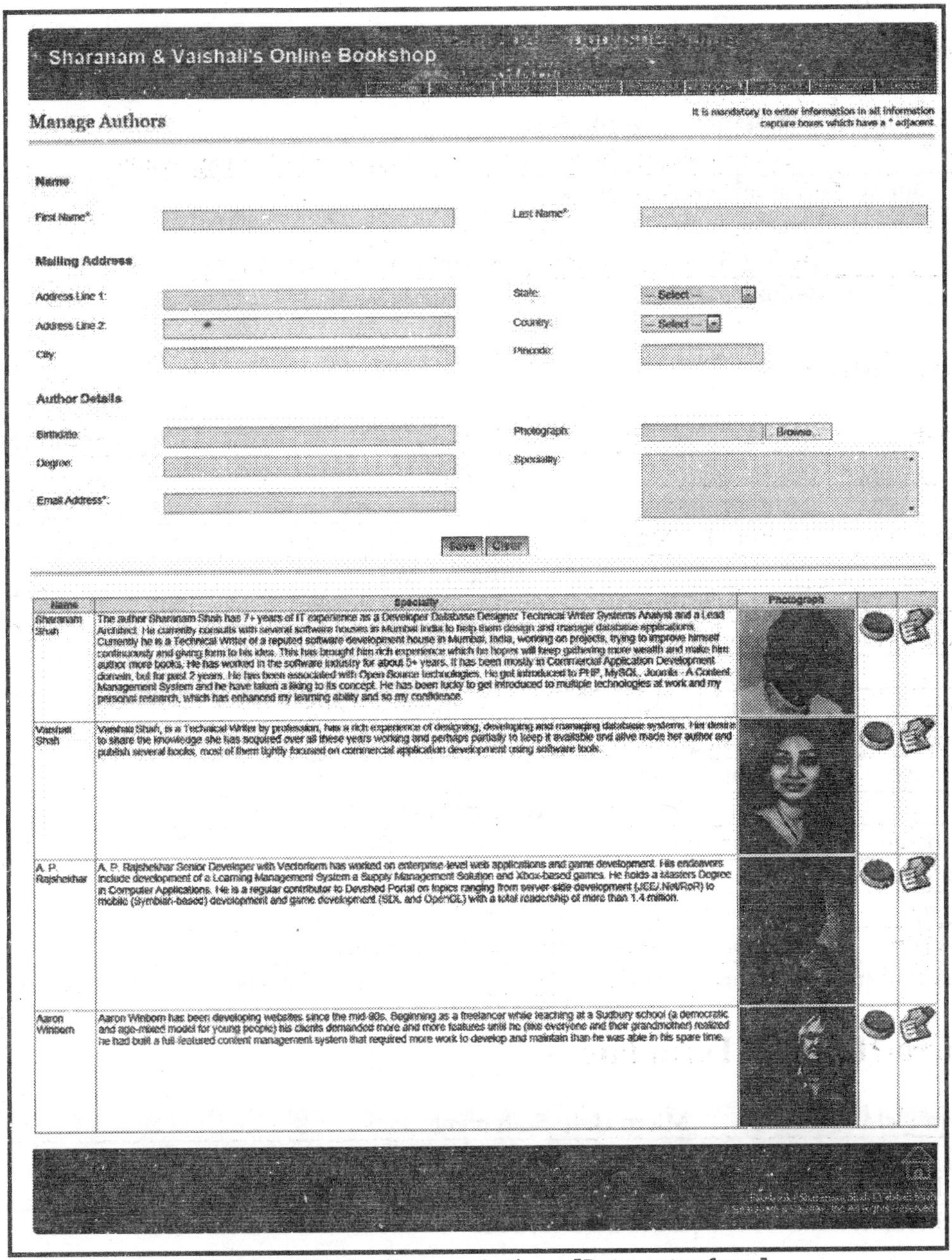

Diagram 35.1: Manage Authors [Data entry form]

This is a JSP which holds a data entry form, as shown in diagram 35.1. This form appears when the user clicks **Authors** .

Form Specifications

File Name	manageAuthors.jsp
Title	BookShop[Sharanam & Vaishali Shah] - Manage Authors
Bound To Table	bms.Authors
Command Name	author
Action	${pageContext.request.contextPath}/admin/saveAuthor
Method	POST

Data Fields

Label	Name	Bound To	Validation Rules
		Name	
First Name	Author.firstName	Authors.FirstName	Cannot be left blank
Last Name	Author.lastName	Authors.LastName	Cannot be left blank
		Mailing Address	
Address Line 1	Author.address1	Authors.Address1	- -
Address Line 2	Author.address2	Authors.Address2	- -
City	Author.city	Authors.City	- -
State	Author.stateNo	Authors.StateNo	- -
Country	Author.countryNo	Authors.CountryNo	- -
Pincode	Author.pincode	Authors.Pincode	- -
		Author Details	
Birthdate	Author.dob	Authors.DOB	- -
Photograph	- -	Authors.Photograph	- -
Degree	Author.degree	Authors.Degree	- -
Speciality	Author.speciality	Authors.Speciality	- -
Email Address	Author.emailAddress	Authors.EmailAddress	Cannot be left blank

Micro-Help For Form Fields

Form Field	Micro Help Statement
	Name
Author.firstName	Enter the first name
Author.lastName	Enter the last name

Mailing Address	
Author.address1	Enter the street address
Author.address2	Enter the street address
Author.city	Enter the city
Author.stateNo	- -
Author.countryNo	- -
Author.pincode	Enter the pincode
Author Details	
Author.dob	Enter the birthdate
Photograph	Select a photograph for this author
Author.degree	Enter the degree
Author.speciality	Enter the speciality
Author.emailAddress	Enter the email address

Data Controls

Object	Label
Submit	Save
Reset	Clear

Code Spec

```
1   <%@page contentType="text/html" pageEncoding="UTF-8"%>
2   <%@taglib uri="http://www.springframework.org/tags/form" prefix="form"%>
3   <%@taglib uri="http://java.sun.com/jsp/jstl/core" prefix="c"%>
4   <!DOCTYPE HTML PUBLIC "-//W3C//DTD HTML 4.01 Transitional//EN"
5     "http://www.w3.org/TR/html4/loose.dtd">
6   <html>
7     <head>
8       <meta http-equiv="Content-Type" content="text/html; charset=UTF-8">
9       <title>BookShop[Sharanam & Vaishali Shah] - Manage Authors</title>
10      <link rel="stylesheet" href="/BookShop/css/admin.css" type="text/css">
11    </head>
12    <body>
13      <%@ include file="/WEB-INF/jsp/adminHeader.jsp" %>
14      <br/>
15      <form:form method="post"
        action="${pageContext.request.contextPath}/admin/saveAuthor"
        commandName="author" enctype="multipart/form-data">
16        <form:hidden path="authorNo" />
17        <table width="100%" border="0" align="center" cellpadding="0"
          cellspacing="0">
18          <tr>
19            <td>
20              <table border="0" cellpadding="0" cellspacing="0" width="100%">
```

```
21                          <tr>
22                              <td class="manageForms">Manage Authors</td>
23                              <td align="center" class="error">${dbError}</td>
24                              <td class="information">
25                                  It is mandatory to enter information in all information
                                    <br>capture boxes which have a <span
                                    class="mandatory">*</span> adjacent
26                              </td>
27                          </tr>
28                      </table>
29                  </td>
30              </tr>
31              <tr><td class="hrLine"> </td></tr>
32              <tr>
33                  <td>
34                      <table width="100%" border="0" align="center" cellpadding="0"
                        cellspacing="0">
35                          <tr>
36                              <td>
37                                  <table width="100%" border="0" cellpadding="4"
                                    cellspacing="4">
38                                      <tr>
39                                          <td class="sectionName" colspan="4">
40                                              <br />Name<br /><br />
41                                          </td>
42                                      </tr>
43                                      <tr>
44                                          <td width="15%">First Name<span
                                            class="mandatory">*</span>:</td>
45                                          <td width="40%">
46                                              <form:input path="firstName" title="Enter the first
                                                name" maxlength="25" size="55"/><br>
47                                              <form:errors path="firstName" cssClass="error" />
48                                          </td>
49                                          <td width="15%">Last Name<span
                                            class="mandatory">*</span>:</td>
50                                          <td width="40%">
51                                              <form:input path="lastName" title="Enter the last
                                                name" maxlength="25" size="55"/><br>
52                                              <form:errors path="lastName" cssClass="error" />
53                                          </td>
54                                      </tr>
55                                      <tr>
56                                          <td class="sectionName" colspan="4">
57                                              <br />Mailing Address<br /><br />
58                                          </td>
59                                      </tr>
60                                      <tr>
61                                          <td width="15%">Address Line 1:</td>
62                                          <td width="40%">
63                                              <form:input path="address1" title="Enter the
                                                street address" maxlength="50" size="55"/>
64                                          </td>
```

```
65      <td width="15%">State:</td>
66      <td width="40%">
67         <form:select path="stateNo">
68            <form:option value="" label="--- Select ---"/>
69            <form:options title="Select the state"
               items="${stateList}" itemValue="stateNo"
               itemLabel="state" />
70         </form:select>
71      </td>
72   </tr>
73   <tr>
74      <td width="15%">Address Line 2:</td>
75      <td width="40%">
76         <form:input path="address2" title="Enter the
            street address" maxlength="50" size="55"/>
77      </td>
78      <td width="15%">Country:</td>
79      <td width="40%">
80         <form:select path="countryNo">
81            <form:option value="" label="--- Select ---"/>
82            <form:options title="Select the country"
               items="${countryList}" itemValue="countryNo"
               itemLabel="country" />
83         </form:select>
84      </td>
85   </tr>
86   <tr>
87      <td width="15%">City:</td>
88      <td width="40%">
89         <form:input path="city" title="Enter the city"
            maxlength="50" size="55"/>
90      </td>
91      <td width="15%">Pincode:</td>
92      <td width="40%">
93         <form:input path="pincode" title="Enter the
            pincode" maxlength="15" size="20"/>
94      </td>
95   </tr>
96   <tr>
97      <td class="sectionName" colspan="4">
98         <br />Author Details<br /><br />
99      </td>
100  </tr>
101  <tr>
102     <td width="15%">Birthdate:</td>
103     <td width="40%">
104        <form:input path="dob" title="Enter the birthdate"
            maxlength="25" size="55"/>
105     </td>
106     <td width="15%">Photograph:</td>
107     <td width="40%">
108        <input type="file" id="file" name="file"
            title="Select a photograph for this author" />
109     </td>
```

```
110                          </tr>
111                          <tr>
112                            <td width="15%">Degree: </td>
113                            <td width="40%">
114                              <form:input path="degree" title="Enter the degree"
                                 maxlength="25" size="55"/>
115                            </td>
116                            <td width="15%" rowspan="2"
                               valign="top">Speciality: </td>
117                            <td width="40%" rowspan="2">
118                              <form:textarea path="speciality" title="Enter the
                                 speciality" cols="55" rows="5"/>
119                            </td>
120                          </tr>
121                          <tr>
122                            <td width="15%">Email Address<span
                               class="mandatory">*</span>: </td>
123                            <td width="40%">
124                              <form:input path="emailAddress" title="Enter the
                                 email address" maxlength="50" size="55"/><br>
125                              <form:errors path="emailAddress" cssClass="error"
                                 />
126                            </td>
127                          </tr>
128                        </table>
129                      </td>
130                    </tr>
131                    <tr><td> </td></tr>
132                    <tr>
133                      <td colspan="2" class="centerAlign">
134                        <input type="submit" class="groovybutton" value="Save"
                           />
135                        <input type="reset" value="Clear" class="groovybutton"
                           onclick="javascript:document.location.href='/BookShop/admi
                           n/manageAuthors'" />
136                      </td>
137                    </tr>
138                  </table>
139                </td>
140              </tr>
141              <tr><td> </td></tr>
142              <tr><td class="hrLine"> </td></tr>
143              <tr><td><br></td></tr>
144            </table>
145          </form:form>
146          <c:if test="${!empty authorList}">
147            <table class="data" width="100%">
148              <tr>
149                <th width="10%">Name</th>
150                <th width="74%">Specialty</th>
151                <th width="10%">Photograph</th>
152                <th width="3%"> </th>
153                <th width="3%"> </th>
```

```
154                </tr>
155                <c:forEach items="${authorList}" var="author">
156                   <tr>
157                      <td>${author.firstName} ${author.lastName}</td>
158                      <td>${author.speciality}</td>
159                      <td><a
                         href="/BookShop/admin/downloadAuthorPhotograph/${author.author
                         No}"><img
                         src="/BookShop/admin/downloadAuthorPhotograph/${author.authorN
                         o}" width="150px"/></a></td>
160                      <td><a
                         href="/BookShop/admin/deleteAuthor/${author.authorNo}"><img
                         title="Click to delete"
                         src="/BookShop/images/delete.jpg"/></a></td>
161                      <td><a
                         href="/BookShop/admin/editAuthor/${author.authorNo}"><img
                         title="Click to edit" src="/BookShop/images/edit.jpg"/></a></td>
162                   </tr>
163                </c:forEach>
164             </table>
165          </c:if>
166          <%@ include file="/WEB-INF/jsp/adminFooter.jsp" %>
167       </body>
168  </html>
```

Explanation:

This is a standard data entry form, which captures the author details. By default when the form loads, it's in the **INSERT** and **VIEW** mode. The form also has Delete and Edit options to delete and edit a particular author record.

Controller [AuthorController.java]

This is a controller class with the following specifications.

Controller Specifications

Class Name	Package	
AuthorController	com.sharanamvaishali.controllers	
Objects		
Object Name	Class Name	Object Type
authorService	AuthorService	Service Layer
countryService	CountryService	Service Layer
stateService	StateService	Service Layer
commonService	CommonService	Service Layer

Methods	
Method Name	Request Mapping
showManageAuthors()	/admin/manageAuthors
downloadAuthorPhotograph()	/admin/downloadAuthorPhotograph/${authorNo}
saveAuthor()	/admin/saveAuthor
deleteAuthor()	/admin/deleteAuthor/${authorNo}
editAuthor()	/admin/editAuthor/${authorNo}

Code Spec

```
1   package com.sharanamvaishali.controllers;
2
3   import com.sharanamvaishali.model.Author;
4   import com.sharanamvaishali.service.AuthorService;
5   import com.sharanamvaishali.service.CommonService;
6   import com.sharanamvaishali.service.CountryService;
7   import com.sharanamvaishali.service.StateService;
8   import java.io.IOException;
9   import java.io.OutputStream;
10  import java.sql.SQLException;
11  import java.util.Map;
12  import javax.servlet.http.HttpServletResponse;
13  import javax.validation.Valid;
14  import org.apache.commons.io.IOUtils;
15  import org.hibernate.exception.ConstraintViolationException;
16  import org.springframework.beans.factory.annotation.Autowired;
17  import org.springframework.dao.DataIntegrityViolationException;
18  import org.springframework.stereotype.Controller;
19  import org.springframework.validation.BindingResult;
20  import org.springframework.web.bind.annotation.*;
21  import org.springframework.web.multipart.MultipartFile;
22
23  @Controller
24  @RequestMapping("/admin")
25  public class AuthorController {
26      @Autowired
27      private CommonService commonService;
28
29      @Autowired
30      private AuthorService authorService;
31
32      @Autowired
33      private CountryService countryService;
34
35      @Autowired
36      private StateService stateService;
37
38      @RequestMapping("/manageAuthors")
39      public String showManageAuthors(Map<String, Object> map) {
40          map.put("author", new Author());
```

```
41        map.put("authorList", authorService.listAuthor());
42        map.put("countryList", countryService.listCountry());
43        map.put("stateList", stateService.listState());
44        return "manageAuthors";
45    }
46
47    @RequestMapping("/downloadAuthorPhotograph/{authorNo}")
48    public String downloadAuthorPhotograph(@PathVariable("authorNo") Integer
       authorNo, HttpServletResponse response) {
49        Author author = authorService.getAuthorById(authorNo);
50        try {
51            if (author.getPhotograph()!=null) {
52                response.setHeader("Content-Disposition", "inline;filename=\"" +
                   author.getFirstName() + "\"");
53                OutputStream out = response.getOutputStream();
54                response.setContentType("image/gif");
55                IOUtils.copy(author.getPhotograph().getBinaryStream(), out);
56                out.flush();
57                out.close();
58            }
59        } catch (IOException e) {
60            e.printStackTrace();
61        } catch (SQLException e) {
62            e.printStackTrace();
63        }
64        return null;
65    }
66
67    @RequestMapping(value = "/saveAuthor", method = RequestMethod.POST)
68    public String saveAuthor(Map<String, Object> map, @ModelAttribute("author")
       Author author, @Valid Author authorValid, BindingResult result,
       @RequestParam("file") MultipartFile file) throws IOException {
69        if (result.hasErrors()) {
70            map.put("countryList", countryService.listCountry());
71            map.put("stateList", stateService.listState());
72            return "manageAuthors";
73        } else {
74            if(!file.isEmpty()) {
75                author.setPhotograph(commonService.getBlob(file.getBytes()));
76            }
77            else {
78                if (author.getAuthorNo() != null) {
79                    author.setPhotograph(authorService.getAuthorById(author.getAuthorNo(
                       )).getPhotograph());
80                }
81            }
82            try {
83                authorService.saveAuthor(author);
84                return "redirect:/admin/manageAuthors";
85            } catch (ConstraintViolationException exp) {
86                map.put("dbError", exp.getMessage());
87                return "manageAuthors";
88            }
89        }
```

```
90      }
91
92      @RequestMapping("/deleteAuthor/{authorNo}")
93      public String deleteAuthor(Map<String, Object> map, @PathVariable("authorNo")
        Integer authorNo) {
94          try {
95              authorService.removeAuthor(authorNo);
96              return "redirect:/admin/manageAuthors";
97          } catch (DataIntegrityViolationException exp) {
98              map.put("dbError", "Cannot delete a parent row.");
99              map.put("author", new Author());
100             return "manageAuthors";
101         }
102     }
103
104     @RequestMapping("/editAuthor/{authorNo}")
105     public String editAuthor(Map<String, Object> map, @PathVariable("authorNo")
        Integer authorNo) {
106         map.put("author", authorService.getAuthorById(authorNo));
107         map.put("countryList", countryService.listCountry());
108         map.put("stateList", stateService.listState());
109         return "manageAuthors";
110     }
111 }
```

Explanation:

The following section describes the above code spec.

showManageAuthors()

AuthorController holds a mapping to help the viewing.

This means the list of author details are retrieved by **AuthorController**'s **showManageAuthors()**.

showManageAuthors() is invoked every time Manage Authors is served.

showManageAuthors():

❑   Makes a provision for adding a new author [if the user chooses to] by instantiating an object of the Author entity class

❑   Retrieves the details of all the author by invoking **listAuthor()** of AuthorService

❑   Retrieves the state names by invoking **listState()** of StateService, which is displayed in the drop down list box of State field

❑   Retrieves the country names by invoking **listCountry()** of CountryService, which is displayed in the drop down list box of Country field

❑ Returns the author, state and country details that **listAuthor()**, **listState()** and **listCountry()** return respectively, to the View to render it, using **map.put()**

downloadAuthorPhotograph()

AuthorController holds a mapping for displaying the photographs of each author in the data grid.

downloadAuthorPhotograph():

❑ Retrieves the appropriate Author's details using **AuthorNo** as the reference. It calls AuthorService's **getAuthorById()** which returns the details of the author as an Author object. **AuthorNo** is made available through **@PathVariable** [in the list of Author rendered by the View]

❑ Checks whether the Authors database table has a photograph for that particular author

o If there is photograph available in the database, then the photograph is retrieved from the Authors database table

o Otherwise returns null

saveAuthor()

AuthorController holds a mapping to help the adding of authors.

```
public String showManageAuthors(Map<String, Object> map) {
    map.put("author", new Author());
    map.put("authorList", authorService.listAuthor());
    map.put("countryList", countryService.listCountry());
    map.put("stateList", stateService.listState());
    return "manageAuthors";
}
```

As soon as Manage Authors is served, an object of the Author entity class is instantiated to make a provision for adding a new author. The user may view, edit, delete or choose to add a new author.

In case, the user chooses to add a new author, keys in the required author details and clicks [Save], **AuthorController** holds a mapping to help the saving of the newly captured author details.

saveAuthor():

❑ Ensures that the captured data is valid

❑ Returns the control to the View along with the error messages [available in the BindingResult object], if the captured data is found to be invalid.

If the View is rendered along with the error messages, then the state and country names in the drop down list boxes are filled up by invoking listState() of StateService and listCountry() of CountryService respectively

❑ Saves the author details using AuthorService's **saveAuthor()**, if the captured data is valid and returns the control to the View to render Manage Authors

deleteAuthor()

In case, the user chooses to delete an author and clicks ⬤, **AuthorController** holds a mapping to help delete an author record from Manage Authors.

deleteAuthor():

❑ Passes **AuthorNo** of the author to be deleted [available as a @PathVariable] to AuthorService's **removeAuthor()**

❑ Checks whether the record to be deleted is used by other database table and accordingly displays the error message indicating that this record cannot be deleted. This is done by catching the DataIntegrityViolation exception

❑ Returns the control to the View which renders Manage Authors with the updated data

editAuthor()

AuthorController holds a mapping to help the editing of existing authors. In case, the user chooses to edit an author and clicks 📝, **AuthorController** holds a mapping to help fill up the Manage Authors form with author details.

editAuthor():

❑ Retrieves the appropriate Author's details using **AuthorNo** as the reference. It calls AuthorService's **getAuthorById()** which returns the details of the author to be edited as an Author object. **AuthorNo** is made available through **@PathVariable** [in the list of

Author rendered by the View] when the user clicks 📝 to edit a particular author

❑ Retrieves the state names by invoking **listState()** of StateService, which is displayed in the drop down list box of the State field

❑ Retrieves the country names by invoking **listCountry()** of CountryService, which is displayed in the drop down list box of the Country field

❑ Returns the control to the View along with the data to be populated in the form. The data to be populated is made available using Map's **put()**, which is used to populate the authors object with the data that **getAuthorById()** of AuthorService returns. The same happens with the countryList and StateList objects

Service Class

Interface

AuthorService.java

This is a service interface with the following specifications.

Service Interface Specifications

Class Name	Package
AuthorService	com.sharanamvaishali.service

Code Spec

```
1  package com.sharanamvaishali.service;
2
3  import com.sharanamvaishali.model.Author;
4  import java.util.List;
5
6  public interface AuthorService {
7      public void saveAuthor(Author author);
8      public List<Author> listAuthor();
9      public void removeAuthor(Integer authorNo);
10     public Author getAuthorById(Integer authorNo);
11 }
```

CommonService.java

This is a service interface with the following specifications.

Service Interface Specifications

Class Name	Package
CommonService	com.sharanamvaishali.service

Code Spec

```
1  package com.sharanamvaishali.service;
2
3  import java.sql.Blob;
4
5  public interface CommonService {
6      public Blob getBlob(byte[] is);
7  }
```

Implementation Class

AuthorServiceImpl.java

This is a service class with the following specifications.

Service Implementation Specifications

Class Name	Package	Implements
AuthorServiceImpl	com.sharanamvaishali.service	AuthorService
Objects		
Object Name	Class Name	Object Type
authorDAO	AuthorDAO	Data Access Object Layer
Methods		
Method Name		Arguments
saveAuthor()		Author author
listAuthor()		- -
removeAuthor()		Integer authorNo
getAuthorById()		Integer authorNo

Code Spec

```
1  package com.sharanamvaishali.service;
2
3  import com.sharanamvaishali.dao.AuthorDAO;
4  import com.sharanamvaishali.model.Author;
5  import java.util.List;
6  import org.springframework.beans.factory.annotation.Autowired;
7  import org.springframework.stereotype.Service;
8  import org.springframework.transaction.annotation.Transactional;
9
10 @Service
11 public class AuthorServiceImpl implements AuthorService {
12     @Autowired
13     private AuthorDAO authorDAO;
14
15     @Transactional
```

```
16      @Override
17      public void saveAuthor(Author author) {
18          authorDAO.saveAuthor(author);
19      }
20
21      @Transactional
22      @Override
23      public List<Author> listAuthor() {
24          return authorDAO.listAuthor();
25      }
26
27      @Transactional
28      @Override
29      public void removeAuthor(Integer authorNo) {
30          authorDAO.removeAuthor(authorNo);
31      }
32
33      @Transactional
34      @Override
35      public Author getAuthorById(Integer authorNo) {
36          return authorDAO.getAuthorById(authorNo);
37      }
38 }
```

Explanation:

The following section describes the above code spec.

saveAuthor()

saveAuthor() holds the business logic to save the captured author details.

This method in turn invokes AuthorDAO's **saveAuthor()**.

listAuthor()

listAuthor() holds the business logic to return the appropriate list of the available authors.

This method in turn invokes AuthorDAO's **listAuthor()**.

removeAuthor()

removeAuthor() holds the business logic to delete author details based on AuthorNo.

This method in turn invokes AuthorDAO's **removeAuthor()**.

getAuthorById()

getAuthorById() holds the business logic to retrieve author details based on AuthorNo.

This method in turn invokes AuthorDAO's **getAuthorById()**.

CommonServiceImpl.java

This is a service class with the following specifications.

Service Implementation Specifications

Class Name	Package	Implements
CommonServiceImpl	com.sharanamvaishali.service	CommonService
Objects		
Object Name	Class Name	Object Type
commonDAO	CommonDAO	Data Access Object Layer
Methods		
Method Name		Arguments
getBlob()		byte[] is

Code Spec

```
1  package com.sharanamvaishali.service;
2
3  import com.sharanamvaishali.dao.CommonDAO;
4  import java.sql.Blob;
5  import org.springframework.beans.factory.annotation.Autowired;
6  import org.springframework.stereotype.Service;
7  import org.springframework.transaction.annotation.Transactional;
8
9  @Service
10 public class CommonServiceImpl implements CommonService {
11     @Autowired
12     private CommonDAO commonDAO;
13
14     @Transactional
15     @Override
16     public Blob getBlob(byte[] is) {
17         return commonDAO.getBlob(is);
18     }
19 }
```

Explanation:

The following section describes the above code spec.

getBlob()

getBlob() holds the business logic to convert the image or the PDF into the Blob data type.

This method in turn invokes CommonDAO's **getBlob()**.

REMINDER

CountryService's **listCountry()** is explained in the *Chapter 31: Manage Countries*, which retrieves the list of country names to be filled in the Country drop down list box.

StateService's **listState()** is explained in the *Chapter 32: Manage States*, which retrieves the list of state names to be filled in the State drop down list box.

DAO Class

Interface

AuthorDAO.java

This is a Data Access Object interface with the following specifications.

DAO Interface Specifications

Class Name	Package
AuthorDAO	com.sharanamvaishali.dao

Code Spec

```
1  package com.sharanamvaishali.dao;
2
3  import com.sharanamvaishali.model.Author;
4  import java.util.List;
5
6  public interface AuthorDAO {
7      public void saveAuthor(Author author);
8      public List<Author> listAuthor();
9      public void removeAuthor(Integer authorNo);
10     public Author getAuthorById(Integer authorNo);
11 }
```

CommonDAO.java

This is a Data Access Object interface with the following specifications.

DAO Interface Specifications

Class Name	Package
CommonDAO	com.sharanamvaishali.dao

Code Spec

```
1  package com.sharanamvaishali.dao;
2
3  import java.sql.Blob;
4
5  public interface CommonDAO {
6      public Blob getBlob(byte[] is);
7  }
```

Implementation Class

AuthorDAOImpl.java

This is a Data Access Object class with the following specifications.

DAO Implementation Specifications

Class Name	Package	Implements
AuthorDAOImpl	com.sharanamvaishali.dao	AuthorDAO
Objects		
Object Name		**Class Name**
sessionFactory		SessionFactory
Methods		
Method Name	**Arguments**	**Return Values**
saveAuthor()	Author author	void
listAuthor()	- -	List <Author>
removeAuthor()	Integer authorNo	void
getAuthorById()	Integer authorNo	Author

Code Spec

```
1  package com.sharanamvaishali.dao;
2
3  import com.sharanamvaishali.model.Author;
```

```
4  import java.util.List;
5  import org.hibernate.SessionFactory;
6  import org.springframework.beans.factory.annotation.Autowired;
7  import org.springframework.stereotype.Repository;
8
9  @Repository
10 public class AuthorDAOImpl implements AuthorDAO {
11     @Autowired
12     private SessionFactory sessionFactory;
13
14     @Override
15     public void saveAuthor(Author author) {
16         sessionFactory.getCurrentSession().merge(author);
17     }
18
19     @Override
20     public List<Author> listAuthor() {
21         return sessionFactory.getCurrentSession().createQuery("from Author").list();
22     }
23
24     @Override
25     public void removeAuthor(Integer authorNo) {
26         Author author = (Author) sessionFactory.getCurrentSession().load(Author.class,
                authorNo);
27         if (null != author) {
28             sessionFactory.getCurrentSession().delete(author);
29         }
30     }
31
32     @Override
33     public Author getAuthorById(Integer authorNo) {
34         return (Author) sessionFactory.getCurrentSession().get(Author.class, authorNo);
35     }
36 }
```

Explanation:

The following section describes the above code spec.

saveAuthor()

saveAuthor() does the actual saving of the author in the Authors database table.

This method uses **merge()** of SessionFactory, which takes care of adding as well as updating the author details, in case the user had edited an existing author and clicked **Save**.

listAuthor()

listAuthor() does the actual retrieval of the available authors.

This method fires a SELECT query that attempts to retrieve records from the Authors database table.

All the records that the query retrieves are extracted and returned as a **List** object.

This List object is returned to the calling method i.e. Service Layer's **listAuthor()**:

```
public List<Author> listAuthor() {
    return authorDAO.listAuthor();
}
```

This method in turn returns it to the AuthorController's **showManageAuthors()**:

```
public String showManageAuthors(Map<String, Object> map) {
    map.put("author", new Author());
    map.put("authorList", authorService.listAuthor());
    map.put("countryList", countryService.listCountry());
```

Finally, AuthorController returns this List object to the View which renders it.

manageAuthors.jsp on taking charge uses the **iterator** tag to iterate over the contents of the List object **authorList**.

```
<c:forEach items="${authorList}" var="author">
    <tr>
        <td>${author.firstName} ${author.lastName}</td>
        <td>${author.speciality}</td>
        <td><a
```

The authorList object holds all those records retrieved by the SQL query.

Each record's column values are extracted using $.

```
<td>${author.firstName} ${author.lastName}</td>
<td>${author.speciality}</td>
```

removeAuthor()

removeAuthor() deletes the appropriate author based on **AuthorNo** received as a reference.

This method uses:

- **load()** of SessionFactory, which retrieves the appropriate Author to be deleted using AuthorNo as a reference
- **delete()** of SessionFactory, which deletes the author from Authors database table

getAuthorById() returns the appropriate author's object from the Authors database table using **AuthorNo** as the reference.

This method uses **get()** of SessionFactory, which returns the appropriate Author from Authors database table.

After editing the author details, when the user clicks **Save**, saveAuthor() of AuthorController, followed by saveAuthor() of AuthorService, followed by saveAuthor() of AuthorDAO takes care of saving the updated author's details.

CommonDAOImpl.java

This is a **D**ata **A**ccess **O**bject class with the following specifications.

DAO Implementation Specifications

Class Name	Package	Implements
CommonDAOImpl	com.sharanamvaishali.dao	CommonDAO
Objects		
Object Name		**Class Name**
sessionFactory		SessionFactory
Methods		
Method Name	**Arguments**	**Return Values**
getBlob()	byte[] is	Blob

Code Spec

```
1   package com.sharanamvaishali.dao;
2
3   import java.sql.Blob;
4   import org.hibernate.SessionFactory;
5   import org.springframework.beans.factory.annotation.Autowired;
6   import org.springframework.stereotype.Repository;
7
8   @Repository
9   public class CommonDAOImpl implements CommonDAO {
10      @Autowired
11      private SessionFactory sessionFactory;
12
13      @Override
14      public Blob getBlob(byte[] is) {
15          Blob blob = sessionFactory.getCurrentSession().getLobHelper().createBlob(is);
```

```
16        return blob;
17    }
18 }
```

Explanation:

The following section describes the above code spec.

getBlob()

getBlob() does the actual conversion of images or the PDFs into Blob data type.

This method uses **getLobHelper()** of SessionFactory, which retrieves a particular session's helper/delegate for creating LOB instances.

This method uses **createBlob()** of SessionFactory, which creates a new Blob from bytes.

REMINDER

CountryDAO's **listCountry()** is explained in the *Chapter 31: Manage Countries*, which retrieves the list of country names to be filled in the Country drop down list box.

StateDAO's **listState()** is explained in the *Chapter 32: Manage States*, which retrieves the list of state names to be filled in the State drop down list box.

Domain Class [Author.java]

This is a domain class with the following specifications.

Domain Specifications

Class Name	Package	Implements
Author	com.sharanamvaishali.model	java.io.Serializable
Properties		
Property Name	Property Type	Methods
authorNo	Integer	getAuthorNo ()	setAuthorNo ()
firstName	String	getFirstName ()	setFirstName ()
lastName	String	getLastName ()	setLastName ()
address1	String	getAddress1 ()	setAddress1 ()
address2	String	getAddress2 ()	setAddress2 ()
city	String	getCity ()	setCity ()

Properties			
Property Name	**Property Type**	\multicolumn{2}{c}{**Methods**}	
stateNo	Integer	getStateNo()	setStateNo()
pincode	String	getPincode(0	setPincode()
countryNo	Integer	getCountryNo()	setCountryNo()
degree	String	getDegree()	setDegree()
emailAddress	String	getEmailAddress()	setEmailAddress()
photograph	Blob	getPhotograph()	setPhotograph()
speciality	String	getSpeciality()	setSpeciality()
dob	String	getDob()	setDob()

Code Spec

```
1   package com.sharanamvaishali.model;
2
3   import java.sql.Blob;
4   import javax.persistence.*;
5   import org.hibernate.validator.constraints.Email;
6   import org.hibernate.validator.constraints.NotEmpty;
7
8   @Entity
9   @Table(name="AUTHORS")
10  public class Author implements java.io.Serializable {
11      @Id
12      @GeneratedValue
13      @Column(name="AUTHORNO")
14      private Integer authorNo;
15      @Column(name="FIRSTNAME")
16      @NotEmpty(message="First name is mandatory")
17      private String firstName;
18      @Column(name="LASTNAME")
19      @NotEmpty(message="Last name is mandatory")
20      private String lastName;
21      @Column(name="ADDRESS1")
22      private String address1;
23      @Column(name="ADDRESS2")
24      private String address2;
25      @Column(name="CITY")
26      private String city;
27      @Column(name="STATENO")
28      private Integer stateNo;
29      @Column(name="PINCODE")
30      private String pincode;
31      @Column(name="COUNTRYNO")
32      private Integer countryNo;
33      @Column(name="DEGREE")
34      private String degree;
35      @Column(name="EMAILADDRESS")
36      @NotEmpty(message="Email address is mandatory")
37      @Email(message="Invalid email address")
```

```
38    private String emailAddress;
39    @Column(name="PHOTOGRAPH")
40    @Lob
41    private Blob photograph;
42    @Column(name="SPECIALITY")
43    private String speciality;
44    @Column(name="DOB")
45    private String dob;
46
47    public String getAddress1() {
48        return address1;
49    }
50    public void setAddress1(String address1) {
51        this.address1 = address1;
52    }
53
54    public String getAddress2() {
55        return address2;
56    }
57    public void setAddress2(String address2) {
58        this.address2 = address2;
59    }
60
61    public Integer getAuthorNo() {
62        return authorNo;
63    }
64    public void setAuthorNo(Integer authorNo) {
65        this.authorNo = authorNo;
66    }
67
68    public String getCity() {
69        return city;
70    }
71    public void setCity(String city) {
72        this.city = city;
73    }
74
75    public Integer getStateNo() {
76        return stateNo;
77    }
78    public void setStateNo(Integer stateNo) {
79        this.stateNo = stateNo;
80    }
81
82    public Integer getCountryNo() {
83        return countryNo;
84    }
85    public void setCountryNo(Integer countryNo) {
86        this.countryNo = countryNo;
87    }
88
89    public String getDegree() {
90        return degree;
91    }
```

```
 92        public void setDegree(String degree) {
 93            this.degree = degree;
 94        }
 95
 96        public String getDob() {
 97            return dob;
 98        }
 99        public void setDob(String dob) {
100            this.dob = dob;
101        }
102
103        public String getEmailAddress() {
104            return emailAddress;
105        }
106        public void setEmailAddress(String emailAddress) {
107            this.emailAddress = emailAddress;
108        }
109
110        public String getFirstName() {
111            return firstName;
112        }
113        public void setFirstName(String firstName) {
114            this.firstName = firstName;
115        }
116
117        public String getLastName() {
118            return lastName;
119        }
120        public void setLastName(String lastName) {
121            this.lastName = lastName;
122        }
123
124        public Blob getPhotograph() {
125            return photograph;
126        }
127        public void setPhotograph(Blob photograph) {
128            this.photograph = photograph;
129        }
130
131        public String getPincode() {
132            return pincode;
133        }
134        public void setPincode(String pincode) {
135            this.pincode = pincode;
136        }
137
138        public String getSpeciality() {
139            return speciality;
140        }
141        public void setSpeciality(String speciality) {
142            this.speciality = speciality;
143        }
144 }
```

REMINDER

 Country.java [the model class] is explained in the *Chapter 31: Manage Countries*. State.java [the model class] is explained in the *Chapter 32: Manage States*.

Chapter

36

SECTION V: BACKEND [ADMINISTRATION] SOFTWARE DESIGN DOCUMENTATION

Manage Books

This module allows performing the following operations:

❑   Adding new books

❑   Editing existing books

❑   Viewing across existing books

❑   Deleting existing books

This module uses the bms.Books table to perform the above operations.

This module is made up of the following:

Type	Name	Description
JSP	manageBooks.jsp	The data entry form.
Spring		
Controller	BookController.java	The controller class that facilitates data operations.
Service Class	BookService.java	The interface for the service layer.
	PublisherService.java	
	CategoryService.java	
	AuthorService.java	
	UserService.java	
	CommonService.java	
	BookServiceImpl.java	The implementation class for the service layer.
	PublisherServiceImpl.java	
	CategoryServiceImpl.java	
	AuthorServiceImpl.java	
	UserServiceImpl.java	
	CommonServiceImpl.java	
	MailService.java	The class for the service layer.
DAO Class	BookDAO.java	The interface for the DAO layer.
	PublisherDAO.java	
	CategoryDAO.java	
	AuthorDAO.java	
	UserDAO.java	
	CommonDAO.java	
	BookDAOImpl.java	The implementation class that performs the actual data operations.
	PublisherDAOImpl.java	
	CategoryDAOImpl.java	
	AuthorDAOImpl.java	
	UserDAOImpl.java	
	CommonDAOImpl.java	
DispatcherServlet	bookshopdispatcher-servlet.xml	Central dispatcher for HTTP request handlers/controllers.
Hibernate		
Mapping	hibernate.cfg.xml	The mapping file that holds Model class mapping.
Model Class	Book.java	The model class.
	Publisher.java	
	Catgeory.java	
	Author.java	

JSP [manageBooks.jsp]

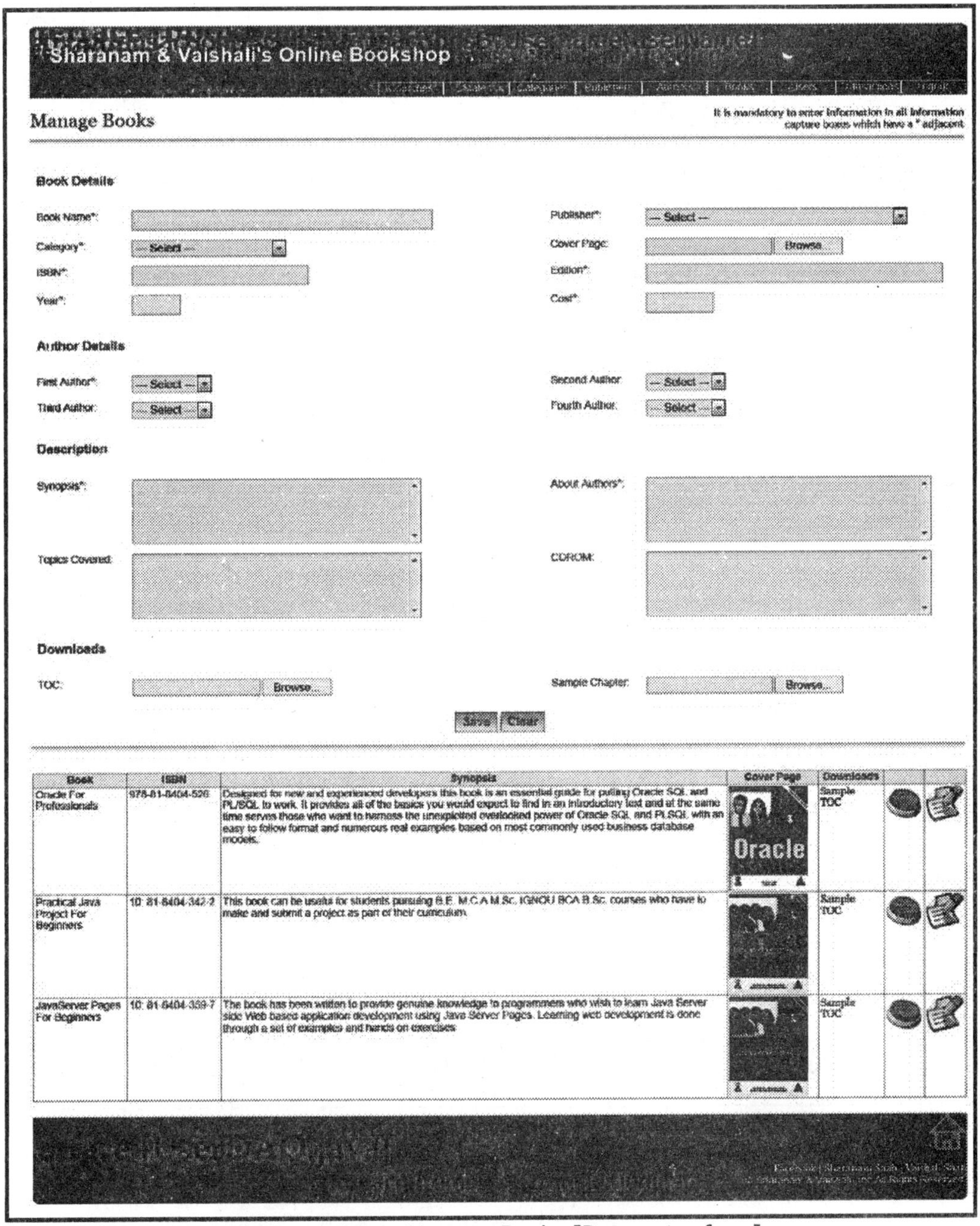

Diagram 35.1: Manage Books [Data entry form]

This is a JSP which holds a data entry form, as shown in diagram 35.1. This form appears when the user clicks ▊ Books ▊.

Form Specifications

File Name	manageBooks.jsp
Title	BookShop[Sharanam & Vaishali Shah] - Manage Books
Bound To Table	bms.Books
Command Name	book
Action	${pageContext.request.contextPath}/admin/saveBook
Method	POST

Data Fields

Label	Name	Bound To	Validation Rules
Book Details			
Book Name	Book.bookName	Books.BookName	Cannot be left blank
Publisher	Book.publisherNo	Books.PublisherNo	Cannot be left blank
Category	Book.categoryNo	Books.CategoryNo	Cannot be left blank
Cover Page	- -	Books.CoverPage	- -
ISBN	Book.isbn	Books.ISBN	Cannot be left blank
Edition	Book.edition	Books.Edition	Cannot be left blank
Year	Book.year	Books.Year	Cannot be left blank
Cost	Book.cost	Books.Cost	Cannot be left blank
Author Details			
First Author	Book.author1No	Books.Author1No	Cannot be left blank
Second Author	Book.author2No	Books.Author2No	- -
Third Author	Book.author3No	Books.Author3No	- -
Fourth Author	Book.author4No	Books.Author4No	- -
Description			
Synopsis	Book.synopsis	Books.Synopsis	Cannot be left blank
About Authors	Book.aboutAuthors	Books.AboutAuthors	- -
Topics Covered	Book.topicsCovered	Books.TopicsCovered	- -
CDROM	Book.contentsCDROM	Books.ContentsCDROM	- -
Downloads			
TOC	- -	Books.TOC	- -
Sample Chapter	- -	Books.SampleChapter	- -

Micro-Help For Form Fields

Form Field	Micro Help Statement
Book Details	
Book.bookName	Enter the book name
Book.publisherNo	Select the publisher
Book.categoryNo	Select the category
Cover Page	Select a cover page for this book
Book.isbn	Enter the isbn
Book.edition	Enter the edition
Book.year	Enter the year
Book.cost	Enter the cost of the book
Author Details	
Book.author1No	Select the author
Book.author2No	Select the author
Book.author3No	Select the author
Book.author4No	Select the author
Description	
Book.synopsis	Enter the synopsis
Book.aboutAuthors	Enter the about the authors
Book.topicsCovered	Enter the topics covered in the book
Book.contentsCDROM	Enter the contents CDROM
Downloads	
TOC	Select the TOC
Sample Chapter	Select the Sample Chapter

Data Controls

Object	Label
Submit	Save
Reset	Clear

Code Spec

```
1  <%@page contentType="text/html" pageEncoding="UTF-8"%>
2  <%@taglib uri="http://www.springframework.org/tags/form" prefix="form"%>
3  <%@taglib uri="http://java.sun.com/jsp/jstl/core" prefix="c"%>
4  <!DOCTYPE HTML PUBLIC "-//W3C//DTD HTML 4.01 Transitional//EN"
5     "http://www.w3.org/TR/html4/loose.dtd">
6  <html>
7    <head>
8      <meta http-equiv="Content-Type" content="text/html; charset=UTF-8">
```

```
 9        <title>BookShop[Sharanam & Vaishali Shah] - Manage Books</title>
10        <link rel="stylesheet" href="/BookShop/css/admin.css" type="text/css">
11    </head>
12    <body>
13        <%@ include file="/WEB-INF/jsp/adminHeader.jsp" %>
14        <br/>
15        <form:form method="post"
          action="${pageContext.request.contextPath}/admin/saveBook"
          commandName="book" enctype="multipart/form-data">
16            <form:hidden path="bookNo" />
17            <table width="100%" border="0" align="center" cellpadding="0"
              cellspacing="0">
18                <tr>
19                    <td>
20                        <table border="0" cellpadding="0" cellspacing="0" width="100%">
21                            <tr>
22                                <td class="manageForms">Manage Books</td>
23                                <td align="center" class="error">${dbError}</td>
24                                <td class="information">
25                                    It is mandatory to enter information in all information
                                    <br>capture boxes which have a <span
                                    class="mandatory">*</span> adjacent
26                                </td>
27                            </tr>
28                        </table>
29                    </td>
30                </tr>
31                <tr><td class="hrLine"> </td></tr>
32                <tr>
33                    <td>
34                        <table width="100%" border="0" align="center" cellpadding="0"
                          cellspacing="0">
35                            <tr>
36                                <td>
37                                    <table width="100%" border="0" cellpadding="4"
                                      cellspacing="4">
38                                        <tr>
39                                            <td class="sectionName" colspan="4">
40                                                <br />Book Details<br /><br />
41                                            </td>
42                                        </tr>
43                                        <tr>
44                                            <td width="10%">Book Name<span
                                              class="mandatory">*</span>:</td>
45                                            <td width="45%">
46                                                <form:input path="bookName" title="Enter the
                                                book name" maxlength="25" size="55"/><br>
47                                                <form:errors path="bookName" cssClass="error"
                                                />
48                                            </td>
49                                            <td width="10%">Publisher<span
                                              class="mandatory">*</span>:</td>
50                                            <td width="45%">
51                                                <form:select path="publisherNo">
```

```
52        <form:option value="" label="--- Select ---"/>
53        <form:options title="Select the publisher"
          items="${publisherList}"
          itemValue="publisherNo"
          itemLabel="publisherName" />
54      </form:select><br>
55      <form:errors path="publisherNo" cssClass="error"
          />
56    </td>
57  </tr>
58  <tr>
59    <td width="10%">Category<span
      class="mandatory">*</span>:</td>
60    <td width="45%">
61      <form:select path="categoryNo">
62        <form:option value="" label="--- Select ---"/>
63        <form:options title="Select the category"
          items="${categoryList}"
          itemValue="categoryNo" itemLabel="category"
          />
64      </form:select><br>
65      <form:errors path="categoryNo" cssClass="error"
          />
66    </td>
67    <td width="10%">Cover Page:</td>
68    <td width="45%">
69      <input type="file" id="coverPageFile"
      name="coverPageFile" title="Select a cover page
      for this book" />
70    </td>
71  </tr>
72  <tr>
73    <td width="10%">ISBN<span
      class="mandatory">*</span>:</td>
74    <td width="45%">
75      <form:input path="isbn" title="Enter the isbn"
      maxlength="15" size="30"/><br>
76      <form:errors path="isbn" cssClass="error" />
77    </td>
78    <td width="10%">Edition<span
      class="mandatory">*</span>:</td>
79    <td width="45%">
80      <form:input path="edition" title="Enter the
      edition" maxlength="25" size="55"/><br>
81      <form:errors path="edition" cssClass="error" />
82    </td>
83  </tr>
84  <tr>
85    <td width="10%">Year<span
      class="mandatory">*</span>:</td>
86    <td width="45%">
87      <form:input path="year" title="Enter the year"
      maxlength="4" size="4"/><br>
88      <form:errors path="year" cssClass="error" />
```

```
89              </td>
90              <td width="10%">Cost<span
                class="mandatory">*</span>:</td>
91              <td width="45%">
92                  <form:input path="cost" title="Enter the cost of
                    the book" maxlength="8" size="8"/><br>
93                  <form:errors path="cost" cssClass="error" />
94              </td>
95          </tr>
96          <tr>
97              <td class="sectionName" colspan="4">
98                  <br />Author Details<br /><br />
99              </td>
100         </tr>
101         <tr>
102             <td width="10%">First Author<span
                class="mandatory">*</span>:</td>
103             <td width="45%">
104                 <form:select path="author1No">
105                     <form:option value="" label="--- Select ---"/>
106                     <form:options title="Select the author"
                        items="${authorList}" itemValue="authorNo"
                        itemLabel="firstName" />
107                 </form:select><br>
108                 <form:errors path="author1No" cssClass="error"
                    />
109             </td>
110             <td width="10%">Second Author:</td>
111             <td width="45%">
112                 <form:select path="author2No">
113                     <form:option value="" label="--- Select ---"/>
114                     <form:options title="Select the author"
                        items="${authorList}" itemValue="authorNo"
                        itemLabel="firstName" />
115                 </form:select>
116             </td>
117         </tr>
118         <tr>
119             <td width="10%">Third Author:</td>
120             <td width="45%">
121                 <form:select path="author3No">
122                     <form:option value="" label="--- Select ---"/>
123                     <form:options title="Select the author"
                        items="${authorList}" itemValue="authorNo"
                        itemLabel="firstName" />
124                 </form:select>
125             </td>
126             <td width="10%">Fourth Author:</td>
127             <td width="45%">
128                 <form:select path="author4No">
129                     <form:option value="" label="--- Select ---"/>
130                     <form:options title="Select the author"
                        items="${authorList}" itemValue="authorNo"
                        itemLabel="firstName" />
```

```
131             </form:select>
132           </td>
133         </tr>
134         <tr>
135           <td class="sectionName" colspan="4">
136             <br />Description<br /><br />
137           </td>
138         </tr>
139         <tr>
140           <td width="10%">Synopsis<span
              class="mandatory">*</span>:</td>
141           <td width="45%">
142             <form:textarea path="synopsis" title="Enter the
                synopsis" cols="55" rows="5"/><br>
143             <form:errors path="synopsis" cssClass="error" />
144           </td>
145           <td width="10%">About Authors<span
              class="mandatory">*</span>:</td>
146           <td width="45%">
147             <form:textarea path="aboutAuthors" title="Enter
                the about the authors" cols="55" rows="5"/><br>
148             <form:errors path="aboutAuthors"
                cssClass="error" />
149           </td>
150         </tr>
151         <tr>
152           <td width="10%">Topics Covered:</td>
153           <td width="45%">
154             <form:textarea path="topicsCovered" title="Enter
                the topics covered in the book" cols="55"
                rows="5"/>
155           </td>
156           <td width="10%">CDROM:</td>
157           <td width="45%">
158             <form:textarea path="contentsCDROM"
                title="Enter the contents CDROM" cols="55"
                rows="5"/>
159           </td>
160         </tr>
161         <tr>
162           <td class="sectionName" colspan="4">
163             <br />Downloads<br /><br />
164           </td>
165         </tr>
166         <tr>
167           <td width="10%">TOC:</td>
168           <td width="45%">
169             <input type="file" id="tocFile" name="tocFile"
                title="Select the TOC" />
170           </td>
171           <td width="10%">Sample Chapter:</td>
172           <td width="45%">
173             <input type="file" id="sampleChapterFile"
                name="sampleChapterFile" title="Select the
```

```
                                        Sample Chapter" />
174                              </td>
175                          </tr>
176                      </table>
177                  </td>
178              </tr>
179              <tr><td> </td></tr>
180              <tr>
181                  <td colspan="2" class="centerAlign">
182                      <input type="submit" class="groovybutton" value="Save"
                          />
183                      <input type="reset" value="Clear" class="groovybutton"
                          onclick="javascript:document.location.href='/BookShop/ad
                          min/manageBooks'" />
184                  </td>
185              </tr>
186          </table>
187      </td>
188  </tr>
189  <tr><td> </td></tr>
190  <tr><td class="hrLine"> </td></tr>
191  <tr><td><br></td></tr>
192  </table>
193  </form:form>
194  <c:if test="${!empty bookList}">
195      <table class="data" width="100%">
196          <tr>
197          <th width="10%">Book</th>
198          <th width="10%">ISBN</th>
199          <th width="54%">Synopsis</th>
200          <th width="10%">Cover Page</th>
201          <th>Downloads</th>
202          <th width="3%"> </th>
203          <th width="3%"> </th>
204          </tr>
205          <c:forEach items="${bookList}" var="book">
206          <tr>
207              <td>${book.bookName}</td>
208              <td>${book.isbn}</td>
209              <td>${book.synopsis}</td>
210              <td><a
                href="/BookShop/admin/downloadBookPhotograph/${book.bookNo}"
                ><img
                src="/BookShop/admin/downloadBookPhotograph/${book.bookNo}"
                width="100px"/></a></td>
211              <td><a
                href="/BookShop/admin/downloadBookSampleChapter/${book.book
                No}">Sample</a><br><a
                href="/BookShop/admin/downloadBookTOC/${book.bookNo}">TOC
                </a></td>
212              <td><a
                href="/BookShop/admin/deleteBook/${book.bookNo}"><img
                title="Click to delete"
                src="/BookShop/images/delete.jpg"/></a></td>
```

```
213              <td><a href="/BookShop/admin/editBook/${book.bookNo}"><img
                 title="Click to edit" src="/BookShop/images/edit.jpg"/></a></td>
214              </tr>
215            </c:forEach>
216          </table>
217        </c:if>
218        <%@ include file="/WEB-INF/jsp/adminFooter.jsp" %>
219      </body>
220   </html>
```

Explanation:

This is a standard data entry form, which captures the book details. By default when the form loads, it's in the **INSERT** and **VIEW** mode. The form also has Delete and Edit options to delete and edit a particular book record.

Controller [BookController.java]

This is a controller class with the following specifications.

Controller Specifications

Class Name	Package
BookController	com.sharanamvaishali.controllers
Objects		
Object Name	**Class Name**	**Object Type**
bookService	BookService	Service Layer
publisherService	PublisherService	Service Layer
categoryService	CategoryService	Service Layer
authorService	AuthorService	Service Layer
commonService	CommonService	Service Layer
Methods	
Method Name	**Request Mapping**
showManageBooks()	/admin/manageBooks
downloadBookPhotograph()	/admin/downloadBookPhotograph/${bookNo}
downloadBookTOC()	/admin/downloadBookTOC/${bookNo}
downloadBookSampleChapter()	/admin/downloadBookSampleChapter/${bookNo}
saveBook()	/admin/saveBook
deleteBook()	/admin/deleteBook/${bookNo}
editBook()	/admin/editBook/${bookNo}

Code Spec

```
1  package com.sharanamvaishali.controllers;
2
```

```
3   import com.sharanamvaishali.model.Book;
4   import com.sharanamvaishali.service.*;
5   import java.io.IOException;
6   import java.io.OutputStream;
7   import java.sql.SQLException;
8   import java.util.Map;
9   import javax.servlet.http.HttpServletResponse;
10  import javax.validation.Valid;
11  import org.apache.commons.io.IOUtils;
12  import org.hibernate.exception.ConstraintViolationException;
13  import org.springframework.beans.factory.annotation.Autowired;
14  import org.springframework.stereotype.Controller;
15  import org.springframework.validation.BindingResult;
16  import org.springframework.web.bind.annotation.*;
17  import org.springframework.web.multipart.MultipartFile;
18
19  @Controller
20  @RequestMapping("/admin")
21  public class BookController {
22      @Autowired
23      private CommonService commonService;
24
25      @Autowired
26      private BookService bookService;
27
28      @Autowired
29      private PublisherService publisherService;
30
31      @Autowired
32      private CategoryService categoryService;
33
34      @Autowired
35      private AuthorService authorService;
36
37      @RequestMapping("/manageBooks")
38      public String showManageBooks(Map<String, Object> map) {
39          map.put("book", new Book());
40          map.put("bookList", bookService.listBook());
41          map.put("publisherList", publisherService.listPublisher());
42          map.put("categoryList", categoryService.listCategory());
43          map.put("authorList", authorService.listAuthor());
44          return "manageBooks";
45      }
46
47      @RequestMapping("/downloadBookPhotograph/{bookNo}")
48      public String downloadBookPhotograph(@PathVariable("bookNo") Integer bookNo,
        HttpServletResponse response) {
49          Book book = bookService.getBookById(bookNo);
50          try {
51              if (book.getCoverPage()!=null) {
52                  response.setHeader("Content-Disposition", "inline;filename=\""
                    +book.getBookName()+ "\"");
53                  OutputStream out = response.getOutputStream();
54                  response.setContentType("image/gif");
```

```
55              IOUtils.copy(book.getCoverPage().getBinaryStream(), out);
56              out.flush();
57              out.close();
58          }
59      } catch (IOException e) {
60          e.printStackTrace();
61      } catch (SQLException e) {
62          e.printStackTrace();
63      }
64      return null;
65  }
66
67  @RequestMapping("/downloadBookTOC/{bookNo}")
68  public String downloadBookTOC(@PathVariable("bookNo") Integer bookNo,
    HttpServletResponse response) {
69      Book book = bookService.getBookById(bookNo);
70      try {
71          if (book.getToc()!=null) {
72              response.setHeader("Content-Disposition", "inline;filename=\""
                +book.getBookName()+ "\"");
73              OutputStream out = response.getOutputStream();
74              response.setContentType("application/pdf");
75              IOUtils.copy(book.getToc().getBinaryStream(), out);
76              out.flush();
77              out.close();
78          }
79      } catch (IOException e) {
80          e.printStackTrace();
81      } catch (SQLException e) {
82          e.printStackTrace();
83      }
84      return null;
85  }
86
87  @RequestMapping("/downloadBookSampleChapter/{bookNo}")
88  public String downloadBookSampleChapter(@PathVariable("bookNo") Integer
    bookNo, HttpServletResponse response) {
89      Book book = bookService.getBookById(bookNo);
90      try {
91          if (book.getSampleChapter()!=null) {
92              response.setHeader("Content-Disposition", "inline;filename=\""
                +book.getBookName()+ "\"");
93              OutputStream out = response.getOutputStream();
94              response.setContentType("application/pdf");
95              IOUtils.copy(book.getSampleChapter().getBinaryStream(), out);
96              out.flush();
97              out.close();
98          }
99      } catch (IOException e) {
100         e.printStackTrace();
101     } catch (SQLException e) {
102         e.printStackTrace();
103     }
104     return null;
```

```
105     }
106
107     @RequestMapping(value = "/saveBook", method = RequestMethod.POST)
108     public String saveBook(Map<String, Object> map, @ModelAttribute("book") Book
        book, @Valid Book bookValid, BindingResult result,
        @RequestParam("coverPageFile") MultipartFile coverPageFile,
        @RequestParam("tocFile") MultipartFile tocFile,
        @RequestParam("sampleChapterFile") MultipartFile sampleChapterFile) throws
        IOException {
109         if (result.hasErrors()) {
110             map.put("bookList", bookService.listBook());
111             map.put("publisherList", publisherService.listPublisher());
112             map.put("categoryList", categoryService.listCategory());
113             map.put("authorList", authorService.listAuthor());
114             return "manageBooks";
115         } else {
116             if(!coverPageFile.isEmpty()) {
117                 book.setCoverPage(commonService.getBlob(coverPageFile.getBytes()));
118             }
119             else {
120                 if (book.getBookNo() != null) {
121                     book.setCoverPage(bookService.getBookById(book.getBookNo()).getCov
                    erPage());
122                 }
123             }
124             if(!tocFile.isEmpty()) {
125                 book.setToc(commonService.getBlob(tocFile.getBytes()));
126             }
127             else {
128                 if (book.getBookNo() != null) {
129                     book.setToc(bookService.getBookById(book.getBookNo()).getToc());
130                 }
131             }
132             if(!sampleChapterFile.isEmpty()) {
133                 book.setSampleChapter(commonService.getBlob(sampleChapterFile.getByt
                    es()));
134             }
135             else {
136                 if (book.getBookNo() != null) {
137                     book.setSampleChapter(bookService.getBookById(book.getBookNo()).ge
                    tSampleChapter());
138                 }
139             }
140             try {
141                 bookService.saveBook(book);
142                 bookService.notifyCustomersByMail(book);
143                 return "redirect:/admin/manageBooks";
144             } catch (ConstraintViolationException exp) {
145                 map.put("dbError", exp.getMessage());
146                 return "manageBooks";
147             }
148         }
149     }
```

```
150
151    @RequestMapping("/deleteBook/{bookNo}")
152    public String deleteBook(@PathVariable("bookNo") Integer bookNo) {
153        bookService.removeBook(bookNo);
154        return "redirect:/admin/manageBooks";
155    }
156
157    @RequestMapping("/editBook/{bookNo}")
158    public String editBook(Map<String, Object> map, @PathVariable("bookNo") Integer
       bookNo) {
159        map.put("book", bookService.getBookById(bookNo));
160        map.put("publisherList", publisherService.listPublisher());
161        map.put("categoryList", categoryService.listCategory());
162        map.put("authorList", authorService.listAuthor());
163        return "manageBooks";
164    }
165 }
```

Explanation:

The following section describes the above code spec.

showManageBooks()

BookController holds a mapping to help the viewing.

This means the list of book details are retrieved by the **BookController** class's **showManageBooks()**.

showManageBooks() is invoked every time Manage Books is served.

showManageBooks():

❑ Makes a provision for adding a new book [if the user chooses to] by instantiating an object of the Book entity class

❑ Retrieves the book details by invoking **listBook()** of BookService

❑ Retrieves the publisher names by invoking **listPublisher()** of PublisherService, which is displayed in the drop down list box of Publisher field

❑ Retrieves the category names by invoking **listCategory()** of CategoryService, which is displayed in the drop down list box of Category field

❑ Retrieves the author names by invoking **listAuthor()** of AuthorService, which is displayed in the drop down list box of Author field

❑ Returns the book, publisher, category and author details that **listBook()**, **listPublisher()**, **listCategory()** and **listAuthor()** return respectively, to the View to render it, using **map.put()**

downloadBookPhotograph()

BookController holds a mapping for displaying the photographs of each book in the data grid.

downloadBookPhotograph():

- ❑ Retrieves the appropriate Book's details using **BookNo** as the reference. It calls BookService's **getBookById()** which returns the details of the book as an Book object. **BookNo** is made available through **@PathVariable** [in the list of Book rendered by the View]
- ❑ Checks whether the Books database table has photograph for the book
- ❑ If there is photograph in the database, then the photograph is retrieved from the Books database table
- ❑ If there are no photographs in the database, then downloadBookPhotograph() retrieves **null** value

downloadBookTOC()

BookController holds a mapping for displaying the TOC of each book in the data grid in the form of PDF.

downloadBookTOC():

- ❑ Retrieves the appropriate Book's details using **BookNo** as the reference. It calls BookService's **getBookById()** which returns the details of the book as an Book object. **BookNo** is made available through **@PathVariable** [in the list of Book rendered by the View]
- ❑ Checks whether the Books database table has TOC for the book
- ❑ If there is TOC in the database, then the TOC is retrieved from the Books database table
- ❑ If there is no TOC in the database, then downloadBookTOC() retrieves **null** value

downloadBookSampleChapter()

BookController holds a mapping for displaying the Sample Chapter of each book in the data grid in the form of PDF.

downloadBookSampleChapter():

❏ Retrieves the appropriate Book's details using **BookNo** as the reference. It calls BookService's **getBookById()** which returns the details of the book as an Book object. **BookNo** is made available through **@PathVariable** [in the list of Book rendered by the View]

❏ Checks whether the Books database table has sample chapter for the book

❏ If there is sample chapter in the database, then the sample chapter is retrieved from the Books database table

❏ If there is no sample chapter in the database, then downloadBookSampleChapter() retrieves **null** value

saveBook()

BookController holds a mapping to help the adding of books.

```
public String showManageBooks(Map<String, Object> map) {
    map.put("book", new Book());
    map.put("bookList", bookService.listBook());
```

As soon as Manage Books is served, an object of the Book entity class is instantiated to make a provision for adding a new book. The user may view, edit, delete or choose to add a new book.

In case, the user chooses to add a new book, keys in the required book details and clicks **Save**, BookController holds a mapping to help the saving of the newly captured book details.

saveBook():

❏ Ensures that the captured data is valid

❏ Returns the control to the View along with the error messages [available in the BindingResult object], if the captured data is found to be invalid.

    If the View is rendered along with the error messages, then the publisher, category and author names in the drop down list boxes are filled up by invoking listPublisher() of PublisherService, listCategory() of CategoryService and listAuthor() of AuthorService respectively

❏ Saves the book details using BookService's **saveBook()**, if the captured data is valid and returns the control to the View to render Manage Books

❏ Notifies the users i.e. the registered users, by sending them mail about the newly released books or the books recently updated using BookService's **notifyCustomersByMail()**

deleteBook()

In case, the user chooses to delete an book and clicks , **BookController** holds a mapping to help delete an book record from Manage Books.

deleteBook():

❑ Passes **BookNo** of the book to be deleted [available as a @PathVariable] to BookService's **removeBook()**

❑ Returns the control to the View which renders Manage Books with the updated data

editBook()

BookController holds a mapping to help the editing of existing books. In case, the user chooses to edit an book and clicks , **BookController** holds a mapping to help fill up the Manage Books form with book details.

editBook():

❑ Retrieves the appropriate Book's details using **BookNo** as the reference. It calls BookService's **getBookById()** which returns the details of the book to be edited as an Book object. **BookNo** is made available through **@PathVariable** [in the list of Book rendered by the View] when the user clicks to edit a particular book

❑ Retrieves the publisher names by invoking **listPublisher()** of PublisherService, which is displayed in the drop down list box of Publisher field

❑ Retrieves the category names by invoking **listCategory()** of CategoryService, which is displayed in the drop down list box of Category field

❑ Retrieves the author names by invoking **listAuthor()** of AuthorService, which is displayed in the drop down list box of Author field

❑ Returns the control to the View along with the data to be populated in the form. The data to be populated is made available using Map's **put()**, which is used to populate the books object with the data that **getBookById()** of BookService returns. The same happens with the publisherList, categoryList and authorList objects

Service Class

Interface [BookService.java]

This is a service interface with the following specifications.

Service Interface Specifications

Class Name	Package
BookService	com.sharanamvaishali.service

Code Spec

```
1  package com.sharanamvaishali.service;
2
3  import com.sharanamvaishali.model.Book;
4  import java.util.List;
5
6  public interface BookService {
7      public void saveBook(Book book);
8      public List<Book> listBook();
9      public void removeBook(Integer bookNo);
10     public Book getBookById(Integer bookNo);
11     public void notifyCustomersByMail(Book book);
12 }
```

Implementation Class

BookServiceImpl.java

This is a service class with the following specifications.

Service Implementation Specifications

Class Name	Package	Implements
BookServiceImpl	com.sharanamvaishali.service	BookService

Properties		
Property Name	Data Type	Value
emailFrom	String	${emailFrom}

Objects		
Object Name	Class Name	Object Type
bookDAO	BookDAO	Data Access Object Layer
userService	UserService	Service Layer
mailService	MailService	Service Layer

Methods	
Method Name	Arguments
saveBook()	Book book
listBook()	- -
removeBook()	Integer bookNo
getBookById()	Integer bookNo
notifyCustomersByMail()	Book book

Code Spec

```
1  package com.sharanamvaishali.service;
2
3  import com.sharanamvaishali.dao.BookDAO;
4  import com.sharanamvaishali.model.Book;
5  import com.sharanamvaishali.model.User;
6  import java.util.List;
7  import org.springframework.beans.factory.annotation.Autowired;
8  import org.springframework.beans.factory.annotation.Value;
9  import org.springframework.stereotype.Service;
10 import org.springframework.transaction.annotation.Transactional;
11
12 @Service
13 public class BookServiceImpl implements BookService {
14     @Value("${emailFrom}")
15     String emailFrom;
16
17     @Autowired
18     private UserService userService;
19
20     @Autowired
21     private MailService mailService;
22
23     @Autowired
24     private BookDAO bookDAO;
25
26     @Transactional
27     @Override
28     public void saveBook(Book book) {
29         bookDAO.saveBook(book);
30     }
31
32     @Transactional
33     @Override
34     public List<Book> listBook() {
35         return bookDAO.listBook();
```

```
36      }
37
38      @Transactional
39      @Override
40      public void removeBook(Integer bookNo) {
41          bookDAO.removeBook(bookNo);
42      }
43
44      @Transactional
45      @Override
46      public Book getBookById(Integer bookNo) {
47          return bookDAO.getBookById(bookNo);
48      }
49
50      @Override
51      public void notifyCustomersByMail(Book book) {
52          List<User> users = userService.listUser();
53          for (User user : users) {
54              String emailMessage = "<table width='100%' border='0' align='center'
                cellpadding='0' cellspacing='0' "
55                  + "style='font-family: Verdana, Arial, Helvetica, sans-serif; "
56                  + "font-size: 12pt; color:#5a5a5a;'><tr><td align='left'>"
57                  + "<p>Dear " + user.getFirstName() + ",</p></td></tr><tr>"
58                  + "<td align='left'>"
59                  + "<p>ISBN: " + book.getIsbn() + "<br /><br />"
60                  + "Edition: " + book.getEdition() + "<br /><br />"
61                  + "Synopsis: " + book.getSynopsis() + "<br /><br />"
62                  + "Topics covered: " + book.getTopicsCovered() + "<br /><br /></p>"
63                  + "<p>Thank you for using  this site.<br /></p><br/><br/><p>"
64                  + "Regards,<br />Sharanam & Vaishali's Online Bookshop<br /></p><p><br
                    />"
65                  + "<br />THIS IS AN AUTOMATED MESSAGE; PLEASE DO NOT REPLY.
                    </p></td></tr></table>";
66              if(user.getAuthority().equals("CUSTOMER") && user.isNewRelease()) {
67                  if(book.getBookNo() == null) {
68                      String emailSubject = "Sharanam & Vaishali's Online Bookshop: " +
                        book.getBookName() + " has been added.";
69                      mailService.sendMail(emailFrom, user.getEmailAddress(), emailSubject,
                        emailMessage);
70                  }
71              }
72              if(user.getAuthority().equals("CUSTOMER") && user.isBookUpdates()) {
73                  if(book.getBookNo()!=null) {
74                      String emailSubject = "Sharanam & Vaishali's Online Bookshop: " +
                        book.getBookName() + " has been updated.";
75                      mailService.sendMail(emailFrom, user.getEmailAddress(), emailSubject,
                        emailMessage);
76                  }
77              }
78          }
79      }
80  }
```

Explanation:

The following section describes the above code spec.

saveBook()

saveBook() holds the business logic to save the captured book details.

This method in turn invokes BookDAO's **saveBook()**.

listBook()

listBook() holds the business logic to return the appropriate list of the available books.

This method in turn invokes BookDAO's **listBook()**.

removeBook()

removeBook() holds the business logic to delete book details based on BookNo.

This method in turn invokes BookDAO's **removeBook()**.

getBookById()

getBookById() holds the business logic to retrieve book details based on BookNo.

This method in turn invokes BookDAO's **getBookById()**.

notifyCustomersByMail()

notifyCustomerByMail() is called by BookController's saveBook(). This method sends an email to the registered customers regarding the newly released books or the books updated.

notifyCustomersByMail():
- Retrieves the user details by invoking **listUser()** of UserService [explained in the next *Chapter 37: Manage Users*]
- For each user:
  - A message is created regarding the book details
  - A check is made whether the registered customer had selected the option for New Releases or Updated Book subscription
  - Accordingly the mail is send for the newly released books or updated books

MailService.java

This is a service class with the following specifications.

Service Implementation Specifications

Class Name	Package	
MailService	com.sharanamvaishali.service	
Properties		
Property Name	Data Type	Value
sendMail	String	${sendMail}
Objects		
Object Name	Class Name	Method
mailSender	JavaMailSender	setMailSender()
Methods		
Method Name	Arguments	
sendMail()	String from String to String subject String msg	

Code Spec

```
1  package com.sharanamvaishali.service;
2  import java.net.MalformedURLException;
3  import java.util.logging.Level;
4  import java.util.logging.Logger;
5  import javax.mail.MessagingException;
6  import javax.mail.internet.MimeMessage;
7  import org.springframework.beans.factory.annotation.Value;
8  import org.springframework.core.io.UrlResource;
9  import org.springframework.mail.MailParseException;
10 import org.springframework.mail.javamail.JavaMailSender;
11 import org.springframework.mail.javamail.MimeMessageHelper;
12
13 public class MailService {
14     @Value("${sendMail}")
15     String sendMail;
16
17     private JavaMailSender mailSender;
18
19     public void setMailSender(JavaMailSender mailSender) {
20         this.mailSender = mailSender;
21     }
22
23     public void sendMail(String from, String to, String subject, String msg) {
24         MimeMessage message = mailSender.createMimeMessage();
```

```
25
26        try{
27            MimeMessageHelper helper = new MimeMessageHelper(message, true);
28
29            helper.setFrom(from);
30            helper.setTo(to);
31            helper.setSubject(subject);
32            helper.setText(msg, true);
33
34            UrlResource file;
35            try {
36                file = new UrlResource("http://localhost:8080/BookShop/images/logo.png");
37                helper.addAttachment(file.getFilename(), file);
38            } catch (MalformedURLException ex) {
39                Logger.getLogger(MailService.class.getName()).log(Level.SEVERE, null, ex);
40            }
41        }catch (MessagingException e) {
42            throw new MailParseException(e);
43        }
44
45        if(sendMail.equals("true")) {
46            mailSender.send(message);
47        }
48    }
49 }
```

Explanation:

The following section describes the above code spec.

sendMail()

sendMail() holds the business logic to send an email to the customers regarding successful registration or newly released book or updated books or forgotten password.

sendMail() takes four parameters:

❑ Email address of the sender

❑ Email address of the recipient

❑ Subject of the Email

❑ Message of the Email

sendMail():

❑ Initializes the MimeMessage class, which represents a MIME style email message

REMINDER

JavaMailSender extends MailSender interface for JavaMail, supporting MIME messages both as direct arguments and through preparation callbacks. JavaMailSender is typically used in conjunction with the MimeMessageHelper class for convenient creation of JavaMail MimeMessages, including attachments and so on.

❑ Initializes MimeMessageHelper class and assigns the following values:

    o MimeMessage to work on

    o Multipart, whether to create a multipart message that supports alternative texts, inline elements and attachments

❑ Sets all the parameters of sendMail() in the MimeMessageHelper class

❑ Initializes UrlResource, which is a Resource implementation for java.net.URL locators. It supports resolution as URL and as File in case of the "file:" protocol

❑ Creates a new UrlResource

❑ Attaches the file i.e. addAttachment() of MimeMessageHelper

❑ Finally, dispatches the mail to the recipient

REMINDER

CommonService.java and CommonServiceImpl.java have been explained in the previous *Chapter 35: Manage Authors.*

PublisherService's **listPublisher()** is explained in the *Chapter 34: Manage Publishers,* which retrieves the list of publisher names to be filled in the Publisher drop down list box.

CategoryService's **listCategory()** is explained in the *Chapter 33: Manage Categories,* which retrieves the list of category names to be filled in the Category drop down list box.

AuthorService's **listAuthor()** is explained in the *Chapter 35: Manage Authors,* which retrieves the list of author names to be filled in the First Author, Second Author, Third Author and Fourth Author drop down list boxes.

DAO Class

Interface [BookDAO.java]

This is a Data Access Object interface with the following specifications.

DAO Interface Specifications

Class Name	Package
BookDAO	com.sharanamvaishali.dao

Code Spec

```
1  package com.sharanamvaishali.dao;
2
3  import com.sharanamvaishali.model.Book;
4  import java.util.List;
5
6  public interface BookDAO {
7      public void saveBook(Book book);
8      public List<Book> listBook();
9      public void removeBook(Integer bookNo);
10     public Book getBookById(Integer bookNo);
11 }
```

Implementation Class [BookDAOImpl.java]

This is a **Data Access Object** class with the following specifications.

DAO Implementation Specifications

Class Name	Package	Implements
BookDAOImpl	com.sharanamvaishali.dao	BookDAO

Objects		
Object Name		Class Name
sessionFactory		SessionFactory

Methods		
Method Name	Arguments	Return Values
saveBook()	Book book	void
listBook()	- -	List <Book>
removeBook()	Integer bookNo	void
getBookById()	Integer bookNo	Book

Code Spec

```
1  package com.sharanamvaishali.dao;
2
3  import com.sharanamvaishali.model.Book;
4  import com.sharanamvaishali.service.BookService;
5  import java.util.List;
6  import org.hibernate.SessionFactory;
```

```java
7  import org.springframework.beans.factory.annotation.Autowired;
8  import org.springframework.stereotype.Repository;
9
10 @Repository
11 public class BookDAOImpl implements BookDAO {
12     @Autowired
13     private SessionFactory sessionFactory;
14
15     @Override
16     public void saveBook(Book book) {
17         sessionFactory.getCurrentSession().merge(book);
18     }
19
20     @Override
21     public List<Book> listBook() {
22         return sessionFactory.getCurrentSession().createQuery("from Book").list();
23     }
24
25     @Override
26     public void removeBook(Integer bookNo) {
27         Book book = (Book) sessionFactory.getCurrentSession().load(Book.class,
           bookNo);
28         if (null != book) {
29             sessionFactory.getCurrentSession().delete(book);
30         }
31     }
32
33     @Override
34     public Book getBookById(Integer bookNo) {
35         return (Book) sessionFactory.getCurrentSession().get(Book.class, bookNo);
36     }
37 }
```

Explanation:

The following section describes the above code spec.

saveBook()

saveBook() does the actual saving of the book in the Books database table.

This method uses **merge()** of SessionFactory, which takes care of adding as well as updating the book details, in case the user had edited an existing book and clicked **Save**.

listBook()

listBook() does the actual retrieval of the available books.

This method fires a SELECT query that attempts to retrieve records from the Books database table.

All the records that the query retrieves are extracted and returned as a **List** object.

This List object is returned to the calling method i.e. Service Layer's **listBook()**:

```
public List<Book> listBook() {
    return bookDAO.listBook();
}
```

This method in turn returns it to the BookController's **showManageBooks()**:

```
public String showManageBooks(Map<String, Object> map) {
    map.put("book", new Book());
    map.put("bookList", bookService.listBook());
    map.put("publisherList", publisherService.listPublisher());
```

Finally, BookController returns this List object to the View which renders it.

manageBooks.jsp on taking charge uses the **iterator** tag to iterate over the contents of the List object **bookList**.

```
<c:forEach items="${bookList}" var="book">
    <tr>
        <td>${book.bookName}</td>
        <td>${book.isbn}</td>
        <td>${book.synopsis}</td>
```

The bookList object holds all those records retrieved by the SQL query.

Each record's column values are extracted using $.

```
<td>${book.bookName}</td>
<td>${book.isbn}</td>
<td>${book.synopsis}</td>
```

removeBook()

removeBook() deletes the appropriate book based on **BookNo** received as a reference.

This method uses:

- **load()** of SessionFactory, which retrieves the appropriate Book to be deleted using BookNo as a reference

- **delete()** of SessionFactory, which deletes the book from Books database table

getBookById()

getBookById() returns the appropriate book's object from the Books database table using **BookNo** as the reference.

This method uses **get()** of SessionFactory, which returns the appropriate Book from Books database table.

After editing the book details, when the user clicks , saveBook() of BookController, followed by saveBook() of BookService, followed by saveBook() of BookDAO takes care of saving the updated book's details.

REMINDER

CommonDAO.java and CommonDAOImpl.java have been explained in the previous *Chapter 35: Manage Authors*.

PublisherDAO's **listPublisher()** is explained in the *Chapter 34: Manage Publishers*, which retrieves the list of publisher names to be filled in the Publisher drop down list box.

CategoryDAO's **listCategory()** is explained in the *Chapter 33: Manage Categories*, which retrieves the list of category names to be filled in the Category drop down list box.

AuthorDAO's **listAuthor()** is explained in the *Chapter 35: Manage Authors*, which retrieves the list of author names to be filled in the First Author, Second Author, Third Author and Fourth Author drop down list boxes.

Domain Class [Book.java]

This is a domain class with the following specifications.

Domain Specifications

Class Name	Package	Implements
Book	com.sharanamvaishali.model	java.io.Serializable

Properties			
Property Name	**Property Type**	**Methods**	
bookNo	Integer	getBookNo()	setBookNo()
bookName	String	getBookName()	setBookName()
author1No	Integer	getAuthor1No()	setAuthor1No()
author2No	Integer	getAuthor2No()	setAuthor2No()
author3No	Integer	getAuthor3No()	setAuthor3No()
author4No	Integer	getAuthor4No()	setAuthor4No()
publisherNo	Integer	getPublisherNo()	setPublisherNo()
categoryNo	Integer	getCategoryNo()	setCategoryNo()
coverPage	Blob	getCoverPage()	setCoverPage()
isbn	String	getIsbn()	setIsbn()
edition	String	getEdition()	setEdition()
year	Integer	getYear()	setYear()
cost	Integer	getCost()	setCost()
synopsis	String	getSynopsis()	setSynopsis()
aboutAuthors	String	getAboutAuthors()	setAboutAuthors()
topicsCovered	String	getTopicsCovered()	setTopicsCovered()
contentsCDROM	String	getContentsCDROM()	setContentsCDROM()
toc	Blob	getToc()	setToc()
sampleChapter	Blob	getSampleChapter()	setSampleChapter()
hits	Integer	getHits()	setHits()

Code Spec

```
1   package com.sharanamvaishali.model;
2
3   import java.sql.Blob;
4   import javax.persistence.*;
5   import javax.validation.constraints.NotNull;
6   import org.hibernate.validator.constraints.NotEmpty;
7
8   @Entity
9   @Table(name="BOOKS")
10  public class Book implements java.io.Serializable {
11      @Id
12      @GeneratedValue
13      @Column(name="BOOKNO")
14      private Integer bookNo;
15      @Column(name="BOOKNAME")
16      @NotEmpty(message="Book name is mandatory")
17      private String bookName;
18      @Column(name="AUTHOR1NO")
19      @NotNull(message="Author name is mandatory")
20      private Integer author1No;
21      @Column(name="AUTHOR2NO")
22      private Integer author2No;
```

```
23      @Column(name="AUTHOR3NO")
24      private Integer author3No;
25      @Column(name="AUTHOR4NO")
26      private Integer author4No;
27      @Column(name="PUBLISHERNO")
28      @NotNull(message="Publisher name is mandatory")
29      private Integer publisherNo;
30      @Column(name="CATEGORYNO")
31      @NotNull(message="Category is mandatory")
32      private Integer categoryNo;
33      @Column(name="COVERPAGE")
34      @Lob
35      private Blob coverPage;
36      @Column(name="ISBN")
37      @NotEmpty(message="ISBN is mandatory")
38      private String isbn;
39      @Column(name="EDITION")
40      @NotEmpty(message="Edition is mandatory")
41      private String edition;
42      @Column(name="YEAR")
43      @NotNull(message="Year is mandatory")
44      private Integer year;
45      @Column(name="COST")
46      @NotNull(message="Cost is mandatory")
47      private Integer cost;
48      @Column(name="SYNOPSIS")
49      @NotEmpty(message="Synopsis is mandatory")
50      private String synopsis;
51      @Column(name="ABOUTAUTHORS")
52      @NotEmpty(message="About Authors is mandatory")
53      private String aboutAuthors;
54      @Column(name="TOPICSCOVERED")
55      private String topicsCovered;
56      @Column(name="CONTENTSCDROM")
57      private String contentsCDROM;
58      @Column(name="TOC")
59      @Lob
60      private Blob toc;
61      @Column(name="SAMPLECHAPTER")
62      @Lob
63      private Blob sampleChapter;
64      @Column(name="HITS")
65      private Integer hits;
66
67      public String getAboutAuthors() {
68          return aboutAuthors;
69      }
70      public void setAboutAuthors(String aboutAuthors) {
71          this.aboutAuthors = aboutAuthors;
72      }
73
74      public Integer getAuthor1No() {
```

```
75          return author1No;
76      }
77      public void setAuthor1No(Integer author1No) {
78          this.author1No = author1No;
79      }
80
81      public Integer getAuthor2No() {
82          return author2No;
83      }
84      public void setAuthor2No(Integer author2No) {
85          this.author2No = author2No;
86      }
87
88      public Integer getAuthor3No() {
89          return author3No;
90      }
91      public void setAuthor3No(Integer author3No) {
92          this.author3No = author3No;
93      }
94
95      public Integer getAuthor4No() {
96          return author4No;
97      }
98      public void setAuthor4No(Integer author4No) {
99          this.author4No = author4No;
100     }
101
102     public String getBookName() {
103         return bookName;
104     }
105     public void setBookName(String bookName) {
106         this.bookName = bookName;
107     }
108
109     public Integer getBookNo() {
110         return bookNo;
111     }
112     public void setBookNo(Integer bookNo) {
113         this.bookNo = bookNo;
114     }
115
116     public Integer getCategoryNo() {
117         return categoryNo;
118     }
119     public void setCategoryNo(Integer categoryNo) {
120         this.categoryNo = categoryNo;
121     }
122
123     public String getContentsCDROM() {
124         return contentsCDROM;
125     }
126     public void setContentsCDROM(String contentsCDROM) {
```

```
127        this.contentsCDROM = contentsCDROM;
128    }
129
130    public Integer getCost() {
131        return cost;
132    }
133    public void setCost(Integer cost) {
134        this.cost = cost;
135    }
136
137    public Blob getCoverPage() {
138        return coverPage;
139    }
140    public void setCoverPage(Blob coverPage) {
141        this.coverPage = coverPage;
142    }
143
144    public String getEdition() {
145        return edition;
146    }
147    public void setEdition(String edition) {
148        this.edition = edition;
149    }
150
151    public Integer getHits() {
152        return hits;
153    }
154    public void setHits(Integer hits) {
155        this.hits = hits;
156    }
157
158    public String getIsbn() {
159        return isbn;
160    }
161    public void setIsbn(String isbn) {
162        this.isbn = isbn;
163    }
164
165    public Integer getPublisherNo() {
166        return publisherNo;
167    }
168    public void setPublisherNo(Integer publisherNo) {
169        this.publisherNo = publisherNo;
170    }
171
172    public Blob getSampleChapter() {
173        return sampleChapter;
174    }
175    public void setSampleChapter(Blob sampleChapter) {
176        this.sampleChapter = sampleChapter;
177    }
178
179    public String getSynopsis() {
```

```
180          return synopsis;
181      }
182      public void setSynopsis(String synopsis) {
183          this.synopsis = synopsis;
184      }
185
186      public Blob getToc() {
187          return toc;
188      }
189      public void setToc(Blob toc) {
190          this.toc = toc;
191      }
192
193      public String getTopicsCovered() {
194          return topicsCovered;
195      }
196      public void setTopicsCovered(String topicsCovered) {
197          this.topicsCovered = topicsCovered;
198      }
199
200      public Integer getYear() {
201          return year;
202      }
203      public void setYear(Integer year) {
204          this.year = year;
205      }
206  }
```

REMINDER

Publisher.java [the model class] is explained in the *Chapter 34: Manage Publishers*.

Category.java [the model class] is explained in the *Chapter 33: Manage Categories*.

Author.java [the model class] is explained in the *Chapter 35: Manage Authors*.

Chapter

37

SECTION V: BACKEND [ADMINISTRATION] SOFTWARE DESIGN DOCUMENTATION

Manage Users

This module allows performing the following operations:

- ❑ Adding new users
- ❑ Editing existing users
- ❑ Viewing across existing users
- ❑ Deleting existing users

This module uses the bms.Users table to perform the above operations.

This module is made up of the following:

Type	Name	Description
JSP	manageUsers.jsp	The data entry form.
Spring		
Controller	UserController.java	The controller class that facilitates data operations.
Service Class	UserService.java	The interface for the service layer.
	CountryService.java	
	StateService.java	
	UserServiceImpl.java	The implementation class for the service layer.
	CountryServiceImpl.java	
	StateServiceImpl.java	
DAO Class	UserDAO.java	The interface for the DAO layer.
	CountryDAO.java	
	StateDAO.java	
	UserDAOImpl.java	The implementation class that performs the actual data operations.
	CountryDAOImpl.java	
	StateDAOImpl.java	
DispatcherServlet	bookshopdispatcher-servlet.xml	Central dispatcher for HTTP request handlers/controllers.
Hibernate		
Mapping	hibernate.cfg.xml	The mapping file that holds Model class mapping.
Model Class	User.java	The model class.
	Country.java	
	State.java	

JSP [manageUsers.jsp]

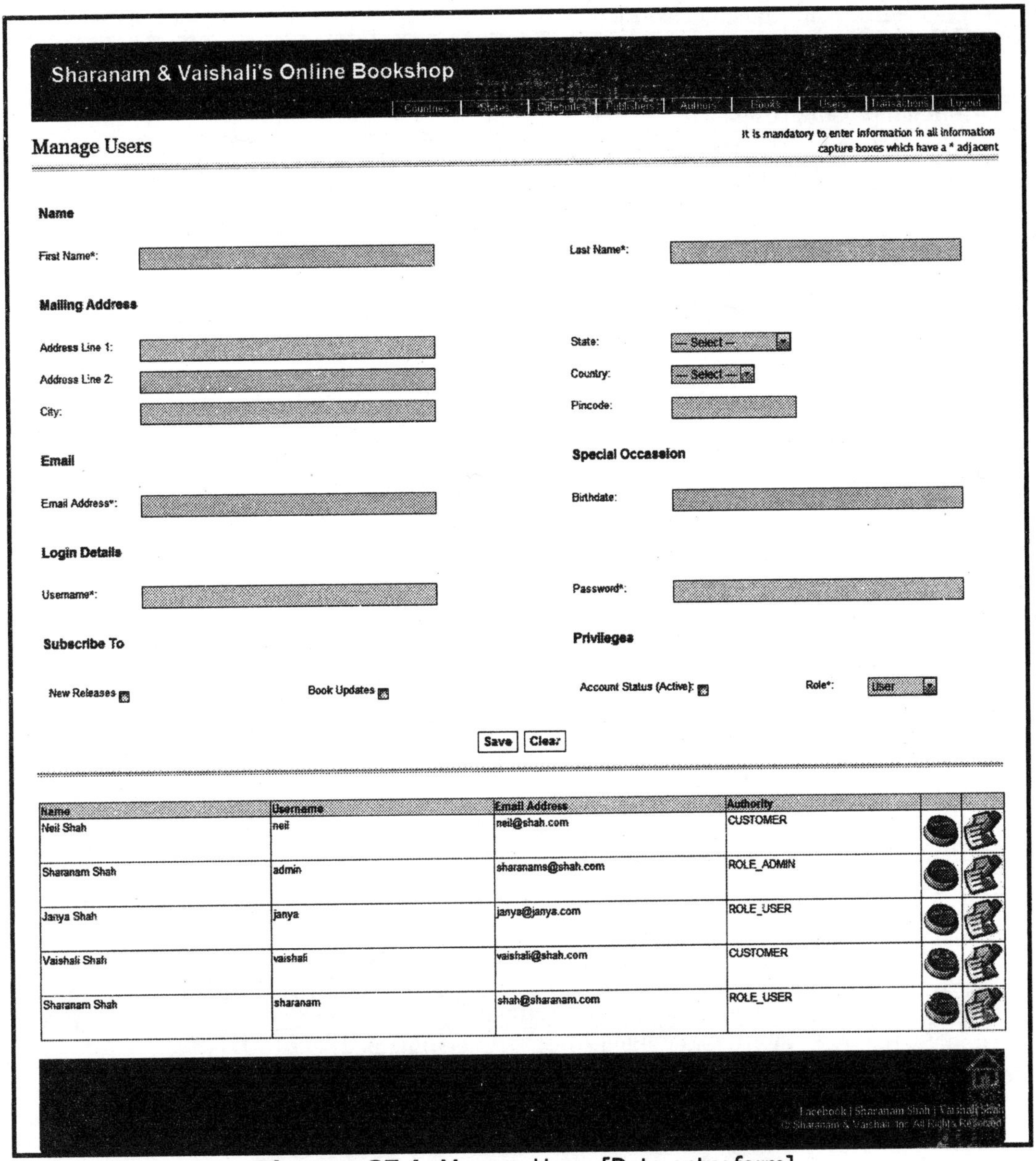

Diagram 37.1: Manage Users [Data entry form]

This is a JSP which holds a data entry form, as shown in diagram 37.1. This form appears when the user clicks [Users].

Form Specifications

File Name	manageUsers.jsp
Title	BookShop[Sharanam & Vaishali Shah] - Manage Users
Bound To Table	bms.Users
Command Name	user
Action	${pageContext.request.contextPath}/admin/saveUser
Method	POST

Data Fields

Label	Name	Bound To	Validation Rules
Name			
First Name	User.firstName	Users.FirstName	Cannot be left blank
Last Name	User.lastName	Users.LastName	Cannot be left blank
Mailing Address			
Address Line 1	User.address1	Users.Address1	- -
Address Line 2	User.address2	Users.Address2	- -
City	User.city	Users.City	- -
State	User.stateNo	Users.StateNo	- -
Country	User.countryNo	Users.CountryNo	- -
Pincode	User.pincode	Users.Pincode	- -
Email			
Email Address	User.emailAddress	Users.EmailAddress	Cannot be left blank
Special Occassion			
Birthdate	User.dob	Users.DOB	- -
Login Details			
Username	User.userName	Users.Username	Cannot be left blank
Password	User.password	Users.Password	Cannot be left blank
Subscribe To			
New Releases	User.newRelease	Users.NewRelease	- -
Book Updates	User.bookUpdates	Users.BookUpdates	- -
Privileges			
Account Status (Active)	User.enabled	Users.Enabled	- -
Role	User.authority	Users.Authority	- -

Micro-Help For Form Fields

Form Field	Micro Help Statement
Name	
User.firstName	Enter the first name
User.lastName	Enter the last name
Mailing Address	
User.address1	Enter the street address
User.address2	Enter the street address
User.city	Enter the city
User.stateNo	--
User.countryNo	--
User.pincode	Enter the pincode
Email	
User.emailAddress	Enter the email address
Special Occassion	
User.dob	Enter the birthdate
Login Details	
User.userName	Enter the username
User.password	Enter the password
Subscribe To	
User.newRelease	Select to new releases
User.bookUpdates	Select to book updates
Privileges	
User.enabled	Select the status
User.authority	Select the role of the user

Data Controls

Object	Label
Submit	Save
Reset	Clear

Code Spec

```
1  <%@page contentType="text/html" pageEncoding="UTF-8"%>
2  <%@taglib uri="http://www.springframework.org/tags/form" prefix="form"%>
3  <%@taglib uri="http://java.sun.com/jsp/jstl/core" prefix="c"%>
4  <!DOCTYPE HTML PUBLIC "-//W3C//DTD HTML 4.01 Transitional//EN"
5     "http://www.w3.org/TR/html4/loose.dtd">
6  <html>
7     <head>
```

```
8         <meta http-equiv="Content-Type" content="text/html; charset=UTF-8">
9         <title>BookShop[Sharanam & Vaishali Shah] - Manage Users</title>
10        <link rel="stylesheet" href="/BookShop/css/admin.css" type="text/css">
11     </head>
12     <body>
13        <%@ include file="/WEB-INF/jsp/adminHeader.jsp" %>
14        <br/>
15        <form:form method="post"
           action="${pageContext.request.contextPath}/admin/saveUser"
           commandName="user">
16           <form:hidden path="userNo" />
17           <table width="100%" border="0" align="center" cellpadding="0"
              cellspacing="0">
18              <tr>
19                 <td>
20                    <table border="0" cellpadding="0" cellspacing="0" width="100%">
21                       <tr>
22                          <td class="manageForms">Manage Users</td>
23                          <td align="center" class="error">${dbError}</td>
24                          <td class="information">
25                             It is mandatory to enter information in all information
                                <br>capture boxes which have a <span
                                class="mandatory">*</span> adjacent
26                          </td>
27                       </tr>
28                    </table>
29                 </td>
30              </tr>
31              <tr><td class="hrLine"> </td></tr>
32              <tr>
33                 <td>
34                    <table width="100%" border="0" align="center" cellpadding="0"
                       cellspacing="0">
35                       <tr>
36                          <td>
37                             <table width="100%" border="0" cellpadding="4"
                                cellspacing="4">
38                                <tr>
39                                   <td class="sectionName" colspan="4">
40                                      <br />Name<br /><br />
41                                   </td>
42                                </tr>
43                                <tr>
44                                   <td width="10%">First Name<span
                                      class="mandatory">*</span>:</td>
45                                   <td width="45%">
46                                      <form:input path="firstName" title="Enter the first
                                         name" maxlength="25" size="55"/><br>
47                                      <form:errors path="firstName" cssClass="error" />
48                                   </td>
49                                   <td width="10%">Last Name<span
                                      class="mandatory">*</span>:</td>
50                                   <td width="45%">
```

```
51        <form:input path="lastName" title="Enter the last
          name" maxlength="25" size="55"/><br>
52        <form:errors path="lastName" cssClass="error" />
53      </td>
54    </tr>
55    <tr>
56      <td class="sectionName" colspan="4">
57        <br />Mailing Address<br /><br />
58      </td>
59    </tr>
60    <tr>
61      <td width="10%">Address Line 1:</td>
62      <td width="45%">
63        <form:input path="address1" title="Enter the
          street address" maxlength="50" size="55"/>
64      </td>
65      <td width="10%">State:</td>
66      <td width="45%">
67        <form:select path="stateNo">
68          <form:option value="" label="--- Select ---"/>
69          <form:options title="Select the state"
            items="${stateList}" itemValue="stateNo"
            itemLabel="state" />
70        </form:select>
71      </td>
72    </tr>
73    <tr>
74      <td width="10%">Address Line 2:</td>
75      <td width="45%">
76        <form:input path="address2" title="Enter the
          street address" maxlength="50" size="55"/>
77      </td>
78      <td width="10%">Country:</td>
79      <td width="45%">
80        <form:select path="countryNo">
81          <form:option value="" label="--- Select ---"/>
82          <form:options title="Select the country"
            items="${countryList}" itemValue="countryNo"
            itemLabel="country" />
83        </form:select>
84      </td>
85    </tr>
86    <tr>
87      <td width="10%">City:</td>
88      <td width="45%">
89        <form:input path="city" title="Enter the city"
          maxlength="50" size="55"/>
90      </td>
91      <td width="10%">Pincode:</td>
92      <td width="45%">
93        <form:input path="pincode" title="Enter the
          pincode" maxlength="15" size="20"/>
94      </td>
```

```
95          </tr>
96          <tr>
97              <td class="sectionName" colspan="2">
98                  <br />Email<br /><br />
99              </td>
100             <td class="sectionName" colspan="2">
101                 <br />Special Occassion<br /><br />
102             </td>
103         </tr>
104         <tr>
105             <td width="10%">Email Address<span
                class="mandatory">*</span>:</td>
106             <td width="45%">
107                 <form:input path="emailAddress" title="Enter the
                    email address" maxlength="50" size="55"/><br>
108                 <form:errors path="emailAddress" cssClass="error"
                    />
109             </td>
110             <td width="10%">Birthdate:</td>
111             <td width="45%">
112                 <form:input path="dob" title="Enter the birthdate"
                    maxlength="25" size="55"/>
113             </td>
114         </tr>
115         <tr>
116             <td class="sectionName" colspan="4">
117                 <br />Login Details<br /><br />
118             </td>
119         </tr>
120         <tr>
121             <td width="10%">Username<span
                class="mandatory">*</span>:</td>
122             <td width="45%">
123                 <form:input path="userName" title="Enter the
                    username" maxlength="25" size="55"/><br>
124                 <form:errors path="userName" cssClass="error" />
125             </td>
126             <td width="10%">Password<span
                class="mandatory">*</span>:</td>
127             <td width="45%">
128                 <form:password path="password" title="Enter the
                    password" maxlength="8" size="55"/><br>
129                 <form:errors path="password" cssClass="error" />
130             </td>
131         </tr>
132         <tr>
133             <td class="sectionName" colspan="2">
134                 <br />Subscribe To<br /><br />
135             </td>
136             <td class="sectionName" colspan="2">
137                 <br />Privileges<br /><br />
138             </td>
139         </tr>
140         <tr>
```

```
141                                    <td colspan="2">
142                                        <table width="100%" border="0" cellpadding="4"
                                           cellspacing="4">
143                                            <tr>
144                                                <td>New Releases<form:checkbox
                                                   path="newRelease" title="Select to new
                                                   releases"/></td>
145                                                <td>Book Updates<form:checkbox
                                                   path="bookUpdates" title="Select to book
                                                   updates"/></td>
146                                            </tr>
147                                        </table>
148                                    </td>
149                                    <td colspan="2">
150                                        <table width="100%" border="0" cellpadding="4"
                                           cellspacing="4">
151                                            <tr>
152                                                <td>Account Status (Active):<form:checkbox
                                                   path="enabled" title="Select the
                                                   status"/></td>
153                                                <td>Role<span
                                                   class="mandatory">*</span>:</td>
154                                                <td>
155                                                    <form:select path="authority"
                                                   title="Select the role of the user">
156                                                        <form:option value="ROLE_USER"
                                                   label="User"/>
157                                                        <form:option value="ROLE_ADMIN"
                                                   label="Admin" />
158                                                        <form:option value="CUSTOMER"
                                                   label="Customer" />
159                                                    </form:select>
160                                                </td>
161                                            </tr>
162                                        </table>
163                                    </td>
164                                </tr>
165                            </table>
166                        </td>
167                    </tr>
168                    <tr><td> </td></tr>
169                    <tr>
170                        <td colspan="2" class="centerAlign">
171                            <input type="submit" class="groovybutton" value="Save"
                               />
172                            <input type="reset" value="Clear" class="groovybutton"
                               onclick="javascript:document.location.href='/BookShop/admi
                               n/manageUsers'" />
173                        </td>
174                    </tr>
175                </table>
176            </td>
177        </tr>
```

```
178              <tr><td> </td></tr>
179              <tr><td class="hrLine"> </td></tr>
180              <tr><td><br></td></tr>
181            </table>
182         </form:form>
183         <c:if test="${!empty userList}">
184            <table class="data" width="100%">
185               <tr>
186                  <th width="24%">Name</th>
187                  <th width="23%">Username</th>
188                  <th width="24%">Email Address</th>
189                  <th width="23">Authority</th>
190                  <th width="3%"> </th>
191                  <th width="3%"> </th>
192               </tr>
193               <c:forEach items="${userList}" var="user">
194                  <tr>
195                     <td>${user.firstName} ${user.lastName}</td>
196                     <td>${user.userName}</td>
197                     <td>${user.emailAddress}</td>
198                     <td>${user.authority}</td>
199                     <td><a href="/BookShop/admin/deleteUser/${user.userNo}"><img
                         title="Click to delete"
                         src="/BookShop/images/delete.jpg"/></a></td>
200                     <td><a href="/BookShop/admin/editUser/${user.userNo}"><img
                         title="Click to edit" src="/BookShop/images/edit.jpg"/></a></td>
201                  </tr>
202               </c:forEach>
203            </table>
204         </c:if>
205         <%@ include file="/WEB-INF/jsp/adminFooter.jsp" %>
206      </body>
207 </html>
```

Explanation:

This is a standard data entry form, which captures the user details. By default when the form loads, it's in the **INSERT** and **VIEW** mode. The form also has Delete and Edit options to delete and edit a particular user record.

Controller [UserController.java]

This is a controller class with the following specifications.

Controller Specifications

Class Name	Package
UserController	com.sharanamvaishali.controllers

| Objects | | |
Object Name	Class Name	Object Type
userService	UserService	Service Layer
countryService	CountryService	Service Layer
stateService	StateService	Service Layer

| Methods | |
Method Name	Request Mapping
showManageUsers()	/admin/manageUsers
saveUser()	/admin/saveUser
deleteUser()	/admin/deleteUser/${userNo}
editUser()	/admin/editUser/${userNo}

Code Spec

```
1  package com.sharanamvaishali.controllers;
2
3  import com.sharanamvaishali.model.User;
4  import com.sharanamvaishali.service.CountryService;
5  import com.sharanamvaishali.service.StateService;
6  import com.sharanamvaishali.service.UserService;
7  import java.util.Map;
8  import javax.validation.Valid;
9  import org.hibernate.exception.ConstraintViolationException;
10 import org.springframework.beans.factory.annotation.Autowired;
11 import org.springframework.beans.factory.annotation.Value;
12 import org.springframework.stereotype.Controller;
13 import org.springframework.validation.BindingResult;
14 import org.springframework.web.bind.annotation.ModelAttribute;
15 import org.springframework.web.bind.annotation.PathVariable;
16 import org.springframework.web.bind.annotation.RequestMapping;
17 import org.springframework.web.bind.annotation.RequestMethod;
18
19 @Controller
20 @RequestMapping("/admin")
21 public class UserController {
22     @Autowired
23     private UserService userService;
24
25     @Autowired
26     private CountryService countryService;
27
28     @Autowired
29     private StateService stateService;
30
31     @RequestMapping("/manageUsers")
32     public String showManageUsers(Map<String, Object> map) {
33         map.put("user", new User());
34         map.put("userList", userService.listUser());
35         map.put("countryList", countryService.listCountry());
36         map.put("stateList", stateService.listState());
```

```
37          return "manageUsers";
38      }
39
40      @RequestMapping(value = "/saveUser", method = RequestMethod.POST)
41      public String saveUser(Map<String, Object> map, @ModelAttribute("user") User
        user, @Valid User userValid, BindingResult result) {
42          if (result.hasErrors()) {
43              map.put("countryList", countryService.listCountry());
44              map.put("stateList", stateService.listState());
45              return "manageUsers";
46          } else {
47              try {
48                  userService.saveUser(user);
49                  return "redirect:/admin/manageUsers";
50              } catch (ConstraintViolationException exp) {
51                  map.put("dbError", exp.getMessage());
52                  return "manageUsers";
53              }
54          }
55      }
56
57      @RequestMapping("/deleteUser/{userNo}")
58      public String deleteUser(Map<String, Object> map, @PathVariable("userNo") Integer
        userNo) {
59          User user = userService.getUserById(userNo);
60          if(!user.getUserName().equals("admin")) {
61              userService.removeUser(userNo);
62              return "redirect:/admin/manageUsers";
63          }
64          else {
65              map.put("dbError", "You cannot delete the admin user.");
66              map.put("user", new User());
67              map.put("userList", userService.listUser());
68              map.put("countryList", countryService.listCountry());
69              map.put("stateList", stateService.listState());
70              return "manageUsers";
71          }
72      }
73
74      @RequestMapping("/editUser/{userNo}")
75      public String editUser(Map<String, Object> map, @PathVariable("userNo") Integer
        userNo) {
76          map.put("user", userService.getUserById(userNo));
77          map.put("countryList", countryService.listCountry());
78          map.put("stateList", stateService.listState());
79          return "manageUsers";
80      }
81  }
```

Explanation:

The following section describes the above code spec.

showManageUsers()

UserController holds a mapping to help the viewing.

This means the list of user details are retrieved by the **UserController** class's **showManageUsers()**.

showManageUsers() is invoked every time Manage Users is served.

showManageUsers():

❑ Makes a provision for adding a new user [if the user chooses to] by instantiating an object of the User entity class

❑ Retrieves the user details by invoking **listUser()** of UserService

❑ Retrieves the state names by invoking **listState()** of StateService, which is displayed in the drop down list box of the State field

❑ Retrieves the country names by invoking **listCountry()** of CountryService, which is displayed in the drop down list box of the Country field

❑ Returns the user, state and country details that **listUser()**, **listState()** and **listCountry()** return respectively, to the View to render it, using **map.put()**

saveUser()

UserController holds a mapping to help the adding of users.

```
public String showManageUsers(Map<String, Object> map) {
    map.put("user", new User());
    map.put("userList", userService.listUser());
```

As soon as Manage Users is served, an object of the User entity class is instantiated to make a provision for adding a new user. The user may view, edit, delete or choose to add a new user.

In case, the user chooses to add a new user, keys in the required user details and clicks **Save**, **UserController** holds a mapping to help the saving of the newly captured user details.

saveUser():

❑ Ensures that the captured data is valid

❑ Returns the control to the View along with the error messages [available in the BindingResult object], if the captured data is found to be invalid

If the View is rendered along with the error messages, then the state and country names in the drop down list boxes are filled up by invoking listState() of StateService and listCountry() of CountryService respectively

❑ Saves the user details using UserService's **saveUser()**, if the captured data is valid and returns the control to the View to render Manage Users

deleteUser()

In case, the user chooses to delete a user and clicks , **UserController** holds a mapping to help delete a user record from Manage Users.

deleteUser():

❑ Retrieves the appropriate User's details using **UserNo** as the reference. It calls UserService's **getUserById()** which returns the details of the user to be edited as a User object. **UserNo** is made available through **@PathVariable** [in the list of User rendered by the View] when the user clicks to delete a particular user

❑ Passes **UserNo** of the user to be deleted [available as a @PathVariable] to UserService's **removeUser()**

❑ Checks whether the record being deleted is not an **admin** user and accordingly displays the error message indicating that this record cannot be deleted

❑ Returns the control to the View which renders Manage Users with the updated data

editUser()

UserController holds a mapping to help the editing of existing users. In case, the user chooses to edit a user and clicks , **UserController** holds a mapping to help fill up the Manage Users form with user details.

editUser():

❑ Retrieves the appropriate User's details using **UserNo** as the reference. It calls UserService's **getUserById()** which returns the details of the user to be edited as a User object. **UserNo** is made available through **@PathVariable** [in the list of User rendered by the View] when the user clicks to edit a particular user

❑ Retrieves the state names by invoking **listState()** of StateService, which is displayed in the drop down list box of the State field

❑ Retrieves the country names by invoking **listCountry()** of CountryService, which is displayed in the drop down list box of the Country field

❑ Returns the control to the View along with the data to be populated in the form. The data to be populated is made available using Map's **put()**, which is used to populate the users object with the data that **getUserById()** of UserService returns. The same happens with the countryList and StateList objects

Service Class

Interface [UserService.java]

This is a service interface with the following specifications.

Service Interface Specifications

Class Name	Package
UserService	com.sharanamvaishali.service

Code Spec

```
1  package com.sharanamvaishali.service;
2
3  import com.sharanamvaishali.model.User;
4  import java.util.List;
5
6  public interface UserService {
7      public void saveUser(User User);
8      public List<User> listUser();
9      public void removeUser(Integer userNo);
10     public User getUserById(Integer userNo);
11 }
```

Implementation Class [UserServiceImpl.java]

This is a service class with the following specifications.

Service Implementation Specifications

Class Name	Package	Implements
UserServiceImpl	com.sharanamvaishali.service	UserService

Objects		
Object Name	**Class Name**	**Object Type**
userDAO	UserDAO	Data Access Object Layer

Methods	
Method Name	**Arguments**
saveUser()	User user
listUser()	- -
removeUser()	Integer userNo
getUserById()	Integer userNo

Code Spec

```
1  package com.sharanamvaishali.service;
2
3  import com.sharanamvaishali.dao.UserDAO;
4  import com.sharanamvaishali.model.User;
5  import java.util.List;
6  import org.springframework.beans.factory.annotation.Autowired;
7  import org.springframework.stereotype.Service;
8  import org.springframework.transaction.annotation.Transactional;
9
10 @Service
11 public class UserServiceImpl implements UserService {
12     @Autowired
13     private UserDAO userDAO;
14
15     @Transactional
16     @Override
17     public void saveUser(User User) {
18         userDAO.saveUser(User);
19     }
20
21     @Transactional
22     @Override
23     public List<User> listUser() {
24         return userDAO.listUser();
25     }
26
27     @Transactional
28     @Override
29     public void removeUser(Integer userNo) {
30         userDAO.removeUser(userNo);
31     }
32
33     @Transactional
34     @Override
35     public User getUserById(Integer userNo) {
36         return userDAO.getUserById(userNo);
37     }
38 }
```

Explanation:

The following section describes the above code spec.

saveUser()

saveUser() holds the business logic to save the captured user details.

This method in turn invokes UserDAO's **saveUser()**.

listUser()

listUser() holds the business logic to return the appropriate list of the available users.

This method in turn invokes UserDAO's **listUser()**.

removeUser()

removeUser() holds the business logic to delete user details based on UserNo.

This method in turn invokes UserDAO's **removeUser()**.

getUserById()

getUserById() holds the business logic to retrieve user details based on UserNo.

This method in turn invokes UserDAO's **getUserById()**.

REMINDER

CountryService's **listCountry()** is explained in the *Chapter 31: Manage Countries,* which retrieves the list of country names to be filled in the Country drop down list box.

StateService's **listState()** is explained in the *Chapter 32: Manage States,* which retrieves the list of state names to be filled in the State drop down list box.

DAO Class

Interface [UserDAO.java]

This is a Data Access Object interface with the following specifications.

DAO Interface Specifications

Class Name	Package
UserDAO	com.sharanamvaishali.dao

Code Spec

```
 1  package com.sharanamvaishali.dao;
 2
 3  import com.sharanamvaishali.model.User;
 4  import java.util.List;
 5
 6  public interface UserDAO {
 7      public void saveUser(User User);
 8      public List<User> listUser();
 9      public void removeUser(Integer userNo);
10      public User getUserById(Integer userNo);
11  }
```

Implementation Class [UserDAOImpl.java]

This is a Data Access Object class with the following specifications.

DAO Implementation Specifications

Class Name	Package	Implements
UserDAOImpl	com.sharanamvaishali.dao	UserDAO

Objects	
Object Name	Class Name
sessionFactory	SessionFactory

Methods		
Method Name	Arguments	Return Values
saveUser()	User user	void
listUser()	- -	List <User>
removeUser()	Integer userNo	void
getUserById()	Integer userNo	User

Code Spec

```
 1  package com.sharanamvaishali.dao;
 2
 3  import com.sharanamvaishali.model.User;
 4  import java.util.List;
 5  import org.hibernate.SessionFactory;
 6  import org.springframework.beans.factory.annotation.Autowired;
```

```
 7  import org.springframework.stereotype.Repository;
 8
 9  @Repository
10  public class UserDAOImpl implements UserDAO {
11      @Autowired
12      private SessionFactory sessionFactory;
13
14      @Override
15      public void saveUser(User User) {
16          sessionFactory.getCurrentSession().merge(User);
17      }
18
19      @Override
20      public List<User> listUser() {
21          return sessionFactory.getCurrentSession().createQuery("from User").list();
22      }
23
24      @Override
25      public void removeUser(Integer userNo) {
26          User User = (User) sessionFactory.getCurrentSession().load(User.class, userNo);
27          if (null != User) {
28              sessionFactory.getCurrentSession().delete(User);
29          }
30      }
31
32      @Override
33      public User getUserById(Integer userNo) {
34          return (User) sessionFactory.getCurrentSession().get(User.class, userNo);
35      }
36  }
```

Explanation:

The following section describes the above code spec.

saveUser()

saveUser() does the actual saving of the user in the Users database table.

This method uses **merge()** of SessionFactory, which takes care of adding as well as updating the user details, in case the user had edited an existing user and clicked **Save**.

listUser()

listUser() does the actual retrieval of the available users.

This method fires a SELECT query that attempts to retrieve records from the Users database table.

All the records that the query retrieves are extracted and returned as a **List** object.

This List object is returned to the calling method i.e. Service Layer's **listUser()**:

```
public List<User> listUser() {
    return userDAO.listUser();
}
```

This method in turn returns it to the UserController's **showManageUsers()**:

```
public String showManageUsers(Map<String, Object> map) {
    map.put("user", new User());
    map.put("userList", userService.listUser());
    map.put("countryList", countryService.listCountry());
```

Finally, UserController returns this List object to the View which renders it.

manageUsers.jsp on taking charge uses the **iterator** tag to iterate over the contents of the List object **userList**.

```
<c:forEach items="${userList}" var="user">
    <tr>
        <td>${user.firstName} ${user.lastName}</td>
        <td>${user.userName}</td>
        <td>${user.emailAddress}</td>
        <td>${user.authority}</td>
```

The userList object holds all those records retrieved by the SQL query.

Each record's column values are extracted using **$**.

```
<td>${user.firstName} ${user.lastName}</td>
<td>${user.userName}</td>
<td>${user.emailAddress}</td>
<td>${user.authority}</td>
```

removeUser()

removeUser() deletes the appropriate user based on **UserNo** received as a reference.

This method uses:

❑ **load()** of SessionFactory, which retrieves the appropriate User to be deleted using UserNo as a reference

❏   **delete()** of SessionFactory, which deletes the user from Users database table

getUserById()

getUserById() returns the appropriate user's object from the Users database table using **UserNo** as the reference.

This method uses **get()** of SessionFactory, which returns the appropriate User from Users database table.

After editing the user details, when the user clicks , saveUser() of UserController, followed by saveUser() of UserService, followed by saveUser() of UserDAO takes care of saving the updated user's details.

REMINDER

CountryDAO's **listCountry()** is explained in the *Chapter 31: Manage Countries*, which retrieves the list of country names to be filled in the Country drop down list box.

StateDAO's **listState()** is explained in the *Chapter 32: Manage States*, which retrieves the list of state names to be filled in the State drop down list box.

Domain Class [User.java]

This is a domain class with the following specifications.

Domain Specifications

Class Name	Package	Implements
User	com.sharanamvaishali.model	java.io.Serializable

Properties			
Property Name	**Property Type**	**Methods**	
userNo	Integer	getUserNo ()	setUserNo ()
userName	String	getUserName ()	setUserName ()
password	String	getPassword ()	setPassword ()
emailAddress	String	getEmailAddress ()	setEmailAddress ()
firstName	String	getFirstName ()	setFirstName ()
lastName	String	getLastName ()	setLastName ()
address1	String	getAddress1 ()	setAddress1 ()
address2	String	getAddress2 ()	setAddress2 ()

Properties			
Property Name	Property Type	Methods	
city	String	getCity()	setCity()
stateNo	Integer	getStateNo()	setStateNo()
pincode	String	getPincode(0	setPincode()
countryNo	Integer	getCountryNo()	setCountryNo()
dob	String	getDob()	setDob()
newRelease	boolean	isNewRelease()	setNewRelease()
bookUpdates	boolean	isBookUpdates()	setBookUpdates()
enabled	boolean	isEnabled()	setEnabled()
authority	String	getAuthority()	setAuthority()

Code Spec

```
1   package com.sharanamvaishali.model;
2
3   import javax.persistence.*;
4   import org.hibernate.validator.constraints.Email;
5   import org.hibernate.validator.constraints.NotEmpty;
6
7   @Entity
8   @Table(name="USERS")
9   public class User implements java.io.Serializable {
10      @Id
11      @GeneratedValue
12      @Column(name="USERNO")
13      private Integer userNo;
14      @Column(name="USERNAME")
15      @NotEmpty(message="Username is mandatory")
16      private String userName;
17      @Column(name="PASSWORD")
18      @NotEmpty(message="Password is mandatory")
19      private String password;
20      @Column(name="EMAILADDRESS")
21      @NotEmpty(message="Email address is mandatory")
22      @Email(message="Invlaid email address")
23      private String emailAddress;
24      @Column(name="FIRSTNAME")
25      @NotEmpty(message="First name is mandatory")
26      private String firstName;
27      @Column(name="LASTNAME")
28      @NotEmpty(message="Last name is mandatory")
29      private String lastName;
30      @Column(name="ADDRESS1")
31      private String address1;
32      @Column(name="ADDRESS2")
33      private String address2;
34      @Column(name="CITY")
35      private String city;
```

```
36      @Column(name="STATENO")
37      private Integer stateNo;
38      @Column(name="PINCODE")
39      private String pincode;
40      @Column(name="COUNTRYNO")
41      private Integer countryNo;
42      @Column(name="DOB")
43      private String dob;
44      @Column(name="NEWRELEASE")
45      private boolean newRelease;
46      @Column(name="BOOKUPDATES")
47      private boolean bookUpdates;
48      @Column(name="ENABLED")
49      private boolean enabled;
50      @Column(name="AUTHORITY")
51      private String authority;
52
53      public String getEmailAddress() {
54          return emailAddress;
55      }
56      public void setEmailAddress(String emailAddress) {
57          this.emailAddress = emailAddress;
58      }
59
60      public String getFirstName() {
61          return firstName;
62      }
63      public void setFirstName(String firstName) {
64          this.firstName = firstName;
65      }
66
67      public String getLastName() {
68          return lastName;
69      }
70      public void setLastName(String lastName) {
71          this.lastName = lastName;
72      }
73
74      public String getPassword() {
75          return password;
76      }
77      public void setPassword(String password) {
78          this.password = password;
79      }
80
81      public String getUserName() {
82          return userName;
83      }
84      public void setUserName(String userName) {
85          this.userName = userName;
86      }
87
88      public Integer getUserNo() {
```

```
89              return userNo;
90          }
91          public void setUserNo(Integer userNo) {
92              this.userNo = userNo;
93          }
94
95          public String getAuthority() {
96              return authority;
97          }
98          public void setAuthority(String authority) {
99              this.authority = authority;
100         }
101
102         public boolean isEnabled() {
103             return enabled;
104         }
105         public void setEnabled(boolean enabled) {
106             this.enabled = enabled;
107         }
108
109         public String getAddress1() {
110             return address1;
111         }
112         public void setAddress1(String address1) {
113             this.address1 = address1;
114         }
115
116         public String getAddress2() {
117             return address2;
118         }
119         public void setAddress2(String address2) {
120             this.address2 = address2;
121         }
122
123         public boolean isBookUpdates() {
124             return bookUpdates;
125         }
126         public void setBookUpdates(boolean bookUpdates) {
127             this.bookUpdates = bookUpdates;
128         }
129
130         public String getCity() {
131             return city;
132         }
133         public void setCity(String city) {
134             this.city = city;
135         }
136
137         public Integer getCountryNo() {
138             return countryNo;
139         }
140         public void setCountryNo(Integer countryNo) {
141             this.countryNo = countryNo;
```

```
142     }
143
144     public String getDob() {
145         return dob;
146     }
147     public void setDob(String dob) {
148         this.dob = dob;
149     }
150
151     public boolean isNewRelease() {
152         return newRelease;
153     }
154     public void setNewRelease(boolean newRelease) {
155         this.newRelease = newRelease;
156     }
157
158     public String getPincode() {
159         return pincode;
160     }
161     public void setPincode(String pincode) {
162         this.pincode = pincode;
163     }
164
165     public Integer getStateNo() {
166         return stateNo;
167     }
168     public void setStateNo(Integer stateNo) {
169         this.stateNo = stateNo;
170     }
171 }
```

REMINDER

Country.java [the model class] is explained in the *Chapter 31: Manage Countries*.
State.java [the model class] is explained in the *Chapter 32: Manage States*.

Chapter

38

SECTION V: BACKEND [ADMINISTRATION] SOFTWARE DESIGN DOCUMENTATION

Manage Transactions

This module allows performing the following operations:

- ❑ Viewing across transactions according to the username
- ❑ Viewing across date wise transactions
- ❑ Viewing across all the transactions
- ❑ Updating the Google Order Number

This module uses the bms.Transactions table to perform the above operations.

This module is made up of the following:

Type	Name	Description
JSP	manageTransactions.jsp	The data entry form.
Spring		
Controller	TransactionController.java	The controller class that facilitates data operations.
Service Class	TransactionService.java	The interface for the service layer.
	TransactionServiceImpl.java	The implementation class for the service layer.
DAO Class	TransactionDAO.java	The interface for the DAO layer.
	TransactionDAOImpl.java	The implementation class that performs the actual data operations.
DispatcherServlet	bookshopdispatcher-servlet.xml	Central dispatcher for HTTP request handlers/controllers.
Hibernate		
Mapping	hibernate.cfg.xml	The mapping file that holds Model class mapping.
Model Class	Transaction.java	The model class.

JSP [manageTransactions.jsp]

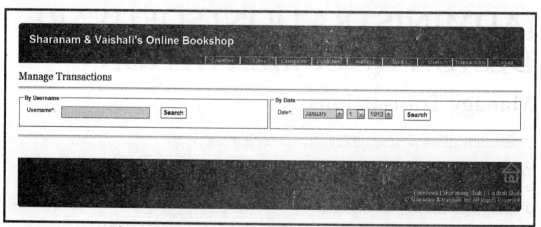

Diagram 38.1: Manage Transactions [Data entry form]

This is a JSP which holds a data entry form, as shown in diagram 38.1. This form appears when the user clicks Transactions.

Form Specifications

File Name	manageTransactions.jsp
Title	BookShop[Sharanam & Vaishali Shah] - Manage Transactions
Bound To Table	bms.Transactions
Method	POST

Data Fields

Label	Name	Bound To	Validation Rules
By Username			
Username	- -	Transactions.Username	- -
By Date			
Date	- -	Transactions.TransactionDate	- -
Google Order No.			
Google Order No.	- -	Transactions.GoogleOrderNo	- -

Micro-Help For Form Fields

Form Field	Micro Help Statement
By Username	
Username	Enter the username
By Date	
Date	Select the month Select the day Select the year
Google Order No.	
Google Order No.	Enter the google order number here

Data Controls

Object	Label
By Username	
Button	Search
By Date	
Button	Search
Google Order No.	
Button	Update

Code Spec

```
1   <%@page contentType="text/html" pageEncoding="UTF-8"%>
2   <%@taglib uri="http://www.springframework.org/tags/form" prefix="form"%>
3   <%@taglib uri="http://java.sun.com/jsp/jstl/core" prefix="c"%>
4   <!DOCTYPE HTML PUBLIC "-//W3C//DTD HTML 4.01 Transitional//EN"
5       "http://www.w3.org/TR/html4/loose.dtd">
6   <html>
7       <head>
8           <meta http-equiv="Content-Type" content="text/html; charset=UTF-8">
9           <title>BookShop[Sharanam & Vaishali Shah] - Manage Transactions</title>
10          <link rel="stylesheet" href="/BookShop/css/admin.css" type="text/css">
11      </head>
12      <body>
13          <%@ include file="/WEB-INF/jsp/adminHeader.jsp" %>
14          <br/>
15          <table width="100%" border="0" align="center" cellpadding="0"
            cellspacing="0">
16              <tr>
17                  <td>
18                      <table border="0" cellpadding="0" cellspacing="0" width="100%">
19                          <tr>
20                              <td class="manageForms">Manage Transactions</td>
21                              <td class="information"> </td>
22                          </tr>
23                      </table>
24                  </td>
25              </tr>
26              <tr><td class="hrLine"> </td></tr>
27              <tr>
28                  <td>
29                      <form method="post">
30                          <table width="100%" border="0" align="center" cellpadding="0"
                            cellspacing="0">
31                              <tr>
32                                  <td width="50%">
33                                      <fieldset class="fieldsetHieght">
34                                          <legend><b>By Username</b></legend>
35                                          <table width="100%" border="0" cellpadding="4"
                                            cellspacing="4">
36                                              <tr>
37                                                  <td width="10%">Username<span
                                                    class="mandatory">*</span>:</td>
38                                                  <td width="42%">
39                                                      <input name="userName" title="Enter the
                                                        username" maxlength="25" size="30"/>
40                                                  </td>
41                                                  <td>
42                                                      <input type="button"
                                                        onclick="document.location.href='${pageContext
                                                        .request.contextPath}/admin/searchTransactions
                                                        ByUsername/' +
                                                        document.forms[0].userName.value"
```

```
                              class="groovybutton" value="Search" />
43                        </td>
44                      </tr>
45                    </table>
46                  </fieldset>
47                </td>
48                <td>
49                  <fieldset class="fieldsetHieght">
50                    <legend><b>By Date</b></legend>
51                    <table width="100%" border="0" cellpadding="4"
                      cellspacing="4">
52                      <tr>
53                        <td width="10%">Date<span
                          class="mandatory">*</span>:</td>
54                        <td width="42%">
55                          <select title="Select the month"
                            name="month">
56                            <option value="1">January</option>
57                            <option value="2">February</option>
58                            <option value="3">March</option>
59                            <option value="4">April</option>
60                            <option value="5">May</option>
61                            <option value="6">June</option>
62                            <option value="7">July</option>
63                            <option value="8">August</option>
64                            <option value="9">September</option>
65                            <option value="10">October</option>
66                            <option value="11">November</option>
67                            <option value="12">December</option>
68                          </select>
69                          <select title="Select the day" name="day">
70                            <option value="1">1</option>
71                            <option value="2">2</option>
72                            <option value="3">3</option>
73                            <option value="4">4</option>
74                            <option value="5">5</option>
75                            <option value="6">6</option>
76                            <option value="7">7</option>
77                            <option value="8">8</option>
78                            <option value="9">9</option>
79                            <option value="10">10</option>
80                            <option value="11">11</option>
81                            <option value="12">12</option>
82                            <option value="13">13</option>
83                            <option value="14">14</option>
84                            <option value="15">15</option>
85                            <option value="16">16</option>
86                            <option value="17">17</option>
87                            <option value="18">18</option>
88                            <option value="19">19</option>
39                            
90                            <option value="21">21</option>
91                            <option value="22">22</option>
92                            <option value="23">23</option>
```

```
93          <option value="24">24</option>
94          <option value="25">25</option>
95          <option value="26">26</option>
96          <option value="27">27</option>
97          <option value="28">28</option>
98          <option value="29">29</option>
99          <option value="30">30</option>
100         <option value="31">31</option>
101       </select>
102       <select title="Select the year" name="year">
103         <%
104           for(int i = (year-100); i <= year; i++) {
105             if(String.valueOf(i).equals(request.getP
                  arameter("year"))) {
106                 out.println("<option selected value="
                      + i + ">" + i + "</option>");
107             }
108             out.println("<option value=" + i + ">"
                  + i + "</option>");
109           }
110         %>
111       </select>
112     </td>
113     <td>
114       <input type="button"
                onclick="document.location.href='${pageContext
                .request.contextPath}/admin/searchTransactions
                ByDate/' + document.forms[0].year.value + '/' +
                + document.forms[0].month.value + '/' +
                document.forms[0].day.value"
                class="groovybutton" value="Search" />
115     </td>
116   </tr>
117 </table>
118 </fieldset>
119   </td>
120 </tr>
121 <tr><td colspan="2"> </td></tr>
122 </table>
123 </form>
124   </td>
125 </tr>
126 <tr><td class="hrLine"> </td></tr>
127 <tr>
128   <td>
129     <br>
130     <c:if test="${!empty transactionGroupedList}">
131       <c:forEach items="${transactionGroupedList}" var="transaction">
132         <table cellspacing="1" cellpadding="2" width="20%"
                style="float:left;">
133           <tr>
134             <td width="50%" class="transactionGroupHeading">
135               Transaction No.:
136             </td>
```

```
137              <td class="transactionGroupContent">
138                 ${transaction[0]}
139              </td>
140           </tr>
141           <tr>
142              <td class="transactionGroupHeading">
143                 Transaction Date:
144              </td>
145              <td class="transactionGroupContent">
146                 ${transaction[1]}
147              </td>
148           </tr>
149           <tr>
150              <td class="transactionGroup">
151                 Username:
152              </td>
153              <td>
154                 ${transaction[2]}
155              </td>
156           </tr>
157        </table>
158        <fieldset class="transactionFieldset">
159           <legend><b>Google Order No.</b></legend>
160           <c:choose>
161              <c:when test="${empty transaction[5]}">
162                 <form method="post">
163                    <input name="googleOrderNo" title="Enter the google
                       order number here" maxlength="25" size="30"/>
164                    <input type="button"
                       onclick="document.location.href='${pageContext.requ
                       est.contextPath}/admin/updateGoogleOrderNo/' +
                       ${transaction[0]} + '/' +
                       document.forms[1].googleOrderNo.value"
                       class="groovybutton" value="Update" />
165                 </form>
166              </c:when>
167              <c:otherwise>
168                 <span
                    class="transactionGoogleOrder">${transaction[5]}</spa
                    n>
169              </c:otherwise>
170           </c:choose>
171        </fieldset>
172        <br/>
173        <table class="data" width="100%">
174           <tr>
175              <th width="10%">Detail No.</th>
176              <th width="60%">Book Name</th>
177              <th width="15%">Cost</th>
178              <th width="15%">Qty.</th>
179           </tr>
180           <c:forEach items="${transactionList}"
              var="transactionDetail">
```

```
181        <c:if test="${transactionDetail.transactionNo ==
                   transaction[0]}">
182            <tr>
183                <td>${transactionDetail.transactionDetailNo}</td>
184                <td>${transactionDetail.bookName}</td>
185                <td>${transactionDetail.qty}</td>
186                <td>${transactionDetail.cost}</td>
187            </tr>
188        </c:if>
189      </c:forEach>
190      <tr>
191          <th colspan="2" class="rightAlign">Total:</th>
192          <th class="leftAlign">${transaction[4]}</th>
193          <th class="leftAlign">${transaction[3]}</th>
194      </tr>
195    </table>
196    <br/><hr/><br/>
197  </c:forEach>
198  </c:if>
199  </td>
200  </tr>
201  </table>
202  <%@ include file="/WEB-INF/jsp/adminFooter.jsp" %>
203  </body>
204 </html>
```

Explanation:

This is a standard data entry form, which captures the username or date to display the transactions made by that particular user or on that particular date. The form also allows updating the Google Order No. for a particular transaction.

Controller [TransactionController.java]

This is a controller class with the following specifications.

Controller Specifications

Class Name	Package	
TransactionController	com.sharanamvaishali.controllers	
Objects		
Object Name	Class Name	Object Type
transactionService	TransactionService	Service Layer
Methods		
Method Name	Request Mapping	
showManageTransactions()	/admin/manageTransactions	
showTransactionsByDate()	/admin/searchTransactionsBy...e	
showTransactionsByUsername()	/admin/searchTransactionsByUsername/${userName}	

Method Name	Request Mapping
showTransactionsByDate()	/admin/searchTransactionsByDate /${year}/${month}/${day}
updateGoogleOrderNo()	/admin//updateGoogleOrderNo /${transactionNo}/${orderNo}

Code Spec

```
1  package com.sharanamvaishali.controllers;
2
3  import com.sharanamvaishali.service.TransactionService;
4  import java.text.ParseException;
5  import java.text.SimpleDateFormat;
6  import java.util.Map;
7  import java.util.logging.Level;
8  import java.util.logging.Logger;
9  import org.springframework.beans.factory.annotation.Autowired;
10 import org.springframework.stereotype.Controller;
11 import org.springframework.web.bind.annotation.PathVariable;
12 import org.springframework.web.bind.annotation.RequestMapping;
13
14 @Controller
15 @RequestMapping("/admin")
16 public class TransactionController {
17     @Autowired
18     private TransactionService transactionService;
19
20     @RequestMapping("/manageTransactions")
21     public String showManageTransactions() {
22         return "manageTransactions";
23     }
24
25     @RequestMapping("/searchTransactionsByUsername")
26     public String showTransactions(Map<String, Object> map) {
27         map.put("transactionGroupedList", transactionService.listGroupedTransactions());
28         map.put("transactionList", transactionService.listTransactions());
29         return "manageTransactions";
30     }
31
32     @RequestMapping("/searchTransactionsByUsername/{userName}")
33     public String showTransactionsByUsername(Map<String, Object> map,
           @PathVariable("userName") String userName) {
34         map.put("transactionGroupedList",
           transactionService.listGroupedTransactionsByUsername(userName));
35         map.put("transactionList",
           transactionService.listTransactionsByUsername(userName)):
36         return "manageTransactions";
37
38
39     @RequestMapping("/searchTransactionsByDate/{year}/{month}/{day}")
```

```
40    public String showTransactionsByDate(Map<String, Object> map,
      @PathVariable("day") String day, @PathVariable("year") String year,
      @PathVariable("month") String month) {
41        SimpleDateFormat sdf = new SimpleDateFormat("yyyy-MM-dd");
42        try {
43            map.put("transactionGroupedList",
              transactionService.listGroupedTransactionsByDate(sdf.parse(year + "-" +
              month + "-" + day)));
44            map.put("transactionList",
              transactionService.listTransactionsByDate(sdf.parse(year + "-" + month + "-"
              + day)));
45        } catch (ParseException ex) {
46            Logger.getLogger(TransactionController.class.getName()).log(Level.SEVERE,
              null, ex);
47        }
48        return "manageTransactions";
49    }
50
51    @RequestMapping("/updateGoogleOrderNo/{transactionNo}/{orderNo}")
52    public String updateGoogleOrderNo(Map<String, Object> map,
      @PathVariable("transactionNo") Integer transactionNo, @PathVariable("orderNo")
      String orderNo) {
53        transactionService.updateGoogleOrderNo(transactionNo, orderNo);
54        return "manageTransactions";
55    }
56 }
```

Explanation:

The following section describes the above code spec.

showManageTransactions()

UserController holds a mapping to display the Manage Transactions form, where the user can view the transactions based on Username or Date.

showManageUsers() is invoked every time Manage Transactions is served.

showTransactions()

TransactionController holds a mapping to help the viewing of all the transactions.

As soon as Manage Transactions is served, the user can view all the transactions by clicking
`Search`.

In case, the user directly clicks `Search`, **TransactionController** holds a mapping to help the viewing of all the transactions irrespective of username/date.

This means the list of transactions are retrieved by the **TransactionController** class's **showTransactions()**.

showTransactions():

❑ Retrieves the details of all the transactions by invoking **listTransactions()** of TransactionService

❑ Retrieves the transactions by **TransactionNo** by invoking **listGroupedTransactions()** of TransactionService

❑ Returns the transaction details that **listTransactions()** and **listGroupedTransactions()** return respectively, to the View to render it, using **map.put()**

showTransactionsByUsername()

TransactionController holds a mapping to help the viewing of the transactions by username.

As soon as Manage Transactions is served, the user can view the transactions by entering the username and then clicking **Search**.

In case, the user enters the username and then clicks **Search**, **TransactionController** holds a mapping to help the viewing of the transactions according to the username.

This means the list of transactions according to the username are retrieved by the **TransactionController** class's **showTransactionsByUsername()**.

showTransactionsByUsername():

❑ Passes **Username** [available as a @PathVariable] to TransactionService's **listTransactionsByUsername()** and **listGroupedTransactionsByUsername()**

❑ Retrieves the details of the appropriate Transactions using **Username** as the reference. It calls TransactionService's **listTransactionsByUsername()** and **listGroupedTransactionsByUsername()** which return the transactions and the details of the retrieved transactions. **Username** is made available through **@PathVariable** [in the list of Transaction rendered by the View]

❑ Returns the transaction details that **listTransactions()** and **listGroupedTransactions()** return respectively, to the View to render it, using **map.put()**

showTransactionsByDate()

TransactionController holds a mapping to help the viewing of the transactions on a particular date.

As soon as Manage Transactions is served, the user can view the transactions by entering the date and then clicking ⌷**Search**⌷.

In case, the user enters the date and then clicks ⌷**Search**⌷, **TransactionController** holds a mapping to help the viewing of the transactions for that particular date.

This means the list of transactions according to that date are retrieved by the **TransactionController** class's **showTransactionsByDate()**.

showTransactionsByDate():

❑ Passes **SimpleDateFormat** date [available as a @PathVariable] to TransactionService's **listTransactionsByDate()** and **listGroupedTransactionsByDate()**

❑ **Year**, **Month** and **Day** is parsed in the format **yyyy-MM-dd** through **SimpleDateFormat**

❑ Retrieves the appropriate Transaction's details using **Year**, **Month** and **Day** as the reference. It calls TransactionService's **listTransactionsByDate()** and **listGroupedTransactionsByDate()** which return the transactions and the details of the retrieved transactions. **Year, Month** and **Day** are made available through **@PathVariable** [in the list of Transaction rendered by the View]

❑ Returns the transaction details that **listTransactions()** and **listGroupedTransactions()** return respectively, to the View to render it, using **map.put()**

updateGoogleOrderNo()

TransactionController holds a mapping to help updating the Google Order Number.

In case, the user chooses to update the Google Order Number, the user has to enter the Google Order Number from the email received from Google Wallet and click ⌷**Update**⌷, **TransactionController** holds a mapping to help update the Google Order Number.

updateGoogleOrderNo():

❑ Passes **TransactionNo** and **OrderNo** [available as a @PathVariable] to TransactionService's **updateGoogleOrderNo()**

❑ Updates the appropriate Transaction's order number using **TransactionNo** and **OrderNo** as the reference. It calls TransactionService's **updateGoogleOrderNo()** which updates Transaction details

❑ Returns the control to the View

Service Class

Interface [TransactionService.java]

This is a service interface with the following specifications.

Service Interface Specifications

Class Name	Package
TransactionService	com.sharanamvaishali.service

Code Spec

```
1   package com.sharanamvaishali.service;
2
3   import com.sharanamvaishali.model.Transaction;
4   import java.util.Date;
5   import java.util.List;
6
7   public interface TransactionService {
8       public List<Transaction> listTransactions();
9       public List<Transaction> listGroupedTransactions();
10      public List<Transaction> listTransactionsByUsername(String userName);
11      public List<Transaction> listGroupedTransactionsByUsername(String userName);
12      public List<Transaction> listTransactionsByDate(Date date);
13      public List<Transaction> listGroupedTransactionsByDate(Date date);
14      public void updateGoogleOrderNo(Integer transactionNo, String orderNo);
15  }
```

Implementation Class [TransactionServiceImpl.java]

This is a service class with the following specifications.

Service Implementation Specifications

Class Name	Package	Implements
TransactionServiceImpl	com.sharanamvaishali.service	TransactionService

Objects		
Object Name	**Class Name**	**Object Type**
transactionDAO	TransactionDAO	Data Access Object Layer

Methods	
Method Name	**Arguments**
listTransactions()	– –
listGroupedTransactions()	– –
listTransactionsByUsername()	String userName
listGroupedTransactionsByUsername()	String userName
listTransactionsByDate()	Date date
listGroupedTransactionsByDate()	Date date
updateGoogleOrderNo()	Integer transactionNo String orderNo

Code Spec

```
1   package com.sharanamvaishali.service;
2
3   import com.sharanamvaishali.dao.TransactionDAO;
4   import com.sharanamvaishali.model.Transaction;
5   import java.util.Date;
6   import java.util.List;
7   import org.springframework.beans.factory.annotation.Autowired;
8   import org.springframework.stereotype.Service;
9   import org.springframework.transaction.annotation.Transactional;
10
11  @Service
12  public class TransactionServiceImpl implements TransactionService {
13      @Autowired
14      private TransactionDAO transactionDAO;
15
16      @Transactional
17      @Override
18      public List<Transaction> listTransactions() {
19          return transactionDAO.listTransactions();
20      }
21
22      @Transactional
23      @Override
24      public List<Transaction> listGroupedTransactions() {
25          return transactionDAO.listGroupedTransactions();
26      }
27
28      @Transactional
29      @Override
30      public List<Transaction> listTransactionsByUsername(String userName) {
31          return transactionDAO.listTransactionsByUsername(userName);
32      }
33
34      @Transactional
35      @Override
36      public List<Transaction> listGroupedTransactionsByUsername(String userName) {
37          return transactionDAO.listGroupedTransactionsByUsername(userName);
38      }
```

```
39
40     @Transactional
41     @Override
42     public List<Transaction> listTransactionsByDate(Date date) {
43         return transactionDAO.listTransactionsByDate(date);
44     }
45
46     @Transactional
47     @Override
48     public List<Transaction> listGroupedTransactionsByDate(Date date) {
49         return transactionDAO.listGroupedTransactionsByDate(date);
50     }
51
52     @Transactional
53     @Override
54     public void updateGoogleOrderNo(Integer transactionNo, String orderNo) {
55         transactionDAO.updateGoogleOrderNo(transactionNo, orderNo);
56     }
57 }
```

Explanation:

The following section describes the above code spec.

listTransactions()

listTransactions() holds the business logic to return the appropriate list of the available transactions.

This method in turn invokes TransactionDAO's **listTransactions()**.

listGroupedTransactions()

listGroupedTransactions() holds the business logic to return the appropriate list of the available transactions as a group [grouped by TransactionNo].

This method in turn invokes TransactionDAO's **listGroupedTransactions()**.

listTransactionsByUsername()

listTransactionsByUsername() holds the business logic to return the appropriate list of the available transactions according to the username.

This method in turn invokes TransactionDAO's **listTransactionsByUsername()**.

listGroupedTransactionsByUsername()

listGroupedTransactionsByUsername() holds the business logic to return the appropriate list of the available transactions as a group [grouped by TransactionNo] according to the username.

This method in turn invokes TransactionDAO's **listGroupedTransactionsByUsername()**.

listTransactionsByDate()

listTransactionsByDate() holds the business logic to return the appropriate list of the available transactions according to the date.

This method in turn invokes TransactionDAO's **listTransactionsByDate()**.

listGroupedTransactionsByDate()

listGroupedTransactionsByDate() holds the business logic to return the appropriate list of the available transactions as a group [grouped by TransactionNo] according to the date.

This method in turn invokes TransactionDAO's **listGroupedTransactionsByDate()**.

updateGoogleOrderNo()

updateGoogleOrderNo() holds the business logic to update the Google Order No of a particular transaction based on **TransactionNo** and **OrderNo**.

This method in turn invokes TransactionDAO's **updateGoogleOrderNo()**.

DAO Class

Interface [TransactionDAO.java]

This is a Data Access Object interface with the following specifications.

DAO Interface Specifications

Class Name	Package
TransactionDAO	com.sharanamvaishali.dao

Code Spec

```
1  package com.sharanamvaishali.dao;
2
3  import com.sharanamvaishali.model.Transaction;
4  import java.util.Date;
5  import java.util.List;
6
7  public interface TransactionDAO {
8      public List<Transaction> listGroupedTransactions();
9      public List<Transaction> listTransactions();
10     public List<Transaction> listGroupedTransactionsByUsername(String userName);
11     public List<Transaction> listTransactionsByUsername(String userName);
12     public List<Transaction> listGroupedTransactionsByDate(Date date);
13     public List<Transaction> listTransactionsByDate(Date date);
14     public void updateGoogleOrderNo(Integer transactionNo, String orderNo);
15 }
```

Implementation Class [TransactionDAOImpl.java]

This is a **D**ata **A**ccess **O**bject class with the following specifications.

DAO Implementation Specifications

Class Name	Package	Implements
TransactionDAOImpl	com.sharanamvaishali.dao	TransactionDAO

Objects	
Object Name	**Class Name**
sessionFactory	SessionFactory

Methods		
Method Name	**Arguments**	**Return Values**
listGroupedTransactions()	- -	List <Transaction>
listTransactions()	- -	List <Transaction>
listGroupedTransactionsByUsername()	String userName	List <Transaction>
listTransactionsByUsername()	String userName	List <Transaction>
listGroupedTransactionsByDate()	Date date	List <Transaction>
listTransactionsByDate()	Date date	List <Transaction>
updateGoogleOrderNo()	Integer transactionNo String orderNo	void

Code Spec

```
1  package com.sharanamvaishali.dao;
2
3  import com.sharanamvaishali.model.Transaction;
4  import java.util.Date;
```

```
 5  import java.util.List;
 6  import org.hibernate.SessionFactory;
 7  import org.springframework.beans.factory.annotation.Autowired;
 8  import org.springframework.stereotype.Repository;
 9
10  @Repository
11  public class TransactionDAOImpl implements TransactionDAO {
12      @Autowired
13      private SessionFactory sessionFactory;
14
15      @Override
16      public List<Transaction> listGroupedTransactions() {
17          return sessionFactory.getCurrentSession().createQuery("select transactionNo,
            transactionDate, userName, sum(qty*cost), sum(qty), googleOrderNo from
            Transaction group by transactionNo").list();
18      }
19
20      @Override
21      public List<Transaction> listTransactions() {
22          return sessionFactory.getCurrentSession().createQuery("from Transaction").list();
23      }
24
25      @Override
26      public List<Transaction> listGroupedTransactionsByUsername(String userName) {
27          return sessionFactory.getCurrentSession().createQuery("select transactionNo,
            transactionDate, userName, sum(qty*cost), sum(qty), googleOrderNo from
            Transaction where userName = '" + userName + "' group by
            transactionNo").list();
28      }
29
30      @Override
31      public List<Transaction> listTransactionsByUsername(String userName) {
32          return sessionFactory.getCurrentSession().createQuery("from Transaction where
            userName = '" + userName + "'").list();
33      }
34
35      @Override
36      public List<Transaction> listGroupedTransactionsByDate(Date date) {
37          return sessionFactory.getCurrentSession().createQuery("select transactionNo,
            transactionDate, userName, sum(qty*cost), sum(qty), googleOrderNo from
            Transaction where date(transactionDate) = :date group by transactionNo")
38              .setDate("date", date)
39              .list();
40      }
41
42      @Override
43      public List<Transaction> listTransactionsByDate(Date date) {
44          return sessionFactory.getCurrentSession().createQuery("from Transaction where
            date(transactionDate) = :date")
45              .setDate("date", date)
46              .list();
47      }
48
49      @Override
```

```
50      public void updateGoogleOrderNo(Integer transactionNo, String orderNo) {
51         sessionFactory.getCurrentSession().createQuery("update Transaction set
           googleOrderNo = :orderNo where transactionNo = :transactionNo")
52             .setString("orderNo", orderNo)
53             .setInteger("transactionNo", transactionNo)
54             .executeUpdate();
55      }
56 }
```

Explanation:

The following section describes the above code spec.

listGroupedTransactions()

listGroupedTransactions() does the actual retrieval of the available transactions.

This method fires a SELECT query that attempts to retrieve records from the Transactions database table grouped by **TransactionNo**.

All the records that the query retrieves are extracted and returned as a **List** object.

This List object is returned to the calling method i.e. Service Layer's **listGroupedTransactions():**

```
public List<Transaction> listGroupedTransactions() {
    return transactionDAO.listGroupedTransactions();
}
```

This method in turn returns it to the TransactionController's **showTransactions():**

```
public String showTransactions(Map<String, Object> map) {
    map.put("transactionGroupedList", transactionService.listGroupedTransactions());
    map.put("transactionList", transactionService.listTransactions());
    return "manageTransactions";
}
```

Finally, TransactionController returns this List object to the View which renders it.

manageTransactions.jsp on taking charge uses the **iterator** tag to iterate over the contents of the List object **transactionGroupedList**.

```
<c:forEach items="${transactionGroupedList}" var="transaction">
    <table cellspacing="1" cellpadding="2" width="20%"
    style="float:left;">
        <tr>
            <td width="50%" class="transactionGroupHeading">
                Transaction No.:
            </td>
            <td class="transactionGroupContent">
                ${transaction[0]}
```

The transactionGroupedList object holds all those records retrieved by the SQL query.

Each record's column values are extracted using $.

```
<td class="transactionGroupContent">
    ${transaction[0]}
</td>
```

listTransactions()

listTransactions() does the actual retrieval of the available transactions.

This method fires a SELECT query that attempts to retrieve records from the Transactions database table.

All the records that the query retrieves are extracted and returned as a **List** object.

This List object is returned to the calling method i.e. Service Layer's **listTransactions()**:

```
public List<Transaction> listTransactions() {
    return transactionDAO.listTransactions();
}
```

This method in turn returns it to the TransactionController's **showTransactions()**:

```
public String showTransactions(Map<String, Object> map) {
    map.put("transactionGroupedList", transactionService.listGroupedTransactions());
    map.put("transactionList", transactionService.listTransactions());
    return "manageTransactions";
}
```

Finally, TransactionController returns this List object to the View which renders it.

manageTransactions.jsp on taking charge uses the **iterator** tag to iterate over the contents of the List object **transactionList**.

```
<c:forEach items="${transactionList}"
var="transactionDetail">
    <c:if test="${transactionDetail.transactionNo ==
    transaction[0]}">
        <tr>
            <td>${transactionDetail.transactionDetailNo}</td>
            <td>${transactionDetail.bookName}</td>
            <td>${transactionDetail.qty} </td>
            <td>${transactionDetail.cost}</td>
```

The transactionList object holds all those records retrieved by the SQL query.

The inner loop retrieves the matching transactions, by comparing the TransactionNo with the outer loop.

Each record's column values are extracted using $.

```
<td>${transactionDetail.transactionDetailNo}</td>
<td>${transactionDetail.bookName}</td>
<td>${transactionDetail.qty}</td>
<td>${transactionDetail.cost}</td>
```

listGroupedTransactionsByUsername()

listGroupedTransactionsByUsername() does the actual retrieval of the available transactions of a particular user [i.e. the username entered in the **By Username** section].

This method fires a SELECT query that attempts to retrieve records from the Transactions database table grouped by **TransactionNo** based on **Username**.

All the records that the query retrieves are extracted and returned as a **List** object.

This List object is returned to the calling method i.e. Service Layer's **listGroupedTransactionsByUsername()**:

```
public List<Transaction> listGroupedTransactionsByUsername(String userName) {
    return transactionDAO.listGroupedTransactionsByUsername(userName);
}
```

This method in turn returns it to the TransactionController's showTransactionsByUsername():

```
public String showTransactionsByUsername(Map<String, Object> map,
@PathVariable("userName") String userName) {
    map.put("transactionGroupedList",
    transactionService.listGroupedTransactionsByUsername(userName));
    map.put("transactionList",
    transactionService.listTransactionsByUsername(userName));
    return "manageTransactions";
}
```

Finally, TransactionController returns this List object to the View which renders it.

manageTransactions.jsp on taking charge uses the **iterator** tag to iterate over the contents of the List object **transactionGroupedList**.

```
<c:forEach items="${transactionGroupedList}" var="transaction">
    <table cellspacing="1" cellpadding="2" width="20%"
    style="float:left;">
        <tr>
            <td width="50%" class="transactionGroupHeading">
                Transaction No.:
            </td>
            <td class="transactionGroupContent">
                ${transaction[0]}
```

The transactionGroupedList object holds all those records retrieved by the SQL query.

Each record's column values are extracted using **$**.

```
<td class="transactionGroupContent">
    ${transaction[0]}
</td>
```

listTransactionsByUsername()

listTransactionsByUsername() does the actual retrieval of the available transactions of a particular user.

This method fires a SELECT query that attempts to retrieve records from the Transactions database table based on **Username**.

All the records that the query retrieves are extracted and returned as a **List** object.

This List object is returned to the calling method i.e. Service Layer's
listTransactionsByUsername():

```
public List<Transaction> listTransactionsByUsername(String userName) {
    return transactionDAO.listTransactionsByUsername(userName);
}
```

This method in turn returns it to the TransactionController's
showTransactionsByUsername():

```
public String showTransactionsByUsername(Map<String, Object> map,
@PathVariable("userName") String userName) {
    map.put("transactionGroupedList",
    transactionService.listGroupedTransactionsByUsername(userName));
    map.put("transactionList",
    transactionService.listTransactionsByUsername(userName));
    return "manageTransactions";
}
```

Finally, TransactionController returns this List object to the View which renders it.

manageTransactions.jsp on taking charge uses the **iterator** tag to iterate over the contents of the List object **transactionList**.

```
<c:forEach items="${transactionList}"
var="transactionDetail">
    <c:if test="${transactionDetail.transactionNo ==
    transaction[0]}">
        <tr>
            <td>${transactionDetail.transactionDetailNo}</td>
            <td>${transactionDetail.bookName}</td>
            <td>${transactionDetail.qty}</td>
            <td>${transactionDetail.cost}</td>
```

The transactionList object holds all those records retrieved by the SQL query.

The inner loop retrieves the matching transactions, by comparing the TransactionNo with the outer loop.

Each record's column values are extracted using $.

```
<td>${transactionDetail.transactionDetailNo}</td>
<td>${transactionDetail.bookName}</td>
<td>${transactionDetail.qty}</td>
<td>${transactionDetail.cost}</td>
```

listGroupedTransactionsByDate()

listGroupedTransactionsByDate() does the actual retrieval of the available transactions made on a particular date [i.e. the date entered in the **By Date** section].

This method fires a SELECT query that attempts to retrieve records from the Transactions database table grouped by **TransactionNo** based on **TransactionDate**.

All the records that the query retrieves are extracted and returned as a **List** object.

This List object is returned to the calling method i.e. Service Layer's **listGroupedTransactionsByDate()**:

```
public List<Transaction> listGroupedTransactionsByDate(Date date) {
    return transactionDAO.listGroupedTransactionsByDate(date);
}
```

This method in turn returns it to the TransactionController's **showTransactionsByDate()**:

```
public String showTransactionsByDate(Map<String, Object> map,
@PathVariable("day") String day, @PathVariable("year") String year,
@PathVariable("month") String month) {
    SimpleDateFormat sdf = new SimpleDateFormat("yyyy-MM-dd");
    try {
        map.put("transactionGroupedList",
        transactionService.listGroupedTransactionsByDate(sdf.parse(year + "-" +
        month + "-" + day)));
        map.put("transactionList",
        transactionService.listTransactionsByDate(sdf.parse(year + "-" + month + "-"
        + day)));
    } catch (ParseException ex) {
```

Finally, TransactionController returns this List object to the View which renders it.

manageTransactions.jsp on taking charge uses the **iterator** tag to iterate over the contents of the List object **transactionGroupedList**.

```
<c:forEach items="${transactionGroupedList}" var="transaction">
    <table cellspacing="1" cellpadding="2" width="20%"
    style="float:left;">
        <tr>
            <td width="50%" class="transactionGroupHeading">
            Transaction No.:
            </td>
            <td class="transactionGroupContent">
                ${transaction[0]}
```

The transactionGroupedList object holds all those records retrieved by the SQL query.

Each record's column values are extracted using $.

```
<td class="transactionGroupContent">
    ${transaction[0]}
</td>
```

listTransactionsByDate()

listTransactionsByDate() does the actual retrieval of the available transactions made on a particular date.

This method fires a SELECT query that attempts to retrieve records from the Transactions database table based on **TransactionDate**.

All the records that the query retrieves are extracted and returned as a **List** object.

This List object is returned to the calling method i.e. Service Layer's **listTransactionsByDate()**:

```
public List<Transaction> listTransactionsByDate(Date date) {
    return transactionDAO.listTransactionsByDate(date);
}
```

This method in turn returns it to the TransactionController's **showTransactionsByDate()**:

```
public String showTransactionsByDate(Map<String, Object> map,
@PathVariable("day") String day, @PathVariable("year") String year,
@PathVariable("month") String month) {
    SimpleDateFormat sdf = new SimpleDateFormat("yyyy-MM-dd");
    try {
        map.put("transactionGroupedList",
        transactionService.listGroupedTransactionsByDate(sdf.parse(year + "-" +
        month + "-" + day)));
        map.put("transactionList",
        transactionService.listTransactionsByDate(sdf.parse(year + "-" + month + "-"
        + day)));
```

Finally, TransactionController returns this List object to the View which renders it.

manageTransactions.jsp on taking charge uses the **iterator** tag to iterate over the contents of the List object **transactionList**.

```
<c:forEach items="${transactionList}"
var="transactionDetail">
    <c:if test="${transactionDetail.transactionNo ==
    transaction[0]}">
        <tr>
            <td>${transactionDetail.transactionDetailNo}</td>
            <td>${transactionDetail.bookName}</td>
            <td>${transactionDetail.qty} </td>
            <td>${transactionDetail.cost}</td>
```

The transactionList object holds all those records retrieved by the SQL query.

The inner loop retrieves the matching transactions, by comparing the TransactionNo with the outer loop.

Each record's column values are extracted using $.

```
<td>${transactionDetail.transactionDetailNo}</td>
<td>${transactionDetail.bookName}</td>
<td>${transactionDetail.qty}</td>
<td>${transactionDetail.cost}</td>
```

updateGoogleOrderNo()

updateGoogleOrderNo() updates the appropriate transaction based on **TransactionNo** and **OrderNo** received as a reference.

This method uses:

❑ **setString()** of Query, which sets the value of OrderNo received from the user as the query parameter

❑ **setInteger()** of Query, which sets the value of TransactionNo received from the user as the query parameter

❑ **executeUpdate()** of Query, which updates the Transactions database table

Domain Class [Transaction.java]

This is a domain class with the following specifications.

Domain Specifications

Class Name	Package	Implements
Transaction	com.sharanamvaishali.model	java.io.Serializable

Properties		

Property Name	Property Type	Methods	
transactionDetailNo	Integer	getTransactionDetailNo()	setTransactionDetailNo()
transactionNo	Integer	getTransactionNo()	setTransactionNo()
googleOrderNo	String	getGoogleOrderNo()	setGoogleOrderNo()
transactionDate	Date	getTransactionDate()	setTransactionDate()
userName	String	getUserName()	setUserName()
bookName	String	getBookName()	setBookName()
cost	Integer	getCost()	setCost()
qty	Integer	getQty()	setQty()

Code Spec

```
1  package com.sharanamvaishali.model;
2
3  import java.sql.Date;
4  import javax.persistence.*;
5
6  @Entity
7  @Table(name="TRANSACTIONS")
8  public class Transaction implements java.io.Serializable {
9      @Id
10     @GeneratedValue
```

```
11      @Column(name="TRANSACTIONDETAILNO")
12      private Integer transactionDetailNo;
13      @Column(name="TRANSACTIONNO")
14      private Integer transactionNo;
15      @Column(name="GOOGLEORDERNO")
16      private String googleOrderNo;
17      @Column(name="TRANSACTIONDATE")
18      private Date transactionDate;
19      @Column(name="USERNAME")
20      private String userName;
21      @Column(name="BOOKNAME")
22      private String bookName;
23      @Column(name="COST")
24      private Integer cost;
25      @Column(name="QTY")
26      private Integer qty;
27
28      public String getGoogleOrderNo() {
29          return googleOrderNo;
30      }
31      public void setGoogleOrderNo(String googleOrderNo) {
32          this.googleOrderNo = googleOrderNo;
33      }
34
35      public String getBookName() {
36          return bookName;
37      }
38      public void setBookName(String bookName) {
39          this.bookName = bookName;
40      }
41
42      public Integer getCost() {
43          return cost;
44      }
45      public void setCost(Integer cost) {
46          this.cost = cost;
47      }
48
49      public Integer getQty() {
50          return qty;
51      }
52      public void setQty(Integer qty) {
53          this.qty = qty;
54      }
55
56      public Integer getTransactionDetailNo() {
57          return transactionDetailNo;
58      }
59      public void setTransactionDetailNo(Integer transactionDetailNo) {
60          this.transactionDetailNo = transactionDetailNo;
61      }
62
63      public Integer getTransactionNo() {
64          return transactionNo;
```

```
65    }
66    public void setTransactionNo(Integer transactionNo) {
67        this.transactionNo = transactionNo;
68    }
69
70    public String getUserName() {
71        return userName;
72    }
73    public void setUserName(String userName) {
74        this.userName = userName;
75    }
76
77    public Date getTransactionDate() {
78        return transactionDate;
79    }
80    public void setTransactionDate(Date transactionDate) {
81        this.transactionDate = transactionDate;
82    }
83 }
```

Chapter

39

SECTION V: BACKEND [ADMINISTRATION] SOFTWARE DESIGN DOCUMENTATION

Common Includes

Administration Header

This module is made up of the following:

Type	Name	Description
JSP	adminHeader.jsp	The header of the administration section.

JSP [adminHeader.jsp]

Sharanam & Vaishali's Online Bookshop

Countries | States | Categories | Publishers | Authors | Books | Users | Transactions | Logout

Diagram 39.1: Header of the Administration Section

This is a JSP which holds the header of the administration section, as shown in diagram 39.1.

This file is included in the beginning of the BODY section in all the Manage forms:

```
<body>
   <%@ include file="/WEB-INF/jsp/adminHeader.jsp" %>
```

Code Spec

```
1   <%@ page language="java" contentType="text/html" import="java.util.*,
    java.text.SimpleDateFormat" %>
2   <%
3      Date d = new Date();
4      Calendar c = Calendar.getInstance();
5      c.setTime(d);
6      int year = c.get(Calendar.YEAR);
7      int month = c.get(Calendar.MONTH) + 1;
8      int day = c.get(Calendar.DATE);
9      String curDate = null;
10     curDate = year + "-" + month + "-" + day;
11  %>
12  <div id="headerDiv">
13     <table class="headerTable" border="0" width="100%">
14        <tr>
15           <td>
16              <h1>Sharanam & Vaishali's Online Bookshop</h1>
17           </td>
18        </tr>
19     </table>
20     <br/>
21     <table border="0" cellspacing="0" cellpadding="0" width="100%">
22        <tr>
23           <td width="37%">
24               
25           </td>
26           <td class="menuborder" width="7%">
27              <a href="${pageContext.request.contextPath}/admin/manageCountries"
                 title="Manage Countries">Countries</a>
28           </td>
29           <td class="menuborder" width="7%">
30              <a href="${pageContext.request.contextPath}/admin/manageStates"
                 title="Manage States">States</a>
31           </td>
32           <td class="menuborder" width="7%">
33              <a href="${pageContext.request.contextPath}/admin/manageCategories"
                 title="Manage Categories">Categories</a>
34           </td>
35           <td class="menuborder" width="7%">
36              <a href="${pageContext.request.contextPath}/admin/managePublishers"
                 title="Manage Publishers">Publishers</a>
37           </td>
38           <td class="menuborder" width="7%">
```

```
39                 <a href="${pageContext.request.contextPath}/admin/manageAuthors"
                   title="Manage Authors">Authors</a>
40           </td>
41           <td class="menuborder" width="7%">
42                 <a href="${pageContext.request.contextPath}/admin/manageBooks"
                   title="Manage Books">Books</a>
43           </td>
44           <td class="menuborder" width="7%">
45                 <a href="${pageContext.request.contextPath}/admin/manageUsers"
                   title="Manage Users">Users</a>
46           </td>
47           <td class="menuborder" width="7%">
48                 <a href="${pageContext.request.contextPath}/admin/manageTransactions"
                   title="Manage Transactions">Transactions</a>
49           </td>
50           <td class="menuborder" width="7%">
51                 <a href='<c:url value="/admin/j_spring_security_logout" />'
                   title="Logout">Logout</a>
52           </td>
53        </tr>
54     </table>
55  </div>
```

Explanation:

This JSP is the header file of the administration section.

This JSP holds:

❑   The current date

❑   The name of the Shop owner

❑   The links of all the Manage forms

❑   The link to logout i.e. return to the admin login page

Administration Footer

This module is made up of the following:

Type	Name	Description
JSP	adminFooter.jsp	The footer of the administration section.

JSP [adminFooter.jsp]

Diagram 39.2: Footer of the Administration Section

This is a JSP which holds the footer of the administration section, as shown in diagram 39.2.

This file is included at the end of the BODY section in all the Manage forms:

```
<%@ include file="/WEB-INF/jsp/adminFooter.jsp" %>
</body>
```

Code Spec

```
1  <table id="footer" width="100%" border="0" cellpadding="0" cellspacing="0">
2    <tr>
3      <td class="footerIconAlgin">
4        <a href="/BookShop/home"><img src="/BookShop/images/home.png"
           title="Home(End User)"/></a>
5      </td>
6    </tr>
7    <tr>
8      <td class="footerTextAlgin" width="25%">
9        <br/>
10       <span><a href="http://www.facebook.com/sharanamvaishali"
           target="_blank">
11       Facebook</a> | </span><span><a
           href="http://www.sharanamshah.com"
12       target="_blank">Sharanam Shah</a></span> | <span><a
           href="http://www.vaishalishahonline.com"
13       target="_blank">Vaishali Shah</a></span><br/><span>&copy; Sharanam &
           Vaishali, Inc All Rights Reserved </span>
14     </td>
15   </tr>
16 </table>
```

Explanation:

This JSP is the footer file of the administration section.

This JSP holds:

❑ The link to the home page of the application i.e. the customer facing home page

❑ The name of the creator of the application

Administration Access Denied Page

This module is made up of the following:

Type	Name	Description
JSP	adminAccessDenied.jsp	The access denied page of the administration section.

JSP [adminAccessDenied.jsp]

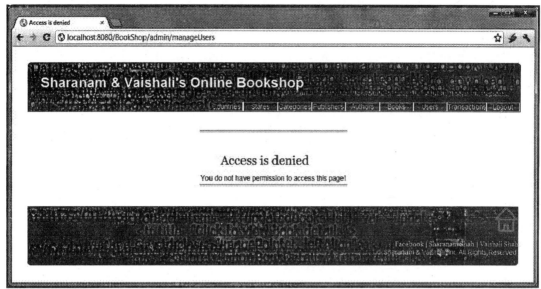

Diagram 39.3: Access Denied Page of the Administration Section

This is a JSP which holds the access denied information of the administration section, as shown in diagram 39.3.

Code Spec

```
1   <%@page contentType="text/html" pageEncoding="UTF-8"%>
2   <%@taglib uri="http://java.sun.com/jsp/jstl/core" prefix="c"%>
3   <!DOCTYPE HTML PUBLIC "-//W3C//DTD HTML 4.01 Transitional//EN"
4       "http://www.w3.org/TR/html4/loose.dtd">
5   <html>
6     <head>
7       <meta http-equiv="Content-Type" content="text/html; charset=UTF-8">
8       <title>Access is denied</title>
9       <link rel="stylesheet" href="/BookShop/css/admin.css" type="text/css">
10    </head>
11    <body>
12      <%@ include file="/WEB-INF/jsp/adminHeader.jsp" %>
13      <br/>
14      <table border="0" cellspacing="0" cellpadding="2" align="center">
15        <tr><td> </td></tr>
16        <tr><td class="hrLine"> </td></tr>
17        <tr><td class="accessDenied">Access is denied</td></tr>
18        <tr>
19          <td style="errorAccessDenied">
20            You do not have permission to access this page!
```

```
21    ·              </td>
22              </tr>
23              <tr><td class="hrLine"> </td></tr>
24          </table>
25          <%@ include file="/WEB-INF/jsp/adminFooter.jsp" %>
26      </body>
27  </html>
```

Explanation:

This JSP is the access denied page of the administration section.

This page is called, when a user other than the ADMIN tries to enter the Manage Users data entry form.

This JSP holds the information that indicates that the access is denied to the clicked link.

Stylesheet

This module is made up of the following:

Type	Name	Description
CSS	admin.css	The stylesheet for the administration section.

Code Spec

```
 1  a {
 2      text-decoration: none;
 3      color: #660000;
 4      font-family: Georgia, serif;
 5  }
 6
 7  a:hover {
 8      text-decoration: none;
 9      color: #FF0000;
10      font-family: Georgia, serif;
11  }
12
13  body {
14      font-family: helvetica, arial, sans-serif;
15      font-size: 13px;
16      color: #333;
17      text-decoration: none;
18      margin: 30px;
19      padding: 0;
20  }
21
22  img {
23      border: none;
24  }
```

```
25
26  td {
27      text-align: left;
28      vertical-align: top;
29  }
30
31  .groovybutton {
32      font-size:15px;
33      font-weight:bold;
34      color:#CC0000;
35      background-color:#FFFFFF;
36      filter:progid:DXImageTransform.Microsoft.Gradient(GradientType=0,StartColorStr='
        #ffCC99FF',EndColorStr='#ffFFFFCC');
37      border-top-style:groove;
38      border-top-color:#FF0099;
39      border-bottom-style:groove;
40      border-bottom-color:#FF0099;
41      border-left-style:groove;
42      border-left-color:#FF0099;
43      border-right-style:groove;
44      border-right-color:#FF0099;
45      height: 25px;
46  }
47
48  INPUT, SELECT {
49      font: 14px/20px Arial, Helvetica, sans-serif;
50      color: #0b0b0b;
51      border: #c3bca4 1px solid;
52      height: 22px;
53      background-color: #efebde;
54  }
55
56  TEXTAREA {
57      font: 14px/20px Arial, Helvetica, sans-serif;
58      color: #0b0b0b;
59      border: #c3bca4 1px solid;
60      background-color: #efebde;
61  }
62
63  .hrLine {
64      height: 20px;
65      background: url('../images/hr.jpg') repeat-x;
66  }
67
68  .information {
69      font-weight: normal;
70      font-size: 13px;
71      color: #333333;
72      font-family: "Trebuchet MS";
73      text-decoration: none;
74      text-align: right;
75      vertical-align: top;
76  }
77
```

```
78   .manageForms {
79       font: 24px Georgia;
80       color: #786e4e;
81       height: 37px;
82   }
83
84   .sectionName {
85       font-family: "Arial", Times, serif;
86       font-size: 16px;
87       font-weight: bold;
88       color: #990000;
89   }
90
91   .data, .data td {
92       border-collapse: collapse;
93       border: 1px solid #c3bca4;
94       margin: 2px;
95       padding: 2px;
96       text-align: left;
97       vertical-align: top;
98   }
99
100  .data th {
101      font-weight: bold;
102      border: 1px solid #c3bca4;
103      background-color: #efebde;
104      color: #990000;
105  }
106
107  .menuborder {
108      border: 1px solid #ffffff;
109      font-family: Geneva, Arial, Helvetica, sans-serif;
110      text-align: center;
111  }
112
113  .menuborder a {
114      font-family: Geneva, Arial, Helvetica, sans-serif;
115      text-align: center;
116      color: white;
117  }
118
119  .menuborder:hover {
120      font-family: Geneva, Arial, Helvetica, sans-serif;
121      background-color: #ffffff;
122      text-align: center;
123  }
124
125  .menuborder:hover a{
126      font-family: Geneva, Arial, Helvetica, sans-serif;
127      color: #000000;
128      text-align: center;
129  }
```

```
130
131  .mandatory {
132     font-weight: bold;
133     font-size: 13px;
134     color: #0099ff;
135     font-family: "Trebuchet MS";
136  }
137
138  .error {
139     color: red;
140  }
141
142  .accessDenied {
143     font: 24px/30px Georgia, serif;
144     width:100px;
145     color: #786e4e;
146     height:37px;
147     text-align: left;
148     vertical-align: top;
149     padding-top: 20px;
150     padding-left: 40px;
151  }
152
153  .errorAccessDenied {
154     vertical-align: top;
155     text-align: center;
156     width: 100px;
157  }
158
159  #headerDiv {
160     height:88px;
161     background-image: url(/BookShop/images/transparent-bg.png);
162     width:100%;
163     border: 2px solid #000;
164     -moz-border-radius: 8px;
165     border-radius: 8px;
166     -moz-border-bottom-left-radius: 0px;
167     -moz-border-bottom-right-radius: 0px;
168     border-bottom-left-radius: 0px;
169     border-bottom-right-radius: 0px;
170     color: white;
171  }
172
173  #footer {
174     color:white;
175     margin-top: 20px;
176     float:left;
177     position:relative;
178     width: 100%;
179     height:88px;
180     background-image: url(/BookShop/images/transparent-bg.png);
181     border-radius: 8px;
182     -moz-border-top-left-radius: 0px;
183     -moz-border-top-right-radius: 0px;
```

```
184        border-top-left-radius: 0px;
185        border-top-right-radius: 0px;
186        padding-bottom: 18px;
187    }
188
189    #footer a{
190        text-decoration: none;
191        color: #fff;
192    }
193
194    .centerAlign {
195        text-align: center;
196    }
197
198    .rightAlign {
199        text-align: right;
200    }
201
202    .leftAlign {
203        text-align: left;
204    }
205
206    .footerTextAlgin {
207        text-align:right;
208        vertical-align: bottom;
209    }
210
211    .footerIconAlgin {
212        text-align:right;
213        vertical-align: bottom;
214    }
215
216    .headerTable {
217        float:left;
218        color:white;
219        padding-left: 20px;
220    }
221
222    .loginButtonAlign {
223        text-align: right;
224    }
225
226    .loginButton {
227        background: url('/BookShop/images/login.jpg') no-repeat;
228        border: 0;
229        cursor: pointer;
230        width: 68px;
231        height: 40px;
232    }
233
234    .fieldsetHieght {
235        height: 60px;
236    }
```

```
237
238  .transactionGroupHeading {
239      font-weight: bold;
240      text-align: right;
241      border-bottom: 2px #786e4e dashed;
242      border-right: 2px #786e4e dashed;
243  }
244
245  .transactionGroupContent {
246      border-bottom: 2px #786e4e dashed;
247  }
248
249  .transactionGroup {
250      font-weight: bold;
251      text-align: right;
252      border-right: 2px #786e4e dashed;
253  }
254
255  .transactionFieldset {
256      float: right;
257      text-align: center;
258  }
259
260  .transactionGoogleOrder {
261      line-height: 30px;
262      font-size: 20px;
263      color: red;
264  }
```

Chapter 40

SECTION VI: FRONTEND [CUSTOMER FACING] SOFTWARE DESIGN DOCUMENTATION

Home Page

This is the entry point to this application.

This module allows performing the following operations:

- **Login as a customer**
- **Search Books**
- **View**
    - New Releases
    - Updated Books
    - Top Titles
    - Authors
    - Publishers

- o   Popular Searches
- o   Categories
- o   Category wise books
- ❏   **Add books to cart**
- ❏   **Show Cart** [If the user is logged in]
- ❏   **Sign Up**
- ❏   **Logout** [If the user is logged in]

This module uses the following tables to perform the above operations:

- ❏   bms.Authors
- ❏   bms.Publishers
- ❏   bms.Books
- ❏   bms.PopularSearches
- ❏   bms.Users
- ❏   bms.Categories

This module is made up of the following:

Type	Name	Description
JSP	home.jsp	The home page.
	leftMenu.jsp	The list of New Releases, Updated Books, Our Authors, Our Publishers, Top Titles.
	allCategories.jsp	The list of categories and category wise books.
	login.jsp	The Login form for the registered users.
	popularSearches.jsp	The list of Popular Searches.
Spring		
Controller	HomeController.java	The controller class that facilitates data operations.
Service Class	BookService.java	The interfaces for the service layer.
	AuthorService.java	
	PublisherService.java	
	CategoryService.java	
	SearchService.java	
	UserService.java	

Spring		
Service Class	BookServiceImpl.java	The implementation classes for the service layer.
	AuthorServiceImpl.java	
	PublisherServiceImpl.java	
	CategoryServiceImpl.java	
	SearchServiceImpl.java	
	UserServiceImpl.java	
DAO Class	BookDAO.java	The interfaces for the DAO layer.
	AuthorDAO.java	
	PublisherDAO.java	
	CategoryDAO.java	
	SearchDAO.java	
	UserDAO.java	
	BookDAOImpl.java	The implementation classes that perform the actual data operations.
	AuthorDAOImpl.java	
	PublisherDAOImpl.java	
	CategoryDAOImpl.java	
	SearchDAOImpl.java	
	UserDAOImpl.java	
DispatcherServlet	bookshopdispatcher-servlet.xml	Central dispatcher for HTTP request handlers/controllers.
Hibernate		
Mapping	hibernate.cfg.xml	The mapping file that holds Model class mapping.
Model Class	Book.java	The model classes.
	Author.java	
	Publisher.java	
	Catgeory.java	
	PopularSearch.java	
	User.java	

JSP

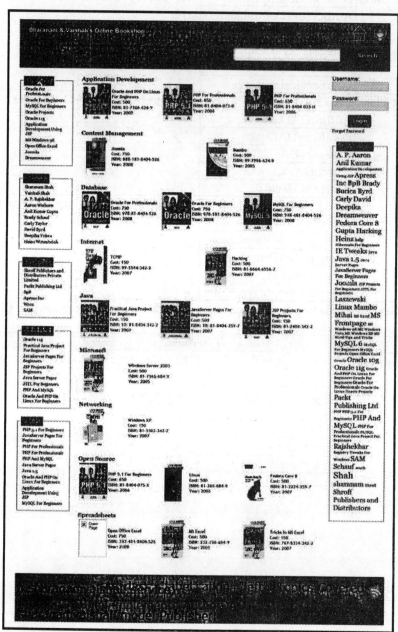

Diagram 40.1: Home page

home.jsp

This is a JSP [the default page] which appears when the user invokes the application, as shown in diagram 40.1.

Form Specifications

File Name	home.jsp
Title	BookShop[Sharanam & Vaishali Shah] - Home Page

Code Spec

```
1   <%@page contentType="text/html" pageEncoding="UTF-8"%>
2   <%@taglib uri="http://java.sun.com/jsp/jstl/core" prefix="c"%>
3   <%@taglib prefix="sec" uri="http://www.springframework.org/security/tags" %>
4   <!DOCTYPE HTML PUBLIC "-//W3C//DTD HTML 4.01 Transitional//EN"
5     "http://www.w3.org/TR/html4/loose.dtd">
6   <html>
7     <head>
8       <meta http-equiv="X-UA-Compatible" content="IE=8" />
9       <meta http-equiv="Content-Type" content="text/html; charset=UTF-8">
10      <title>BookShop[Sharanam & Vaishali Shah] - Home Page</title>
11      <link rel="stylesheet" href="/BookShop/css/frontend.css" type="text/css">
12    </head>
13    <body>
14      <%@ include file="/WEB-INF/jsp/header.jsp" %>
15      <div id="bodyDiv">
16        <table width="100%" border="0" cellpadding="0" cellspacing="0">
17          <tr>
18            <td width="15%" class="topAlign">
19              <br>
20              <%@ include file="/WEB-INF/jsp/leftMenu.jsp" %>
21            </td>
22            <td width="70%" class="topAlign, centerAlign">
23              <table width="100%" cellpadding="10" cellspacing="0">
24                <tr>
25                  <td>
26                    <%@ include file="/WEB-INF/jsp/allCategories.jsp" %>
27                  </td>
28                </tr>
29              </table>
30            </td>
31            <td width="15%" class="topAlign">
32              <table border="0" width="100%" cellpadding="0" cellspacing="0">
33                <tr>
34                  <td>
35                    <br>
36                    <sec:authorize access="isAnonymous()">
37                      <%@ include file="/WEB-INF/jsp/login.jsp" %>
38                    </sec:authorize>
```

```
39                            </td>
40                           </tr>
41                          </table>
42                          <br/>
43                          <table width="100%" border="0" cellpadding="0" cellspacing="0">
44                           <tr>
45                            <td class="topAlign">
46                              <%@ include file="/WEB-INF/jsp/popularSearches.jsp" %>
47                            </td>
48                           </tr>
49                          </table>
50                         </td>
51                       </tr>
52                     </table>
53                     <%@ include file="/WEB-INF/jsp/footer.jsp" %>
54                 </div>
55             </body>
56 </html>
```

Explanation:

This is the JSP file of the home page. This JSP includes other JSP files such as the Login JSP, the Popular Searches JSP and so on.

This is the startup point when the application is called.

leftMenu.jsp

This is a JSP, which includes the following sections, as shown in the diagram 40.2:

❑   New Releases

❑   Updated Books

❑   Our Authors

❑   Our Publishers

❑   Top Titles

This JSP is included in the home page.

New Releases

Spring 3 For Beginners
Oracle For Professionals
Oracle For Beginners
MySQL For Beginners
Oracle Projects
Oracle 11g
Application
Development Using JSP
MS Windows 98
Open Office Excel
Joomla

Our Authors

Sharanam Shah
Vaishali Shah
A. P. Rajshekhar
Aaron Winborn
Anil Kumar Gupta
Brady Schauf
Carly Taylor
David Byrd
Deepika Vohra
Heinz Wittenbrink

Our Publishers

Shroff Publishers and
Distributors Private
Limited
Packt Publishing Ltd
BpB
Apress Inc
Wrox
SAM

Updated Books

Oracle 11g
Practical Java Project
For Beginners
JavaServer Pages For
Beginners
JSP Projects For
Beginners
Java Server Pages
JSTL For Beginners
PHP And MySQL
Oracle And PHP On
Linux For Beginners

Top Titles

PHP 5.1 For Beginners
JavaServer Pages For
Beginners
PHP For Professionals
PHP For Professionals
PHP And MySQL
Java Server Pages
Java 1.5
Oracle And PHP On
Linux For Beginners
Oracle For Beginners
Application
Development Using JSP

Diagram 40.2: Left Menu page

Code Spec

```
1   <table width="100%" cellpadding="0" cellspacing="0">
2      <tr>
3         <td class="topAlign">
4            <fieldset>
5               <legend>New Releases</legend>
6               <table cellspacing="4" cellpadding="0" width="100%">
7                  <c:forEach items="${newReleasesList}" var="newReleases">
8                     <tr title="Click to view book details">
9                        <td class="imagePointer, leftAlign">
10                          <a href="showBookDetails/${newReleases.bookNo}">
11                             ${newReleases.bookName}
12                          </a>
13                       </td>
14                    </tr>
15                 </c:forEach>
16              </table>
17           </fieldset>
18        </td>
19     </tr>
20  </table>
21  <br>
22  <table width="100%" cellpadding="0" cellspacing="0">
23     <tr>
24        <td class="topAlign">
25           <fieldset>
26              <legend>Our Authors</legend>
27              <table cellspacing="4" cellpadding="0" width="100%">
28                 <c:forEach items="${ourAuthorsList}" var="ourAuthors">
29                    <tr title="Click to view author details">
30                       <td class="imagePointer, leftAlign">
31                          <a href="showAuthorDetails/${ourAuthors.authorNo}">
32                             ${ourAuthors.firstName} ${ourAuthors.lastName}
33                          </a>
34                       </td>
35                    </tr>
36                 </c:forEach>
37              </table>
38           </fieldset>
39        </td>
40     </tr>
41  </table>
42  <br>
43  <table width="100%" cellpadding="0" cellspacing="0">
44     <tr>
45        <td class="topAlign">
46           <fieldset>
47              <legend>Our Publishers</legend>
48              <table cellspacing="4" cellpadding="0" width="100%">
49                 <c:forEach items="${ourPublishersList}" var="ourPublishers">
50                    <tr title="Click to view publisher details">
```

```
51                        <td class="imagePointer, leftAlign">
52                            <a href="showPublisherDetails/${ourPublishers.publisherNo}">
53                                ${ourPublishers.publisherName}
54                            </a>
55                        </td>
56                    </tr>
57                </c:forEach>
58            </table>
59          </fieldset>
60       </td>
61    </tr>
62 </table>
63 <br>
64 <table width="100%" cellpadding="0" cellspacing="0">
65    <tr>
66       <td class="topAlign">
67          <fieldset>
68             <legend>Updated Books</legend>
69             <table cellspacing="4" cellpadding="0" width="100%">
70                <c:forEach items="${updatedBooksList}" var="updatedBooks">
71                    <tr title="Click to view book details">
72                        <td class="imagePointer, leftAlign">
73                            <a href="showBookDetails/${updatedBooks.bookNo}">
74                                ${updatedBooks.bookName}
75                            </a>
76                        </td>
77                    </tr>
78                </c:forEach>
79            </table>
80          </fieldset>
81       </td>
82    </tr>
83 </table>
84 <br>
85 <table width="100%" cellpadding="0" cellspacing="0">
86    <tr>
87       <td class="topAlign">
88          <fieldset>
89             <legend>Top Titles</legend>
90             <table cellspacing="4" cellpadding="0" width="100%">
91                <c:forEach items="${topTitlesList}" var="topTitles">
92                    <tr title="Click to view book details">
93                        <td class="imagePointer, leftAlign">
94                            <a href="showBookDetails/${topTitles.bookNo}">
95                                ${topTitles.bookName}
96                            </a>
97                        </td>
98                    </tr>
99                </c:forEach>
100           </table>
101         </fieldset>
102      </td>
103   </tr>
104 </table>
```

Explanation:

This is the JSP, which is included in the home page.

allCategories.jsp

This is a JSP, which includes the Categories section and the books available under each category, as shown in diagram 40.3.

This JSP is included in the home page.

Application Development

 Oracle And PHP On Linux For
Beginners
Cost: 500
ISBN: 81-7366-624-9
Year: 2005

 PHP For Professionals
Cost: 650
ISBN: 81-8404-073-D
Year: 2006

 PHP For Professionals
Cost: 650
ISBN: 81-8404-035-H
Year: 2006

Content Management

 Joomla
Cost: 750
ISBN: 888-181-8404-526
Year: 2008

Mambo
Cost: 500
ISBN: 99-7996-624-9
Year: 2005

Database

 Oracle For Professionals
Cost: 750
ISBN: 978-81-8404-526
Year: 2008

 Oracle For Beginners
Cost: 750
ISBN: 978-181-8404-526
Year: 2008

 MySQL For Beginners
Cost: 750
ISBN: 978-481-8404-526
Year: 2008

Internet

 TCPIP
Cost: 150
ISBN: 99-5544-342-2
Year: 2007

Hacking
Cost: 500
ISBN: 81-6664-6556-7
Year: 2007

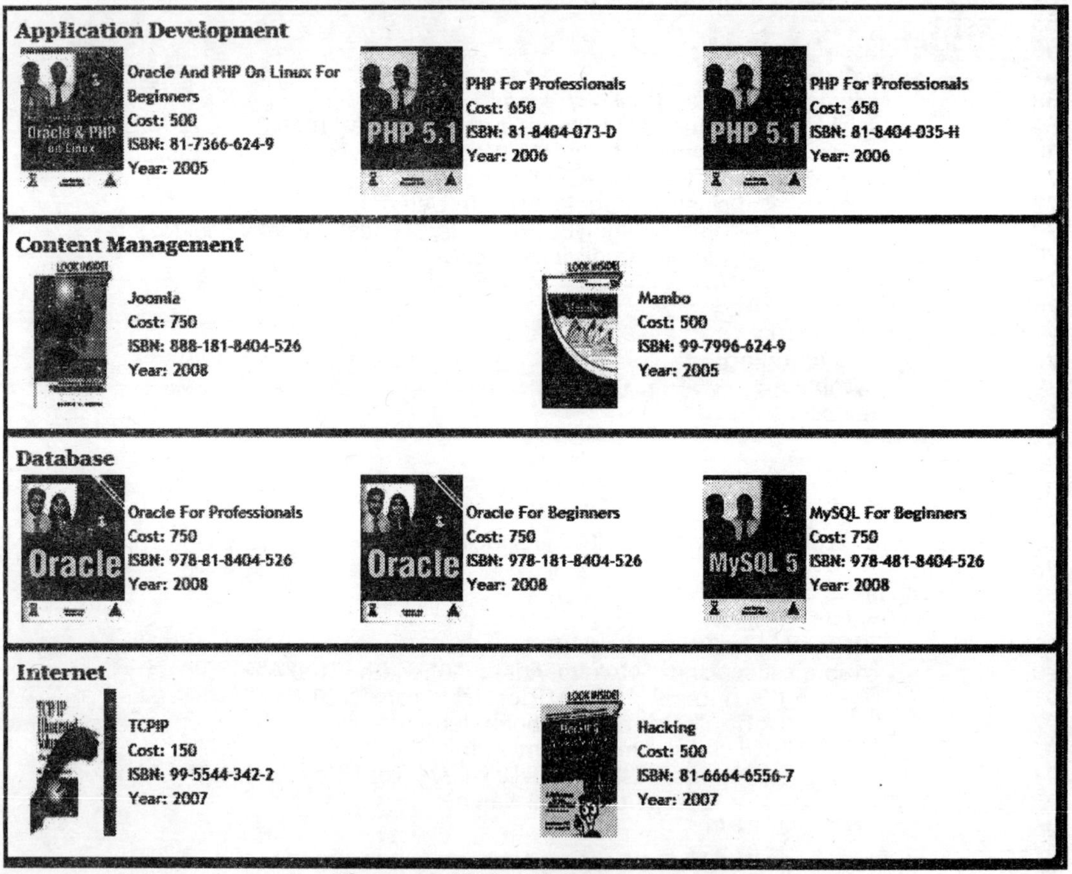

Diagram 40.3: All Categories page

Code Spec

```
1  <%! int ctr = 0; %>
2  <c:forEach items="${allCategoriesList}" var="allCategories">
```

```
3     <table id="portlets-content-main" align="center" border="0" cellspacing="1"
      cellpadding="1" width="100%" class="allCategoriesTable">
4        <tr>
5          <td class="categoriesNames">
6             <a href="showCategoryDetails/${allCategories.categoryNo}"
                title="${allCategories.description}" >
7               ${allCategories.category}
8             </a>
9             <table align="left" border="0" cellspacing="1" cellpadding="1"
                width="100%" class="allCategoriesTable">
10               <tr>
11                  <% ctr = 0; %>
12                  <c:forEach items="${allBooksList}" var="categoryWiseBooks">
13                     <c:if test="${categoryWiseBooks.categoryNo ==
                          allCategories.categoryNo}">
14                        <% ctr++;
15                        if (ctr<4) { %>
16                        <td width="33%">
17                           <table align="left" border="0" cellspacing="1"
                                cellpadding="1" width="100%" class="allCategoriesTable">
18                              <tr>
19                                 <td width="20%">
20                                    <a
                                      href="showBookDetails/${categoryWiseBooks.bookN
                                      o}" title="${categoryWiseBooks.synopsis}">
21                                       <img alt="Cover Page"
                                         src="admin/downloadBookPhotograph/${category
                                         WiseBooks.bookNo}" height="110px"
                                         width="80px"/>
22                                    </a>
23                                 </td>
24                                 <td align="left" class="heading" >
25                                    ${categoryWiseBooks.bookName}<br>
26                                    Cost: ${categoryWiseBooks.cost}<br>
27                                    ISBN: ${categoryWiseBooks.isbn}<br>
28                                    Year: ${categoryWiseBooks.year}<br>
29                                    <sec:authorize access="isAuthenticated()">
30                                       <a href="addToCart/<sec:authorize
                                         access='isAuthenticated()'><sec:authentication
                                         property='principal.username'
                                         /></sec:authorize>/${categoryWiseBooks.bookN
                                         o}">
31                                          <img src="/BookShop/images/cart.jpg"
                                            class="imagePointer" border="0"/>
32                                       </a> 
33                                       <a
                                         href="admin/downloadBookSampleChapter/${cate
                                         goryWiseBooks.bookNo}">Sample</a>
                                          |  <a
                                         href="admin/downloadBookTOC/${categoryWiseB
                                         ooks.bookNo}">TOC</a>
34                                    </sec:authorize>
35                                 </td>
36                              </tr>
```

```
37                          </table>
38                          </td>
39                          <% } %>
40                      </c:if>
41                  </c:forEach>
42              </tr>
43          </table>
44      </td>
45  </tr>
46  </table>
47  </c:forEach>
```

Explanation:

This is the JSP, which is included in the home page.

login.jsp

This is a JSP, which includes the login form, as shown in diagram 40.4.

This JSP is included in the home page.

Diagram 40.4: Login page

Form Specifications

File Name	login.jsp
Form Name	loginForm
Bound To Table	bms.Users
Action	<c:url value='j_spring_security_check'/>
Method	POST

Data Fields

Login Details			
Label	Name	Bound To	Validation Rules
Username	j_username	Users.Username	Cannot be left blank
Password	j_password	Users.Password	Cannot be left blank

Data Controls

Object	Label
Submit	Submit

Code Spec

```
1  <form name='loginForm' action="<c:url value='j_spring_security_check'/>"
   method='POST'>
2    <table width="100%" border="0" cellpadding="0" cellspacing="0">
3      <tr>
4        <td>
5          <c:if test="${not empty error}">
6            <div class="error">
7              Your login attempt was not successful, try again.<br />
8              Invalid username or password
9            </div>
10         </c:if>
11       </td>
12     </tr>
13     <tr>
14       <td class="leftAlign, content">Username:</td>
15     </tr>
16     <tr>
17       <td class="leftAlign">
18         <input type='text' name='j_username' value='' maxlength="8">
19       </td>
20     </tr>
21     <tr><td> </td></tr>
22     <tr>
23       <td class="leftAlign, content">Password:</td>
24     </tr>
25     <tr>
26       <td class="leftAlign">
27         <input type='password' name='j_password' maxlength="8"/>
28       </td>
29     </tr>
30     <tr><td> </td></tr>
31     <tr>
32       <td class="centerAlign">
33         <input type="submit" name="submit" class="loginButton" value="" />
34       </td>
```

```
35        </tr>
36        <tr>
37          <td class="leftAlign">
38            <a href="/BookShop/admin/forgotPassword">Forgot Password</a>
39          </td>
40        </tr>
41      </table>
42  </form>
```

Explanation:

This is a simple JSP page which holds a HTML form to capture the login credentials. These credentials are passed to the Spring Security check which takes care of authenticating the user credentials and if found valid takes the user in.

The login data entry form allows the registered users to login to the frontend application.

After a user logs in to the frontend application, the user is allowed to:

❑ Add books to the cart

❑ See a list of books added to the cart

❑ Make payments for the books added to the cart

❑ Download the TOC and Sample Chapter of the desired books

popularSearches.jsp

This is a JSP, which includes the popular searches, as shown in diagram 40.5.

This JSP is included in the home page.

Popular Searches

A. P. Aaron Anil Kumar Application Development Using JSP Apress Inc BpB Brady Bucica Byrd Carly David Deepika Dreamweaver Fedora Core 8 Gupta Hacking Heinz help Hibernate For Beginners IE Tweaks java Java 1.5 Java Server Pages JavaServer Pages For Beginners Joomla JSP Projects For Beginners JSTL For Beginners Laszewski Linux Mambo Mihai MS Excel MS Frontpage MS Windows 98 MS Windows Vista MS Windows XP MS Word Tips and Tricks MySQL 6 MySQL For Beginners MySQL Projects Open Office Excel Oracle Oracle 10g Oracle 11g Oracle And PHP On Linux For Beginners Oracle For Beginners Oracle For Professionals Oracle On Linux Oracle Projects Packt Publishing Ltd PHP PHP 5.1 For Beginners PHP And MySQL PHP For Professionals Practical Java Project For Beginners Rajshekhar Registry Tweaks For Windows SAM Schauf seach Shah Sharanam shroff Shroff Publishers and Distributors Private Limited SPD Star Office Struts For Beginners Suse Linux Taylor TCPIP Tom Tricks In MS Excel Vaishali Vaishali Shah Vohra Winborn Windows Server 2003 Windows Tricks Windows XP Wittenbrink Wrox

Diagram 40.5: Popular Searches page

Code Spec

```
1   <fieldset>
2      <legend>Popular Searches</legend>
3      <c:forEach items="${popularSearchList}" var="popularSearch">
4         <c:if test="${popularSearch[1]>=1 && popularSearch[1]<5}">
5            <a href="searchResults/${popularSearch[0]}" class="popularSearch1"
               title="Click to search for ${popularSearch[0]}">
6                ${popularSearch[0]}
7            </a>
8         </c:if>
9         <c:if test="${popularSearch[1]>=5 && popularSearch[1]<10}">
10           <a href="searchResults/${popularSearch[0]}" class="popularSearch2"
               title="Click to search for ${popularSearch[0]}">
11               ${popularSearch[0]}
12           </a>
13        </c:if>
14        <c:if test="${popularSearch[1]>=10 && popularSearch[1]<15}">
15           <a href="searchResults/${popularSearch[0]}" class="popularSearch3"
               title="Click to search for ${popularSearch[0]}">
16               ${popularSearch[0]}
17           </a>
18        </c:if>
19        <c:if test="${popularSearch[1]>=15 && popularSearch[1]<20}">
20           <a href="searchResults/${popularSearch[0]}" class="popularSearch4"
               title="Click to search for ${popularSearch[0]}">
21               ${popularSearch[0]}
22           </a>
23        </c:if>
24        <c:if test="${popularSearch[1]>=20}">
25           <a href="searchResults/${popularSearch[0]}" class="popularSearch5"
               title="Click to search for ${popularSearch[0]}">
26               ${popularSearch[0]}
27           </a>
28        </c:if>
29     </c:forEach>
30  </fieldset>
```

Explanation:

The words of popular searches are displayed according to the weightage of the popular search values. The more popular keywords are displayed bigger whereas the less popular words are displayed smaller.

Controller [HomeController.java]

This is a controller class with the following specifications.

Controller Specifications

Class Name	Package	
HomeController	com.sharanamvaishali.controllers	
Objects		
Object Name	Class Name	Object Type
userService	UserService	Service Layer
searchService	SearchService	Service Layer
bookService	BookService	Service Layer
authorService	AuthorService	Service Layer
publisherService	PublisherService	Service Layer
categoryService	CategoryService	Service Layer
Methods		
Method Name	Request Mapping	
startHome()	/	
showHome()	/home	

Code Spec

```
1   package com.sharanamvaishali.controllers;
2
3   import com.sharanamvaishali.model.Search;
4   import com.sharanamvaishali.service.*;
5   import java.util.Map;
6   import javax.servlet.http.HttpServletRequest;
7   import org.springframework.beans.factory.annotation.Autowired;
8   import org.springframework.security.core.context.SecurityContextHolder;
9   import org.springframework.stereotype.Controller;
10  import org.springframework.web.bind.annotation.RequestMapping;
11
12  @Controller
13  public class HomeController {
14      @Autowired
15      private UserService userService;
16
17      @Autowired
18      private SearchService searchService;
19
20      @Autowired
21      private BookService bookService;
22
23      @Autowired
24      private AuthorService authorService;
25
26      @Autowired
27      private PublisherService publisherService;
28
29      @Autowired
```

```
30    private CategoryService categoryService;
31
32    @RequestMapping("/")
33    public String startHome() {
34        return "redirect:/home";
35    }
36
37    @RequestMapping("/home")
38    public String showHome(Map<String, Object> map, HttpServletRequest request) {
39        map.put("newReleasesList", bookService.listNewReleases());
40        map.put("ourAuthorsList", authorService.listOurAuthors());
41        map.put("ourPublishersList", publisherService.listOurPublishers());
42        map.put("allCategoriesList", categoryService.listCategory());
43        map.put("allBooksList", bookService.listBook());
44        map.put("popularSearchList", searchService.listPopularSearches());
45        map.put("updatedBooksList", bookService.listUpdatedBooks());
46        map.put("topTitlesList", bookService.listTopTitles());
47        if(SecurityContextHolder.getContext().getAuthentication().isAuthenticated()) {
48            map.put("userDetails",
                 userService.getUserByUsername(SecurityContextHolder.getContext().getAuthen
                 tication().getName()));
49        }
50        map.put("search", new Search());
51        return "home";
52    }
53 }
```

Explanation:

The following section describes the above code spec.

startHome()

HomeController holds a mapping to help the redirection.

Using this mapping the control shifts to the home.jsp page via the **/home** request mapping and the homepage is served, as shown in diagram 40.1.

showHome()

As soon as the application loading completes home.jsp is served based on HomeController configuration.

showHome() is invoked <u>every time</u> **home.jsp** is served. It populates the List objects with the appropriate data. These List objects are made available to home.jsp.

showHome():

❑ Retrieves the appropriate New Releases. It calls BookService class's **listNewReleases()** which returns the details of the newly released books

❑ Retrieves the appropriate Our Author's details. It calls AuthorService class's **listOurAuthors()** which returns the details of the authors

❑ Retrieves the appropriate Our Publisher's details. It calls PublisherService class's **listOurPublishers()** which returns the details of the publishers

❑ Retrieves the appropriate Category's details. It calls CategoryService class's **listCategories()** which returns the details of the categories

❑ Retrieves all the Books. It calls BookService class's **listBook()** which returns the details of all the available books

❑ Retrieves the Popular Searches. It calls SearchService class's **listPopularSearches()** which returns the values of the popular searches

❑ Retrieves the Updated Books. It calls BookService class's **listUpdatedBooks()** which returns the details of the updated books

❑ Retrieves the Top Titles. It calls BookService class's **listTopTitles()** which returns the details of the top books

❑ Populates the userDetails object with the username of the logged in user. This is only done if the user has logged in. This object is used to show the welcome message after the user has logged in

❑ Initializes the search form as the search form is a part of the view

❑ Returns the control to the View along with the data to be populated in the browser. The data that is retrieved is made available using Map's **put()**

Service Classes

Interface

This is a service interface with the following specifications.

BookService.java

Service Interface Specifications

Class Name	Package
BookService	com.sharanamvaishali.service

Code Spec

```
1  package com.sharanamvaishali.service;
2
3  import com.sharanamvaishali.model.Book;
4  import java.util.List;
5
6  public interface BookService {
7      public List<Book> listBook();
8      public List<Book> listNewReleases();
9      public List<Book> listUpdatedBooks();
10     public List<Book> listTopTitles();
11 }
```

AuthorService.java

Service Interface Specifications

Class Name	Package
AuthorService	com.sharanamvaishali.service

Code Spec

```
1  package com.sharanamvaishali.service;
2
3  import com.sharanamvaishali.model.Author;
4  import java.util.List;
5
6  public interface AuthorService {
7      public List<Author> listOurAuthors();
8  }
```

PublisherService.java

Service Interface Specifications

Class Name	Package
PublisherService	com.sharanamvaishali.service

Code Spec

```
1  package com.sharanamvaishali.service;
2
3  import com.sharanamvaishali.model.Publisher;
4  import java.util.List;
5
6  public interface PublisherService {
```

```
7    public List<Publisher> listOurPublishers();
8 }
```

CategoryService.java

Service Interface Specifications

Class Name	Package
CategoryService	com.sharanamvaishali.service

Code Spec

```
1  package com.sharanamvaishali.service;
2
3  import com.sharanamvaishali.model.Category;
4  import java.util.List;
5
6  public interface CategoryService {
7     public List<Category> listCategory();
8  }
```

SearchService.java

Service Interface Specifications

Class Name	Package
SearchService	com.sharanamvaishali.service

Code Spec

```
1  package com.sharanamvaishali.service;
2
3  import java.util.List;
4
5  public interface SearchService {
6     public List listPopularSearches();
7  }
```

UserService.java

Service Interface Specifications

Class Name	Package
UserService	com.sharanamvaishali.service

Code Spec

```
1  package com.sharanamvaishali.service;
2
3  import com.sharanamvaishali.model.User;
4
5  public interface UserService {
6      public User getUserByUsername(String userName);
7  }
```

Implementation Class

This is a service class with the following specifications.

BookServiceImpl.java

Service Implementation Specifications

Class Name	Package	Implements
BookServiceImpl	com.sharanamvaishali.service	BookService

Objects		
Object Name	Class Name	Object Type
bookDAO	BookDAO	Data Access Object Layer

Methods	
Method Name	Arguments
listBook()	- -
listNewReleases()	- -
listUpdatedBooks()	- -
listTopTitles()	- -

Code Spec

```
1  package com.sharanamvaishali.service;
2
3  import com.sharanamvaishali.dao.BookDAO;
4  import com.sharanamvaishali.model.Book;
5  import java.util.List;
6  import org.springframework.beans.factory.annotation.Autowired;
7  import org.springframework.stereotype.Service;
8  import org.springframework.transaction.annotation.Transactional;
9
10 @Service
11 public class BookServiceImpl implements BookService {
12     @Autowired
13     private BookDAO bookDAO;
14
15     @Transactional
```

```
16     @Override
17     public List<Book> listBook() {
18         return bookDAO.listBook();
19     }
20
21     @Transactional
22     @Override
23     public List<Book> listNewReleases() {
24         return bookDAO.listNewReleases();
25     }
26
27     @Transactional
28     @Override
29     public List<Book> listUpdatedBooks() {
30         return bookDAO.listUpdatedBooks();
31     }
32
33     @Transactional
34     @Override
35     public List<Book> listTopTitles() {
36         return bookDAO.listTopTitles();
37     }
38 }
```

Explanation:

The following section describes the above code spec.

listBook()

listBook() holds the business logic to retrieve the book details.

This method in turn invokes the DAO Layer's [BookDAO] **listBook()**.

listNewReleases()

listNewReleases() holds the business logic to retrieve the newly released book details.

This method in turn invokes the DAO Layer's [BookDAO] **listNewReleases()**.

listUpdatedBooks()

listUpdatedBooks() holds the business logic to retrieve the updated book details.

This method in turn invokes the DAO Layer's [BookDAO] **listUpdatedBooks()**.

listTopTitles()

listTopTitles() holds the business logic to retrieve the top titled book details.

This method in turn invokes the DAO Layer's [BookDAO] **listTopTitles()**.

AuthorServiceImpl.java

Service Implementation Specifications

Class Name	Package	Implements
AuthorServiceImpl	com.sharanamvaishali.service	AuthorService
Objects		
Object Name	**Class Name**	**Object Type**
authorDAO	AuthorDAO	Data Access Object Layer
Methods		
Method Name		**Arguments**
listOurAuthors()		- -

Code Spec

```
1  package com.sharanamvaishali.service;
2
3  import com.sharanamvaishali.dao.AuthorDAO;
4  import com.sharanamvaishali.model.Author;
5  import java.util.List;
6  import org.springframework.beans.factory.annotation.Autowired;
7  import org.springframework.stereotype.Service;
8  import org.springframework.transaction.annotation.Transactional;
9
10 @Service
11 public class AuthorServiceImpl implements AuthorService {
12     @Autowired
13     private AuthorDAO authorDAO;
14
15     @Transactional
16     @Override
17     public List<Author> listOurAuthors() {
18         return authorDAO.listOurAuthors();
19     }
20 }
```

Explanation:

The following section describes the above code spec.

<u>*listOurAuthors()*</u>

listOurAuthors() holds the business logic to retrieve the author details.

This method in turn invokes the DAO Layer's [AuthorDAO] **listOurAuthors()**.

PublisherServiceImpl.java

Service Implementation Specifications

Class Name	Package	Implements
PublisherServiceImpl	com.sharanamvaishali.service	PublisherService

Objects		
Object Name	**Class Name**	**Object Type**
publisherDAO	PublisherDAO	Data Access Object Layer

Methods	
Method Name	**Arguments**
listOurPublishers()	- -

Code Spec

```
1  package com.sharanamvaishali.service;
2
3  import com.sharanamvaishali.dao.PublisherDAO;
4  import com.sharanamvaishali.model.Publisher;
5  import java.util.List;
6  import org.springframework.beans.factory.annotation.Autowired;
7  import org.springframework.stereotype.Service;
8  import org.springframework.transaction.annotation.Transactional;
9
10 @Service
11 public class PublisherServiceImpl implements PublisherService {
12     @Autowired
13     private PublisherDAO publisherDAO;
14
15     @Transactional
16     @Override
17     public List<Publisher> listOurPublishers() {
18         return publisherDAO.listOurPublishers();
19     }
20 }
```

Explanation:

The following section describes the above code spec.

listOurPublishers()

listOurPublishers() holds the business logic to retrieve the publisher details.

This method in turn invokes the DAO Layer's [PublisherDAO] **listOurPublishers()**.

CategoryServiceImpl.java

Service Implementation Specifications

Class Name	Package	Implements
CategoryServiceImpl	com.sharanamvaishali.service	CategoryService

Objects		
Object Name	**Class Name**	**Object Type**
categoryDAO	CategoryDAO	Data Access Object Layer

Methods	
Method Name	**Arguments**
listCategory()	- -

Code Spec

```
1  package com.sharanamvaishali.service;
2
3  import com.sharanamvaishali.dao.CategoryDAO;
4  import com.sharanamvaishali.model.Category;
5  import java.util.List;
6  import org.springframework.beans.factory.annotation.Autowired;
7  import org.springframework.stereotype.Service;
8  import org.springframework.transaction.annotation.Transactional;
9
10 @Service
11 public class CategoryServiceImpl implements CategoryService {
12     @Autowired
13     private CategoryDAO categoryDAO;
14
15     @Transactional
16     @Override
17     public List<Category> listCategory() {
18         return categoryDAO.listCategory();
19     }
20 }
```

Explanation:

The following section describes the above code spec.

listCategory()

listCategory() holds the business logic to retrieve the category details.

This method in turn invokes the DAO Layer's [CategoryDAO] listCategory().

SearchServiceImpl.java

Service Implementation Specifications

Class Name	Package	Implements
SearchServiceImpl	com.sharanamvaishali.service	SearchService

Objects		
Object Name	Class Name	Object Type
searchDAO	SearchDAO	Data Access Object Layer

Methods	
Method Name	Arguments
listPopularSearches()	- -

Code Spec

```
1  package com.sharanamvaishali.service;
2
3  import com.sharanamvaishali.dao.SearchDAO;
4  import java.util.List;
5  import org.springframework.beans.factory.annotation.Autowired;
6  import org.springframework.stereotype.Service;
7  import org.springframework.transaction.annotation.Transactional;
8
9  @Service
10 public class SearchServiceImpl implements SearchService {
11     @Autowired
12     private SearchDAO searchDAO;
13
14     @Transactional
15     @Override
16     public List listPopularSearches() {
17         return searchDAO.listPopularSearches();
18     }
19 }
```

Explanation:

The following section describes the above code spec.

listPopularSearches()

listPopularSearches() holds the business logic to retrieve the popular searches details.

This method in turn invokes the DAO Layer's [SearchDAO] **listPopularSearches()**.

UserServiceImpl.java

Service Implementation Specifications

Class Name	Package	Implements
UserServiceImpl	com.sharanamvaishali.service	UserService

Objects		
Object Name	**Class Name**	**Object Type**
userDAO	UserDAO	Data Access Object Layer

Methods	
Method Name	**Arguments**
getUserByUsername()	String username

Code Spec

```
1   package com.sharanamvaishali.service;
2
3   import com.sharanamvaishali.dao.UserDAO;
4   import com.sharanamvaishali.model.User;
5   import org.springframework.beans.factory.annotation.Autowired;
6   import org.springframework.stereotype.Service;
7   import org.springframework.transaction.annotation.Transactional;
8
9   @Service
10  public class UserServiceImpl implements UserService {
11      @Autowired
12      private UserDAO userDAO;
13
14      @Transactional
15      @Override
16      public User getUserByUsername(String userName) {
17          return userDAO.getUserByUserName(userName);
18      }
19  }
```

Explanation:

The following section describes the above code spec.

getUserByUsername()

getUserByUsername() holds the business logic to retrieve user details based on Username.

This method in turn invokes UserDAO's **getUserByUsername()**.

DAO Classes

Interface

This is a Data Access Object interface with the following specifications.

BookDAO.java

DAO Interface Specifications

Class Name	Package
BookDAO	com.sharanamvaishali.dao

Code Spec

```
1  package com.sharanamvaishali.dao;
2
3  import com.sharanamvaishali.model.Book;
4  import java.util.List;
5
6  public interface BookDAO {
7      public List<Book> listBook();
8      public List<Book> listNewReleases();
9      public List<Book> listUpdatedBooks();
10     public List<Book> listTopTitles();
11 }
```

AuthorDAO.java

DAO Interface Specifications

Class Name	Package
AuthorDAO	com.sharanamvaishali.dao

Code Spec

```
1  package com.sharanamvaishali.dao;
2
```

```
3  import com.sharanamvaishali.model.Author;
4  import java.util.List;
5
6  public interface AuthorDAO {
7      public List<Author> listOurAuthors();
8  }
```

PublisherDAO.java

DAO Interface Specifications

Class Name	Package
PublisherDAO	com.sharanamvaishali.dao

Code Spec

```
1  package com.sharanamvaishali.dao;
2
3  import com.sharanamvaishali.model.Publisher;
4  import java.util.List;
5
6  public interface PublisherDAO {
7      public List<Publisher> listOurPublishers();
8  }
```

CategoryDAO.java

DAO Interface Specifications

Class Name	Package
CategoryDAO	com.sharanamvaishali.dao

Code Spec

```
1  package com.sharanamvaishali.dao;
2
3  import com.sharanamvaishali.model.Category;
4  import java.util.List;
5
6  public interface CategoryDAO {
7      public List<Category> listCategory();
8  }
```

SearchDAO.java

DAO Interface Specifications

Class Name	Package
SearchDAO	com.sharanamvaishali.dao

Code Spec

```
1  package com.sharanamvaishali.dao;
2
3  import java.util.List;
4
5  public interface SearchDAO {
6      public List listPopularSearches();
7  }
```

UserDAO.java

DAO Interface Specifications

Class Name	Package
UserDAO	com.sharanamvaishali.dao

Code Spec

```
1  package com.sharanamvaishali.dao;
2
3  import com.sharanamvaishali.model.User;
4  import java.util.List;
5
6  public interface UserDAO {
7      public User getUserByUserName(String userName);
8  }
```

Implementation Class

This is a **Data Access Object** class with the following specifications.

BookDAOImpl.java

DAO Implementation Specifications

Class Name	Package	Implements
BookDAOImpl	com.sharanamvaishali.dao	BookDAO

Objects	
Object Name	**Class Name**
sessionFactory	SessionFactory

Methods		
Method Name	**Arguments**	**Return Values**
listBook()	- -	List <Book>
listNewReleases()	- -	List <Book>
listUpdatedBooks()	- -	List <Book>
listTopTitles()	- -	List <Book>

Code Spec

```
1   package com.sharanamvaishali.dao;
2
3   import com.sharanamvaishali.model.Book;
4   import java.util.List;
5   import org.hibernate.SessionFactory;
6   import org.springframework.beans.factory.annotation.Autowired;
7   import org.springframework.stereotype.Repository;
8
9   @Repository
10  public class BookDAOImpl implements BookDAO {
11      @Autowired
12      private SessionFactory sessionFactory;
13
14      @Override
15      public List<Book> listBook() {
16          return sessionFactory.getCurrentSession().createQuery("from Book").list();
17      }
18
19      @Override
20      public List<Book> listNewReleases() {
21          return sessionFactory.getCurrentSession().createQuery("from Book ORDER BY year
            DESC").setMaxResults(10).list();
22      }
23
24      @Override
25      public List<Book> listUpdatedBooks() {
26          return sessionFactory.getCurrentSession().createQuery("from Book WHERE edition
            <> 'First' ORDER BY year DESC").setMaxResults(10).list();
27      }
28
29      @Override
30      public List<Book> listTopTitles() {
31          return sessionFactory.getCurrentSession().createQuery("from Book ORDER BY hits
            DESC").setMaxResults(10).list();
32      }
33  }
```

Explanation:

The following section describes the above code spec.

listBook()

listBook() does the actual retrieval of the available books.

This method fires a SELECT query that attempts to retrieve records from the Books database table.

All the records that the query retrieves are extracted and returned as a **List** object.

This List object is returned to the calling method i.e. Service Layer's **listBook():**

```
public List<Book> listBook() {
    return bookDAO.listBook();
}
```

This method in turn returns it to the HomeController class's **showHome():**

```
@RequestMapping("/home")
public String showHome(Map<String, Object> map, HttpServletRequest request) {
    map.put("allBooksList", bookService.listBook());
```

Finally, the HomeController returns this List object to the View which renders it.

The JSP i.e. allCategories.jsp [a .jsp file included in home.jsp] on taking charge uses the **iterator** tag to iterate over the contents of the List object **allBooksList**.

```
<c:forEach items="${allBooksList}" var="categoryWiseBooks">
    <c:if test="${categoryWiseBooks.categoryNo == allCategories.categoryNo}">
        <% ctr++;
        if (ctr<4) { %>
        <td width="33%">
            <table align="left" border="0" cellspacing="1" cellpadding="1" width="100%"
            class="allCategoriesTable">
                <tr>
                    <td width="20%">
                        <a href="showBookDetails/${categoryWiseBooks.bookNo}"
                        title="${categoryWiseBooks.synopsis}">
                            <img alt="Cover Page"
                            src="admin/downloadBookPhotograph/${categoryWiseBooks.bookNo}" height="110px"
                            width="80px"/>
                        </a>
```

The allBooksList object holds all those records retrieved by the SQL query.

Each record's column values are extracted using $.

listNewReleases()

listNewReleases() does the actual retrieval of the available newly released books.

This method fires a SELECT query that attempts to retrieve the records from the Books database table.

All the records that the query retrieves are extracted and returned as a **List** object.

This List object is returned to the calling method i.e. Service Layer's **listNewReleases()**:

```
public List<Book> listNewReleases() {
    return bookDAO.listNewReleases();
}
```

This method in turn returns it to the HomeController class's **showHome()**:

```
@RequestMapping("/home")
public String showHome(Map<String, Object> map, HttpServletRequest request) {
    map.put("newReleasesList", bookService.listNewReleases());
```

Finally, the HomeController returns this List object to the View which renders it.

The JSP i.e. leftMenu.jsp [a .jsp file included in home.jsp] on taking charge uses the **iterator** tag to iterate over the contents of the List object **newReleasesList**.

```
<c:forEach items="${newReleasesList}" var="newReleases">
  <tr title="Click to view book details">
    <td class="imagePointer, leftAlign">
      <a href="showBookDetails/${newReleases.bookNo}">
        ${newReleases.bookName}
      </a>
```

The newReleasesList object holds all those records retrieved by the SQL query.

Each record's column values are extracted using $.

listUpdatedBooks()

listUpdatedBooks() does the actual retrieval of the available updated books.

This method fires a SELECT query that attempts to retrieve records from the Books database table.

All the records that the query retrieves are extracted and returned as a **List** object.

This List object is returned to the calling method i.e. Service Layer's **listUpdatedBooks()**:

```
public List<Book> listUpdatedBooks() {
    return bookDAO.listUpdatedBooks();
}
```

This method in turn returns it to the HomeController class's **showHome()**:

```
@RequestMapping("/home")
public String showHome(Map<String, Object> map, HttpServletRequest request) {
    map.put("updatedBooksList", bookService.listUpdatedBooks());
```

Finally, the HomeController returns this List object to the View which renders it.

The JSP i.e. leftMenu.jsp [a .jsp file included in home.jsp] on taking charge uses the **iterator** tag to iterate over the contents of the List object **updatedBooksList**.

```
<c:forEach items="${updatedBooksList}" var="updatedBooks">
    <tr title="Click to view book details">
        <td class="imagePointer, leftAlign">
            <a href="showBookDetails/${updatedBooks.bookNo}">
            ${updatedBooks.bookName}
            </a>
```

The updatedBooksList object holds all those records retrieved by the SQL query.

Each record's column values are extracted using **$**.

listTopTitles()

listTopTitles() does the actual retrieval of the available top titled books.

This method fires a SELECT query that attempts to retrieve records from the Books database table.

All the records that the query retrieves are extracted and returned as a **List** object.

This List object is returned to the calling method i.e. Service Layer's **listTopTitles()**:

```
public List<Book> listTopTitles() {
    return bookDAO.listTopTitles();
}
```

This method in turn returns it to the HomeController class's **showHome()**:

```
@RequestMapping("/home")
public String showHome(Map<String, Object> map, HttpServletRequest request) {
    map.put("topTitlesList", bookService.listTopTitles());
```

Finally, the HomeController returns this List object to the View which renders it.

The JSP i.e. leftMenu.jsp [a .jsp file included in home.jsp] on taking charge uses the **iterator** tag to iterate over the contents of the List object **topTitlesList.**

```
<c:forEach items="${topTitlesList}" var="topTitles">
    <tr title="Click to view book details">
        <td class="imagePointer, leftAlign">
            <a href="showBookDetails/${topTitles.bookNo}">
                ${topTitles.bookName}
            </a>
```

The topTitlesList object holds all those records retrieved by the SQL query.

Each record's column values are extracted using $.

AuthorDAOImpl.java

DAO Implementation Specifications

Class Name	Package	Implements
AuthorDAOImpl	com.sharanamvaishali.dao	AuthorDAO
Objects		
Object Name		Class Name
sessionFactory		SessionFactory
Methods		
Method Name	Arguments	Return Values
listOurAuthors()	- -	List <Author>

Code Spec

```
1  package com.sharanamvaishali.dao;
2
3  import com.sharanamvaishali.model.Author;
4  import java.util.List;
5  import org.hibernate.SessionFactory;
6  import org.springframework.beans.factory.annotation.Autowired;
7  import org.springframework.stereotype.Repository;
8
9  @Repository
10 public class AuthorDAOImpl implements AuthorDAO {
11     @Autowired
12     private SessionFactory sessionFactory;
13
14     @Override
15     public List<Author> listOurAuthors() {
```

```
16        return sessionFactory.getCurrentSession().createQuery("from
          Author").setMaxResults(10).list();
17  }
18 }
```

Explanation:

The following section describes the above code spec.

listOurAuthors()

listOurAuthors() does the actual retrieval of the available authors.

This method fires a SELECT query that attempts to retrieve records from the Authors database table.

All the records that the query retrieves are extracted and returned as a **List** object.

This List object is returned to the calling method i.e. Service Layer's **listOurAuthors()**:

```
public List<Author> listOurAuthors() {
    return authorDAO.listOurAuthors();
}
```

This method in turn returns it to the HomeController class's **showHome()**:

```
@RequestMapping("/home")
public String showHome(Map<String, Object> map, HttpServletRequest request) {
    map.put("ourAuthorsList", authorService.listOurAuthors());
```

Finally, the HomeController returns this List object to the View which renders it.

The JSP i.e. leftMenu.jsp [a .jsp file included in home.jsp] on taking charge uses the **iterator** tag to iterate over the contents of the List object **ourAuthorsList**.

```
<c:forEach items="${ourAuthorsList}" var="ourAuthors">
    <tr title="Click to view author details">
        <td class="imagePointer, leftAlign">
            <a href="showAuthorDetails/${ourAuthors.authorNo}">
            ${ourAuthors.firstName} ${ourAuthors.lastName}
        </a>
```

The ourAuthorsList object holds all those records retrieved by the SQL query.

Each record's column values are extracted using $.

PublisherDAOImpl.java

DAO Implementation Specifications

Class Name	Package	Implements
PublisherDAOImpl	com.sharanamvaishali.dao	PublisherDAO
Objects		
Object Name	**Class Name**	
sessionFactory	SessionFactory	
Methods		
Method Name	**Arguments**	**Return Values**
listOurPublishers()	- -	List <Publisher>

Code Spec

```
1  package com.sharanamvaishali.dao;
2
3  import com.sharanamvaishali.model.Publisher;
4  import java.util.List;
5  import org.hibernate.SessionFactory;
6  import org.springframework.beans.factory.annotation.Autowired;
7  import org.springframework.stereotype.Repository;
8
9  @Repository
10 public class PublisherDAOImpl implements PublisherDAO {
11     @Autowired
12     private SessionFactory sessionFactory;
13
14     @Override
15     public List<Publisher> listOurPublishers() {
16         return sessionFactory.getCurrentSession().createQuery("from
           Publisher").setMaxResults(10).list();
17     }
18 }
```

Explanation:

The following section describes the above code spec.

listOurPublishers()

listOurPublishers() does the actual retrieval of the available publishers.

This method fires a SELECT query that attempts to retrieve records from the Publishers database table.

All the records that the query retrieves are extracted and returned as a **List** object.

This List object is returned to the calling method i.e. Service Layer's **listOurPublishers()**:

```
public List<Publisher> listOurPublishers() {
    return publisherDAO.listOurPublishers();
}
```

This method in turn returns it to the HomeController class's **showHome()**:

```
@RequestMapping("/home")
public String showHome(Map<String, Object> map, HttpServletRequest request) {
    map.put("ourPublishersList", publisherService.listOurPublishers());
```

Finally, the HomeController returns this List object to the View which renders it.

The JSP i.e. leftMenu.jsp [a .jsp file included in home.jsp] on taking charge uses the **iterator** tag to iterate over the contents of the List object **ourPublishersList**.

```
<c:forEach items="${ourPublishersList}" var="ourPublishers">
    <tr title="Click to view publisher details">
        <td class="imagePointer, leftAlign">
            <a href="showPublisherDetails/${ourPublishers.publisherNo}">
                ${ourPublishers.publisherName}
            </a>
```

The ourPublishersList object holds all those records retrieved by the SQL query.

Each record's column values are extracted using $.

CategoryDAOImpl.java

DAO Implementation Specifications

Class Name	Package	Implements
CategoryDAOImpl	com.sharanamvaishali.dao	CategoryDAO
Objects		
Object Name	**Class Name**	
sessionFactory	SessionFactory	
Methods		
Method Name	**Arguments**	**Return Values**
listCategory()	- -	List <Category>

Code Spec

```
1  package com.sharanamvaishali.dao;
2
3  import com.sharanamvaishali.model.Category;
```

```
 4  import java.util.List;
 5  import org.hibernate.SessionFactory;
 6  import org.springframework.beans.factory.annotation.Autowired;
 7  import org.springframework.stereotype.Repository;
 8
 9  @Repository
10  public class CategoryDAOImpl implements CategoryDAO {
11      @Autowired
12      private SessionFactory sessionFactory;
13
14      @Override
15      public List<Category> listCategory() {
16          return sessionFactory.getCurrentSession().createQuery("from Category ORDER BY
            category").list();
17      }
18  }
```

Explanation:

The following section describes the above code spec.

listCategory()

listCategory() does the actual retrieval of the available categories.

This method fires a SELECT query that attempts to retrieve records from the Categories database table.

All the records that the query retrieves are extracted and returned as a **List** object.

This List object is returned to the calling method i.e. Service Layer's **listCategory()**:

```
public List<Category> listCategory() {
    return categoryDAO.listCategory();
}
```

This method in turn returns it to the HomeController class's **showHome()**:

```
@RequestMapping("/home")
public String showHome(Map<String, Object> map, HttpServletRequest request) {
    map.put("allCategoriesList", categoryService.listCategory());
```

Finally, the HomeController returns this List object to the View which renders it.

The JSP i.e. allCategories.jsp [a .jsp file included in home.jsp] on taking charge uses the **iterator** tag to iterate over the contents of the List object **allCategoriesList**.

```
<c:forEach items="${allCategoriesList}" var="allCategories">
    <table id="portlets-content-main" align="center" border="0" cellspacing="1"
    cellpadding="1" width="100%" class="allCategoriesTable">
        <tr>
            <td class="categoriesNames">
                <a href="showCategoryDetails/${allCategories.categoryNo}"
                title="${allCategories.description}" >
                    ${allCategories.category}
            </a>
```

The allCategoriesList object holds all those records retrieved by the SQL query.

Each record's column values are extracted using $.

SearchDAOImpl.java

DAO Implementation Specifications

Class Name	Package	Implements
SearchDAOImpl	com.sharanamvaishali.dao	SearchDAO

Objects	
Object Name	**Class Name**
sessionFactory	SessionFactory

Methods		
Method Name	**Arguments**	**Return Values**
listPopularSearches()	- -	List

Code Spec

```
1   package com.sharanamvaishali.dao;
2
3   import java.util.List;
4   import org.hibernate.SessionFactory;
5   import org.springframework.beans.factory.annotation.Autowired;
6   import org.springframework.stereotype.Repository;
7
8   @Repository
9   public class SearchDAOImpl implements SearchDAO {
10      @Autowired
11      private SessionFactory sessionFactory;
12
13      @Override
14      public List listPopularSearches() {
15          return sessionFactory.getCurrentSession().createSQLQuery("SELECT Value,
            COUNT(*) AS Weight FROM PopularSearches GROUP BY Value").list();
```

```
16    }
17 }
```

Explanation:

The following section describes the above code spec.

listPopularSearches()

listPopularsearches() does the actual retrieval of the available popular searches.

This method fires an SELECT query that attempts to retrieve records from the PopularSearches database table.

All the records that the query retrieves are extracted and returned as a **List** object.

This List object is returned to the calling method i.e. Service Layer's **listPopularSearches():**

```
public List listPopularSearches() {
    return searchDAO.listPopularSearches();
}
```

This method in turn returns it to the HomeController class's **showHome():**

```
@RequestMapping("/home")
public String showHome(Map<String, Object> map, HttpServletRequest request) {
    map.put("popularSearchList", searchService.listPopularSearches());
```

Finally, the HomeController returns this List object to the View which renders it.

The JSP i.e. popularSearches.jsp [a .jsp file included in home.jsp] on taking charge uses the **iterator** tag to iterate over the contents of the List object **popularSearchList**.

```
<c:forEach items="${popularSearchList}" var="popularSearch">
    <c:if test="${popularSearch[1]>=1 && popularSearch[1]<5}">
        <a href="searchResults/${popularSearch[0]}" class="popularSearch1"
        title="Click to search for ${popularSearch[0]}">
            ${popularSearch[0]}
        </a>
```

The popularSearchList object holds all those records retrieved by the SQL query.

Each record's column values are extracted using $.

UserDAOImpl.java

DAO Implementation Specifications

Class Name	Package	Implements
UserDAOImpl	com.sharanamvaishali.dao	UserDAO

Objects	
Object Name	**Class Name**
sessionFactory	SessionFactory

Methods		
Method Name	**Arguments**	**Return Values**
getUserByUserName()	String userName	User

Code Spec

```
1  package com.sharanamvaishali.dao;
2
3  import com.sharanamvaishali.model.User;
4  import org.hibernate.Query;
5  import org.hibernate.SessionFactory;
6  import org.springframework.beans.factory.annotation.Autowired;
7  import org.springframework.stereotype.Repository;
8
9  @Repository
10 public class UserDAOImpl implements UserDAO {
11     @Autowired
12     private SessionFactory sessionFactory;
13
14     @Override
15     public User getUserByUserName(String userName) {
16         Query query = sessionFactory.getCurrentSession().createQuery("from User WHERE
           userName = :UserName");
17         query.setString("UserName", userName);
18         return (User) query.uniqueResult();
19     }
20 }
```

Explanation:

The following section describes the above code spec.

getUserByUsername()

getUserByUsername() returns the appropriate user's object from the Users database table using **Username** as the reference.

This method uses **get()** of SessionFactory, which returns the appropriate Country from Countries database table.

This method uses:

❏ **setString()** of Query, which sets the value of userName received from the user as the query parameter

❏ **uniqueResult()** of Query, which returns a single instance that matches the query from the Users database table

REMINDER

Search.java [the model class] is explained in the *Chapter 45: Search Results*.

User.java [the model class] is explained in the *Chapter 37: Manage Users*.

Book.java [the model class] is explained in the *Chapter 36: Manage Books*.

Publisher.java [the model class] is explained in the *Chapter 34: Manage Publishers*.

Category.java [the model class] is explained in the *Chapter 33: Manage Categories*.

Author.java [the model class] is explained in the *Chapter 35: Manage Authors*.

Spring Security [spring-security.xml]

The login form embedded in the home page also uses Spring Security file similar to the Administration Login form.

Code Spec

```
1   <beans:beans xmlns="http://www.springframework.org/schema/security"
2      xmlns:beans="http://www.springframework.org/schema/beans"
3      xmlns:xsi="http://www.w3.org/2001/XMLSchema-instance"
4      xsi:schemaLocation="http://www.springframework.org/schema/beans
5      http://www.springframework.org/schema/beans/spring-beans-3.1.xsd
6      http://www.springframework.org/schema/security
7      http://www.springframework.org/schema/security/spring-security-3.1.xsd">
8      <http auto-config="true" use-expressions="true">
9         <form-login login-page="/login" login-processing-url="/j_spring_security_check"
           default-target-url="/home" authentication-failure-url="/loginFailed" />
10        <logout logout-url="/j_spring_security_logout" logout-success-url="/home" />
11     </http>
12     <authentication-manager>
```

```
13        <authentication-provider>
14            <jdbc-user-service data-source-ref="dataSource"
15            users-by-username-query="select username, password, enabled from Users
              where username=?"
16  ·         authorities-by-username-query="select username, authority from Users where
              username=?" />
17        </authentication-provider>
18     </authentication-manager>
19  </beans:beans>
```

Explanation:

The following section describes the above code spec.

use-expressions Attribute Of <http>

The use-expressions attribute when set to true, enables EL-expressions.

login-page Attribute Of <form-login>

login-page indicates that the login form resides at **/login**. This is ultimately handled by a Spring MVC controller, which holds a method with an appropriate request mapping.

authentication-failure-url Attribute Of <form-login>

Likewise, if authentication fails, **authentication-failure-url** is set to send the user back to the same administration login page.

login-processing-url Attribute Of <form-login>

login-processing-url is set to **/j_spring_security_check**, which indicates the URL to which the login form will submit back to authenticate the user.

default-target-url Attribute Of <form-login>

default-target-url is set to **/home**, which indicates the URL to which the user will be send to if the authentication is valid.

logout-url Attribute Of <logout>

logout-url is internally mapped to **/j_spring_security_logout**, which indicates the URL to invalidate a user session.

logout-success-url Attribute Of <logout>

logout-success-url is set to /home, which indicates the URL to which the user is sent to, on a successful logout.

Chapter

41

SECTION VI: FRONTEND [CUSTOMER FACING] SOFTWARE DESIGN DOCUMENTATION

Book Details

This module allows viewing the details of the book. This page is invoked when a user clicks a book name or the book image from the frontend.

This module uses the bms.Books table to retrieve that particular book's data.

This module is made up of the following:

Type	Name	Description
JSP	showBookDetails.jsp	The details of a particular book.
Spring		
Controller	HomeController.java	The controller class that facilitates data operations.
	BookController.java	
Service Class	BookService.java	The interfaces for the service layer.
	UserSerice.java	

Spring		
Service Class	BookServiceImpl.java	The implementation classes for the service layer.
	UserServiceImpl.java	
DAO Class	BookDAO.java	The interfaces for the DAO layer.
	UserDAO.java	
	BookDAOImpl.java	The implementation classes that perform the actual data operations.
	UserDAOImpl.java	
DispatcherServlet	bookshopdispatcher-servlet.xml	Central dispatcher for HTTP request handlers/controllers.
Hibernate		
Mapping	hibernate.cfg.xml	The mapping file that holds Model class mapping.
Model Class	Book.java	The model classes.
	User.java	

JSP [showBookDetails.jsp]

Book Details Without Logging In

A link identified by a book name in one of these sections when clicked, displays book details of the selected book, as shown in diagram 41.1.

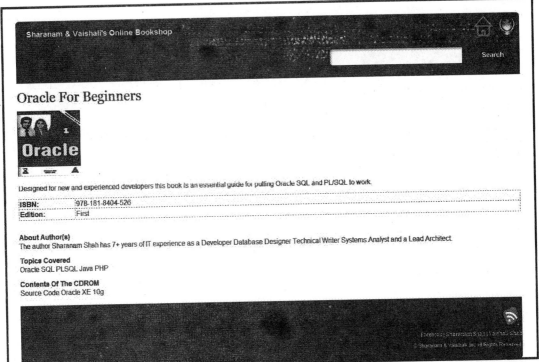

Diagram 41.1: Book Details page [without logged in]

Book Details After Logging In

If the customer has logged in and is viewing the book details page, then the page appears with additional options that allow adding the book to the cart, downloading sample chapters and TOC, as shown in diagram 41.2.

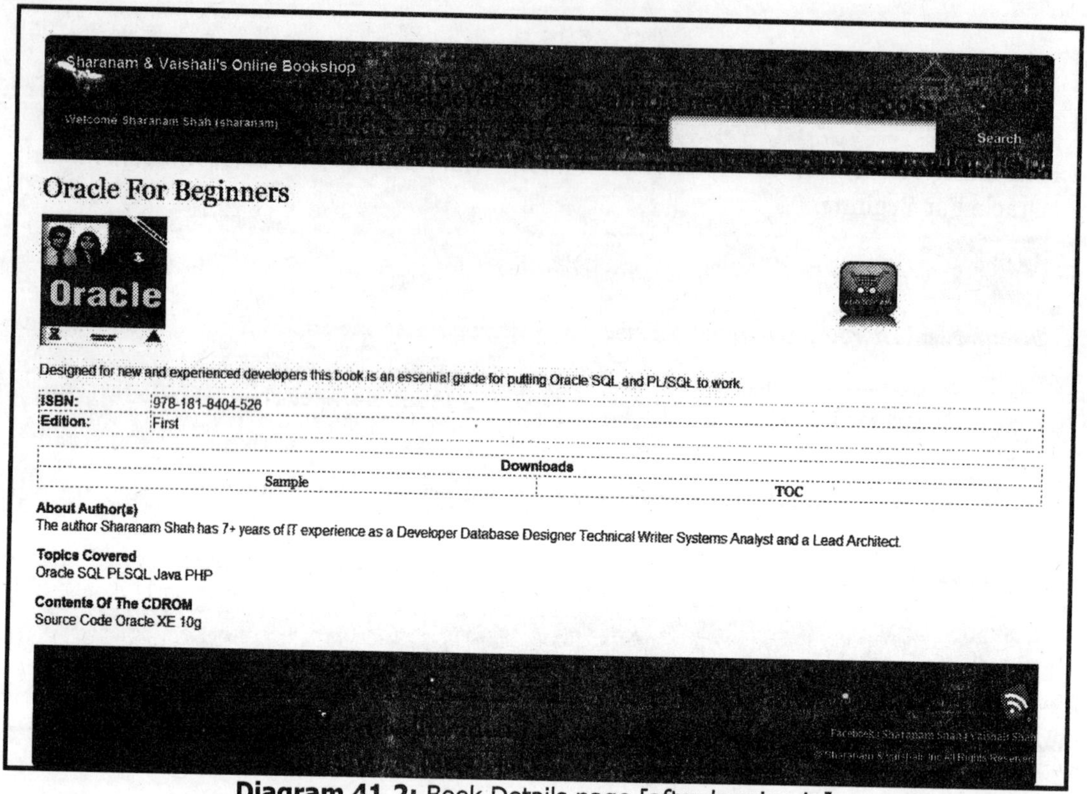

Diagram 41.2: Book Details page [after logging in]

Form Specifications

File Name	showBookDetails.jsp
Title	${bookList.bookName}

Code Spec

```
1    <%@page contentType="text/html" pageEncoding="UTF-8"%>
2    <%@taglib prefix="sec" uri="http://www.springframework.org/security/tags" %>
3    <!DOCTYPE HTML PUBLIC "-//W3C//DTD HTML 4.01 Transitional//EN"
4      "http://www.w3.org/TR/html4/loose.dtd">
5    <html>
6      <head>
7        <meta http-equiv="Content-Type" content="text/html; charset=UTF-8">
8        <title>${bookList.bookName}</title>
9        <link rel="stylesheet" href="/BookShop/css/frontend.css" type="text/css">
10     </head>
11     <body>
```

```
12    <%@ include file="/WEB-INF/jsp/header.jsp" %>
13    <div id="bodyDiv">
14        <table border="0" width="100%" cellspacing="0" cellpadding="0">
15            <tr>
16                <td colspan="2" align="left" class="topAlign">
17                    <br />
18                    <span class="spanShowDetails">${bookList.bookName}</span>
19                    <br />
20                    <br />
21                </td>
22            </tr>
23            <tr>
24                <td align="left" class="topAlign">
25                    <img
                    src="/BookShop/admIn/downloadBookPhotograph/${bookList.bookNo
                    }" height="150px" width="150px"/>
26                </td>
27                <td align="center">
28                    <sec:authorize access="isAuthenticated()">
29                        <a href="/BookShop/addToCart/<sec:authentication
                        property='principal.username' />/${bookList.bookNo}">
30                            <img src="/BookShop/images/addToCart.jpg" width="74px"
                            height="74px" class="imagePointer" border="0"/>
31                        </a> 
32                    </sec:authorize>
33                </td>
34            </tr>
35            <tr>
36                <td align="left" class="content" colspan="2"><br
                />${bookList.synopsis}</td>
37            </tr>
38            <tr><td colspan="2"> </td></tr>
39            <tr>
40                <td align="left" colspan="2">
41                    <table border="0" cellspacing="2" cellpadding="0" width="100%"
                    style="border: 1px dashed #0099ff;">
42                        <tr>
43                            <td class="label" width="10%" align="left"
                            style="border-right: 1px dashed #0099ff; border-bottom: 1px
                            dashed #0099ff;">ISBN: </td>
44                            <td valign="top" class="content" colspan="2" width="80%"
                            style="border-bottom: 1px dashed
                            #0099ff;">${bookList.isbn}</td>
45                        </tr>
46                        <tr>
47                            <td class="label" width="10%" align="left"
                            style="border-right: 1px dashed
                            #0099ff;">Edition: </td>
48                            <td valign="top" class="content" colspan="2"
                            width="80%">${bookList.edition}</td>
49                        </tr>
50                    </table>
51                    <br>
```

```
52              <sec:authorize access="isAuthenticated()">
53                  <table border="0" cellspacing="2" cellpadding="0" width="100%"
                    style="border: 1px dashed #0099ff;">
54                      <tr>
55                          <td class="label" colspan="3" width="20%" align="center"
                            style="border-bottom: 1px dashed
                            #0099ff;">Downloads</td>
56                      </tr>
57                      <tr>
58                          <td valign="top" colspan="2" class="content" width="50%"
                            align="center" style="border-right: 1px dashed #0099ff;">
59                              <a
                            href="/BookShop/admin/downloadBookSampleChapter/${
                            bookList.bookNo}">Sample</a>
60                          </td>
61                          <td valign="top" class="content" width="50%"
                            align="center">
62                              <a
                            href="/BookShop/admin/downloadBookTOC/${bookList.bo
                            okNo}">TOC</a>
63                          </td>
64                      </tr>
65                  </table>
66              </sec:authorize>
67          </td>
68      </tr>
69      <tr><td colspan="2"> </td></tr>
70      <tr>
71          <td colspan="2">
72              <table width="100%" border="0" cellspacing="0" cellpadding="0"
                align="center">
73                  <tr>
74                      <td class="label" align="left">About Author(s)</td>
75                  </tr>
76                  <tr>
77                      <td class="content"
                        align="left">${bookList.aboutAuthors}</td>
78                  </tr>
79              </table>
80          </td>
81      </tr>
82      <tr><td colspan="2"> </td></tr>
83      <tr>
84          <td colspan="2">
85              <table width="100%" border="0" cellspacing="0" cellpadding="0"
                align="center">
86                  <tr>
87                      <td class="label" align="left">Topics Covered</td>
88                  </tr>
89                  <tr>
90                      <td class="content"
                        align="left">${bookList.topicsCovered}</td>
91                  </tr>
92              </table>
```

```
93              </td>
94            </tr>
95            <tr><td colspan="2"> </td></tr>
96            <tr>
97              <td colspan="2">
98                <table width="100%" border="0" cellspacing="0" cellpadding="0"
                  align="center">
99                  <tr>
100                   <td class="label" align="left">Contents Of The CDROM</td>
101                 </tr>
102                 <tr>
103                   <td class="content"
                      align="left">${bookList.contentsCDROM}</td>
104                 </tr>
105               </table>
106             </td>
107           </tr>
108         </table>
109         <%@ include file="/WEB-INF/jsp/footer.jsp" %>
110       </div>
111     </body>
112 </html>
```

Explanation:

The JSP displays the details of the book.

Whilst populating the book details in JSP, the system checks if the user has logged in. Only if the user has logged in, additional links to the following are displayed:

❑   Add To Cart

❑   TOC and Sample Chapter download

Controller [HomeController.java]

This is a controller class with the following specifications.

Controller Specifications

Class Name	Package	
HomeController	com.sharanamvaishali.controllers	
Objects		
Object Name	Class Name	Object Type
userService	UserService	Service Layer
bookService	BookService	Service Layer

Methods	
Method Name	Request Mapping
showBookDetails()	/showBookDetails/${bookNo}

Code Spec

```
1   package com.sharanamvaishali.controllers;
2
3   import com.sharanamvaishali.model.Search;
4   import com.sharanamvaishali.service.BookService;
5   import java.util.Map;
6   import org.springframework.beans.factory.annotation.Autowired;
7   import org.springframework.security.core.context.SecurityContextHolder;
8   import org.springframework.stereotype.Controller;
9   import org.springframework.web.bind.annotation.PathVariable;
10  import org.springframework.web.bind.annotation.RequestMapping;
11
12  @Controller
13  public class HomeController {
14      @Autowired
15      private UserService userService;
16
17      @Autowired
18      private BookService bookService;
19
20      @RequestMapping("/showBookDetails/{bookNo}")
21      public String showBookDetails(Map<String, Object> map, @PathVariable("bookNo")
        int bookNo) {
22          map.put("bookList", bookService.getBookById(bookNo));
23          bookService.updateHits(bookNo);
24          map.put("search", new Search());
25          if(SecurityContextHolder.getContext().getAuthentication().isAuthenticated()) {
26              map.put("userDetails",
                userService.getUserByUsername(SecurityContextHolder.getContext().getAuthen
                tication().getName()));
27          }
28          return "showBookDetails";
29      }
30  }
```

Explanation:

The following section describes the above code spec.

showBookDetails()

showBookDetails() is invoked for every book hyperlink in the following sections of **home.jsp**:

❑   New Releases

- ❏ Update Books
- ❏ Top Titles
- ❏ Books available under each Category

showBookDetails():

- ❏ Retrieves the appropriate Book's details using **BookNo** as the reference. It calls BookService class's **getBookById()** which returns the details of the book as a Book object. **BookNo** is made available through **@PathVariable** [in the list of Book rendered by the View] when the user clicks /showBookDetails/${bookNo} to view a particular book details. This data is made available to the view using Map's **put()**
- ❏ Updates the Book object's Hits column by calling BookService's **updateHits()**, based on which the Top Titles section on the homepage is served
- ❏ Initializes the search form as the search form is a part of the view
- ❏ Populates the userDetails object with the username of the logged in user. This is only done, if the user has logged in. This object is used to show the welcome message after the user has logged in
- ❏ Returns the control to the View along with the data to be populated in the browser. The data that is retrieved is made available using Map's **put()**

REMINDER

BookController's **downloadBookPhotograph()** is explained in the *Chapter 36: Manage Books*, which is used to display the cover page of the book.

Service Class

Interface [BookService.java]

This is a service interface with the following specifications.

Service Interface Specifications

Class Name	Package
BookService	com.sharanamvaishali.service

Code Spec

```
1  package com.sharanamvaishali.service;
2
```

```
3  public interface BookService {
4      public void updateHits(Integer bookNo);
5  }
```

Implementation Class [BookServiceImpl.java]

This is a service class with the following specifications.

Service Implementation Specifications

Class Name	Package	Implements
BookServiceImpl	com.sharanamvaishali.service	BookService
Objects		
Object Name	Class Name	Object Type
bookDAO	BookDAO	Data Access Object Layer
Methods		
Method Name	Arguments	
getBookById()	Integer bookNo	
updateHits()	Integer bookNo	

Code Spec

```
1  package com.sharanamvaishali.service;
2
3  import com.sharanamvaishali.dao.BookDAO;
4  import org.springframework.beans.factory.annotation.Autowired;
5  import org.springframework.stereotype.Service;
6  import org.springframework.transaction.annotation.Transactional;
7
8  @Service
9  public class BookServiceImpl implements BookService {
10     @Autowired
11     private BookDAO bookDAO;
12
13     @Transactional
14     @Override
15     public void updateHits(Integer bookNo) {
16         bookDAO.updateHits(bookNo);
17     }
18 }
```

Explanation:

The following section describes the above code spec.

REMINDER

> BookService's **getBookById()** is explained in the *Chapter 36: Manage Books,* which retrieves the book details based on BookNo.

updateHits()

updateHits() holds the business logic to update the Hits column of the Book object whenever a book is clicked for viewing its details.

This method in turn invokes the DAO Layer's [BookDAO] **updateHits()**.

REMINDER

> UserService's **getUserByUsername()** is explained in the *Chapter 40: Home Page*, which retrieves the user who has logged in.

DAO Class

Interface [BookDAO.java]

This is a Data Access Object interface with the following specifications.

DAO Interface Specifications

Class Name	Package
BookDAO	com.sharanamvaishali.dao

Code Spec

```
1  package com.sharanamvaishali.dao;
2
3  public interface BookDAO {
4      public void updateHits(Integer bookNo);
5  }
```

Implementation Class [BookDAOImpl.java]

This is a **Data Access Object** class with the following specifications.

DAO Implementation Specifications

Class Name	Package	Implements
BookDAOImpl	com.sharanamvaishali.dao	BookDAO

Objects	
Object Name	Class Name
sessionFactory	SessionFactory
bookService	BookService

Methods		
Method Name	Arguments	Return Values
getBookById()	Integer bookNo	Book
updateHits()	Integer bookNo	Void

Code Spec

```
1  package com.sharanamvaishali.dao;
2
3  import com.sharanamvaishali.model.Book;
4  import com.sharanamvaishali.service.BookService;
5  import org.hibernate.SessionFactory;
6  import org.springframework.beans.factory.annotation.Autowired;
7  import org.springframework.stereotype.Repository;
8
9  @Repository
10 public class BookDAOImpl implements BookDAO {
11     @Autowired
12     private SessionFactory sessionFactory;
13
14     @Autowired
15     private BookService bookService;
16
17     @Override
18     public void updateHits(Integer bookNo) {
19         Book book = bookService.getBookById(bookNo);
20         book.setHits(book.getHits()+1);
21         sessionFactory.getCurrentSession().merge(book);
22     }
23 }
```

Explanation:

The following section describes the above code spec.

REMINDER

 BookDAO's **getBookById()** is explained in the *Chapter 36: Manage Books*, which retrieves the book details based on BookNo.

updateHits()

updateHits() updates the Hits column of the appropriate Book's object from the Books database table using BookNo as the reference.

This method uses **merge()** of SessionFactory, which takes care of adding as well as updating the book details.

REMINDER

UserDAO's **getUserByUsername()** is explained in the *Chapter 40: Home Page*, which retrieves the user who has logged in.

REMINDER

Search.java [the model class] is explained in the *Chapter 45: Search Results*.
User.java [the model class] is explained in the *Chapter 37: Manage Users*.
Book.java [the model class] is explained in the *Chapter 36: Manage Books*.

Chapter

42

SECTION VI: FRONTEND [CUSTOMER FACING] SOFTWARE DESIGN DOCUMENTATION

Author Details

This module allows viewing the details of the author and the books written by that particular author along with its details. This page is invoked when a user clicks the author name from the frontend.

This module uses bms.Authors table to retrieve that particular author's data and bms.Books table to retrieve the books written by that author.

This module is made up of the following:

Type	Name	Description
JSP	showAuthorDetails.jsp	The details of a particular author along with the book details written by that particular author.

Spring		
Controller	HomeController.java	The controller class that facilitates data operations.
	AuthorController.java	
	BookController.java	
Service Class	AuthorService.java	The interfaces for the service layer.
	UserSerice.java	
	BookService.java	
	AuthorServiceImpl.java	The implementation classes for the service layer.
	UserServiceImpl.java	
	BookServiceImpl.java	
DAO Class	AuthorDAO.java	The interfaces for the DAO layer.
	UserDAO.java	
	BookDAO.java	
	AuthorDAOImpl.java	The implementation classes that perform the actual data operations.
	UserDAOImpl.java	
	BookDAOImpl.java	
DispatcherServlet	bookshopdispatcher-servlet.xml	Central dispatcher for HTTP request handlers/controllers.
Hibernate		
Mapping	hibernate.cfg.xml	The mapping file that holds Model class mapping.
Model Class	Author.java	The model classes.
	User.java	
	Search.java	
	Book.java	

JSP [showAuthorDetails.jsp]

Author Details Without Logging In

A link identified by an author name in the section **Our Authors** when clicked, displays author details of the selected author, as shown in diagram 42.1.

Diagram 42.1: Author Details page

Author Details After Logging In

This page shows the Add to cart link for every book written by that particular author, as shown in diagram 42.2, for the logged in users.

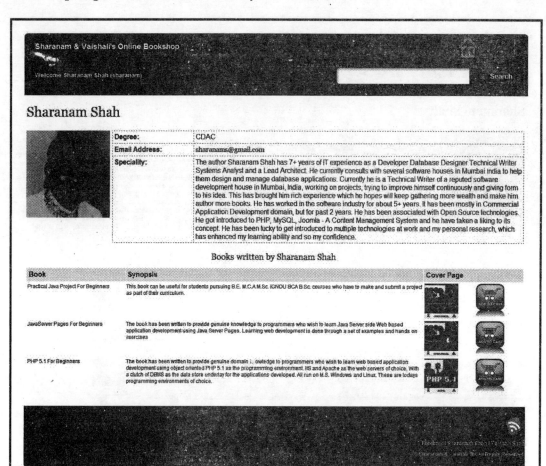

Diagram 42.2: Author Details page [Logged in user]

Clicking an entry from the list displays that book's details [explained in the *Chapter 41: Book Details*].

Form Specifications

File Name	showAuthorDetails.jsp
Title	${authorList.firstName} ${authorList.lastName}'s Profile

Code Spec

```
1  <%@page contentType="text/html" pageEncoding="UTF-8"%>
2  <%@taglib uri="http://java.sun.com/jsp/jstl/core" prefix="c"%>
3  <%@taglib prefix="sec" uri="http://www.springframework.org/security/tags" %>
```

```
4   <!DOCTYPE HTML PUBLIC "-//W3C//DTD HTML 4.01 Transitional//EN"
5     "http://www.w3.org/TR/html4/loose.dtd">
6   <html>
7     <head>
8       <meta http-equiv="Content-Type" content="text/html; charset=UTF-8">
9       <title>${authorList.firstName} ${authorList.lastName}'s Profile</title>
10      <link rel="stylesheet" href="/BookShop/css/frontend.css" type="text/css">
11    </head>
12    <body>
13      <%@ include file="/WEB-INF/jsp/header.jsp" %>
14      <div id="bodyDiv">
15        <table width="100%" border="0" cellspacing="4" cellpadding="1">
16          <tr>
17            <td colspan="2" align="left" class="topAlign">
18              <br />
19              <span class="spanShowDetails">${authorList.firstName}
                   ${authorList.lastName}</span>
20            </td>
21          </tr>
22          <tr><td colspan="2"> </td></tr>
23          <tr>
24            <td align="left" class="topAlign">
25              <img
                   src="/BookShop/admin/downloadAuthorPhotograph/${authorList.autho
                   rNo}" height="200px" width="200px"/>
26            </td>
27            <td align="left" class="topAlign">
28              <table cellspacing="0" border="0" cellpadding="4" width="100%"
                   style="border:1px dashed #0099ff;">
29                <tr>
30                  <td class="label" width="20%" align="left"
                       style="border-right:1px dashed #0099ff; border-bottom:1px
                       dashed #0099ff;">
31                    Degree: 
32                  </td>
33                  <td class="content" valign="top" width="80%"
                       style="border-bottom:1px dashed #0099ff;">
34                    ${authorList.degree}
35                  </td>
36                </tr>
37                <tr>
38                  <td class="label" width="20%" align="left"
                       style="border-right:1px dashed #0099ff; border-bottom:1px
                       dashed #0099ff;">
39                    Email Address: 
40                  </td>
41                  <td class="content" valign="top" width="80%"
                       style="border-bottom:1px dashed #0099ff;">
42                    <a href='mailto:${authorList.emailAddress}'>
43                      ${authorList.emailAddress}
44                    </a>
45                  </td>
46                </tr>
47                <tr>
```

```
48          <td class="label" width="20%" valign="top" align="left"
            style="border-right:1px dashed #0099ff;">
49             Speciality: 
50          </td>
51          <td class="content" valign="top" width="80%">
52             ${authorList.speciality}
53          </td>
54       </tr>
55    </table>
56  </td>
57  </tr>
58  <tr>
59    <td colspan="2">
60       <br><center>
61       <span style="font:20px/22px Georgia, serif; text-align:center;
         width:300px; color:#990000; height:37px;">Books written by
         ${authorList.firstName} ${authorList.lastName}</span>
62       </center><br>
63          <table class="view" align="center" cellspacing="0" cellpadding="6"
            width="100%">
64             <tr>
65                <th width="20%" class="label" align="left">Book</th>
66                <th width="60%" class="label" align="left">Synopsis</th>
67                <th width="10%" class="label" align="left">Cover
                  Page</th>
68                <th width="10%" class="label" align="left"> </th>
69             </tr>
70          <c:forEach items="${bookList}" var="book">
71             <tr title="Click to view">
72                <td width="20%" class="showBookList"
                  onclick="javascript:location.href='/BookShop/showBookDetail
                  s/${book.bookNo}'">
73                   ${book.bookName}
74                </td>
75                <td width="60%" class="showBookList"
                  onclick="javascript:location.href='/BookShop/showBookDetail
                  s/${book.bookNo}'">
76                   ${book.synopsis}
77                </td>
78                <td width="10%" class="showBookList"
                  onclick="javascript:location.href='/BookShop/showBookDetail
                  s/${book.bookNo}'">
79                   <img
                     src="../admin/downloadBookPhotograph/${book.bookNo}"
                     height="80px" width="80px"/>
80                </td>
81                <td width="10%" class="showBookList">
82                   <sec:authorize access="isAuthenticated()">
83                      <a href="/BookShop/addToCart/<sec:authentication
                        property='principal.username' />/${book.bookNo}">
84                         <img src="/BookShop/images/addToCart.jpg"
                           width="74px" height="74px" style="cursor:pointer;"
                           border="0"/>
85                      </a> 
```

```
86                          </sec:authorize>
87                        </td>
88                      </tr>
89                    </c:forEach>
90                  </table>
91                </td>
92              </tr>
93            </table>
94            <%@ include file="/WEB-INF/jsp/footer.jsp" %>
95          </div>
96        </body>
97    </html>
```

Explanation:

The JSP displays the details of the author and books written by that author.

Whilst populating these details in JSP, the system checks if the user has logged in. Only if the user has logged in, the additional link i.e. Add To Cart is displayed.

Controller [HomeController.java]

This is a controller class with the following specifications.

Controller Specifications

Class Name	Package	
HomeController	com.sharanamvaishali.controllers	
Objects		
Object Name	Class Name	Object Type
userService	UserService	Service Layer
authorService	AuthorService	Service Layer
Methods		
Method Name	Request Mapping	
showAuthorDetails()	/showBookDetails/${bookNo}	

Code Spec

```
1   package com.sharanamvaishali.controllers;
2
3   import com.sharanamvaishali.model.Search;
4   import com.sharanamvaishali.service.*;
5   import java.util.Map;
```

```
 6  import org.springframework.beans.factory.annotation.Autowired;
 7  import org.springframework.security.core.context.SecurityContextHolder;
 8  import org.springframework.stereotype.Controller;
 9  import org.springframework.web.bind.annotation.PathVariable;
10  import org.springframework.web.bind.annotation.RequestMapping;
11
12  @Controller
13  public class HomeController {
14      @Autowired
15      private UserService userService;
16
17      @Autowired
18      private AuthorService authorService;
19
20      @RequestMapping("/showAuthorDetails/{authorNo}")
21      public String showAuthorDetails(Map<String, Object> map,
        @PathVariable("authorNo") Integer authorNo) {
22          map.put("authorList", authorService.getAuthorById(authorNo));
23          map.put("bookList", authorService.getAllBooksByAuthor(authorNo));
24          map.put("search", new Search());
25          if(SecurityContextHolder.getContext().getAuthentication().isAuthenticated()) {
26              map.put("userDetails",
                userService.getUserByUsername(SecurityContextHolder.getContext().getAuthen
                tication().getName()));
27          }
28          return "showAuthorDetails";
29      }
30  }
```

Explanation:

The following section describes the above code spec.

showAuthorDetails()

showAuthorDetails() is invoked for every author hyperlink in the **Our Authors** section of **home.jsp**.

showAuthorDetails():

❑ Retrieves the appropriate Author's details using **AuthorNo** as the reference. It calls AuthorService's **getAuthorById()** which returns the details of the author as an Author object. **AuthorNo** is made available through @PathVariable [in the list of Authors rendered by the View] when the user clicks /showAuthorDetails/${authorNo} to view a particular author details. This data is made available to the view using Map's **put()**

❑ Retrieves the books using **AuthorNo** as the reference. It calls AuthorService's **getAllBooksByAuthor()** which returns the books for that particular author as a Book List object. **AuthorNo** is made available through **@PathVariable** [in the list of Authors rendered by the View] when the user clicks /showAuthorDetails/${authorNo} to view a particular author's details

❑ Initializes the search form as the search form is a part of the view

❑ Populates the userDetails object with the username of the logged in user. This is only done, if the user has logged in. This object is used to show the welcome message after the user has logged in

❑ Returns the control to the View along with the data to be populated in the browser. The data that is retrieved is made available using Map's **put()**

REMINDER

AuthorController's **downloadAuthorPhotograph()** is explained in the *Chapter 35: Manage Authors*, which is used to display the photograph of the author.

BookController's **downloadBookPhotograph()** is explained in the *Chapter 36: Manage Books*, which is used to display the cover page of the book written by that particular author.

Service Class

Interface [AuthorService.java]

This is a service interface with the following specifications.

Service Interface Specifications

Class Name	Package
AuthorService	com.sharanamvaishali.service

Code Spec

```
1  package com.sharanamvaishali.service;
2
3  import com.sharanamvaishali.model.Book;
4  import java.util.List;
5
6  public interface AuthorService {
7      public List<Book> getAllBooksByAuthor(Integer authorNo);
8  }
```

Implementation Class [BookServiceImpl.java]

This is a service class with the following specifications.

Service Implementation Specifications

Class Name	Package	Implements
AuthorServiceImpl	com.sharanamvaishali.service	AuthorService

Objects		
Object Name	**Class Name**	**Object Type**
authorDAO	AuthorDAO	Data Access Object Layer

Methods	
Method Name	**Arguments**
getAuthorById()	Integer authorNo
getAllBooksByAuthor()	Integer authorNo

Code Spec

```
1  package com.sharanamvaishali.service;
2
3  import com.sharanamvaishali.dao.AuthorDAO;
4  import com.sharanamvaishali.model.Book;
5  import java.util.List;
6  import org.springframework.beans.factory.annotation.Autowired;
7  import org.springframework.stereotype.Service;
8  import org.springframework.transaction.annotation.Transactional;
9
10 @Service
11 public class AuthorServiceImpl implements AuthorService {
12     @Autowired
13     private AuthorDAO authorDAO;
14
15     @Transactional
16     @Override
17     public List<Book> getAllBooksByAuthor(Integer authorNo) {
18         return authorDAO.getAllBooksByAuthor(authorNo);
19     }
20 }
```

Explanation:

The following section describes the above code spec.

REMINDER

 AuthorService's **getAuthorById()** is explained in the *Chapter 35: Manage Authors*, which retrieves the author details based on AuthorNo.

getAllBooksByAuthor()

getAllBooksByAuthor() holds the business logic to retrieve the books of a particular author.

This method in turn invokes the DAO Layer's [AuthorDAO] **getAllBooksByAuthor()**.

REMINDER

UserService's **getUserByUsername()** is explained in the *Chapter 40: Home Page*, which retrieves the details of the logged in user.

BookService's **getBookById()** is explained in the *Chapter 36: Manage Books*, which is called by BookController's downloadBookPhotograph().

DAO Class

Interface [AuthorDAO.java]

This is a Data Access Object interface with the following specifications.

DAO Interface Specifications

Class Name	Package
AuthorDAO	com.sharanamvaishali.dao

Code Spec

```
1  package com.sharanamvaishali.dao;
2
3  import com.sharanamvaishali.model.Book;
4  import java.util.List;
5
6  public interface AuthorDAO {
7      public List<Book> getAllBooksByAuthor(Integer authorNo);
8  }
```

Implementation Class [AuthorDAOImpl.java]

This is a Data Access Object class with the following specifications.

DAO Implementation Specifications

Class Name	Package	Implements
AuthorDAOImpl	com.sharanamvaishali.dao	AuthorDAO

Objects	
Object Name	**Class Name**
sessionFactory	SessionFactory

Methods		
Method Name	**Arguments**	**Return Values**
getAuthorById()	Integer authorNo	Author
getAllBooksByAuthor()	Integer authorNo	List<Book>

Code Spec

```
1   package com.sharanamvaishali.dao;
2
3   import com.sharanamvaishali.model.Book;
4   import java.util.List;
5   import org.hibernate.SessionFactory;
6   import org.springframework.beans.factory.annotation.Autowired;
7   import org.springframework.stereotype.Repository;
8
9   @Repository
10  public class AuthorDAOImpl implements AuthorDAO {
11      @Autowired
12      private SessionFactory sessionFactory;
13
14      @Override
15      public List<Book> getAllBooksByAuthor(Integer authorNo) {
16          return sessionFactory.getCurrentSession().createQuery("FROM Book WHERE
            author1No = " + authorNo + " OR author2No = " + authorNo + " OR author3No =
            " + authorNo + " OR author4No = " + authorNo).list();
17      }
18  }
```

Explanation:

The following section describes the above code spec.

REMINDER

 AuthorDAO's **getAuthorById()** is explained in the *Chapter 35: Manage Authors*, which retrieves the author details based on AuthorNo.

getAllBooksByAuthor()

getAllBooksByAuthor() returns the appropriate books List object from the Books database table using **AuthorNo** as the reference.

This method uses **list()** of Query, which returns the appropriate books from the Books database table belonging to a particular author.

REMINDER

UserService's **getUserByUsername()** is explained in the *Chapter 40: Home Page*, which retrieves the details of the logged in user.

BookDAO's **getBookById()** is explained in the Chapter 36: Manage Books, which is called by BookService's getBookById().

REMINDER

Search.java [the model class] is explained in the *Chapter 45: Search Results*.
User.java [the model class] is explained in the *Chapter 37: Manage Users*.
Book.java [the model class] is explained in the *Chapter 36: Manage Books*.

Chapter

43

SECTION VI: FRONTEND [CUSTOMER FACING] SOFTWARE DESIGN DOCUMENTATION

Publisher Details

This module allows viewing the details of the publisher and the books published by that publisher along with its details. This page is invoked when a user clicks the publisher name from the frontend.

This module uses bms.Publishers table to retrieve that particular publisher's data and bms.Books to retrieve the books published by that publisher.

This module is made up of the following:

Type	Name	Description
JSP	showPublisherDetails.jsp	The details of a particular publisher along with the book details published by that particular publisher.

Spring		
Controller	HomeController.java	The controller class that facilitates data operations.
	PublisherController.java	
	BookController.java	
Service Class	PublisherService.java	The interfaces for the service layer.
	UserSerice.java	
	BookService.java	
	PublisherServiceImpl.java	The implementation classes for the service layer.
	UserServiceImpl.java	
	BookServiceImpl.java	
DAO Class	PublisherDAO.java	The interfaces for the DAO layer.
	UserDAO.java	
	BookDAOImpl.java	
	PublisherDAOImpl.java	The implementation classes that perform the actual data operations.
	UserDAOImpl.java	
	BookDAOImpl.java	
DispatcherServlet	bookshopdispatcher-servlet.xml	Central dispatcher for HTTP request handlers/controllers.
Hibernate		
Mapping	hibernate.cfg.xml	The mapping file that holds the Model class mapping.
Model Class	Publisher.java	The model classes.
	User.java	
	Search.java	
	Book.java	

JSP [showPublisherDetails.jsp]

Publisher Details Without Logging In

A link identified by a publisher name in the section **Our Publishers** when clicked, displays publisher details of the selected publisher, as shown in diagram 43.1.

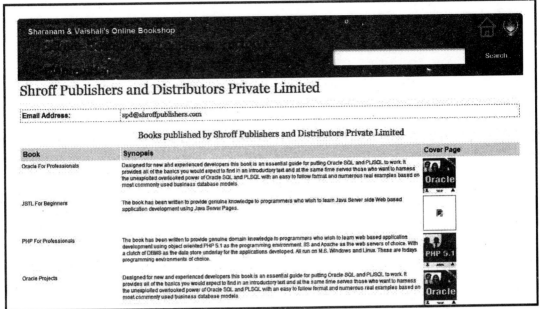

Diagram 43.1: Publisher Details page

Publisher Details After Logging In

This page shows the Add to cart link for every book published by that particular publisher, as shown in diagram 43.2, for the logged in users.

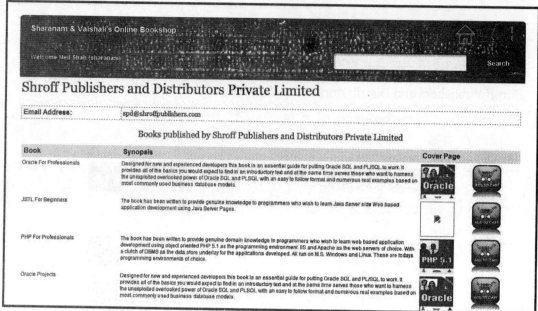

Diagram 43.2: Publisher Details page [after logging in]

Clicking an entry from the list displays that book's details [explained in the *Chapter 41: Book Details*].

Form Specifications

File Name	showPublisherDetails.jsp
Title	${publisherList.publisherName}'s Profile

Code Spec

```
1   <%@page contentType="text/html" pageEncoding="UTF-8"%>
2   <%@taglib uri="http://java.sun.com/jsp/jstl/core" prefix="c"%>
3   <%@taglib prefix="sec" uri="http://www.springframework.org/security/tags" %>
4   <!DOCTYPE HTML PUBLIC "-//W3C//DTD HTML 4.01 Transitional//EN"
5      "http://www.w3.org/TR/html4/loose.dtd">
6   <html>
7     <head>
8       <meta http-equiv="Content-Type" content="text/html; charset=UTF-8">
9       <title>${publisherList.publisherName}'s Profile</title>
10      <link rel="stylesheet" href="/BookShop/css/frontend.css" type="text/css">
11    </head>
12    <body>
13      <%@ include file="/WEB-INF/jsp/header.jsp" %>
```

```
14    <div id="bodyDiv">
15       <table width="100%" border="0" cellspacing="4" cellpadding="1">
16          <tr>
17             <td align="left" class="topAlign">
18                <span
                  class="spanShowDetails">${publisherList.publisherName}</span>
19             </td>
20          </tr>
21          <tr><td> </td></tr>
22          <tr>
23             <td align="left" class="topAlign">
24                <table cellspacing="0" border="0" cellpadding="4" width="100%"
                  style="border:1px dashed #0099ff;">
25                   <tr>
26                      <td class="label" width="20%" align="left"
                       style="border-right:1px dashed #0099ff;">
27                         Email Address: 
28                      </td>
29                      <td class="content" valign="top" width="80%">
30                         <a href='mailto:${publisherList.emailAddress}'>
31                            ${publisherList.emailAddress}
32                         </a>
33                      </td>
34                   </tr>
35                </table>
36             </td>
37          </tr>
38          <tr>
39             <td>
40                <br><center>
41                <span style="font:20px/22px Georgia, serif; text-align:center;
                  width:300px; color:#990000; height:37px;">Books published by
                  ${publisherList.publisherName}</span>
42                </center><br>
43                <table class="view" align="center" cellspacing="0" cellpadding="6"
                  width="100%">
44                   <tr>
45                      <th width="20%" class="label" align="left">Book</th>
46                      <th width="60%" class="label" align="left">Synopsis</th>
47                      <th width="10%" class="label" align="left">Cover Page</th>
48                      <th width="10%" class="label" align="left"> </th>
49                   </tr>
50                   <c:forEach items="${bookList}" var="book">
51                      <tr title="Click to view">
52                         <td width="20%" class="showBookList"
                          onclick="javascript:location.href='/BookShop/showBookDetail
                          s/${book.bookNo}'">
53                            ${book.bookName}
54                         </td>
55                         <td width="60%" class="showBookList"
                          onclick="javascript:location.href='/BookShop/showBookDetail
                          s/${book.bookNo}'">
56                            ${book.synopsis}
```

```
57                                    </td>
58                                    <td width="10%" class="showBookList"
                                      onclick="javascript:location.href='/BookShop/showBookDetail
                                      s/${book.bookNo}'">
59                                        <img
                                          src="/BookShop/admin/downloadBookPhotograph/${book.b
                                          ookNo}" height="80px" width="80px"/>
60                                    </td>
61                                    <td width="10%" class="showBookList">
62                                        <sec:authorize access="isAuthenticated()">
63                                            <a href="/BookShop/addToCart/<sec:authentication
                                              property='principal.username' />/${book.bookNo}">
64                                                <img src="/BookShop/images/addToCart.jpg"
                                                  width="74px" height="74px" style="cursor:pointer;"
                                                  border="0"/>
65                                            </a> 
66                                        </sec:authorize>
67                                    </td>
68                                </tr>
69                            </c:forEach>
70                        </table>
71                    </td>
72                </tr>
73            </table>
74            <%@ include file="/WEB-INF/jsp/footer.jsp" %>
75        </div>
76    </body>
77 </html>
```

Explanation:

The JSP displays the details of the publisher and books published by that publisher.

Whilst populating these details in JSP, the system checks if the user has logged in. Only if the user has logged in, an additional link i.e. Add To Cart is displayed.

Controller [HomeController.java]

This is a controller class with the following specifications.

Controller Specifications

Class Name	Package	
HomeController	com.sharanamvaishali.controllers	
Objects		
Object Name	Class Name	Object Type
userService	UserService	Service Layer
publisherService	PublisherService	Service Layer

Methods	
Method Name	**Request Mapping**
showPublisherDetails()	/showPublisherDetails/${publisherNo}

Code Spec

```
1  package com.sharanamvaishali.controllers;
2
3  import com.sharanamvaishali.model.Search;
4  import com.sharanamvaishali.service.*;
5  import java.util.Map;
6  import org.springframework.beans.factory.annotation.Autowired;
7  import org.springframework.security.core.context.SecurityContextHolder;
8  import org.springframework.stereotype.Controller;
9  import org.springframework.web.bind.annotation.PathVariable;
10 import org.springframework.web.bind.annotation.RequestMapping;
11
12 @Controller
13 public class HomeController {
14     @Autowired
15     private UserService userService;
16
17     @Autowired
18     private PublisherService publisherService;
19
20     @RequestMapping("/showPublisherDetails/{publisherNo}")
21     public String showPublisherDetails(Map<String, Object> map,
       @PathVariable("publisherNo") Integer publisherNo) {
22         map.put("publisherList", publisherService.getPublisherById(publisherNo));
23         map.put("bookList", publisherService.getAllBooksByPublisher(publisherNo));
24         map.put("search", new Search());
25         if(SecurityContextHolder.getContext().getAuthentication().isAuthenticated()) {
26             map.put("userDetails",
               userService.getUserByUsername(SecurityContextHolder.getContext().getAuthen
               tication().getName()));
27         }
28         return "showPublisherDetails";
29     }
30 }
```

Explanation:

The following section describes the above code spec.

showPublisherDetails()

showPublisherDetails() is invoked for every publisher hyperlink in the **Our Publishers** section of **home.jsp**.

showPublisherDetails():

☐ Retrieves the appropriate Publisher's details using **PublisherNo** as the reference. It calls PublisherService's **getPublisherById()** which returns the details of the publisher as a Publisher object. **PublisherNo** is made available through **@PathVariable** [in the list of Publishers rendered by the View] when the user clicks /showPublisherDetails/${publisherNo} to view a particular publisher details. This data is made available to the view using Map's **put()**

☐ Retrieves the books using **PublisherNo** as the reference. It calls PublisherService's **getAllBooksByPublisher()** which returns the books for that particular publisher as a Book List object. **PublisherNo** is made available through **@PathVariable** [in the list of Publishers rendered by the View] when the user clicks /showPublisherDetails/${publisherNo} to view a particular publisher's details

☐ Initializes the search form as the search form is a part of the view

☐ Populates the userDetails object with the username of the logged in user. This is only done if the user has logged in. This object is used to show the welcome message after the user has logged in

☐ Returns the control to the View along with the data to be populated in the browser. The data that is retrieved is made available using Map's **put()**

REMINDER

    BookController's **downloadBookPhotograph()** is explained in the *Chapter 36: Manage Books*, which is used to display the cover page of the book published by that particular publisher.

Service Class

Interface [PublisherService.java]

This is a service interface with the following specifications.

Service Interface Specifications

Class Name	Package
PublisherService	com.sharanamvaishali.service

Code Spec

```
1  package com.sharanamvaishali.service;
2
```

```
3  import com.sharanamvaishali.model.Book;
4  import java.util.List;
5
6  public interface PublisherService {
7      public List<Book> getAllBooksByPublisher(Integer publisherNo);
8  }
```

Implementation Class [PublisherServiceImpl.java]

This is a service class with the following specifications.

Service Implementation Specifications

Class Name	Package	Implements
PublisherServiceImpl	com.sharanamvaishali.service	PublisherService

Objects		
Object Name	Class Name	Object Type
publisherDAO	PublisherDAO	Data Access Object Layer

Methods	
Method Name	Arguments
getPublisherById()	Integer publisherNo
getAllBooksByPublisher()	Integer publisherNo

Code Spec

```
1   package com.sharanamvaishali.service;
2
3   import com.sharanamvaishali.dao.PublisherDAO;
4   import com.sharanamvaishali.model.Book;
5   import java.util.List;
6   import org.springframework.beans.factory.annotation.Autowired;
7   import org.springframework.stereotype.Service;
8   import org.springframework.transaction.annotation.Transactional;
9
10  @Service
11  public class PublisherServiceImpl implements PublisherService {
12      @Autowired
13      private PublisherDAO publisherDAO;
14
15      @Transactional
16      @Override
17      public List<Book> getAllBooksByPublisher(Integer publisherNo) {
18          return publisherDAO.getAllBooksByPublisher(publisherNo);
19      }
20  }
```

Explanation:

The following section describes the above code spec.

<u>**REMINDER**</u>

 PublisherService's **getPublisherById()** is explained in the *Chapter 34: Manage Publishers*, which retrieves the publisher details based on PublisherNo.

getAllBooksByPublisher()

getAllBooksByPublisher() holds the business logic to retrieve the books published by a particular publisher.

This method in turn invokes the DAO Layer's [PublisherDAO] **getAllBooksByPublisher()**.

<u>**REMINDER**</u>

 UserService's **getUserByUsername()** is explained in the *Chapter 40: Home Page*, which retrieves the details of the logged in user.

BookService's **getBookById()** is explained in the *Chapter 36: Manage Books*, which is called by BookController's downloadBookPhotograph().

DAO Class

Interface [PublisherDAO.java]

This is a Data Access Object interface with the following specifications.

DAO Interface Specifications

Class Name	Package
PublisherDAO	com.sharanamvaishali.dao

Code Spec

```
1  package com.sharanamvaishali.dao;
2
3  import com.sharanamvaishali.model.Book;
4  import java.util.List;
5
6  public interface PublisherDAO {
```

```
7      public List<Book> getAllBooksByPublisher(Integer publisherNo);
8  }
```

Implementation Class [PublisherDAOImpl.java]

This is a **Data Access Object** class with the following specifications.

DAO Implementation Specifications

Class Name	Package	Implements
PublisherDAOImpl	com.sharanamvaishali.dao	PublisherDAO

Objects	
Object Name	**Class Name**
sessionFactory	SessionFactory

Methods		
Method Name	**Arguments**	**Return Values**
getPublisherById()	Integer publisherNo	Publisher
getAllBooksByPublisher()	Integer publisherNo	List<Book>

Code Spec

```
1  package com.sharanamvaishali.dao;
2
3  import com.sharanamvaishali.model.Book;
4  import java.util.List;
5  import org.hibernate.SessionFactory;
6  import org.springframework.beans.factory.annotation.Autowired;
7  import org.springframework.stereotype.Repository;
8
9  @Repository
10 public class PublisherDAOImpl implements PublisherDAO {
11     @Autowired
12     private SessionFactory sessionFactory;
13
14     @Override
15     public List<Book> getAllBooksByPublisher(Integer publisherNo) {
16         return sessionFactory.getCurrentSession().createQuery("FROM Book WHERE
           publisherNo = " + publisherNo).list();
17     }
18 }
```

Explanation:

The following section describes the above code spec.

REMINDER

PublisherDAO's **getPublisherById()** is explained in the *Chapter 34: Manage Publishers*, which retrieves the publisher details based on PublisherNo.

getAllBooksByPublisher()

getAllBooksByPublisher() returns the appropriate books List object from the Books database table using **PublisherNo** as the reference.

This method uses **list()** of Query, which returns the appropriate books from the Books database table published by a particular publisher.

REMINDER

UserDAO's **getUserByUsername()** is explained in the *Chapter 40: Home Page*, which retrieves the details of the logged in user.

BookDAO's **getBookById()** is explained in the Chapter 36: Manage Books, which is called by BookService's getBookById().

REMINDER

Search.java [the model class] is explained in the *Chapter 45: Search Results*.
User.java [the model class] is explained in the *Chapter 37: Manage Users*.
Book.java [the model class] is explained in the *Chapter 36: Manage Books*.

Chapter

44

SECTION VI: FRONTEND [CUSTOMER FACING] SOFTWARE DESIGN DOCUMENTATION

Category Details

This module allows viewing the details of the category and the books for that category along with its details. This page is invoked when a user clicks the category name from the frontend.

This module uses bms.Categories table to retrieve that particular category's data and bms.Books to retrieve the books for that category.

This module is made up of the following:

Type	Name	Description
JSP	showCategoryDetails.jsp	The details of a particular category along with the details of the books under that particular category.

Spring		
Controller	HomeController.java	The controller class that facilitates data operations.
	BookController.java	
Service Class	CategoryService.java	The interfaces for the service layer.
	UserSerice.java	
	BookService.java	
	CategoryServiceImpl.java	The implementation classes for the service layer.
	UserServiceImpl.java	
	BookServiceImpl.java	
DAO Class	CategoryDAO.java	The interfaces for the DAO layer.
	UserDAO.java	
	BookDAOImpl.java	
	CategoryDAOImpl.java	The implementation classes that perform the actual data operations.
	UserDAOImpl.java	
	BookDAOImpl.java	
DispatcherServlet	bookshopdispatcher-servlet.xml	Central dispatcher for HTTP request handlers/controllers.
Hibernate		
Mapping	hibernate.cfg.xml	The mapping file that holds Model class mapping.
Model Class	Category.java	The model classes.
	User.java	
	Search.java	
	Book.java	

JSP [showCategoryDetails.jsp]

Category Details Without Logging In

A link identified by a category name in the section **Categories** when clicked, displays category details of the selected category, as shown in diagram 44.1.

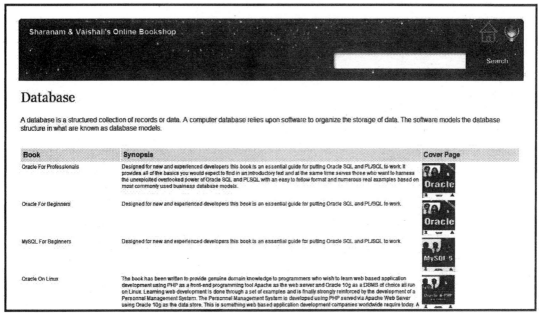

Diagram 44.1: Category Details page

Category Details After Logging In

This page shows Add to cart link for every book categorized under that particular category, as shown in diagram 44.2, for the logged in users.

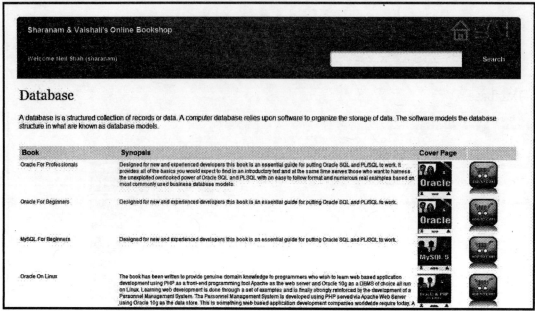

Diagram 44.2: Category Details page [after logging in]

Clicking an entry from the list displays that book's details [explained in the *Chapter 41: Book Details*].

Form Specifications

File Name	showCategoryDetails.jsp
Title	${categoryList.category}

Code Spec

```
1  <%@page contentType="text/html" pageEncoding="UTF-8"%>
2  <%@taglib uri="http://java.sun.com/jsp/jstl/core" prefix="c"%>
3  <%@taglib prefix="sec" uri="http://www.springframework.org/security/tags" %>
4  <!DOCTYPE HTML PUBLIC "-//W3C//DTD HTML 4.01 Transitional//EN"
5     "http://www.w3.org/TR/html4/loose.dtd">
6  <html>
7    <head>
8      <meta http-equiv="Content-Type" content="text/html; charset=UTF-8">
9      <title>${categoryList.category}</title>
10     <link rel="stylesheet" href="/BookShop/css/frontend.css" type="text/css">
11   </head>
12   <body>
13     <%@ include file="/WEB-INF/jsp/header.jsp" %>
14     <div id="bodyDiv">
```

```
15    <table width="100%" border="0" cellspacing="4" cellpadding="1">
16       <tr>
17          <td align="left" class="topAlign">
18             <br />
19             <span class="spanShowDetails">${categoryList.category}</span>
20          </td>
21       </tr>
22       <tr><td> </td></tr>
23       <tr>
24          <td align="left" valign="top" class="content">
25             ${categoryList.description}
26          </td>
27       </tr>
28       <tr>
29          <td>
30             <br><br>
31             <table class="view" align="center" cellspacing="0" cellpadding="6"
                  width="100%">
32                <tr>
33                   <th width="20%" class="label" align="left">Book</th>
34                   <th width="60%" class="label" align="left">Synopsis</th>
35                   <th width="10%" class="label" align="left">Cover Page</th>
36                   <th width="10%" class="label" align="left"> </th>
37                </tr>
38                <c:forEach items="${bookList}" var="book">
39                   <tr title="Click to view">
40                      <td width="20%" class="showBookList"
                         onclick="javascript:location.href='/BookShop/showBookDetail
                         s/${book.bookNo}'">
41                         ${book.bookName}
42                      </td>
43                      <td width="60%" class="showBookList"
                         onclick="javascript:location.href='/BookShop/showBookDetail
                         s/${book.bookNo}'">
44                         ${book.synopsis}
45                      </td>
46                      <td width="10%" class="showBookList"
                         onclick="javascript:location.href='/BookShop/showBookDetail
                         s/${book.bookNo}'">
47                         <img
                            src="/BookShop/admin/downloadBookPhotograph/${book.b
                            ookNo}" height="80px" width="80px"/>
48                      </td>
49                      <td width="10%" class="showBookList">
50                         <sec:authorize access="isAuthenticated()">
51                            <a href="/BookShop/addToCart/<sec:authentication
                               property='principal.username' />/${book.bookNo}">
52                               <img src="/BookShop/images/addToCart.jpg"
                                  width="74px" height="74px" style="cursor:pointer;"
                                  border="0"/>
53                            </a> 
54                         </sec:authorize>
55                      </td>
56                   </tr>
```

```
57                        </c:forEach>
58                      </table>
59                    </td>
60                  </tr>
61                </table>
62                <%@ include file="/WEB-INF/jsp/footer.jsp" %>
63              </div>
64          </body>
65    </html>
```

Explanation:

The JSP displays the details of the category and books available under that category.

Whilst populating these details in JSP, the system checks if the user has logged in. Only if the user has logged in, additional link of Add To Cart is displayed.

Controller [HomeController.java]

This is a controller class with the following specifications.

Controller Specifications

Class Name	Package	
HomeController	com.sharanamvaishali.controllers	
Objects		
Object Name	Class Name	Object Type
userService	UserService	Service Layer
categoryService	CategoryService	Service Layer
Methods		
Method Name	Request Mapping	
showCategoryDetails()	/showCategoryDetails/${categoryNo}	

Code Spec

```
1    package com.sharanamvaishali.controllers;
2
3    import com.sharanamvaishali.model.Search;
4    import com.sharanamvaishali.service.*;
5    import java.util.Map;
6    import org.springframework.beans.factory.annotation.Autowired;
7    import org.springframework.security.core.context.SecurityContextHolder;
8    import org.springframework.stereotype.Controller;
9    import org.springframework.web.bind.annotation.PathVariable;
10   import org.springframework.web.bind.annotation.RequestMapping;
11
```

```
12  @Controller
13  public class HomeController {
14      @Autowired
15      private UserService userService;
16
17      @Autowired
18      private CategoryService categoryService;
19
20      @RequestMapping("/showCategoryDetails/{categoryNo}")
21      public String showCategoryDetails(Map<String, Object> map,
        @PathVariable("categoryNo") Integer categoryNo) {
22          map.put("categoryList", categoryService.getCategoryById(categoryNo));
23          map.put("bookList", categoryService.getAllBooksByCategory(categoryNo));
24          map.put("search", new Search());
25          if(SecurityContextHolder.getContext().getAuthentication().isAuthenticated()) {
26              map.put("userDetails",
                userService.getUserByUsername(SecurityContextHolder.getContext().getAuthen
                tication().getName()));
27          }
28          return "showCategoryDetails";
29      }
30  }
```

Explanation:

The following section describes the above code spec.

showCategoryDetails()

showCategoryDetails() is invoked for every hyperlink in the Categories section of **home.jsp**.

showCategoryDetails():

❑ Retrieves the appropriate Category's details using **CategoryNo** as the reference. It calls CategoryService's **getCategoryById()** which returns the details of the category as a Category object. **CategoryNo** is made available through **@PathVariable** [in the list of Categories rendered by the View] when the user clicks /showCategoryDetails/${categoryNo} to view a particular category details. This data is made available to the view using Map's **put()**

❑ Retrieves the books using **CategoryNo** as the reference. It calls CategoryService's **getAllBooksByCategory()** which returns the books for that particular category as a Book List object. **CategoryNo** is made available through **@PathVariable** [in the list of Categories rendered by the View] when the user clicks /showCategoryDetails/${categoryNo} to view a particular category details

❑ Initializes the search form as the search form is a part of the view

❏ Populates the userDetails object with the username of the logged in user. This is only done, if the user has logged in. This object is used to show the welcome message after the user has logged in

❏ Returns the control to the View along with the data to be populated in the browser. The data that is retrieved is made available using Map's **put()**

REMINDER

 BookController's **downloadBookPhotograph()** is explained in the *Chapter 36: Manage Books*, which is used to display the cover page of the book categorized under that particular category.

Service Class

Interface [CategoryService.java]

This is a service interface with the following specifications.

Service Interface Specifications

Class Name	Package
CategoryService	com.sharanamvaishali.service

Code Spec

```
1  package com.sharanamvaishali.service;
2
3  import com.sharanamvaishali.model.Book;
4  import java.util.List;
5
6  public interface CategoryService {
7      public List<Book> getAllBooksByCategory(Integer categoryNo);
8  }
```

Implementation Class [CategoryServiceImpl.java]

This is a service class with the following specifications.

Service Implementation Specifications

Class Name	Package	Implements
CategoryServiceImpl	com.sharanamvaishali.service	CategoryService

Objects		
Object Name	**Class Name**	**Object Type**
categoryDAO	CategoryDAO	Data Access Object Layer
Methods		
Method Name		**Arguments**
getCategoryById()		Integer categoryNo
getAllBooksByCategory()		Integer categoryNo

Code Spec

```
1  package com.sharanamvaishali.service;
2
3  import com.sharanamvaishali.dao.CategoryDAO;
4  import com.sharanamvaishali.model.Book;
5  import java.util.List;
6  import org.springframework.beans.factory.annotation.Autowired;
7  import org.springframework.stereotype.Service;
8  import org.springframework.transaction.annotation.Transactional;
9
10 @Service
11 public class CategoryServiceImpl implements CategoryService {
12     @Autowired
13     private CategoryDAO categoryDAO;
14
15     @Transactional
16     @Override
17     public List<Book> getAllBooksByCategory(Integer categoryNo) {
18         return categoryDAO.getAllBooksByCategory(categoryNo);
19     }
20 }
```

Explanation:

The following section describes the above code spec.

REMINDER

 CategoryService's **getCategoryById()** is explained in the *Chapter 33: Manage Categories*, which retrieves the category details based on CategoryNo.

getAllBooksByCategory()

getAllBooksByCategory() holds the business logic to retrieve the books belonging to a particular category.

This method in turn invokes the DAO Layer's [CategoryDAO] **getAllBooksByCategory()**.

REMINDER

UserService's **getUserByUsername()** is explained in the *Chapter 40: Home Page*, which retrieves the details of the logged in user.

BookService's **getBookById()** is explained in the *Chapter 36: Manage Books*, which is called by BookController's downloadBookPhotograph().

DAO Class

Interface [CategoryDAO.java]

This is a Data Access Object interface with the following specifications.

DAO Interface Specifications

Class Name	Package
CategoryDAO	com.sharanamvaishali.dao

Code Spec

```
1  package com.sharanamvaishali.dao;
2
3  import com.sharanamvaishali.model.Book;
4  import java.util.List;
5
6  public interface CategoryDAO {
7      public List<Book> getAllBooksByCategory(Integer categoryNo);
8  }
```

Implementation Class [CategoryDAOImpl.java]

This is a Data Access Object class with the following specifications.

DAO Implementation Specifications

Class Name	Package	Implements
CategoryDAOImpl	com.sharanamvaishali.dao	CategoryDAO
Objects		
Object Name	**Class Name**	
sessionFactory	SessionFactory	

Methods		
Method Name	**Arguments**	**Return Values**
getCategoryById()	Integer categoryNo	Category
getAllBooksByCategory()	Integer categoryNo	List<Book>

Code Spec

```
1  package com.sharanamvaishali.dao;
2
3  import com.sharanamvaishali.model.Book;
4  import java.util.List;
5  import org.hibernate.SessionFactory;
6  import org.springframework.beans.factory.annotation.Autowired;
7  import org.springframework.stereotype.Repository;
8
9  @Repository
10 public class CategoryDAOImpl implements CategoryDAO {
11     @Autowired
12     private SessionFactory sessionFactory;
13
14     @Override
15     public List<Book> getAllBooksByCategory(Integer categoryNo) {
16         return sessionFactory.getCurrentSession().createQuery("FROM Book WHERE
           categoryNo = " + categoryNo).list();
17     }
18 }
```

Explanation:

The following section describes the above code spec.

REMINDER

 CategoryDAO's **getCategoryById()** is explained in the *Chapter 33: Manage Categories*, which retrieves the category details based on CategoryNo.

getAllBooksByCategory()

getAllBooksByCategory() returns the appropriate books List object from the Books database table using **CategoryNo** as the reference.

This method uses **list()** of Query, which returns the appropriate books from the Books database table belonging to a particular category.

REMINDER

UserDAO's **getUserByUsername()** is explained in the *Chapter 40: Home Page*, which retrieves the details of the logged in user.

BookDAO's **getBookById()** is explained in the Chapter 36: Manage Books, which is called by BookService's getBookById().

REMINDER

Category.java [the model class] is explained in the *Chapter 33: Manage Categories*.

Search.java [the model] class is explained in the *Chapter 45: Search Results*.

User.java [the model class] is explained in the *Chapter 37: Manage Users*.

Book.java [the model class] is explained in the *Chapter 36: Manage Books*.

Chapter

45

SECTION VI: FRONTEND [CUSTOMER FACING] SOFTWARE DESIGN DOCUMENTATION

Search Results

This module allows viewing the details of the search criteria such as the book name, ISBN and so on. This page is invoked when a user either clicks **Search** after entering the search criteria or directly clicks the words available under the Popular Searches section of the home page.

This module uses bms.Books, bms.Authors and bms.Publishers tables to retrieve the particular search criteria's data and bms.PopularSearches to add and delete the search criteria values.

This module is made up of the following:

Type	Name	Description
JSP	searchResults.jsp	The list of search criteria along with its details.

Spring		
Controller	SearchController.java	The controller class that facilitates data operations.
	BookController.java	
Service Class	SearchService.java	The interfaces for the service layer.
	UserService.java	
	BookService.java	
	SearchServiceImpl.java	The implementation classes for the service layer.
	UserServiceImpl.java	
	BookServiceImpl.java	
DAO Class	SearchDAO.java	The interfaces for the DAO layer.
	UserDAO.java	
	BookDAO.java	
	SearchDAOImpl.java	The implementation classes that perform the actual data operations.
	UserDAOImpl.java	
	BookDAOImpl.java	
DispatcherServlet	bookshopdispatcher-servlet.xml	Central dispatcher for HTTP request handlers/controllers.
Hibernate		
Mapping	hibernate.cfg.xml	The mapping file that holds Model class mapping.
Model Class	Book.java	The model classes.
	Author.java	
	Publisher.java	
	User.java	
	Search.java	
	PopularSearch.java	

JSP [searchResults.jsp]

When ▮ Search ▮ is clicked or when the Popular Searches word is clicked, the search result page appears, as shown in diagram 45.1.

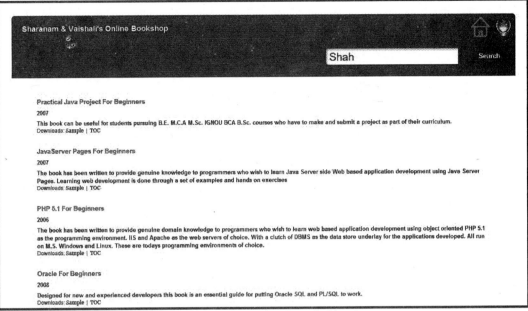

Diagram 45.1: The Search Results

Clicking an entry from the list displays that book's details [explained in the *Chapter 41: Book Details*].

Form Specifications

File Name	searchResults.jsp
Title	BookShop[Sharanam & Vaishali Shah] - Search Results

Code Spec

```
1   <%@page contentType="text/html" pageEncoding="UTF-8"%>
2   <%@taglib uri="http://java.sun.com/jsp/jstl/core" prefix="c"%>
3   <!DOCTYPE HTML PUBLIC "-//W3C//DTD HTML 4.01 Transitional//EN"
4     "http://www.w3.org/TR/html4/loose.dtd">
5   <html>
6     <head>
7       <meta http-equiv="Content-Type" content="text/html; charset=UTF-8">
8       <title>BookShop[Sharanam & Vaishali Shah] - Search Results</title>
9       <link rel="stylesheet" href="/BookShop/css/frontend.css" type="text/css">
10    </head>
11    <body>
12      <%@ include file="/WEB-INF/jsp/header.jsp" %>
13      <div id="bodyDiv">
14        <table align="center" cellpadding="0" cellspacing="0" width="90%">
```

```
15              <tr>
16                <td>
17                  <c:forEach items="${searchResultsList}" var="result">
18                    <br /><br /><br />
19                    <a class="searchName"
                       href="/BookShop/showBookDetails/${result[0]}">${result[1]}</a
                       ><br>
20                    <span class="searchYear">${result[2]}</span><br>
21                    <span class="searchSynopsis">${result[3]}</span><br>
22                    Downloads: <a
                       href="/BookShop/admin/downloadBookSampleChapter/${result[0]
                       }">Sample</a>  |  <a
                       href="/BookShop/admin/downloadBookTOC/${result[0]}">TOC</a
                       >
23                  </c:forEach>
24                </td>
25              </tr>
26            </table>
27            <%@ include file="/WEB-INF/jsp/footer.jsp" %>
28          </div>
29        </body>
30      </html>
```

Explanation:

The JSP displays the details of the book for the word searched for.

Controller [SearchController.java]

This is a controller class with the following specifications.

Controller Specifications

Class Name	Package	
SearchController	com.sharanamvaishali.controllers	
Objects		
Object Name	Class Name	Object Type
userService	UserService	Service Layer
searchService	SearchService	Service Layer
Methods		
Method Name	Request Mapping	
showSearchResultsByCriteria()	/searchResults/${searchCriteria}	
showSearchResults()	/searchResults	

Code Spec

```
 1  package com.sharanamvaishali.controllers;
 2
 3  import com.sharanamvaishali.model.PopularSearch;
 4  import com.sharanamvaishali.model.Search;
 5  import com.sharanamvaishali.service.SearchService;
 6  import com.sharanamvaishali.service.UserService;
 7  import java.util.Map;
 8  import org.springframework.beans.factory.annotation.Autowired;
 9  import org.springframework.security.core.context.SecurityContextHolder;
10  import org.springframework.stereotype.Controller;
11  import org.springframework.web.bind.annotation.PathVariable;
12  import org.springframework.web.bind.annotation.RequestMapping;
13
14  @Controller
15  public class SearchController {
16      @Autowired
17      private UserService userService;
18
19      @Autowired
20      private SearchService searchService;
21
22      @RequestMapping("/searchResults/{searchCriteria}")
23      public String showSearchResultsByCriteria(Map<String, Object> map,
          @PathVariable("searchCriteria") String searchCriteria) {
24          map.put("searchResultsList", searchService.searchResults(searchCriteria));
25          Search search = new Search(searchCriteria);
26          map.put("search", search);
27          PopularSearch ps = new PopularSearch();
28          ps.setSearchValue(searchCriteria);
29          searchService.savePopularSearch(ps);
30          if(SecurityContextHolder.getContext().getAuthentication().isAuthenticated()) {
31              map.put("userDetails",
                  userService.getUserByUsername(SecurityContextHolder.getContext().getAuthen
                  tication().getName()));
32          }
33          return "searchResults";
34      }
35
36      @RequestMapping("/searchResults")
37      public String showSearchResults(Map<String, Object> map) {
38          map.put("searchResultsList", searchService.searchAllResults());
39          Search search = new Search();
40          map.put("search", search);
41          if(SecurityContextHolder.getContext().getAuthentication().isAuthenticated()) {
42              map.put("userDetails",
                  userService.getUserByUsername(SecurityContextHolder.getContext().getAuthen
                  tication().getName()));
43          }
44          return "searchResults";
45      }
46  }
```

Explanation:

The following section describes the above code spec.

showSearchResultsByCriteria()

showSearchResultsByCriteria() is invoked when [Search] is clicked [with a search criteria] in the Search section of the header or when the desired hyperlink is clicked in the Popular Searches section of **home.jsp**.

showSearchResultsByCriteria():

❑ Retrieves the appropriate search results using **SearchCriteria** as the reference. It calls SearchService's **searchResults()** which returns the search results as a Search object. **SearchCriteria** is made available through **@PathVariable** [in the list of Search Results rendered by the View] when the user clicks Search [/searchResults/${searchCriteria}] to view the search results. This data is made available to the view using Map's **put()**

❑ Initializes the search form as the search form is a part of the view

❑ Creates an object of **PopularSearch** entity to set the search criteria

❑ Calls SearchService's **savePopularSearch()**, which inserts the **SearchCriteria** into **PopularSearch**

❑ Populates the userDetails object with the username of the logged in user. This is only done, if the user has logged in. This object is used to show the welcome message after the user has logged in

❑ Returns the control to the View along with the data to be populated in the browser. The data that is retrieved is made available using Map's **put()**

showSearchResults()

showSearchResults() is invoked when [Search] is clicked [without a search criteria] in the Search section of the header.

showSearchResults():

❑ Retrieves the appropriate search results. It calls SearchService's **searchAllResults()** which returns the search results as a Search object. This data is made available to the view using Map's **put()**

❑ Initializes the search form as the search form is a part of the view

❑ Populates the userDetails object with the username of the logged in user. This is only done, if the user has logged in. This object is used to show the welcome message after the user has logged in

❑ Returns the control to the View along with the data to be populated in the browser. The data that is retrieved is made available using Map's **put()**

REMINDER

BookController's **downloadBookSampleChapter()** and **downloadBookTOC()** is explained in the *Chapter 36: Manage Books*, which is used to download the sample chapter and TOC.

Service Class

Interface [SearchService.java]

This is a service interface with the following specifications.

Service Interface Specifications

Class Name	Package
SearchService	com.sharanamvaishali.service

Code Spec

```
1  package com.sharanamvaishali.service;
2
3  import com.sharanamvaishali.model.PopularSearch;
4  import java.util.List;
5
6  public interface SearchService {
7      public List searchResults(String searchCriteria);
8      public List searchAllResults();
9      public void savePopularSearch(PopularSearch popularSeacrh);
10 }
```

Implementation Class [SearchServiceImpl.java]

This is a service class with the following specifications.

Service Implementation Specifications

Class Name	Package	Implements
SearchServiceImpl	com.sharanamvaishali.service	SearchService

Objects		
Object Name	**Class Name**	**Object Type**
searchDAO	SearchDAO	Data Access Object Layer
Methods		
Method Name		**Arguments**
searchResults()		String searchCriteria
searchAllResults()		- -
savePopularSearch()		PopularSearch popularSearch

Code Spec

```
1  package com.sharanamvaishali.service;
2
3  import com.sharanamvaishali.dao.SearchDAO;
4  import com.sharanamvaishali.model.PopularSearch;
5  import java.util.List;
6  import org.springframework.beans.factory.annotation.Autowired;
7  import org.springframework.stereotype.Service;
8  import org.springframework.transaction.annotation.Transactional;
9
10 @Service
11 public class SearchServiceImpl implements SearchService {
12     @Autowired
13     private SearchDAO searchDAO;
14
15     @Transactional
16     @Override
17     public List searchResults(String searchCriteria) {
18         return searchDAO.searchResults(searchCriteria);
19     }
20
21     @Transactional
22     @Override
23     public List searchAllResults() {
24         return searchDAO.searchAllResults();
25     }
26
27     @Transactional
28     @Override
29     public void savePopularSearch(PopularSearch popularSearch) {
30         searchDAO.savePopularSearch(popularSearch);
31         searchDAO.deletePopularSearches();
32     }
33 }
```

Explanation:

The following section describes the above code spec.

searchResults()

searchResults() holds the business logic to retrieve the search results.

This method in turn invokes the DAO Layer's [SearchDAO] **searchResults()**.

searchAllResults()

searchAllResults() holds the business logic to retrieve all the search results.

This method in turn invokes the DAO Layer's [SearchDAO] **searchAllResults()**.

savePopularSearch()

savePopularSearch() holds the business logic to:

❑ Save the SearchCriteria in the PopularSearch

❑ Delete the old PopularSearch entries for house keeping

This method in turn invokes the DAO Layer's [SearchDAO] **savePopularSearch()** and **deletePopularSearches()**.

REMINDER

UserService's **getUserByUsername()** is explained in the *Chapter 40: Home Page*, which retrieves the details of the logged in user.

BookService's **getBookById()** is explained in the *Chapter 36: Manage Books*, which is called by BookController's downloadBookPhotograph().

DAO Class

Interface [SearchDAO.java]

This is a Data Access Object interface with the following specifications.

DAO Interface Specifications

Class Name	Package
SearchDAO	com.sharanamvaishali.dao

Code Spec

```
1  package com.sharanamvaishali.dao;
2
3  import com.sharanamvaishali.model.PopularSearch;
4  import java.util.List;
5
6  public interface SearchDAO {
7      public List searchResults(String searchCriteria);
8      public List searchAllResults();
9      public void savePopularSearch(PopularSearch popularSeacrh);
10     public int getTotalPopularSearches();
11     public void deletePopularSearches();
12 }
```

Implementation Class [SearchDAOImpl.java]

This is a **D**ata **A**ccess **O**bject class with the following specifications.

DAO Implementation Specifications

Class Name	Package	Implements
SearchDAOImpl	com.sharanamvaishali.dao	SearchDAO
Objects		
Object Name		**Class Name**
sessionFactory		SessionFactory
Methods		
Method Name	**Arguments**	**Return Values**
searchResults()	String searchCriteria	List
searchAllResults()	– –	List
savePopularSearch()	PopularSearch popularSearch	void
getTotalPopularSearches()	– –	int
deletePopularSearches()	– –	void

Code Spec

```
1  package com.sharanamvaishali.dao;
2
3  import com.sharanamvaishali.model.PopularSearch;
4  import java.util.Iterator;
5  import java.util.List;
6  import org.hibernate.SessionFactory;
7  import org.springframework.beans.factory.annotation.Autowired;
8  import org.springframework.stereotype.Repository;
9
```

```java
10  @Repository
11  public class SearchDAOImpl implements SearchDAO {
12      @Autowired
13      private SessionFactory sessionFactory;
14
15      @Override
16      public List searchResults(String searchCriteria) {
17          return sessionFactory.getCurrentSession().createSQLQuery("SELECT DISTINCT
            BookNo, BookName, Year, Synopsis"
18                  + " FROM Books, Authors, Publishers "
19                  + "WHERE Authors.AuthorNo = Books.Author1No "
20                  + "OR Authors.AuthorNo = Books.Author2No "
21                  + "OR Authors.AuthorNo = Books.Author3No "
22                  + "OR Authors.AuthorNo = Books.Author4No "
23                  + "OR Publishers.PublisherNo = Books.PublisherNo "
24                  + "AND (BookName LIKE '%"+ searchCriteria + "%' "
25                  + "OR ISBN LIKE '%"+ searchCriteria + "%' "
26                  + "OR Edition LIKE '%"+ searchCriteria + "%' "
27                  + "OR Year LIKE '%"+ searchCriteria + "%' "
28                  + "OR Synopsis LIKE '%"+ searchCriteria + "%' "
29                  + "OR AboutAuthors LIKE '%"+ searchCriteria + "%' "
30                  + "OR TopicsCovered LIKE '%"+ searchCriteria + "%' "
31                  + "OR ContentsCDROM LIKE '%"+ searchCriteria + "%' "
32                  + "OR Cost LIKE '%"+ searchCriteria + "%' "
33                  + "OR FirstName LIKE '%"+ searchCriteria + "%' "
34                  + "OR LastName LIKE '%"+ searchCriteria + "%' "
35                  + "OR PublisherName LIKE '%"+ searchCriteria + "%')")
36                  .list();
37      }
38
39      @Override
40      public List searchAllResults() {
41          return sessionFactory.getCurrentSession().createSQLQuery("SELECT DISTINCT
            BookNo, BookName, Year, Synopsis"
42                  + " FROM Books, Authors, Publishers "
43                  + "WHERE Authors.AuthorNo = Books.Author1No "
44                  + "OR Authors.AuthorNo = Books.Author2No "
45                  + "OR Authors.AuthorNo = Books.Author3No "
46                  + "OR Authors.AuthorNo = Books.Author4No "
47                  + "OR Publishers.PublisherNo = Books.PublisherNo")
48                  .list();
49      }
50
51      @Override
52      public void savePopularSearch(PopularSearch popularSearch) {
53          sessionFactory.getCurrentSession().save(popularSearch);
54      }
55
56      @Override
57      public int getTotalPopularSearches() {
58          Object TransactionNo =
            sessionFactory.getCurrentSession().createSQLQuery("SELECT COUNT(*) AS Total
            FROM PopularSearches").addScalar("Total").uniqueResult();
59          return Integer.parseInt(TransactionNo.toString());
```

```
60    }
61
62    @Override
63    public void deletePopularSearches() {
64        if(getTotalPopularSearches()>600) {
65            List<PopularSearch> ps =
                  sessionFactory.getCurrentSession().createQuery("FROM
                  PopularSearch").setMaxResults(10).list();
66            for (Iterator i = ps.iterator(); i.hasNext();) {
67                Object objPs = i.next();
68                sessionFactory.getCurrentSession().delete(objPs);
69            }
70        }
71    }
72 }
```

Explanation:

The following section describes the above code spec.

searchResults()

searchResults() returns the appropriate search results from the database table using **SearchCriteria** as the reference.

This method uses **createSQLQuery()** of SessionFactory, which returns the List of Object arrays with scalar values for each column in the Books, Authors and Publishers table.

This method uses **list()** of Query, which returns the appropriate search results from the Books table.

searchAllResults()

searchAllResults() returns all the search results from the database table.

This method uses **createSQLQuery()** of SessionFactory, which returns the List of Object arrays with scalar values for each column in the Books, Authors and Publishers table.

This method uses **list()** of Query, which returns all the search results from the Books table.

savePopularSearch()

savePopularSearch() does the actual saving of the SearchCriteria in the PopularSearches database table.

This method uses **save()** of SessionFactory, which takes care of adding the SearchCriteria.

getTotalPopularSearches()

getTotalPopularSearch() retrieves the total number of records available in the PopularSearches database table.

This method uses:

☐   **addScalar()** of Query, which declares a scalar query

☐   **uniqueResult()** of Query, which returns single instance of a persistence object. If no result are found, then it returns a null value

deletePopularSearches()

deletePopularSearch() deletes the PopularSearch entries, if the total records in the PopularSearch cross 600 entries.

This method uses **delete()** of SessionFactory, which deletes the 10 records from the PopularSearches database table.

REMINDER

UserDAO's **getUserByUsername()** is explained in the *Chapter 40: Home Page*, which retrieves the details of the logged in user.

BookDAO's **getBookById()** is explained in the Chapter 36: Manage Books, which is called by BookService's getBookById().

Domain Class

This is a domain class with the following specifications.

PopularSearch.java

Domain Specifications

Class Name	Package	Implements
PopularSearch	com.sharanamvaishali.model	java.io.Serializable

Properties			
Property Name	Property Type	Methods	
searchNo	Integer	getSearchNo()	setSearchNo()
searchValue	String	getSearchValue()	setSearchValue()

Code Spec

```
1   package com.sharanamvaishali.model;
2
3   import javax.persistence.*;
4
5   @Entity
6   @Table(name="POPULARSEARCHES")
7   public class PopularSearch implements java.io.Serializable {
8       @Id
9       @GeneratedValue
10      @Column(name="SEARCHNO")
11      private Integer searchNo;
12      @Column(name="VALUE")
13      private String searchValue;
14
15      public Integer getSearchNo() {
16          return searchNo;
17      }
18      public void setSearchNo(Integer searchNo) {
19          this.searchNo = searchNo;
20      }
21
22      public String getSearchValue() {
23          return searchValue;
24      }
25      public void setSearchValue(String searchValue) {
26          this.searchValue = searchValue;
27      }
28  }
```

Search.java

Domain Specifications

Class Name	Package	Implements
Search	com.sharanamvaishali.model	java.io.Serializable

Constructor	
Name	Arguments
Search()	- -
Search()	String searchCriteria

Properties		
Property Name	**Property Type**	**Methods**
searchCriteria	String	getSearchCriteria () setSearchCriteria ()

Code Spec

```
1   package com.sharanamvaishali.model;
2
3   public class Search implements java.io.Serializable {
4       private String searchCriteria;
5
6       public Search() {
7       }
8
9       public Search(String searchCriteria) {
10          this.searchCriteria = searchCriteria;
11      }
12
13      public String getSearchCriteria() {
14          return searchCriteria;
15      }
16      public void setSearchCriteria(String searchCriteria) {
17          this.searchCriteria = searchCriteria;
18      }
19  }
```

REMINDER

User.java [the model class] is explained in the *Chapter 37: Manage Users*.

Book.java [the model class] is explained in the *Chapter 36: Manage Books*.

Author.java [the model class] is explained in the *Chapter 35: Manage Authors*.

Publisher.java [the model class] is explained in the *Chapter 34: Manage Publishers*.

Chapter

46

SECTION VI: FRONTEND [CUSTOMER FACING] SOFTWARE DESIGN DOCUMENTATION

Cart

This module allows adding the books to the cart and then viewing the details of the books purchased along with the total amount to be paid.

When the user logs in:

appears in the home page in the Catgeories section

appears in the Show Book Details, ShowAuthor Details, Show Publisher Details and Show Category Details pages

To add a book to the cart, the user needs to log in and either click or .

The home page holds a link to the Shopping Cart. The link appears only if the user has logged in.

After the books are added using the **Add To Cart** link, the details about the books purchased are displayed in the **Show Cart** page.

This module uses bms.Books table to retrieve a particular book details.

This module is made up of the following:

Type	Name	Description
JSP	showCart.jsp	The list of books in the cart with its details.
Spring		
Controller	CartController.java	The controller class that facilitates data
	BookController.java	operations.
Service Class	CartService.java	The interfaces for the service layer.
	BookService.java	
	UserService.java	
	AuthorService.java	
	PublisherService.java	
	CategoryService.java	
	SearchService.java	
	CartServiceImpl.java	The implementation classes for the service
	BookServiceImpl.java	layer.
	UserServiceImpl.java	
	AuthorServiceImpl.java	
	PublisherServiceImpl.java	
	CategoryServiceImpl.java	
	SearchServiceImpl.java	
DAO Class	BookDAO.java	The interfaces for the DAO layer.
	UserDAO.java	
	AuthorDAO.java	
	PublisherDAO.java	
	CategoryDAO.java	
	SearchDAO.java	
	BookDAOImpl.java	The implementation classes that perform
	UserDAOImpl.java	the actual data operations.
	AuthorDAOImpl.java	
	PublisherDAOImpl.java	
	CategoryDAOImpl.java	
	SearchDAOImpl.java	

Spring		
DispatcherServlet	bookshopdispatcher-servlet.xml	Central dispatcher for HTTP request handlers/controllers.
Hibernate		
Mapping	hibernate.cfg.xml	The mapping file that holds Model class mapping.
Model Class	Book.java	The model classes.
	Author.java	
	Publisher.java	
	User.java	
	Search.java	
	CartItem.java	
	Category.java	

JSP [showCart.jsp]

When the user clicks 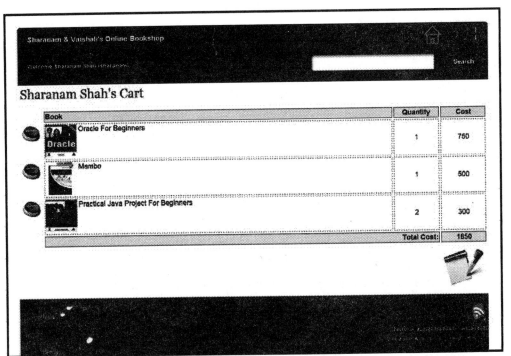, showCart.jsp is served, as shown in diagram 46.1.

Diagram 46.1: Show Cart

Clicking an entry from the list displays that book's details [explained in the *Chapter 41: Book Details*].

If the customer has not added any books to the cart it appears empty, as shown in diagram 46.2.

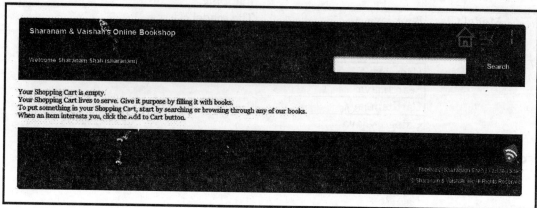

Diagram 46.2: The Empty Cart

Form Specifications

File Name	showCart.jsp
Title	BookShop[Sharanam & Vaishali Shah] - <sec:authorize access='isAuthenticated()'><sec:authentication property='principal.username' /></sec:authorize>'s Cart

Code Spec

```
1  <%@page contentType="text/html" pageEncoding="UTF-8"%>
2  <%@taglib uri="http://java.sun.com/jsp/jstl/core" prefix="c"%>
3  <%@taglib prefix="sec" uri="http://www.springframework.org/security/tags" %>
4  <!DOCTYPE HTML PUBLIC "-//W3C//DTD HTML 4.01 Transitional//EN"
5    "http://www.w3.org/TR/html4/loose.dtd">
6  <html>
7    <head>
8      <meta http-equiv="Content-Type" content="text/html; charset=UTF-8">
9      <title>BookShop[Sharanam & Vaishali Shah] - <sec:authorize
    access='isAuthenticated()'><sec:authentication property='principal.username'
    /></sec:authorize>'s Cart</title>
10     <link rel="stylesheet" href="/BookShop/css/frontend.css" type="text/css">
11   </head>
12   <body>
13     <%@ include file="/WEB-INF/jsp/header.jsp" %>
```

```
14        <div id="bodyDiv">
15        <c:choose>
16           <c:when test="${!empty cartList}">
17              <table width="100%" border="0" cellspacing="4" cellpadding="1"
              style="font-size:18px;">
18                 <tr>
19                    <td colspan="2" align="left" class="topAlign">
20                       <span class="spanShowDetails">${userDetails.firstName}
                       ${userDetails.lastName}'s Cart</span><br/><br/>
21                    </td>
22                 </tr>
23                 <tr>
24                    <td align="center" class="topAlign" width="5%"> </td>
25                    <td align="left" class="showCartList">
26                       <strong>Book</strong>
27                    </td>
28                    <td align="center" class="showCartList" width="10%">
29                       <strong>Quantity</strong>
30                    </td>
31                    <td align="center" class="showCartList" width="10%">
32                       <strong>Cost</strong>
33                    </td>
34                 </tr>
35                 <c:forEach items="${cartList}" var="cart">
36                    <c:set var="totalCost" value="${totalCost+(cart.qty*cart.cost)}"/>
37                       <tr>
38                          <td align="center" class="topAlign">
39                             <a href="/BookShop/removeFromCart/<sec:authorize
                             access='isAuthenticated()'><sec:authentication
                             property='principal.username'
                             /></sec:authorize>/${cart.bookNo}">
40                                <img src="/BookShop/images/delete.jpg" alt="Click to
                                remove the Book from the cart">
41                             </a>
42                          </td>
43                          <td align="left" class="topAlign" style="border:1px dashed
                          #990033;">
44                             <a href="/BookShop/showBookDetails/${cart.bookNo}">
45                                <img
                                src="/BookShop/admin/downloadBookPhotograph/${cart.b
                                ookNo}" height="80px" width="80px"/>
46                             </a>
47                             ${cart.bookName}
48                          </td>
49                          <td align="center" style="border:1px dashed #990033;">
50                             ${cart.qty}
51                          </td>
52                          <td align="center" style="border:1px dashed #990033;">
53                             ${cart.cost}
54                          </td>
55                       </tr>
56                 </c:forEach>
57                 <tr>
58                    <td> </td>
```

```
59              <td colspan="2" align="right" style="border:1px solid #990033;
                background-color:#FFFF99;">
60                  <b>Total Cost:</b>
61              </td>
62              <td align="center" style="border:1px solid #990033;
                background-color:#FFFF99;">
63                  <b>${totalCost}</b>
64              </td>
65          </tr>
66      </table>
67      <br/>
68      <c:if test='${!googleMerchantID.equals("")}'>
69          <a href="/BookShop/saveCart/<sec:authorize
            access='isAuthenticated()'><sec:authentication
            property='principal.username' /></sec:authorize>">
70              <img align="right" src="/BookShop/images/checkOut.jpg"
                title="Check out using Google Wallet" />
71          </a>
72      </c:if>
73  </c:when>
74  <c:otherwise>
75      <span style="font:16px/18px Georgia, serif; width:300px;
        color:#990000; height:37px;"><br/>Your Shopping Cart is
        empty.<br>Your Shopping Cart lives to serve. Give it purpose by filling it
        with books.<br>To put something in your Shopping Cart, start by
        searching or browsing through any of our books.<br>When an item
        interests you, click the Add to Cart button.</span>
76  </c:otherwise>
77  </c:choose>
78  <%@ include file="/WEB-INF/jsp/footer.jsp" %>
79  </div>
80  </body>
81 </html>
```

Explanation:

The JSP displays the details of the books added to the cart by the customer.

This JSP also allows the user to delete/remove a book from the cart using .

Spring Security Tags

In the above code spec, Spring Security Tags are used to retrieve the username of the logged in user.

<sec:authorize> is used to determine whether its contents should be evaluated or not. **isAuthenticated()** returns true if the user is not anonymous.

<sec:authentication> allows access to the current Authentication object stored in the security context. It renders a property of the object directly in the JSP. So, for example, if the principal property of the Authentication is an instance of Spring Security's UserDetails object, then using:

<sec:authentication property='principal.username' />

will render the name of the current user.

Controller [CartController.java]

This is a controller class with the following specifications.

Controller Specifications

Class Name	Package	
CartController	com.sharanamvaishali.controllers	
Properties		
Property Name	Data Type	Value
googleMerchantID	String	${googleMerchantID}
Objects		
Object Name	Class Name	Object Type
searchService	SearchService	Service Layer
bookService	BookService	Service Layer
authorService	AuthorService	Service Layer
publisherService	PublisherService	Service Layer
categoryService	CategoryService	Service Layer
cartService	CartService	Service Layer
userService	UserService	Service Layer
Methods		
Method Name	Request Mapping	
showCart()	/showCart/${userName}	
addToCart()	/addToCart/${userName}/${bookNo}	
removeFromCart()	/removeFromCart/${userName}/${bookNo}	

Code Spec

```
1  package com.sharanamvaishali.controllers;
2
3  import com.sharanamvaishali.model.CartItem;
4  import com.sharanamvaishali.model.Search;
5  import com.sharanamvaishali.service.*;
6  import java.util.List;
```

```
7   import java.util.Map;
8   import javax.servlet.http.HttpSession;
9   import org.springframework.beans.factory.annotation.Autowired;
10  import org.springframework.beans.factory.annotation.Value;
11  import org.springframework.security.core.context.SecurityContextHolder;
12  import org.springframework.stereotype.Controller;
13  import org.springframework.web.bind.annotation.PathVariable;
14  import org.springframework.web.bind.annotation.RequestMapping;
15
16  @Controller
17  public class CartController {
18      @Value("${googleMerchantID}")
19      String googleMerchantID;
20
21      @Autowired
22      private SearchService searchService;
23
24      @Autowired
25      private BookService bookService;
26
27      @Autowired
28      private AuthorService authorService;
29
30      @Autowired
31      private PublisherService publisherService;
32
33      @Autowired
34      private CategoryService categoryService;
35
36      @Autowired
37      private CartService cartService;
38
39      @Autowired
40      private UserService userService;
41
42      @RequestMapping("/showCart/{userName}")
43      public String showCart(Map<String, Object> map, @PathVariable("userName") String
        userName, HttpSession session) {
44          map.put("cartList", (List<CartItem>) session.getAttribute(userName));
45          map.put("search", new Search());
46          map.put("googleMerchantID", googleMerchantID);
47          if(SecurityContextHolder.getContext().getAuthentication().isAuthenticated()) {
48              map.put("userDetails",
                userService.getUserByUsername(SecurityContextHolder.getContext().getAuthen
                tication().getName()));
49          }
50          return "showCart";
51      }
52
53      @RequestMapping("/addToCart/{userName}/{bookNo}")
54      public String addToCart(Map<String, Object> map, @PathVariable("bookNo") Integer
        bookNo, @PathVariable("userName") String userName, HttpSession session) {
55          cartService.addBookToCart(bookNo, userName, session);
56          map.put("newReleasesList", bookService.listNewReleases());
```

```
57        map.put("ourAuthorsList", authorService.listOurAuthors());
58        map.put("ourPublishersList", publisherService.listOurPublishers());
59        map.put("allCategoriesList", categoryService.listCategory());
60        map.put("allBooksList", bookService.listBook());
61        map.put("popularSearchList", searchService.listPopularSearches());
62        map.put("updatedBooksList", bookService.listUpdatedBooks());
63        map.put("topTitlesList", bookService.listTopTitles());
64        map.put("search", new Search());
65        return "redirect:/home";
66    }
67
68    @RequestMapping("/removeFromCart/{userName}/{bookNo}")
69    public String removeFromCart(Map<String, Object> map, @PathVariable("bookNo")
       Integer bookNo, @PathVariable("userName") String userName, HttpSession session)
       {
70        cartService.removeBookFromCart(bookNo, userName, session);
71        map.put("newReleasesList", bookService.listNewReleases());
72        map.put("ourAuthorsList", authorService.listOurAuthors());
73        map.put("ourPublishersList", publisherService.listOurPublishers());
74        map.put("allCategoriesList", categoryService.listCategory());
75        map.put("allBooksList", bookService.listBook());
76        map.put("popularSearchList", searchService.listPopularSearches());
77        map.put("updatedBooksList", bookService.listUpdatedBooks());
78        map.put("topTitlesList", bookService.listTopTitles());
79        map.put("search", new Search());
80        return "redirect:/showCart/{userName}";
81    }
82 }
```

Explanation:

The following section describes the above code spec.

showCart()

showCart():

❑ Retrieves the appropriate CartItem's details using **Username** as the reference. It calls Session's **getAttribute()** which returns the details of the CartItem as a List object. **Username** is made available through **@PathVariable** [in the list of User rendered by the View] when the user clicks Show Cart [/showCart/${userName}] to view the cart. This data is made available to the view using Map's **put()**

❑ Initializes the search form as the search form is a part of the view

❑ Makes the Google Merchant ID available to the View

❑ Populates the userDetails object with the username of the logged in user. This is only done, if the user has logged in. This object is used to show the welcome message after the user has logged in

❑ Returns the control to the View along with the data to be populated in the browser. The data that is retrieved is made available using Map's **put()**

addToCart()

addToCart():

❑ Calls CartService's addBookToCart(), which adds the book details such as the book name, cost, quantity to the CartList along with the session and username

Username and **BookNo** is made available through **@PathVariable** when the user clicks Add To Cart [/addToCart/${userName}/${bookNo}] to add the book to the cart.

❑ Retrieves the appropriate New Releases details. It calls BookService class's **listNewReleases()** which returns the details of the newly released books

❑ Retrieves the appropriate Our Author's details. It calls AuthorService class's **listOurAuthors()** which returns the details of the authors

❑ Retrieves the appropriate Our Publisher's details. It calls PublisherService class's **listOurPublishers()** which returns the details of the publishers

❑ Retrieves the appropriate Category's details. It calls CategoryService class's **listCategory()** which returns the details of the categories

❑ Retrieves the appropriate Book's details. It calls BookService class's **listBook()** which returns the details of all the books

❑ Retrieves the Popular Searches values. It calls SearchService class's **listPopularSearches()** which returns the values of popular searches

❑ Retrieves the appropriate Updated Book's details. It calls BookService class's **listUpdatedBooks()** which returns the details of the updated books

❑ Retrieves the appropriate Top Title Book's details. It calls BookService class's **listTopTitles()** which returns the details of the top titled books

❑ Initializes the search form as the search form is a part of the view

❑ Redirects the user to the View. The data that is retrieved is made available using Map's **put()**

removeFromCart()

removeFromCart():

❏ Removes the appropriate CartItem's details using **Username** and **BookNo** as the reference. It calls CartService's **removeBookFromCart()** which removes the CartItem. **Username** and **BookNo** are made available through **@PathVariable** [in the list of CartItem rendered by the View] when the user clicks /removeFromCart/${userName}/${bookNo} to remove the book from the cart

❏ Initializes the search form as the search form is a part of the view

❏ Returns the control to the View along with the data to be populated in the browser

REMINDER

    BookController's **downloadBookSampleChapter()** and **downloadBookTOC()** is explained in the *Chapter 36: Manage Books*, which is used to download the sample chapter and TOC.

Service Class

Interface [CartService.java]

This is a service interface with the following specifications.

Service Interface Specifications

Class Name	Package
CartService	com.sharanamvaishali.service

Code Spec

```
1  package com.sharanamvaishali.service;
2
3  import javax.servlet.http.HttpSession;
4
5  public interface CartService {
6      public void addBookToCart(Integer bookNo, String userName, HttpSession session);
7      public void removeBookFromCart(Integer bookNo, String userName, HttpSession
       session);
8  }
```

Implementation Class [CartServiceImpl.java]

This is a service class with the following specifications.

Service Implementation Specifications

Class Name	Package	Implements
CartServiceImpl	com.sharanamvaishali.service	CartService
Methods		
Method Name	Arguments	
addBookToCart()	Integer bookNo String username HttpSession session	
Methods		
Method Name	Arguments	
removeBookFromCart()	Integer bookNo String username HttpSession session	

Code Spec

```
1   package com.sharanamvaishali.service;
2
3   import com.sharanamvaishali.model.Book;
4   import com.sharanamvaishali.model.CartItem;
5   import java.util.ArrayList;
6   import java.util.List;
7   import javax.servlet.http.HttpSession;
8   import org.springframework.beans.factory.annotation.Autowired;
9   import org.springframework.stereotype.Service;
10  import org.springframework.transaction.annotation.Transactional;
11
12  @Service
13  public class CartServiceImpl implements CartService {
14      @Autowired
15      private BookService bookService;
16
17      @Transactional
18      @Override
19      public void addBookToCart(Integer bookNo, String userName, HttpSession session) {
20          List<CartItem> cartList;
21          if((List<CartItem>) session.getAttribute(userName)!=null) {
22              cartList = (List<CartItem>) session.getAttribute(userName);
23          }
24          else {
25              cartList = new ArrayList();
```

```
27        Book book = bookService.getBookById(bookNo);
28        boolean itemExists = false;
29        for (CartItem item : cartList) {
30            if (item.getBookNo().equals(bookNo)) {
31                item.setQty(item.getQty()+1);
32                item.setCost(item.getCost() * item.getQty());
33                itemExists = true;
34            }
35        }
36        if (!itemExists) {
37            CartItem cartItem = new CartItem(userName, book.getBookNo(),
                  book.getBookName(), book.getSynopsis(), book.getCost(), 1);
38            cartList.add(cartItem);
39        }
40        session.setAttribute(userName, cartList);
41    }
42
43    @Override
44    public void removeBookFromCart(Integer bookNo, String userName, HttpSession
       session) {
45        List<CartItem> cartList;
46        if((List<CartItem>) session.getAttribute(userName)!=null) {
47            cartList = (List<CartItem>) session.getAttribute(userName);
48        }
49        else {
50            cartList = new ArrayList();
51        }
52        for (int i=0; i<cartList.size(); i++) {
53            if (cartList.get(i).getBookNo().equals(bookNo)) {
54                cartList.remove(i);
55            }
56        }
57        session.setAttribute(userName, cartList);
58    }
59 }
```

Explanation:

The following section describes the above code spec.

addBookToCart()

addBookToCart() takes three parameters:

□ BookNo i.e. the book that is clicked for purchase

□ The Username i.e. the user who is purchasing the book

□ The Session

addBookToCart():

❑   Determines if there are already cart items available for the logged in user via the Session's getAttribute()

   o   If the cart already exists in the session, then the cart items belonging to that user are retrieved from the session

   o   If not, then a new CartItem List of type ArrayList is created

❑   Retrieves the appropriate Book's details using **BookNo** as the reference. It calls BookService's **getBookById()** which returns the details of the Book as an Book object

❑   Determines if the same book is being added to the cart again

   o   If yes, then the quantity is increased by 1 and the cost is also increased accordingly

❑   Adds all the book data i.e. username, book number, book name, synopsis, cost to the CartItem

❑   Finally, sets all the data in the Session via its **setAttribute()**

removeBookFromCart()

removeBookFromCart() holds the business logic to remove the book details from the CartItem.

REMINDER

UserService's **getUserByUsername()** is explained in the *Chapter 40: Home Page*, which retrieves the user who has logged in.

BookService's **getBookById()** is explained in the *Chapter 36: Manage Books*, which is called by BookController's downloadBookPhotograph() and CartService's addBookToCart().

AuthorService's **listOurAuthors()**, PublisherService's **listOurPublilshers()**, CategoryService's **listCategory()**, SearchService's **listPopularSearches()** and BookService's **listNewReleases()**, **listBook()**, **listUpdatedBooks()** and **listTopTitles()** are explained in the *Chapter 40: Home Page*.

REMINDER

UserDAO's **getUserByUsername()** is explained in the *Chapter 40: Home Page*, which retrieves the user who has logged in.

BookDAO's **getBookById()** is explained in the Chapter 36: Manage Books, which is called by BookService's getBookById().

AuthorDAO's **listOurAuthors()**, PublisherDAO's **listOurPublilshers()**, CategoryDAO's **listCategory()**, SearchDAO's **listPopularSearches()** and BookDAO's **listNewReleases()**, **listBook()**, **listUpdatedBooks()** and **listTopTitles()** are explained in the *Chapter 40: Home Page*.

Domain Class [CartItem.java]

This is a domain class with the following specifications.

Domain Specifications

Class Name	Package	Implements
CartItem	com.sharanamvaishali.model	java.io.Serializable

Constructor	
Name	**Arguments**
CartItem()	- -
CartItem()	String username Integer bookNo String bookName String synopsis Integer cost Integer qty

Properties			
Property Name	**Property Type**	**Methods**	
userName	String	getUserName()	setUserName()
bookNo	Integer	getBookNo()	setBookNo()
bookName	String	getBookName()	setBookName()
synopsis	String	getSynopsis()	setSynopsis()
cost	Integer	getCost()	setCost()
qty	Integer	getQty()	setQty()

Code Spec

```
1  package com.sharanamvaishali.model;
2
```

```java
3  public class CartItem implements java.io.Serializable {
4      private String userName;
5      private Integer bookNo;
6      private String bookName;
7      private String synopsis;
8      private Integer cost;
9      private Integer qty;
10
11     public CartItem() {
12     }
13
14     public CartItem(String userName, Integer bookNo, String bookName, String synopsis,
       Integer cost, Integer qty) {
15         this.userName = userName;
16         this.bookNo = bookNo;
17         this.bookName = bookName;
18         this.synopsis = synopsis;
19         this.cost = cost;
20         this.qty = qty;
21     }
22
23     public Integer getBookNo() {
24         return bookNo;
25     }
26     public void setBookNo(Integer bookNo) {
27         this.bookNo = bookNo;
28     }
29
30     public String getUserName() {
31         return userName;
32     }
33     public void setUserName(String userName) {
34         this.userName = userName;
35     }
36
37     public String getBookName() {
38         return bookName;
39     }
40     public void setBookName(String bookName) {
41         this.bookName = bookName;
42     }
43
44     public String getSynopsis() {
45         return synopsis;
46     }
47     public void setSynopsis(String synopsis) {
48         this.synopsis = synopsis;
49     }
50
51     public Integer getCost() {
52         return cost;
53     }
54     public void setCost(Integer cost) {
           this.cost = cost;
```

```
56      }
57
58      public Integer getQty() {
59          return qty;
60      }
61      public void setQty(Integer qty) {
62          this.qty = qty;
63      }
64  }
```

REMINDER

User.java [the model class] is explained in the *Chapter 37: Manage Users*.

Book.java [the model class] is explained in the *Chapter 36: Manage Books*.

Author.java [the model class] is explained in the *Chapter 35: Manage Authors*.

Publisher.java [the model class] is explained in the *Chapter 34: Manage Publishers*.

Category.java [the model class] is explained in the *Chapter 33: Manage Categories*.

PopularSearch.java and Search.java [the model classes] are explained in the *Chapter 45: Search Results*.

Chapter

47

SECTION VI: FRONTEND [CUSTOMER FACING] SOFTWARE DESIGN DOCUMENTATION

Checkout

This module is invoked when a user clicks available in showCart.jsp.

This sends the cart details to Google Wallet for further processing and payment.

This module is made up of the following:

Type	Name	Description
JSP	checkOut.jsp	The page which redirects the user to Google Wallet page for payment.
Spring		
Controller	CartController.java	The controller class that facilitates data operations.
Service Class	CartService.java	The interfaces for the service layer.
	TransactionService.java	
	CartServiceImpl.java	The implementation classes for the service layer.
	TransactionServiceImpl.java	
DAO Class	TransactionDAO.java	The interfaces for the DAO layer.
	TransactionDAOImpl.java	The implementation class that performs the actual data operations.
DispatcherServlet	bookshopdispatcher-servlet.xml	Central dispatcher for HTTP request handlers/controllers.
Hibernate		
Mapping	hibernate.cfg.xml	The mapping file that holds Model class mapping.
Model Class	Transaction.java	The model classes.
	CartItem.java	

JSP [checkOut.jsp]

When the user clicks ![icon], the user is first directed to checkOut.jsp which in turn redirects to the Google Wallet.

Form Specifications

File Name	checkOut.jsp
Title	BookShop - Performing Transaction - Please wait....
Action	https://sandbox.google.com/checkout/cws/v2/Merchant/${google MerchantID}/checkoutForm
Method	POST

Data Fields

Type	Name	Value
Hidden	item_name_${loop.index+1}	${cartItem.bookName}
Hidden	item_description_${loop.index+1}	${cartItem.synopsis}
Hidden	item_quantity_${loop.index+1}	${cartItem.qty}
Hidden	item_price_${loop.index+1}	${cartItem.cost}
Hidden	checkout-flow-support.merchant-checkout-flow-support.continue-shopping-url	http://localhost:8080/BookShop/home
Hidden	_charset_	- -

Code Spec

```
1  <%@page contentType="text/html" pageEncoding="UTF-8"%>
2  <%@taglib uri="http://java.sun.com/jsp/jstl/core" prefix="c"%>
3  <!DOCTYPE html>
4  <html>
5    <head>
6      <meta http-equiv="Content-Type" content="text/html; charset=UTF-8">
7      <title>BookShop - Performing Transaction - Please wait....</title>
8    </head>
9    <body class="checkoutBody">
10     <form method="POST"
          action="https://sandbox.google.com/checkout/cws/v2/Merchant/${googleMerchan
          tID}/checkoutForm" accept-charset="utf-8">
11       <c:if test="${!empty cartList}">
12         <c:forEach items="${cartList}" var="cartItem" varStatus="loop">
13           <input type="hidden" name="item_name_${loop.index+1}"
                value="${cartItem.bookName}">
```

```
14              <input type="hidden" name="item_description_${loop.index+1}"
                value="${cartItem.synopsis}">
15              <input type="hidden" name="item_quantity_${loop.index+1}"
                value="${cartItem.qty}">
16              <input type="hidden" name="item_price_${loop.index+1}"
                value="${cartItem.cost}">
17          </c:forEach>
18      </c:if>
19      <input type="hidden"
        name="checkout-flow-support.merchant-checkout-flow-support.continue-shoppi
        ng-url" value="http://localhost:8080/BookShop/home"/>
20          <input type="hidden" name="_charset_"/>
21      </form>
22      <script>
23      <!--
24          document.forms[0].submit();
25      -->
26      </script>
27      </body>
28  </html>
```

Explanation:

The JSP is invoked after the book data is added in the bms.Transactions table.

This JSP dynamically generates the **FORM** for submission to the Google Wallet.

```
<form method="POST"
action="https://sandbox.google.com/checkout/cws/v2/Merchant/${googleMerchan
tID}/checkoutForm" accept-charset="utf-8">
    <c:if test="${!empty cartList}">
        <c:forEach items="${cartList}" var="cartItem" varStatus="loop">
            <input type="hidden" name="item_name_${loop.index+1}"
            value="${cartItem.bookName}">
            <input type="hidden" name="item_description_${loop.index+1}"
            value="${cartItem.synopsis}">
            <input type="hidden" name="item_quantity_${loop.index+1}"
            value="${cartItem.qty}">
            <input type="hidden" name="item_price_${loop.index+1}"
            value="${cartItem.cost}">
        </c:forEach>
    </c:if>
    <input type="hidden"
    name="checkout-flow-support.merchant-checkout-flow-support.continue-shoppi
    ng-url" value="http://localhost:8080/BookShop/home"/>
    <input type="hidden" name="_charset_"/>
</form>
```

This helps sending all the books data from the cart to the Google Wallet for billing and calculation.

After the FORM is generated the same is automatically submitted to Google Wallet [sandbox] using:

```
<script>
  <!--
    document.forms[0].submit();
  -->
</script>
```

Controller [CartController.java]

This is a controller class with the following specifications.

Controller Specifications

Class Name	Package	
CartController	com.sharanamvaishali.controllers	
Properties		
Property Name	Data Type	Value
googleMerchantID	String	${googleMerchantID}
Objects		
Object Name	Class Name	Object Type
cartService	CartService	Service Layer
Methods		
Method Name	Request Mapping	
saveCart()	/saveCart/${userName}	
checkOut()	/checkOut/${userName}	

Code Spec

```
1   package com.sharanamvaishali.controllers;
2
3   import com.sharanamvaishali.service.CartService;
4   import java.util.List;
5   import java.util.Map;
6   import javax.servlet.http.HttpSession;
7   import org.springframework.beans.factory.annotation.Autowired;
8   import org.springframework.beans.factory.annotation.Value;
9   import org.springframework.stereotype.Controller;
10  import org.springframework.web.bind.annotation.PathVariable;
11  import org.springframework.web.bind.annotation.RequestMapping;
12
13  @Controller
14  public class CartController {
15      @Value("${googleMerchantID}")
16      String googleMerchantID;
```

```
17
18      @Autowired
19      private CartService cartService;
20
21      @RequestMapping("/saveCart/{userName}")
22      public String saveCart(Map<String, Object> map, @PathVariable("userName") String
        userName, HttpSession session) {
23          cartService.saveCart(userName, session);
24          return "redirect:/checkOut/{userName}";
25      }
26
27      @RequestMapping("/checkOut/{userName}")
28      public String checkOut(Map<String, Object> map, @PathVariable("userName") String
        userName, HttpSession session) {
29          map.put("cartList", (List<CartItem>) session.getAttribute(userName));
30          map.put("googleMerchantID", googleMerchantID);
31          session.removeAttribute(userName);
32          return "checkOut";
33      }
34  }
```

Explanation:

The following section describes the above code spec.

saveCart()

saveCart():

❏ Calls CartService's saveCart(), which adds the book details such as the book name, cost, quantity to the Transactions database table

❏ Redirects along with the data to the Google Wallet page

checkOut()

checkOut() is called by **savecart()** using the request mapping **/checkOut/${userName}**.

checkOut():

❏ Retrieves the appropriate Cart details using **Username** as the reference. It calls Session's **getAttribute()** which returns the details of the CartItem as a List object. **Username** is made available through **@PathVariable** [in the list of User rendered by the View] when the user is redirected to /checkOut/${userName} to send the book details to Google Wallet. This data is made available to the view using Map's **put()**

❏ Makes the Google Merchant ID available to the View

❏ Deletes the Cart Items from the Session

❏ Returns the control to the View along with the data to be sent to Google Wallet

Service Class

Interface

This is a service interface with the following specifications.

CartService.java

Service Interface Specifications

Class Name	Package
CartService	com.sharanamvaishali.service

Code Spec

```
1  package com.sharanamvaishali.service;
2
3  import javax.servlet.http.HttpSession;
4
5  public interface CartService {
6      public void saveCart(String userName, HttpSession session);
7  }
```

TransactionService.java

Service Interface Specifications

Class Name	Package
TransactionService	com.sharanamvaishali.service

Code Spec

```
1  package com.sharanamvaishali.service;
2
3  import com.sharanamvaishali.model.Transaction;
4
5  public interface TransactionService {
6      public void saveTransaction(Transaction transaction);
7  }
```

Implementation Class

This is a service class with the following specifications.

CartServiceImpl.java

Service Implementation Specifications

Class Name	Package	Implements
CartServiceImpl	com.sharanamvaishali.service	CartService

Objects		
Object Name	Class Name	Object Type
transactionService	TransactionService	Service Layer
transactionDAO	TransactionDAO	Data Access Object Layer

Methods	
Method Name	Arguments
saveCart()	String username HttpSession session

Code Spec

```
1   package com.sharanamvaishali.service;
2
3   import com.sharanamvaishali.dao.TransactionDAO;
4   import com.sharanamvaishali.model.CartItem;
5   import com.sharanamvaishali.model.Transaction;
6   import java.util.ArrayList;
7   import java.util.List;
8   import javax.servlet.http.HttpSession;
9   import org.springframework.beans.factory.annotation.Autowired;
10  import org.springframework.stereotype.Service;
11  import org.springframework.transaction.annotation.Transactional;
12
13  @Service
14  public class CartServiceImpl implements CartService {
15      @Autowired
16      private TransactionService transactionService;
17
18      @Autowired
19      private TransactionDAO transactionDAO;
20
21      @Transactional
22      @Override
23      public void saveCart(String userName, HttpSession session) {
24          List<CartItem> cartList = (List<CartItem>) session.getAttribute(userName);
25          Integer nextTransactionNo = transactionDAO.getNextTransactionNo();
26          for (CartItem cartItem : cartList) {
27              if (cartItem.getUserName().equals(userName)) {
28                  Transaction transaction = new Transaction();
29                  transaction.setTransactionNo(nextTransactionNo);
30                  transaction.setBookName(cartItem.getBookName());
31                  transaction.setCost(cartItem.getCost());
32                  transaction.setQty(cartItem.getQty());
```

```
33              transaction.setUserName(userName);
34              transactionService.saveTransaction(transaction);
35          }
36      }
37  }
38 }
```

Explanation:

The following section describes the above code spec.

saveCart()

saveCart() holds the business logic to save the cart details as transactions.

saveCart():

❑ Retrieves the cart details using Username as the reference

❑ Increments **TransactionNo** by invoking the DAO Layer's [TransactionDAO] **getNextTransactionNo()**

❑ Iterates over the Cart Items. For every iteration:

   o A new Transaction object is initialized

   o Book details are set in the Transaction object

   o TransactionService's saveTransaction() is invoked to save the transaction data

TransactionServiceImpl.java

Service Implementation Specifications

Class Name	Package	Implements
TransactionServiceImpl	com.sharanamvaishali.service	TransactionService
Objects		
Object Name	Class Name	Object Type
transactionDAO	TransactionDAO	Data Access Object Layer
Methods		
Method Name		Arguments
saveTransantion()	.	Transaction transaction

Code Spec

```
1  package com.sharanamvaishali.service;
2
3  import com.sharanamvaishali.dao.TransactionDAO;
4  import com.sharanamvaishali.model.Transaction;
```

```
 5  import org.springframework.beans.factory.annotation.Autowired;
 6  import org.springframework.stereotype.Service;
 7  import org.springframework.transaction.annotation.Transactional;
 8
 9  @Service
10  public class TransactionServiceImpl implements TransactionService {
11      @Autowired
12      private TransactionDAO transactionDAO;
13
14      @Transactional
15      @Override
16      public void saveTransaction(Transaction transaction) {
17          transactionDAO.saveTransaction(transaction);
18      }
19  }
```

Explanation:

The following section describes the above code spec.

saveTransaction()

saveTransaction() holds the business logic to save the cart details.

This method in turn invokes the DAO Layer's [TransactionDAO] **saveTransaction()**.

DAO Class

Interface [TransactionDAO.java]

This is a Data Access Object interface with the following specifications.

DAO Interface Specifications

Class Name	Package
TransactionDAO	com.sharanamvaishali.dao

Code Spec

```
1  package com.sharanamvaishali.dao;
2
3  import com.sharanamvaishali.model.Transaction;
4
5  public interface TransactionDAO {
6      public void saveTransaction(Transaction transaction);
7      public Integer getNextTransactionNo();
8  }
```

Implementation Class [TransactionDAOImpl.java]

This is a **Data Access Object** class with the following specifications.

DAO Implementation Specifications

Class Name	Package	Implements
TransactionDAOImpl	com.sharanamvaishali.dao	TransactionDAO

Objects	
Object Name	Class Name
sessionFactory	SessionFactory

Methods		
Method Name	Arguments	Return Values
saveTransaction()	Transaction transaction	void
getNextTransactionNo()	- -	Integer

Code Spec

```
1  package com.sharanamvaishali.dao;
2
3  import com.sharanamvaishali.model.Transaction;
4  import org.hibernate.SessionFactory;
5  import org.springframework.beans.factory.annotation.Autowired;
6  import org.springframework.stereotype.Repository;
7
8  @Repository
9  public class TransactionDAOImpl implements TransactionDAO {
10     @Autowired
11     private SessionFactory sessionFactory;
12
13     @Override
14     public void saveTransaction(Transaction transaction) {
15        sessionFactory.getCurrentSession().merge(transaction);
16     }
17
18     @Override
19     public Integer getNextTransactionNo() {
20        return
           Integer.parseInt(sessionFactory.getCurrentSession().createSQLQuery("SELECT
           MAX(TransactionNo)+1 AS NextTransactionNo FROM
           Transactions").list().get(0).toString());
21     }
22  }
```

Explanation:

The following section describes the above code spec.

saveTransaction()

save**Transaction()** does the actual saving of the transaction [CartItem] in the Transactions database table.

This method uses **merge()** of SessionFactory, which takes care of adding when the user clicks

getNextTransactionNo()

getNextTransactionNo() retrieves the next TransactionNo from the Transactions database table.

This method uses:

❑ **createSQLQuery()** of SessionFactory, which creates the Query object using the native SQL syntax

❑ **get()** of SessionFactory, which returns the persistent instance with the given identifier

REMINDER

Transaction.java [the model class] is explained in the *Chapter 38: Manage Transactions.*

CartItem.java [the model class] is explained in the *Chapter 46: Cart.*

Chapter

48

SECTION VI: FRONTEND [CUSTOMER FACING] SOFTWARE DESIGN DOCUMENTATION

Sign Up

This module allows registering the customers. After signing up, the customers can purchase books and download the TOC and the sample chapter.

This module uses the bms.Users table to perform the above operations.

This module is made up of the following:

Type	Name	Description
JSP	signUp.jsp	The data entry form.
	signUpThankYou.jsp	The thank you page of registration.
Spring		
Controller	SignUpController.java	The controller class that facilitates data operations.

Spring		
Service Class	UserService.java	The interface for the service layer.
	CountryService.java	
	StateService.java	
	MailService.java	
	UserServiceImpl.java	The implementation class for the service layer.
	CountryServiceImpl.java	
	StateService.java	
DAO Class	UserDAO.java	The interface for the DAO layer.
	CountryDAO.java	
	StateDAO.java	
	UserDAOImpl.java	The implementation classes that perform the actual data operations.
	CountryDAOImpl.java	
	StateDAOImpl.java	
DispatcherServlet	bookshopdispatcher-servlet.xml	Central dispatcher for HTTP request handlers/controllers
Hibernate		
Mapping	hibernate.cfg.xml	The mapping file that holds Model class mapping
Model Class	User.java	The model class
	Country.java	
	State.java	
	Search.java	

JSP

signUp.jsp

Visitors can sign up to the site using on the homepage.

 when clicked delivers the Signup page, as shown in diagram 48.1.

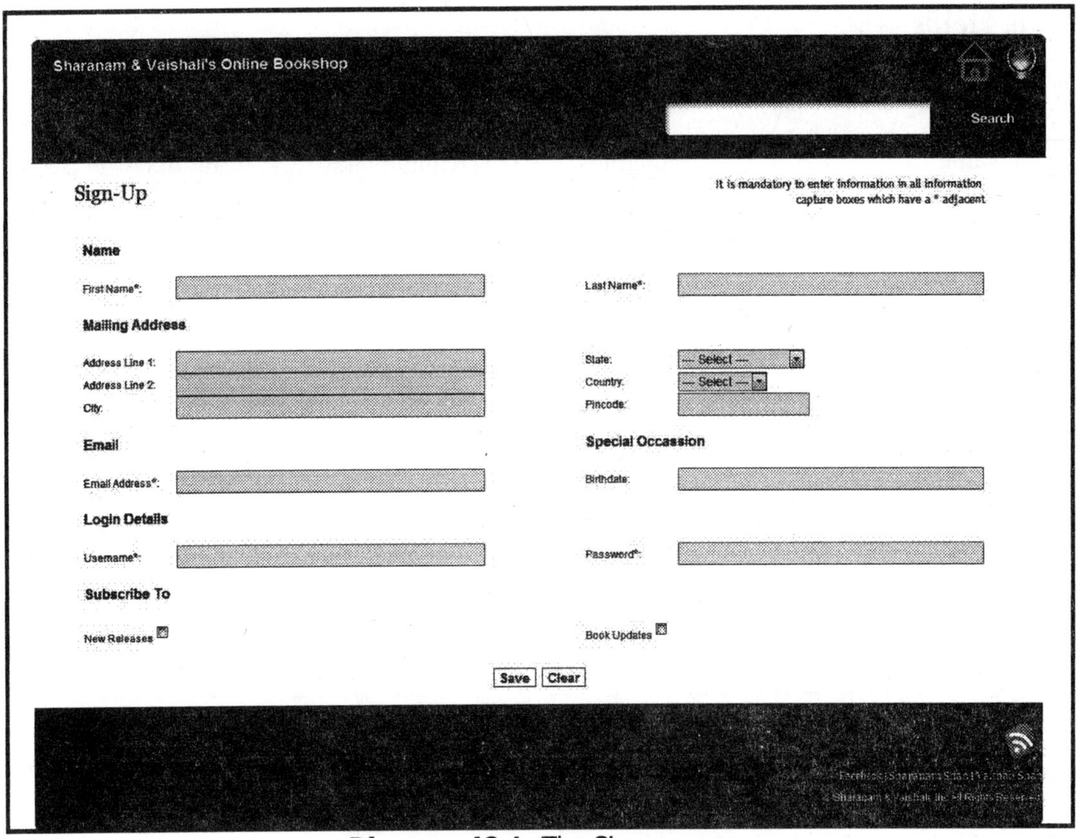

Diagram 48.1: The Signup page

This is a JSP which holds a data entry form, as shown in diagram 48.1.

Form Specifications

File Name	signUp.jsp
Title	BookShop[Sharanam & Vaishali Shah] - Sign Up
Bound To Table	bms.Users
Command Name	User
Action	${pageContext.request.contextPath}/saveSignUp
Method	POST

Data Fields

Label	Name	Bound To	Validation Rules
Name			
First Name	User.firstName	Users.FirstName	Cannot be left blank
Last Name	User.lastName	Users.LastName	Cannot be left blank
Mailing Address			
Address Line 1	User.address1	Users.Address1	- -
Address Line 2	User.address2	Users.Address2	- -
City	User.city	Users.City	- -
State	User.stateNo	Users.StateNo	- -
Country	User.countryNo	Users.CountryNo	- -
Pincode	User.pincode	Users.Pincode	- -
Email			
Email Address	User.emailAddress	Users.EmailAddress	Cannot be left blank
Special Occasion			
Birthdate	User.dob	Users.DOB	- -
Login Details			
Username	User.userName	Users.Username	Cannot be left blank
Password	User.password	Users.Password	Cannot be left blank
Subscribe To			
New Releases	User.newRelease	Users.NewRelease	- -
Book Updates	User.bookUpdates	Users.BookUpdates	- -

Micro-Help For Form Fields

Form Field	Micro Help Statement
Name	
User.firstName	Enter the first name
User.lastName	Enter the last name
Mailing Address	
User.address1	Enter the street address
User.address2	Enter the street address
User.city	Enter the city
User.stateNo	Select the state
User.countryNo	Select the country
User.pincode	Enter the pincode
Email	
User.emailAddress	Enter the email address
Special Occasion	
User.dob	Enter the birthdate

Form Field	Micro Help Statement
Login Details	
User.userName	Enter the username
User.password	Enter the password
Subscribe To	
User.newRelease	Select to new releases
User.bookUpdates	Select to book updates

Data Controls

Object	Label
Submit	Save
Reset	Clear

Code Spec

```
1  <%@page contentType="text/html" pageEncoding="UTF-8"%>
2  <%@taglib uri="http://www.springframework.org/tags/form" prefix="form"%>
3  <%@taglib uri="http://java.sun.com/jsp/jstl/core" prefix="c"%>
4  <!DOCTYPE HTML PUBLIC "-//W3C//DTD HTML 4.01 Transitional//EN"
5    "http://www.w3.org/TR/html4/loose.dtd">
6  <html>
7    <head>
8      <meta http-equiv="Content-Type" content="text/html; charset=UTF-8">
9      <title>BookShop[Sharanam & Vaishali Shah] - Sign Up</title>
10     <link rel="stylesheet" href="/BookShop/css/frontend.css" type="text/css">
11   </head>
12   <body>
13     <%@ include file="/WEB-INF/jsp/header.jsp" %>
14     <div id="bodyDiv">
15       <form:form method="post"
         action="${pageContext.request.contextPath}/saveSignUp"
         commandName="user">
16         <form:hidden path="userNo" />
17         <table width="100%" border="0" align="center" cellpadding="0"
           cellspacing="0">
18           <tr>
19             <td>
20               <table border="0" cellpadding="0" cellspacing="0"
                 width="100%">
21                 <tr>
22                   <td class="spanHeader">Sign-Up</td>
23                   <td align="center" class="error">${dbError}</td>
24                   <td class="information">
25                     It is mandatory to enter information in all information
                     <br>capture boxes which have a <span
                     class="mandatory">*</span> adjacent
26                   </td>
```

```
27                        </tr>
28                      </table>
29                    </td>
30                  </tr>
31                  <tr><td> </td></tr>
32                  <tr>
33                    <td>
34                      <table width="90%" border="0" align="center" cellpadding="0"
                         cellspacing="0">
35                        <tr>
36                          <td>
37                            <table width="100%" border="0" cellpadding="0"
                               cellspacing="0">
38                              <tr>
39                                <td class="label" colspan="4">
40                                  <br />Name<br /><br />
41                                </td>
42                              </tr>
43                              <tr>
44                                <td width="10%">First Name<span
                                   class="mandatory">*</span>:</td>
45                                <td width="45%">
46                                  <form:input path="firstName" title="Enter the
                                   first name" maxlength="25" size="55"/><br>
47                                  <form:errors path="firstName" cssClass="error"
                                   />
48                                </td>
49                                <td width="10%">Last Name<span
                                   class="mandatory">*</span>:</td>
50                                <td width="45%">
51                                  <form:input path="lastName" title="Enter the
                                   last name" maxlength="25" size="55"/><br>
52                                  <form:errors path="lastName" cssClass="error"
                                   />
53                                </td>
54                              </tr>
55                              <tr>
56                                <td class="label" colspan="4">
57                                  <br />Mailing Address<br /><br />
58                                </td>
59                              </tr>
60                              <tr>
61                                <td width="10%">Address Line 1:</td>
62                                <td width="45%">
63                                  <form:input path="address1" title="Enter the
                                   street address" maxlength="50" size="55"/>
64                                </td>
65                                <td width="10%">State:</td>
66                                <td width="45%">
67                                  <form:select path="stateNo">
68                                    <form:option value="" label="--- Select
                                     ---"/>
69                                    <form:options title="Select the state"
```

```
                              items="${stateList}" itemValue="stateNo"
                              itemLabel="state" />
70                          </form:select>
71                        </td>
72                      </tr>
73                      <tr>
74                        <td width="10%">Address Line 2:</td>
75                        <td width="45%">
76                          <form:input path="address2" title="Enter the
                            street address" maxlength="50" size="55"/>
77                        </td>
78                        <td width="10%">Country:</td>
79                        <td width="45%">
80                          <form:select path="countryNo">
81                            <form:option value="" label="--- Select
                              ---"/>
82                            <form:options title="Select the country"
                              items="${countryList}"
                              itemValue="countryNo" itemLabel="country"
                              />
83                          </form:select>
84                        </td>
85                      </tr>
86                      <tr>
87                        <td width="10%">City:</td>
88                        <td width="45%">
89                          <form:input path="city" title="Enter the city"
                            maxlength="50" size="55"/>
90                        </td>
91                        <td width="10%">Pincode:</td>
92                        <td width="45%">
93                          <form:input path="pincode" title="Enter the
                            pincode" maxlength="15" size="20"/>
94                        </td>
95                      </tr>
96                      <tr>
97                        <td class="label" colspan="2">
98                          <br />Email<br /><br />
99                        </td>
100                       <td class="label" colspan="2">
101                         <br />Special Occassion<br /><br />
102                       </td>
103                     </tr>
104                     <tr>
105                       <td width="10%">Email Address<span
                          class="mandatory">*</span>:</td>
106                       <td width="45%">
107                         <form:input path="emailAddress" title="Enter
                            the email address" maxlength="50"
                            size="55"/><br>
108                         <form:errors path="emailAddress"
                            cssClass="error" />
109                       </td>
110                       <td width="10%">Birthdate:</td>
```

```
111                                        <td width="45%">
112                                            <form:input path="dob" title="Enter the
                                               birthdate" maxlength="25" size="55"/>
113                                        </td>
114                                    </tr>
115                                    <tr>
116                                        <td class="label" colspan="4">
117                                            <br />Login Details<br /><br />
118                                        </td>
119                                    </tr>
120                                    <tr>
121                                        <td width="10%">Username<span
                                           class="mandatory">*</span>:</td>
122                                        <td width="45%">
123                                            <form:input path="userName" title="Enter the
                                               username" maxlength="25" size="55"/><br>
124                                            <form:errors path="userName" cssClass="error"
                                               />
125                                        </td>
126                                        <td width="10%">Password<span
                                           class="mandatory">*</span>:</td>
127                                        <td width="45%">
128                                            <form:password path="password" title="Enter
                                               the password" maxlength="8" size="55"/><br>
129                                            <form:errors path="password" cssClass="error"
                                               />
130                                        </td>
131                                    </tr>
132                                    <tr>
133                                        <td class="label" colspan="4">
134                                            <br />Subscribe To<br /><br />
135                                        </td>
136                                    </tr>
137                                    <tr>
138                                        <td colspan="2">New Releases<form:checkbox
                                           path="newRelease" title="Select to new
                                           releases"/></td>
139                                        <td colspan="2">Book Updates<form:checkbox
                                           path="bookUpdates" title="Select to book
                                           updates"/></td>
140                                    </tr>
141                                </table>
142                            </td>
143                        </tr>
144                        <tr>
145                            <td colspan="2" class="centerAlign">
146                                <br /><br />
147                                <input type="submit" class="groovybutton" value="Save"
                                   />
148                                <input type="reset" value="Clear" class="groovybutton"
                                   onclick="javascript:document.location.href='/BookShop/si
                                   gnUp'" />
```

```
149                              </td>
150                            </tr>
151                          </table>
152                        </td>
153                      </tr>
154                    </table>
155                  </form:form>
156                  <%@ include file="/WEB-INF/jsp/footer.jsp" %>
157              </div>
158          </body>
159  </html>
```

Explanation:

This is a standard data entry form. By default when the form loads, it's in the **INSERT** mode.

After JSP loads, the user can simply key in the required data and click **Save**. After saving the data in the database, an email is sent to the user indicating a successful sign up and the user is taken to the Sign up Thank You page.

signUpThankYou.jsp

Once **Save** is clicked, after entering the correct data in the sign up form, the Signup Thank You page is delivered, as shown in diagram 48.2.

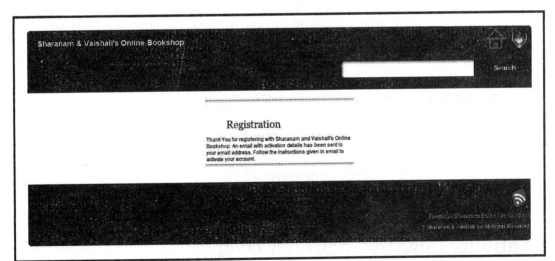

Diagram 48.2: The Signup Thank You page

This is a JSP which holds a thank you message indicating a successful sign up, as shown in diagram 48.2.

Form Specifications

File Name	signUpThankYou.jsp
Title	BookShop[Sharanam & Vaishali Shah] - Sign Up Thank You

Code Spec

```
1  <%@page contentType="text/html" pageEncoding="UTF-8"%>
2  <!DOCTYPE HTML PUBLIC "-//W3C//DTD HTML 4.01 Transitional//EN"
3    "http://www.w3.org/TR/html4/loose.dtd">
4  <html>
5    <head>
6      <meta http-equiv="Content-Type" content="text/html; charset=UTF-8">
7      <title>BookShop[Sharanam & Vaishali Shah] - Sign Up Thank You</title>
8      <link rel="stylesheet" href="/BookShop/css/frontend.css" type="text/css">
9    </head>
10   <body>
11     <%@ include file="/WEB-INF/jsp/header.jsp" %>
12     <div id="bodyDiv">
13       <table border="0" cellspacing="0" cellpadding="2" align="center">
14         <tr><td> </td></tr>
15         <tr><td class="hrLine"> </td></tr>
16         <tr><td class="spanHeader">Registration</td></tr>
17         <tr>
18           <td class="thankYouContent">
19             Thank You for registering with Sharanam and Vaishali's Online
             Bookshop. An email with activation details has been sent to your
             email address. Follow the instructions given in email to activate your
             account.
20           </td>
21         </tr>
22         <tr><td class="hrLine"> </td></tr>
23       </table>
24       <%@ include file="/WEB-INF/jsp/footer.jsp" %>
25     </div>
26   </body>
27 </html>
```

Explanation:

This is a thank you of the sign up form. This page appears once the user registers successfully.

Controller [SignUpController.java]

This is a controller class with the following specifications.

Controller Specifications

Class Name	Package	
SignUpController	com.sharanamvaishali.controllers	
Properties		
Property Name	Data Type	Value
emailDFrom	String	${emailFrom}
Objects		
Object Name	Class Name	Object Type
userService	UserService	Service Layer
countryService	CountryService	Service Layer
stateService	StateService	Service Layer
mailService	MailService	Service Layer
Methods		
Method Name	Request Mapping	
showSignUp()	/signUp	
registerCustomer()	/saveSignUp	
showSignUpThankYou()	/signUpThankYou	

Code Spec

```
1   package com.sharanamvaishali.controllers;
2
3   import com.sharanamvaishali.model.Search;
4   import com.sharanamvaishali.model.User;
5   import com.sharanamvaishali.service.CountryService;
6   import com.sharanamvaishali.service.MailService;
7   import com.sharanamvaishali.service.StateService;
8   import com.sharanamvaishali.service.UserService;
9   import java.util.Map;
10  import javax.validation.Valid;
11  import org.hibernate.exception.ConstraintViolationException;
12  import org.springframework.beans.factory.annotation.Autowired;
13  import org.springframework.beans.factory.annotation.Value;
14  import org.springframework.stereotype.Controller;
15  import org.springframework.validation.BindingResult;
16  import org.springframework.web.bind.annotation.ModelAttribute;
17  import org.springframework.web.bind.annotation.RequestMapping;
18  import org.springframework.web.bind.annotation.RequestMethod;
19
20  @Controller
21  public class SignUpController {
22      @Value("${emailFrom}")
23      String emailFrom;
24
25      @Autowired
26      private MailService mailService;
```

```
27
28     @Autowired
29     private UserService userService;
30
31     @Autowired
32     private CountryService countryService;
33
34     @Autowired
35     private StateService stateService;
36
37     @RequestMapping("/signUp")
38     public String showSignUp(Map<String, Object> map) {
39         map.put("user", new User());
40         map.put("countryList", countryService.listCountry());
41         map.put("stateList", stateService.listState());
42         map.put("search", new Search());
43         return "signUp";
44     }
45
46     @RequestMapping(value = "/saveSignUp", method = RequestMethod.POST)
47     public String registerCustomer(Map<String, Object> map, @ModelAttribute("user")
       User user, @Valid User signUpValid, BindingResult result) {
48         if (result.hasErrors()) {
49             map.put("countryList", countryService.listCountry());
50             map.put("stateList", stateService.listState());
51             map.put("search", new Search());
52             return "signUp";
53         } else {
54             try {
55                 user.setAuthority("CUSTOMER");
56                 user.setEnabled(true);
57                 userService.saveUser(user);
58                 mailService.sendMail(emailFrom,
59                 user.getEmailAddress(),
60                 "Sharanam & Vaishali's Online Bookshop: Registration mail",
61                 "<table width='100%' border='0' align='center' cellpadding='15'
                   cellspacing='0' "
62                     + "style='font-family:Verdana, Arial, Helvetica, sans-serif;
                       font-size:12pt; color:#5a5a5a;'>"
63                     + "<tr><td align='left'>Dear " + user.getFirstName() +
                       ",</td></tr><tr>"
64                     + "<td align='left'>Your login details are:<br/><br/>"
65                     + "Username: " + user.getUserName() + "<br />"
66                     + "Password: " + user.getPassword() + "<br /><br/>"
67                     + "<p>Thank you for using  this site.<br />"
68                     + "</p><br/><br/><p>Regards,<br />Sharanam & Vaishali's Online
                       Bookshop<br />"
69                     + "</p><p> <br /><br />THIS IS AN AUTOMATED MESSAGE; PLEASE
                       DO NOT REPLY. </p>"
70                     + "</td></tr></table>");
71                 return "redirect:/signUpThankYou";
72             } catch (ConstraintViolationException exp) {
73                 map.put("dbError", exp.getMessage());
```

```
74          return "signUp";
75        }
76      }
77    }
78
79    @RequestMapping("/signUpThankYou")
80    public String showSignUpThankYou(Map<String, Object> map) {
81        map.put("search", new Search());
82        return "signUpThankYou";
83    }
84 }
```

Explanation:

The following section describes the above code spec.

showSignUp()

showSignUp():

❑ Makes a provision for adding a new user by instantiating an object of the User entity class

❑ Retrieves the country details by invoking CountryService's **listCountry()**

❑ Retrieves the state details by invoking StateService's **listState()**

❑ Initializes the search form as the search form is a part of the view

registerCustomer()

registerCustomer():

❑ Checks if result [BindingResult] has any errors [validation's errors]

❑ If the captured data is found to be invalid, then:

   o Retrieves the country details by invoking CountryService's listCountry()

   o Retrieves the state details by invoking StateService's listState()

   o Initializes the search form as the search form is a part of the view

   o Returns the control to the View along with the error messages [available in the BindingResult object]

❑ If the captured data is found to be valid, then:

   o Sets the Authority column to CUSTOMER to indicate that this is a customer signing up

   o Sets the Enabled column to TRUE to allow the customer to Login

   o Saves the user details using **UserService**'s **saveUser()**

o   Sends an email to the registered customer via **MailService**'s **sendMail()**, after the data is inserted in the appropriate tables. This email informs the customer about the successful sign up

o   Redirects the control to the View to render the signUpThankYou page

showSignUpThankYou()

showSignUpThankYou():

❑   Initializes the search form as the search form is a part of the view

❑   Returns the control to the View to render the signUpThankYou page

REMINDER

UserService's **saveUser()** is explained in the *Chapter 37: Manage Users*, which saves the user details entered in the Sign Up form.

CountryService's **listCountry()** is explained in the *Chapter 31: Manage Countries*, which retrieves the list of country names to be filled in the Country drop down list box.

StateService's **listState()** is explained in the *Chapter 32: Manage States*, which retrieves the list of state names to be filled in the State drop down list box.

MailService's **sendMail()** is explained in the *Chapter 36: Manage Books*, which sends an email to the users who have successfully registered.

REMINDER

UserDAO's **saveUser()** is explained in the *Chapter 37: Manage Users*, which saves the user details entered in the Sign Up form.

CountryDAO's **listCountry()** is explained in the *Chapter 31: Manage Countries*, which retrieves the list of country names to be filled in the Country drop down list box.

StateDAO's **listState()** is explained in the *Chapter 32: Manage States*, which retrieves the list of state names to be filled in the State drop down list box.

REMINDER

User.java [the model class] is explained in the *Chapter 37: Manage Users*.
Country.java [the model class] is explained in the *Chapter 31: Manage Countries*.
State.java [the model class] is explained in the *Chapter 32: Manage States*.
Search.java [the model class] is explained in the *Chapter 45: Search Results*.

Chapter

49

SECTION VI: FRONTEND [CUSTOMER FACING] SOFTWARE DESIGN DOCUMENTATION

Forgot Password

Forgot Password is a data entry form which retrieves the password and sends the same via an email when the appropriate username is entered.

This module uses the bms.Users table to perform the above operation.

This module is made up of the following:

Type	Name	Description
JSP	forgotPassword.jsp	The data entry form.
Spring		
Controller	UserController.java	The controller class that facilitates data operations.
Service Class	UserService.java	The interface for the service layer.
	MailService.java	

Spring		
Service Class	UserServiceImpl.java	The implementation class for the service layer.
DAO Class	UserDAO.java	The interface for the DAO layer.
	UserDAOImpl.java	The implementation class that performs the actual data operations.
DispatcherServlet	bookshopdispatcher-servlet.xml	Central dispatcher for HTTP request handlers/controllers.
Hibernate		
Mapping	hibernate.cfg.xml	The mapping file that holds Model class mapping.
Model Class	User.java	The model class.
	Search.java	

JSP [forgotPassword.jsp]

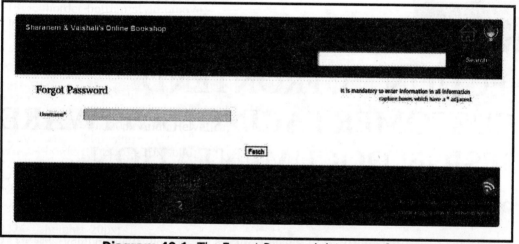

Diagram 49.1: The Forgot Password data entry form

This is a JSP which holds a data entry form, as shown in diagram 49.1. This form appears when the user clicks **Forgot Password** link available on the home page of the application.

Form Specifications

File Name	forgotPassword.jsp
Title	BookShop[Sharanam & Vaishali Shah] - Forgot Password
Bound To Table	bms.Users
Form Name	forgotPassword
Method	POST

Data Fields

Label	Name	Bound To	Validation Rules
Username	- -	Users.Username	Cannot be left blank

Micro-Help For Form Fields

Form Field	Micro Help Statement
Username	Enter the username

Data Controls

Object	Label
Button	Fetch

Code Spec

```
1  <%@page contentType="text/html" pageEncoding="UTF-8"%>
2  <%@taglib uri="http://java.sun.com/jsp/jstl/core" prefix="c"%>
3  <!DOCTYPE HTML PUBLIC "-//W3C//DTD HTML 4.01 Transitional//EN"
4   "http://www.w3.org/TR/html4/loose.dtd">
5  <html>
6    <head>
7      <meta http-equiv="X-UA-Compatible" content="IE=8" />
8      <meta http-equiv="Content-Type" content="text/html; charset=UTF-8">
9      <title>BookShop[Sharanam & Vaishali Shah] - Forgot Password</title>
10     <link rel="stylesheet" href="/BookShop/css/frontend.css" type="text/css">
11   </head>
12   <body>
13     <%@ include file="/WEB-INF/jsp/header.jsp" %>
14     <div id="bodyDiv">
15       <form name="forgotPassword" method="post">
16         <table width="100%" border="0" cellspacing="0" cellpadding="2"
           align="center">
17           <tr>
18             <td>
19               <table border="0" cellpadding="0" cellspacing="0" width="100%">
20                 <tr>
21                   <td class="spanHeader">Forgot Password</td>
22                   <td class="information">
23                     It is mandatory to enter information in all information
                       <br>capture boxes which have a <span
                       class="mandatory">*</span> adjacent
24                   </td>
25                 </tr>
26               </table>
27             </td>
```

```
28              </tr>
29              <tr><td> </td></tr>
30              <tr>
31                <td>
32                  <table width="90%" border="0" align="center" cellpadding="0"
                    cellspacing="0">
33                    <tr>
34                      <td>
35                        <table width="100%" border="0" cellpadding="0"
                          cellspacing="0">
36                          <tr>
37                            <td width="10%">Username<span
                              class="mandatory">*</span>:</td>
38                            <td>
39                              <input name="userName" maxlength="55"
                                title="Enter the username" size="55"/>
40                            </td>
41                          </tr>
42                          <tr>
43                            <td width="10%"> </td>
44                            <td>
45                              <br/><br/><strong
                                class="error">${message}</strong>
46                            </td>
47                          </tr>
48                          <tr>
49                            <td colspan="2" class="centerAlign">
50                              <br /><br />
51                              <input class="groovybutton" type="button"
                                onclick="if(document.forgotPassword.userName.v
                                alue!='')
                                {document.location.href='${pageContext.request.
                                contextPath}/admin/retrievePassword/' +
                                document.forgotPassword.userName.value}"
                                title="Retrieve Password" value="Fetch" />
52                            </td>
53                          </tr>
54                        </table>
55                      </td>
56                    </tr>
57                  </table>
58                </td>
59              </tr>
60            </table>
61          </form>
62          <%@ include file="/WEB-INF/jsp/footer.jsp" %>
63        </div>
64      </body>
65    </html>
```

Explanation:

The Forgot password data entry form retrieves the password for the customers who have forgotten their password.

The password of the customer is send via an email, if the user enters the correct username.

Controller [UserController.java]

This is a controller class with the following specifications.

Controller Specifications

Class Name	Package
UserController	com.sharanamvaishali.controllers

Properties		
Property Name	**Data Type**	**Value**
emailDFrom	String	${emailFrom}

Objects		
Object Name	**Class Name**	**Object Type**
userService	UserService	Service Layer
mailService	MailService	Service Layer

Methods	
Method Name	**Request Mapping**
showForgotPassword()	/admin/forgotPassword
retrievePassword()	/admin/retrievePassword/${userName}

Code Spec

```
1   package com.sharanamvaishali.controllers;
2
3   import com.sharanamvaishali.model.Search;
4   import com.sharanamvaishali.model.User;
5   import com.sharanamvaishali.service.MailService;
6   import com.sharanamvaishali.service.UserService;
7   import java.util.Map;
8   import org.springframework.beans.factory.annotation.Autowired;
9   import org.springframework.beans.factory.annotation.Value;
10  import org.springframework.stereotype.Controller;
11  import org.springframework.web.bind.annotation.PathVariable;
12  import org.springframework.web.bind.annotation.RequestMapping;
13
14  @Controller
15  @RequestMapping("/admin")
16  public class UserController {
17      @Value("${emailFrom}")
18      String emailFrom;
19
20      @Autowired
21      private MailService mailService;
```

```
22
23    @Autowired
24    private UserService userService;
25
26    @RequestMapping("/forgotPassword")
27    public String showForgotPassword(Map<String, Object> map) {
28        Search search = new Search();
29        map.put("search", search);
30        return "forgotPassword";
31    }
32
33    @RequestMapping("/retrievePassword/{userName}")
34    public String retrievePassword(Map<String, Object> map,
      @PathVariable("userName") String userName) {
35        User user = userService.getUserByUsername(userName);
36        String message;
37        if (user != null) {
38            map.put("userDetails", user);
39            mailService.sendMail(emailFrom,
40            user.getEmailAddress(),
41            "Sharanam & Vaishali's Online Bookshop: Forgot Password mail",
42            "<table width='100%' border='0' align='center' cellpadding='0' cellspacing='0'
              "
43                  + "style='font-family:Verdana, Arial, Helvetica, sans-serif;
                    font-size:12pt; color:#5a5a5a;'>"
44                  + "<tr><td align='left'><p>Dear " + user.getFirstName() +
                    ",</p></td></tr><tr>"
45                  + "<td align='left'><p>As requested, please find your login details
                    below:</p><br/>"
46                  + "<br/><p>Username: " + user.getUserName() + "<br />Password: " +
                    user.getPassword() +
47                  "<br /></p><br/><p>Thank you for using  this site.<br
                    /></p><br/><br/><p>"
48                  + "Regards,<br />Sharanam & Vaishali's Online Bookshop<br
                    /></p><p><br /><br />"
49                  + "THIS IS AN AUTOMATED MESSAGE; PLEASE DO NOT REPLY.
                    </p></td></tr></table>");
50            message = "Password sent to " + user.getEmailAddress();
51        } else {
52            message = "Invalid Username. Please try again";
53        }
54        map.put("message", message);
55        Search search = new Search();
56        map.put("search", search);
57        return "forgotPassword";
58    }
59 }
```

Explanation:

The following section describes the above code spec.

showForgotPassword()

showForgotPassword():

❑ Initializes the search form as the search form will be part of the view

❑ Returns the control to the View. The data of the search form that is retrieved is made available using Map's **put()**

retrievePassword()

retrievePassword():

❑ Retrieves the appropriate User's details using **Username** as the reference. It calls UserService's **getUserByUsername()** which returns the details of the user as an User object. **Username** is made available through **@PathVariable** [in the list of Users rendered by the View] when the user clicks Forgot Password [/retrievePassword/${userName}] to retrieve the password. This data is made available for the email to be send to the recipient who has forgotten the password using Map's **put()**

❑ Sends an email to the customer who has forgotten the password along with the password via **MailService**'s **sendMail()**, if the username is entered correctly

❑ Returns the control to the View along with the error messages, if the username entered by the customer is not valid

❑ Initializes the search form as the search form is a part of the view

❑ Shifts control to the View to render the forgotPassword page

REMINDER

UserService's **getUserByUsername()** is explained in the *Chapter 40: Home Page*.

MailService's **sendMail()** is explained in the *Chapter 36: Manage Books*, which sends an email to the users.

REMINDER

UserDAO's **getUserByUsername()** is explained in the *Chapter 40: Home Page*.

REMINDER

User.java [the model class] is explained in the *Chapter 37: Manage Users*.
Search.java [the model class] is explained in the *Chapter 45: Search Results*.

Chapter

50

SECTION VI: FRONTEND [CUSTOMER FACING] SOFTWARE DESIGN DOCUMENTATION

Common Includes

Frontend Header

This module is made up of the following:

Type	Name	Description
JSP	header.jsp	The header of the frontend [customer facing] section.

JSP [header.jsp]

When the user is not logged in, the header appears, as shown in diagram 50.1.

Diagram 50.1: Header of the Frontend Section [User not logged in]

When the user is logged in, the header appears, as shown in diagram 50.2.

Diagram 50.2: Header of the Frontend Section [User logged in]

This file is included in the beginning of the BODY section in all the frontend files:

```
<body>
    <%@ include file="/WEB-INF/jsp/header.jsp" %>
```

Form Specifications

File Name	header.jsp
Bound To Table	bms.PopularSearches
Command Name	search
Method	POST

Data Fields

Label	Name	Bound To	Validation Rules
--	Search.searchCriteria	--	--

Micro-Help For Form Fields

Form Field	Micro Help Statement
Search.searchCriteria	Enter the search criteria

Data Controls

Object	Label
Button	Search

Code Spec

```
1  <%@taglib uri="http://www.springframework.org/tags/form" prefix="form"%>
2  <%@taglib prefix="sec" uri="http://www.springframework.org/security/tags" %>
3  <div id="headerDiv">
4      <table border="0" cellpadding="0" cellspacing="0" width="100%">
5          <tr>
6              <td width="45%" class="topAlign" align="left">
7                  <table id="welcome" border="0" width="100%">
8                      <tr>
9                          <td>
10                             <h2>Sharanam & Vaishali's Online Bookshop</h2>
11                         </td>
12                     </tr>
13                     <tr>
14                         <td>
15                             <sec:authorize access="isAuthenticated()">
16                                 <br/>
17                                 <h3 class="welcomeMessage">Welcome
                                   ${userDetails.firstName} ${userDetails.lastName}
                                   (<sec:authentication property="principal.username" />)</h3>
18                             </sec:authorize>
19                         </td>
20                     </tr>
21                 </table>
22             </td>
23             <td width="55%">
24                 <table border="0" width="100%">
25                     <tr>
26                         <td>
27                             <table border="0" class="topAlign" align="right" cellpadding="0"
                                   cellspacing="0">
28                                 <tr>
29                                     <td>
30                                         <a href="/BookShop/home"><img
                                           src="/BookShop/images/home.png" title="Home (End
                                           User)"/></a>
31                                     </td>
32                                     <sec:authorize access="isAnonymous()">
33                                         <td>
34                                               
35                                             <a href="/BookShop/signUp"><img
                                               src="/BookShop/images/signup.png" title="Sign
                                               Up"/></a>
36                                         </td>
37                                     </sec:authorize>
38                                     <sec:authorize access="isAuthenticated()">
39                                         <td>
40                                               
41                                             <a href="/BookShop/showCart/<sec:authorize
                                               access='isAuthenticated()'><sec:authentication
                                               property='principal.username'
```

```
              />"></sec:authorize>"><img
              src="/BookShop/images/showCart.png" title="Show
              Cart"/></a>
42            </td>
43          </sec:authorize>
44          <sec:authorize access="isAuthenticated()">
45            <td>
46              
47            <a href="/BookShop/j_spring_security_logout"><img
              src="/BookShop/images/logout.png"
              title="Logout"/></a>
48            </td>
49          </sec:authorize>
50        </tr>
51      </table>
52    </td>
53    </tr>
54    <tr>
55      <td>
56        <br/>
57        <table class="rightAlign" border="0" cellspacing="0"
          cellpadding="0" width="100%">
58          <tr>
59            <td>
60              <form:form commandName="search" method="post">
61                <form:input path="searchCriteria"
                  cssClass="search-text" title="Enter the search criteria"
                  /><input id="button-search" class="search-button"
                  type="button"
                  onclick="document.location.href='${pageContext.reque
                  st.contextPath}/searchResults/' +
                  document.forms[0].searchCriteria.value" title="Search"
                  name="fulltext" value="" />
62              </form:form>
63            </td>
64          </tr>
65        </table>
66      </td>
67    </tr>
68  </table>
69  </td>
70  </tr>
71  </table>
72  </div>
```

Explanation:

This is a JSP which holds the header of the frontend section. It also holds the search form, where the user can search for books.

When the user is logged in, the links Home, Show Cart and Logout are displayed along with the name of the user who has logged in, as shown in diagram 50.2.

When the user is not logged in, the links Home and Sign Up are displayed, as shown in diagram 50.1.

Frontend Footer

This module is made up of the following:

Type	Name	Description
JSP	footer.jsp	The footer of the frontend section.

JSP [footer.jsp]

Diagram 50.3: Footer of the Frontend Section

This is a JSP which holds the footer of the frontend section, as shown in diagram 50.3.

This file is included at the end of the BODY section in all the frontend files:

```
<%@ include file="/WEB-INF/jsp/footer.jsp" %>
</body>
```

Code Spec

```
1   <div class="footer" id="footer">
2       <div id="footerContainer">
3           <div id="copyright">
4                 
5               <a href="/BookShop/admin/adminLogin"><img
                 src="/BookShop/images/admin.png" title="Administration"/></a>
6               <br/>
7               <span><a href="http://www.facebook.com/sharanamvaishali"
                 target="_blank">
8               Facebook</a> | </span><span><a
                 href="http://www.sharanamshah.com"
9               target="_blank">Sharanam Shah</a></span> | <span><a
                 href="http://www.vaishalishahonline.com"
10              target="_blank">Vaishali Shah</a></span><br/><span>&copy; Sharanam &
                 Vaishali, Inc All Rights Reserved </span>
11          </div>
12      </div>
13  </div>
```

Explanation:

This JSP is the footer file of the frontend section.

This JSP holds:

❑ The link to the administration section

❑ The name of the creator of the application

Stylesheet

This module is made up of the following:

Type	Name	Description
CSS	frontend.css	The stylesheet for the frontend section.

Code Spec

```
1  html {
2      overflow-y: scroll;
3      overflow-x: auto;
4      height:100%;
5  }
6
7  body {
8      width: 95%;
9      height:100%;
10     font-family: helvetica, arial, sans-serif;
11     font-size: 12px;
12     color: #333;
13     text-decoration: none;
14     margin: 30px;
15     padding: 0;
16     background: url(../images/chess.jpg) no-repeat center center fixed;
17     -webkit-background-size: cover;
18     -moz-background-size: cover;
19     -o-background-size: cover;
20     background-size: cover;
21 }
22
23 img {
24     border: none;
25 }
26
27 fieldset {
28     padding: 10px 10px;
29     border: 1px solid #663366;
30     -moz-border-radius: 8px;
31     border-radius: 8px;
32 }
```

```
33
34   legend {
35       background: #663366;
36       color:#fff;
37       border: solid 1px black;
38       -webkit-border-radius: 8px;
39       -moz-border-radius: 8px;
40       border-radius: 8px;
41       padding: 6px;
42   }
43
44   #bodyDiv {
45       position: absolute;
46       background-image: url(../images/mainbg.png);
47       background-repeat:repeat;
48       width:95%;
49   }
50
51   #maincontentDiv {
52       float:left;
53       height:100%;
54       width:100%;
55       background: white;
56       margin:0px;padding:0px;
57       margin-left:15px;
58       padding-left:0px;
59       padding-top:15px;
60       padding-bottom:15px;
61   }
62
63   #headerDiv {
64       height:138px;
65       background-image: url(../images/transparent-bg.png);
66       width:100%;
67       border: 2px solid #000;
68       -moz-border-radius: 8px;
69       border-radius: 8px;
70       -moz-border-bottom-left-radius: 0px;
71       -moz-border-bottom-right-radius: 0px;
72       border-bottom-left-radius: 0px;
73       border-bottom-right-radius: 0px;
74   }
75
76   #welcome {
77       float:left;
78       color:white;
79       padding-left: 20px;
80   }
81
82   #searchBar {
83       text-align: right;
84       height: 50px;
85       width:100%;
86       line-height: 5px;
```

```
 87  }
 88
 89  .search-text {
 90      padding: 0 30px 0 10px; margin: 0; border: 0;
 91      line-height:40px;
 92      background: #ffffff;
 93      height:43px;
 94      background:url(../images/text-input-bg.png)  no-repeat;
 95      font-family: sans-serif; font-size: 25px; color: #333333;
 96  }
 97
 98  .search-button {
 99      height: 28px; padding: 0 30px 0 10px; margin: 0; border: 0;
100      width:135px;
101      height:43px;
102      font-family: sans-serif; font-size: 14px; color: #333333;
103      background: #ffffff;
104      line-height:28px;
105      vertical-align: top;
106      background:url(../images/search-button.png)  no-repeat center;
107  }
108
109  #portlets-head-main {
110      text-align: left;
111      font-size: 16px!important;
112      color: #333333;
113
114      background: #D8D8D8;
115      filter: progid:DXImageTransform.Microsoft.gradient(startColorstr='#ffffff', endColors
116
117      background: -webkit-gradient(linear, left top, left bottom, from(#ffffff), to(#D8D8D8
118      background: -moz-linear-gradient(top,  #ffffff,  #D8D8D8); /* for firefox 3.6+ */
119      border: 1px solid #D8D8D8;
120      -moz-border-top-right-radius: 4px;
121      border-top-right-radius: 4px;
122
123      padding: 5px 0px 5px 5px;
124  }
125
126  #portlets-content-main {
127      padding: 10px 10px;
128
129      border: 2px;
130      -moz-box-shadow: 4px 4px 4px #663366;
131      -webkit-box-shadow: 4px 4px 4px #663366;
132      box-shadow: 4px 4px 4px #663366;
133
134      -moz-border-radius: 4px;
135      border-radius: 4px;
136  }
137
138  #footer {
139      color:white;
140      margin-top: 20px;
```

```css
141    float:left;
142    position:relative;
143    width: 100%;
144    background-image: url(../images/transparent-bg.png);
145    border-radius: 8px;
146    -moz-border-top-left-radius: 0px;
147    -moz-border-top-right-radius: 0px;
148    border-top-left-radius: 0px;
149    border-top-right-radius: 0px;
150 }
151
152 #footer a{
153    text-decoration: none;
154    color: #fff;
155 }
156
157 #copyright {
158    text-align:right;
159 }
160
161 #copyright span {
162    line-height:25px;
163 }
164
165 #footerContainer {
166    width:100%;
167    padding: 20px 0 20px 0;
168    margin-left:auto;
169    margin-right:auto;
170 }
171
172 a {
173    text-decoration: none;
174    color: #660000;
175    font-family: Georgia, serif;
176 }
177
178 a:hover {
179    text-decoration: none;
180    color: #FF0000;
181    font-family: Georgia, serif;
182 }
183
184 .label {
185    font-family: "Arial", Times, serif;
186    font-size: 16px;
187    font-weight: bold;
188    color: #990000;
189 }
190
191 .content {
192    font-family: "Arial", Times, serif;
193    font-size: 16px;
194    font-weight: normal;
```

```
195      color: #666666;
196    }
197
198    .categoriesNames {
199      font-family: Verdana,Arial,Helvetica,sans-serif;
200      font-size: 16px;
201      font-weight: bold;
202      color: #990000;
203      text-align: left;
204      vertical-align: top;
205    }
206
207    .groovybutton {
208      font-size:15px;
209      font-weight:bold;
210      color:#CC0000;
211      background-color:#FFFFFF;
212      filter:progid:DXImageTransform.Microsoft.Gradient(GradientType=0,StartColorStr='#
213      border-top-style:groove;
214      border-top-color:#FF0099;
215      border-bottom-style:groove;
216      border-bottom-color:#FF0099;
217      border-left-style:groove;
218      border-left-color:#FF0099;
219      border-right-style:groove;
220      border-right-color:#FF0099;
221    }
222
223    INPUT, SELECT {
224      font: 14px/20px Arial, Helvetica, sans-serif;
225      color: #0b0b0b;
226      border: #c3bca4 1px solid;
227      height: 22px;
228      background-color: #efebde;
229    }
230
231    .hrLine {
232      height: 20px;
233      background: url('../images/hr.jpg') repeat-x;
234    }
235
236    .view {
237      border: 0px solid blue;
238      border-collapse: collapse;
239    }
240
241    .view th {
242      background-color: #EFEBDE;
243      color: #666;
244      text-align: left;
245      border: 1px solid white;
246      padding: 5px;
247    }
248
```

```css
249  .view td {
250     padding: 3px;
251  }
252
253  .view tr.odd {
254     background-color: #fafbff;
255  }
256
257  .view tr.even {
258     background-color: #EFEBDE;
259  }
260
261  .heading {
262     font-weight: bold;
263     font-size: 12px;
264     color: #663366;
265     font-family: "Trebuchet MS";
266  }
267
268  .spanHeader {
269     font: 24px/30px Georgia, serif;
270     width:300px;
271     color: #786e4e;
272     height:37px;
273     text-align: left;
274     vertical-align: top;
275     padding-top: 20px;
276     padding-left: 50px;
277  }
278
279  .thankYouContent {
280     vertical-align: top;
281     text-align: left;
282     width: 300px;
283  }
284
285  .information {
286     font-weight: normal;
287     font-size: 13px;
288     color: #333333;
289     font-family: "Trebuchet MS";
290     text-decoration: none;
291     text-align: right;
292     vertical-align: top;
293     padding-top: 20px;
294     padding-right: 70px;
295  }
296
297  .mandatory {
298     font-weight: bold;
299     font-size: 13px;
300     color: #0099ff;
301     font-family: "Trebuchet MS";
302  }
```

```
303
304  .error {
305      color: red;
306  }
307
308  .searchName {
309      font-family: "Arial", Times, serif;
310      font-size: 15px;
311      font-weight: bold;
312      color: blue;
313      line-height: 20px;
314  }
315
316  .searchYear {
317      font-family: "Arial", Times, serif;
318      font-size: 13px;
319      font-weight: bold;
320      color: green;
321      line-height: 30px;
322  }
323
324  .searchSynopsis {
325      font-family: "Arial", Times, serif;
326      font-size: 13px;
327      font-weight: bold;
328      color: #666666;
329      line-height: 18px;
330  }
331
332  .centerAlign {
333      text-align: center;
334  }
335
336  .allCategoriesTable {
337      position: relative;
338      float: left;
339  }
340
341  .imagePointer {
342      cursor: pointer;
343  }
344
345  .checkoutBody {
346      background-color: red;
347  }
348
349  .welcomeMessage {
350      color: aqua;
351  }
352
353  .rightAlign {
354      text-align: right;
```

```
355  }
356
357  .topAlign {
358      vertical-align: top;
359  }
360
361  .leftAlign {
362      text-align: left;
363  }
364
365  .loginButton {
366      background: url('/BookShop/images/login.jpg') no-repeat;
367      border: 0;
368      cursor: pointer;
369      width: 68px;
370      height: 40px;
371  }
372
373  .popularSearch1 {
374      font-size: 10px;
375      cursor: pointer;
376  }
377
378  .popularSearch2 {
379      font-size: 12px;
380      cursor: pointer;
381  }
382
383  .popularSearch3 {
384      font-size: 15px;
385      cursor: pointer;
386  }
387
388  .popularSearch4 {
389      font-size: 20px;
390      cursor: pointer;
391  }
392
393  .popularSearch5 {
394      font-size: 25px;
395      cursor: pointer;
396  }
397
398  .spanShowDetails {
399      font: 32px/34px Georgia,serif;
400      width: 300px;
401      color: #990000;
402      height: 37px;
403  }
404
405  .showBookList {
406      vertical-align: top;
407      text-align: left;
```

```
408    cursor: pointer;
409  }
410
411  .showCartList {
412      vertical-align: top;
413      border: 1px solid #990033;
414      background-color: #FFFF99;
415  }
```

Chapter

51

SECTION VII: PROJECT CONFIGURATION FILES

Dispatcher Servlet [bookshopdispatcher-servlet.xml]

Using Web based application information is submitted to the server.

Every time a user clicks a link or submits a form using a Web browser, a request is initiated. This request indicates what the user is asking for by holding information such as the requested URL and the data submitted by the user via a form.

The front controller receives such requests and to serve them, calls the appropriate handler.

In Spring, all such requests go through DispatcherServlet. DispatcherServlet is Spring's front controller servlet. The front controller servlet delegates responsibility for a request to other components of an application to perform the actual processing.

DispatcherServlet sends these requests on to a Spring MVC controller which processes the request.

Usually an application may have several controllers. To decide which controller to send a request to, DispatcherServlet refers to handler mappings.

The handler mapping uses the URL that the request holds to determine the appropriate controller.

DispatcherServlet then sends the request to the controller indicated by the handler mapping.

In order to package and send the information to the user who requested it, the controller identifies the View that will render this information.

The controller then sends the request, along with the model [raw information] and view name, back to DispatcherServlet. This way the controller does not get coupled to a particular view.

DispatcherServlet consults a View resolver to map the view name to a specific view implementation, which may or may not be a JSP.

Diagram 51.1 displays the flow of request in the Spring Web MVC Framework.

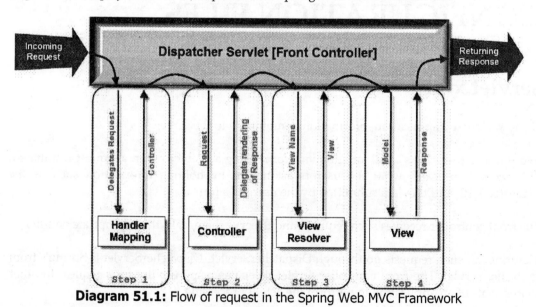

Diagram 51.1: Flow of request in the Spring Web MVC Framework

bookshopdispatcher-servlet.xml

As mentioned earlier, DispatcherServlet consults one or more handler mappings in order to know which controller to dispatch a request to. It learns this from the bookshopdispatcher-servlet.xml file.

DispatcherServlet thus loads the **Application Context** from bookshopdispatcher-servlet.xml.

Code Spec

```
1   <?xml version="1.0" encoding="UTF-8"?>
2   <beans xmlns="http://www.springframework.org/schema/beans"
3          xmlns:context="http://www.springframework.org/schema/context"
4          xmlns:aop="http://www.springframework.org/schema/aop"
5          xmlns:xsi="http://www.w3.org/2001/XMLSchema-instance"
6          xmlns:tx="http://www.springframework.org/schema/tx"
7          xmlns:mvc="http://www.springframework.org/schema/mvc"
8          xsi:schemaLocation="http://www.springframework.org/schema/beans
9          http://www.springframework.org/schema/beans/spring-beans-3.1.xsd
10         http://www.springframework.org/schema/aop
11         http://www.springframework.org/schema/aop/spring-aop-3.1.xsd
12         http://www.springframework.org/schema/context
13         http://www.springframework.org/schema/context/spring-context-3.1.xsd
14         http://www.springframework.org/schema/tx
15         http://www.springframework.org/schema/tx/spring-tx-3.1.xsd
16         http://www.springframework.org/schema/mvc
17         http://www.springframework.org/schema/mvc/spring-mvc-3.0.xsd">
18
19     <context:annotation-config />
20     <context:component-scan base-package="com.sharanamvaishali" />
21     <context:property-placeholder location="classpath*:bookshop.properties"/>
22
23     <bean id="properties"
       class="org.springframework.beans.factory.config.PropertiesFactoryBean">
24         <property name="locations">
25            <list><value>classpath*:bookshop.properties</value></list>
26         </property>
27     </bean>
28
29     <bean id="viewResolver"
       class="org.springframework.web.servlet.view.InternalResourceViewResolver">
30         <property name="viewClass"
       value="org.springframework.web.servlet.view.JstlView" />
31         <property name="prefix" value="/WEB-INF/jsp/" />
32         <property name="suffix" value=".jsp" />
33         <property name="exposedContextBeanNames">
34            <list>
35               <value>properties</value>
36            </list>
37         </property>
```

```
38     </bean>
39
40     <bean id="dataSource" destroy-method="close"
       class="org.apache.commons.dbcp.BasicDataSource">
41         <property name="driverClassName" value="${dbDriverClassName}"/>
42         <property name="url" value="${dbURL}"/>
43         <property name="username" value="${dbUsername}"/>
44         <property name="password" value="${dbPassword}"/>
45     </bean>
46
47     <bean id="sessionFactory"
       class="org.springframework.orm.hibernate4.LocalSessionFactoryBean">
48         <property name="dataSource" ref="dataSource" />
49         <property name="configLocation">
50            <value>classpath:hibernate.cfg.xml</value>
51         </property>
52         <property name="hibernateProperties">
53            <props>
54               <prop key="hibernate.dialect">org.hibernate.dialect.MySQLDialect</prop>
55               <prop key="hibernate.show_sql">${showHQL}</prop>
56            </props>
57         </property>
58     </bean>
59
60     <bean id="multipartResolver"
       class="org.springframework.web.multipart.commons.CommonsMultipartResolver">
61         <property name="maxUploadSize" value="10000000" />
62     </bean>
63
64     <tx:annotation-driven />
65
66     <bean id="transactionManager"
       class="org.springframework.orm.hibernate4.HibernateTransactionManager">
67         <property name="sessionFactory" ref="sessionFactory" />
68     </bean>
69
70     <mvc:annotation-driven/>
71     <mvc:resources mapping="/css/**" location="/WEB-INF/css/*" />
72     <mvc:resources mapping="/images/**" location="/WEB-INF/images/*" />
73
74     <bean id="mailSender"
       class="org.springframework.mail.javamail.JavaMailSenderImpl">
75         <property name="host" value="${emailHost}" />
76         <property name="port" value="${emailPort}" />
77         <property name="username" value="${emailFrom}" />
78         <property name="password" value="${emailPasswd}" />
79         <property name="javaMailProperties">
80            <props>
81               <prop key="mail.smtp.auth">true</prop>
82               <prop key="mail.smtp.starttls.enable">true</prop>
83            </props>
84         </property>
85     </bean>
86
```

```
87     <bean id="mailService" class="com.sharanamvaishali.service.MailService">
88        <property name="mailSender" ref="mailSender" />
89     </bean>
90  </beans>
```

Explanation:

This is the Spring XML configuration file. The following section describes the above code spec.

<context:annotation-config>

<context:annotation-config> informs Spring that the application uses annotation-based wiring.

<context:component-scan>

<context:component-scan> informs Spring to automatically discover and declare beans.

<context:property-placeholder>

<context:property-placeholder> informs Spring to where to locate the properties file, in this case the properties file being bookshop.properties.

properties

This bean defines the properties for Spring MVC.

For this bean **locations** is set, whose value is where the bookshop properties file is located. Thus, Spring automatically picks up the values of the properties stated in the controllers and bookshopdispatcher-servlet.xml.

viewResolver

This bean defines the view resolver for Spring MVC.

For this bean:

- **viewClass** is set as org.springframework.web.servlet.view.JstlView
- **/WEB-INF/jsp/** is set as prefix
- **.jsp** is set as suffix
- **exposedContextBeanNames** is set as properties

JstlView dispatches the request to JSP, just like InternatResourceView. But it also exposes JSTL-specific request attributes so that one can take advantage of JSTL's internationalization support.

Thus, Spring automatically resolves the JSP from WEB-INF/jsp folder and assigned suffix .jsp to it.

Spring is informed about existence of the properties file.

dataSource

This is the Java datasource used to connect to bms database in MySQL. The following configuration information is provided in the dataSource in the form of properties:

❑ JDBC driver class name

❑ JDBC URL

❑ Database username

❑ Database password

sessionFactory

This is the Hibernate configuration where the following Hibernate settings are defined:

❑ **hibernate.cfg.xml** is set as a configuration file which contains entity class mappings

❑ **org.hibernate.dialect.MySQLDialect** is set as a dialect, which informs Hibernate that MySQL database is used in the application

❑ **hibernate.show_sql** is set to true, which means that all SQL statements are written to console

multipartResolver

When a multi-part request is detected by Spring, it activates the resolver that has been declared in DispatcherServlet and hands over the request. The resolver then wraps the current HttpServletRequest into a MultipartHttpServletRequest that supports multipart file uploads. Using MultipartHttpServletRequest, information can be retrieved about the multiparts contained by this request and actually get access to the multipart files themselves in the controllers.

Here, the maximum size for the file uploads is 10000000 bytes

transactionManager

Hibernate transaction manager is used to manage the transactions of the BookShop application.

HibernateTransactionManager class is used for the transaction manager. This class binds a Hibernate Session from the specified factory to the thread, potentially allowing for one thread Session per factory.

<mvc:annotation-driven>

<mvc:annotation-driven> informs Spring to allow MVC based annotations.

<mvc:resources>

<mvc:resources> allows resource requests following a particular URL pattern to be served by a ResourceHttpRequestHandler from any of a list of Resource locations. This provides a convenient way to serve resources from locations other than the web application root, including locations on the classpath.

Here, the CSS and images requests are mapped i.e. the location of the CSS and image files are mentioned.

mailSender

This bean defines the JavaMailSender for the Spring MVC.

This is the JavaMailSender configuration where the following settings are defined in the form properties:
- The host of the email
- The port of the email
- The username of the sender
- The password of the sender
- The JavaMail properties

mailService

This bean defines the MailService for Spring MVC.

Whenever Spring encounters mailSender, it instantiates MailService located in the package com.sharanamvaishali.service in the application.

Chapter 52

SECTION VII: PROJECT CONFIGURATION FILES
Standard Deployment Descriptor [web.xml]

In Java EE, a standard deployment descriptor describes how a component, module or an application [such as a web application or enterprise application] should be deployed. It directs a deployment tool to deploy a module or application with specific container options, security settings and describes specific configuration requirements. XML is used for the syntax of these deployment descriptor files.

For web applications, the deployment descriptor must be called web.xml and must reside in the WEB-INF directory in the web application root.

web.xml

All incoming requests flow through DispatcherServlet. Hence, like any other Servlet in a Java EE application, the Java EE container needs to be informed, to load this Servlet at web app startup time via an in the web app's WEB-INF/web.xml.

Code Spec

```
 1  <?xml version="1.0" encoding="UTF-8"?>
 2  <web-app version="3.0" xmlns="http://java.sun.com/xml/ns/javaee"
 3      xmlns:xsi="http://www.w3.org/2001/XMLSchema-instance"
 4      xsi:schemaLocation="http://java.sun.com/xml/ns/javaee
 5      http://java.sun.com/xml/ns/javaee/web-app_3_0.xsd">
 6      <servlet>
 7          <servlet-name>bookshopdispatcher</servlet-name>
 8          <servlet-class>org.springframework.web.servlet.DispatcherServlet</servlet-clas
            s>
 9          <load-on-startup>1</load-on-startup>
10      </servlet>
11      <servlet-mapping>
12          <servlet-name>bookshopdispatcher</servlet-name>
13          <url-pattern>/</url-pattern>
14      </servlet-mapping>
15      <listener>
16          <listener-class>org.springframework.web.context.ContextLoaderListener</listen
            er-class>
17      </listener>
18      <context-param>
19          <param-name>contextConfigLocation</param-name>
20          <param-value>
21              /WEB-INF/bookshopdispatcher-servlet.xml,
22              /WEB-INF/spring-security.xml
23          </param-value>
24      </context-param>
25      <filter>
26          <filter-name>springSecurityFilterChain</filter-name>
27          <filter-class>org.springframework.web.filter.DelegatingFilterProxy</filter-class>
28      </filter>
29      <filter-mapping>
30          <filter-name>springSecurityFilterChain</filter-name>
31          <url-pattern>/*</url-pattern>
32      </filter-mapping>
33      <welcome-file-list>
34          <welcome-file>home</welcome-file>
35      </welcome-file-list>
36      <session-config>
37          <session-timeout>30</session-timeout>
38      </session-config>
39  </web-app>
```

Explanation:

In web.xml:

❑ DispatcherServlet is registered as a Servlet called **bookshopdispatcher,** which is the name of DispatcherServlet

❑ DispatcherServlet is mapped to handle all incoming requests that end with **/**

- The following contexts are loaded into the Web application context:
  - bookshopdispatcher-servlet.xml
  - spring-security.xml
- This application needs the Spring Security filter. So, this application has an entry for the Spring Security filter

  The declarations for the Spring Security filter causes every web request to be passed through to the bean called springSecurityFilterChain, which is usually an instance of Spring Security's FilterChainProxy.

  FilterChainProxy is a generally-useful class that enables web requests to be passed to different filters based on URL patterns. Those delegated filters are managed inside the application context, so they can benefit from dependency injection.
- As soon as the user requests for the BookShop web application using http://localhost:8080/BookShop/, the request hits the servlet engine which routes the call to the deployed **BookShop** web application

  web.xml holds a welcome file that serves up.

  home matches the URL pattern that has been registered for DispatcherServlet and the request is routed to it.

  DispatcherServlet needs to decide what to do with the request. Based on the configuration available in **bookshopdispatcher-servlet.xml**, the request is routed to a specific Controller.

  Here, **home** is declared as a bean and maped to HomeController. This means, if a URL with **home** is requested, it will ask HomeController to handle the request.

Chapter

53

SECTION VII: PROJECT CONFIGURATION FILES

Properties File [bookshop.properties]

The Properties file represents a persistent set of properties.

.properties is a file extension for files mainly used in Java related technologies to store the configurable parameters of an application.

They can also be used for storing strings for Internationalization and localization, which are known as Property Resource Bundles.

Each parameter is stored as a pair of strings, one storing the name of the parameter [called the key] and the other storing the value.

bookshop.properties

Code Spec

```
1  googleMerchantID=<Google Merchant ID>
2  emailFrom=<Google Email Address>
3  emailUser=<Google Email Address>
4  emailPasswd=<Google Email Password>
5  emailHost=smtp.gmail.com
6  emailPort=587
7  dbUsername=<MySQL Username>
8  dbPassword=<MySQL User Password>
9  dbURL=jdbc:mysql://localhost:3306/<MySQL Database Name>
10 dbDriverClassName=com.mysql.jdbc.Driver
11 showHQL=false
12 sendMail=true
```

Explanation:

bookshop.properties contains the following sensitive information:

❑ The Google merchant ID

❑ The email address of the sender

❑ The email address/username of the sender

❑ The password of the sender

❑ The host of the email

❑ The port of the email

❑ MySQL database username

❑ MySQL database password

❑ MySQL database name

❑ MySQL driver class name

❑ A flag to show or hide HQL

❑ A flag to send mail or not

Chapter

54

SECTION VII: PROJECT CONFIGURATION FILES

Hibernate Configuration File [hibernate.cfg.xml]

Hibernate is configured with hibernate.cfg.xml, which is widely used.

Hibernate consults hibernate.cfg.xml file for its operating properties such as database dialect, connection string and mapping files. These files are searched on class path.

hibernate.cfg.xml

Code Spec

```
1  <?xml version="1.0" encoding="UTF-8"?>
2  <!DOCTYPE hibernate-configuration PUBLIC "-//Hibernate/Hibernate Configuration DTD
   3.0//EN" "http://www.hibernate.org/dtd/hibernate-configuration-3.0.dtd">
3  <hibernate-configuration>
4     <session-factory>
```

```
5          <mapping class="com.sharanamvaishali.model.Country" />
6          <mapping class="com.sharanamvaishali.model.Category" />
7          <mapping class="com.sharanamvaishali.model.State" />
8          <mapping class="com.sharanamvaishali.model.Publisher" />
9          <mapping class="com.sharanamvaishali.model.User" />
10         <mapping class="com.sharanamvaishali.model.Author" />
11         <mapping class="com.sharanamvaishali.model.Book" />
12         <mapping class="com.sharanamvaishali.model.Transaction" />
13         <mapping class="com.sharanamvaishali.model.PopularSearch" />
14      </session-factory>
15   </hibernate-configuration>
```

Explanation:

Hibernate needs to be informed about the mapping classes to refer to.

The mapping class that is needed for the application is defined and referenced in the Hibernate configuration file using <mapping>.

Let's take an example.

In the *Chapter 31: Manage Countries,* a domain **Country** was created. There is a table **Countries** in the database bms.

So the domain **Country** is mapped in the Hibernate Configuration file.

Chapter

55

SECTION VIII: RUNNING THE PROJECT

Assembling And Deploying The Project Using NetBeans IDE

This chapter depicts the steps to assemble the code spec explained so far into a project called **BookShop** and then finally deploy the project using the NetBeans IDE.

Prerequisites

NetBeans IDE 7.1.2

Since the BookShop application is build using the NetBeans IDE, install the NetBeans IDE and then assemble and deploy the project. *The setup file is available in this book's accompanying CDROM.*

MySQL 5.5.25

This application uses MySQL as the data store, install it prior proceeding. *The setup file is available in this book's accompanying CDROM.*

An Important Note!!!

A completely ready to use project assembled in NetBeans IDE is available on this book's CDROM. This chapter only helps understanding the assembling steps.

If you want to learn to assemble a fresh copy of this project, follow the steps indicated hereafter.

You can skip the assembling section and choose to directly run the application that's available on this book's accompanying CDROM, in which case, **it is required:**

❑   To have the MySQL database engine up and running

❑   To have **bms** database loaded on the MySQL database engine. For more information on how to do this, refer to the *Loading The BMS Database In MySQL* topic of this chapter

❑   To fill up the values in the application's properties file for the application to run. For more information on how to do this, refer to the *Modifying bookshop.properties* topic of this chapter

Creating A Web Application

To begin the assembling exercise, open NetBeans IDE. This book's accompanying CDROM holds the setup file for the NetBeans IDE 7.1.

Select **File → New Project**, to create a new **Web Application**. **New Project** dialog box appears, as shown in diagram 55.1.1.

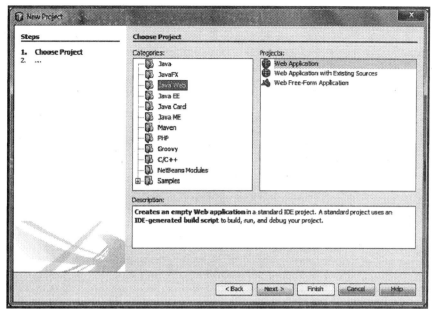

Diagram 55.1.1: New Project dialog box

Select **Java Web** → **Web Application**, as shown in diagram 55.1.1. Click Next >.

New Web Application dialog box appears, as shown in diagram 55.1.2.

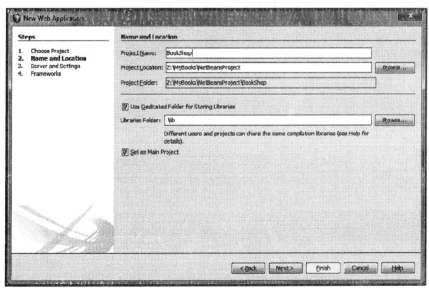

Diagram 55.1.2: New Web Application dialog box

Enter the name of the Web application as **BookShop** and keep the defaults, as shown in diagram 55.1.2. Click [Next >]. **Server and Settings** dialog box appears, as shown in diagram 55.1.3.

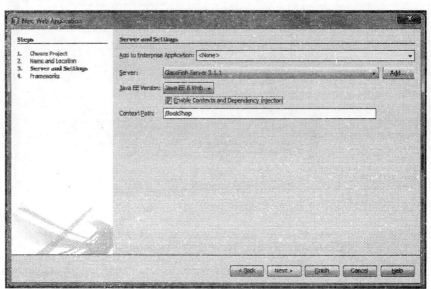

Diagram 55.1.3: Server and Settings

Keep the defaults and check the **Enable Contexts and Dependency Injection** option, as shown in diagram 55.1.3. Click [Next >]. **Frameworks** dialog box appears, as shown in diagram 55.1.4.

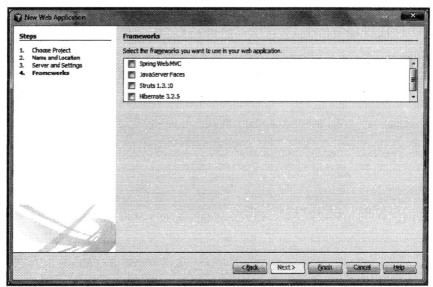

Diagram 55.1.4: Frameworks

Do not select any frameworks, as shown in diagram 55.1.4. Click [FINISH]. **BookShop** application is created in the NetBeans IDE.

Adding The Libraries To The Project

Right-click on the **BookShop** application, select **Properties**.

Project Properties - BookShop dialog box appears, as shown in diagram 55.2.1.

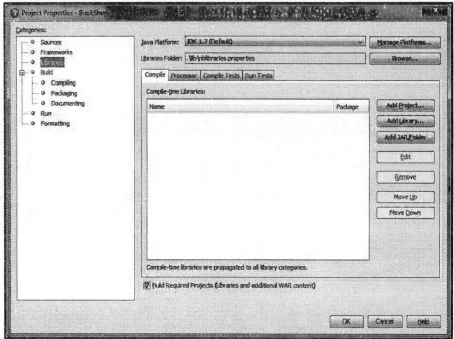

Diagram 55.2.1: Project Properties - BookShop

Select **Libraries** available in the **Categories** list, as shown in diagram 55.2.1.

Click **Add JAR/Folder**. This displays the dialog box that allows choosing the JAR files, as shown in diagram 55.2.2.

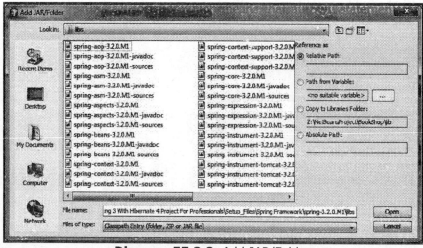

Diagram 55.2.2: Add JAR/Folder

Add the following library files:

1. **Spring Libraries:**

   a) From <Drive>:\spring-3.2.0.M1**libs:**

      i)   spring-aop-3.2.0.M1.jar

      ii)   spring-asm-3.2.0.M1.jar

      iii) spring-beans-3.2.0.M1.jar

      iv) spring-context-3.2.0.M1.jar

      v)   spring-context-support-3.2.0.M1.jar

      vi) spring-core-3.2.0.M1.jar

      vii) spring-expression-3.2.0.M1.jar

      viii)spring-jdbc-3.2.0.M1.jar

      ix) spring-orm-3.2.0.M1.jar

      x)   spring-tx-3.2.0.M1.jar

      xi) spring-web-3.2.0.M1.jar

      xii) spring-webmvc-3.2.0.M1.jar

2. **Spring Security Libraries:**

   a) From <Drive>:\spring-security-3.1.0.RELEASE**dist:**

      i)   spring-security-config-3.1.0.RELEASE.jar

      ii)   spring-security-core-3.1.0.RELEASE.jar

      iii) spring-security-web-3.1.0.RELEASE.jar

      iv) spring-security-taglibs-3.1.0.RELEASE.jar

3. **Hibernate Libraries:**

   a) From <Drive>:\hibernate-release-4.1.4.Final\lib**required:**

      i)   dom4j-1.6.1.jar

      ii)   hibernate-commons-annotations-4.0.1.FINAL.jar

      iii) hibernate-core-4.1.4.FINAL.jar

      iv) hibernate-jpa-2.0-api-1.0.1.FINAL.jar

      v)   javassist-3.15.0.GA.jar

      vi) jboss-logging-3.1.0.GA.jar

      vii) jboss-transaction-api_1.1_spec-1.0.0.FINAL.jar

    b) From <Drive>:\hibernate-release-4.1.4.Final\lib**jpa:**

        i)   hibernate-entitymanager-4.1.4.FINAL.jar

4. **Additional Libraries:**

    a) From <Drive>:**mysql-connector-java-5.1.14:**

        i)   mysql-connector-java-5.1.14-bin.jar

    b) AOP Alliance

        i)   com.springsource.org.aopalliance-1.0.0.jar

    c) ANTLR

        i)   antlr-runtime-3.0.1.jar

    d) From <Drive>:**commons-dbcp-1.4:**

        i)   commons-dbcp-1.4.jar

    e) From <Drive>:**commons-pool-1.6:**

        i)   commons-pool-1.6.jar

    f) From <Drive>:**slf4j-1.6.4:**

        i)   slf4j-api-1.6.4.jar

        ii) slf4j-simpl-1.6.4.jar

    g) Commons

        i)   commons-collections-3.1.jar

        ii) commons-io-2.3.jar

        iii) commons-fileupload-1.2.2.jar

        iv) commons-logging-1.1.1.jar

    h) Mails

        i)   mail.jar

After adding all the JAR files, click **OK**. This adds all the libraries to the project.

Building The Code Spec

Create the following .java class files:

Model Classes

Country.java

To create this class, right-click the **BookShop** project and select **New → Java Class...** as shown in diagram 55.3.1.

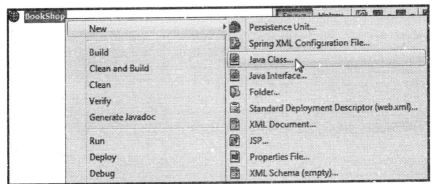

Diagram 55.3.1: Selecting Java Class...

New Java Class dialog box appears, as shown in diagram 55.3.2.

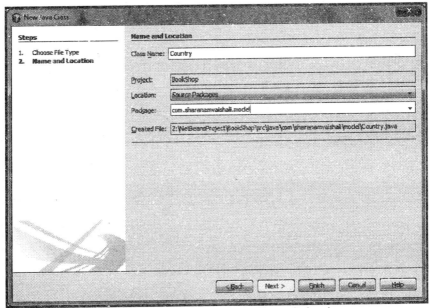

Diagram 55.3.2: New Java Class dialog box

Enter **Country** as the **Class Name** and **com.sharanamvaishali.model** as the **Package**, as shown in diagram 55.3.2.

Click **Finish**. Country.java is created in the NetBeans IDE. Key in the appropriate code.

Similarly create the following model classes:

- State.java
- Category.java
- Publisher.java
- Author.java
- Book.java
- User.java
- Transaction.java
- PopularSearch.java
- Search.java
- CartItem.java

Data Access Object [DAO] Layer

Interfaces

CountryDAO.java

To create this interface, right-click the **BookShop** project and select **New → Java Interface...** as shown in diagram 55.4.1.

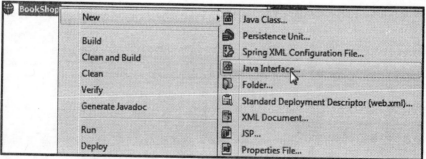

Diagram 55.4.1: Selecting Java Interface...

New Java Interface dialog box appears, as shown in diagram 55.4.2.

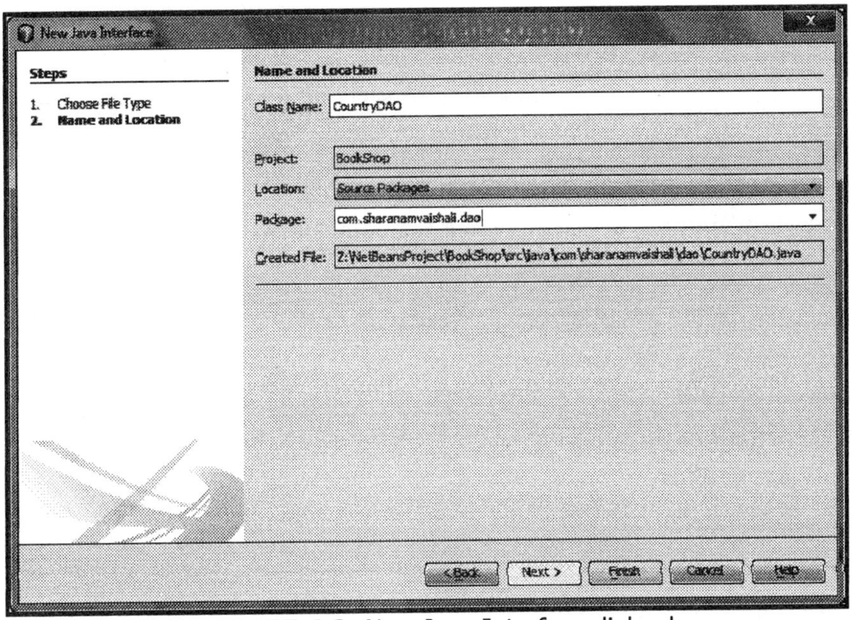

Diagram 55.4.2: New Java Interface dialog box

Enter **CountryDAO** as the **Class Name** and **com.sharanamvaishali.dao** as the **Package**, as shown in diagram 55.4.2.

Click **Finish**. CountryDAO.java is created in the NetBeans IDE. Key in the appropriate code.

Similarly create the following DAO interface:

- ❑ StateDAO.java
- ❑ CategoryDAO.java
- ❑ PublisherDAO.java
- ❑ AuthorDAO.java
- ❑ BookDAO.java
- ❑ UserDAO.java
- ❑ TransactionDAO.java
- ❑ SearchDAO.java
- ❑ CommonDAO.java

Implementations

CountryDAOImpl.java

To create this class, right-click the **BookShop** project and select **New → Java Class....**.

New Java Class dialog box appears.

Enter **CountryDAOImpl** as the **Class Name** and **com.sharanamvaishali.dao** as the **Package**.

Click **Finish**. CountryDAOImpl.java is created in the NetBeans IDE. Key in the appropriate code.

Similarly create the following DAO implementation classes:
- StateDAOImpl.java
- CategoryDAOImpl.java
- PublisherDAOImpl.java
- AuthorDAOImpl.java
- BookDAOImpl.java
- UserDAOImpl.java
- TransactionDAOImpl.java
- SearchDAOImpl.java
- CommonDAOImpl.java

Service Layer

Interfaces

CountryService.java

To create this interface, right-click the **BookShop** project and select **New → Java Interface....**.

New Java Interface dialog box appears.

Enter **CountryService** as the **Class Name** and **com.sharanamvaishali.service** as the **Package**.

Click **Finish**. CountryService.java is created in the NetBeans IDE. Key in the appropriate code.

Similarly create the following Service interface:

- ☐ StateService.java
- ☐ CategoryService.java
- ☐ PublisherService.java
- ☐ AuthorService.java
- ☐ BookService.java
- ☐ UserService.java
- ☐ TransactionService.java
- ☐ SearchService.java
- ☐ CommonService.java
- ☐ CartService.java

Implementations

CountryServiceImpl.java

To create this class, right-click the **BookShop** project and select **New → Java Class....**

New Java Class dialog box appears.

Enter **CountryServiceImpl** as the **Class Name** and **com.sharanamvaishali.service** as the **Package**.

Click **Finish**. CountryServiceImpl.java is created in the NetBeans IDE. Key in the appropriate code.

Similarly create the following Service implementation classes:

- ☐ StateServiceImpl.java
- ☐ CategoryServiceImpl.java
- ☐ PublisherServiceImpl.java
- ☐ AuthorServiceImpl.java
- ☐ BookServiceImpl.java
- ☐ UserServiceImpl.java
- ☐ TransactionServiceImpl.java
- ☐ SearchServiceImpl.java
- ☐ CommonServiceImpl.java

❏   CartServiceImpl.java
❏   MailService.java

Controllers

AuthenticationController.java

To create this class, right-click the **BookShop** project and select **New → Java Class....**

New Java class dialog box appears.

Enter **AuthenticationController** as the **Class Name** and **com.sharanamvaishali.controllers** as the **Package**.

Click **Finish**. AuthenticationController.java is created in the NetBeans IDE. Key in the appropriate code.

Similarly create the following Controllers:
❏   CountryController.java
❏   StateController.java
❏   CategoryController.java
❏   PublisherController.java
❏   AuthorController.java
❏   BookController.java
❏   UserController.java
❏   TransactionController.java
❏   SearchController.java
❏   CartController.java
❏   HomeController.java
❏   SignUpController.java

Views

login.jsp

To create this JSP, right-click the **BookShop** project and select **New → JSP...**, as shown in diagram 55.5.1.

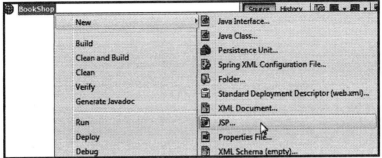

Diagram 55.5.1: Selecting JSP...

New JSP dialog box appears, as shown in diagram 55.5.2.

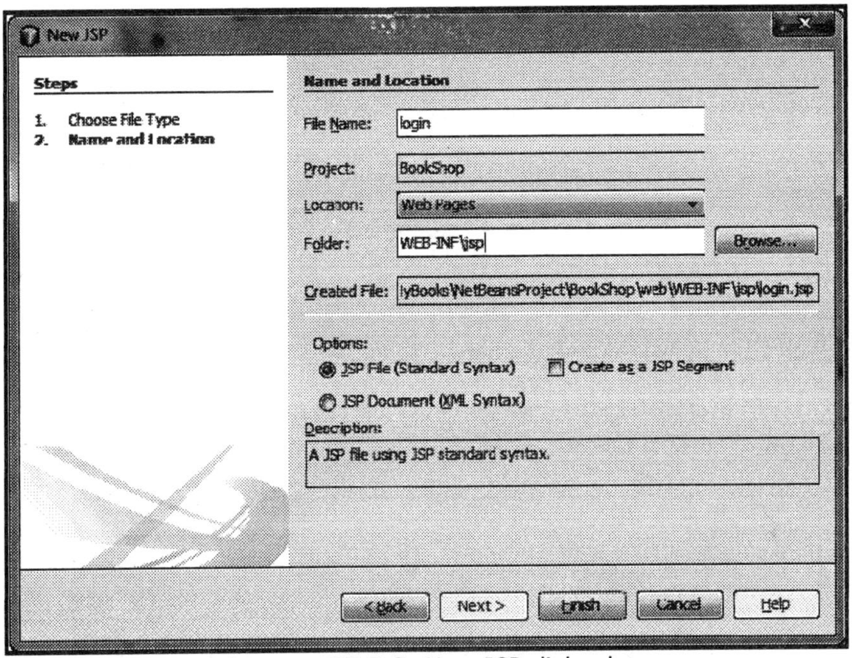

Diagram 55.5.2: New JSP dialog box

Enter **login** as the **File Name** and **WEB-INF/jsp** as the **Folder**, as shown in diagram 55.5.2.

Click **Finish**. login.jsp is created under the folder /WEB-INF/jsp in the NetBeans IDE. Key in the appropriate code.

Similarly create the following views:

- adminAccessDenied.jsp
- adminFooter.jsp
- adminHeader.jsp
- adminLogin.jsp
- manageAuthors.jsp
- manageBooks.jsp
- manageCategories.jsp
- manageCountries.jsp
- managePublishers.jsp
- manageStates.jsp
- manageTransactions.jsp
- manageUsers.jsp
- signUp.jsp
- signUpThankYou.jsp

- allCategories.jsp
- checkOut.jsp
- footer.jsp
- forgotPassword.jsp
- header.jsp
- home.jsp
- leftMenu.jsp
- popularSearches.jsp
- searchResults.jsp
- showAuthorDetails.jsp
- showBookDetails.jsp
- showCart.jsp
- showCategoryDetails.jsp
- showPublisherDetails.jsp

Spring XML Configuration Files

bookshopdispatcher-servlet.xml

To create the configuration file, right-click the **WEB-INF** folder available in **BookShop** application and select **New → Other...**, as shown in diagram 55.6.1.

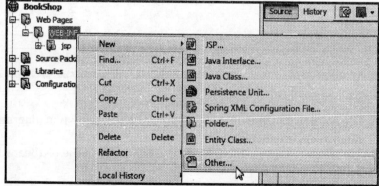

Diagram 55.6.1: Selecting Other...

New File dialog box appears, as shown in diagram 55.6.2.

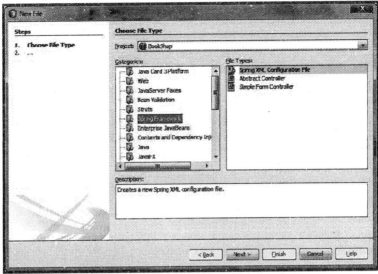

Diagram 55.6.2: New File dialog box

Select **Spring Framework** available under the **Categories** list and **Spring XML Configuration File** available under the **File types,** as shown in diagram 55.6.2.

Click **Next. New Spring XML Configuration File** dialog box appears, as shown in diagram 55.6.3.

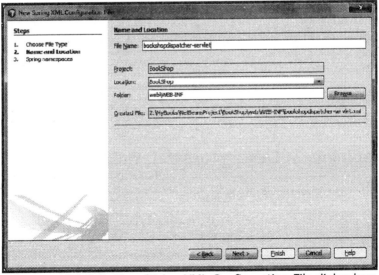

Diagram 55.6.3: New Spring XML Configuration File dialog box

Enter **File Name** as **bookshopdispatcher-servlet**, as shown in diagram 55.6.3.

Click **Next**. **New File** dialog box prompts for the Spring namespace, as shown in diagram 55.6.4.

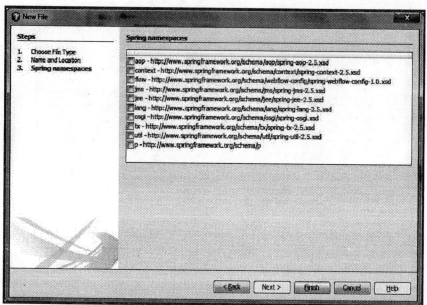

Diagram 55.6.3: Spring namespaces

Do not select any namespace, as shown in diagram 55.6.4. As this book uses Spring 3.2.0, so the namespaces are added manually.

Click **Finish**. The NetBeans IDE creates bookshopdispatcher-servlet.xml. Key in the appropriate code.

Similarly create spring-security.xml.

Standard Deployment Descriptor [web.xml]

To create web.xml, right-click the **Bookshop** project and select **New → Other...**, as shown in diagram 55.7.1.

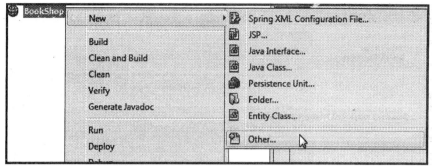

Diagram 55.7.1: Selecting Other...

New File dialog box appears, as shown in diagram 55.7.2.

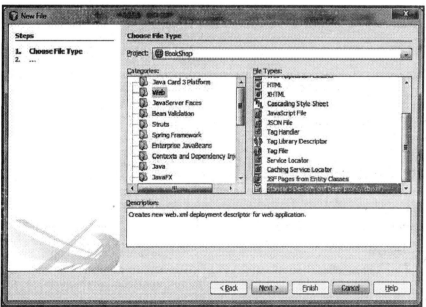

Diagram 55.7.2: New File dialog box

Select **Web** available under the **Categories** list and **Standard Deployment Descriptor (web.xml)** available under the **File Type** list, as shown in diagram 55.7.2.

Click **Next**. The details of web.xml are shown in the dialog box, as shown in diagram 55.7.3, which is not editable.

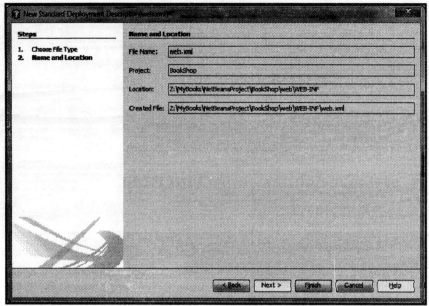

Diagram 55.7.3: New File dialog box

Click **Finish**. web.xml is created under the folder /WEB-INF in the NetBeans IDE. Key in the appropriate code.

Hibernate Configuration File [hibernate.cfg.xml]

To create the configuration file, right-click the **BookShop** application and select **New →
Other...**, as shown in diagram 55.8.1.

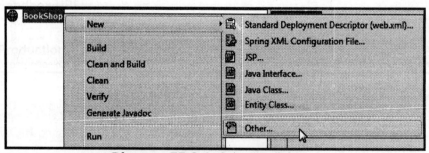

Diagram 55.8.1: Selecting Other...

New File dialog box appears, as shown in diagram 55.8.2.

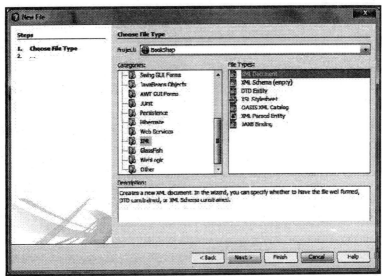

Diagram 55.8.2: New File dialog box

Select **XML** available under the **Categories** list and **XML Document** available under the **File types**, as shown in diagram 55.8.2.

Click **Next**. **New XML Document** dialog box appears, as shown in diagram 55.8.3.

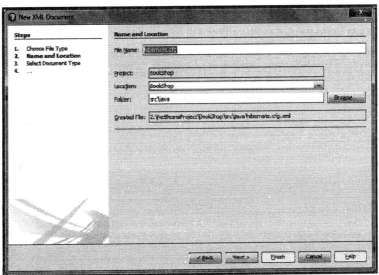

Diagram 55.8.3: New XML Document dialog box

Enter **hibernate.cfg** as the **File Name** and **src\java** as the **Folder**, as shown in diagram 55.8.3.

Click **Next**. **New File** dialog box appears, as shown in diagram 55.8.4.

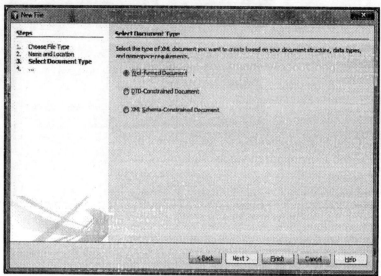

Diagram 55.8.4: New File dialog box

Keep the defaults.

Click **Finish**. The NetBeans IDE creates hibernate.cfg.xml. Key in the appropriate code.

Properties File [bookshop.properties]

To create the configuration file, right-click the **BookShop** application and select **New →
Other...**.

New File dialog box appears, as shown in diagram 55.9.1.

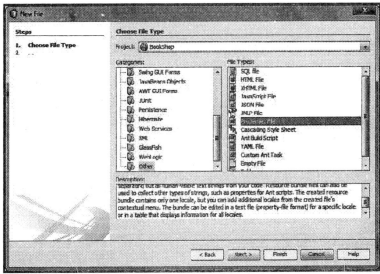

Diagram 55.9.1: New File dialog box

Select **Other** available under the **Categories** list and **Properties File** available under the **File types,** as shown in diagram 55.9.1.

Click **Next. New Properties File** dialog box appears, as shown in diagram 55.9.2.

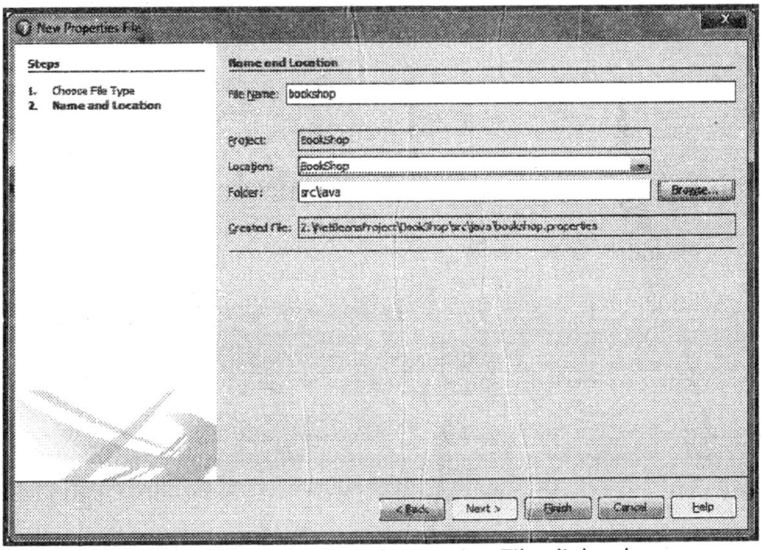

Diagram 55.9.2: New Properties File dialog box

Enter **bookshop** as the **File Name** and **src\java** as the **Folder**, as shown in diagram 55.9.2.

Click **Finish**. The NetBeans IDE creates bookshop.properties. Key in the appropriate code.

Images And CSS

After the source packages, views and configuration files are in place, create the following images and CSS under **/WEB-INF**.

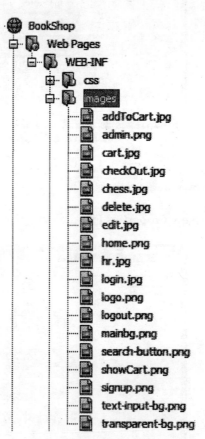

Modifying bookshop.properties

After all the project files are in place, before compiling and running the application, modify the properties file.

This file holds the mail, the Google checkout and MySQL database attributes. Key in the appropriate details for properties indicated by **<>**.

```
googleMerchantID=<The Google Merchant ID>
emailFrom=<Username>@gmail.com
emailUser=<Username>
emailPasswd=<Password>
emailHost=smtp.gmail.com
emailPort=587
dbUsername=<MySQL Username>
dbPassword=<MySQL Password>
dbURL=jdbc:mysql://localhost:3306/bms
dbDriverClassName=com.mysql.jdbc.Driver
showHQL=false
sendMail=true
```

REMINDER

MySQL attributes i.e. **dbUsername** and **dbPassword** are a must for the application to function.

Follow the steps indicated in *Appendix A: Understanding Google Wallet*, to obtain a Google Merchant ID that can be used with this project.

This project uses Gmail as the email host. Hence use the username and password of a Gmail account. The host can be changed to some other email provider by changing **emailHost** and **emailPort**.

sendMail can be set to **false** which will disable mail dispatching throughout the application.

Loading The BMS Database In MySQL

Creating The MySQL Database

Assuming that the MySQL database is up and running, log into the database using the **MySQL Command Line Client** utility.

Create a database called **bms**.

Switch to that database.

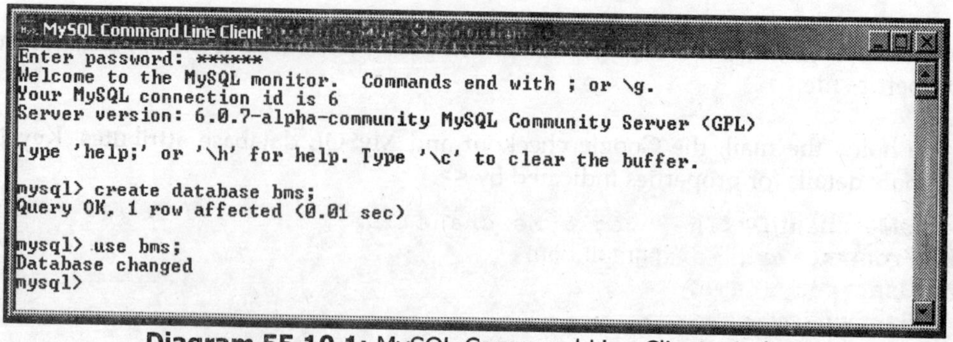

Diagram 55.10.1: MySQL Command Line Client window

Creating Tables With Sample Data

This book's accompanying CDROM [<CDROM Drive>:/Code/BookShop] holds a SQL script with the tables and sample data that can be used to quickly begin using this application.

To do so, copy the SQL script called **bms.sql** to the local hard disk drive and issue the source command, as shown in diagram 55.10.2.

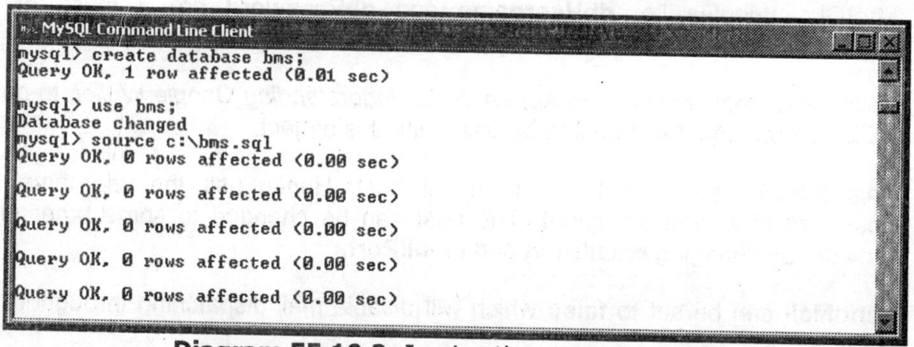

Diagram 55.10.2: Issuing the source command

This will import all the tables along with the sample data.

Building The Project

Now that the files, the database tables and the data is in place, **build** the project **BookShop** using the NetBeans IDE, as shown in diagram 55.11.1.

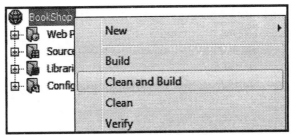

Diagram 55.11.1: Building the project

This compiles all the project files and the builds the WAR file, as shown in diagram 55.11.2.

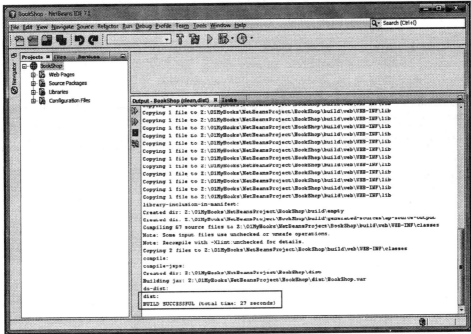

Diagram 55.11.2: Project build successfully

Running The Project

After a successful build the project is ready to run.

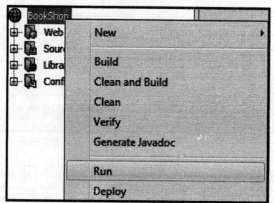

Diagram 55.12.1: Running the project

Clicking **Run deploys** the project's WAR file to the **Glassfish V2 server** [the one that was chosen when creating the BookShop project using the NetBeans IDE] and brings up the application's homepage in the system's default Web browser.

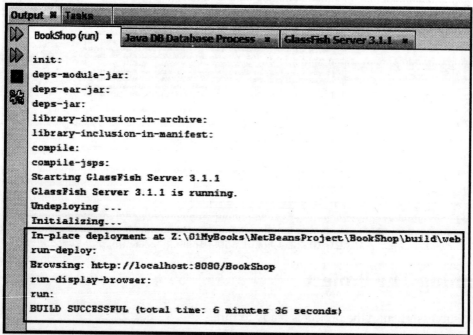

Diagram 55.12.2: Deploying the application and browsing the BookShop index file

Diagram 55.12.3: The home page of the BookShop project

This chapter only shows how to assemble this application using the NetBeans IDE. This is useful for those who wish to learn the steps involved in creating such an application from scratch.

Appendix

A

SECTION IX: APPENDIX

Understanding Google Wallet

Google Wallet is a fast, convenient checkout process that allows:

❑ Customers to buy products from the website with a single login

❑ Seller to process their orders and charge their credit or debit cards for free

In order to use the Google checkout with the project, it is required to sign-up with Google as a merchant/seller.

Point the web browser to http://sandbox.google.com/checkout/seller/. This displays the homepage as shown in diagram A.1.

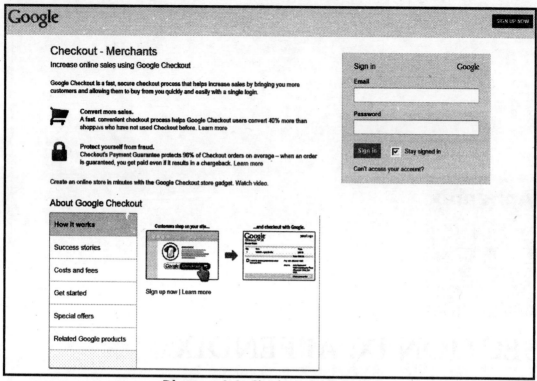

Diagram A.1: Checkout - Merchants

The seller holds the following email account with Google:
s.v.onlinebookshop@gmail.com

If an email account is not available, then create one with Google before proceeding.

Enter the email address and the password in the Sign in section and click ![Sign in]. Google prompts for business information, as shown in diagram A.2.

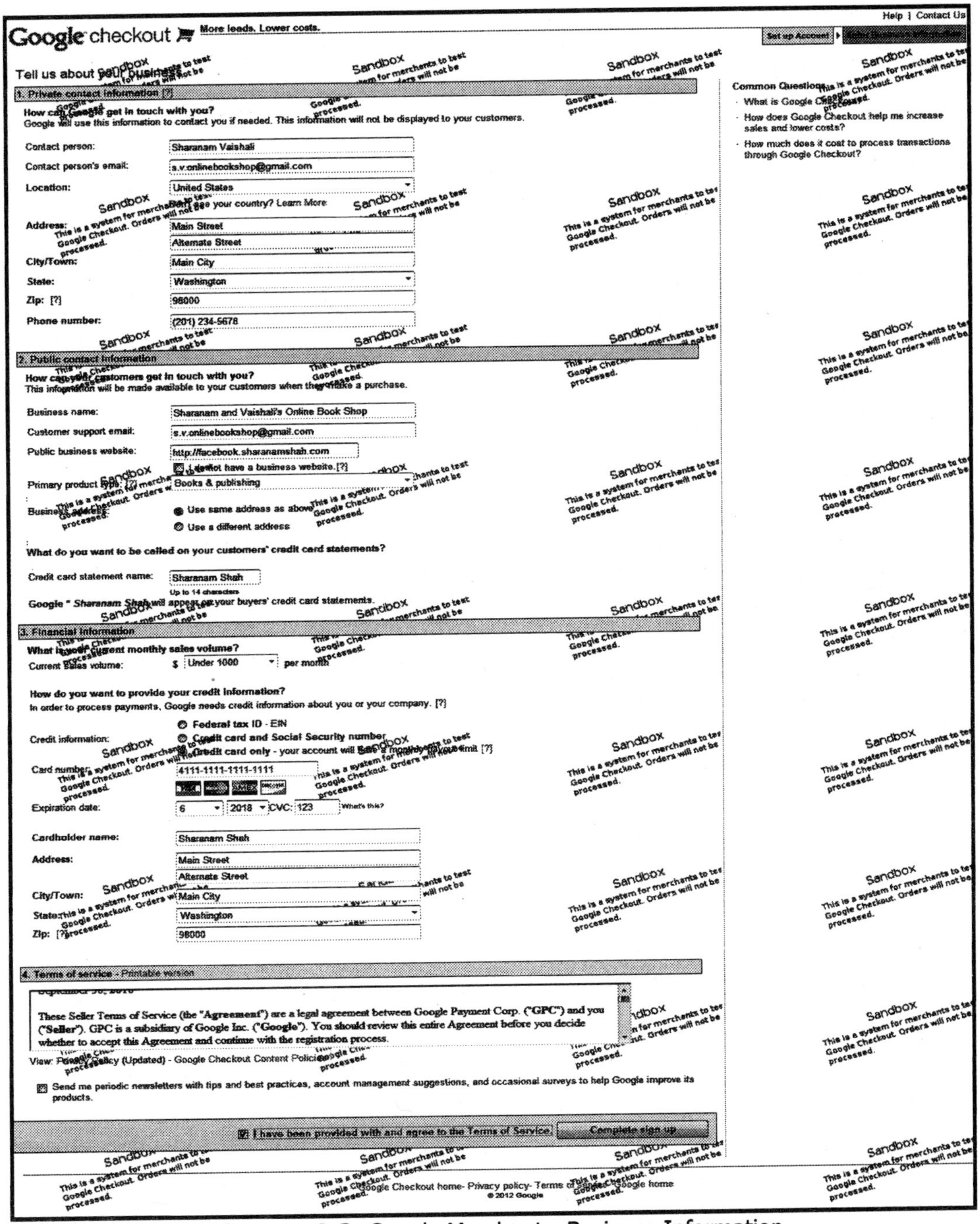

Google checkout 🏷 More leads, Lower costs.

Help | Contact Us

Set up Account ▶

Tell us about your business

1. Private contact information [?]

How can we best get in touch with you?
Google will use this information to contact you if needed. This information will not be displayed to your customers.

Contact person: Sharanam Vaishali

Contact person's email: s.v.onlinebookshop@gmail.com

Location: United States
Don't see your country? Learn More

Address: Main Street
Alternate Street

City/Town: Main City

State: Washington

Zip: [?] 98000

Phone number: (201) 234-5678

2. Public contact information

How can your customers get in touch with you?
This information will be made available to your customers when they make a purchase.

Business name: Sharanam and Vaishali's Online Book Shop

Customer support email: s.v.onlinebookshop@gmail.com

Public business website: http://facebook.sharanamshah.com
☐ I do not have a business website. [?]

Primary product type: Books & publishing

Business address: ● Use same address as above
○ Use a different address

What do you want to be called on your customers' credit card statements?

Credit card statement name: Sharanam Shah
Up to 14 characters

Google * *Sharanam Shah* will appear on your buyers' credit card statements.

3. Financial Information

What is your current monthly sales volume?
Current sales volume: $ Under 1000 per month

How do you want to provide your credit information?
In order to process payments, Google needs credit information about you or your company. [?]

Credit information: ○ Federal tax ID - EIN
● Credit card and Social Security number
○ Credit card only - your account will have a monthly payout limit [?]

Card number: 4111-1111-1111-1111

Expiration date: 6 ▼ 2018 ▼ CVC: 123 What's this?

Cardholder name: Sharanam Shah

Address: Main Street
Alternate Street

City/Town: Main City

State: Washington

Zip: [?] 98000

4. Terms of service - Printable version

These Seller Terms of Service (the "Agreement") are a legal agreement between Google Payment Corp. ("GPC") and you ("Seller"). GPC is a subsidiary of Google Inc. ("Google"). You should review this entire Agreement before you decide whether to accept this Agreement and continue with the registration process.

View: Privacy policy (Updated) - Google Checkout Content Policies

☑ Send me periodic newsletters with tips and best practices, account management suggestions, and occasional surveys to help Google improve its products.

☑ I have been provided with and agree to the Terms of Service. [Complete sign up]

Common Questions
· What is Google Checkout?
· How does Google Checkout help me increase sales and lower costs?
· How much does it cost to process transactions through Google Checkout?

Google Checkout home - Privacy policy- Terms - Google home
© 2012 Google

Diagram A.2: Google Merchant - Business Information

Since this is a sandbox, enter dummy information, as shown in diagram A.3.

Once done, click **Complete sign up**. This displays the merchant account homepage, as shown in diagram A.3.

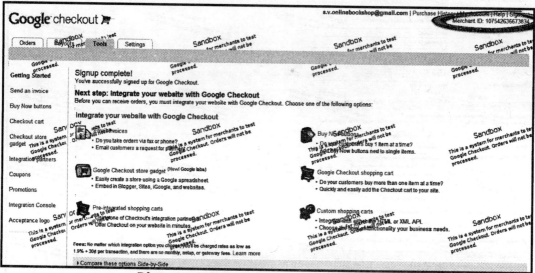

Diagram A.3: Google Merchant - Homepage

This completes the signup process. Make a note of the merchant ID, as shown in diagram A.9. This ID will be required when integrating Google checkout with the shopping cart.

Click **Settings**. This shows a page, as shown in diagram A.4.

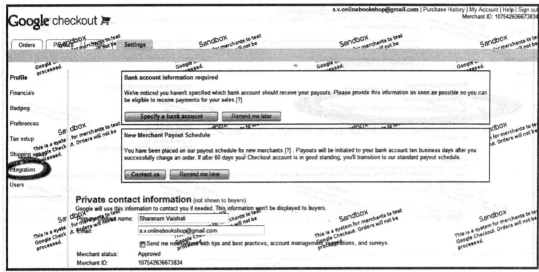

Diagram A.4: Settings

Click **Integration**. This brings up the Integration settings, as shown in diagram A.5.

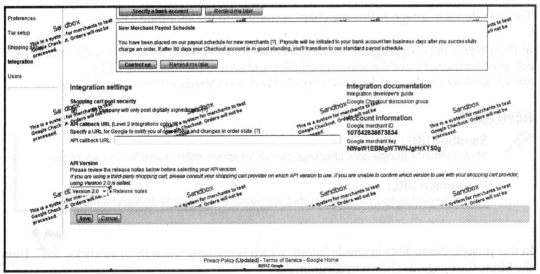

Diagram A.5: Integration settings

Change **Shopping cart post security** to accept unsigned carts by unchecking ☑ **My company will only post digitally signed carts**, as shown in diagram A.6.

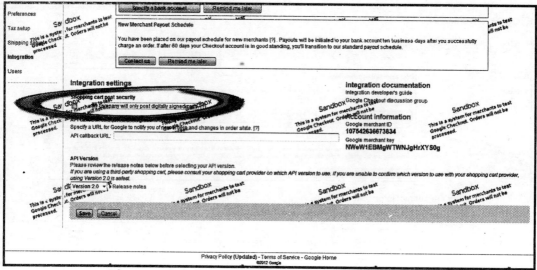

Diagram A.6: Changing the Shopping cart post security

Click .

The next step is to integrate this merchant account with the shopping cart.

In this project, the shopping cart holds the books in the session. This information needs to be collected/extracted from the session variables and sent to the following URL:
https://sandbox.google.com/checkout/cws/v2/Merchant/**<MerchantID>**/checkoutForm

REMINDER

Sandbox URL:
https://sandbox.google.com/checkout/cws/v2/Merchant/**<MerchantID>**/checkoutForm

Production URL:
https://checkout.google.com/api/checkout/v2/checkoutForm/Merchant/**<MerchantID>**

In this project, this is done in checkOut.jsp, which is invoked when the user clicks ![icon] from the **Show Cart** page, as shown in diagram A.7.

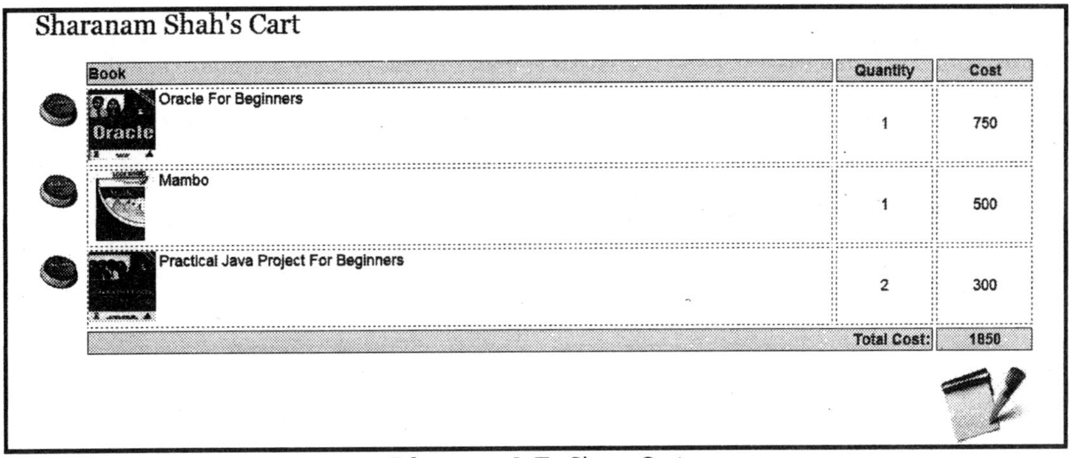

Diagram A.7: Show Cart

Clicking  submits the cart to checkOut.jsp.

This script extracts the cart data from the session variables and holds it in a <FORM>.

Finally, the form is submitted to Google checkout's sandbox URL along with the Merchant ID.

The code spec that extracts the cart details from the session and holds it using a set of pre-defined [by Google checkout] hidden form fields in the <FORM> element is as follows:

```
<form method="POST"
action="https://sandbox.google.com/checkout/cws/v2/Merchant/${googleMerchantID}/checkoutForm"
accept-charset="utf-8">
    <c:if test="${!empty cartList}">
        <c:forEach items="${cartList}" var="cartItem" varStatus="loop">
            <input type="hidden" name="item_name_${loop.index+1}" value="${cartItem.bookName}">
            <input type="hidden" name="item_description_${loop.index+1}"
            value="${cartItem.synopsis}">
            <input type="hidden" name="item_quantity_${loop.index+1}" value="${cartItem.qty}">
            <input type="hidden" name="item_price_${loop.index+1}" value="${cartItem.cost}">
        </c:forEach>
    </c:if>
    <input type="hidden"
name="checkout-flow-support.merchant-checkout-flow-support.continue-shopping-url"
value="http://localhost:8080/BookShop/home"/>
    <input type="hidden" name="_charset_"/>
</form>
```

Explanation:

A for each loop is used to traverse through the items in the cartList object. Every item that is extracted is made part of the FORM tag, using a hidden input tag.

Code spec:

```
<input type="hidden" name="item_name_${loop.index+1}"
    value="${cartItem.bookName}">
```

Explanation:

Assigning book name to the Google pre-defined hidden form field named item_name_<No>. Here, for every book name being assigned in the **Iterator**, the hidden form field will be named as:

item_name_1
item_name_2
item_name_3
. . .

Code spec:

```
<input type="hidden" name="item_description_${loop.index+1}"
    value="${cartItem.synopsis}">
```

Explanation:

Assigning book synopsis to the Google pre-defined hidden form field named item_description_<No>. Here, for every book synopsis being assigned in the **Iterator**, the hidden form field will be named as:

item_description_1
item_ description _2
item_ description _3
. . .

Code spec:

```
<input type="hidden" name="item_quantity_${loop.index+1}"
    value="${cartItem.qty}">
```

Explanation:

Assigning book quantity to the Google pre-defined hidden form field named item_quantity_<No>. Here, for every book quantity being assigned in the **Iterator**, the hidden form field will be named as:

item_quantity_1
item_ quantity_2

item_ quantity_3

...

Code spec:

```
<input type="hidden" name="item_price_${loop.index+1}"
    value="${cartItem.cost}">
```

Explanation:

Assigning book cost to the Google pre-defined hidden form field named item_price_<No>. Here, for every book cost being assigned in the **Iterator**, the hidden form field will be named as:

item_ price_1

item_ price_2

item_ price_3

...

Code spec:

```
<input type="hidden" name="checkout-flow-support.merchant-checkout-flow-
    support.continue-shopping-url"
        value="http://localhost:8080/BookShop/home"/>
<input type="hidden" name="_charset_"/>
```

Explanation:

Assigning the homepage URL to which the user can go by clicking **Return to Sharanam & Vaishali's Online Bookshop »** link on the Google checkout's thank you page.

This completes the cart integration with Google checkout.

WARNING

For demonstration/learning purpose, the cart is integrated with the Google checkout Sandbox URL.

The sandbox is a Google Checkout environment that allows testing the cart integration without affecting real transactions.

Points to keep in mind:

The sandbox sign-up process is identical to the production environment signup process. However, because the sandbox is a test system, it is not required to enter real credit card numbers, Social Security numbers or other information.

The only thing that is needed is to provide a valid email address, which becomes the username.

Creating an account for the sandbox environment does not create an account for the production environment and vice versa. It is required to sign up for each environment separately.

The sandbox account will have a different Merchant ID and Merchant Key compared to the production account.

Index

SHROFF PUBLISHERS & DISTRIBUTORS PVT. LTD.

Shroff Reprints & Original Titles

The X Team Series
(An Imprint of Shroff Publishers)

Computers

ISBN	Title	Author	Year	Price
9789350236321	**.NET Interview Q&A, 164 Pages**	**Harwani**	**2012**	**225.00**
9788184041569	Ajax for Beginners (B/CD), 452 Pages	Bayross	2006	375.00
9788184041972	Application Development with Oracle & PHP on Linux for Beginners, 2/ed (B/CD), 940 Pages	Bayross	2007	650.00
9789350233733	Blogging for Beginners, 268 Pages	Harwani	2011	350.00
9788184046397	C for Beginners, 532 Pages	Mothe	2009	375.00
9789350233900	C Interviews Q&A, 119 Pages [Forthcoming]	Thorat	2011	150.00
9788184046564	C++ for Beginners, 403 Pages	Harwani	2009	375.00
9789350231012	Core Java for Beginners, (B/CD), 892 Pages	Shah	2010	500.00
9788184046694	Database Concepts and Systems for Students, 3/ed, 428 Pgs	Bayross	2009	325.00
9788184048780	HTML for Beginners, 2/ed, 416 Pages	Aibara	2010	500.00
9789350236475	**HTML5 for Beginners, 564 Pages**	**Aibara**	**2012**	**450.00**
9788184047059	Hibernate 3 for Beginners - Covers Java Persistence API (B/CD), 680 Pages	Shah	2009	500.00
9788184045697	Java EE 5 for Beginners, 2/ed **(B/CD)**, 1,192 Pages	Bayross	2008	575.00
9788184049398	Java EE 6 for Beginners, (B/CD), 1092 Pages	Shah	2009	825.00
9788184049411	Java EE 6 Server Programming for Professionals (B/DVD), 1,328 Pages (H/B)	Shah	2010	750.00
9788184048063	Java EE Project using EJB 3, JPA and Struts 2 for Beginners, (B/CD), 1,258 Pages	Shah	2009	1,025.00
9788184043174	Java for Beginners **(B/CD)**, Covers Java SE 6 JDK, 600 Pages	Chavan	2007	450.00
9788184045932	Java for Professionals: A Practical Approach to Java Programming (Covers Java SE 6), 790 Pages	Harwani	2008	525.00
9788184046670	Java for Students, 690 Pages	Pherwani	2009	475.00
9789350233719	Java for Students, 2/ed, 850 Pages	Pherwani	2011	600.00
9788184047097	Java Persistence API in EJB 3 for Professionals, (B/CD) 756 Pgs	Shah	2009	550.00
9788184045925	JavaServer Pages Project for Beginners, **(B/CD)**, 746 Pages	Shah	2008	550.00
9788184045598	Java Server Programming for Professionals, Revised & Enlarged 2/ed (Covers Java EE 5) (B/CD), 1,612 Pages	Bayross	2008	700.00
9788184043594	Java Server Pages for Beginners **(B/CD)**, 872 Pages	Bayross	2007	500.00
9788184048438	Lamp Programming for Professionals, (B/CD), 1,284	Shah	2009	1,275.00
9789350233986	**Mobile Computing for Beginners, 782 Pages**	**Shende**	**2012**	**750.00**
9789350235188	MySQL 5.1 for Professionals (B/CD), 772 Pages	Bayross	2011	650.00

ISBN	Title	Author	Year	Price
9788184045260	Oracle for Professionals **(B/CD)**, 1,420 Pgs	Shah	2008	750.00
9788184043228	PC Hardware for Beginners, 308 Pages	Sangia	2007	225.00
9788184040753	PHP 5.1 for Beginners **(B/CD)**, 1,284 Pages	Bayross	2006	650.00
9788184048445	PHP Project for Beginners, (B/CD), 1,200 Pages	Shah	2010	600.00
9788184047073	Practical ASP.NET 3.5 Projects for Beginners, (B/CD), 550 Pgs	Harwani	2009	450.00
9788184048070	Practical EJB Project for Beginners, 312 Pages	Harwani	2009	325.00
9788184043426	Practical Java Project for Beginners **(B/CD)**, 164 Pages	Harwani	2007	150.00
9788184043419	Practical Web Services for Beginners, 168 Pages	Harwani	2007	150.00
9789350234907	Programming with Pl/SQL for Beginners, 236 Pages	Patil	2011	300.00
9788184049725	QuickTest Professional (QTP) Version 10, 116 Pages	Mallepally	2010	125.00
9789350231241	QTP for Professionals, 480 Pages	Reddy	2010	450.00
9789350236499	**SAP MM for Beginners, 384 Pages**	**Rakshit**	**2012**	**600.00**
9788184048100	SAP SD for Beginners, 324 Pages	Samad	2009	450.00
9789350233894	SAP SD for Beginners 2/ed, 260 Pages	Samad	2011	350.00
9789350236482	**Software Automation Testing Tools for Beginners, 1110 Pages**	**Shende**	**2012**	**1000.00**
9789350236901	**Spring 3 for Beginners, Pages 612**	**Shah**	**2012**	**575.00**
9788184047448	Struts 2 for Beginners, 2/ed, (B/CD), 566 Pages	Shah	2009	450.00
9788184046960	Struts 2 with Hibernate 3 Project for Beginners, (B/CD), 1,042 Pages	Shah	2009	675.00
9788184041071	Visual Basic 2005 for Beginners **(B/CD)**, 1,172 Pages	Bayross	2006	150.00

Other Computer Titles

ISBN	Title	Author	Year	Price
9789350230237	A Primer on Software Quality Models & Project Management, 640 Pages	Mehta	2010	600.00
9788184048827	Art of Creative Destruction: Illustarted Software Testing, Test Automation & Agile Testing, 2/ed, 348 Pages	Puranik	2010	425.00
9788173660030	AS/400 Architecture & Applications, 332 Pages	Lawrence	1993	250.00
9788173660047	AS/400: A Practical Guide to Programming & Operations, 284 Pgs	Zeilenga	1993	225.00
9789350232859	Beginning Web Development for Smartphones Developing Web Applications with PHP, MySQL and jQTouch, 252 Pages	Harwani	2011	300.00
9789350231029	C# 4.0 Programming Made Easy, 624 Pages	Kadam	2011	425.00
9789350230244	Computer Architecture and Maintenance, 320 Pages	Kadam	2010	250.00
9788173660016	CICS: A How-To for Cobol Programmers, 428 Pages	Kirk	1993	300.00
9789350235553	**Data Structure and Algorithm, 492 Pages**	**Rukadikar**	**2012**	**400.00**
9788184048957	FAQ's in MFC and MFC Solutions, Vol I (B/CD) 510 Pages	P. G. Naik	2010	425.00
9788173666810	First Encounter with Java Including BlueJ, 386 Pages	Bhutta	2006	225.00
9789350230275	Instant Oracle, 100 Pages	Shah	2010	75.00
9788173664632	Introducing MySQL, 96 Pages	Oak	2005	50.00
9789350230251	Management Information System (MIS), 176 Pages	Kadam	2010	200.00
9789350231258	Maximum Oracle with Oracle Best Practices, 772 Pages	Puranik	2011	675.00
9788173660023	MVS / VSAM for the Application Programmer, 504 Pages	Brown	1993	325.00
9788184047899	Operating Systems, 2/ed, 408 Pages	Sumitradevi	2009	500.00
9789350236918	**Oracle Financials 11i: A Practical Guide for the Beginners, 2nd Edition, 436 Pgs**	**Peri**	**2012**	**725.00**
9788173668012	Software Defect Prevention Concepts and Implementation, 180 Pages **(H/B)**	Kane & Bajaj	2003	300.00
9789350236307	**Software Testing: Interview Questions, 176 Pages**	**Reddy**	**2012**	**175.00**

ISBN	Title	Author	Year	Price
9788173668814	Strategic Bidding: A Successful Approach, 192 Pgs	Garg	2004	250.00
9788173660078	TCP/IP Companion: A Guide For The Common User, 284 Pages	Arick	1993	225.00
9789350231005	Testing in 30$^+$ Open Source Tools (B/CD), 1,080 Pages	Shende	2010	900.00
9788173660429	Vijay Mukhi's ERP Odyssey: Implementing PeopleSoft Financials 7.0/7.5, 528 Pages	Mukhi	1999	350.00

Business, Management & Finance

ISBN	Title	Author	Year	Price
9788184046977	An Introduction to Foreign Exchange & Financial Risk Management, **(B/CD)**, 348 Pages	Lakshman	2009	400.00
9789350230268	Bootstrapping A Software Company, 348 Pages	Yadav	2010	425.00
9788184044287	Breaking the Black Box, **(B/CD)**, 276 Pages	Pring	2008	500.00
9788184044249	Break Your Negative Attitude, 114 Pages	Dr. Mishra	2007	125.00
9789350230220	Complete Guide to Technical Analysis: An Indian Perspective, 612 Pages	Pring	2010	650.00
9788184040425	Developing Analytical Skills: Case Studies in Management, 636 Pages	Dr. Natarajan	2008	500.00
9788173660993	Doing Business with the French, 150 Pages	Jhangiani	1999	150.00
9788184044959	Enabling Event-ful Experiences, 250 Pages	Balachandran	2008	200.00
9788184044744	Ethics, Indian Ethos and Management, 252 Pages	Balachandran	2008	175.00
9789350231227	Financial Decision Modeling Operations Research & Business Statistics (Group II, Paper 5 C.A. Final), 696 Pages	Sridhar	2010	350.00
9789350230794	Financial Management: Problems & Solutions, 4/ed, 1,228 Pgs	Sridhar	2010	750.00
9789350232965	Futures & Options: Equities & Commodities, 4/ed, 392 Pgs	Sridhar	2011	475.00
9789350233917	Globally Distributed Work, 280 Pages	Mehta	2011	425.00
9789350233887	Hospitality Management, 304 pages	Shirke	2011	525.00
9788184040432	How to Eat The Elephant? The CEO's Guide To An Enterprise System Implementation, 104 Pages	Tulsyan	2007	325.00
9789350230459	How to Learn Management from your wife (PB), 96 Pages	Rangnekar	2010	125.00
9789350233108	How to Learn Management from your wife (HB), 96 Pages	Rangnekar	2010	275.00
9788184044447	How to Select Stocks Using Technical Analysis, (B/CD), 338 Pages	Pring	2008	500.00
9788184044164	Logistics in International Business, 2/ed, 428 Pages	Aserkar	2007	450.00
9788184047547	Magic and Logic of Elliott Waves, The, 204 Pages	Kale	2009	500.00
9788184048568	Management Accounting & Financial Analysis for C.A.Final (June 2009), 9/ed, 540 Pages	Sridhar	2009	400.00
9789350235126	Management of Services, 348 Pages	Jain	2011	450.00
9788184044454	Momentum Explained, Volume I (B/CD), 366 Pages	Pring	2008	600.00
9788184044461	Momentum Explained, Volume II (B/CD), 338 Pages	Pring	2008	550.00
9788184047066	Purchasing and Inventory Management, 338 Pages	Menon	2009	475.00
9789350233870	Quantitative Techniques for Project Management, 256 Pages	Velayoudam	2011	600.00
9788173666797	Rules of Origin in International Trade, 238 Pages	Dr. Sathpathy	2005	300.00
9789350233580	Services Marketing, 448 Pages	Balachandran	2011	450.00
9789350233115	Soft Skills In Management, 148 Pages	Rangnekar	2011	125.00
9789350237847	**Strategic Financial Management For C. A. Final, 9/Ed, 904 Pgs.**	**Sridhar**	**2012**	**650.00**
9788173668814	Strategic Bidding: A Successful Approach, 192 Pages	Garg	2004	250.00
9788184043211	Time Your Trades With Technical Analysis **(B/CD)**, 348 Pages	Pradhan	2007	600.00

Catering & Hotel Management

9788173668739	Careers in Hospitality - Hotel Management Entrance Exam Guide, 332 Pages	Rego	2004	200.00
9789350233887	Hospitality Management, 303 Pages [Forthcoming]	Shirke	2011	525.00
9789350230817	Marvels of Indian Snacks, 264 Pages	Shankaran	2011	350.00
9788184044751	Marvels of South Indian Cuisine, 220 Pages	Shankaran	2008	250.00
9788184046687	Marvels of North Indian Cuisine, 196 Pages	Shankaran	2009	325.00

Civil Engineering

9789350233252	Concrete for High Performance Sustainable Infrastructure, 312 Pages	Newlands	2011	750.00
9789350233245	New Developments in Concrete Construction, 296 Pages	Dhir	2011	750.00
9788173663772	Principles of Environmental Science Engineering and Maintenance, 288 Pages	Dr. Thirumurthy	2004	175.00
9788184048056	Raina's Concrete Bridge Practice: Construction, Maintenance and Rehabiliation 2/ed, 452 Pages (H/B) [14 Full Color Inserts]	Dr. Raina	2010	625.00
9788184048049	Raina's Concrete Bridge: Inspection, Repair, Strengthening, Testing, Load Capacity Evaluation 2/ed, 800 Pages (H/B) [32 Full Color Inserts]	Dr. Raina	2010	1,200.00
9788184047530	Raina's Concrete for Construction: Facts & Practice, 400 Pgs (H/B)	Dr. Raina	2009	650.00
9788184047875	Raina's Construction & Contract Management, 2/ed Inside Story, 585 Pages (H/B)	Dr. Raina	2009	750.00
9788184043785	Raina's Concrete Bridge Practice, 3/ed : Analysis, Design & Economics, 856 Pages	Dr. Raina	2007	1,000.00
9788184046618	Raina's Field Manual for Highway and Bridge Engineers, 3/ed,1,404 Pages	Dr. Raina	2009	1,800.00
9789350231418	Raina's Handbook for Concrete Bridges, 1500 Pages (H/B) [Forthcoming]	Dr. Raina	2011	TBA
9788184040135	The World of Bridges, 300 Pages (H/B) [4 color]	Dr. Raina	2006	500.00
9789350231180	Using Primavera 6: Planning, Executing, Monitoring and Controlling Projects, 228 Pages	Al-Saridi	2010	275.00

Communication

9789350231265	Knowing Your Word's Worth: A Practical Guide to Communicating Effectively in English, 180 Pages	Shirodkar	2011	175.00

Dental / Health / Medical

9788173669798	The Balancing Act "A Win Over Obesity", 296 Pages	Dr. Gadkari	2005	225.00
9788184049480	The Balancing Act "Know Your Heart", 368 Pages	Dr. Gadkari	2010	250.00
9788173668975	Splinting Management of MOBILE & Migrating Teeth, 104 Pgs	Dr. Kakar	2004	150.00

Economics

9788184043266	Analysing Macroeconomics: A Toolkit for Managers, Executives & Students **(H/B)**, 156 Pages	Rakesh Singh	2007	50ʋ
9788184044171	Analysing Macroeconomics: A Toolkit for Managers, Executives & Students **(P/B)**, 156 Pages	Rakesh Singh	2007	250.00

Electrical Engineering

9788184043235	Basic Electrical Circuits, 2/ed, 368 Pages	Dr. Salam	2007	250.00

Electronics & Communication

9788173669002	Electronic Components and Materials, 3/ed, 404 Pages	Joshi	2004	175.00

Environmental Engineering

9788173663772	Principles of Environmental Science Engineering and Maintenance, 288 Pgs	Dr. Thirumurthy	2004	175.00

Event Management

9788184044959	Enabling Event-ful Experiences, 250 Pages	Balachandran	2008	250.00

General Titles

9788184045642	Hello Police Station (Marathi), 118 Pages	Shinde	2008	100.00
9789350231760	Mom Don't Spoil Me, 140 Pages	Dr. Mishra	2010	150.00

HRD

9788184047080	Departmental Enquiries: Concept, Procedure & Practice, 534 Pages	Goel	2009	475.00
9788184046229	How To Improve Trainer Effectiveness, 170 Pages	Balachandran	2008	200.00

Law

9789350230800	A Handbook on the Maintenance & Welfare of Parents and Senior Citizens Act, 2007.	Gracias	2010	150.00
9788173664151	Customs Valuation in India 3/ed, 262 Pages	Satapathy	2002	375.00
9788184042481	Laws Of Carriage Of Goods By Sea & Multimodal Transport In India, 92 Pages	Hariharan	2007	60.00
9788173661426	Law of Sale of Goods & Partnership, 228 Pages	Chandiramani	2000	150.00
9789350231289	Social Security, Insurance & The Law, 460 Pgs	Gopalakrishna	2011	600.00

Learning Disability

9789350233924	On the wave of Brain: A Broad Perspective of Learning Disability 300 Pages	Jain	2011	450.00

Marine

9788184043242	Containerisation, Multimodal Transport and Infrastructure Development in India, 5/ed, 852 Pages	Hariharan	2007	650.00
9788173660375	M.S. (STCW) Rules, 1998 incl. Training & Assessment Programme - 1,216 Pages	DG Shipping	1998	225.00
9788173661419	Maritime Education, Training & Assessment Manual (TAP) - Vol II, 474 Pages	DG Shipping	1999	400.00
9788184043136	Marine Control Technology, 336 Pages	Majumder	2007	400.00
9788173669279	Marine Diesel Engines, 428 Pages	Aranha	2004	250.00
9788184048544	Marine Electrical Technology, 5/ed, 1,250 Pages	Fernandes	2010	750.00
9788173660801	Marine Internal Combustion Engines, 272 Pages	Kane	2003	150.00
9788173660146	Safety Management Systems - An Underconstruction Activity, 98 Pages	Capt. Singhal	1998	95.00
9788173665516	A Textbook on Container & Multimodal Transport Management, 522 Pages	Dr. Hariharan	2002	500.00

Mechanical Engineering

9789350236192	**A Glance On Transformer Oil, 96 Pages**	**Pandey**	**2012**	**125.00**

Motivation

9788184044249	Break Your Negative Attitude, 114 Pages	Dr. Mishra	2007	125.00
9788173665271	Heads You Win, Tails You Win, 2/ed, 200 Pages	Dr.Mishra	2005	200.00
9789350236208	**Life is Fundamentally Management!, 200 Pages**	**Senthival**	**2012**	**250.00**
9789350230206	Nothing Is Absolute, 274 Pages	Balachandran	2010	300.00

Parenting

9789350231760	Mom Don't Spoil Me, 140 Pages	Dr. Mishra	2010	150.00

Patent

9788184047882	Breeding Innovation and Intellectual Capital, 2/ed 196 Pgs	Dr.Batra	2009	600.00

Physics

9788184043259	Gravitation Demythicised: An Introduction to Einstein's General Relativity and Cosmology for Common Man, 258 Pages	Shenoy	2007	250.00
9788184047929	Study Aid Theoretical Physics - Volume I: Relativistic Theory and Electrodynamics, 418 Pgs	Prof Fai	2010	300.00
9788184047912	Theoretical Physics - Volume I: Relativistic Theory and Electrodynamics, 490 Pages	Prof Fai	2010	400.00

Project Management

9789350230237	A Primer on Software Quality Models & Project Management, 640 Pages	Mehta	2010	600.00
9788184048568	Management Accounting & Financial Analysis for C.A.Final 9/ed, 540 Pages	Sridhar	2009	400.00

Self-Help

		Author	Year	Price
9788184047905	Enhancing Soft Skills, 346 Pages	Biswas	2009	375.00
9789350237113	**Secrets of Your Leadership Success, 212 Pages**	**Rao**	**2012**	**350.00**

- All Prices are in Indian Rupees
- Titles Released after January 2012 are marked in Bold.